History of the World

in Christian Perspective
Third Edition

Jerry H. Combee, Ph.D.

Contributors: *Kurt Grussendorf, Beka Horton,*
Brian Ashbaugh, Susan Etheridge

A Beka Book®
A MINISTRY OF
PENSACOLA CHRISTIAN COLLEGE
PENSACOLA, FLORIDA 32523-9160

Contents

Pronunciation Key . . . . inside front cover

PART 1
ANCIENT HISTORY AND THE MIDDLE AGES

UNIT 1

From Eden to Israel

THE BEGINNING OF WORLD HISTORY: THE ANCIENT MIDDLE EAST 3

1 The Beginning 4
Creation • Fall of man • Flood • Dispersion

2 From Sumer to Canaan 12
Sumerian Civilization • Call of Abraham
Hammurabi and Babylon • Patriarchs in Canaan

3 Down to Egypt 26
Egyptian Civilization • Hebrew Exodus

4 Israel in Its Land 40
Ten Commandments • Conquest of Canaan
David and Solomon • Phoenicians • Hittites

Unit Summary From Eden to Israel 53

NEW EMPIRES AND CULTURES:
THE MIDDLE EAST, GREECE, AND ROME 55

5 According to His Will: Assyria, Babylon, and Persia 56
Assyrian Empire • Chaldean Empire • Nebuchadnezzar
Persian Empire • Cyrus the Great

6 Greece—A Drama in Two Acts 68
Early Greek Civilization • Homer and the Olympian Gods
Athens and Sparta • Alexander the Great

7 Rome before Christ 88
Foundation of Rome • Roman Republic
Punic Wars • Julius Caesar • Caesar Augustus

8 Rome after Christ 114
Gospel of Christ • Persecution of Early Church
Constantine the Great • Fall of Rome

Unit Summary Preparation for Christ 129

UNIT 2
Preparation for Christ

THE MIDDLE AGES AND
THE DISTORTION OF CHRISTIANITY 133

9 Early Church History 134
New Testament • Early Church
Rise of Roman Church and Popes

10 Islam versus Christendom 148
Mohammed and Islam • Europe's Crusades

11 From Empire to Feudalism 158
Charlemagne and His Empire • Feudalism

12 An Age of Darkness 174
Distorted Christianity • Holy Roman Empire • Renaissance

Unit Summary Response to Christ 192

UNIT 3
Response to Christ

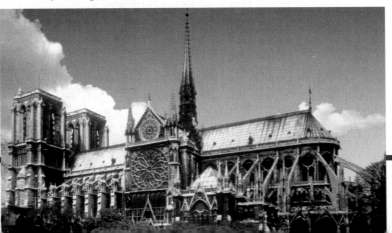

PART 2
THE MODERN AGE
AND THE TWENTIETH CENTURY

UNIT 4

The World Changes

BEGINNING OF THE MODERN AGE 201

13 The Protestant Reformation 202
  Forerunners of the Reformation • John Wycliffe
  John Huss • Inquisition • Gutenberg and the
  Printing Press • Erasmus • Martin Luther

14 Post-Reformation Europe 218
  Peasants' Revolt • State Churches • Counter Reformation
  Thirty Years' War • Seventeenth-century Europe

15 The English Nation 236
  Alfred the Great • Norman Conquest • Magna Carta
  Parliament • Hundred Years' War • Wars of the Roses
  Henry VIII • English Reformation • Elizabeth I
  Defeat of the Spanish Armada • English Civil War
  Restoration of Monarchy • Glorious Revolution

16 An Age of Exploration: Asia and the Americas 264
  Prince Henry the Navigator • Marco Polo
  Christopher Columbus • America • India
  China • Japan, Korea, Indonesia

17 The United States—A New Kind of Nation 294
  Pilgrims • Great Awakening • War for Independence
  Constitution of the United States • Expansion and Progress
  Rise as a World Power • Revival and Missions

18 France in the Modern Age 324
  Huguenots • Louis XIV • Age of Enlightenment
  French Revolution • Reign of Terror • Napoleon Bonaparte
  Congress of Vienna • July Revolution

Unit Summary The World Changes 356

PROGRESS IN THE MODERN AGE 361

19 Science and Industry in the Modern Age 362
  Founders of Modern Science • Darwin and Evolution
  Agricultural Advancement • Industrial Revolution
  Inventors and Captains of Industry • Triumph of Capitalism
20 The New World of Classics 392
  Music • Art • Literature
21 The British Empire: Asia, Africa, and Australia 408
  Queen Victoria • The British Empire • India and
  the Far East • Africa • Australia and New Zealand
  Canada • Christianity in Victorian England

Unit Summary Mankind Advances 436

UNIT 5
Mankind Advances

THE TWENTIETH CENTURY 438

22 World War I and the Rise of Communism 440
  World War I • Czarist Russia • Karl Marx and
  Communism • Bolshevik Revolution
  Nikolai Lenin • Joseph Stalin • Soviet Union
23 Before and During World War II 464
  1920s • Great Depression • Mussolini and Fascist Italy
  Hitler and Nazi Germany • Militaristic Japan • World War II
24 The Cold War Era 490
  United Nations • Cold War • Communist Revolution
  in China • Korean War • Communism in Cuba • Third World
  Nations • Vietnam Conflict • Détente • Space Race
25 Era of Change 520
  Ronald Reagan • Collapse of Soviet Union • Persian Gulf War
  European Union • South Africa • Bill Clinton

Unit Summary Philosophies Clash 542

Index 546

Credits 551

UNIT 6
Philosophies Clash

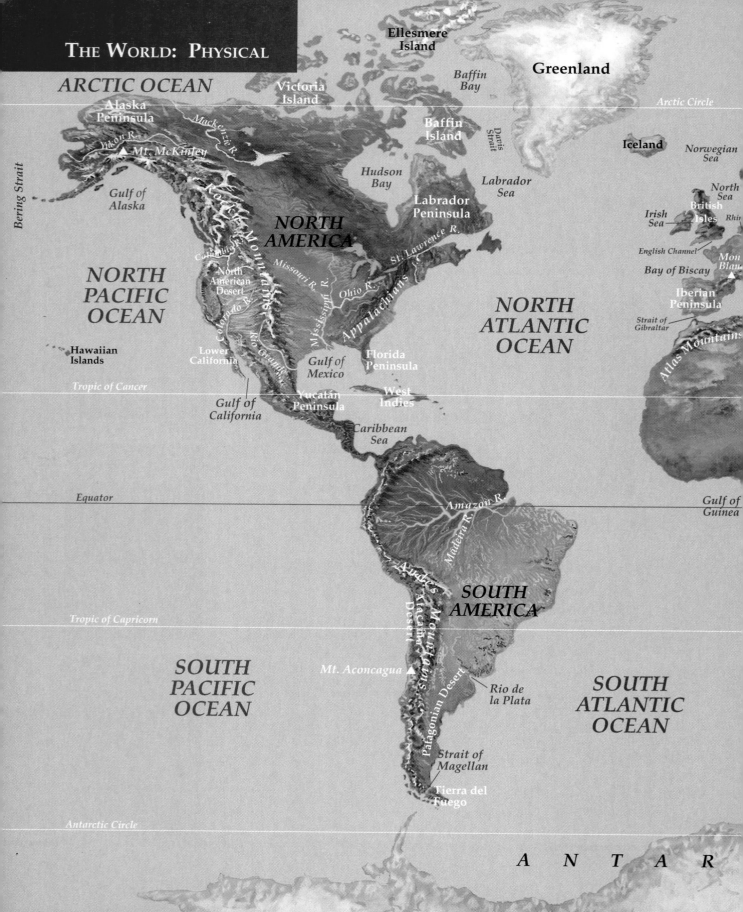

THE WORLD: PHYSICAL

ARCTIC OCEAN

Ellesmere Island

Greenland

Arctic Circle

Victoria Island

Baffin Bay

Alaska Peninsula

Mackenzie R.

Baffin Island

Davis Strait

Iceland

Norwegian Sea

Yukon R.

▲ *Mt. McKinley*

Hudson Bay

Labrador Sea

North Sea

Irish Sea

British Isles

Rhin

Bering Strait

Gulf of Alaska

Rocky Mountains

NORTH AMERICA

Labrador Peninsula

English Channel

Mon Blan ▲

NORTH PACIFIC OCEAN

Columbia R.

North American Desert

Missouri R.

St. Lawrence R.

Bay of Biscay

Mississippi R.

Ohio R.

Appalachians

NORTH ATLANTIC OCEAN

Iberian Peninsula

Colorado R.

Rio Grande

Strait of Gibraltar

Atlas Mountains

Hawaiian Islands

Lower California

Florida Peninsula

Tropic of Cancer

Gulf of Mexico

West Indies

Gulf of California

Yucatán Peninsula

Caribbean Sea

Equator

Amazon R.

Gulf of Guinea

Madeira R.

SOUTH AMERICA

Andes Mountains

Atacama Desert

Tropic of Capricorn

SOUTH PACIFIC OCEAN

Mt. Aconcagua ▲

Patagonian Desert

Rio de la Plata

SOUTH ATLANTIC OCEAN

Strait of Magellan

Tierra del Fuego

Antarctic Circle

ANTAR

ARCTIC OCEAN

Barents
Sea

Arctic Circle

*Scandinavian
Peninsula*

Bering
Sea

Baltic Sea

Ural Mountains

ASIA

Sea of
Okhotsk

*Kamchatka
Peninsula*

EUROPE

*Lake
Baikal*

Danube R.

Volga R.

Gobi
Desert

Black Sea
Bosporus

▲ Mt.
Elbrus

Caucasus Mts.

Kyzyl Kum
Desert

Caspian Sea

Sea of
Japan

Korean Pen.

Balkan
Pen.

Asia
Minor

▲ Mt.
Ararat

Kara Kum
Desert

Takla Makan
(desert)

Hwang Ho R.

Yellow
Sea

Honshu (Japan)

▲ Mt. Fuji

Dardanelles

Tigris R.

Mediterranean Sea

Euphrates R.

Persian Gulf

Mt. Everest
29,028 ft.

▲

Himalayas

Yangtze R.

East
China
Sea

Sinai
Pen.

Indus R.

Gulf of
Oman

Thar
Desert

Tropic of Cancer

Nile R.

Red Sea

*Arabian
Peninsula*

Taiwan

Sahara
(desert)

Nubian
Desert

Gulf of Aden

Arabian
Sea

Peninsula
of
India

Bay of
Bengal

Indochina
Peninsula

South China
Sea

Philippine
Sea

AFRICA

Malay Pen.

Philippines

Congo R.

Equator

Lake
Victoria

▲ Mt. Kenya

Borneo

Lake
Tanganyika

▲ Mt. Kilimanjaro

INDIAN
OCEAN

Sumatra

Celebes

New Guinea

SOUTH
PACIFIC
OCEAN

Java

Malay Archipelago

Mozambique Channel

Madagascar

Coral
Sea

Kalahari
Desert

Tropic of Capricorn

AUSTRALIA

Australian
Desert

Great Dividing Range

Tasman
Sea

Great
Australian
Bight

Murray R.

Darling R.

New Zealand

Tasmania

Antarctic Circle

C   T   I   C   A

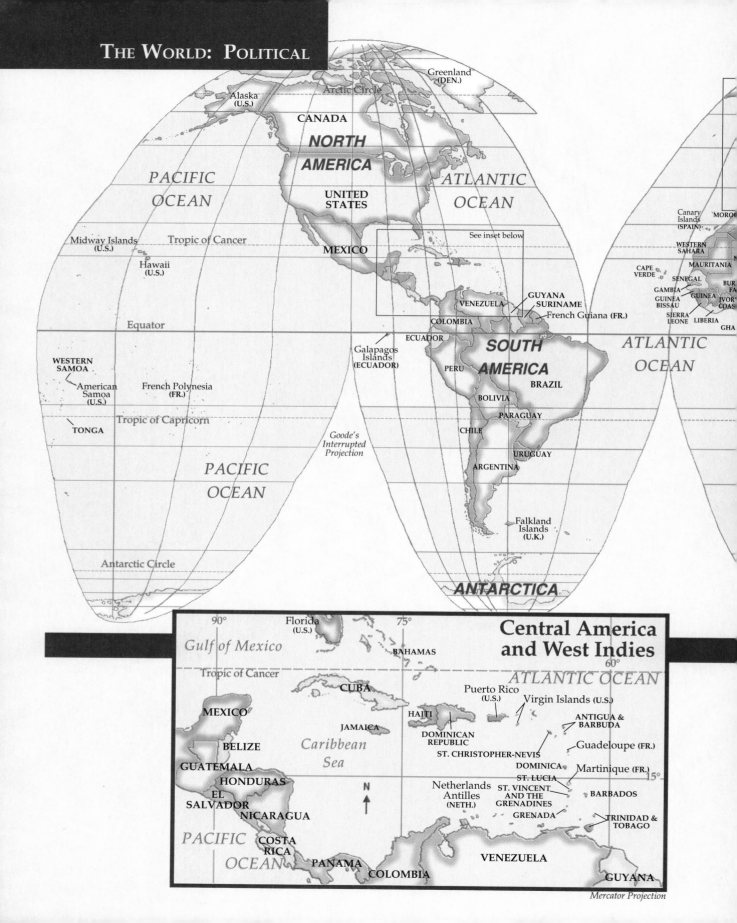

Greenland (DEN.)
Arctic Circle
Alaska (U.S.)

CANADA

NORTH AMERICA

PACIFIC OCEAN

UNITED STATES

ATLANTIC OCEAN

Midway Islands (U.S.)
Tropic of Cancer

MEXICO

See inset below

Hawaii (U.S.)

Canary Islands (SPAIN)
MOROCCO
WESTERN SAHARA
CAPE VERDE
MAURITANIA
SENEGAL
GAMBIA
GUINEA BISSAU
GUINEA
SIERRA LEONE
LIBERIA
IVORY COAST
GHA
BUR FA

VENEZUELA
GUYANA
SURINAME
French Guiana (FR.)

Equator

COLOMBIA

ECUADOR

Galapagos Islands (ECUADOR)

SOUTH AMERICA

ATLANTIC OCEAN

WESTERN SAMOA
American Samoa (U.S.)
French Polynesia (FR.)

PERU

BRAZIL

BOLIVIA

Tropic of Capricorn

TONGA

PARAGUAY

CHILE

URUGUAY

Goode's Interrupted Projection

PACIFIC OCEAN

ARGENTINA

Falkland Islands (U.K.)

Antarctic Circle

ANTARCTICA

Central America and West Indies

90°
Florida (U.S.)
75°
Gulf of Mexico
BAHAMAS
60°
Tropic of Cancer
ATLANTIC OCEAN
CUBA
Puerto Rico (U.S.)
Virgin Islands (U.S.)
MEXICO
HAITI
ANTIGUA & BARBUDA
JAMAICA
DOMINICAN REPUBLIC
Guadeloupe (FR.)
BELIZE
Caribbean Sea
ST. CHRISTOPHER-NEVIS
DOMINICA
Martinique (FR.)
GUATEMALA
ST. LUCIA
15°
HONDURAS
N
Netherlands Antilles (NETH.)
ST. VINCENT AND THE GRENADINES
BARBADOS
EL SALVADOR
NICARAGUA
GRENADA
TRINIDAD & TOBAGO
PACIFIC OCEAN
COSTA RICA
PANAMA
VENEZUELA
COLOMBIA
GUYANA

Mercator Projection

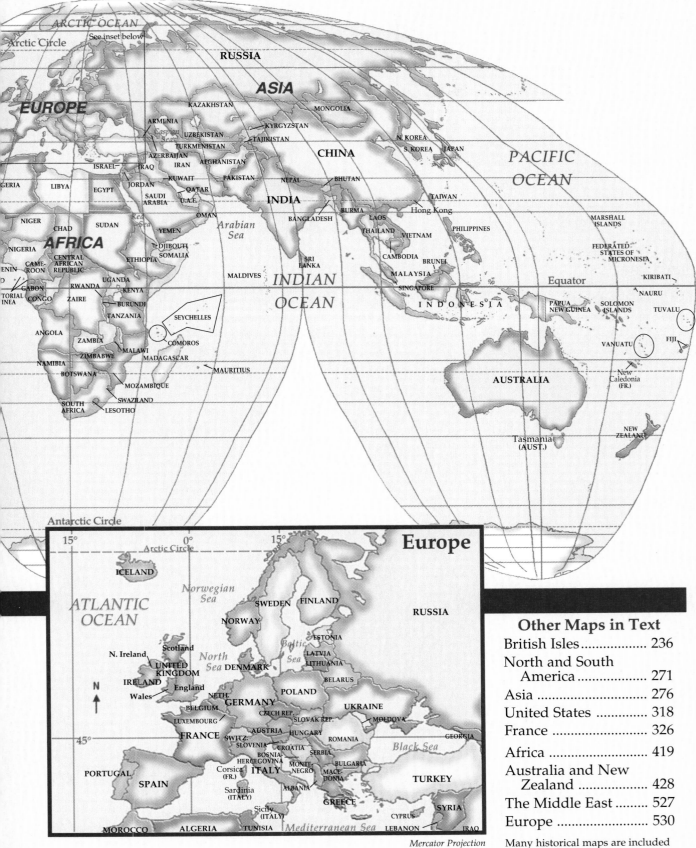

ARCTIC OCEAN

Arctic Circle

See inset below

RUSSIA

EUROPE

ASIA

KAZAKHSTAN

MONGOLIA

ARMENIA

KYRGYZSTAN

Caspian Sea

UZBEKISTAN

TURKMENISTAN

TAJIKISTAN

N. KOREA

CHINA

S. KOREA

JAPAN

AZERBAIJAN

IRAN

AFGHANISTAN

PACIFIC

ISRAEL

IRAQ

KUWAIT

PAKISTAN

NEPAL

BHUTAN

OCEAN

GERIA

LIBYA

EGYPT

JORDAN

QATAR

INDIA

TAIWAN

SAUDI
ARABIA

U.A.E.

BURMA

Hong Kong

NIGER

CHAD

SUDAN

OMAN

Arabian
Sea

BANGLADESH

LAOS

MARSHALL
ISLANDS

Red
Sea

YEMEN

THAILAND

VIETNAM

AFRICA

DJIBOUTI

SRI
LANKA

CAMBODIA

BRUNEI

FEDERATED
STATES OF
MICRONESIA

NIGERIA

CENTRAL
AFRICAN
REPUBLIC

CAME-
ROON

ETHIOPIA

SOMALIA

MALDIVES

INDIAN

MALAYSIA

ENIN

UGANDA

SINGAPORE

Equator

KIRIBATI

TORIAL
INEA

GABON

CONGO

RWANDA

KENYA

OCEAN

INDONESIA

PAPUA
NEW GUINEA

SOLOMON
ISLANDS

NAURU

ZAIRE

BURUNDI

TUVALU

TANZANIA

SEYCHELLES

ANGOLA

COMOROS

VANUATU

FIJI

ZAMBIA

MALAWI

NAMIBIA

ZIMBABWE

MADAGASCAR

MAURITIUS

New
Caledonia
(FR.)

BOTSWANA

AUSTRALIA

MOZAMBIQUE

NEW
ZEALAND

SOUTH
AFRICA

SWAZILAND

LESOTHO

Antarctic Circle

Tasmania
(AUST.)

15°   0°   15°

Europe

Arctic Circle

ICELAND

Norwegian
Sea

SWEDEN

FINLAND

RUSSIA

ATLANTIC
OCEAN

NORWAY

ESTONIA

Baltic
Sea

LATVIA

N. Ireland

Scotland

North
Sea

LITHUANIA

UNITED
KINGDOM

DENMARK

BELARUS

N

IRELAND

Wales

England

NETH.

POLAND

UKRAINE

BELGIUM

GERMANY

LUXEMBOURG

CZECH REP.

SLOVAK REP.

MOLDOVA

45°

FRANCE

SWITZ.

AUSTRIA

HUNGARY

ROMANIA

GEORGIA

SLOVENIA

CROATIA

SERBIA

Black Sea

BOSNIA-
HERCEGOVINA

MONTE-
NEGRO

BULGARIA

PORTUGAL

SPAIN

Corsica
(FR.)

ITALY

MACE-
DONIA

TURKEY

Sardinia
(ITALY)

ALBANIA

GREECE

SYRIA

Sicily
(ITALY)

CYPRUS

LEBANON

MOROCCO

ALGERIA

TUNISIA

Mediterranean Sea

IRAQ

Mercator Projection

Other Maps in Text

British Isles 236

North and South
  America 271

Asia 276

United States 318

France 326

Africa 419

Australia and New
  Zealand 428

The Middle East 527

Europe 530

Many historical maps are included
throughout the book.

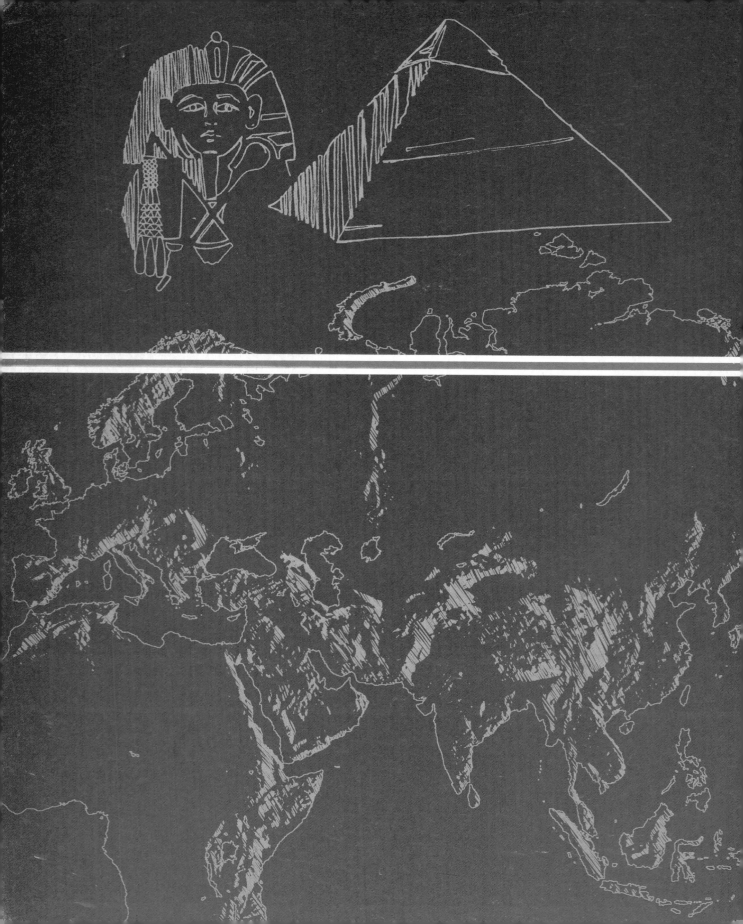

PART 1

ANCIENT HISTORY AND THE MIDDLE AGES

(CREATION–A.D. 1500)

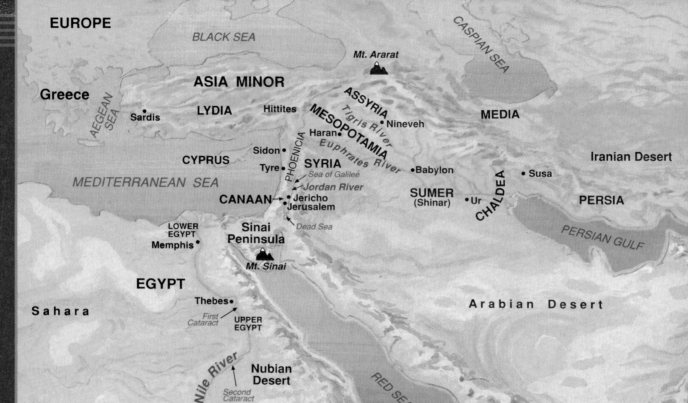

THE ANCIENT MIDDLE EAST

EUROPE

BLACK SEA

Mt. Ararat

ASIA MINOR

Greece

Sardis

LYDIA

Hittites

ASSYRIA

CASPIAN SEA

MESOPOTAMIA

Tigris River

Nineveh

MEDIA

Haran

Euphrates River

CYPRUS

Sidon

PHOENICIA

SYRIA

Iranian Desert

MEDITERRANEAN SEA

Tyre

Sea of Galilee

Babylon

Susa

Jordan River

CANAAN

Jericho

SUMER
(Shinar)

Ur

CHALDEA

PERSIA

Jerusalem

Dead Sea

LOWER EGYPT

Memphis

Sinai Peninsula

PERSIAN GULF

Mt. Sinai

EGYPT

Arabian Desert

Sahara

Thebes

First Cataract

UPPER EGYPT

Nile River

RED SEA

Nubian Desert

Second Cataract

GULF OF ADEN

Flood **2300**
Tower of Babel
Dispersion of mankind

2000 Call of Abraham/Golden Age of Ur
Rise of Minoan (Greece) and
Indus Valley (India) civilizations

? 4000   3000   2500   2000

Rise of Sumerian
and Egyptian
civilizations

1700 Jacob and family
journey to Egypt

1800 Hammurabi and Babylon

Note: Dates given are approximate.

Unit 1

THE BEGINNING OF WORLD HISTORY: THE ANCIENT MIDDLE EAST

(CREATION–C. 500 B.C.)

From Eden to Israel

1 The Beginning
2 From Sumer to Canaan
3 Down to Egypt
4 Israel in Its Land

• **1500** Exodus/Ten Commandments
Rise of Chinese civilization

• **1000** Israel's first king

• **722** Fall of Samaria (Israel)
to Assyrians

1500   **1000**   **500**

• **1450** Israel's conquest of Canaan

Rise of Hittite empire
Rise of Assyrian empire

• **586** Fall of Jerusalem (Judah)
to Chaldeans

1
The Beginning

Creation

The Beginning of the World

World history is a story: it had a beginning, and it will have an end. What we believe about the beginning affects how we understand history. The patterns we see, the lessons we learn, the estimates we make of the goodness or badness of men and situations—these things and more depend upon our beliefs about the beginning.

Genesis, the first book of the Bible, is the most reliable source for what we need to know about the beginning of world history. If you have read it, you have already begun to study history. The word *Genesis* means "beginning" or "origin." The book of Genesis tells us that "in the beginning God created the heaven and the earth," including the universe and man.

The Beginning of Man

Adam, whose name means "man," and **Eve,** whose name means "mother of all," were the last creations of God. In order of importance, however, they were first. God had made everything else—even the sun, moon, and stars—within view of man's habitation on Earth.

Man is special to God because he alone was created in the image of God. Man is definitely not God or "a god." Man is man. But man possesses some characteristics similar to God's that permit fellowship with God. Man's special characteristics include: **(1)** language and thought, **(2)** awareness of the difference between right and wrong, and **(3)** freedom to make choices.

We must never forget man's special characteristics in our study of world history. No plant or animal possesses these characteristics. We can have a kind of relationship with one another that no other creatures can share. Most important, we can relate to God in a way that no other part of creation can.

Our freedom to make choices is also important. Men are responsible for what they have done in history. How we choose to use language and thought and how we choose between right and wrong make "all the difference in the world."

The first human beings were highly intelligent. Adam, for example, classified all the varieties of animals, giving each kind a name. He knew language well; it was he who named his wife so appropriately as the mother of all. Of course, the pair could have learned much more. Because of their direct and frequent fellowship with God, what God might have chosen to reveal to them about the workings of the universe can only be imagined.

Adam and Eve lived at peace with one another and in a relationship of perfect equality. They were not disturbed with quarrels provoked by jealousy and selfishness, for they did not know these sins.

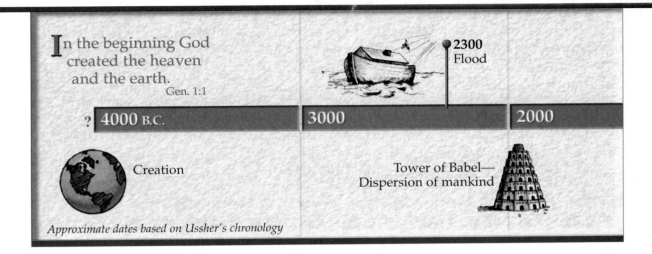

In the beginning God created the heaven and the earth.
Gen. 1:1

2300 Flood

? **4000** B.C.   **3000**   **2000**

Creation

Tower of Babel—
Dispersion of mankind

Approximate dates based on Ussher's chronology

They could always reach complete agreement on any matter because evil desires did not interfere with their cool powers of reason. They could share equally in all matters of decision.

God placed all of creation under the dominion of man. The world was his to rule, not to waste or destroy, but to develop for the benefit of mankind. God expected this dominion to be great, for He specifically commanded Adam and Eve to be fruitful and multiply and fill (populate) the earth.

We can only guess what the results would have been had Adam and Eve continued to obey God. World history as we know it resulted from a choice that Adam and Eve made.

Rebellion

The Beginning of Human Sin

God the Creator laid down but one command to Adam and Eve. They were not to eat the fruit of the tree of the knowledge of good and evil. If they ate the fruit, they would die.

But Satan appeared to Eve in the form of a serpent and tempted her to eat of the forbidden fruit. She yielded to the temptation, and Adam followed suit. Adam and

Eve had committed <u>the first human sin</u>. They had rebelled against God. Discontented with being creatures made in the image of God, they wanted to be as God themselves.

God could not turn His back on what had happened. As a just God—and, as we will see, a loving God—He punished the man and the woman.

Paradise was lost, and the world took on many important characteristics familiar to us. Perfect equality ended; now the husband would rule his wife. Childbirth would be painful. Work would be tedious and difficult. Rather than leisurely plucking fruit from the limbs of trees in a thriving garden, man would have to plow and plant in ground that more easily grew weeds and thorns than food. Man's greatest punishment was to be driven from the garden and from the fruit of the tree of eternal life. Henceforth, men would die.

From this original choice of sin has flowed a story of crimes and tears, the actual world history we have known. All who have lived have also sinned. The work of evil has continued, and Satan's power through temptation has grown. In the beginning, there was perfection. Since the beginning, man has fallen to ever greater depths of rebellion against God.

A Different Story of the Beginning

The story of evolution. The extreme of man's rebellion against God is the denial of the Bible's teaching that God is the Creator of man. According to the story of **evolution,** man was not created directly by God but instead "evolved" from the animals. Evolutionists say that at some point in history certain animals began accidentally changing in ways that eventually produced a man. This idea has many weaknesses, however. It cannot explain the beginning of world history, and it gives a false impression of man.

Logic's traps for evolution. We have seen that man differs from animals in that man possesses language and thought. Anyone who believes that man evolved from animals must explain how language and reason began. But such an explanation cannot be given, for it is a question of "chickens and eggs—which came first?"

Human thought requires language. Much of our thinking is in words. When we think, it is as if we listen to ourselves talk inside our heads. Language, on the other hand, requires thought. Unless there is thought behind the sounds called language or speech, what comes out is mere gibberish. Which came first, language or thought?

Without language and the ability to communicate with one another, there would be no truly human society. Instead of society, we would have a mere herd or swarm. But language and communication assumes men living together in society. Which came first, society or language?

Genesis, of course, does not have these problems of logic. It presents man as <u>the direct creation of God</u> and from the very first having all three—language, thought, and society.

Evolution, humanism, and the destruction of man. The evolutionist's only escape from logic is to downplay man's special characteristics. Thus, he will underrate man's speech and reason. As for language, the evolutionist will say that the animals have it, or at least something very close. Thought, he says, is really nothing more than a process of electricity and chemistry. The evolutionist will also attack man's awareness of the difference between right and wrong and man's freedom to choose, for he cannot explain the evolution of these characteristics. The awareness of right and wrong is just something we learn, he says, not something we are born with, and man's freedom to choose is just an illusion. To an evolutionist, man is really nothing more than a computer made of flesh and bone, and not a very fast one at that.

Do you begin to see the consequences of rebelling against God? Do you begin to see the result of **humanism,** *putting man in place of or above God?* Not God but man is hurt. When man tries to be God, he only succeeds in making himself like an animal or a machine.

The Bible's account of the beginning elevates God. It also elevates man, but not at God's expense. Humanism, whether in the guise of evolution or of some other view, tries to build man up by downplaying or ignoring God. It rebels against God but utterly destroys man by making him no different from an animal or a machine.

Cain and the First Murder

Cain's crime. The evil consequences of rebellion against God became obvious even in the first two sons of Adam and Eve when **Cain,** who placed his own opinion of what is good above God's, killed his brother **Abel** in a fit of jealousy and hatred. God was quick to punish Cain by sending him away from the land of his father to live as a wanderer. God had not yet laid down the penalty of capital punishment for murder, the requirement that a man who murders should himself suffer death.

Cain's culture. Cain lived on to father a line of descendants who built a culture in rebellion against God. A **culture** is *the way of life of a group of people.* Cultures include how people make a living for themselves. Cain's descendants engaged in a variety of occupations, learning, for example, how to use the earth's metals to make tools of iron and bronze (a mixture of copper and tin). Cultures also include art and music. Cain's descendants learned to make and play musical instruments. Their accomplishments were indeed very impressive.

The most important part of culture is <u>how people relate to God</u>. The descendants of Cain were growing in knowledge and abilities, but they were also growing in rebellion against God—a pattern we will often see in world history. Their evil deeds toward one another were increasingly violent. By the fourth generation, a man named **Lamech** bragged openly of killing a man who had wounded him and a boy who had merely struck him.

Seth and Continued Hope

Cain's descendants continued to grow in numbers and in evil, but they did not have the entire earth to themselves. After the murder of Abel and God's banishment of Cain, Adam and Eve had another son named **Seth.** Seth and his descendants were not perfect, but some of them were at least aware of their sin and inclined to repent. They recognized that God is God and that man is man, the creation of God.

In world history, however, *Cain's way or culture tends to be the stronger among men.* Fifteen hundred years after Seth's birth, God could find but one man that He could view with favor. This man, **Noah,** became the only hope for the continued existence of the human race.

---CHECK UP---

1. Why do we begin our study of world history with the book of Genesis?
2. Why is man special to God?
3. List three special characteristics of man.
4. What was the first human sin? What impact did it have on world history?
5. What is a culture?
6. What is the most important part of a culture?
7. Which culture tends to be stronger in world history, Cain's or Seth's?

Identify: Adam and Eve, evolution, humanism, Cain, Abel, Seth

A Chance for a New Beginning

The Flood

By the time of Noah, the earth was so filled with evil that God in His justice could no longer tolerate it. Thus, God decided to destroy mankind with a great flood.

The human race exists today only because God warned Noah of the coming destruction. God instructed Noah to build an ark so that he and his wife and his three sons and their wives could escape the Flood. In faith, Noah obeyed the Word of

Mt. Ararat: After the Flood, Noah's ark came to rest on this mountain in modern Turkey.

Shortly after the dispersion of mankind from the tower of Babel, civilizations arose in Europe, Asia, and Africa.

God and became one of the greatest figures of world history, for without Noah's faith, world history would have come to an abrupt end.

After the Flood, Noah and his family came out of the ark, together with the animals God had instructed Noah to save. Man had a chance for a new beginning, but it was not a return to paradise. Living conditions were worse than ever before. Great changes had occurred in the land and the climate. There was hostility between man and the animals. Most important, men, even Noah, still had a sin nature.

God placed a beautiful rainbow in the sky as a symbol of the promise He made to Noah and his descendants that He would never again destroy all life on the earth with a great flood. At the same time, God also reassured man of his special place in the creation. God had not forgotten that man is the one creature He made in His own image. To teach man the sanctity of human life, God Himself established the law of *capital punishment* (the death penalty) for murder and ordained that man set up systems of law and justice for the restraint of evil.

Man had another chance to build a culture in submission to God. As the population increased rapidly, however, the vast majority of men chose to build not with God but against Him. Men had learned little from the Flood, the greatest catastrophe the human race has ever known. Many ancient writings from all over the world affirm the reality of the Flood, but only the Bible makes it clear why the Flood took place: it says that *the Flood was God's punishment for the height of evil man had reached.* Rebellion against God reached a new peak soon after the Flood, and God again intervened with enormous consequences for world history.

The Beginning of Nations

The tower of Babel. All human beings born after the flood are descendants of Noah's three sons—**Shem, Ham,** and

8

Japheth. The survivors of the Flood and their descendants gradually migrated southeastward from the mountains in which the ark had come to rest and settled in a plain called **Shinar** [shī'nẽr], also known in world history as *Sumer.*

Nimrod, a descendant of Noah's son Ham, emerged as the leader of the group. With his reputation as a mighty hunter and as a rebel against God, ambitious Nimrod "began to be a mighty one in the earth" (Gen. 10:8). He eventually became the supreme ruler of eight cities. At a time when "the whole earth was of one language" (Gen. 11:1) and all people lived in one small area, Nimrod in effect ruled the world.

Under Nimrod's leadership, the people who had come together in Shinar began to build the city of **Babel,** later known as **Babylon.** In the midst of it, they began to construct a tower reaching far up into the sky. Nimrod and his followers were humanists. Defying God's commandment to replenish the earth, they declared "let us make us a name, lest we be scattered abroad upon the face of the whole earth" (Gen. 11:4).

Many languages. God's response to these men was simply to confuse their one language. Miraculously, He <u>caused all the people</u> (except perhaps within extended families) <u>to speak different languages</u>. Nimrod's dominion collapsed without the bond of a common language, for the people were no longer able to live and work together. Thus, the people dispersed across the earth, taking their many languages with them.

Many nations. Language is one of the chief sources of difference and division in the human race. A common language encourages a group of people to think of themselves as a unit or a nation and not just a collection of individuals. A **nation** is *a large group of people who think of themselves as one and act in history as a unit.*

The division of the human race into many nations has had many consequences. World history has been marked with wars and international strife. Imagine what the human race could have accomplished if, from the Flood until now, all men had worked together for their mutual good.

Because of the fall into sin at the beginning of world history, however, it is good that God saw fit to slow down the growth of human power. Without the division of mankind into nations, nothing would have been "restrained from them, which they have imagined to do" (Gen. 11:6).

Check Up

1. Why did God send the Flood?
2. How much did man learn from the Flood?
3. What are two names for the place where the survivors of the Flood settled?
4. What event resulted in the confusion of languages and the dispersion of people into many nations?
5. What is a nation?

Identify: Noah, Babel, Nimrod

The Legacy of Babel

After the dispersion from Babel, towerlike structures arose in several different areas of the world. In Sumer, the location of the original tower, huge ziggurats [zĭg′ o͞o·răts] reached into the sky at a very early date. Not long after, in Egypt, towering pyramids began to be erected. Even in faraway South America the ancient Mayas [mä′yɑz] built soaring structures combining the basic shape of pyramids with features of ziggurats such as stairways.

The striking similarity of such buildings is just what we would expect to find, based on the Bible's teaching that all of the cultures on the earth are the result of a dispersion from one original center of culture.

The Bible gives no details about the design of the tower of Babel. With the actual structure having long ago vanished into the mists of the past, we can only guess about its appearance. To many people, it seems likely that the tower resembled the later ziggurats in the same area, but no one knows for sure. Perhaps the tower looked more like the Egyptian pyramids or even the Mayan buildings. On the other hand, nothing in the Bible's description of the tower rules out the possibility that it resembled some of our modern skyscrapers or even the gantry for a rocket launching!

CHAPTER 1 REVIEW

COMPLETION *Choose the correct name to complete each sentence and write the letter in the blank.*

a Abel	*e* Ham	*i* Noah
b Adam	*f* Japheth	*j* Seth
c Cain	*g* Lamech	*k* Shem
d Eve	*h* Nimrod	*l* Shinar

1. The very first man was ____; his name means "man."

2. The first woman was ____; her name means "mother of all."

3. The first person murdered was ____.

4. God doomed ____ to live as a wanderer because of his sin.

5. Man's rebellion against God can be well seen in the life of ____, who bragged about the murders he had committed.

6. Some of the descendants of ____ were at least aware of their sins.

7. The man who obeyed God, built the ark, and with his family escaped God's judgment of the world was ____.

8. Three brothers who repopulated the world after the Flood were ____, ____, and ____.

9. A mighty hunter named ____ encouraged the people to build the tower of Babel.

10. The city of Babylon was located on the plain of ____.

CONCEPT TO CONSIDER *On a separate sheet of paper, answer the following question using complete sentences.*

Why do you suppose God confused man's language and dispersed mankind across the face of the earth?

MULTIPLE CHOICE *Write the letter of the answer that best completes each sentence.*

1. *Genesis* means ____.
   a creation   *c* history
   b beginning   *d* out of nothing

2. The idea that denies that God created man is called ____.
   a origins   *c* history
   b evolution   *d* logic

3. Putting man in place of or above God is called ____.
   a evolution   *c* humanism
   b history   *d* logic

4. The way of life of a group of people is called a ____.
   a culture   *c* city
   b society   *d* nation

5. A group of people who think of themselves as one and act in history as a unit may be called a ____.
   a culture   *c* city
   b society   *d* nation

TIME LINE CHALLENGE *Number the events in the order in which they happened.*

____ Beginning of nations

____ The first murder

____ Creation of the world

____ Building of the tower of Babel

____ The first human sin

____ Birth of Adam's third son

____ Creation of man

2
From Sumer to Canaan
(c. 2300–1700 B.C.)

HIGHLIGHTS

Sumerian Civilization • Call of Abraham
Hammurabi and Babylon • Patriarchs in Canaan

Sumer

Abraham's Call

Man's rebellion during the earliest times, from the fall into sin to the tower of Babel, did not cause God to stop loving the creatures made in His image. God planned to save man from sin and its consequences.

God's plan for mankind provides a thread to follow through history.

We need guidance because the **dispersion** of mankind, *the scattering of people over the earth,* complicates the study of world history. So many people in so many places cannot all be studied at the same time. By focusing on God's plan, we see how history leads to Jesus Christ. God first chose a special nation out of which Christ would come.

The story begins in the ancient **Middle East,** a part of the world where the continents of Africa, Asia, and Europe meet, when God selected one man, **Abraham,** to become <u>the father of the nation of Israel.</u> Abraham, a descendent of Noah's son Shem, was living with his wife and other relatives in the city of **Ur** around 2000 B.C. when God told him to leave and journey to a new land. Ur was one of the most important cities in the land of **Sumer.**

The Land of Sumer

The fertile crescent. Sumer was part of an area in the Middle East known as the **fertile crescent** because of *its ability to grow crops and because its shape resembles a crescent moon.* Its fertility contrasted greatly with the desert in the south and the mountains and plateaus in the north. (The Mediterranean Sea lay on its the western side, the Persian Gulf on its eastern side.)

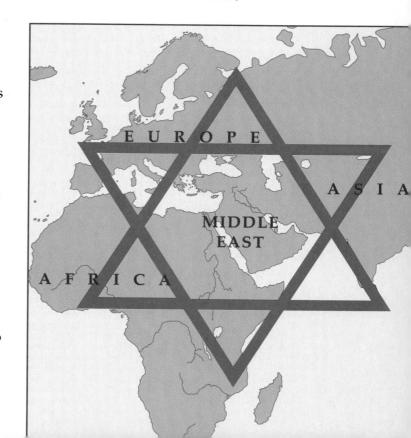

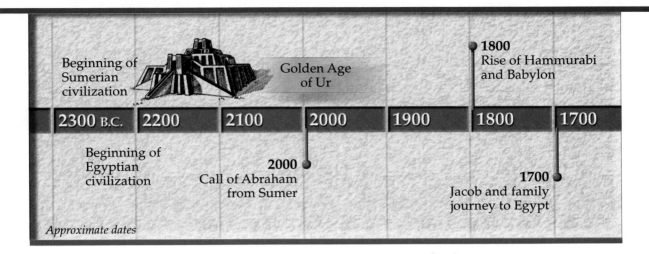

Beginning of
Sumerian
civilization

Golden Age
of Ur

1800
Rise of Hammurabi
and Babylon

2300 B.C.	2200	2100	2000	1900	1800	1700

Beginning of
Egyptian
civilization

2000
Call of Abraham
from Sumer

1700
Jacob and family
journey to Egypt

Approximate dates

The eastern part of the crescent, where Sumer lay, did not owe its fertility to great rainfall. The average rainfall in Sumer provided far too little water for growing crops. Two great rivers, the **Tigris** [tī′grĭs] and the **Euphrates** [û·frā′tēz], made the land fertile. *Tigris* means "arrow"; the river got its name because it flows almost as "straight as an arrow" out of the mountains of the north until it empties into the Persian Gulf. *Euphrates* means "that makes fruitful," certainly an appropriate name for this river.

What Are Years B.C.?

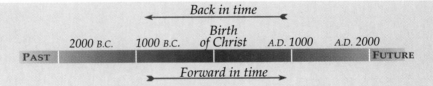

Back in time

2000 B.C.   1000 B.C.   *Birth of Christ*   A.D. 1000   A.D. 2000

PAST   FUTURE

Forward in time

The main division in history is between years B.C. and years A.D. **B.C.** means *before the birth of Christ.* The further *back* in history before the birth of Christ, the higher the B.C. year numbers will be. **A.D.** is an abbreviation for the Latin words ANNO DOMINI, meaning *"in the year of our Lord."* The further *forward* in history after the birth of Christ, the higher the A.D. year numbers will be.

It is sometimes difficult to pick a specific year marking a great change or dividing line in history. Things do not always "happen in a day." Also, our information about history may not be complete. We may have to say "about" or "around" for a date. The *c.* that you will often see before dates stands for *circa* [sûr′kə], Latin for "approximately."

The division of time into years B.C. and years A.D. reflects the fact that Christ's first coming was the greatest turning point in world history.

HARAN

CARCHEMISH

EBLA

UGARIT

MEDITERRANEAN SEA

SIDON

TYRE

DAN

MEGIDDO

SEA OF GALILEE

CANAAN

JORDAN R.

JERICHO

DEAD SEA

BEER-SHEBA

EGYPT

NILE R.

SINAI

RED SEA

FROM SUMER
TO CANAAN
THE
FERTILE CRESCENT

CITIES

FERTILE LAND

Mesopotamia. The 180,000 square mile area between and immediately around these rivers became known as **Mesopotamia** [měs′ō·pŏ·tā′mĭ·ə], meaning "land between the rivers." At the time of Abraham, lower Mesopotamia consisted of Akkad and Sumer. Sumer lay between Akkad and the Persian Gulf in a region the Bible calls *Shinar,* where the tower of Babel was built.

The People of Sumer

The Sumerians were probably the descendants of those who stayed in the general vicinity of the tower after the dispersion. Perhaps the ambitious Nimrod remained, stubbornly refusing to depart from what had been his kingdom of cities. If Nimrod, a descendant of Ham, was their ancestor, the Sumerians were a **Hamitic** people.

The Akkadian king **Sargon** [sär′gŏn] the Great conquered the Sumerians. The Akkadians ruled Sumer for about 200 years. The Sumerians were the real conquerors, however, for their way of life so impressed the Akkadians that they adopted everything but the Sumerian language.

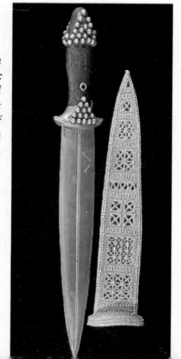

Sumerian Gold Dagger: This dagger and its sheath exhibit the great skill of Sumerian craftsmen.

---CHECK UP---

1. What is the thread that we can follow through world history?
2. How does the dispersion make studying history more difficult?
3. Where was Abraham living when God called him to a new land around 2000 B.C.?
4. What does B.C. stand for? What does A.D. mean? What does a *c.* before a date indicate?
5. What event is the greatest turning point of history?
6. Explain the term *fertile crescent.* What made the eastern part of the region fertile?
7. Why was Mesopotamia a good name for the eastern part of the fertile crescent? Explain the names of two main rivers in this region.

Identify: dispersion, Middle East, Shinar, Hamitic, Sargon

A Cradle of Culture

Sumer became a cradle for culture after the dispersion. The few people who stayed in Sumer after the dispersion no doubt retained old knowledge and skills. The Sumerians, building upon the past, could quickly develop an impressive culture.

Irrigation, cooperation, and kingship. By constructing canals, dams, and dikes for irrigation and flood control, the Sumerians conquered the Tigris and Euphrates rivers and made the land fertile. Only by working together could they construct such complex water-control systems. The organization of many people into cities gave the strength, skill, and knowledge that come from cooperation. As in earlier construction projects such as the tower of Babel, successful cooperation in irrigation required discipline and leadership. Some people had to rule, and others had to be ruled. Kingship was the earliest form of government; one-man government provided the greatest unity. Sumerian kings

Sumerian Wheel: Few modern machines do not in some way depend upon the wheel. The Sumerians were the first people in world history known to have used it.

Sumerian Measurements and Statistics: Writing was the Sumerians' greatest accomplishment. Thousands of their clay tablets with cuneiform writing have survived the centuries.

naturally took much credit themselves for the great benefits of the canals.

Other accomplishments. Few machines do not in some way depend upon the **wheel,** and the Sumerians were the first people in world history known to have used it. Our system of dividing time also comes from the Sumerians. Their numbering system, based on the number 60, underlies our division of hours into 60 minutes and minutes into 60 seconds. The Sumerians carefully observed the skies. Studying the phases of the moon in relation to the sun's different positions in the sky, they discovered what months and years are. In the arts and crafts, too, the Sumerians reached far beyond the simple or primitive. Their workmanship in some things has never been surpassed.

Writing—the greatest accomplishment. Writing was the Sumerians' greatest accomplishment. Whether men before the Flood could write is not certain, but the Sumerians appear to have been <u>the first people *after* the Flood to have used writing</u>. Abraham may have taken some knowledge of writing with him when he left Ur. The Sumerians wrote on clay tablets with a stick or *stylus* shaped in such a way that the markings had a wedgelike appearance. This *wedge-shaped writing* is called **cuneiform** [kŭ·nē′*i*·fôrm]. Cuneiform writing remained dominant in much of the Middle East long after the Sumerians had ceased to exist as an independent people.

The Sumerians left a written record of their way of life which greatly impressed and influenced later peoples. Thousands of clay tablets record business transactions, taxation, and other civil affairs. Some reveal the Sumerians' basic beliefs about God and themselves.

Basic Beliefs of the Sumerians

A polytheistic religion. However impressive Sumerian culture might have been, the Sumerians had not learned the lessons of the Flood or of the tower of Babel. They had lost the knowledge of the one true God and His purposes. When God called Abraham out of the land of Sumer, it was a summons to separate from the many false beliefs of the Sumerians.

The Sumerians were **polytheists** [pŏl′ĭ·thē·ĭsts: *worshipers of many gods*]. Unlike the **monotheist** [mŏn′ō·thē·ĭst: *worshiper of one god*] Abraham, they believed in the existence of more than one god, indeed of very many gods. Forgetting that the one personal God created everything in nature, the Sumerians personified (thought of as persons) forces of nature such as wind and rain or objects of nature such as the sky, sun, and moon, and worshiped them as gods.

Sumerian humanism. The Sumerians were also **humanists,** for they had <u>made men into gods</u>, changing "the glory of the uncorruptible God into an image made like corruptible man . . ." (Rom. 1:23). Abraham believed that men were created in the image of God by God, but the Sumerian gods were created in the image of men by men.

The Sumerians made their gods resemble humans in actions as well as in appearance. Unlike Abraham's God of infinite perfection and power, the Sumerian gods displayed petty jealousy, envy, and fear. **Anu** [ä′nōō], the god of the sky, supposedly ruled the other gods but, much like a human ruler, was constantly threatened by rebellion. These imagined gods met annually to decide what they would cause to happen on the earth for the rest of the year. A dissenting god might plot against a decision. These false beliefs had a powerful influence on the lives of the Sumerian people.

How the Sumerians Tried to Serve Their Gods

Cities and ziggurats. Believing that men had been created to serve these powerful gods who could bring good or bad things upon them, the Sumerians strove to please their gods. Each Sumerian city supposedly belonged to a god; the purpose of a city was to serve its god.

The most important parts of Sumerian cities were the **ziggurats** [zĭg′ōō·răts], *towers built in tiers or stages, each stage smaller than the one beneath, all atop a large mound of clay or debris.* Atop the ziggurats, Sumerians tried to reach up to heaven to offer thanks, praises, and sacrifices to their gods. The ziggurats were large and designed to impress the imaginary Sumerian gods. The ziggurat at Ur during Abraham's day was 200 feet long, 150 feet wide, 70 feet high, and crowned with a shrine to the moon god *Nanna.*

Kings, religion, and politics. Each city had a king who ruled over the people of the city but also served as a slave of the city's god. Pictures of King **Ur-Nammu** [ōōr′năm′mōō] of Ur, for example, show him as a worker building the ziggurat. The source of the king's power over other men was the special relationship that he was believed to have with the god of the city. Using religion as a political tool, the king demanded obedience by claiming to be the particular slave favored by the god. Anyone who refused to support the king risked bringing the god's wrath upon the whole city.

Business, commerce, taxes. Sumerian temples also served as commercial and business centers. The god of the city owned everything, including agricultural production. Farmers brought offerings to the temple, while a host of craftsmen worked in the temple making things to please the god and, of course, the god's chief servant.

Struggle between cities. The Sumerians also tried to imitate their gods. For example, kings often aspired to rule over other cities, just as some gods wished to rule over other gods. As a result, there was continual warfare between the cities of Sumer.

Hope. The Sumerians' vain efforts to elevate themselves by building a great society without God was the first of world history's many repetitions of the mistake made at the tower of Babel. Yet Sumer

Ziggurat of Ur: Ur's ziggurat may have looked like this in Abraham's day.

was the scene of an event in a new chain of hope. One man in Sumer, Abraham, believed in and obeyed the one true God and began a journey toward the land of God's promise.

Abraham's Faith

Although Abraham left behind an impressive culture, he received from God much more. God promised Abraham that his name would be great, for he would be the father of a great nation—a nation that would be a blessing to the whole world. God would protect and defend it, cursing its enemies and blessing its friends.

Abraham believed God and began a journey of faith. He did not know precisely where he would settle, and he must have feared the unknown dangers of the land he was entering. There were to be many trials of Abraham's faith, as indeed there have been for the faith of the nation he fathered. But Abraham's faith would lay the foundation for a new alternative to the Sumerian pattern of rebellion against God that continued in Mesopotamia.

Hammurabi's Babylonian Empire

Empires in Babylonia

A few hundred years after Abraham's departure from Mesopotamia, the city of **Babylon** became the center of a new **empire** (*rule by one city or people over other cities or peoples*). So impressive was this and later empires centered there that Sumer and the surrounding lands became known as *Babylonia* [băb′ĭ•lō′nĭ•ə].

Babylon, the city of the original tower of Babel, has always symbolized the world's alternative to building a culture on foundations of godly obedience and faith.

Before we follow Abraham around the fertile crescent to Canaan, let us see what happened in Babylonia from about 2000 B.C. to 1500 B.C.

Hammurabi

The rise of Babylon. Since the dispersion of mankind, Babylon had not been a very important city. Other cities such as Ur had commanded empires. The Sumerian empire centered at Ur ended around the 1900s B.C. when Amorites from the west and Elamites from the east invaded. Some time after the fall of Ur, a group of Amorites established a kingdom at Babylon and began to extend their power over nearby cities. With the great cities of *Mari* to the north and *Larsa* to the south, however, Babylon's future remained uncertain.

An extraordinary man. The city's situation changed drastically around 1800 B.C. when a king named **Hammurabi** [häm′ oo•rä′bē] came to the throne of Babylon. In just 31 years, this extraordinary leader conquered the surrounding kingdoms and united all of Mesopotamia under his rule.

Hammurabi's bureaucracy. Hammurabi personally supervised the details of his vast empire with the help of his bureaucracy. A **bureaucracy** is *an organized group of people appointed by a ruler to help him govern.* Knowing he could not be in more than one place at a time, Hammurabi appointed men to act as his representatives throughout the empire. He stayed in constant touch with these officials through the writing of letters.

Deceitful politics. Hammurabi's letters also played a role in the building of his empire. He often wrote to other kings who were not yet under his control. "Smart like a fox," Hammurabi built his empire through lies and deceit. For example, for 20 years he kept the king of Larsa off guard with letters expressing great affection for him. When the opportunity came to conquer Larsa, however, Hammurabi enjoyed a quick victory.

Hammurabi:
This clay figure
is believed to
represent the
crafty king of
Babylon.

HAMMURABI'S BABYLONIAN EMPIRE

Hammurabi's pride. Hammurabi's empire did benefit many people. Living conditions improved in many ways, business and trade increased through construction of highways and the establishment of a postal service, and improved canals increased the amount of land available for farming. However, Hammurabi's real goal was to increase his own power, to elevate and glorify himself. We can see Hammurabi's selfishness in the collection of laws for which he is best remembered.

CHECK UP

1. What was the Sumerians' greatest accomplishment?
2. What is the difference between a polytheist and a monotheist?
3. How did the Sumerian gods differ from the one true God?
4. Why did the Sumerians strive to please their gods?
5. How could a Sumerian king demand the obedience of his subjects?
6. Why did war and struggle exist between Sumerian cities?
7. What was God's promise to Abraham, and what did Abraham's faith begin?
8. Which city was the center of the great empire that rose up a few hundred years after Abraham's time?
9. Who became king of Babylon and united all of Mesopotamia under his rule?

Identify: wheel, stylus, cuneiform, humanist, Anu, Nanna, Ur-Nammu, ziggurat, empire, Babylonia, bureaucracy

---

Hammurabi's Laws

Laws with divine support. Hammurabi had his laws carved on a large stone pillar about six feet high. Toward the top was a picture of Hammurabi receiving the right to give laws from the sun god *Shamash* [shä'mäsh]. In words under the picture, Hammurabi confirmed that indeed the gods had chosen him to give these laws to the people. Hammurabi was one of the first lawgivers to see the importance of claiming divine authority for his work, but he was certainly not the last.

Laws that were written down. Beneath the introductory words on the stone, Hammurabi had almost 300 laws carved. **Laws** are <u>rules people follow in living together</u>. Without such rules people could not live together at all. Living without laws would be like trying to play a game without rules. Consider how important it is that all the players in a game know the rules. It is unfair to blame anyone for not following a rule if he was not told the rules in advance of the game. Also, unless everyone knows and agrees upon the rules in advance, there will likely be many quarrels. The worst thing, of course, is to try to play a game and make up the rules as you go along.

By having the laws written down for the people, Hammurabi showed great wisdom and understanding about the nature of laws. He wisely saw the necessity of **promulgation,** <u>making the laws known</u>. Hammurabi had the laws written down and set up in a place where everyone could see them. Ignorance of the law could not be an excuse for disobedience.

Imperfect laws. Just as it is not enough in games to have merely *any* rules, it is not enough in life to have merely *any* laws. We need *right* and *just* rules and laws. In this respect, Hammurabi's laws were far from perfect. This is obvious when they are compared to the laws that God gave his people through Moses centuries later.

God always makes the punishment fit the crime, but Hammurabi did not. Hammurabi put a much lower value on human life; in his laws, material possessions were the most important things. Hammurabi also failed to recognize the necessity for **equality under the law,** which means that <u>all people who commit the same crime should be punished in the same way</u>. Hammurabi's laws called for different punishments according to whether the criminal was rich or poor or whether the victim of a crime was rich or poor. Later in our study of world history, we will see *why* the laws God gave through Moses were so much better than Hammurabi's laws.

Hammurabi and the Gods

The culture of Sumer changed little during Hammurabi's Babylonian empire. Some advances were made in arithmetic and astronomy, elaborate new dictionaries improved the language, and Babylon became an impressive city, with great palaces and temples. But most of the Sumerians' basic beliefs about the gods continued, in spite of the foreign conquests that had occurred and would occur again. The invading peoples adopted the same gods, merely renaming them. For example, the Sumerian goddess of love, *Inanna* [ən·än′ə], was renamed *Ishtar* [ĭsh′tär]. The gods remained basically the same; therefore, the people's behavior, based on belief in these gods, also remained much the same.

One extremely important change in the beliefs about the gods did occur. *Marduk* [mär′dook], the chief god of the city of Babylon, suddenly became the king of all

Hammurabi's Laws: Hammurabi had this picture of himself and the sun god Shamash carved atop the stone pillar with his laws.

the gods. This change did much to elevate Babylon in the eyes of the people. To oppose Babylon or Hammurabi invited disfavor in the eyes of Marduk, the king of the gods.

The Fall of Hammurabi's Babylonian Empire

Hammurabi ruled for 42 years, beginning around 1800 B.C. But the kings that followed were unable to hold on to the empire that Hammurabi had built and maintained. Attackers from the outside struck repeatedly. In the 1500s B.C., the city of Babylon itself fell into enemy hands.

The great rock upon which Hammurabi's laws were carved was eventually buried and forgotten. Not until A.D. 1901 was it uncovered. This rock stands in a museum today as one of the few reminders of the great Hammurabi and his empire. How very different are the reminders we have of Abraham, who followed God's call to a strange land, believing the promise that he would father a great nation.

The Patriarchs in Canaan

The Land of Canaan

The land to which God led Abraham was called **Canaan.** Located at the western end of the fertile crescent beside the Mediterranean Sea, Canaan was the center of the ancient world. Through it passed the trade routes between Mesopotamia and Egypt and also the road between Egypt and Asia Minor. Canaan was a main route of conquest as well as of trade. Armies of competing world powers often crossed through it or met in battle there.

Canaan's central location shows God's awareness of the importance of geography in history. From ancient times, through the time of Christ, and to the present day, Canaan (also known as Israel or Palestine) has had a central and strategic position in the world. It has always been subject to invasion and has had a history of wars and strife. The Bible points to a valley in Israel called **Megiddo** [mĕ·gĭd′ō], or **Armageddon** [är′mə·gĕd′un], as the last battleground of world history.

Israel's Founding Fathers

The **Patriarchs** [pā′trĭ·ärks]—*Abraham,* his son *Isaac,* and his grandson *Jacob*—lived in Canaan for a total of 230 years. God's promises to Abraham passed first to Isaac and then to Jacob. These three men were the founding fathers of Israel, the most unusual and important nation in world history.

During the time of the Patriarchs, **Israel,** as Abraham's descendants came to be known, was simply a large family. Before becoming a **nation-state,** *a nation or a people living in its own land with its own government,* Israel would endure a long period of slavery in Egypt, where it would grow from a large family into a nation.

The People of Canaan

Many peoples in Canaan. Canaan was named after one of its inhabitants, Canaan the son of Ham. The Canaanites consisted of many peoples such as the *Amorites, Hittites, Kenites, Jebusites,* and others. Canaan had no single center of political or military power. This lack of a central unified government in Canaan made it easier for Israel to develop as a nation during the time of the Patriarchs and to establish a nation-state after her years in Egypt.

Worshipers of pleasure. In spite of all their diversity, the Canaanites had in common the worship of a host of false deities, some 70 in number. The gods of the Canaanites were, if possible, worse than those that Abraham had left behind in Sumer and Mesopotamia. **Baal** was *the chief god of the Canaanites.* They imagined him as a rider in the clouds, identifying him with storms, and associated him with sex. The Canaanites' "worship" consisted of wild dances and rituals, including the sacrifice of human beings, even babies.

The Canaanites were worshipers of pleasure. Their gods inspired a life devoted to the satisfaction of lust. In the

The Valley of Megiddo (Jezreel): The last great battle of history will take place in this valley.

cities of *Sodom* and *Gomorrah,* the evils of the flesh reached such extremes that God destroyed the cities with fire and brimstone. Over time, the evils of the Canaanites grew worse. When the Israelites returned from Egypt, God would, with full justice, take the land away from the evil Canaanites and give it to His chosen people.

The Godliness of the Patriarchs

Like most of the people in Canaan, the Patriarchs were *nomads,* wandering herdsmen with no permanent home. They also followed many of the same customs as the Canaanites in matters of inheritance, marriage contracts, children, and land.

Only their recognition of the one true God made the Patriarchs stand out from the Canaanites.

Although some members of their families began following the Canaanite religion of pleasure, the Patriarchs themselves always maintained their faith in the promises of God and enjoyed a unique relationship with God. Everyone who dealt with them quickly saw that the Patriarchs were special people, to be harmed only at great risk. Abraham, for example, used a few hundred men to defeat the armies of kings from the east who had previously devastated the Canaanites in battle.

The Humanity of the Patriarchs

It should not be surprising that the Patriarchs and their children were humans who sinned and suffered the consequences.

Our study of the Patriarchs in Canaan closes with terrible sin among the 12 sons of Jacob, the fathers of the 12 tribes of Israel. As a consequence of their great jealousy for Jacob's favorite son **Joseph,** ten of the brothers sold him into slavery.

Abraham, Isaac, and Jacob were nevertheless three of the most important men in history. They are not remembered for superhuman perfection, or for achievements such as Hammurabi's, but for their godly lives and their special legacy to mankind through Israel. From Sumer to Canaan, the Patriarchs were shining examples of faith to a world in rebellion against God.

CHECK UP

1. Who supposedly authorized Hammurabi to be a lawgiver?
2. What are laws? Why is it important that laws be written down?
3. Did Hammurabi's laws treat the rich and poor the same? Explain.
4. How did Hammurabi use religion as a political tool?
5. Who are the Patriarchs? How long did they live in Canaan?
6. What is a nation-state?
7. How did the lack of a central, unified government in Canaan help Israel?
8. Give one example of God's judgment on the lustful people of Canaan.
9. What one thing made the Patriarchs stand out from the Canaanites?
10. How were the Patriarchs similar to the Canaanites? How did they differ?

Identify: promulgation, Megiddo, Armageddon, Baal, Joseph

CHAPTER 2 REVIEW

MULTIPLE CHOICE Write the letter of the answer that best completes each sentence.

1. God chose _____ to become the father of the nation of Israel.
   a Moses   c Isaac
   b Abraham   d Jacob

2. Abraham lived in the Sumerian city of _____ until God told him to start his journey.
   a Babylon   c Mari
   b Ur   d Larsa

3. The people of _____ irrigated their land with canals and developed written language.
   a Israel   c Canaan
   b Damascus d Sumer

4. The Biblical name for the region of Sumer is _____.
   a Akkad   c Babel
   b Shinar   d Tigris

5. The name of the _____ River means "arrow."
   a Tigris   c Jordan
   b Euphrates d Nile

6. The name of the _____ River means "that makes fruitful."
   a Tigris   c Jordan
   b Euphrates d Nile

7. The name _____ means "land between rivers."
   a Sumer   c Babel
   b Akkad   d Mesopotamia

8. Sargon was the king of _____.
   a Mari   c Akkad
   b Larsa   d Sumer

9. The god of the sky, _____, supposedly ruled all the other Sumerian gods.
   a Baal   c Marduk
   b Anu   d Haran

10. The god _____ supposedly owned the city of Ur.
    a Namu   c Anu
    b Larsa   d Nanna

11. King _____ is pictured as the builder of a ziggurat.
    a Larsa   c Hammurabi
    b Ur-Nammu d Mari

12. An invasion by the _____ brought the Sumerian empire to an end in the 1900s B.C.
    a Hittites c Akkadians
    b Chaldeans d Amorites and Elamites

13. King _____ united all of Mesopotamia under a single empire.
    a Ur-Nammu c Hammurabi
    b Sargon   d Marduk

14. The city of _____ was the capital of this empire.
    a Babylon c Gomorrah
    b Sodom   d Ur

15. The sun god _____ supposedly gave Hammurabi authority to make his code of laws.
    a Shamash c Marduk
    b Nanna   d Ishtar

16. The chief god of Babylon who became the king of all the gods was _____.
    a Anu   c Marduk
    b Ishtar   d Shamash

17. The valley of _____, also called Armageddon, will be the last battleground of world history.
    a Canaan   c Akkad
    b Megiddo d Sumer

18. The chief god of the Canaanites was _____.
    a Anu   c Marduk
    b Baal   d Shamash

COMPLETION Write the term(s) that will best complete each sentence.

1. The study of history is complicated by the _____ of mankind which occurred after the confusion of tongues at Babel.

2. The _____ was an arch-shaped stretch of land that was an excellent place for growing crops.

3. The Sumerians were the first people known to have used the _____, a simple device which is now used by everyone almost every day.

4. Wedge-shaped _____ writing provided the world with perhaps the first written language.

5. The land of _____ was the center of the ancient world.

6. Abraham, Isaac, and Jacob are called the _____, the "founding fathers" of the Jewish nation.

7. Jacob's son _____ was sold into slavery by his brothers.

8. A nation or people living in its own land with its own government is called a _____.

CONCEPTS TO CONSIDER On a separate sheet of paper, answer the following questions using complete sentences.

1. Why is the call of Abraham considered an important event in human history?

2. Explain the division of history between years B.C. and years A.D.

MATCHING Match each description with the correct term and write the letter in the blank.

a bureaucracy f humanist
b cuneiform g laws
c dispersion h monotheist
d empire i nation-state
e equality j polytheist
  under the law k promulgation

_____ 1. rules people follow in living together

_____ 2. making the laws known

_____ 3. all people who commit the same crime should be punished in the same way

_____ 4. the rule of one city or people over other cities or peoples

_____ 5. one who worships many gods

_____ 6. one who worships only one god

_____ 7. one who makes men into gods

_____ 8. a group of people appointed by a ruler to help him govern

3
Down to Egypt
(c. 2300–1400 B.C.)

HIGHLIGHTS
Egyptian Civilization • Hebrew Exodus

Egypt in World History

Impressions of Ancient Egypt

Herodotus. Soon after Ham's son **Mizraim** settled in Egypt, this land in northeastern Africa became the site of a people that in many respects equaled or excelled the accomplishments of Mesopotamia. Unlike Hammurabi's Babylonian Empire, Egypt was not an empire of cities. The Egyptians thought of themselves as one people, calling themselves by the same name regardless of the particular cities in which they lived. For more than a thousand years, Egypt ruled an empire that extended all the way to the Euphrates River. Even after 1000 B.C., when one foreign conqueror after another ruled the land, many massive ruins remained as evidence of Egypt's former greatness.

The Greek historian **Herodotus** [hĕ·rŏd′ŏ·*tus*] viewed the ruins of Egypt in the fifth century B.C. and wrote of his impressions. He marveled at the huge tombs called **pyramids** and the mysterious **sphinxes** [sfĭngk′sĕz: *large stone statues with the heads of men, rams, or hawks and the bodies of lions*]. He also saw the **hieroglyphics** [hī′ĕr·ŏ·glĭf′ĭks: "*sacred carvings*"], the strange writing of the ancient Egyptians.

The Bible. Impressive Egypt also played an important role in Bible history. God planned that Israel, before it became a nation-state, would first spend many years down in Egypt. During this time, Israel grew from a large family of 70 persons to a nation of over 2 million. Two Israelites held positions of great power in Egypt.

Joseph became the chief assistant to an Egyptian king when he interpreted the king's dreams. Under Joseph's leadership, Egypt prepared for a seven-year worldwide famine, foretold in the king's dreams, by storing enough grain to feed all of Egypt and even Canaan during the famine. It was during this famine that Jacob sent some of his sons from Canaan to Egypt to buy grain, beginning a chain of events which reconciled Joseph to his brothers, who had sold him into slavery, and brought Jacob with all of his family to live in Egypt.

Sometime after Joseph's death, a new Egyptian king began to fear the Israelite foreigners because of their rapid increase in numbers. He enslaved them with hard construction and field work. The Israelite population continued to increase, however, and suffering together as slaves only made them more aware of themselves as a distinct nation with a special relationship to God. In desperation, the king commanded that all of the male infants born to the Israelites be drowned.

The story of how one of these male infants, **Moses,** was saved from drowning is perhaps one of the most familiar parts of the Bible. As the adopted son of the king's daughter, Moses probably received the best education available in Egypt and might even have become an Egyptian king himself.

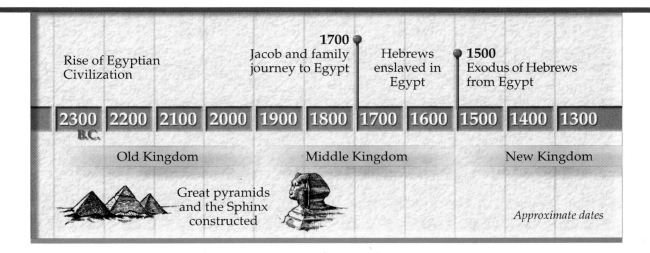

Rise of Egyptian Civilization					1700 Jacob and family journey to Egypt		Hebrews enslaved in Egypt	1500 Exodus of Hebrews from Egypt		
2300 B.C.	2200	2100	2000	1900	1800	1700	1600	1500	1400	1300
Old Kingdom				Middle Kingdom				New Kingdom		

Great pyramids and the Sphinx constructed

Approximate dates

Instead, he became the leader of the Israelites as God delivered the nation from slavery. In His deliverance, God gave Israel ample evidence that she was indeed His chosen nation and demonstrated His power to all the world in His judgment of mighty and impressive Egypt.

Hieroglyphics—the Riddle of Egypt

For a long time, almost everything known about ancient Egypt came from the works of Herodotus and from the Bible, because knowledge of how to read the Egyptian hieroglyphics had been lost. For about 15 centuries (until the 19th century A.D.), these puzzling pictures of birds, snakes, bottles, jugs, and other things were believed to be a part of Egyptian religion.

In A.D. 1799, French soldiers in Egypt accidentally uncovered a broken slab of black basalt (a fine-grained rock) near the town of Rosetta. This stone, later dubbed the **Rosetta Stone,** contained a message carved in three languages: hieroglyphics, demotic (another ancient Egyptian language), and Greek. It soon became obvious that the hieroglyphics were indeed writing and that the Greek carvings could be used to decipher them. The French scholar *Jean Francis Champollion* [shän′-pô·lyôn′] worked for 14 years until he had solved the riddle of the Rosetta Stone. After the results of Champollion's work were announced in 1822, scholars were able to read other hieroglyphics that the ancient Egyptians had left behind.

Pyramid after Pyramid: Many pyramids still stand in Egypt today.

27

A Storehouse of Relics

Many ancient Egyptian artifacts survive today after thousands of years, including delicate fabrics and wooden objects that ordinarily would have decayed. We now know much about ancient Egypt because so many perishable things have survived the centuries. Egypt has been a storehouse for relics of the past because the land is so hot and dry and almost never receives any rain. Except for the great river that flows through it, Egypt would be a desert wasteland.

Egypt's Great River

The Nile River and Its Gifts

An oasis in the desert. The **Nile River,** the longest river in the world and one of the few that flow south to north, made ancient Egypt an oasis in a desert. Every year in June, the Nile began to rise and flood the valley. The water level peaked in the middle of September, and the floodwaters began to recede. By December, the life-giving waters had returned to their normal channels, leaving behind more than 10,000 square miles of cultivable soil. An approximately 650-mile strip of rich and moist soil two to thirty miles wide began in the south and stretched northward. For the last 100 miles or so of its course through Egypt toward the Mediterranean Sea, the Nile fanned out into many streams to form the **delta** region, named for its resemblance to the Greek letter *delta* (Δ). The strip, and especially the delta, was one of the most fertile areas in the world— more so than even Mesopotamia, where the Tigris and Euphrates rivers made what was otherwise a desert into part of the fertile crescent.

Irrigation (canals, dikes, reservoirs) played an important role in Egypt just as in Mesopotamia. But rather than redirect the Nile, the Egyptians simply adapted to its natural flood cycle. They saw the Nile as

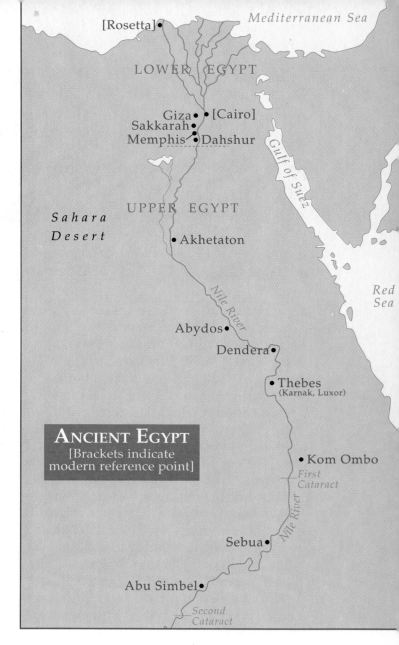

more of a friend than a foe and eagerly received the "gifts" it brought to Egypt each year. Herodotus, in fact, called Egypt the "gift of the Nile."

The gifts of the Nile. The greatest gift of the Nile to Egypt was the fertile soil it left behind. Agriculture provided a solid foundation for great wealth in Egypt, making the land a breadbasket for the ancient world. Even when the Nile failed to follow its cycle during the time of Joseph, the Egyptians had stored enough grain to carry them through the seven-year famine.

Egypt's Fertile Strip: *This photograph shows the Nile River in modern Egypt.*

The Nile also provided transportation for trade and communication. Boats could move northward with the current and return south by raising sails to catch the winds that almost always blew out of the north.

The Nile was a plentiful source for building materials. From the **papyrus** [pə·pī′r*u*s] plants that grew along the river banks, the Egyptians made boats, baskets, boxes, mats, sandals, and furniture, as well as paper. They used mud from the Nile to make bricks, with which they built dwellings ranging from huts to palaces.

The valley through which the Nile flowed was surrounded by natural barriers to foreign invasion. Desert sands lay to the east, west, and south. Rapids called **cataracts** in the south prevented the Nile from being used to invade Egypt. Invaders could come into the north from the Mediterranean Sea, but this area was easy to defend. The only real weaknesses were to the northeast from the direction of Canaan.

Archaeology

Much of what we know about the ancient civilizations of Mesopotamia and Egypt has been learned through **archaeology** [är′kē·ŏl′ō·jē], *the study of the relics and ruins of ancient cultures.* Using these clues, archaeologists try to reconstruct how the people of the past lived.

Archaeology can be useful in the study of world history. It is sometimes necessary, however, to sift out the influence of evolutionary thought. Archaeologists often take the idea of evolution for granted rather than as something to be proved, resulting in many one-sided, questionable, and even fanciful interpretations of relics. Actually, the more that archaeologists discover about ancient people, the less crude, primitive, or simple they appear to have been—just the opposite of what the evolutionist expects.

Archaeology is at its best when it puts away pottery chunks and lets ancient men speak for themselves through the remains of their writing.

Egypt's Confusion

False Beliefs about Creation

The ancient Egyptians believed that the Nile gushed up from an underground sea at the first set of rapids. They explained the river's flood cycle with stories about their gods. They also had myths for the sun's daily cycle of rising and setting. The Egyptians' belief in false gods prevented them from seeing nature as it really is.

Ancient Egypt confused the Creator with His creation. Although "that which may be known of God is manifest in them, for God hath shown it unto them" (Rom. 1:19), the Egyptians did not recognize the one true God. They did not see that nature operates according to basic laws of matter and energy established by God. Neither did they see that nature is subject to miracles when God chooses to interrupt the routine operation of the basic laws.

Forgetting that nature *is not* God, the Egyptians were overly impressed with it. Everywhere they looked, they saw awesome powers and forces to be worshiped as gods.

Results of Egypt's Confusion

Medical advances. Their concern for practical things led the Egyptians to make great advances in medicine. Egyptian doctors were famous in the ancient world, particularly for their treatment of physical injuries. For many ailments, however, Egyptian doctors used magic. Belief that evil spirits cause disease naturally accompanied the belief that the powers of nature are gods.

Strict guidelines in art. Egypt also excelled in the arts. The beauty of Egyptian architecture and sculpture has impressed men for centuries. Egyptian painters had no rivals in the ancient world. Unfortunately, Egypt's artists were hindered by their belief in natural cycles.

Egyptian art was beautiful, but because change was not acceptable, it was all very much alike.

The Confusing Gods of the Egyptians

The Egyptians worshiped many gods, possibly hundreds. Some of their most interesting gods were animals such as cats, crocodiles, cows, and frogs. They were so serious about their worship of animals that they even buried some animals in the same elaborate manner in which they buried their own people. According to an old story, some Egyptians once killed a foreigner because he had killed one of their sacred cats.

Other Egyptian gods were pictured as men or as combinations of animals and men. Horus, for example, had the body of a man and the head of a falcon. The Egyptians also worshiped their kings, called **pharaohs** [fâr′ŏz], as gods. In making gods of "man, and . . . birds, and four-footed beasts, and creeping things" (Rom. 1:23), the Egyptians showed that they had no clear idea of the important differences between man and animals. In a sense, Egyptian beliefs lowered men to the level of animals and elevated animals to the level of gods.

Sacred Animals: The Egyptians worshiped cats and other animals as gods.

Horus: This god, with the head of a falcon and the body of a man, well illustrates the confusing Egyptian religion.

Papyrus Painting: Wealthy Egyptians offer gifts to the god Osiris.

The Egyptians' Belief in the Afterlife

Assurance of an afterlife. From the earliest times, Egyptians believed with certainty in life after death but were very confused about what this afterlife would be like. It supposedly resembled *this* life in many ways. The soul, they thought, could leave the body at death, but it had to be able to return to the body periodically. This belief in an afterlife explains why the Egyptians were so concerned about building tombs to protect their bodies. A well-equipped tomb had such articles as food, sandals, and jewels. It might also be decorated with paintings and wooden models relating to the afterlife.

Mummification. The Egyptians' belief in an afterlife also led them to preserve bodies through a process known as **mummification.** First, they would soak a dead body in mixtures of salts, spices, and resins to preserve it. After the body had dried into a shriveled shape, they stuffed it and wrapped it with linen. The entire process could take as long as 70 days.

Cycle of the god-kings. At first, the afterlife was limited to the pharaohs and their families. The Egyptians believed that every pharaoh ruled on earth as the god Horus and in the underworld after death

as his father, Osiris. Later, access to the afterlife was extended to all Egyptians. The cycle of the god-kings gave the Egyptians great incentive to obey their pharaohs.

CHECK UP

1. What are the huge tombs of ancient Egypt called?
2. Why did the king of Egypt fear the Israelites and eventually enslave them?
3. What discovery led to the deciphering of hieroglyphics? Who deciphered them?
4. Why have so many relics of ancient Egypt survived for thousands of years?
5. How did the Nile make Egypt fertile?
6. Name some gifts of the Nile. What was the most important gift? Why?
7. What natural barriers helped to prevent foreign invasions of Egypt?
8. In what areas did the Egyptians make great advances?
9. What did the Egyptians believe about life after death?
10. Why were Egyptian tombs well stocked with everyday household items?

Identify: Egypt, Mizraim, Herodotus, Moses, Joseph, sphinxes, hieroglyphics, archaeology, delta, papyrus, pharaoh, mummification

Mummification: In the process of mummification, the body was embalmed, wrapped in linen, and placed inside a coffin, such as the one shown here open. Often these coffins were then placed in other more elaborate containers.

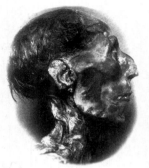

A Mummified Head:
This is the shriveled head of the mummy of the pharaoh Ramses II.

The God-Kings of Egypt

The First Pharaoh and the Dynasties

Two kingdoms. Early Egypt was divided into two main parts: **Lower Egypt** (in the north) included the delta area, and **Upper Egypt** (in the south) extended to the first cataract. Both parts of Egypt were divided into what the Greeks later called *nomes.* Each nome probably had a king. First, the nomes of Lower Egypt united under one king, and then the nomes of Upper Egypt united under another king. **Menes** [mē′nēz] united the two kingdoms and became the first pharaoh of all Egypt. He had the city of *Memphis* built as his capital near where Lower and Upper Egypt met.

The dynasties of Egypt. Beginning with Menes, Egypt was ruled by a series of *dynasties (families within which the right to be king passed from one member to the other).* So important were these dynasties that many people divide ancient Egypt's history into three parts: the **Old Kingdom,** the **Middle Kingdom,** and the **New Kingdom.** This division reflects the fact that before 1000 B.C. the dynasties were interrupted twice for periods of several hundred years. Internal turmoil caused the first interruption and marked the end of

the Old Kingdom and the beginning of the Middle Kingdom. The second interruption was due to foreign conquest by the **Hyksos** [hĭk′sōs], a people from the east about whom little is known. The Hyksos were finally driven out, and the New Kingdom began.

Egypt ceased to be a major world power after about 1000 B.C. Other pharaohs ruled, but many foreign conquerors also came to the throne. Foreign powers ruled Egypt from the fourth century B.C. to the 20th century A.D.

The Building Projects of the Pharaohs

Irrigation and flood control. The pharaohs used their power over the Egyptians to command great building projects. Some projects were of practical value. Canals, dikes, and reservoirs, for example, enhanced the Nile's gift of fertility and helped eliminate the disadvantages of yearly flooding. However, the building projects most important to the pharaohs were their eternal homes, their tombs.

Royal tombs. The earliest tombs the pharaohs had built for themselves were simple brick structures called *mastabas* [măs′tə·bəz] with flat tops and sloping sides. Over time, larger and larger mastabas were built until the pharaoh

Djoser [d'jō'sĕr] had six mastabas stacked together, each smaller than the one beneath it. This **Step Pyramid** may have been the first structure in world history made entirely of stone.

Less than two centuries later, the first true pyramids were built. These massive structures were made of large stone blocks arranged to rise evenly to a point. The three most famous pyramids were built in the area of **Giza** [gē'zə: also spelled *Gizeh*]. The first and largest pyramid, called the **Great Pyramid,** was built for the pharaoh **Khufu** (also known as Cheops [kē'äps]).

Khufu's pyramid covered 13 acres. More than 2,300,000 stone blocks were used, for a total estimated weight of 5,700,000 tons. The average weight of each block was two and one-half tons, but some of the blocks weighed 60 tons each. The pyramid originally stood 480 feet high. No one knows for certain how this or any of the other pyramids were constructed, except that much human muscle power was used. One guess is that it took 100,000 men 20 years (probably laboring while the Nile was flooded, when it was impossible to farm the land) to build Khufu's pyramid.

The second largest pyramid at Giza was built for the pharaoh **Khafre** [käf'rā]. Of more interest, however, is the mysterious structure that stands near his pyramid. The **Great Sphinx,** a gigantic statue carved in limestone, has a lion's body 240 feet long and 66 feet high, with a 13-foot-wide human face in the likeness of a pharaoh—possibly Khafre.

The third pyramid at Giza was built for the pharaoh **Menkaure** [mɛn·kou'r]. All three pyramids, as well as the Great Sphinx, can still be seen at Giza today.

Temples. Several large pyramids were built during the Old Kingdom, followed by the construction of many smaller pyramids, until pharaohs began to show a preference for **mortuary temples.** Many mortuary temples were built when Egypt ruled an empire. One of the most famous and beautiful belonged to **Hatshepsut** [hăt·shĕp'sōōt], the only female pharaoh. Hatshepsut respected the tradition that only men were pharaohs by wearing a man's clothes and a false beard.

Many ancient structures still standing in Egypt were built under the direction of **Ramses II** [răm'sĕz]. Ramses preferred large structures, particularly images of himself. At his mortuary temple in Thebes, he had a 57-foot-high statue of himself that weighed 1,000 tons. At another temple, he had four statues of himself, each more than 60 feet tall.

Ramses II: *This pharaoh loved large structures, especially images of himself.*

Great Sphinx: *This huge statue guards the pyramids at Giza.*

"King Tut"

Over the centuries, most of the ancient tombs of Egypt were plundered by robbers, but some remained hidden. One of the few tombs that were little disturbed was that of the teenaged pharaoh **Tutankhamen** [tōōt′ängk·ä′men], better known as "King Tut." Discovered in A.D. 1922 by two Englishmen, Lord Carnarvon and Howard Carter, Tut's tomb revealed a wealth of beautiful treasures, some of which are pictured here.

Tut and His Queen: This scene from the back of King Tut's throne gives a picture of the king and his wife. Notice how the sun is beaming down on them.

Model Boat: This model boat of painted wood was buried with Tutankhamen.

Funeral Mask: This detail of Tutankhamen's funeral mask gives a close-up of the young king' face. The mask is of gold inlaid with lapis lazuli, a rich blue stone.

Child's Chair: A small chair, decorated with ivory and gold, was buried with Tutankhamen in his tomb.

The Empire of the Pharaohs

Motives. The building projects of the pharaohs required an enormous number of laborers. The pharaohs also desired ever greater amounts of material wealth. The desire for more laborers and more wealth through **tribute** *(a payment from one nation to another)* gave the pharaohs strong motives for building an empire.

Peak of Egyptian power. Under **Thutmose III** [thoot·mō′se], the Egyptian empire reached its greatest extent—to the Euphrates River in the north and deep into Africa in the south. Egypt held this territory for 150 years, making her the strongest power in the world.

Egypt's military power consisted mainly of chariots. The pharaohs learned the importance of chariots from the conquest of Egypt by the Hyksos. The advantage of the Hyksos, who had chariots while the Egyptians did not, was something like the advantage a tank force has today against a field of foot soldiers. Only when the Egyptians had mastered the art of chariot warfare were they able to drive the Hyksos out. The pharaohs of the empire made certain that Egypt possessed a large supply of chariots and professional chariot fighters.

The pharaohs eventually lost their empire because the territory was too vast and cumbersome to maintain. Egypt could not match the ambitious military powers arising in the north and east. Also, like almost everything else about Egypt, the success of the empire depended on the pharaoh. Only the most able men could manage the difficult tasks of holding onto such an empire; to rule Egypt alone was a challenge.

Egyptian Society

The pharaoh of Egypt had many assistants. His chief assistant, the *vizier* [vĭ·zēr′], acted in the name of the pharaoh and supervised the administration of justice, tax collection, military excursions, and construction projects. The Israelite slave Joseph became a vizier. Various governors and other officials also assisted the pharaoh with the responsibilities of government. Priests had much influence in the government because they controlled the tremendous amount of wealth provided for the gods of Egypt. This ruling class of **nobles** and **priests** made up the upper class of Egyptian society.

The middle class consisted of **craftsmen, scribes,** and **soldiers.** The pharaohs (and their more important assistants) employed brick masons, chariot-makers, boat-builders, jewelry-makers, painters, sculptors, and many other kinds of craftsmen. These men made the many objects of beauty that the pharaohs enjoyed and took with them to their tombs. Scribes kept written records for the pharaoh and other government officials. Soldiers protected Egypt from invasion and maintained order within the realm. As we move down the organization of the pharaoh's assistants to the vast majority, we find that really all

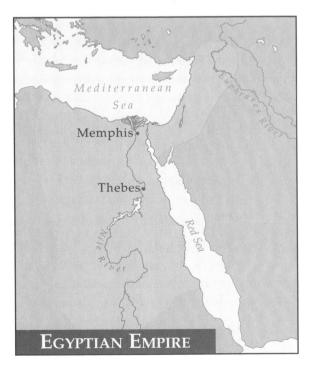

EGYPTIAN EMPIRE

Working the Fields: Most Egyptians were farmers. They worked the land for the pharaoh and gave the greatest part of their crops to him.

Egyptians were in a sense the pharaoh's assistants. *Egypt was one huge bureaucracy.*

At the bottom of the social scale were the *farmers* and *slaves.* Most Egyptians were tenant farmers. They worked the land for the pharaoh and gave the greater part of their crops to him. During the flood season, the farmers were drafted to work on the pharaoh's construction projects. Below the tenant farmers were the slaves. Some worked in gold and copper mines, while others performed menial services directly for the pharaohs and those of the ruling class. The Israelite slaves were forced to build cities.

God's Judgment of Egypt

Moses. When God answered the Israelites' cry for freedom from Egypt, He first called a man to lead His people.

When he was 40 years old, Moses, the adopted son of a pharaoh's daughter, felt pity for his people. He killed an Egyptian who was beating an Israelite. Fearing that the pharaoh might punish him for what he had done, Moses fled from Egypt to a wilderness.

Forty years later, God appeared to Moses and directed him to return to Egypt. The 80-year-old Moses went back to face the pharaoh and all the might of Egypt as the leader of the Israelites in their exodus from Egypt.

The ten plagues and Egyptian religion. Because the pharaoh refused to let Israel go, God brought a series of 10 calamities upon Egypt. Each brought increased destruction, but the pharaoh continued to refuse to let Moses' people go until the last plague. When all the first-born sons of Egypt (including the pharaoh's own son) died, the pharaoh finally changed his mind.

These plagues demonstrated the ridiculousness of the Egyptian religion. The one true God turned the powers of nature against a people that had worshiped them. The Nile became a river of blood. Animals that the Egyptians held in awe brought horrible destruction as the land was filled with swarming frogs, lice, and flies. Animal gods such as cows were struck with a deadly disease. Boils came upon animals, men, and even priests, the special servants of the gods. The "powers of the sky" brought bone-crushing hail and clouds of ravenous locusts. The mighty sun ceased to shine for three days. Through these miracles, God showed that His power knows no limit and can interrupt any natural cycle at any time to work His will.

The stubborn pharaoh. Well before the tenth plague, everyone in Egypt except the pharaoh seems to have been convinced of God's power and the awful consequences of risking His wrathful judgment. But even after he had let the Israelites go, after the tenth disaster, the pharaoh still had not learned his lesson. Perhaps he could see no alternative for rebuilding his kingdom after the plagues except through slave labor. Confident in his army of chariots, and still convinced that he was a god, pharaoh led the mighty armies of Egypt into the wilderness after the Israelites.

There, pharaoh met his final humiliation. Just when he had the Israelites backed against a sea, God parted the sea with a great wind, allowing the Israelites to pass through on dry ground. When the Egyptians followed, the waters of the sea returned and crashed down upon them. Though Egypt was not completely destroyed by these disasters, it had experienced God's judgment in one of world history's most dramatic moments.

CHECK UP

1. Who united Upper and Lower Egypt?
2. What are the three main divisions of ancient Egyptian history?
3. When did Egypt cease to be a major power?
4. Which three pharaohs built pyramids at Giza? Whose is the largest?
5. What type of tomb became popular after the pyramids?
6. Who was the only female pharaoh?
7. What were the pharaohs' main motives for building an empire?
8. Under what pharaoh did the Egyptian empire reach its greatest extent? What were the boundaries of the empire at that time?
9. Explain how Egypt was one huge bureaucracy.
10. How did Moses become the leader of the Israelite slaves?
11. What did the 10 plagues demonstrate about Egyptian religion?
12. Why did the pharaoh chase the Israelites? What happened to the Egyptians in the wilderness?

Identify: nomes, Memphis, dynasties, Hyksos, mastabas, Step Pyramid, Djoser, Great Sphinx, Ramses II, tribute, vizier

CHAPTER 3 REVIEW

MULTIPLE CHOICE Write the letter of the answer that best completes each sentence.

1. Ham's son _____ settled in Egypt.
   a Jacob   *c* Seth
   b Canaan   *d* Mizraim

2. The Greek historian _____ left descriptions of the wonders of ancient Egypt.
   a Horus   *c* Homer
   b Herodotus   *d* Osiris

3. The vizier who prepared Egypt for a seven-year famine was _____.
   a Moses   *c* Jacob
   b Joseph   *d* Israel

4. God delivered Israel from slavery by using _____ as a leader.
   a Moses   *c* Jacob
   b Joseph   *d* Isaac

5. The scholar who deciphered the Rosetta Stone and unlocked the secrets of hieroglyphics was _____.
   a Herodotus   *c* Champollion
   b Napoleon   *d* Moses

6. Egypt is not a barren desert because of _____.
   a the Nile River *c* the Mediterranean
   b large lakes   *d* the fertile crescent

7. The northern section of Egypt, including the delta region, was called _____.
   a Lower Egypt *c* Memphis
   b Upper Egypt *d* Thebes

8. The two kingdoms of Egypt were united by _____.
   a Hatshepsut   *c* Ramses
   b Menes   *d* Djoser

9. The new capital of united Egypt was called _____.
   a Memphis   *c* Thebes
   b Menes   *d* Cairo

10. The Step Pyramid was built for _____.
    a Menes   *c* Khufu
    b Ramses   *d* Djoser

11. The largest of the Giza pyramids was built for _____.
    a Djoser   *c* Khafre
    b Khufu   *d* Thutmose

12. The Great Sphinx stands near the pyramid of _____.
    a Khufu   *c* Ramses
    b Khafre   *d* Menkaure

13. The only female pharaoh was _____.
    a Horus   *c* Hatshepsut
    b Nefertiti   *d* Cleopatra

14. The pharaoh who had many giant statues of himself was _____.
    a Ramses II   *c* Tutankhamen
    b Thutmose III   *d* Hatshepsut

15. Under _____, the Egyptian empire reached its greatest extent.
    a Ramses II   *c* Tutankhamen
    b Thutmose III   *d* Amenhotep III

16. Chariots were used by the _____ to invade and conquer Egypt.
    a Hittites   *c* Babylonians
    b Hyksos   *d* Persians

MATCHING Match each description with the correct term.

   a archaeologist   *f* vizier
   b cataracts   *g* Middle Kingdom
   c dynasties   *h* Old Kingdom
   d hieroglyphics   *i* New Kingdom
   e nomes

_____ 1. Egyptian writing

_____ 2. one who studies the relics of ancient cultures

_____ 3. great families who ruled Egypt

_____ 4. the kingdom that ended during a period of internal turmoil

_____ 5. the kingdom that ended when the Hyksos conquered Egypt

_____ 6. the pharaoh's chief assistant

_____ 7. the small divisions of Upper and Lower Egypt

_____ 8. rapids found in the Nile River

COMPLETION *Choose the correct term to complete each sentence and write the letter in the blank.*

a	delta	*f*	Rosetta Stone
b	mastabas	*g*	sphinx
c	mummification	*h*	Step Pyramid
d	papyrus	*i*	tribute
e	pyramids		

1. Some pharaohs built huge tombs called ____, which are still standing today.
2. A ____ is a mysterious statue with the head of a man, a ram, or a hawk, and the body of a lion.
3. Jean Francis Champollion used the ____ to decipher Egyptian writing.
4. The ancient Egyptians used ____ plants to make paper.
5. The ____ region is the fan-shaped area where the Nile runs into the Mediterranean Sea.
6. The delicate process of ____ has preserved the bodies of some pharaohs for thousands of years.
7. Djoser built the ____, perhaps the first structure in world history made entirely of stone.
8. One of the reasons the pharaohs wanted to conquer other countries was that the conquered nations would have to pay ____ to Egypt.

MAP SKILLS *Use the map on p. 28 to answer the following questions.*

1. What sea formed the northern border of Egypt? The eastern border?

____

2. In which part of Egypt, Upper or Lower, was Giza located?

____

3. What desert lay to the west of Egypt?

____

TIME LINE CHALLENGE *Number each group of events in the order in which they happened. Do each group separately.*

GROUP A
____ Moses leads the people out of Egypt
____ Joseph sold as a slave in Egypt
____ The 10 plagues
____ Moses murders an Egyptian
____ Jacob takes his family to Egypt
____ Joseph becomes a vizier
____ The seven-year famine begins

GROUP B
____ The Middle Kingdom
____ Menes unites Upper and Lower Egypt
____ Egypt declines as a major power
____ The Old Kingdom
____ The New Kingdom
____ The Hyksos invade Egypt

GROUP C
____ Menkaure builds the third great pyramid at Giza
____ Mastabas used as tombs for the pharaohs
____ Djoser builds his Step Pyramid
____ Pyramid and Sphinx built by Khafre
____ Khufu's pyramid built
____ Ramses II builds colossal figures of himself

CONCEPT TO CONSIDER *On a separate sheet of paper, answer the following question using complete sentences.*

How did the 10 plagues demonstrate the ridiculousness of Egyptian religion?

4
Israel in Its Land
(c. 1500–500 B.C.)

HIGHLIGHTS
Ten Commandments • Conquest of Canaan
David and Solomon • Phoenicians • Hittites

Israel as a Nation-State

Through Sinai

Joyful singing filled the wilderness as the Israelites praised God for His power and love. After a miraculous delivery from slavery in Egypt, Israel confidently looked forward to freedom in its own land as a nation-state with its own government.

The southern route to Canaan led through the *Sinai* [sī'nī] *Peninsula*. A barren land of rocks, sand dunes, mountains, and an occasional oasis, Sinai also contained fierce warrior tribes.

God was with His people every step of the way those first days in the wilderness. Food fell from the sky, water gushed from a desert rock, and the powerful *Amalekites* suffered defeat as God's power flowed through Moses' staff. Israel soon arrived safely at Mount Sinai.

Israel would have the chance to build world history's first nation *under* God, an example for a world in rebellion against God.

Earlier peoples had based their cultures on mistaken basic beliefs. The governments and laws of the world had been connected with many false gods, and Israel's neighbors continued this pattern. Now the one true God gave Israel its government, laws, and beliefs.

God's Government for Israel

Covenant. God and Israel made a **covenant** *(solemn agreement)* at **Mount Sinai.** The promises first made to Abraham were extended to the nation he had fathered. *If* Israel obeyed God, He would greatly bless it. Just as certainly, *if* Israel did not obey God, the nation would be severely punished.

Theocracy. When the Israelites fully agreed to this, *God became the King of Israel.* In God's plan, Israel would continue to have human leaders like **Moses,** but these leaders would be chosen, given special abilities, and led by God.

Mount Sinai: *The site chosen by God for the giving of the Ten Commmandments.*

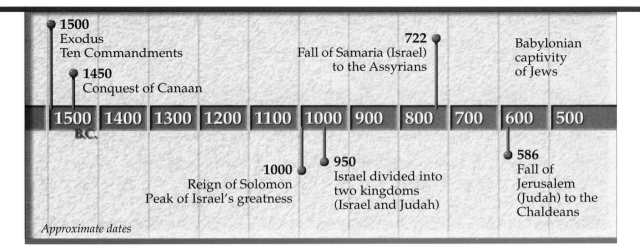

1500
Exodus
Ten Commandments

1450
Conquest of Canaan

722
Fall of Samaria (Israel)
to the Assyrians

Babylonian
captivity
of Jews

| 1500 | 1400 | 1300 | 1200 | 1100 | 1000 | 900 | 800 | 700 | 600 | 500 |
B.C.

1000
Reign of Solomon
Peak of Israel's greatness

950
Israel divided into
two kingdoms
(Israel and Judah)

586
Fall of
Jerusalem
(Judah) to the
Chaldeans

Approximate dates

As a **theocracy** [thē·ŏk′rə·sē: *rule by God*], Israel would be a nation under God's constant care, a nation blessed for doing good and punished for doing evil. To be blessed like no other nation before, Israel had only to obey God's commandments.

God's Laws for Israel

God gave laws to Israel in the form of commandments. To avoid doubt in anyone's mind about what was required, God Himself wrote the laws on stone tablets and directed Moses to write them down as well. God knew that if laws are believed to be merely man-made, men will not respect them. While the laws given at Mount Sinai are sometimes called the **Laws of Moses,** Israel had no doubt that God was the author of the laws and that Moses was merely God's messenger.

God's laws are superior to any made by men. Consider Hammurabi's laws. Unlike God, Hammurabi considered material possessions to be more important than human life. He also failed to achieve equality under the law, equal punishment for all who commit a particular crime. God's laws are perfect and just.

God's Morality for Israel—and Us

God's laws are perfect because He knows the true **principles of morality** (the

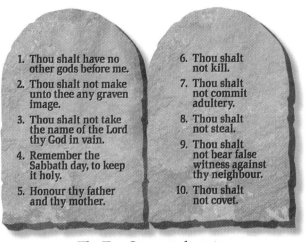

1. Thou shalt have no other gods before me.
2. Thou shalt not make unto thee any graven image.
3. Thou shalt not take the name of the Lord thy God in vain.
4. Remember the Sabbath day, to keep it holy.
5. Honour thy father and thy mother.
6. Thou shalt not kill.
7. Thou shalt not commit adultery.
8. Thou shalt not steal.
9. Thou shalt not bear false witness against thy neighbour.
10. Thou shalt not covet.

The Ten Commandments

basic rules of right and wrong, good and evil). The first ten of God's laws, known as the **Ten Commandments** or the **Decalogue** [dĕk′ə·lŏg: *the ten words*], briefly state the principles of morality. The rest of the laws apply these principles for Israel. The principles of morality are for all people today, but many applications were made solely for ancient Israel.

It was a great moment in world history when God revealed the true principles of morality, at first to the Israelites but eventually to all men through the Bible.

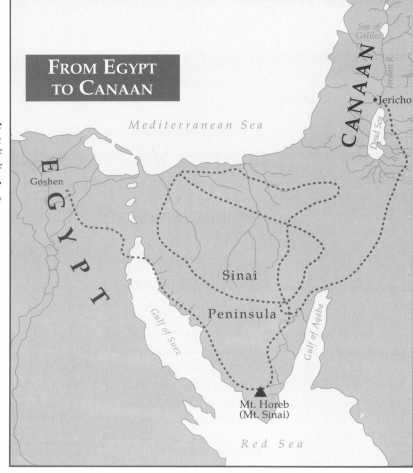

FROM EGYPT TO CANAAN

The Exodus:
This map traces a possible route of the Israelites out of Egypt, across the Red Sea, and into the wilderness.

Having the right relationship to God is the key to having the right relationship to other men and enjoying happiness. The first four commandments cover our relationship with God—knowing Him as the one and only God, worshiping no other "gods," never failing to keep even His name and special day holy. These are the most important principles of morality.

God at Mount Sinai established the basic beliefs for a new kind of culture. With its government and laws, Israel very soon could have been in the promised land beginning its days as a nation-state.

Wilderness Wandering

In spite of all the miracles that the Israelites had seen in their exodus from Egypt, their faith in God quickly faltered. When they reached the southern borders of Canaan, Israel sent spies into the land. Ten of the spies returned with an evil report of fierce giants and great walled cities; two of the spies, Joshua and Caleb, returned with a promising report of a bountiful land ripe for conquest. Rather than trusting in God to fulfill His promise, Israel decided to return to Egypt instead of claiming the Promised Land. As a result of their disobedience, God sentenced the Israelites to wander in the wilderness. Including the time they had already spent in the desert, the Israelites would wander for 40 years before entering Canaan.

The Conquest of Canaan

Israel's victories. When the time finally came for Israel to enter Canaan and for Moses to die, God chose **Joshua** to be the new leader. As a military man, Joshua was well suited for the conquest of Canaan.

Another series of miracles began when Joshua led the people across the *Jordan River* into Canaan while God held the waters back. The heavily fortified city of **Jericho** soon fell at the sound of trumpets and shouts. A great alliance of people in southern Canaan met defeat when God lengthened the day so that the Israelites could finish the battle before nightfall. Northern Canaanites, heavily armed with chariots and other weapons that the Israelites did not have, were the next to be defeated. Within about seven years, nearly all of Canaan was under Israel's control.

Joshua's warning. Before he died, Joshua divided the conquered land among the tribes of Israel. He warned that unless Israel followed the ways of God, she would be severely punished. Unfortunately, for the next 300 years, Israel repeatedly departed from God.

During the conquest of Canaan, Israel had disobeyed God by failing to drive the Canaanites completely out of the land. As a new generation of Israelites settled in the land of plenty, they were exposed to the Canaanites' wicked culture and their religion of pleasure and lust.

CHECK UP
1. Give three indications that God was with the Israelites as they traveled in the wilderness.
2. What is a covenant? Describe Israel's covenant.
3. What is a theocracy? Describe Israel's theocracy.
4. What are the true principles of morality?
5. What is another name for the Ten Commandments?
6. How long did God sentence Israel to wander in the wilderness?
7. What warning did Joshua give before his death?
8. During the conquest of Canaan, how did Israel disobey God? What was the consequence of this disobedience?

Identify: Sinai Peninsula, Amalekites, Mount Sinai, Moses, Jericho

---

More Than a Tent: *Under God's very specific directions, the Israelites constructed the tabernacle which served as their place of worship during the 40 years of wandering and later. It was only a tent, but the presence of God must have made it appear to be much more.*

The Judges of Israel

The Israelites soon began to worship the Canaanite gods. Rather than obeying God, every man tended to do what *he* thought was right. Just as Joshua had warned, the Israelites were punished. God permitted the enemies in the surrounding areas to harass and oppress Israel. Then the people remembered God and cried out for His help. This happened again and again. Each time God answered their pleas by choosing leaders to guide them back to the ways of God and freedom.

These leaders of Israel during its first 300 years in Canaan were called the **judges.** There were 12 judges in all (not counting Samuel), and few if any led all of Israel. Most were responsible for limited areas, sometimes only a tribe or two. There were probably periods during which there were no judges. At other times, there may have been several at once.

As long as the judge lived, the people obeyed God and freedom and prosperity returned to Israel. But after the judge died, the same old cycle of disobedience and punishment would start all over again.

Samuel and the First Earthly King of Israel

Samuel's warning. God had called **Samuel** to lead Israel from the oppression of the Philistines. Since his calling, Samuel had been the accepted leader of Israel. As he grew old, the people began to wonder who would lead them when Samuel died.

Thus, the Israelites demanded a human king. Israel wanted to be rid of the most powerful and just king a nation could have, God Himself. They preferred a king they could always see, just as from time to time they wanted a "god" they could always see.

Through Samuel, God warned Israel of the consequences of granting one such power. The Israelites would eventually carry a heavy burden of taxation. But God granted Israel's persistent request and through Samuel chose the first human king of Israel.

King Saul. God selected **Saul** to be king. At first a very humble man, Saul soon showed other sides of his character when he began to disobey the instructions God gave him. After ruling for 32 years, Saul came to a tragic death on the battlefield.

King David

God chose **David** to be the next king of Israel. David ruled for 40 years and became one of the greatest earthly kings in history. With God's support, King David *led Israel to the peak of its greatness as a nation-state.* Israel thoroughly defeated its enemies and extended its borders to the Euphrates River in the north and to a stream called the Brook of Egypt in the south. The desert marked Israel's eastern boundary, and the Mediterranean Sea its western limit. All of this region belonged to Israel except for Phoenicia, a friendly ally, and a few Philistine cities on the coast.

King Solomon

David's son, **Solomon,** inherited the great kingdom that God had built during David's reign. David's knowledge of war and politics had, with the blessing of God, allowed Israel to become perhaps the greatest world power in the 10th century B.C. It was now Solomon's task to rule this nation-state wisely.

God offered Solomon any gift of his choice. Recognizing his inability to rule God's people, Solomon asked for the wisdom to govern Israel. God granted this wish and also promised Solomon much wealth and honor.

Solomon was honored far and wide for his wisdom and the wealth of his kingdom. Egyptian pharaohs and great queens acknowledged Solomon's greatness and the importance of the nation-state he ruled. Solomon formed alliances with foreign

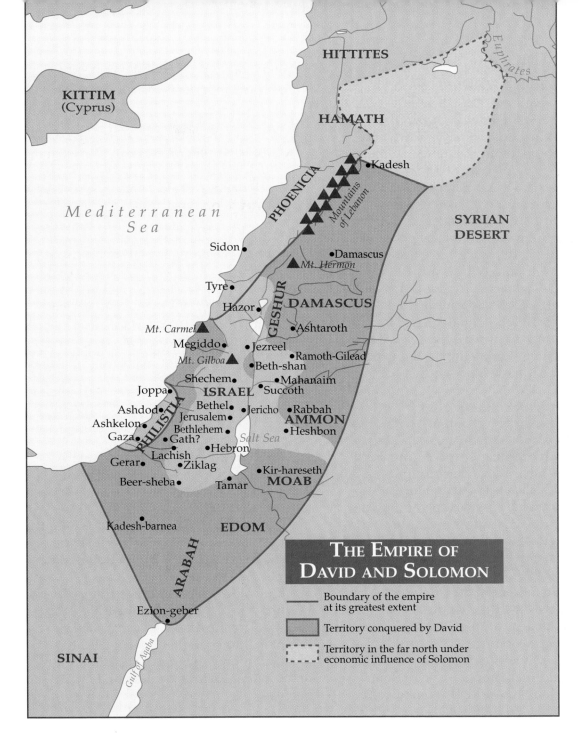

KITTIM
(Cyprus)

HITTITES

Euphrates

HAMATH

•Kadesh

PHOENICIA

*Mediterranean
Sea*

Mountains of Lebanon

SYRIAN
DESERT

Sidon•

•Damascus

▲ *Mt. Hermon*

Tyre•

GESHUR

DAMASCUS

Hazor•

•Ashtaroth

Mt. Carmel ▲

Megiddo•   •Jezreel

Mt. Gilboa ▲   •Ramoth-Gilead

•Beth-shan

Shechem•   •Mahanaim

Joppa•   ISRAEL   •Succoth

Ashdod•   Bethel•   •Jericho   •Rabbah

Ashkelon•   Jerusalem•   AMMON

Gaza•   Bethlehem•   •Heshbon

•Gath?   *Salt Sea*

Lachish   •Hebron

Gerar•   •Ziklag

Beer-sheba•   Tamar•   •Kir-hareseth

MOAB

Kadesh-barnea•   EDOM

ARABAH

Ezion-geber•

SINAI

Gulf of Aqaba

THE EMPIRE OF DAVID AND SOLOMON

—— Boundary of the empire at its greatest extent

▨ Territory conquered by David

- - - Territory in the far north under economic influence of Solomon

powers and used the central location of Israel in the ancient world to bring great riches to his kingdom.

Solomon put much of this wealth into great building projects. Four hundred eighty years after escaping from Egypt, the Israelites began to build a great temple for God. Many pages in the Bible give the details of this temple, describing its furniture and decorations. Solomon had many other buildings constructed as well. He also had new cities built and old cities remodeled. With all of his building projects, Solomon rivaled the pharaohs of Egypt.

However, Solomon's projects required many thousands of laborers. Soon the Israelites were forced to work for the king and pay increasingly heavy taxes to support the lavish lifestyle of the royal family. God's warning about the dangers of human kings had come true. The Israelites had become slaves in their own land under their own government.

The "last straw" came when Solomon himself began to worship false gods. Solomon died after reigning for 40 years, and Israel split into two separate kingdoms: the **Northern Kingdom,** still calling itself **Israel,** and the **Southern Kingdom,** calling itself **Judah.** The two kingdoms continued to turn away from God. First Israel and then Judah fell into the hands of new empires that were rising in the east.

Legacy of Israel as a Nation-State

The first chapter of Israel's history as a nation-state had come to a close. The sadness of its ending, however, must not blind us to what *had* been accomplished. There was still cause for hope for Israel and all mankind. <u>The writing of the Bible had begun</u>. God had inspired some of the great leaders of Israel to write much of the Old Testament. Moses had written the first five books; David, many of the Psalms; and Solomon, the Proverbs.

Israel was the first nation in world history to have a complete written account of its history. A permanent record had been made of the general principles of morality, the basic beliefs for a nation under God. As the Old Testament continued to grow, God indicated that a solution was coming for the spiritual problem that had plagued Israel as a nation-state and, of course, the rest of mankind. The future contained new chapters for Israel as a nation-state and hope for a Kingdom of God. God had promised David that one of his descendants would become an *eternal* King.

1. What pattern or cycle occurred again and again in Israelite history after the death of Joshua?
2. Who led the Israelites during their first 300 years in Canaan?
3. Why did the Israelites want a human king?
4. How long did David rule?
5. What were the boundaries of the nation of Israel during David's reign?
6. What did Solomon ask God for? What did Solomon do with much of his wealth?
7. How were the Israelites slaves in their own land under their own government?
8. What is the great legacy of Israel?

Identify: Samuel, Saul, Northern Kingdom, Israel, Southern Kingdom, Judah

Two Neighbors

The kingdoms of Israel and Judah were ultimately swallowed up in new empires that arose to the north and east of Canaan. Israel, the Northern Kingdom, fell in the 700s B.C. to the **Assyrian** [ə·sĭr′ĭ·an] **Empire,** and Judah, the Southern Kingdom, fell in the 500s B.C. to the **Chaldean** [kăl·dē′an] **Empire.**

The Phoenicians and the Hittites, two neighbors of the Israelites, were also absorbed by these new empires. They compare interestingly to one another and to Israel in how they used their opportunities in world history as independent peoples.

The Phoenicians
A group of independent cities.
Phoenicia was a narrow 200-mile-long strip of land along the Mediterranean Sea in northern Canaan that the Israelites never occupied. The people who lived there are remembered in world history as the **Phoenicians.**

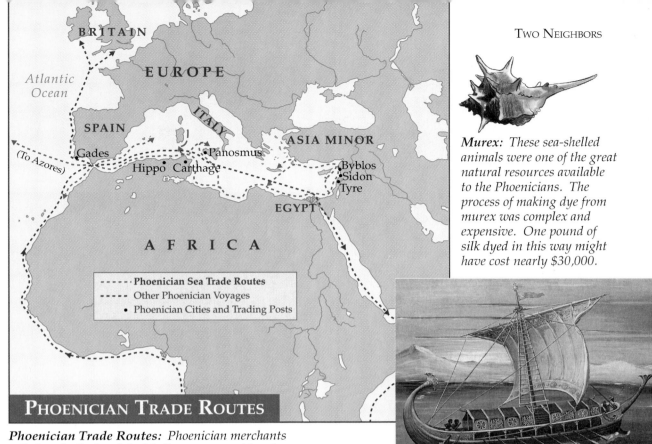

PHOENICIAN TRADE ROUTES

Murex: These sea-shelled animals were one of the great natural resources available to the Phoenicians. The process of making dye from murex was complex and expensive. One pound of silk dyed in this way might have cost nearly $30,000.

Map legend:
- - - - Phoenician Sea Trade Routes
- - - - Other Phoenician Voyages
• Phoenician Cities and Trading Posts

Phoenician Trade Routes: Phoenician merchants sailed to the limits of the Mediteranean world and beyond. Some Phoenicians once sailed around the continent of Africa.

Phoenician Merchant Galley

Actually, the Phoenicians did not think of themselves as one people. The Greeks gave them the name "Phoenician," meaning "blood-red people," because of the red and purple cloth that they became famous for making and selling. The Phoenicians lived in a group of independent cities such as **Tyre** and **Sidon** that never became an empire of cities or a nation-state. They were more interested in business and commerce than in conquest and politics.

Sea traders. The Phoenicians used their central location between Mesopotamia, Egypt, and the world of the Mediterranean Sea to the west to become <u>prosperous sea traders</u>. Along their shores were multitudes of **murex,** a kind of sea snail from which the Phoenicians learned to make dye for their wool and silk cloth. In the mountain forests to the east, fir and **cedar trees** grew; the Phoenicians learned

how to use this beautiful wood to decorate buildings and to make fine furniture and sturdy boats. These boats were fast because they had not only sails but also two rows of oars on each side.

Phoenician cloth became the prized possession of kings in the ancient world (even today purple is a symbolic color of royalty). Egyptian pharaohs bought Phoenician wood, and King Solomon had the temple in Jerusalem lined with Phoenician cedar. The skills of the Phoenician craftsmen were widely sought after. Solomon, for example, traded wheat, olive oil, and gold to the Phoenicians in return for their help in his construction projects. In addition to selling their own products, the Phoenicians also bought and sold the goods of other peoples such as papyrus from Egypt and ivory from northern Africa and India.

47

Cedars of Lebanon: *In the mountain forests of Lebanon grew magnificent cedar trees. Products made from the wood of these trees were greatly valued by royalty, including King Solomon.*

The ever-increasing desire of the Phoenicians for the profits of trade drove them on. They were hard and daring seamen, and their seagoing merchant ventures were far ranging. Once they sailed around the continent of Africa. Most of their ships traveled in the Mediterranean Sea. As they went to the limits of the Mediterranean world, the Phoenicians established a great network of trading posts. Some of these settlements eventually grew into great and important cities such as **Carthage,** over a thousand miles west of Canaan.

The Phoenician alphabet. Strangely, the most important thing that the Phoenicians carried with them on their trading ventures was an **alphabet,** which they simply gave away. The origin of this alphabet is not known, but the Phoenicians wrote with signs that stood for the twenty-two basic sounds of the consonants in their language. The **Greeks** took the free gift of the Phoenicians and developed a *true alphabet* with symbols for the basic sounds of consonants *and* vowels. This alphabet formed the basis for the written Greek language which at the time of Christ was the universal "second language" of the world. The Greek language greatly contributed to the spread of the gospel, for the New Testament was first written in Greek.

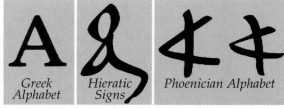

| Greek Alphabet | Hieratic Signs | Phoenician Alphabet |

Letter A—in Greek, Egyptian, and Phoenician.

Phoenician Writing: *Above is an example of ancient Phoenician writing on a pottery chunk.*

The Phoenicians carried their alphabet all over the known world, and yet they wrote nothing of importance for world history. Almost everything they wrote had to do with their business activities.

The Hittites

Asia Minor. The **Hittites,** another interesting neighbor of Israel, were almost completely forgotten in world history. For many centuries, the only knowledge of them came from the few places that they are mentioned in the Bible. In the 19th century A.D., some critics of the Bible claimed that the Hittites never existed. Archaeological discoveries in the 20th century, however, convinced all historians that the Hittites did indeed exist.

Some Hittites were living in Canaan as early as about 2000 B.C., when Abraham arrived. Hittites were still living in Canaan when the Israelites returned from Egypt, and they remained there throughout the time of Israel as a nation-state.

Most of the Hittites, however, lived in an area north of Canaan called **Asia Minor** *(a peninsula of western Asia between the Black Sea, the Mediterranean Sea, and the Euphrates River)*. The Hittites controlled an empire in this region for about a thousand years. They once held power as far as Sumer and even conquered the city of Babylon in the 1500s B.C. At times, they also fought with Egypt for influence in Canaan.

Warriors. Whereas the Phoenicians directed their natural and human resources toward trade, the Hittites <u>used their resources for war and conquest</u>. They learned how to work with the **iron** in their land and were among the first in world history to make iron weapons, which were much stronger than the bronze weapons of their enemies. Hittite craftsmen also learned to make the lightest and fastest chariots of the time.

Hittite conquest and Phoenician trade, however, were both for the same purpose—material wealth. Perhaps Hittites and Phoenicians differed in their basic beliefs only in the emphasis the Hittites placed on war and violence. Images of Hittite gods looked almost identical to images of Hittite kings. In fact, the Hittite gods were glorified Hittite warriors.

Borrowers. The Hittites' way of life produced nothing new in world history. The Hittites were great "borrowers" from the peoples they conquered. Hittite art, for example, took no original approach or form. It resembled the art of the conquered peoples, differing only slightly in emphasis.

Although the Hittites were a major world power for much longer than Israel, they used their opportunity in history merely to loot as much of the world as they could.

Hittite Warrior: *The Hittites used their natural and human resources for war and conquest.*

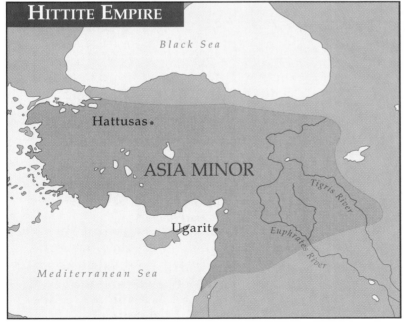

HITTITE EMPIRE

Black Sea

Hattusas•

ASIA MINOR

Ugarit•

Tigris River

Euphrates River

Mediterranean Sea

Hittite Empire: *The Hittites controlled much of Asia Minor for about 1,000 years.*

Toward New Empires and Christ

The Hittites and Phoenicians did not "fall in a day." Hittite power began to decline about 1200 B.C. after invaders burned their capital city, **Hattusas** [кнät′too·shäsh′]. In the 700s B.C., the new Assyrian Empire dealt the final blow to the Hittites. The Phoenician cities in Canaan were subject to repeated harassment by the Assyrians beginning in the 800s B.C. Some of the cities that the Phoenicians had started as trading posts, however, existed independently of the new empires for hundreds of years. Carthage, for example, contended with Rome for power until 146 B.C.

Nevertheless, the main tendency of world history was toward very large empires. Nation after nation such as the Hittites, Phoenicians, and Israelites were engulfed in these massive human organizations. But God's promise to Abraham remained; Israel still had an important role to play in world history. The new empires simply helped prepare the world for the birth of Christ, God's blessing to all mankind through Israel.

CHECK UP

1. What empire conquered the Northern Kingdom of Israel? When?
2. What empire conquered the Southern Kingdom of Judah? When?
3. Where was Phoenicia located?
4. What does the name *Phoenician* mean?
5. Did the Phoenicians consider themselves to be one people? What was their main interest?
6. What was the most important thing the Phoenicians carried with them as they traded throughout the Mediterranean?
7. How did the Hittites differ from the Phoenicians?
8. What was the main purpose of Hittite conquest?
9. When did Hittite power begin to decline? Who finally conquered the Hittites? When?
10. Describe the main tendency of civilizations in world history. How did this pattern fit in with God's plans?

Identify: Tyre and Sidon, murex, cedar, Carthage, Greeks, Asia Minor, iron, Hattusas

---

CHAPTER 4 REVIEW

MULTIPLE CHOICE Write the letter of the answer that best completes each sentence.

1. Because God was with them, the Israelites were able to defeat the _____ while traveling toward Sinai.
   a Assyrians   c Hittites
   b Amalekites   d Phoenicians

2. Moses received the Ten Commandments on Mount _____.
   a Horeb   c Sinai
   b Olivet   d Ararat

3. God chose _____ to lead Israel after Moses' death.
   a Joshua   c Saul
   b Aaron   d Samuel

4. God parted the waters of the _____ so that the Israelites could cross over into Canaan.
   a Mediterranean Sea   c Jordan River
   b Sea of Galilee   d Dead Sea

5. The walls of _____ fell at the sound of trumpets and shouts.
   a Tyre   c Hattusas
   b Jericho   d Sidon

6. The wise leader _____ warned against the dangers of having an earthly king.
   a Moses   c Saul
   b Joseph   d Samuel

CHAPTER 4 REVIEW

7. The first earthly king of Israel was
    _____.
    a Samuel   c David
    b Saul   d Solomon

8. The greatest earthly king of Israel,
   and one of the greatest kings of any
   age, was _____.
    a David   c Samuel
    b Solomon   d Saul

9. King _____ asked God for wisdom.
    a Saul   c Solomon
    b David   d Samuel

10. The Northern Kingdom was called
    _____.
    a Judah   c Phoenicia
    b Israel   d Canaan

11. The Southern Kingdom was called
    _____.
    a Judah   c Phoenicia
    b Israel   d Canaan

12. The Northern Kingdom fell in the
    700s B.C. to the _____.
    a Hittites   c Assyrians
    b Phoenicians d Chaldeans

13. The Southern Kingdom fell in the
    500s B.C. to the _____.
    a Hittites   c Assyrians
    b Phoenicians d Chaldeans

14. The _____ were merchants who
    established trade routes and colonies
    throughout the Mediterranean world.
    a Hittites   c Amalekites
    b Phoenicians d Assyrians

15. Two of the independent Phoenician
    cities were _____.
    a Jericho and Jerusalem
    b Tyre and Sidon
    c Hattusas and Chaldea
    d Sidon and Murex

16. One Phoenician trading post which
    grew into a large city was _____.
    a Jericho   c Carthage
    b Nineveh   d Hattusas

17. Historians who doubted the existence
    of the warlike _____ described in the
    Bible changed their minds because of
    archaeological discoveries in the 20th
    century.
    a Phoenicians c Chaldeans
    b Assyrians   d Hittites

18. The area between the Black Sea, the
    Mediterranean Sea, and the Euphrates
    River is known as _____.
    a Asia Minor   c Assyria
    b Mesopotamia d Canaan

19. The decline of Hittite power began
    when the Assyrians burned _____.
    a Carthage   c Hattusas
    b Tyre   d Sidon

MAP SKILLS *Use the map on pp. 45 and 47
to answer the following questions.*

1. What river marked the northernmost
   extent of Israel's influence?

   _____

2. What natural boundary separated
   Israel from Phoenicia?

   _____

3. Name another of Israel's western
   neighbors.

   _____

4. What body of water marked the
   southernmost extent of Israel's
   influence?

   _____

5. Name two Phoenician trading posts
   on the northern coast of Africa.

   _____

CHAPTER 4 REVIEW (CONTINUED)

COMPLETION Choose the correct term to complete each sentence and write the letter in the blank.

a alphabet   e judges
b covenant   f murex
c Decalogue   g principles of morality
d iron   h theocracy

1. At Mount Sinai, God made a(n) _____ (a solemn agreement) with Israel.
2. A government ruled by God is called a(n) _____.
3. The basic rules of right and wrong, good and evil, are called _____.
4. The Ten Commandments are also known as the _____.
5. God chose leaders called _____ to guide Israel through its first 300 years in Canaan.
6. The Phoenicians used sea snails called _____ to make a valuable purple dye.
7. The Phoenicians' most valuable contribution to world history was the _____ they carried with them as they traded throughout the Mediterranean.
8. The Hittites were aided in battle by strong weapons made of _____.

CONCEPT TO CONSIDER On a separate sheet of paper, answer the following question using complete sentences.

Did the Phoenicians and the Hittites make any lasting contributions to world history? Explain. What contributions did Israel make to mankind?

TIME LINE CHALLENGE Number the events in each group in the order in which they happened. Do each group separately.

GROUP A
_____ The Israelites refuse to go into Canaan.
_____ The Israelites wander in the wilderness for forty years.
_____ Israel defeats the Amalekites.
_____ God makes a covenant with Israel at Sinai.
_____ Moses dies; Joshua takes over.

GROUP B
_____ God parts the waters of the Jordan River.
_____ Samuel serves as judge.
_____ The land of Canaan is divided among the tribes.
_____ The walls of Jericho fall.
_____ Saul becomes king.
_____ The judges begin to rule Israel.

GROUP C
_____ The Temple is built.
_____ King David comes to the throne.
_____ The nation divides into Israel and Judah.
_____ The Assyrians and the Chaldeans overrun Canaan.
_____ Solomon dies.
_____ Solomon becomes king.

After a perfect beginning, mankind rebelled against God and set history on a downward course. Men and cultures, however impressive their accomplishments might be, have fallen deeper and deeper into sin. At such dramatic moments as the expulsion from Eden, the Flood, and the dispersion from Babel, God's judgment for man's choice of sin has wrought enormous consequences for history.

But to save men from sin, God has a plan which provides a thread to follow through history. This thread leads to Jesus Christ. It began in the ancient Middle East in about the year 2000 B.C. when God called Abraham to be the father of Israel, the nation from which Christ would come.

Abraham left behind an impressive culture in Sumer. The Sumerians, through elaborate irrigation systems, took advantage of the Tigris and Euphrates rivers to make a desert bloom. This cradle of culture gave birth to such important accomplishments as writing. Hammurabi, ruler of the vast Babylonian Empire, used writing to set up laws that, along with other methods of government he employed, brought peace and prosperity.

The culture Abraham left behind, however, was in rebellion against God. As humanists, the Sumerians and others who followed in their footsteps in Mesopotamia worshiped false gods that were only glorified human beings. Humanistic beliefs dominated the Sumerians, whose lives revolved around worshiping or imitating their gods. Rulers like Hammurabi cleverly manipulated such beliefs to increase their own power.

It took great faith in God for Abraham to be able to separate himself from the world of his day and travel around the fertile crescent to Canaan. Even in Canaan, Abraham and the other Patriarchs faced great temptations to live as the Canaanites, who worshiped gods of pleasure and lust and accomplished nothing of value in world history.

Soon the developing nation of Israel found itself down in Egypt, where God planned for it to spend several hundred years. Egypt equaled or excelled the culture of Mesopotamia in many respects. Ruins of its massive architecture such as the pyramids still stand today. Thanks to the Nile River, Egypt flowered as an oasis in the desert. But this impressive culture was also in rebellion against God. Confused beliefs about a bewildering variety of gods and the cycles of nature stunted growth in the arts and sciences. The Egyptians took humanism to a new extreme by worshiping their pharaohs as gods. When the pharaohs enslaved the Israelites and refused to let them go, God assured Israel that it was His chosen nation and demonstrated His power to all the world by fiercely judging mighty Egypt.

Free in its own land with its own government, Israel had the chance to build world history's first nation under God. The governments, laws, and basic beliefs of earlier cultures had been dominated by false gods. Israel's neighbors, the Phoenicians and Hittites, had no vision or goal for themselves in world history beyond the profits of their trade and conquest. But the one true God gave Israel its government, laws, and basic beliefs.

The first chapter of Israel's history as a nation-state, however, ended with Israel as another culture in rebellion against God. God's impartial judgment came upon His people, who soon fell captive to new empires. But Moses, David, and other great Israelite leaders had been inspired to write much of the Old Testament. As the Bible grew, God promised that a solution was coming for the spiritual problems that plagued the Jews and the rest of mankind. God would use the massive new empires to prepare the world for the first coming of Jesus Christ.

BRITAIN

ATLANTIC
OCEAN

GAUL

EUROPE

ITALY

• Rome

SPAIN

GREECE

Athens

Carthage •

Mediterranean Sea

AFRICA

Danube

700s B.C.
Rise of Assyrian
Empire/Works
of Homer

600s
Rise of
Chaldean
Empire

500s
Rise of
Persian
Empire

536 Decree of Cyrus/Remnant
of Jews returns to Judah

509 Latins establish Roman Republic

323 Greek empire divided

700 | 600 | 500 | 400 | 300 | 200

721 Assyrians conquer
Northern Kingdom
of Israel

490–480
Persian Wars
(Greeks defeat Persians)

431–404
Peloponnesian Wars
(Sparta defeats Athens)

336–323
Alexander the Great
builds a Greek
empire

246–146 Punic Wars
(Rome defeats Carthage)

586 Chaldeans conquer Southern Kingdom of Judah

Unit 2

NEW EMPIRES AND CULTURES: THE MIDDLE EAST, GREECE, AND ROME

(c. 800 B.C.–A.D. 500)

Preparation for Christ

5 According to His Will:
Assyria, Babylon, and Persia

6 Greece—A Drama in Two Acts

7 Rome before Christ

8 Rome after Christ

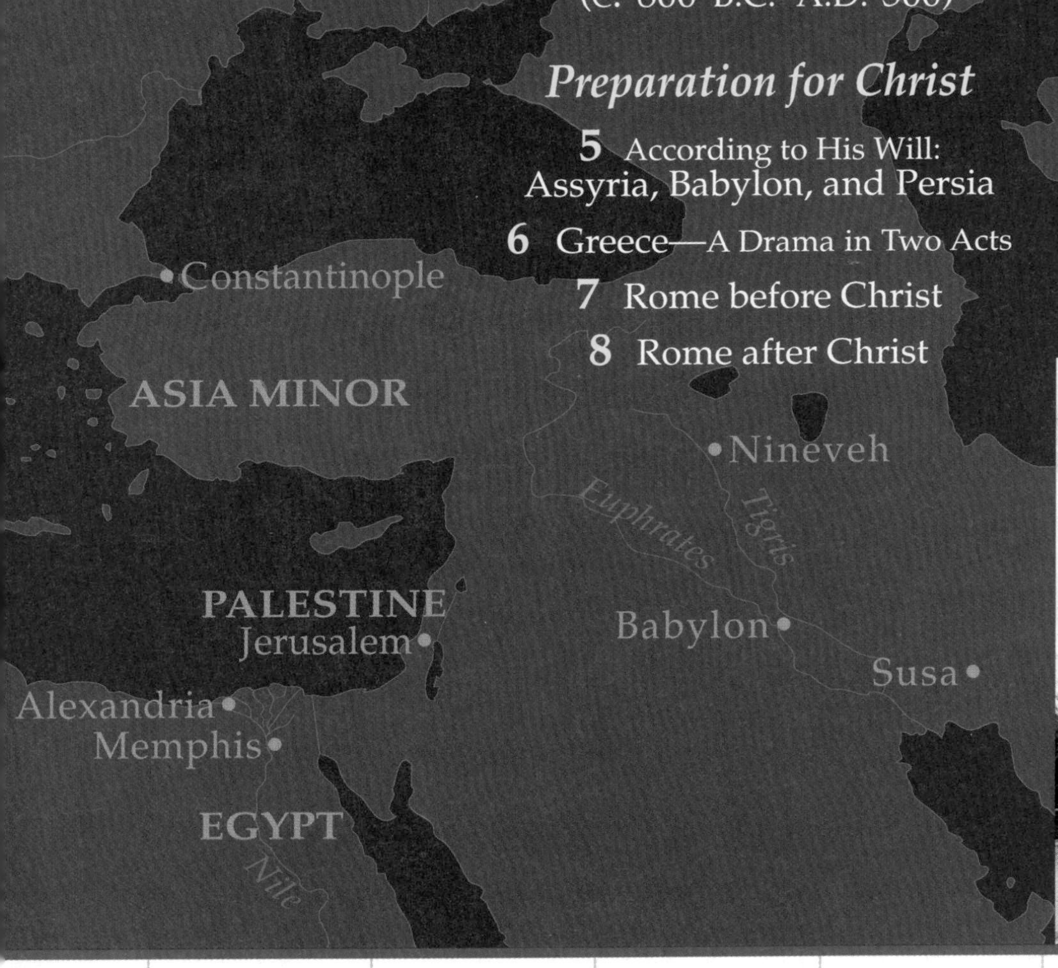

ASIA

Constantinople

ASIA MINOR

Nineveh

Euphrates

Tigris

PALESTINE
Jerusalem

Babylon

Susa

Alexandria
Memphis

EGYPT

Nile

- 30 Caesar Augustus becomes emperor/Pax Romana begins
- 4 B.C.–A.D. 30 Life of Christ
- 64 Rome burns
- 79 Mt. Vesuvius erupts
- 300s Barbarian invasions begin
- 313 Constantine issues Edict of Milan, legalizing Christianity

100		100	200	300	400

- 49–44 Julius Caesar rules Rome
- 54–68 Nero rules Rome Persecution of Christians begins
- Constantine reunites Roman Empire 324
- Christianity becomes official religion of Roman Empire/Empire divided between East and West 395
- Barbarians capture Rome 410

5
According to His Will:
Assyria, Babylon, and Persia
(c. 800–300 B.C.)

HIGHLIGHTS
Assyrian Empire • Chaldean Empire • Nebuchadnezzar
Persian Empire • Cyrus the Great

The Assyrian Empire

Origin of the Assyrian Empire
Assyria and its people. Kings and peoples who aspired to rule the world began rising and falling in the 700s B.C. The first conquerors came from **Assyria,** originally a small area in the rolling hill country of the upper Tigris River valley.

The **Assyrians** were probably named for Shem's son **Asshur** [äs′sho̅o̅r], who built the city of **Assur.** The people who established the Assyrian empire were actually a mixture of Semites and Hamites. Ham's grandson Nimrod had entered Assyria at an early date and led in the building of the city of **Nineveh** [nĭn′*e*·ve], which later replaced Assur as the capital of the Assyrian Empire.

A tool of God's judgment. The Assyrian drive to build a world empire began in earnest during the 700s B.C. under **Tiglath-pileser III** (ruled 745–727 B.C.). By the late 600s B.C., the Assyrians controlled nearly all of the fertile crescent, part of central Asia Minor, and Egypt. Their conquests included the Israelites of the Northern Kingdom, whose time had come to suffer judgment for their sins. Thus, Assyria became God's instrument of judgment. In His word to the Jewish

prophet Isaiah, God describes Assyria as the instrument of His wrath.

. . . the rod of mine anger, and the staff in their hand is mine indignation. I will send him against an hypocritical nation, and against the people of my wrath will I give him a charge, to take the spoil, and to take the prey, and to tread them down like the mire of the streets. (Isa. 10:5–6)

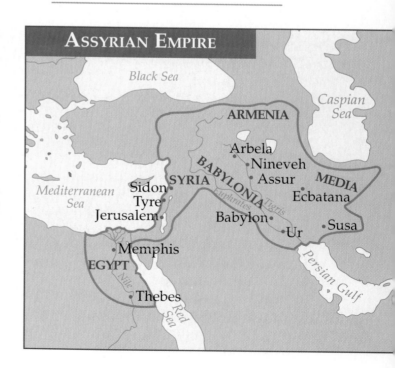

ASSYRIAN EMPIRE

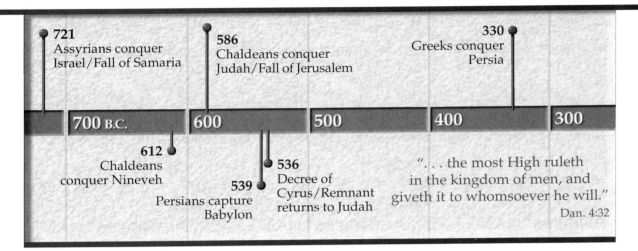

721
Assyrians conquer
Israel/Fall of Samaria

586
Chaldeans conquer
Judah/Fall of Jerusalem

330
Greeks conquer
Persia

700 B.C.   600   500   400   300

612
Chaldeans
conquer Nineveh

539
Persians capture
Babylon

536
Decree of
Cyrus/Remnant
returns to Judah

*". . . the most High ruleth
in the kingdom of men, and
giveth it to whomsoever he will."*
Dan. 4:32

Method of the Assyrian Empire

The Assyrians were among the most feared and hated people of ancient times. Not satisfied to merely destroy and replace governments, they sought a more thorough and complete conquest by attempting to crush the spirit of nationalism among the peoples they conquered. The Assyrians frequently *deported* nations from their lands, sending them to other locations and bringing in new inhabitants from elsewhere. No longer living as a group in a place they could call their own, the conquered peoples stopped thinking of themselves as nations. Around 722 B.C., the Assyrian king **Shalmaneser V** [shăl′mə·nē′zĕr] deported the ten tribes of the Northern Kingdom of Israel. Scattered around the empire, they never returned to their homeland.

Purpose of the Assyrian Empire

Wealth. Through fear and terror, the Assyrians conquered and ruled a great empire that brought them enormous wealth. The peoples they conquered sent a steady stream of tribute to enrich the cities, palaces, and temples of the Assyrian homeland. Assyrian kings held lavish feasts for thousands of guests. Once, in the city of Calah [kā′lə], nearly 70,000 people feasted for ten days, consuming more than 2,000 oxen and 16,000 sheep.

Art and literature. The empire also enabled Assyrian kings to pursue their interests in art and literature. **Ashurbanipal** [ä′shoor·bä′nĕ·päl: ruled 669–626 B.C.], the last great Assyrian king, collected a library of about 100,000 cuneiform clay tablets. The library included records of important events in Assyria's history as well as memorable literature from Mesopotamia such as the story of Gilgamesh.

Records of brutality. Like the Assyrian kings before him, Ashurbanipal had numerous images and inscriptions carved in stone to celebrate his feats. Assyrian kings boasted of the brutality and cruelty they showed to the people they conquered. Nearly bursting with pride, they described

Boasts and Tribute: *Conquered subjects brought tribute, such as these horses, to the Assyrians. The Assyrian kings loved this tribute and often boasted about it.*

themselves as kings of the universe who had brought the "whole world" into submission. The Jewish prophet **Jonah** warned Nineveh of God's coming judgment, and for a while the Assyrians repented and believed in God, but they soon resumed their vain rebellion.

Fall of the Assyrian Empire

Sennacherib's defiance. Standing outside the walls of Jerusalem in the Southern Kingdom, the Assyrian king **Sennacherib** [se·năk′ĕr·ĭb: ruled 705–681 B.C.] boasted that the God of Judah could do no better than the gods of the peoples he had already conquered. Sennacherib had just finished his blasphemy when an angel completely destroyed the Assyrian forces and sent their king running home in shame to Assyria, where he died at the hands of his own children. God punished "the stout heart of the king of Assyria, and the glory of his high looks" (Isa. 10:12).

A quick defeat. Despite their policy of empire-building and maintenance, the Assyrians were unable to conquer Judah or even prevent the fall of their own empire. *Chaldeans* from southern Mesopotamia, *Medes* from the east, and *Scythians* [sĭth′ĭ·anz] from the north combined to attack, using cavalry forces that the Assyrian infantry could not match for mobility and striking power. In fulfillment of the Biblical prophesies in the book of **Nahum,** Nineveh fell in 612 B.C. Now Assyria experienced the kind of cruelty it had inflicted on others. Less than 100 years after reaching its peak in power and size, the Assyrian Empire was wiped from the face of the earth.

A New Babylonian Empire

Origin of the Chaldean Empire

The **Chaldeans** soon came from the southern end of Mesopotamia and established a kingdom at Babylon. **King Nabo-**polassar [năb′ŏ·pŏ·lăs′ĕr: ruled from 625 to 605 B.C.] formed an alliance with the Medes and the Scythians who had overthrown the Assyrian Empire. Under his leadership, the Chaldeans conquered all of Mesopotamia and established the Chaldean Empire, sometimes called the **Second** or **New Babylonian Empire** (Hammurabi's Babylonian Empire was the First or Old Babylonian Empire). The Chaldean Empire eventually extended over the entire fertile crescent, but it never included Egypt as had the Assyrian Empire.

Under Nabopolassar's son **Nebuchadnezzar** [nĕb′ŭ·kad·nĕz′ĕr: ruled 605–562 B.C.], the Chaldeans conquered the western part of the fertile crescent, including the Southern Kingdom of Judah. The time had come for Judah to suffer judgment for her rebellion against God. Thus, Nebuchadnezzar destroyed Jerusalem and carried the inhabitants of Judah away to captivity in Babylon, the capital city of the new empire.

Method of the Chaldean Empire

The Chaldeans had learned important lessons from the Assyrians. By taking the Jews to Babylon and destroying the city of Jerusalem, Nebuchadnezzar demonstrated that he could be as ruthless as any Assyrian. However, the Chaldeans treated their captives much better than the Assyrians had treated theirs. The Jews actually

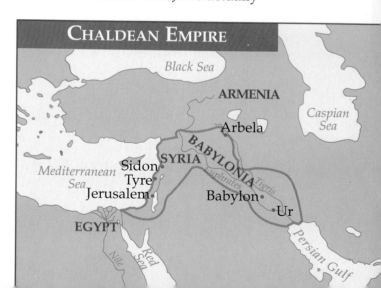

CHALDEAN EMPIRE

Black Sea

ARMENIA

Caspian Sea

Arbela

BABYLONIA

SYRIA

Sidon

Mediterranean Sea

Tyre

Jerusalem

Babylon

Ur

EGYPT

Euphrates

Tigris

Persian Gulf

Nile

Red Sea

Hanging Gardens of Babylon: From a distance, these gardens appeared to hang in the air.

prospered during their captivity in Babylon. **Daniel,** one of the captives, eventually became the chief adviser to Nebuchadnezzar.

Purpose of the New Babylonian Empire

Nebuchadnezzar followed the great tradition of pride in buildings that had characterized Mesopotamia since the days of Nimrod and the tower of Babel. Nebuchadnezzar and other Chaldean kings claimed, as the Assyrians had, to rule the "four corners of the world." But rather than using cruelty to make a name for themselves in history, the Chaldean kings used the impressive city of Babylon, the crown of the empire, as a means of self-glorification.

The city of Babylon. The tribute that poured in from the empire allowed Nebuchadnezzar to glorify himself by making Babylon one of the most beautiful and magnificent cities of all time. The surrounding walls may have been nearly 60 miles around, 100 or more feet high, and wide enough on top for two lanes of chariot traffic. Inside the walls stood great temples, a ziggurat, and a palace perhaps three miles around and hundreds of feet high. Especially striking were the *Hanging Gardens,* a structure of receding terraces supported by arches and columns and filled with flowers

and trees. Nebuchadnezzar built the gardens for his wife, who missed the greenery of her mountainous homeland to the northeast in the land of the Medes. From a distance, the gardens appeared to "hang" in the air. The Hanging Gardens of Babylon were regarded as one of the wonders of the ancient world.

Nebuchadnezzar's dream. In the second year of his reign, Nebuchadnezzar had a dream which foretold the course of world history. God revealed the meaning of this dream to Daniel, who explained to Nebuchadnezzar that the God of Heaven had given him a preview of the great empires that would rule the world. Nebuchadnezzar and his Chaldean Empire, the greatest of these empires, would rule the known world for about 60 years. Other empires would follow, but none would be as great as Babylon.

Daniel and the Future

Daniel's ability to interpret dreams and visions and to foretell the future greatly impressed Nebuchadnezzar, who made Daniel his chief adviser. Just as Joseph's similar gifts had enabled him to rise from a slave to the chief assistant of an Egyptian pharaoh, so Daniel's gifts led to his elevation from prisoner of war to chief adviser of the Chaldean king. Nebuchadnezzar's other "wise men" could not match Daniel's ability to prophesy. They had to rely on magic and the false "science" of astrology, which attempts to predict the course of human affairs according to the position of the stars and planets in the sky.

Daniel's gifts were from God. Few men have been privileged with such visions of the future as God sent Daniel. His prophecies have been a source of hope to God's people throughout the centuries; in fact, we still await the fulfillment of Daniel's prophecy about the end times.

Fall of the Babylonian Empire

God's dealings with Nebuchadnezzar. Unfortunately, Nebuchadnezzar's respect for Daniel and Daniel's God did not last. Consumed with pride, he became convinced that all the world should bow down to the great city of Babylon, its god, and its king. Repeating the mistake made at the tower of Babel, Nebuchadnezzar forgot God and sought instead to exalt his own name. As he proudly boasted about his achievements, God reduced Nebuchadnezzar to a madman who ate grass. After seven years of living like a wild animal, the Chaldean king regained his sanity and praised God for His power to make the proud humble, recognizing Him as the true King of the world. Nebuchadnezzar gave his testimony in his official capacity as king and sent it out to all the peoples of the empire. For a moment, the great world empire of the Chaldeans stood in a right relationship to God.

Just as the repentance of the Assyrians had quickly passed, the Chaldeans' acknowledgment of God did not last. Perhaps Nebuchadnezzar never turned from God again, but by the time of his son **Nabonidus** [năb′ŏ·nī′dus: ruled from 556–539 B.C.], the Chaldeans were openly blaspheming God.

The end of an empire. Because Nabonidus, the last Chaldean king, cared more for travel than for government, he

Ishtar Gate: Among the many wonders of ancient Babylon was the Gate of Ishtar, a beautiful structure decorated with colorful enameled bricks and reliefs of lions, bulls, and dragons. The reconstruction pictured here is located near the ruins of the original gate.

appointed his son **Belshazzar** [bĕl·shăz′ĕr] to handle the actual business of government for him in Babylon. Thus, while Nabonidus remained king in name, Belshazzar actually ruled the Chaldeans.

In 539 B.C., Belshazzar held a great banquet for a thousand people. While he and his guests drank from gold and silver cups taken years before from God's temple in Jerusalem, a hand from heaven appeared and wrote on the wall of the banquet hall. By the time of Belshazzar, Daniel had almost been forgotton, but Belshazzar's queen remembered him. The frightened king summoned Daniel, who came and interpreted the message as a prophecy of doom for Babylon. That same night—in fulfillment of the prophecy—*Medes* and *Persians* invaded the city, and Belshazzar was killed. Less than a hundred years after it began, the Chaldean Empire ended abruptly.

The Persian Empire

Cyrus and the Origin of the Persian Empire

Subservience to the Medes. The Persians lived just east of the Tigris and Euphrates Valley. They probably descended from Noah's son Japheth, whose descendants are sometimes called **Indo-Europeans.** The Indo-Europeans settled the continent of Europe and even reached as far as India in Asia. Even today there are traces of an ancient common language among these people.

The Persians were at first loosely organized and subservient to the Medes. The Medes, much more powerful descendants of Japheth to the north, had played an important role in the fall of the Assyrian Empire. The Persians' situation changed drastically, however, when **Cyrus the Great** [sī′*rus*] began to lead them.

Cyrus's victories. Between 559 and 550 B.C., Cyrus <u>united the Persians</u> and <u>led them to victory</u> over the Medes. Unlike conquerors before him, Cyrus wisely spared the life of the Median king, did no harm to the Medes' capital city, and even left Median officials in charge of the same duties.

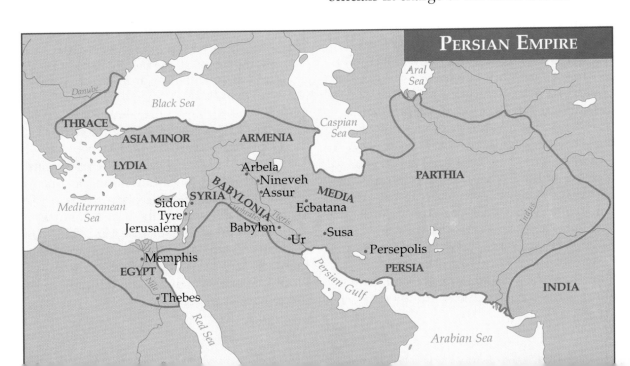

PERSIAN EMPIRE

Cyrus's sudden rise to power stunned the world. The Chaldeans, the Egyptians, and even the distant Greeks feared him. Especially worried were the *Lydians* [lĭd'ĭ·anz], an important people in Asia Minor that the Medes had tried but failed to subdue.

Cyrus as an instrument of God. These fears were well founded. Cyrus was an appealing leader who drew men to him like a magnet.

What even Cyrus did not know, however, was that God had chosen him specifically for the tasks that lay ahead.

The prophet **Isaiah,** hundreds of years before, had written that God would be Cyrus's ally in world conquest. By 539 B.C., Cyrus had conquered both the Lydians and the Chaldeans and as a result controlled all of Asia Minor and the fertile crescent.

Cyrus's Policies of Conquest and Politics

Clever tactics in battle and religion. Cyrus used many clever strategies in his conquests. He surprised the Lydians by going against the usual practice and fighting in the bitter cold of winter. He also had some of his men ride camels in battle, knowing that horses are afraid of camels and that his enemies' mounts would thus be useless for fighting. He surprised the Chaldeans by redirecting a river that flowed through Babylon and entering the city behind the Chaldeans' main defense lines. A quick military victory over the Chaldean army permitted Cyrus's troops to take the city of Babylon without a fight.

Cyrus not only knew how to conquer but also how to hold on to his conquests. He generally honored the gods of the peoples he conquered. When Cyrus entered the city of Babylon, he presented himself not as a distant emperor but as the new king of Babylon, chosen to be king by

Marduk himself, the god of Babylon. Thus he received a generous welcome.

A new approach to empire building. Unlike the Chaldeans, Cyrus did not require the people he conquered to give up their local loyalties to their city, god, and king. He also avoided the Assyrian methods of fear and terror. He wisely restrained his army from harming or frightening the inhabitants of the cities and lands they conquered.

Cyrus, Daniel, and the Freeing of the Jews

As he had first done with the Medes, Cyrus left most of the old Chaldean officials in place, with Persians looking over their shoulders. Daniel was among the Babylonian officials who retained their positions. With his God-given talents, Daniel rose to even greater power under the Persians than he had under the Chaldeans.

Daniel may have told Cyrus of Isaiah's prophecies and showed the king that the power of God had been behind his astounding conquests. In 536 B.C., God moved Cyrus to issue one of the most remarkable commands of any king in world history:

Thus saith Cyrus king of Persia, All the kingdoms of the earth hath the LORD God of heaven given me; and he hath charged me to build a house in Jerusalem, which *is* in Judah. Who *is there* among you of all his people? The LORD, his God, *be* with him, and let him go up (2 Chron. 36:23).

A total of 42,360 Jews returned to Judah. God's plans for Cyrus were finished.

Cyrus died in 529 B.C., but later Persian kings reaffirmed his commandment concerning the Jews. After some of the people around Judah tried to stir up the Persians against the Jews, **Darius** [də·rī'us: 522–486 B.C.] was reminded of Cyrus's commandment. Darius even added that tax money would be used to pay for the rebuilding of the temple.

The Bible as History

The Bible, the most important source for the knowledge of history, is the only completely reliable source because the men who wrote it were inspired by the Holy Spirit. The Bible is the Word of God and therefore contains no mistakes, something that can be said of no other book.

Our study of the beginning showed the importance of the Bible for information about the earliest times. The Bible also provides the student of world history with invaluable information about ancient cultures. Only the Bible, for example, records the moments when the three empires studied in this chapter were briefly in a right relationship to God. Read the books of Jonah and Daniel to learn more about these events in history.

The book of Esther is also a good book to read in this study. It records the life of a brave and beautiful Israelite girl who helped save her people from disaster. This book contains some of the best information available anywhere about the daily life of Persian kings and how some people misused the rule that a Persian king's commandment could never be changed. (Esther married Xerxes I, known in the Bible as Ahasuerus.)

The Bible has also been the source for many of the most important things you have learned about Sumer, Canaan, Egypt, and Israel. If you want to do further reading in ancient history, you could do no better than to read the Old Testament!

Darius and the Royal Road

For about half a century, the Middle East prospered as never before. Darius helped business by making taxation uniform and systematic. People were able to plan ahead in their purchases, savings, and investments because they knew in advance how much they would have to pay for taxes. Darius also standardized weights, measures, and units of money. The use of trading standards throughout the empire made buying, selling, and lending much easier. New roads also aided trade by improving transportation. The great "highway" of the Persian Empire was the **"Royal Road,"** which stretched over 1600 miles from Susa, the Persian capital, to Sardis, a city in Asia Minor. The Royal Road enabled the Persians to develop an excellent postal system much like the

"Pony Express" of American history. Riders carried the mail on horseback, relaying it to new riders at stations along the Royal Road. Thanks to Darius, the entire Middle East became one big market place or "common market." Things made in one place might be sold and used thousands of miles away.

Decline and Fall of the Persian Empire

We will see in the next chapter that, in accordance with Daniel's prophecies, the Persian Empire finally fell to the Greeks around 330 B.C. Long before, the Persian Empire had declined and weakened, as Daniel had foretold. Daniel prophesied that the Persian Empire would be "inferior" to the Chaldean Empire. Even though it was much larger and longer-lasting, it never had a stable "head."

Kings and Coins: Since time immemorial, coins have been minted with the images of rulers. This coin depicts a Persian king riding in a chariot. Coins with such pictures circulated throughout the vast Persian Empire as a constant reminder of the king.

A Stairway to Kings: Foreigners bearing tribute and assistants ready to act the part of a slave marched up this giant staircase to enter the court of the Persian king at Persepolis.

Darius had set up a good organization, but the empire could never be strong without stable leadership. Kings constantly changed. The members of the royal family and the court continually quarreled, plotted, and fought over who would be king.

Consider these kings after Darius I, the years of their kingships, and key events associated with them:

Xerxes [zûrk´sēz: 486–464 B.C.]: murdered in his bed.

Artaxerxes I [är´tag·zûrk´sēz: 464–424 B.C.]: killed his elder brother to acquire the throne.

Darius II (423–404 B.C.): killed several brothers.

Artaxerxes II (404–358 B.C.): all the provinces banded together to attempt his overthrow.

Artaxerxes III (359–338 B.C.): poisoned by a palace assistant.

Arses [är´sēz: 338–336 B.C.]: murdered along with his entire family.

Darius III (336–330 B.C.): killed by his own men as he ran to escape the new world conquerors from the west, Alexander the Great and the Greeks.

Instruments of God's Will

God's greater purposes. God sometimes works in mysterious ways. He has often changed the course of history through the life of one man who did not even realize that he was God's instrument and who may have even been living in rebellion against God. Such a man can still serve God's greater purposes although "he meaneth not so, neither doth his heart think so. . ." (Isa. 10:7). Each of the empires studied in this chapter was for a time an instrument of God's will in this way.

Proud, ambitious kings. The culture of Mesopotamia had changed little since the days of Hammurabi, the Sumerians, and even Nimrod. Like their ancestors, the

Assyrian and Chaldean Empires lived in rebellion against God. Both looked up to the same kind of gods we first encountered in Sumer—glorified human beings, imagined as superhuman warriors and city builders. Each worshiped a special "king of the gods" identified with great cities of their empires. In worship and imitation of their gods, proud Assyrian and Chaldean kings strove to exalt themselves and their empires above the rest of mankind and even above God himself.

Yet, as we have seen, God used the Assyrians and Chaldeans in His judgment of the Northern and Southern Kingdoms of the Jews, who were sinking deeper and deeper into the worship of false gods and rejecting the one true God. Indeed, there were even brief moments when the Assyrians and Chaldeans actually had a right relationship with God. But God's impartial judgment soon came upon each of these empires as well. The Persian Empire was God's instrument to destroy the Chaldean Empire and free the Jews from the Babylonian captivity. Much larger and longer-lasting than the empires of the Assyrians or Chaldeans, the Persian Empire for about 200 years brought *all* the peoples of the Middle East into *one* unit ruled by *one* man. As Cyrus finally realized, the power of God had been behind such astounding conquests.

The roles of God's people in the three empires. God's people played extraordinary roles in these three great empires of ancient times, just as they had in mighty and impressive Egypt. We have seen, for example, the remarkable influence that Daniel exercised in *both* the Chaldean and Persian Empires. He was a right-hand man to the most powerful rulers on the earth of his time. Daniel *consciously* sought God's will for his life. Not even Nebuchadnezzar or Cyrus could match the power that Daniel possessed as God's free instrument.

Continuing thread of hope. Through it all, God continued to work in history with His plan for man's salvation. A remnant of the Jews, spiritually wiser from their years of suffering, had returned to their homeland, where Christ would be born from among them. New peoples were arising to the west who, learning from the great cultures and empires of the ancient Middle East, would establish cultures and empires yet to be exceeded in splendor and glory. Although they knew nothing of God's plans for them, the Greeks and Romans prepared the world for God's greatest intervention in history.

CHECK UP

1. What ruler united the Persians and led them to victory over the Medes?
2. What prophet predicted that God would aid this ruler in his conquests?
3. How did the Persians treat their conquered cities as compared to the Assyrians and Chaldeans?
4. What command did Cyrus make in 536 B.C.?
5. How did Darius help make the Middle East a common market?
6. Why is the Bible the only completely reliable source for history?
7. Why should a person studying Persian history read the book of Esther?
8. Give some examples to show how Persian royalty after Darius I plotted and fought over who would be king.
9. Give an example of an Israelite who had great influence on the empires of the Chaldeans and Persians.
10. Explain how God used the empires of Assyria, Chaldea, and Persia.

Identify: Japheth, Indo-Europeans, Cyrus, Lydians, Darius, "Royal Road"

CHAPTER 5 REVIEW

MULTIPLE CHOICE *Write the letter of the answer that best completes each sentence.*

1. The Assyrians were descendants of Noah's son ____.
   a Japheth   c Ham
   b Shem   d Nimrod

2. Nimrod led in building the Assyrian city of ____, which later became the capital of Assyria.
   a Assur   c Persepolis
   b Nineveh   d Babylon

3. The Assyrian drive to world empire began in earnest under ____.
   a Nimrod   c Tiglath-pileser III
   b Tiglath-pileser I   d Sennacherib

4. The ten tribes of the Northern Kingdom were spread around the Assyrian Empire during the reign of ____.
   a Tiglath-pileser III   c Ashurbanipal
   b Sennacherib   d Shalmaneser V

5. The last great Assyrian king, who collected over 100,000 cuneiform clay tablets, was ____.
   a Ashurbanipal   c Shalmaneser V
   b Tiglath-pileser III   d Sennacherib

6. God defeated ____ because of his pride and defiance.
   a Tiglath-pileser III   c Shalmaneser V
   b Ashurbanipal   d Sennacherib

7. All of the following participated in the invasion and defeat of the Assyrian Empire *except* the ____.
   a Chaldeans   c Greeks
   b Medes   d Scythians

8. The prophet ____ prophesied the destruction of Nineveh.
   a Isaiah   c Daniel
   b Nahum   d Micah

9. The people who came from the southern end of Mesopotamia and established a kingdom at Babylon were the ____.
   a Assyrians   c Babylonians
   b Scythians   d Chaldeans

10. Under the leadership of ____, the Chaldean Empire was established.
    a Nabopolassar   c Nabonidus
    b Nebuchadnezzar   d Belshazzar

11. The king who conquered the western part of the fertile crescent (including the Kingdom of Judah) was ____.
    a Nabopolassar   c Nabonidus
    b Nebuchadnezzar   d Belshazzar

12. Nabonidus, the last Chaldean king, preferred to travel around the empire, leaving the actual business of government under the supervision of his son ____.
    a Nabopolassar   c Cyrus
    b Nebuchadnezzar   d Belshazzar

13. Babylonia was invaded and Belshazzar was killed by ____.
    a Chaldeans and Assyrians
    b Assyrians and Persians
    c Medes and Persians
    d Persians and Scythians

14. The Israelite captive who interpreted Nebuchadnezzar's dream as well as the writing on the wall was ____.
    a Isaiah   c Daniel
    b Nahum   d Jonah

15. The Persian king who allowed the Jews to return to Judah was ____.
    a Belshazzar   c Darius
    b Cyrus   d Nabonidus

16. The prophet ____ foretold that God would assist Cyrus in his conquests.
    a Nahum   c Isaiah
    b Jonah   d Daniel

17. The Persian king who made the Middle East into one big market place was ____.
    a Darius   c Xerxes
    b Cyrus   d Arses

COMPLETION Choose the correct term to complete each sentence and write the letter in the blank.

a Assyrian   c Persian   e Darius
b Chaldean   d Nebuchadnezzar   f Cyrus

1. The king who used camels in battle to frighten his enemy's horses was _____.
2. The "Royal Road" greatly benefitted trade in the _____ Empire.
3. The king who established trading standards was _____.
4. The Southern Kingdom of Judah was conquered by the _____ Empire.
5. The Northern Kingdom of Israel was conquered by the _____ Empire.
6. The king who permitted the Jews to return to Judah was _____.
7. The Assyrian Empire was succeeded by the _____ Empire.
8. The empire known for its cruelty and violence was the _____ Empire.
9. The largest and longest lasting empire was the _____ Empire.
10. The greatest empire was the _____ Empire.

TIME LINE CHALLENGE Choose the letter of the correct date for each event listed below.

745 B.C.	669	625	612	605	559–550	539	536	522	330
A	B	C	D	E	F	G	H	I	J

_____ 1. Reign of Ashurbanipal begins—the last great Assyrian king
_____ 2. Nebuchadnezzar begins his reign
_____ 3. Nabopolassar, who took Mesopotamia from the Assyrians, begins his reign
_____ 4. Assyrian drive for world empire begins under Tiglath-pileser III
_____ 5. Cyrus unites the Persians and defeats the Medes
_____ 6. Persia falls to the Greeks
_____ 7. Darius begins his reign
_____ 8. Nineveh falls, as predicted by the prophet Nahum
_____ 9. Cyrus allows 42,360 Jews to return to Judah
_____ 10. The Medes and Persians invade Babylon

CONCEPT TO CONSIDER On a separate sheet of paper, answer the following question, using complete sentences.

Briefly explain how God's hand in human events is illustrated by the rise and fall of such empires as Assyria, Babylon, and Persia.

6
Greece—A Drama in Two Acts
(c. 800–300 B.C.)

HIGHLIGHTS
Early Greek Civilization • Homer and the Olympian Gods
Athens and Sparta • Alexander the Great

Act One

Appearance on the Stage of World History

A New Scene

As the scene shifts from the Middle East westward toward Europe, Greece comes into sight, jutting into the Mediterranean Sea. The history of Greece is like a drama in two acts. Act one opens with the origin of Greek civilization and leads to the rise of the Athenian empire; Act two begins with the great war between Athens and Sparta which set the stage for the rise of Alexander the Great, the conqueror who came "from the west on the face of the whole earth . . ." (Dan. 8:5) in fulfillment of Biblical prophecy.

The ancient Greeks excelled in poetry, politics, and philosophy and aspired to excellence in the arts, but they desired to exceed man's limits. Some great minds saw through myths and broke free from the kind of man-made gods that had dominated Middle Eastern peoples for centuries. Having recognized such deities as only glorified human beings, "an image made like to corruptible man" (Rom. 1:23), the Greeks might have turned to the one true God. Instead they began to think of themselves as gods. "Professing themselves to be wise, they became fools" (Rom. 1:22), and repeated the mistake of worshiping man, the creature, rather than God, the Creator.

Greek Drama: Many of the tragic plays that brought the ancient Greeks to tears are still performed. These dramas reveal much about how the Greeks viewed life.

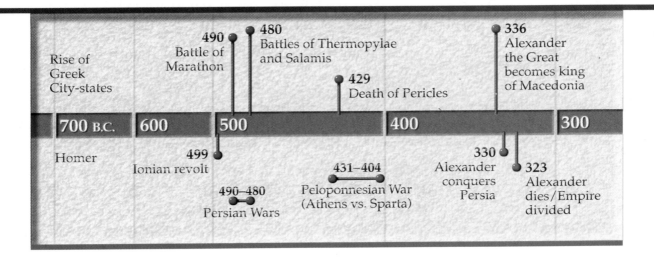

700 B.C.   600   500   400   300

Rise of Greek City-states

490 Battle of Marathon

480 Battles of Thermopylae and Salamis

429 Death of Pericles

336 Alexander the Great becomes king of Macedonia

Homer

499 Ionian revolt

490–480 Persian Wars

431–404 Peloponnesian War (Athens vs. Sparta)

330 Alexander conquers Persia

323 Alexander dies/Empire divided

Origin of the Greeks

Descendants of Japheth. The Greeks were descendants of Japheth's son **Javan** [jă′van]. Perhaps **Japheth** himself went to Greece, for people were already living there very early in world history.

Minoan civilization. The earliest civilization in the vicinity of Greece was that of the **Minoans** [mĭ·nō′anz]. Centered on the island of *Crete,* Minoan civilization produced such impressive structures as the palace at **Knossos** [nŏs′us], which occupied more than four acres and contained an excellent plumbing system. The Minoans crisscrossed the Aegean Sea as sea traders from about 1600 to 1400 B.C., when their culture suddenly and violently ended. Some historians believe that volcanic activity on a nearby island may have destroyed the Minoan civilization on Crete with volcanic ash, earthquakes, and tidal waves.

The warlike Mycenaeans. The **Mycenaeans** [mī′sĕ·nē′anz] flourished on the mainland of Greece between about 1600 and 1200 B.C. The Mycenaeans, like the Minoans, built an impressive culture. The fortress city of **Mycenae** [mī·sē′nē], for which they were named, was surrounded by walls 10 feet thick; royal tombs outside the city also demonstrate great architectural

skill. The Mycenaeans used the sea for adventures in piracy and war that often took them far from home. Some may have joined other pirates in harassing the coast of Asia Minor in the 13th century B.C. Mycenaeans once burned the city of **Troy** on the coast of Asia Minor after a 10-year war.

A dark age. About 1200 B.C., Greece fell into a dark age. Cities were suddenly destroyed and left in ruins, and writing

Forerunners of the Greeks: The Minoans on the island of Crete were the earliest known people in the vicinity of Greece.

69

Temple of the Olympian Zeus

Homer

stopped. Invaders from the north, known in world history as **Dorians** [dō′rĭ·*a*nz], probably hastened the destruction, but the violent Mycenaeans no doubt contributed to their own downfall. The dark age ended with the reappearance of writing in the 700s B.C., and a new Greek culture began to emerge, one that would make a lasting impact on world history. This new culture was greatly influenced by the work of one man, the blind poet **Homer.**

Homer and Greek Mythology

Homer and his poems. Little is known about Homer. He probably lived during the 700s B.C., perhaps on the island of Crete or in the city of **Smyrna.** He seems to have been a bard, a singing poet, and may not have even known how to write. But Homer gets the credit for polishing and refining the old stories of Greek mythology to create the *Iliad* [ĭl′ĭ·*a*d] and the *Odyssey* [ŏd′*i*·sē], two poems still widely read and admired. No poet has ever had such influence on the thinking of a people as Homer had upon the Greeks.

The Olympian gods. From Homer, the Greeks learned of the gods who supposedly lived on **Mount Olympus** [ŏ·lĭm′p*u*s]. These gods closely resembled those of other peoples. **Zeus** [zoos], reminiscent of

Babylon's Marduk, was the king of these gods. Like the Mesopotamian and Egyptian gods, the Greek Olympian gods were associated with the powers of nature. **Apollo** [ə·pŏl′ō] had a close connection with the sun, **Poseidon** [pô·sī′dĕ·ŏn] with the sea, and **Artemis** [är′tĕ·mĭs] with the moon. Other gods or goddesses personified such things as wisdom [Athena: ə·thē′nə], love and beauty [Aphrodite: ăf′rô·dī′tĕ], and marriage [Hera: hē′rə, Zeus's wife].

The Olympian gods differed from all previous gods in one important respect: they were the product of a poetic genius. Homer's gods had individual human personalities unmatched in the myths of other cultures. However, the *Iliad* and the *Odyssey* made it obvious to more thoughtful Greeks that the gods were in reality nothing more than glorified human beings.

Heroes. Human characters also played important roles in Homer's poems. Like the gods of Olympus, these **heroes** were glorified human beings; they differed from the gods only in that they were mortal (they could die) and less powerful. Homer's heroes were men of unusual ability and tremendous bravery such as *Achilles* [ə·kĭl′ēz] and *Odysseus* [ô·dĭs′ūs], both great warriors in Greek mythology.

The Rise of Greek Cities

Long before Homer, Greek families worshiped their ancestors. Ancestor worship made family ties very strong, linking past, present, and future generations. As families branched out, larger groups formed. At first, families came together to form tribes and villages. Later, tribes and villages joined to form the *polis* [pō′lĭs], or city-state. The word *politics* comes from the Greek word *polis*.

The typical polis surrounded a hilltop fortress called the **acropolis** [ə·krŏp′ŏ·lĭs]. In addition to providing refuge from enemy attack, the acropolis served as a seat of government and religion. In the shadow of the acropolis stood the **agora** [ăg′ŏ·rə], or marketplace, a busy place of commerce, conversation, and political debate. Most Greek cities also had a *gymnasium,* a place of physical training and games of skill, and an *amphitheater,* an outdoor theater.

The Greek city had to be small so that all of its citizens could meet together and

The Acropolis of Athens: A large, rocky hill called the Acropolis dominates the horizon of Athens today, just as it did in ancient times. On the Acropolis were built magnificent temples and other public buildings.

The Parthenon: The most famous building on the Acropolis of Athens, the Parthenon, is believed by some people to be the finest building of ancient times.

71

The Agora: The men of Athens met in the Agora to do business and discuss the issues of their day.

Olympic Games: Long-distance running was one of many events at the ancient Olympic games.

know one another personally in order to share common gods and feel the closeness characteristic of the polis. It was therefore impossible for all of the Greeks to gather into one big polis. In Homer's day, more than a hundred independent cities dotted Greece.

Geography also encouraged the formation of many separate cities. Mountains and valleys made travel between cities difficult, and the lack of substantial rivers combined with the moist Mediterranean climate made irrigation projects (such as those that induced cooperation in Mesopotamia and Egypt) impractical and unneccessary.

Greek Unity

Common gods. Most Greeks came to believe in the gods of Homer's poems. These common gods, along with the Greek language, stimulated unity among the people. The Greeks began to distinguish themselves from the rest of mankind, calling non-Greek peoples "barbarians." To the Greeks, barbarians were little different from animals and worthy only of slavery.

Common interests. A common love of sports and an appreciation for beauty also encouraged Greek unity. Sports played an important role in every polis. Greek

athletes enjoyed running, wrestling, and spear- and discus-throwing. To encourage unity among the various city-states, the Greeks began to hold the **Olympic games** every four years in honor of Zeus. The first Olympic games took place in **776 B.C.**, the first recorded date in Greek history. The Olympics became so important that cities would interrupt their warring to attend and then return to the battlefield when the games were over.

The Seven Wonders of the Ancient World

Of the seven wonders of the ancient world, five were products of Greek ingenuity.

1. The Pyramids of Egypt
2. The Hanging Gardens of Babylon
3. The Temple of Artemis at Ephesus
4. The Statue of Zeus at Olympia
5. The Mausoleum at Halicarnassus
6. The Colossus of Rhodes
7. The Lighthouse of Alexandria

The Greeks' love for sports reflected their appreciation of beauty; obsessed with physical perfection, the Greeks practically worshiped their athletes. Greek art and architecture also reflected this appreciation of beauty. Greece became famous in the ancient world for her magnificent temples and her beautiful, lifelike sculptures.

Wars and politics. The Greek sense of unity was still very limited, however. The cities of Greece spent as much time at war with one another as they spent in friendly athletic competition. Only attacks from an outside enemy ever united the Greeks in enterprises of war or politics.

The Greco-Persian Wars

Greek expansion. As many Greek cities grew rapidly beyond what the land could support, people began to move to less crowded areas. Thus Greek colonies appeared on islands in the Aegean Sea, north of the Aegean in *Thrace,* and east of the Aegean in *Ionia* [ī·ō′nĭ·ə], a region along the coast of Asia Minor. Colonists also journeyed westward to Sicily, southern Italy, Gaul, North Africa, and even Spain. As the Greeks spread out, they encountered many "barbarian" peoples who opposed their colonization efforts. They also attracted the attention of the

Persians, whose empire was rapidly expanding in all directions.

Darius and Ionian revolt. Soon after **Cyrus the Great** added Lydia to his Persian Empire in 546 B.C., he conquered Ionia. Neither the Ionians nor the mainland Greeks welcomed the Persian conqueror. Encouraged by the cities of Athens and Eretria [ə·rē′trĭ·ə], the Ionians revolted against the Persians in 499 B.C. **Darius I,** the new Persian king, crushed the Ionian revolt and demanded that the mainland Greeks submit to him. Determined not to be absorbed by the Persian Empire, the cities of *Athens, Eretria,* and *Sparta* refused Darius's demands.

The Battle of Marathon. In the summer of 490 B.C., Darius sent a fleet to Greece. After defeating Eretria, the Persian fleet landed troops at **Marathon** [măr′ə·thŏn], about a day's march north of Athens. Although the Spartans had not yet arrived, the greatly outnumbered Athenians charged, driving the Persians back to their ships. After a second defeat at Athens, the Persians finally returned to their empire in the east. The Battle of Marathon not only proved that the Persian conquerors *could* be defeated, but it also brought great prestige to Athens, beginning her rise to power among the cities of Greece.

Xerxes plots revenge. Ten years after the battle of Marathon, Darius's son **Xerxes I** [zûrk′sēz] determined to avenge his father and conquer the Greeks. With great expectations of extending his empire far to the west, the Persian monarch assembled what may have been the largest military force the world had ever seen—perhaps more than 2,500,000 men and 3,000 ships.

The Battle of Thermopylae. So vast was the Persian army that only a small portion of it could sail by ship; the rest of the mighy host had to march into Greece by land. While the Persians lost time building a bridge across the **Hellespont** [hĕl′əs·pŏnt], a strait where Europe and

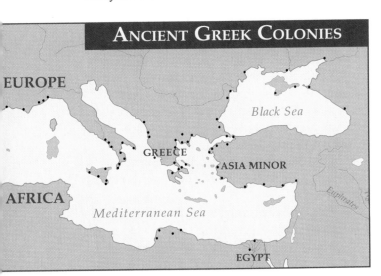

ANCIENT GREEK COLONIES

EUROPE

Black Sea

AFRICA

GREECE

ASIA MINOR

Mediterranean Sea

Euphrates

EGYPT

Asia Minor are less than one mile apart, Sparta organized an alliance of 30 Greek cities. Under the Spartan king *Leonidas* [lĕ·ŏn'ĭ·das], the Greeks decided to block the Persian advance toward Athens at **Thermopylae** [thĕr·mŏp'ĭ·lē], a narrow mountain pass in central Greece about six miles from the Aegean Sea. There, in 480 B.C., the Greeks and Persians met once again. For two days, the Spartans held off the Persian hordes until a traitor informed Xerxes of another way over the mountains. Attacked from both front and rear, Leonidas ordered most of his troops to withdraw. He and about 300 Spartans remained and gave their lives to hold the Persians at the pass long enough for the other Greeks to retreat.

The Battle of Salamis. From Thermopylae, the Persians marched southward without opposition to Athens, only to find the city abandoned. Nearly all of the inhabitants had evacuated to the island of **Salamis** [săl'ə·mĭs]. Xerxes burned Athens's sacred temples and then went down to the shore to watch the huge Persian navy do battle with the much smaller Greek navy in the narrow strait between the island of Salamis and the mainland. There, Xerxes watched in horror as the Greek ships outmaneuvered his crowded fleet and began to ram and sink the Persian ships one by one. After losing most of his navy, Xerxes fled to Persia with two thirds of his army. The other third remained in Greece until they suffered a crushing defeat in 479 B.C.

Greek victory. The defeat of Xerxes' great army ended any hopes the Persians had of conquering Greece. Greek civilization would continue to thrive in the west. However, the political and military unity of the Greek cities soon vanished after the defeat of their common enemy. Before long, Sparta and Athens, the two cities that had most distinguished themselves in the war against the Persians, were at odds with each other.

CHECK UP

1. How did geography encourage the development of separate, independent cities in Greece?
2. Name a few things that contributed to Greek unity.
3. When were the first Olympic games held? How did they encourage unity?
4. Where did the Greeks establish colonies?
5. What Persian ruler conquered Ionia?
6. Which Persian ruler launched the first Persian invasion of mainland Greece?
7. Which emperor started the second Persian invasion of Greece? What natural barrier slowed his army down as they marched toward Greece?
8. Name the narrow pass where the Spartans met the Persians and held them off for two days.
9. Where did the small Athenian fleet defeat the great Persian fleet?

Identify: ancestor worship, polis, acropolis, agora, gymnasium, amphitheater, Athens, Eretria, Sparta, Leonidas

The Drama of Politics

The Changing Governments of the Greek Cities

Importance of family background. Originally, only a small minority enjoyed political freedom and equality in the Greek cities. This inequality in Greek society was rooted in the inequality found within the Greek family structure. The family religion of ancestor worship made fathers very powerful; the passing of this authority—as well as all property—to the eldest son produced considerable inequality within large, extended families. People without a family religion were regarded as inferior or "ignoble."

Precarious monarchy. The first city governments reflected the family structure. One man was responsible for the family religion, and one man was given responsibility for the worship of the city's gods. In the cities, such men became known as kings. This form of government was a **monarchy,** meaning *rule by one.*

In ancient Greece, the powerful heads of the families thought themselves equal to one another and to the king of the city. They resented and resisted any king who tried to dominate them. Rejected by the family heads of the city, a king might turn elsewhere for support. Because the heads of the families could not tolerate this threat to their supremacy, kings were often run out of a city or stripped of all but their priestly power.

Aristocracy and the few "best." The rejection of the kings led to a new form of government. The family heads *as a group* began to rule the cities directly. In this way,

---

the Greeks became the first people in world history to reject one-man rule.

This new form of government was an **aristocracy** [ăr/is·tŏk/rə·sē], meaning *rule by the "best."*

Because of their noble birth and important religious role, the heads of the great families thought themselves better than everyone else in the city. Inheritance arrangements made them the wealthiest men in the city and, therefore, the most powerful. Warriors had to buy their own horses and equipment for the cavalry, at that time the city's most important military force, and only the rich aristocrats [a·rĭs/tŏ·krăts] could afford to do that.

Oligarchy and the new rich. Business and commerce grew so rapidly beginning in the eighth century B.C. that many men who could not claim noble birth became rich from foreign trade. (Foreigners were beginning to highly value the olives and grapes that grew abundantly in Greece.) These new rich could now afford to buy the equipment needed to be a soldier in the

heavily armed infantry, which was becoming more important and required more men than the cavalry did. By this time, worship of the old family gods had grown weak and was less respected. It was difficult for the heads of the great families to claim that they alone were the "best."

The new rich demanded that they be given a voice in the government and be treated like true citizens. Thus a new form of government, an **oligarchy** [ŏl/ĭ·gär/kē], developed. Oligarchy means *rule by a few rather than one or many.* In practice, however, it meant *rule by a few rich men.* Sometimes the few rich men called themselves *aristocrats* and their government an *aristocracy.* It was not long before these few men were claiming that being rich meant being best.

The many poor versus the few rich. By this time, the many poor were making an important contribution to Greek military power and naturally resented the dominance of the few rich. A large number could afford the equipment needed for the new lightly armed infantry, and *anyone* could afford to be part of the navy, now the main military force of some cities. Thus, many poor men refused to fight for the city unless they were recognized as true citizens with a voice in the government. The rest of the history of politics in the Greek cities is primarily a story of bitter struggle between the few rich and the many poor.

Tyranny. One or two of the few rich, wanting all of the power to themselves, encouraged hatred between rich and poor to achieve their goals. They pretended to be friend and protector of the many poor against the few rich. "If you will only trust me with power," said such a man to the many poor, "I will help you by hurting the rich."

Men who succeeded in these schemes established a **tyranny** [tĭr/ə·nē], *a bad form of one-man rule.* These tyrants [tī/rănts] were selfish and interested only in their own good. Unlike the earlier kings, the tyrants had no religious power and could not necessarily pass their position on to their sons. But like the kings, they appealed to the common people as friends.

Democracy and rule by the poor. The people soon learned that tyrants are not the friends they pretend to be. Discontent with tyranny, they rose up and established a democracy. **Democracy** means *rule by the many or the common people.* In practice, however, it meant *rule by the poor.* It did *not* mean rule by all. Even under a democracy, many people, including women and slaves, had no voice in the government and were not true citizens. Slaves alone might number one quarter of a Greek city's population.

A vicious cycle of instability. The triumph of democracy in the cities where it occurred did not stop changes in governments. Believing themselves to be "better," the rich deeply resented the role of the poor in the government. They also feared that the poor would use their political power to steal from the rich. Sometimes the rich managed to reestablish an oligarchy, at least for a while. But there was still no stability. By the time of the Persian Wars and after, many Greek cities were experiencing a vicious cycle of oligarchy, tyranny, and democracy.

Sparta: A Special Case

Oligarchy based on force. Not all Greek cities followed through the complete cycle of governmental changes. Sparta stopped short with oligarchy. A very small circle of men governed Sparta through an assembly, while two so-called kings spent more time keeping tabs on one another than they did ruling.

The members of this small ruling class were the only true citizens of Sparta; they alone had the privilege to participate in the government. These "true Spartans" were very wealthy and owned the best land. A

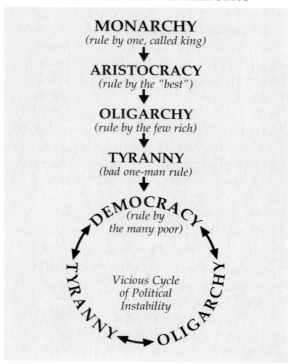

Patterns of Change in Greek Governments

MONARCHY
(rule by one, called king)
↓
ARISTOCRACY
(rule by the "best")
↓
OLIGARCHY
(rule by the few rich)
↓
TYRANNY
(bad one-man rule)
↓
DEMOCRACY
(rule by the many poor)

Vicious Cycle of Political Instability

TYRANNY ← → OLIGARCHY

slightly larger middle class of merchants and businessmen conducted the industry and commerce of the city. Although this class lacked a voice in the government, they did have certain rights and privileges. The largest class of all was that of the **Helots,** the common laborers who farmed the land for the ruling class. While the Helots worked like slaves in the fields, the ruling class spent its time training to fight. Spartan education was extremely harsh and almost entirely physical. It was designed not so much to train citizens for war as to help them control the Helots by force.

Reluctant for war. In spite of their reputation as terrific warriors and their city's image as a big army camp, the Spartans only reluctantly fought wars. True citizens were too few to man an adequate army. People with no part in the government—people who were for all practical purposes foreigners—had to be armed and called upon to fight. War made it harder for the small ruling class to control the Helots.

The Peloponnesian League. To multiply her military strength, Sparta formed an alliance with Corinth [kôr′ĭnth], Megara [mĕg′ə·rə], and other cities in the Peloponnesus [pĕl′ə·pə·nē′sus], a region in southern Greece. During the Persian Wars, this **Peloponnesian League,** as it was called, joined Athens and her allies to ward off the Persian invasion. Just 50 years later, however, Sparta and her Peloponnesian League would be at war with Athens herself.

The Athenian Democracy

Solon's laws. Athens followed the cycle of changing governments beyond oligarchy to democracy. Athens' movement toward democracy began with the laws of **Solon,** an aristocrat who <u>introduced democratic principles to Athenian government</u>. Solon's laws gave all free adult males in Athens the right to participate in the assembly, the body which voted on all new laws and made all major decisions.

Pericles and direct democracy. **Pericles** [pĕr′ə·klēz], an aristocrat who dominated Athens from 461 to 429 B.C., <u>brought the Athenian democracy to its fullest measure</u>. Until Pericles came on the scene, the right to attend the assembly and to hold public office had been of little practical value to the poor. Men who had to work for a living could not afford the time to participate in politics. Pericles called for fees to be paid to those serving in government.

For the first time in world history, political participation became a realistic possibility for the many poor.

Periclean Athens had a complete democracy virtually unknown today. In a

Pericles

modern **representative democracy,** *the people elect a few men who represent them in the government.* Athens was a **direct democracy:** *the people themselves made the big decisions of government directly, rather than indirectly through representatives.* Only relatively small places like the Greek cities can have direct democracy. In ancient Athens, all adult free males could assemble in one place, speak and listen to speeches, and then make decisions for the city. As the history of Athens shows, direct democracy is stable and workable only when it is blessed with extraordinary leaders such as Pericles.

Pericles' leadership and speaking ability. Pericles owed his position of leadership to the great intelligence he displayed in his power of speech. Speaking ability counted for more than anything else when the Athenian assembly met. A man like Pericles who could give beautiful and persuasive speeches almost always carried the day. Pericles used his eloquent speeches to lift the eyes of Athenians above petty selfishness and encourage strong patriotism.

Belief in the gods of the city was no longer enough to unite the city and her citizens. The city's gods were gradually going the way of the old family gods. In his greatest speech, Pericles made no mention of the gods. He tried instead to make the individual and the city one by painting a beautiful word picture of Athens. The great city he described was an ideal, but it was close enough to the real Athens that people really believed in it for a while. The selfish struggle between rich and poor was temporarily suspended as all looked upon Athens as a city worth dying for.

Pericles spoke of a city destined for immortal fame and glory in which all citizens could have a share. Above all there was freedom:

—freedom to have a say in public business,

—freedom to live a private life without undue interference,

—freedom to rise, by one's own merits, from poverty and obscurity to renown and wealth.

Yet this freedom did not mean lawlessness, or so Pericles said. Athenians

—freely obeyed the laws and authorities,

—freely refrained from injuring one another,

—freely displayed the valor necessary to defend the city in war.

Undoubtedly for the average Athenian, the most stirring parts of Pericles' speeches were when he spoke of the Athenian empire.

The Athenian Empire

After the Persian Wars, Athens eagerly became the leading city in Greece. To guard against possible future attacks by the Persians, Athens formed a defensive alliance called the **Delian League.** At its peak, the league contained about 250 Greek cities on the coasts and islands of the Aegean Sea; each member supposedly had an equal voice, but Athens dominated the league. Gradually, the Delian League became an Athenian empire as membership ceased to be voluntary and "members" began to send money, ships, and soldiers to Athens as tribute. Having acquired an empire, the Athenians soon found that they could not live without one. The Athenian democracy depended upon the empire. The empire was a central part of the ideal Athens that inspired rich and poor to temporarily suspend their hostility toward one another. On a more practical level, many people made their living by serving in the Athenian government or navy, and the empire provided the money to pay these people.

Inevitable war. Athens could not enjoy the benefits of empire for long without *increasing* its empire. The more prosperous Athens became, for example, the more wealth it took to maintain the prosperity. Without "new worlds to conquer," what outlet would there be for the great Athenians? The stronger the Athenian empire became, the more cities outside the empire had to fear. Threatened by Athenian expansion, Sparta and the Peloponnesian League began to prepare for the inevitable war with Athens.

─────── CHECK UP ───────

1. How did the government of Greek cities reflect the structure of Greek families?

2. What form of government did Sparta have?

3. What name was given to those in Sparta who did not belong to the ruling class? How did the ruling class spend its time?

4. Describe Spartan education.

5. Why were the Spartans reluctant warriors?

6. Who brought Athenian democracy to its fullest measure?

7. What is the difference between representative and direct democracy? Which form did Athens use?

8. How did Pericles encourage patriotism in Athens?

9. How did Athens become dependent upon its empire?

Identify: monarchy, aristocracy, oligarchy, tyranny, democracy, Peloponnesian League, Delian League

PELOPONNESIAN WAR

(Map labels:) Adriatic Sea, ILLYRIA, MACEDONIA, THRACE, Byzantium, Pella, Propontis, Mt. Olympus▲, EPIRUS, THESSALY, Troy, LEMNOS, Sparta and its allies, Athens and its allies, CORCYRA, Aegean Sea, AEOLIS, LESBOS, LYDIA, Thermopylae×, Sardis, ITHACA, Delphi, EUBOEA, CHIOS, IONIA, ASIA MINOR, Ionian Sea, Thebes, Marathon×, Athens, Salamis, Corinth, SAMOS, Olympia, Mycenae, DELOS, Miletus, SPORADES, Key — ▲ mountain, × battle, • city, PELOPONNESUS, CYCLADES, COS, Pylus, Sparta, MELOS, THERA, RHODES, Mediterranean Sea

Act Two

The Peloponnesian War

Sparta versus Athens

Oligarchy vs. democracy. Greece was split in two. On one side stood oligarchical and reserved Sparta with her Peloponnesian League; on the other side loomed democratic and daring Athens with her empire. War between Sparta and Athens began in 431 B.C. and lasted until 404 B.C., with but a brief period of peace between. Sparta was the first to declare war, but Athens, under Pericles' leadership, was eager to fight. Most of the Greeks and eventually even the Persians became involved in the **Peloponnesian War.**

Pericles' Leadership

Pericles, the leader of Athens, perceived that Athens had the advantage of money and naval power while Sparta had the advantage of land power. He persuaded his fellow citizens to allow Sparta to invade the Athenian countryside. The city could then defend itself behind the walls while Sparta exhausted its resources in vain. In the meantime, the Athenian navy would inflict as much damage as it could.

This policy might have succeeded if Pericles had remained in leadership, for he could persuade the Athenians to sacrifice and see beyond the suffering of the moment. But a plague struck the city, killing many Athenians. In 429 B.C., Pericles died of the plague, and the leadership of Athens fell to inferior men.

By 421 B.C., both Sparta and Athens were ready for a rest and agreed to peace.

Athens' Defeat

As expected, the peace between Sparta and Athens was brief. New leadership soon led the Athenians in a campaign to conquer the Greek colonies of the west and to provide the Athenian empire with a new source of wealth and manpower. Athens did not fare as well as she had hoped, however, and her allies began to abandon her. Sparta formed an alliance with Persia and built a fleet to challenge Athens at sea. In 405 B.C., the Athenian navy was caught off guard and destroyed. In 404 B.C., Athens surrendered, lost her empire and fleet, and was forced to pledge allegiance to Sparta.

Consequences of the War

The war brought nothing good to any of the Greek cities. Sparta's new "leadership" was, if anything, worse than Athens' had been. Sparta tried to set up oligarchies in the cities. While friendly to Sparta, these governments often brutalized their own people. In less than a year, the Athenians cast off their Spartan yoke. By 371 B.C., the city of **Thebes** [thēbs] delivered a decisive defeat to Sparta, and the cities of Greece regained their independence.

Greek Philosophy

The Birth of Greek Philosophy
Philosophers and the gods. The first Greeks to call the false gods into question were the philosophers. *Philosopher* means *"lover of wisdom."* Several things led the philosophers, in their quest for knowledge, to reject the myths about the gods. It was obvious to people of intelligence that the gods of Homer's poems were fictional. **Xenophanes** [zē·nŏf′ə·nēz] spoke for philosophers in general when in the sixth century B.C. he ridiculed Greek polytheism and **anthropomorphism** [ăn′thrŏ·pŏ·môr′-fĭz′m: *ascribing human characteristics to nonhuman things*]. If horses had gods and could make statues, said Xenophanes, their gods would look like horses! Then, in the seventh and sixth centuries B.C., some Greeks who traveled widely began to see the great variety of beliefs about gods in the ancient world. On many points, these beliefs contradicted one another, especially concerning the beginnings. It was only natural to ask which, if any, of these beliefs were correct.

To understand the world around them, the curious Greek philosophers relied on their abilities to think and to observe the here and now. *Man is the measure of all things,* they said. Not content with silly stories about false gods, the philosophers

Socrates

demanded truths that could be explained and defended to any reasonably intelligent man.

Socrates
The first philosopher to insist that morality, or proper conduct, is a part of philosophy was **Socrates** [sŏk′rə·tēz: 470–399 B.C.]. He urged his students to ask questions and to examine their beliefs. "Know thyself," was his sage advice. But lacking knowledge of the absolute moral standards of the one true God as revealed in Scripture, he could not prove his ideas to others or himself. The superstitious Athenians accused Socrates of corrupting the youth of Athens because he encouraged his students to question their beliefs in the gods of the city. Given a choice between exile from Athens or death, Socrates chose to take his own life by drinking hemlock, a poison.

Plato and Aristotle
Plato. Socrates inspired **Plato** [plā′tō: c. 428–347 B.C.], one of his students, to become one of the greatest philosophers of all times. Although Socrates did not record his philosophy, Plato wrote thirty or more works called **dialogues** [dī′ə·lŏgz].

It is difficult to know exactly what Plato believed. His dialogues resembled dramatic plays, although they were not meant to be performed. Plato's dialogues do make one thing clear: answers to the fundamental

Plato and Aristotle: This is how Raphael, a famous artist born in A.D. 1483, depicted Plato and Aristotle. Plato is on the left, Aristotle on the right.

CHECK UP

1. What was the war between Athens and Sparta called?
2. What advantages did the Athenians have over the Spartans? What advantage did the Spartans have over the Athenians?
3. What great catastrophe robbed Athens of its leader?
4. What happened in 405 B.C. that led to Athens' surrender in 404 B.C.?
5. What city defeated Sparta in 371 B.C., enabling the cities of Greece to regain their independence?
6. What does *philosopher* mean? What part of Greek life did the philosophers call into question?
7. What philosopher ridiculed Greek polytheism in the sixth century B.C.? What does *anthropomorphism* mean?

Identify: Pericles, Socrates, Plato, dialogues, Aristotle

---

questions about the basic principles of all things must recognize and explain the obvious order, design, or purpose in the universe. Plato was moving *toward* the truth that God inspired the Apostle Paul to write in the New Testament:

> . . . the invisible things of him [God] from the creation of the world are clearly seen, being understood by the things that are made, even his eternal power and Godhead . . . (Rom. 1:20).

Aristotle. The same may be said of **Aristotle** [ăr′ĭs·tŏt′′l: 384–322 B.C.], Plato's most famous pupil. Aristotle recognized order, design, or purpose in the universe. He knew that no science would be adequate which failed to account for this order. Aristotle concluded that there had to be a single, superhuman, thinking Being called God who gave order to everything in the universe.

A New World Empire

The Rise of Macedonia

Macedonia [măs′ə·dō′nĭ·ə] loomed on the northern fringes of Greece. It was not a land of independent cities but a powerful kingdom. Although the Greeks considered the Macedonians barbarians, the Macedonian kings claimed Greek ancestry and greatly admired Greek culture, including the works of the philosophers.

In 359 B.C., **Philip II** became the king of Macedonia. He was determined to do what no one, Greek or barbarian, had ever done—become the master of all Greece. Soon he had conquered the outlying regions of Macedonia and moved south into Thessaly [thĕs′ə·lĕ] and east into Thrace [thrā·sĕ] as he prepared to take

Philip II: The image of this ancient silver coin is that of Philip II, king of Macedonia and father of Alexander the . Great.

Greece. Turmoil within and among the Greek cities had made them ripe for conquest, but Philip enjoyed special advantages. The gold mines of Macedonia enabled him to equip a large, strong army of full-time soldiers. Philip's soldiers were trained to fight as a **phalanx** [fā′lăngks: *a large group of foot soldiers armed with spears and shields, trained to charge the enemy as a group*]. Fighting like one giant warrior with one great spear and one massive shield, an army in phalanx formation could sweep cavalry or other military forces off the field.

By 338 B.C., Philip had conquered most of Greece. The Macedonian king decided not to treat Greece as empires are usually treated. He did not demand heavy taxes. He hoped that the Greeks whom he admired so much would freely join him in his next adventure—the conquest of the Persian Empire, the Greeks' ancient enemy.

Alexander the Great

Death cut Philip's plans short, however. He was murdered in 336 B.C., the victim of a plot by his jealous wife *Olympias.* Philip's son **Alexander**—known in world history as Alexander the Great—became the new king at the age of 20. Headstrong and daring, Alexander threw himself into action. Through single-minded drive he overcame the fearful risks of world conquest. Just as Daniel had prophesied, Alexander charged like a goat with a single, powerful horn—an enraged animal shattering and trampling everything in its path (Dan. 8:5–7, 21).

Alexander first extended his domains northward into Europe to the Danube River

and westward to the Adriatic Sea. In 334 B.C., Alexander crossed the Hellespont and defeated Persian forces waiting for him. He entered **Babylon** in the autumn of 331 B.C., and by December, he had taken **Susa,** the Persian capital. **Persepolis,** the chief city of the Persian homeland, fell in 330 B.C. Alexander's forces carried out the great treasures of Persepolis on the backs of 20,000 mules and 5,000 camels. Centuries before, the Persians had burned the great public buildings of Athens; now Alexander put the torch to the Persian palace of Persepolis. With the death of Darius III in 330 B.C., Alexander officially became the king of Persia. Within two more years, the easternmost provinces of the Persian Empire all belonged to Alexander.

From his base in Greece (a land area smaller than the state of Florida), Alexander had conquered the Persian Empire without losing a single battle. The world has ever since been amazed. It seemed that nothing could stand in his way, that he had almost supernatural insight into the strategy and tactics of war. Alexander did not realize that the power of God had permitted his conquests.

A new Achilles. Alexander thought of himself as a new Achilles, the great warrior hero of Homer's *Iliad.* Alexander had memorized the *Iliad* as a young boy, finding inspiration in it for strength, courage, endurance, and will power. He learned the value of affections, loyalties, and generosity (even to defeated enemies). He saw Achilles as a model of leadership. Like Achilles, Alexander was always at the front with his troops—fighting, suffering, and triumphing just as they did.

Student of Aristotle. Alexander was also aware of the developments of Greek culture after Homer. As a boy, Alexander had studied under Aristotle, who had come from Athens specifically to be Alexander's teacher. Thus one of the greatest conquerors in world history was a student of one of the greatest

Alexander the Great: This mosaic (a picture made from small pieces of variously colored material) shows Alexander in his usual pose: in the heat of battle.

philosophers of all times. No doubt this relationship contributed to Alexander's respect for **Hellenic** [hĕl·ĕn′ĭk] ideas. *(Hellenic is derived from Hellenes [hĕl′ēnz], another name for the Greeks.)*

A Hellenistic world. In his new empire, Alexander tolerated many local customs. He permitted the Jews around Jerusalem, for example, to worship God in their traditional way. But wherever he conquered, Alexander introduced Greek culture. His successors would continue this practice. The period of several hundred years between Alexander's conquest and the Roman Empire is known as the **Hellenistic Age.** During this time, Greek became the second language of the world. All over the empire, Alexander built cities like those in Greece (especially Athens), with the same architecture and way of life. Alexander named 16 of these cities for himself—"Alexandria." He built the first and most famous **Alexandria** in Egypt. Within a century, it became the most important city in the Hellenistic world.

Alexander's tragic end. Though he ruled all of Greece and Persia, Alexander could not restrain himself from further conquests. He had to possess all of India. Thus Alexander advanced deeper and deeper into India, determined to reach what he believed to be the eastern limit of the world. (Alexander shared the common view of the time that the

Indian subcontinent was a small peninsula jutting eastward into a body of water called "Ocean.") But Alexander's weary men finally refused to go any further, and Alexander agreed to turn around. His conquest of the world was over.

After a long and difficult journey, Alexander reached Babylon by 323 B.C. Still hoping for other conquests, Alexander the Great, not yet 33 years old, died of an intense fever or poison on June 13 of that year. A Greek dramatist could not have written a more tragic ending for this greatest of Greek heroes.

Break-Up of Alexander's Empire

Daniel prophesied a short life for Alexander's empire; as soon as Alexander died, a struggle for power broke out. Alexander had shattered everything in his path; now the time came for his empire to be shattered. Four of Alexander's greatest generals divided the empire among themselves. **Ptolemy** [tŏl′e·mē] took Egypt. **Antipater** [ăn·tĭp′ə·tẽr] took Macedonia. **Laomedon** [lā·ŏm′ê·dŏn] took Syria, the name then used for the western half of the fertile crescent (including all of Canaan). **Seleucus** [sĕ·lū′kʉs] took the eastern part of the fertile crescent, and soon took Syria from Laomedon. The Ptolemies in Egypt and Seleucids in Syria ruled for nearly 200 years.

Under these and other smaller kingdoms of the Hellenistic Age, Greek culture continued to spread. Old ways of life and basic beliefs weakened under the ceaseless, questioning Greek curiosity. Pride had caused the Greeks to turn toward a new extreme of humanism. The old gods of human imagination were "dead," but philosophers like Plato and Aristotle and great men of politics and war like Alexander had begun thinking of themselves as gods. The characteristic curiosity of the Greeks, however, would not permit such beliefs to be held without doubts. Greek culture was better at destroying old beliefs than providing new ones. Many people felt lost. The old gods had been the very foundation of the world for most men. Without the gods, their world was stripped of all meaning.

As hearts broke open, the world became increasingly ready for Jesus Christ.

The Greek Legacy

The ancient Greeks developed a culture that has influenced western civilization for more than 2,000 years. Consider their contribution to the field of government. The concept of democracy originated in ancient Greece. Before the Greeks developed the principles of democracy, the common man had no voice in government; kings and aristocrats ruled nations.

In literature, many of their works remain popular today. One of the best-known Greek authors is **Aesop,** writer of the famous fables. Several Greek historians produced important works, such as **Herodotus,** who wrote a history of the Persian Wars, and **Thucydides,** who wrote the literary masterpiece *History of the Peloponnesian War.*

In art, Greek influence lives on through the stately columns, graceful sculptures, and simple elegance of Greek architecture. Numerous ruins of Greek temples and other structures can still be seen throughout the Mediterranean world. Some of the best examples of Greek architecture are found in Athens, including the **Parthenon,** a beautiful temple to Athena, goddess of wisdom.

Perhaps the most important legacy of the Greeks was their language, for by it the gospel of Jesus Christ spread throughout the Roman world in the first century A.D.

CHECK UP

1. What did Macedonian kings admire about Greece? How did the Greeks feel about the Macedonians?
2. What Macedonian king conquered almost all of Greece?
3. How did Daniel describe Alexander in his prophecy?
4. When did Alexander conquer Susa, the Persian capital?
5. Who was Alexander's tutor?
6. How did Alexander treat the lands and peoples he had conquered?
7. What is the name for the period between Alexander's conquests and the Roman Empire?
8. What name did Alexander give to 16 of the cities he built throughout his empire? Where was the most famous of these cities located?
9. How old was Alexander when he died? Where did he die? When?
10. What four generals divided Alexander's empire after his death? Which section of the empire did each general receive?

Identify: Macedonia, phalanx, Olympias, Babylon, Persepolis, Hellenic

CHAPTER 6 REVIEW

MULTIPLE CHOICE Write the letter of the answer that best completes each sentence.

1. The Greeks were descendants of Japheth's son _____.
   - *a* Canaan
   - *b* Javan
   - *c* Shem
   - *d* Ham

2. The _____ built the earliest civilization in the vicinity of Greece.
   - *a* Mycenaeans
   - *b* Minoans
   - *c* Trojans
   - *d* Ionians

3. These early people lived on the island of _____.
   - *a* Troy
   - *b* Knossos
   - *c* Smyrna
   - *d* Crete

4. The _____ flourished on the mainland of Greece between about 1600 and 1200 B.C.
   - *a* Minoans
   - *b* Dorians
   - *c* Mycenaeans
   - *d* Trojans

5. These early inhabitants of Greece burned the city of _____ after a 10-year war.
   - *a* Crete
   - *b* Troy
   - *c* Knossos
   - *d* Minoa

6. Invaders from the north known as _____ helped bring about a dark age in Greece which started about 1200 B.C.
   - *a* Ionians
   - *b* Olympians
   - *c* Trojans
   - *d* Dorians

7. The blind poet who greatly influenced Greek culture and portrayed the gods as glorified human beings was _____.
   - *a* Homer
   - *b* Herodotus
   - *c* Aesop
   - *d* Thucydides

8. According to Greek mythology, the home of the gods was _____.
   - *a* Mount Olympus
   - *b* Marathon
   - *c* Troy
   - *d* Thrace

9. The Persian emperor _____ conquered Ionia in 546 B.C.
   - *a* Darius I
   - *b* Cyrus the Great
   - *c* Xerxes
   - *d* Darius II

10. The Persian king who crushed the Ionian revolt and demanded that the mainland Greeks submit to him was _____.
    - *a* Darius I
    - *b* Darius II
    - *c* Xerxes
    - *d* Cyrus the Great

11. The greatly outnumbered Athenians surprised the Persians by defeating them at the Battle of _____.
    - *a* Salamis
    - *b* Thermopylae
    - *c* Marathon
    - *d* Hellespont

12. Ten years later, king _____ launched a second Persian invasion of Greece.
    - *a* Darius I
    - *b* Xerxes
    - *c* Leonidus
    - *d* Darius II

13. This second invasion got off to a bad start when the Persian army stopped to build a bridge across the _____.
    - *a* Black Sea
    - *b* Aegean Sea
    - *c* Mediterranean Sea
    - *d* Hellespont

14. The brave Spartan army was betrayed at the Battle of _____.
    - *a* Thermopylae
    - *b* Salamis
    - *c* Marathon
    - *d* Athens

15. The small Greek navy defeated the Persian fleet at the Battle of _____.
    - *a* Thermopylae
    - *b* Themistocles
    - *c* Hellespont
    - *d* Salamis

16. Those in Sparta who did not belong to the ruling class were called _____.
    - *a* oligarchs
    - *b* Helots
    - *c* tyrants
    - *d* aristocrats

17. During the plague in Athens, the city lost one of its greatest leaders in the death of _____.
    - *a* Leonidas
    - *b* Socrates
    - *c* Pericles
    - *d* Thucydides

18. By 371 B.C., Sparta had been soundly defeated by the city of _____.
    - *a* Athens
    - *b* Thebes
    - *c* Macedonia
    - *d* Olympias

19. The Macedonian king who conquered almost all of Greece before he was assassinated was ____.
    a Alexander c Darius III
    b Philip II d Ptolemy

20. After the king's death, his son ____ came to the throne.
    a Philip III c Darius III
    b Ptolemy d Alexander

21. Alexander entered the city of ____ in the autumn of 331 B.C.
    a Persepolis c Gaugamela
    b Thebes d Babylon

22. In 330 B.C., Alexander conquered ____, the chief city of the Persian homeland.
    a Persepolis c Porus
    b Babylon d Issus

23. As Alexander's empire spread, he gave the name ____ to 16 cities, the most famous of which was in Egypt.
    a Cairo c Alexandria
    b Athens d Philippi

24. After Alexander's death, Egypt was taken over by ____.
    a Cleopatra c Seleucus
    b Antipater d Ptolemy

25. Macedonia was ruled after Alexander's death by ____.
    a Ptolemy c Seleucus
    b Antipater d Laomedon

26. Syria (including Canaan) fell under the leadership of ____.
    a Laomedon c Antipater
    b Porus d Ptolemy

COMPLETION *Choose the correct term to complete each sentence and write the answer in the blank.*

a ancestors   e Iliad   i polis   m phalanx
b aristocracy   f monarchy   j Peloponnesian   n philosopher
c Delian   g Odyssey   k tyranny   o barbarians
d democracy   h oligarchy   l Hellenistic

1. Homer's two greatest works are the ____ and the ____.

2. Long before Homer, Greek families worshiped their ____ as gods.

3. The Greek city-state was called a(n) ____.

4. The Greeks viewed all non-Greek people as ____.

5. The term ____ means rule by one.

6. The ____ War between Athens and Sparta lasted from 431 B.C. to 404 B.C.

7. The period between Alexander's conquest and the rise of the Roman Empire is known as the ____ Age.

8. The term ____ means rule by the "best."

9. The term ____ means rule by a few rather than one or many men.

10. A successful military strategy used by the Macedonian army was the ____, a large group of foot soldiers trained to charge the enemy as a group.

11. The bad form of one-man rule that arises when one man seizes power by appealing to the people is called ____.

12. The term ____ means rule by the many or the common people.

13. ____ means "lover of wisdom."

14. To prevent another Persian invasion of Greece, Athens formed the ____ League.

15. To multiply her military strength, Sparta formed the ____ League.

MATCHING Match each description with the correct name.

a Apollo   e Poseidon   h Aristotle
b Artemis   f Zeus   i Plato
c Leonidas   g Athena   j Socrates
d Pericles

_____ 1. King of all the gods

_____ 2. God of the sun

_____ 3. Insisted that morality be a part of philosophy

_____ 4. Wrote in the form of dialogues

_____ 5. Tutored young Alexander the Great

_____ 6. Brought Athenian democracy to its fullest measure

_____ 7. Brave leader of the Spartans at Thermopylae

_____ 8. Goddess of wisdom

CONCEPTS TO CONSIDER Answer the following questions on a separate sheet of paper, using complete sentences.

1. Briefly explain the cycle of change in the government of the Greek city-states.

2. Briefly compare and contrast Athens and Sparta.

3. Give some examples of humanism in Greek society.

TIME LINE CHALLENGE Choose the letter of the correct date for each of the events listed below. Answers may be used more than once.

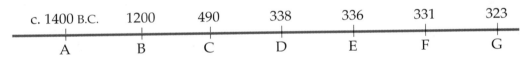

c. 1400 B.C.	1200	490	338	336	331	323
A	B	C	D	E	F	G

_____ 1. Battle of Marathon

_____ 2. End of Minoan civilization

_____ 3. A Greek "dark age" begins

_____ 4. Alexander the Great becomes king of Macedonia

_____ 5. Alexander conquers Babylon

_____ 6. Alexander dies at the age of 32

_____ 7. Alexander captures Susa

_____ 8. Philip conquers most of Greece

7
Rome before Christ
(c. 800 B.C.–Birth of Christ)

HIGHLIGHTS
Foundation of Rome • Roman Republic
Punic Wars • Julius Caesar • Caesar Augustus

Origin of the City of Rome

Beginning in Italy

Italy projects from Europe as the next major peninsula west of Greece. Shaped like a high-heeled boot, it stretches about 600 miles southeastward into the Mediterranean Sea. Two large islands, *Sardinia* [sär·dĭn′ĭ·ə] and *Sicily,* are nearby. The rugged **Alps** Mountains in the north isolate Italy from the rest of Europe. The Alps keep cold winds out of Italy and, with the Mediterranean Sea, furnish a warm climate with ample rainfall, making the land good for growing crops and grazing animals. Just south of the Alps, the great *Po River* flows through a large fertile plain separated from the rest of Italy by the **Apennine Mountains,** a rugged range which stretches from the Po River valley to the tip of the peninsula.

Rome began as an insignificant city along the *Tiber River* in central western Italy, but through force and violence it eventually united Italy and much of the world in an empire as "strong as iron" (Dan. 2:40). Rome made few original contributions to world history; it borrowed from the cultures of Mesopotamia, Egypt, and especially Greece. In building and maintaining its empire, Rome employed methods used in the past by previous empires. But no previous empire had combined all of these things as brilliantly as Rome did.

Rome became the fourth kingdom of Daniel's prophecy and, unknowingly, made final preparation for Christ.

Early Inhabitants of Italy

Gauls. By the fifth century B.C., four groups of Indo-Europeans were living in Italy: Gauls, Greeks, Etruscans, and Latins. The Gauls [gôlz], a Celtic people from western Europe, occupied the Po River valley in the north.

Greeks. The Greeks planted so many colonies on the island of Sicily and the southern Italian mainland that this area

PEOPLES OF ANCIENT ITALY

88

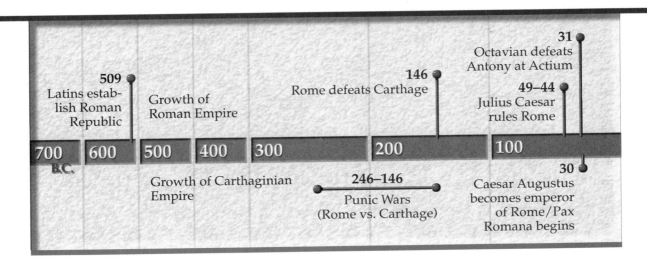

509
Latins establish Roman Republic

Growth of Roman Empire

146
Rome defeats Carthage

31
Octavian defeats Antony at Actium

49–44
Julius Caesar rules Rome

700 | 600 | 500 | 400 | 300 | 200 | 100
B.C.

Growth of Carthaginian Empire

246–146
Punic Wars (Rome vs. Carthage)

30
Caesar Augustus becomes emperor of Rome/Pax Romana begins

The Forum: *The original meeting place grew into a great center of buildings. The Forum's ruins still stand.*

became known as ***Magna Graecia*** [măg′nə grē′shə] or "greater Greece." The culture of Magna Graecia greatly influenced Rome.

Etruscans. The Etruscans [i·trŭs′kænz] occupied central and northern Italy. Their exact origin remains a mystery. The Etruscans <u>built the first cities in Italy</u>. They made good use of Italy's natural resources of copper, lead, and iron; they also engineered bridges, roads, and waterworks (to prevent erosion and flooding). The inhabitants of Rome undoubtedly learned much from the Etruscans. Indeed, the Etruscans were probably the channel for the early influence of Greek culture on Rome.

Latins. The **Latins** lived in central and southern Italy. *Rome*, one of their settlements, soon became a name more important than any previous tribal identification.

The Founding of Rome

Sometime between the tenth and eighth centuries B.C., several Latin villages along the Tiber River united and established the **Forum.** Rome grew atop seven hills around this common meeting place.

Roman Arch: The Romans are famous for using arches in their buildings, many ruins of which stand today. The Romans learned how to make arches from the Etruscans.

This site on the south bank of the Tiber about 15 miles from the sea was a good place for a city. Because the river was navigable, the early Romans had access to the sea for trade without the usual danger that seacoast cities had from pirates. Rome's central location was appropriate for its eventual domination of Italy.

Many legends reflect the ancient Romans' fascination with their city's beginning. The legend of **Romulus** [rŏm′ū·lŭs] and **Remus** [rē′mŭs] tells a story of two brothers who set out to establish a new city but quarreled over the location. They decided that whoever saw the largest number of vultures in the sky could select the city's site. When Romulus claimed to have seen 12 vultures, he proceeded to lay out the city with a sacred ditch. Remus, who saw only six vultures, did not accept Romulus's claim. Feeling cheated, he jumped over the ditch to make fun of Romulus. Romulus killed Remus, finished the city, and named it "Roma" for himself. Whether or not the legend of Romulus and Remus is true, it was obvious from the very beginning that Rome was built upon a foundation of force and violence.

Rome's Religious Foundations

The Romans had many gods, but few if any were purely Roman. Etruscan, Greek, Persian, and Egyptian influences—to name a few—eventually found their place in the Roman religion. As Rome grew in power and dominion, the number of gods increased and the names and myths of old gods changed. Of the many temples erected in ancient Rome, perhaps the best known is the **Pantheon** [păn′thē·ŏn], a temple dedicated to the numerous gods of the empire.

History of the Roman Republic

The Early Republic

Rome was first governed by Latin kings. However, the early Roman monarchy was no more durable than its Greek counterpart had been. The Etruscans eventually conquered the city and installed their own kings. When the Latins revolted in 509 B.C. and removed the last Etruscan king, they established a **republic** (a form of government in which all citizens who are entitled to vote participate in decisions through elected representatives.)

Most Roman citizens belonged to the large class of people known as **plebeians** [plĕ·bē′yǎnz], or **plebs.** This class included the common people of Rome—merchants, businessmen, soldiers, craftsmen, and independent farmers. Wealthier Romans—perhaps descendants of the first three Latin tribes to settle on Rome's hills—were known as **patricians** [pə·trĭsh′-ǎnz]. The patricians resembled the aristocrats of early Greece who used their prominence in the family religion to gain political power.

In the early republic, a body known as the **Assembly** represented the citizens of Rome, including the plebs. To maintain control of the republic, the heads of the patrician families formed the **Senate,** an elite group that originally served as an advisory body to the king. With the end of the monarchy, the Senate became <u>the most powerful body in the Roman republic</u>. In place of a king, the Senate elected two *consuls* [kŏn'sulz] for one-year terms to administer the government and the army.

The Changing Republic

The early republic favored the patricians over the plebs in several ways. For example, the plebs were barred from holding public office and prohibited from marrying into the patrician class. Thus, while the plebs could vote, they actually had little voice in the government. They also paid most of the taxes in Rome and filled the lower ranks of the Roman army, while patricians served as military officers.

For two centuries, the plebs struggled for the right to participate in the government of Rome. Finally, in the early fifth century B.C., the plebs scored a victory with the *concilium plebis* [kon·sĭl'ĭ·um plē'bĭs], an official plebeian assembly. The plebeian assembly elected *tribunes* to represent them; these tribunes had power to block any action by the Senate, the patrician assembly, or the consuls that might hurt the plebs. By the middle of the fifth century, the plebs had scored another victory with the *Law of the Twelve Tables*, demanding that Roman law be written down and displayed in the Forum for everyone to see. Eventually the plebs won the right to serve as consuls and senators, and the plebeian assembly gained the power to make laws for all

Roman citizens, patrician or plebeian. With this victory, the final say in Roman government passed to the plebs, and the patricians fell from power.

The original distinction between patrician and pleb eventually became less important than the distinction between rich and poor. Prosperous times gave ambitious plebs the opportunity to gain great wealth through business ventures; some plebs actually became richer than the patricians. As the rich and poor grew further and further apart, this distinction would bring increasing strife and turmoil to Rome.

CHECK UP

1. What is Italy shaped like? What two large islands lie near Italy?
2. What is Rome's place in Daniel's prophecy?
3. Early in Rome's history, what people occupied the Po River valley in the north?
4. Who established colonies on the island of Sicily and the southern Italian mainland?
5. What people built the first cities in Italy?
6. Which tribe established the city of Rome?
7. Why was the site of Rome such a good place for a city?
8. Where did Rome get most of its gods?
9. What is a republic?
10. Who were the patricians? Who were the plebeians?
11. After the monarchy had come to an end, what body became the most important part of the Roman republic?

Identify: Italy, Po River, Alps, Apennine Mountains, Magna Graecia, Tiber River, Forum, Romulus and Remus, Pantheon

The Early Roman Wars of Foreign Conquest

Roman Conquest of Italy

Rome's empire began with the conquest of the Italian peninsula. After defeating the Etruscans in 509 B.C., Rome became the leader of the Latin tribes. By the beginning of the fourth century B.C., Rome had formed the **Latin League,** a defensive alliance against the Etruscans, and had secured central Italy.

The Roman league soon became an empire just as Athens' Delian League had. As Rome's power increased, members began to fear that their protector would become a master. Finally, war broke out, and Rome won total victory over the Latins in 338 B.C., dissolving the league and forcing the Latin cities to ally themselves to Rome with separate treaties.

Victory over the Greeks in Italy. The Greek colonies of southern Italy began to fear Rome and asked the Greek king **Pyrrhus** [pĭr′əs] of Epirus [ĭ·pī′rəs] to help. Pyrrhus dealt Rome several defeats but lost many warriors each time. Such costly victories became known as "Pyrrhic victories." By 270 B.C., all the Greek cities in southern Italy belonged to Rome. With the conquest of more territory in the north in 266 B.C., Rome controlled all Italy south of the Po River.

Policies for the empire. Rome had conquered Italy by force, and the threat of Roman military power hung over the head of anyone who might be tempted to rebel. But the Romans recognized the limits of force and adopted policies to keep conquered peoples from wanting to rebel. For example, Rome generally permitted old native governments and customs to prevail in purely local matters. The Romans also left local religions undisturbed and kept the burden of tribute low.

Rome encouraged conquered peoples to think of the empire as a source of peace,

CARTHAGINIAN EMPIRE

order, and prosperity. Obedient subjects could hope for Roman citizenship, with its rights and protections; by the first century B.C., all the inhabitants of the Italian peninsula were Roman citizens. Business and trade thrived as Rome built roads to facilitate travel, provided protection from robbers, and established a common system of coins.

The Punic Wars

Carthage. Across the Mediterranean Sea on the northern coast of Africa stood the mighty city of **Carthage** [kär′thĭj], Rome's chief rival. Founded as a Phoenician trading post, Carthage had become the major power of the western Mediterranean Sea by the third century B.C. An excellent natural harbor, a large population, and an impressive navy permitted Carthage to dominate Africa's northern coast, Sardinia, western Sicily, and parts of Spain and Corsica. Massive walls and fortifications protected the city from possible invasion.

Rome naturally feared and resented Carthage. As a result of this rivalry, the two cities fought a series of wars between 264 and 146 B.C. known as the **Punic Wars** [pū′nĭk: from *punicus*, the Latin word for Phoenician].

First Punic War. The First Punic War (264–241 B.C.) began when Carthage grasped for control of the northeastern tip of Sicily. Almost overnight the Romans built a fleet to battle the armies of Carthage. The war at first went badly for Rome, as she lost many ships and perhaps

$^1/_6$ of her citizens. But the Romans built a new fleet and completely defeated the Carthaginians in 241 B.C.

The desire for more tribute-paying lands and peoples now replaced security as Rome's main motive for acquiring an empire. With the addition of *Sardinia* and *Corsica* in 238 B.C., the Roman Empire included all three of the great islands of the western Mediterranean.

Second Punic War. The Second Punic War (218–202 B.C.) resulted from attempts by Carthage to increase her power in *Spain.* Rome declared war when the young Carthaginian general **Hannibal** attacked a town in Spain that Rome considered an ally. At the age of nine, Hannibal had vowed eternal hatred toward Rome; now he had the opportunity to vent that hatred. In 218 B.C., *Hannibal led a large force of men, horses, and African war elephants across the Alps into Italy.* Although most of his elephants and many of his men died in the cold mountains, Hannibal's army remained strong enough to win several important battles during the 16 years it spent in Italy. But Rome's Italian allies remained loyal, and Carthage could not send Hannibal any help across the Roman-controlled Mediterranean.

When the Roman general **Scipio** [sĭp′ĭ·ō] led an attack on Carthage, Hannibal was called home to defend the city. At the Battle of **Zama** [zā′mə: 202 B.C.], Hannibal was defeated and Carthage's power utterly broken. In the treaty of 201 B.C., Carthage gave up Spain and completely disarmed.

Third Punic War. As master of the western Mediterranean, Rome had little to fear. But still some Romans worried that Carthage might somehow regain her power. Thus, in the Third Punic War (149–146 B.C.), <u>Rome annihilated Carthage</u>. After burning the city to the ground, the Romans sowed the fields with salt to make the land uninhabitable.

Eastern Conquests

War with Macedonia. While Rome fought Carthage, she conquered many eastern lands that had once been a part of Alexander the Great's empire. War with Alexander's homeland, *Macedonia,* began in 215 B.C. during the Second Punic War. Another war with Rome during 201–197 B.C. brought a total Macedonian defeat. The Macedonian rulers pledged allegiance to Rome and gave up all claims to foreign territories. To the delight of many Greeks,

Hannibal's Elephants: *During the Second Punic War, the Carthaginian general Hannibal brought war elephants from Africa.*

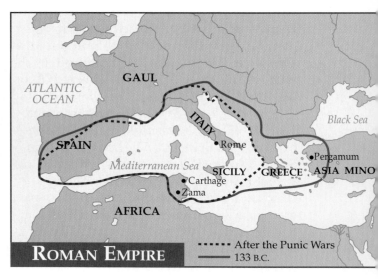

Colosseum: The Colosseum was the site of many cruel spectacles in which men fought men, men fought beasts, and beasts fought beasts—to the death. It was capable of seating over 40,000 spectators.

ROMAN EMPIRE

········· After the Punic Wars
——— 133 B.C.

Rome declared Greece "free" of Macedonian domination.

War with Syria. From 192 to 189 B.C., Rome fought and defeated the Seleucid king **Antiochus III** [ăn·tī'ə·kus] of **Syria,** who in fulfillment of Daniel's prophecy had defiled the temple in Jerusalem. Now it would be much easier for Rome to conquer Egypt, Palestine, and Greece.

Addition of Pergamum. With the addition of the Asian kingdom of **Pergamum** [pĕr'gə·mum] in 133 B.C., the Roman Empire included provinces in Europe, Africa, and Asia. Egypt, Palestine, and Syria were not yet officially provinces of the Roman empire, but their rulers knew better than to displease Rome.

Republican Rome was supreme in the ancient world. Less than 400 years after the beginning of the Republic in 509 B.C., Rome had become master of a huge empire. Through force and violence, it was well on the way to fulfilling Daniel's prophecy of a fourth world empire.

The Collapse of the Republic

As Rome increased in wealth and power, the very foundation of the Republic—the old Roman character traits of simplicity, discipline, and patriotism—began to crumble. Roman conquests corrupted the people with an abundance of slaves and unearned wealth, encouraging immorality, laziness, and an obsession with worldly pleasures. Unable to compete with cheap slave labor, many Romans found themselves unemployed and forced to accept government welfare, while others took advantage of the situation to increase their wealth.

As the rich grew richer and the poor grew poorer, discontent increased steadily among the common masses of Rome. The government tried to appease the people with "bread and circuses"—free food and entertainment. But handouts of bread only squelched republican independence and self-respect, while circuses fed one of the darkest hungers of depraved human nature—to take pleasure in the pain and suffering of others. Thousands of Roman citizens crowded into amphitheaters like the *Colosseum* every day to watch men fight men and beasts to the death. As the gap between the rich and the poor widened, civil wars erupted and military dictators arose to forcefully restore law and order.

The Rise and Fall of Julius Caesar

Pompey versus Caesar

Two strong and ambitious men arose from the continual turmoil of the empire—Pompey [pŏm′pē] and Julius Caesar [sē′zēr]. Elected consul in 70 B.C., **Pompey** sought the support of the many poor in his political career. He later led Rome in several great military victories in the Middle East and captured the city of Jerusalem in 63 B.C. When Pompey returned to Rome, however, the Senate refused to approve arrangements he had made in the eastern empire or to grant land to his troops and the poor.

Meanwhile, **Julius Caesar,** another Roman aristocrat, had become popular as a champion of the poor. Tall, handsome, intelligent, and eloquent, Caesar held many important government offices. Caesar and Pompey struck a bargain. With Pompey's support, the 38-year-old Caesar was elected consul in 59 B.C. Then, as consul, Caesar went over the Senate's head and took Pompey's requests to the Assembly, which approved them.

Julius Caesar

But Caesar's ambitions were far from satisfied. Realizing that he needed an army and an impressive military reputation to climb higher in Roman politics, Caesar sought and obtained appointment to a five-year term as the governor of Gaul (the vicinity of present-day France).

Caesar's conquest of Gaul. Caesar spent nine years conquering Gaul and proved himself to be one of history's most brilliant generals and clever politicians. His conquests extended from the Rhine River to the English Channel, including the modern countries of France, Holland, Switzerland, Belgium, and parts of Germany. Caesar even crossed the channel and conquered Britain as far as the Thames [tĕmz] River. Caesar treated the Gauls well, making them loyal friends of Rome. Through his conquests, Roman culture—which had by now been heavily influenced by Greek culture—spread throughout much of western Europe.

As he had hoped, Caesar's conquests increased his reputation and power. To strengthen his popularity, Caesar wrote several commentaries on his exploits and had them published in Rome; these well-written commentaries kept Caesar's name before the people and built his reputation as a hero. While support for Caesar grew back in Rome, his loyal army grew ever stronger.

Caesar's conquest of Rome. As Caesar's second term as governor of Gaul neared an end, he prepared to return to Rome. The Senate feared Caesar, for he had become popular with the common people. Pompey, having grown jealous of Caesar, joined Caesar's opponents. The Senate sent an order to Caesar to disband his army, but Caesar disobeyed and crossed the **Rubicon** [rōō′bĭ·kŏn] River in 49 B.C.

By crossing the Rubicon into Italy, Caesar had committed himself; he would either be executed as a traitor or be hailed as a conqueror. (Even today, the expression *crossing the Rubicon* means making a decision that can never be reversed.) One by one, the cities of Italy opened their gates to Caesar. As Caesar neared Rome, he seemed impossible to defeat. Pompey, his army, and most of the Senate fled eastward.

The Rule of Julius Caesar

From 49 to 44 B.C., Caesar controlled Rome and therefore much of the world. The Romans called him father and supreme ruler. He had himself declared dictator for life and held absolute power. Caesar turned the Senate into a political joke, filling it with men prepared to follow his orders without question.

Caesar's rule, for all practical purposes, marked the end of the Roman Republic and the beginning of the Roman Empire and one-man rule.

During his five-year rule, Caesar took measures to secure his position. He freely pardoned many old enemies and won admiration as a man of generosity. He proved himself a friend of the poor by reducing debts and providing employment on public construction projects. Everyone found convenient the calendar of 365 ¼ days that Caesar introduced from Egypt with modifications. Called the **Julian calendar,** it is the basis of our present calendar. All of Rome praised the new spirit of efficiency that Caesar brought to the government.

Caesar had many grand visions for Rome. He hoped to rebuild the city with beautiful new public buildings and an altered course for the Tiber River. He planned many new roads and even a sea canal in Greece. Caesar also looked forward to adding vast new lands to the empire in the west and the east.

Death of Julius Caesar

Julius Caesar did not have the chance to do all he had planned to do as absolute ruler of Rome, partly because he spent the first four years of his five-year reign chasing Pompey and his army. Pompey finally suffered a humiliating death on an Egyptian beach in 48 B.C., but not until 45 B.C. did Caesar defeat Pompey's army.

A Source for History

Drama

We can learn much about a period of history from the plays that were written and performed during that period. Dramatists often depict important features of the way of life during their era. Dramas can reflect the most basic beliefs of a culture.

We can also learn about history from plays written by men who lived many hundreds of years after the events they dramatized. The best examples are some of the plays by William Shakespeare, an English dramatist and poet born in A.D. 1564. His plays based on history are still performed and enjoyed today. Many of them concern events in English history, but one, called *Julius Caesar,* depicts the events surrounding that ancient Roman's death. Shakespeare made up some of the details in this play, but it does capture the spirit of the moment in a memorable way.

In the climax of the play, Shakespeare has the dying Caesar say to his friend Brutus who stabbed him, "Et tu, Brute?" ("You too, Brutus?") These words that Shakespeare put into Caesar's mouth are probably more famous than any words the powerful Roman ever actually said.

Some Romans remained unwilling to submit to the rule of one man. After all, Caesar was only a man. Force and violence once again had their way in Rome on March 15, 44 B.C., when Caesar was stabbed to death by a group of Senators who hoped to restore the Senate to power and reestablish the old republic. Forced to flee for their lives, Caesar's assassins soon realized their hopes were in vain. Caesar's death resulted only in more war and bloodshed until the last remnants of the old republic were finally lost forever.

CHECK UP

1. What did Rome form in the fourth century B.C. as a defensive alliance against the Etruscans?
2. Who was Pyrrhus?
3. What attitude did Rome hope its conquered lands would have toward the empire?
4. What city became Rome's chief rival? What three wars were fought against this rival?
5. What daring Carthaginian general led a large group of men, horses, and elephants over the Alps to attack Rome?
6. Explain the collapse of the republic. How did the government try to appease the people?
7. Who led Rome to victory in the Middle East and captured Jerusalem in 63 B.C.?
8. Who conquered Gaul for Rome?
9. What did Julius Caesar do when the Senate ordered him to disband his army?
10. What did Caesar do to secure his position and to improve Rome? What did he have visions of doing?
11. When was Caesar murdered? Why was he murdered?

Identify: Pyrrhic victory, Scipio, Zama, Pergamum, Colosseum, Rubicon, Julian calendar

---

The Early Roman Empire

Antony versus Octavian

The two leading candidates to replace Caesar were **Antony,** Caesar's closest friend, and **Octavian** [ŏk·tā′vĭ·ɑn], Caesar's 18-year-old adopted son and legal heir. At first willing to share power, Antony and Octavian split the dictatorship between them and ruled a divided Roman world from 44 to 31 B.C. Octavian possessed the western part, Antony the east.

Then Antony fell in love with **Cleopatra,** the queen of Egypt and last heir of the old Ptolemaic dynasty. Antony angered many Romans when he began to give away parts of Roman territory to Cleopatra. Octavian cleverly took advantage of Antony's conduct with Cleopatra and incited Rome and Italy against him.

Once again force and violence decided who would rule Rome. Octavian's fleet met Antony's fleet off the coast of Greece near **Actium** [ăk′tĭ·um] in 31 B.C. There, after a fierce battle, Antony abandoned his ships, and the fleet surrendered. Antony and Cleopatra fled to Egypt, where they committed suicide. Octavian conquered Egypt in 30 B.C. and returned to Rome as the undisputed ruler of a vast and powerful empire.

Octavian Becomes Caesar Augustus

In matters of ancient tradition, names sometimes meant as much to people as reality. The Roman Republic had become only a name, but it still stirred many hearts. Octavian wisely claimed to be restoring the Republic. He returned the Senate's power to make laws and even gave the Senate control over Italy and half of the provinces. Yet everyone knew that the Senate did whatever Octavian wanted.

Octavian had many titles. His favorite was **Princeps** [prĭn′sĕps], "first citizen." As leader of the Roman army, Octavian was called **Imperator** [ĭm·pə·rŏt′ẽr]; the

Emperor Augustus:
The image on this silver coin of Antioch is that of Emperor Augustus. Coins such as this were in wide use in Palestine during the life of Christ.

title of *Emperor* came from this. **Caesar** was also an important title of Octavian and later Roman emperors. When Christ said to give to "Caesar the things which are Caesar's" (Matt. 22:21), He was referring to all Roman emperors. The Bible refers to Octavian as "Caesar **Augustus**" (Luke 2:1). Augustus [ə·gŭs′tus] was Octavian's most interesting title. It meant "the Revered." Romans had previously reserved this title for gods.

Accomplishments of Caesar Augustus

Under Caesar Augustus began the **Pax Romana** [păks rō·mä′nə: 30 B.C.–A.D. 180], *two hundred years of the Roman Empire remembered as a time of peace and prosperity.* During this time, Caesar Augustus expanded and strengthened the empire, extending the northern border to the *Danube River.* He established a professional bureaucracy to run the business of the vast empire and organized a permanent, professional army, which he tried to keep out of Roman politics by stationing it in faraway provinces. He eased travel by freeing the empire from the dangers of robbers and by building well-paved roads to the most remote provinces. As a result, business and trade thrived throughout the empire. Caesar Augustus tried to make taxes fair through the **census,** *which counted total population and value of property in each province.* One of Caesar Augustus's censuses brought Joseph and his wife Mary to Bethlehem, where she gave birth to Jesus Christ.

Caesar Augustus knew that many people saw Rome and its emperor as the only hope of a hopeless world. Few people seriously believed in the old gods any longer. Although philosophers were divided into various groups such as the *Stoics* [stō′ĭks], the *Epicureans* [ĕp′i·kū·rē′anz], and the *Skeptics* [skĕp′tĭks], they all agreed that the only happiness possible to men lay in forgetting about and withdrawing from the world. Such a life would bring few pleasures, said the philosophers, but at least it would bring few pains!

The Pax Romana brought such a great improvement in conditions during the centuries after the breakup of Alexander the Great's empire that many people began to look upon the city of Rome and the Roman emperor as a kind of savior of the world. Caesar Augustus naturally encouraged such beliefs, for they strengthened Rome's position and his own. He also knew that *something* had to limit the evil desires that had broken out in Rome since the very beginning. Perhaps Caesar Augustus knew that the respect Rome and its rulers needed could come only if something higher than merely another human being and human city appeared to be at the head of the empire. If the old gods were for all practical purposes "dead," why not let Rome and the Roman emperor be gods? It was such a simple and obviously false belief that it is surprising anyone took it seriously. But they did.

By the time of the birth of Jesus Christ, Rome had become the world's alternative to God.

Preparation for Jesus Christ

God's love for all mankind had never ceased. Throughout history, He had been working to restore the fellowship between Himself and man broken by original sin.

God's amazing plan for the salvation of man required a world in which good news could travel fast. By Caesar Augustus's time, much of the known world was under one government, and two centuries of peace had begun. It was almost as if the city of Rome had become the world. Men could

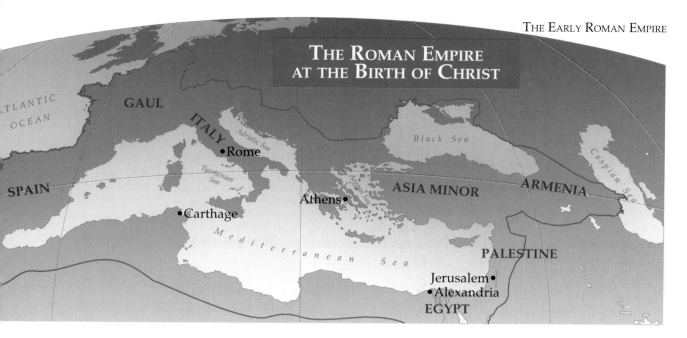

THE ROMAN EMPIRE AT THE BIRTH OF CHRIST

travel throughout the empire without crossing a "foreign" enemy country. A man who had achieved Roman citizenship could expect certain legal protections wherever he went. Travel by land or sea was safer and easier than ever before. Greek was widely spoken and read as a second language. There was even a "second, second" language—Latin.

> Not since the tower of Babel, the confusion of languages, and the dispersion of mankind over the face of the earth had there been such a "one world."

God's plan of salvation also required a world in which good news would be welcomed. By Caesar Augustus's day, Rome and its emperor were the only hope for many men. But these new "gods" offered nothing beyond this life. A few philosophers said, "Be happy by withdrawing from the world and avoiding pain." But most people said, "Be happy by plunging into the world seeking pleasure." The very poor, of course, could afford neither the withdrawal of the philosopher nor the pleasure seeking of the rich. All men lived as if there were no tomorrow. Then, as now, there was "none righteous, no, not one" (Ps. 14:3; Rom. 3:10).

Some of Abraham's descendants, the Jews, placed their hope in God's promise of a coming Savior. The Jews' efforts to build a nation under God had failed. Israel's sin had split the nation in two, and both kingdoms had been swallowed up in successive world empires. By Caesar Augustus's time, the Jews were scattered across the face of the earth. Wherever they lived, however, most Jews gathered on the Sabbath day in places of worship called **synagogues** [sĭn′·ə·gŏgz], where they read the Old Testament. Sometimes they read a Greek version called the **Septuagint** [sĕp·too′·ə·jənt], a translation probably made during the third century B.C. The thirty-nine books of the Old Testament had been written and recognized as the Word of God since perhaps the fifth century B.C. For hundreds of years, Jews had read over and over the passages of the Old Testament in which God promised that a Savior would come. Even some people who did not trace their ancestry to Abraham heard the Word of God and joined the Jews in longing for the "**Messiah**," the "Anointed One." The name *Christ* comes from the Greek word used to translate the Hebrew word *Messiah*.

Since the 500s B.C. and the return from Babylon, Jews had been living around the city of Jerusalem in **Palestine,** as the promised land had come to be called. When world history changed from years before Christ (B.C.) to years after the birth of Christ (A.D.), Palestine was a part of the Roman Empire. **Herod,** who had married into a Jewish family, was ruling Palestine as the local king with Rome's permission. Such kings of the Jews as Herod were appointed by the Roman government.

During the reign of Caesar Augustus, in the days of Herod, God sent His Son Jesus, the true King of the Jews and of all mankind, to be born of a virgin in Bethlehem of Judea.

The thread we have been following through history has at last led us to Jesus Christ and the turning point of history.

Measuring Time

Measuring time, like measuring distance, requires units of measurement and reference points, and God has supplied both in order for man to be able to keep track of time.

God created units for measuring time by putting "lights in the firmament of the heaven to divide the day from the night; and . . . for signs, and for seasons, and for days, and years" (Gen. 1:14). Since the beginning, men have kept track of time by observing the sun, moon, and stars as they travel through the sky like clockwork. By watching the phases of the moon, men discovered the idea of the month. By following the changing positions of the sun, rising and setting on the horizon, men discovered the idea of a **year** which, as we know now, is *the actual length of time it takes the earth to go around the sun.* Calendars divide time into years, and subdivide years into months, weeks, and days.

Few works of man, however, are free from error, and no calendar has ever measured a year exactly. The calendar Julius Caesar took from Egypt, for example, allotted only 365 days per year. The **Julian calendar** came closer with a yearly total of

365 $1/4$ days per year (the additional fraction of a day was included by assigning the month of February one extra day every fourth year, the year we call leap year). Although the Julian calendar was so accurate that people used it for over 1,500 years, it was still off by 11 minutes 14 seconds per year. In a thousand years, this mistake adds up to seven days. The Julian calendar was becoming so out of phase with the seasons that people in A.D. 1582 began switching to the more accurate **Gregorian calendar** (named for Pope Gregory XIII), which we use today. Even the Gregorian calendar is off about 26 seconds per year.

In addition to units of measurement, we also need reference points from which to measure time. We must refer to some moment when counting years and specifying the number of a particular year. The Julian calendar reckoned years from the founding of Rome, specifying year numbers as "Year of Rome" (in Latin, *Anno Urbis Conditae,* abbreviated A.U.C.). After Christ, however, people recognized that God had supplied the great turning point of history. In A.D. 526, *Dionysius Exiguus* introduced the reckoning of years with

Christ's birth as the reference point, the familiar B.C.-A.D. system.

Unfortunately, Exiguus made a mistake of four to six years in calculating the birth of Christ. He used God's error-free information about Christ's birth in chapters 1 and 2 of Matthew. But in trying to match this information with records based on the old "Years of Rome" (A.U.C.), Exiguus went wrong. Christ was actually born between 4–6 B.C., not in A.D. 1. By the time this human error had been discovered, it was impossible to change the dates in all the books and records of the world, and so the dates we use are off four to six years from the actual year of Christ's birth.

CHECK UP

1. Who were the two main candidates to replace the dead Caesar?
2. How did the two rivals cooperate at first?
3. Who eventually took Caesar's place? Where did he defeat his rival?
4. Which title was Octavian's favorite? What did the title mean?
5. Which title did *Emperor* come from?
6. What does the Bible call Octavian? What does this title mean?
7. What was the *Pax Romana*?
8. Give three examples of the many groups of philosophers in ancient Rome.
9. What became the god of the Romans?
10. Why could good news travel so quickly in the Roman Empire? What made it easier for people in different lands to understand each other?
11. Give two names for Jesus that mean "Anointed One."

Identify: census, synagogues, Septuagint, Palestine, Herod, Gregorian Calendar

CHAPTER 7 REVIEW

MATCHING **Match each description with the correct name.**

a Antiochus III   c Hannibal   e Pyrrhus   g Scipio   i Octavian
b Antony   d Julius Caesar   f Romulus   h Pompey   j Cleopatra

_____ 1. A mythical founder of Rome
_____ 2. Greek king whose victories over Rome cost him many men
_____ 3. Used elephants in his march through the Alps during the Second Punic War
_____ 4. Led the Roman attack on Carthage during the Second Punic War
_____ 5. Seleucid king who fought against Rome from 192 to 189 B.C.
_____ 6. Elected consul in 70 B.C.; captured Jerusalem in 63 B.C.
_____ 7. Ruled the Roman Empire from 49 to 44 B.C.
_____ 8. Caesar's closest friend; defeated at Actium
_____ 9. Julius Caesar's adopted son and heir; became known as Caesar Augustus
_____10. Last Ptolemaic ruler of Egypt; committed suicide with Antony in 31 B.C.

CHAPTER 7 REVIEW (CONTINUED)

MULTIPLE CHOICE Write the letter of the answer that best completes each sentence.

1. Two large islands that lie near the Italian peninsula are _____.
   a Crete and Rhodes
   b Cyprus and Sardinia
   c Sardinia and Sicily
   d Sicily and Crete

2. The mountains which isolate Italy from the rest of Europe are the _____.
   a Alps   c Apennines
   b Pyrenees   d Himalayas

3. The great _____ River flows through a large fertile plain just south of the Alps.
   a Tiber   c Rhine
   b Etruscan   d Po

4. The mountain range which stretches from the Po River valley to the tip of the peninsula is the _____.
   a Pyrenees   c Himalayas
   b Alps   d Apennines

5. The city of Rome is located on the _____ River.
   a Po   c Danube
   b Tiber   d Nile

6. The _____ were a Celtic people who occupied the Po River valley in northern Italy.
   a Gauls   c Etruscans
   b Macedonians   d Romans

7. The _____ established colonies in Sicily and southern Italy which greatly influenced the Romans.
   a Gauls   c Greeks
   b Etruscans   d Corsicans

8. These colonies caused southern Italy to be known as _____.
   a Magna Graecia c Carthage
   b Sardinia   d Gaul

9. The _____ built the first Italian cities.
   a Latins   c Gauls
   b Etruscans   d Sardinians

10. Rome was settled by the _____.
    a Etruscans   c Corsicans
    b Latins   d Gauls

11. Between 264 and 146 B.C., Rome fought three wars known as the _____ Wars.
    a Sicilian   c Peloponnesian
    b Etruscan   d Punic

12. Rome's enemy in these three wars was _____.
    a Gaul   c Carthage
    b Phoenicia   d Macedonia

13. Hannibal's defeat at the Battle of _____ ended the Second Punic War.
    a Zama   c Pergamum
    b Actium   d Sardinia

14. With the addition of the Asian kingdom of _____ in 133 B.C., the Roman Empire included provinces in Europe, Africa, and Asia.
    a Pergamum   c Carthage
    b Magna Graecia d Syria

15. Caesar built a reputation for himself by conquering and then governing the land of _____.
    a Pergamum   c Sardinia
    b Gaul   d Magna Graecia

16. Caesar showed his determination to be the ruler of Rome when he crossed the _____ in 49 B.C.
    a Alps   c Po River
    b Tiber River d Rubicon River

17. Octavian defeated Antony's fleet in battle near _____ in 31 B.C.
    a Zama   c Actium
    b Carthage   d Gaul

18. Octavian's favorite title was _____, which means "first citizen."
    a Imperator   c Caesar
    b Augustus   d Princeps

19. As leader of the Roman army, Octavian was called _____, from which we get the term *emperor*.
    a Imperator   c Caesar
    b Augustus   d Princeps

20. Octavian's most interesting title, _____ (meaning "the Revered"), was a title that had previously been reserved for the gods.
    a Imperator   c Caesar
    b Augustus   d Princeps

21. By the time of the Roman Empire, the Promised Land had come to be called _____.
    a Syria   c Jordan
    b Palestine   d Judea

22. The king of the Promised Land when Christ was born was _____.
    a Julius Caesar   c Herod
    b Herodotus   d Pompey

COMPLETION *Choose the correct term to complete each sentence and write the letter in the blank.*

a census   d patricians   f plebeians
b Forum   e Pax Romana   g republic
c Latin League

1. The _____ was a common meeting place which was the heart of the city of Rome.

2. The _____ were the common people of Rome.

3. The _____ was a defensive alliance against the Etruscans.

4. The _____ was the 200-year period of peace and prosperity when Rome was the absolute master of the world.

5. A _____ counted total population and value of property in each province of the Roman Empire.

TIME LINE CHALLENGE *Choose the letter of the correct date for each of the events listed below.*

c. 800 B.C.	509	264–241	218	202	201	49	44	31	30
A	B	C	D	E	F	G	H	I	J

_____ 1. Beginning of the Pax Romana

_____ 2. First Punic War

_____ 3. Hannibal's march through the Alps

_____ 4. Hannibal defeated at the Battle of Zama

_____ 5. End of Roman monarchy; Roman republic begins

_____ 6. Battle of Actium

_____ 7. Beginning of Julius Caesar's reign

_____ 8. Caesar is assassinated

CONCEPTS TO CONSIDER *On a separate sheet of paper, answer the following questions using complete sentences.*

1. How did Alexander's Greek Empire and the Roman Empire help to prepare the world for the coming of Jesus Christ?

2. Explain the collapse of the Roman republic. How did discontent and strife within the republic lead to the rise of dictators?

Chronology of Bible History

On the following pages are many of the events of the Bible arranged in chronological order. There are several methods for determining dates for Biblical events. The Bible itself—the most reliable source for history we have—supplies dates for the events it records through numerous genealogies, as in Genesis 5, for example: "And Adam lived an hundred and thirty years, and begat . . . Seth. . . . And all the days that Adam lived were nine hundred and thirty years. . . . And Seth lived an hundred and five years, and begat Enos . . ." and so on (Gen. 5: 3–6).

The first person to work out a chronology based only on the Bible itself was James Ussher (1581–1656), archbishop of Armagh in Ireland. This well-respected scholar and theologian, an expert in Semitic languages, had earlier published a translation of the works of Ignatius of Antioch, an early Christian bishop. In 1654, Ussher finished his *Annals of the Old and New Testaments,* in which he presented his chronology. This chronology, much of which appears on the following pages, uses only the Bible as its basis. Archbishop Ussher believed that by adding up the years given in the genealogies and other passages in Scripture he could determine the dates for the accompanying events.

The chart also contains dates for other historical events in addition to those in the Bible. With nothing as reliable as the Bible to base their calculations upon, historians are constantly changing their minds about many of these dates, and often disagree among themselves. Today almost no historian would accept several of these dates as accurate—dates that not long ago were regarded as authoritative.

The chronology printed here may serve as a reference for your study of history in this and other books. It will also be helpful to you, when studying the Word of God, to keep in mind the times in which the Scriptural events occurred.

Old Testament Chronology

I. From "The Beginning" to the Deluge

Subjects	Events	Ussher's Dates (B.C.)
Creation and Earliest Man	The Creation of the world.	4004
	The formation of lands and seas.	
	The Creation of plants and animals.	
	The Creation of Man.	
Man in His Earliest Home	The Garden of Eden, in the region of the Tigris and the Euphrates; ancient Mesopotamia and Babylonia.	4004
	The first sin.	
	Expulsion of Adam and Eve from Eden.	
Cain and Abel	Cain born.	4002(?)
	Abel born.	4001(?)
	Cultivation of the soil, and keeping of flocks begun.	
	Abel murdered by his brother Cain.	3875
From the Death of Abel to the Deluge	Seth born, Adam being 130 years old.	3874
	Enoch born.	3382
	Methuselah born.	3317

I. From "The Beginning" to the Deluge (Continued)

Subjects	Events	Ussher's Dates (B.C.)
	Adam dies, being 930 years old.	3074
	Enoch translated, being 365 years old.	3017
	Seth dies, being 912 years old.	2962
	Noah born.	2948
	Methuselah dies, being 969 years old.	2348
The Deluge	Noah enters into the ark, being 600 years old.	2348
	Noah leaves the ark, after dry land appears.	2347
	Traditions of the Deluge are found among all races. The Babylonian story of the Deluge was found, written on clay tablets, in the ruins of Nineveh. It differs little in its main points from that in the Bible.	
The New Start	The Covenant with Noah, immediately following the Deluge.	2347

II. From the Deluge to the Exodus

Events in Scripture History	Places	Ussher's Dates (B.C.)	Other Historical Events
The Deluge.		2348	Seventh ruler of China died 2257.
The confusion of tongues.	Babylonia	2247	
Death of Noah.	Arabia	1998	Nineveh built 2218.
Abram born at Ur.	Chaldea	1996	Zoroaster 2115(?).
Abram moves from Ur to Haran.	Mesopotamia	1926	Celts in Europe about 2000.
The call of Abram.	"	1921	Hyksos in Egypt in time of Abraham, probably.
Abram and Lot move to Canaan.	Canaan	1921	
Abram and Lot separate.	"	1918	Dates vary from 2100–1675.
Lot captured by Chedorlaomer.	Sodom	1913	Sesostris I, Egypt, 1980–1935(?).
The Covenant with Abram.	Hebron	1912	
Birth of Ishmael.	"	1910	
Renewal of Covenant; Change of Abram's name to Abraham.	"	1897	Hammurabi (Amraphel of Gen. 14:1), and his code, contemporary with Abraham. The dates vary from 2300 to 1900 B.C. His Monument discovered at Susa (Shushan) of Persia (in A.D. 1901, 2) contains the earliest known writing on stone, with laws something like those in Leviticus.
Destruction of *Sodom.*	Sodom	1897	
Isaac born.	Moab	1896	
Ishmael sent away.		1892	
Covenant with Abimelech.		1891	
Moab and Ammon born.		1897	
Ishmael marries an Egyptian.			
Sacrifice of Isaac.	Moriah	1871	
Death of Sarah.	Hebron	1860	
Abraham marries Keturah.			
Marriage of Isaac and Rebekah.	Lahai-roi	1857	
Jacob and Esau born.	Beersheba	1837	
Death of Abraham.	"	1822	
Esau sells his birthright.	Lahai-roi	1804	
Isaac forbidden to enter Egypt; goes to	Gerar	1804	
Esau marries Hittite wives.		1796	
Jacob obtains birthright blessing.	Beersheba	1760	
Jacob goes to Padan-aram; his vision at Bethel.		1760	

These dates are only approximate.

II. From the Deluge to the Exodus *(Continued)*

Events in Scripture History	Places	Ussher's Dates (B.C.)	Other Historical Events
Esau's Ishmaelite marriages.		1760	Tel-el-Amarna letters, 15th
Death of Ishmael.		1773	century or earlier: 300
Jacob marries Leah and Rachel.	Padan-aram	1753	letters inscribed on clay
Birth of Jacob's children (except	"	1752–	tablets 2 by 3 inches,
Benjamin).		1739	and sent between
			Palestine and Amarna
Joseph born.	"	1739	in Egypt showing a
Jacob returns to Canaan.			general prevalence of
Jacob wrestles with the angel.	Peniel	1739	dissatisfaction with the
Birth of Benjamin and death of			rule of Egypt.
Rachel.	Bethlehem	1729	
Joseph sold into Egypt from	Dothan	1718	
Joseph put in prison.	Egypt	1718	
Death of Isaac.	Hebron	1716	
Joseph interprets Pharaoh's dream.	Egypt	1716	
Joseph made prime minister.	"	1716	
The seven years of plenty begin.		1716	
Birth of Manasseh and Ephraim.	Egypt		
The seven years of famine begin.		1709	
Jacob and his family move to Goshen.	Egypt	1706	
Death of Jacob.	"	1689	According to Ussher, the
Death of Joseph.	"	1635	Israelites were shep-
Beginning of oppression of Israel.	"	1573	herds in Goshen for 133
			years, 1706–1573. Then
Moses born.	"	1571	they were slaves of the
Exile of Moses begins.	Arabia	1531	Egyptians for 82 years,
Call of Moses; burning bush.	"	1492	1573–1491.
Plagues of Egypt.	Egypt	1492–1	Others make the slavery in
The first Passover.	"	1491	Egypt to continue much
THE EXODUS in April.	"	1491	longer and the date of
			the Exodus to be
			between 1300 and 1200
			B.C.

These dates are only approximate.

III. From Egypt to Palestine *(40 years)*

Persons	Events	Places	Ussher's Dates (B.C.)	
Moses	THE EXODUS, in April.			
	The Pillar of fire.	Arabia	1491	Most scholars incline
	The giving of the manna.	"	1491	to these later dates
	The giving of the law.	Mt. Sinai	1491	and Rameses II as
	The golden calf.	"	1491	the Pharaoh of the
	The Tabernacle set up.	"	1490	Oppression.
Aaron	The ceremonial law given.	"	1490	
	Nadab and Abihu.	Wilderness of Arabia		
	Wandering for 40 years in	Between branches of	1491–	
	Wilderness.	Red Sea	1451	
Caleb	New start for Canaan.	Kadesh		
	Waters from the rock.	Meribah	1452	
Joshua	Death of Aaron on.	Mt. Hor	1452	
	Brazen serpent.	The Arabah	1452	
	Balaam's blessing.	Moab	1452	
	Death of Moses.	Nebo-Pisgah	1451	

IV. The Conquest of Palestine

Persons	Events	Places	Ussher's Dates (B.C.)
	Passing over Jordan.	Near Jericho	1451
	The Fall of Jericho.	"	1451
Joshua	Defeat at Ai.	Near Jericho	1451
	Law read from Ebal and Gerizim.	Shechem	1451
	Conquest of Canaan.		1451–1443
Caleb	Cities of refuge appointed.		1444
	Joshua renews the covenant.	Shechem	1427
	Death of Joshua.	Timnath-serah	1427

V. The Period of the Judges

Judges and Events	Places	Years of Oppression	Years of Peace	Years B.C. from Beecher
Oppression of Chushan-Rishathaim, from Mesopotamia (during the last years of Joshua)	Palestine	8		1441–1434
1. Othniel, Son-in-law of Caleb, Deliverer and Judge (14 years)	Near Hebron			1434
Peace and Prosperity			37	1434–1397
Oppression by Eglon of Moab	So. Palestine	18		1397–1380
2. Ehud of Benjamin	Near Jericho			1380
Peace and Prosperity			10	1380–1370
Oppression by Jabin of Canaan	Northern tribes	} 20		1370–1351
Oppression by the Philistines, during the last 3 years of Jabin's oppression	Southern tribes			1353–1351
3. Deborah of Ephraim } Deliverers from Jabin 4. Balak of Naphtali	No. Palestine			1351
5. Shamgar of Judah, Deliverer from Philistines	S.W. Palestine			1351
Peace and Prosperity			22	1351–1329
Oppression by Midianites	So. Galilee	7		1329–1323
6. *Gideon* of Manasseh, Deliverer and Judge	So. Galilee			1323
Peace and Prosperity			24	1323–1299
7. Abimelech, Prince of Israel (3 years)	Shechem		3	1298–1296
8. Tola of hill country	Ephraim		23	1295–1273
Oppression by Philistines	S.W. Israel			1283
9. Jair, Judge of Israel E. of Jordan	Gilead		22	1272–1251
10. Samson—exploits as judge	S.W. Israel		20	1250–1231
Oppression by Ammonites beyond Jordan	East Israel	18		1230–1213
11. Jephthah, Judge (6 years) beyond Jordan	Gilead		6	1212–1207
12. Ibzan, Judge from Bethlehem 7 m. N.W. of Nazareth	Galilee		7	1206–1200
13. Elon of Zebulun	Galilee		10	1199–1190
14. Abdon, Judge (8 years)	Ephraim		8	1189–1182
Oppression by Philistines	W. Israel			1182
15. Eli, the high priest, acts as judge in Shiloh	Benjamin		40	1182–1142
16. Samuel called to be prophet	Shiloh			1160(?)
Judge of Israel, or chief citizen	Israel			1141–1065(?)

NOTE: The dates given here are from Prof. Willis J. Beecher's *Dated Events of the Old Testament*, and for the most part do not vary very largely from those given by Ussher in many Bibles.

VI. The United Kingdom (120 years: 1103 to 1057 or 983 to 937)

Events in Scripture History	Places	Dates (B.C.) Beecher	Ussher	Other Events
Saul's Kingdom				
Israel asks for a king.		1103(?)	1095	Chou dynasty in
Saul chosen and made king.	Gilgal	1102	1095	China brings us to
Saul's victory over Ammon.		1102	1095	historic ground,
Birth of David.	Bethlehem	1092	1085	1123–255.
Saul's final rejection and break with Samuel.		1078(?)	1079	
Private anointing of David.	Bethlehem	1077(?)	1065	
David becomes Saul's minstrel.		1074(?)	1063	
David and Goliath.	Ephesdammim	1073(?)	1063	
David's marriage to Michal.		1071(?)	1062	
David's outlaw life. 7 years.		1068–1063	1062–1055	
David spares Saul's life (skirt).	Engedi	1066(?)	1060	
Death of Samuel.	Ramah	1065(?)	1060	
David and Nabal.	Carmel	1065(?)	1059	
The spear and the cruse incident.		1065(?)	1058	
David among the Philistines.	Ziklag	1064	1057	
Death of Saul and Jonathan.	Gilboa	1063	1056	
David's Kingdom				
David becomes king of Judah.	Hebron	1063	1056	Hiram, King of Tyre,
War between David and *Ish-bosheth*.		1063–1056	1056–1048	contemporary of
David king over all Israel. Jerusalem becomes capital.		1055	1048	David and Solomon.
Period of war.		1055–1043	1048–1042	
Ark brought to Jerusalem.		1042(?)	1042	Homer thought by
The great promise to David.	Jerusalem	1041(?)	1042	some to be contem-
Birth of Solomon.	"	1041(?)	1033	porary with David.
Preparation for building the Temple.	"			
Absalom's rebellion.		1023	1023	
Solomon anointed and proclaimed.	"	1022	1015	
Death of David.	"	1022	1015	
Solomon's Kingdom				
Solomon becomes real king.	Jerusalem	1022	1015	
Temple foundations laid.	"	1019	1012	Homer, 1000(?)
Temple dedicated.	"	1011	1004	Zoroaster, 1000(?)
Visit of Queen of Sheba to Solomon.	"	995(?)	995	
Jeroboam flees to Shishak in Egypt.		986(?)	980	Shishak in Egypt,
Death of Solomon.	"	983	975	who invades Israel.

NOTE ON THE DIVIDED KINGDOM.

The dates are given according to Prof. Willis J. Beecher in his *Dated Events of the Old Testament History*, the most thorough and scholarly study of the subject including the Assyrian Canon. There are also given the dates of Arbp. James Ussher, as in many Bibles.

THE MOVEMENT OF THE HISTORY. FIVE GREAT PERIODS.

I. The United Kingdom. 3 Kings. 120 years, 1102–982.

II. The Divided Kingdom. { JUDAH. One dynasty: 11 kings, 1 queen. } 260 years { ISRAEL. Nine dynasties: 19 kings. } to 720.

III. Judah, alone. 8 kings. David's dynasty 136 years, 722–586.

IV. The Exile. 70 years, 605–536.

V. The Return. The new nation, 536–400 and on.

VII. The Divided Kingdoms of Judah and Israel

(Periods: Judah nearly 400 years. Israel about 260 years. Judah alone 136 years.)

JUDAH — One dynasty (David's) 11 kings and one queen		Dates B.C.		ISRAEL — 9 dynasties 19 kings		
Prophets	Kings and Events	Beecher	Ussher	Kings and Events	Prophets	Contemporary History
	Rehoboam, 17 years.			**Jeroboam I,** 22 years.		
	Influx of Levites, etc.,			Semi-idolatry established.		
	from Israel.	982	975	Exodus of Levites, etc., to		
	Rehoboam forsakes			Judah.		
	Jehovah.	980				Shishak monument.
	Invasion by Shishak.	978				
	Abijam, 3 years.	965	957			
		962	955		Ahijah	
	Asa, 41 years.	961	954	**Nadab,** parts of 2 years.		
	Land at rest 10 years.	960	953	**Baasha,** 24 years.		
	Invasion by Zerah the					
	Ethiopian.	949	941			
	Great revival and					
	reformation.	948	941			
	War with Israel.	947		Civil war with Judah.		
		937	930	**Elah,** parts of 2 years.		
				Zimri, 7 days.		
		936	929	**Omri,** 12 years.		
				Great enlargement of		Moabite stone naming
				kingdom.		Omri.
	Decline.	925	918	**Ahab,** 22 years.		
				Marries Jezebel.		
	Jehoshaphat, 25 years.	921	917	Idolatry introduced.		Shalmanezer II, Assyria.
	Wide extended revival.			Religious persecution.		
	Outward prosperity.	905	854	**Ahaziah:** co-regnant, 2 years.	Elijah	854, Battle of Karkar,
	Decline through					Assyria.
	alliance with Jezebel.	904	853	**Jehoram,** 12 years.		
	Jehoram: co-regnant,					
	4 years.	900	893			
	Alone, 4 years.	897		Mesha of Moab revolts.		
	Ahaziah, part of one year.	893	885			Black Obelisk naming
	Athaliah, 6 years.	892	884	**Jehu,** 28 years.		Jehu.
	Murder of seed-royal.					907(?) Homer, Hesiod.
son of	Baal worship.			Zealous reformer.	Elisha	
Jehoiada	Temple desecrated.			Destroys house of Ahab.		884, Lycurgus.
						878(?) } Carthage
						858(?) } founded.
	Joash, 40 years	886	878	Tributary to Assyria.		
Zechariah	Temple and its worship					Sheshonk III, Egypt.
	restored.	864	856	**Jehoahaz,** 17 years.		820(?) Lycurgus, Sparta.
		850	842	**Jehoash:** co-regnant, 3 years.		814, Macedonia
				Hazael's expedition.		founded.
	Amaziah, 29 years.	847		Alone, 16 years.		
	Defeat of Edom.	846	840	Death of Elisha.		
	Conquest by Jehoash of			Victories over Damascus.		814(?) Carthage
	Israel.	833		Conquest of Judah.		founded.
	Nominal ruler under					
	suzerainty of Israel.	832	825	**Jeroboam II,** 41 years.		797, Damascus taken
					Hosea	by Assyrians.
	Death of Amaziah.	818		Suzerain of all peoples from		
Amos	INTERREGNUM for 11 years.			Mediterranean to		
				Euphrates.	Jonah	

109

VII. The Divided Kingdoms of Judah and Israel *(Continued)*

JUDAH		Dates B.C.		ISRAEL		
Prophets	Kings and Events	Beecher	Ussher	Kings and Events	Prophets	Contemporary History
	Uzziah, 52 years. (Also called Azariah.)	806	811		Amos	Blank in Assyrian history. Confusion in Egyptian. 776 B.C., First Olympiad.
		792		Death of Jeroboam. INTERREGNUM for 22 years.		
	Succeeds Jeroboam as suzerain of region.	791				
		769	773	**Zechariah,** 6 months.		The Jewish Cyclopedia
	Leprosy of Uzziah (?)	768	772	**Shallum,** 1 month.		gives 2 reigns of
	Jotham: co-regnant, 23 years.	767	772	**Monahem,** 10 years.		Jeroboam II, 825–799 and 788–773; Israel being under Syria 799
		758	761	**Pekahiah,** 2 years.		to 788.
						753, Rome founded. Draco.
		755	759	**Pekah,** 20 years.		
Isaiah	Alone, 16 years.	754	742			733(?) Expedition of Pul, or Tiglath-pileser of Assyria, captures
	Invasion by Israel and Rezin of Damascus.	740		Invasion of Judah.		Damascus and
	Ahaz, 16 years.	739				Samaria.
Micah		738	742	Deportation by Tiglath-pileser. Death of Pekah.		The Jewish Cycl. gives 2 reigns for Pekah, 759–744 and 735–730.
	Tributary to Assyria.	736		Hoshea, governor.		
		726	730	**Hoshea,** king 9 years.		Taylor Cylinder.
		723	726			722, Sargon I, Assyria. 713, Year in Rome begun with January.
	Hezekiah, 29 years. Great Passover.	722				705, Sennacherib, Assyria.
		720 } 718		First siege and capture of Samaria. Fall of Samaria. End of Kingdom of Israel.		

VII. The Divided Kingdoms of Judah and Israel *(Continued)*

JUDAH		Dates B.C.		ISRAEL		
Prophets	Kings and Events	Beecher	Ussher	Kings and Events	Prophets	Contemporary History
Isaiah	First invasion of Sennacherib.	710				660–585, First Mikado in Japan.
	Hezekiah's sickness. Second invasion of Sennacherib.	701				681, Esarhaddon, Assyria.
	Manasseh, 55 years.	694	697			685–668, Second Messenian war.
	Death of Isaiah(?)	679				659, Byzantium founded.
	Manasseh carried to Babylon(?)	648				Scythian invasion.
	Manasseh's return and reformation.	647	642			
Nahum	**Amon,** 2 years.	639				640, Median Empire independent.
Joel			640			
	Josiah, 31 years.	638				624 (621?) Draco's legislation.
	Josiah begins reforms.	627				
		626	*Authorities are practically agreed on these dates.*			623–543, "Buddha," India. Public beginning, July 594.
Zephaniah	Josiah's great reformation. Reformation passover. }	622	609			608, Expedition of Pharaoh Necho.
	Jehoahaz, 3 months.	608				606, Destruction of Nineveh.
			609			
Daniel	**Jehoiakim,** 11 years.					604, Nebuchadnezzar.
	First captivity begins.	607	606			603, Carchemish.
	First deportation.	605	598			605, Daniel in exile. Expounds king's dream, 603.
Jeremiah	Second deportation.	598				
	Jehoiachin, 3 months.	597				604, Phoenicians circumnavigate Africa.
	The great deportation.					
	Zedekiah, 11 years.	597	598			
Habakkuk	Siege of Jerusalem.	588	588			594, Solon's legislation.
Ezekiel	Destruction of Jerusalem and the Temple.	586	586			593, Seven wise men in Greece.
	Beginning of great captivity.	586	586			588, Pythian games begin.

111

VIII. The Captivity to the End of the Old Testament (about 2000 years)

Prophets	Jewish Events	Dates (B.C.)		Contemporary History
		Beecher	Ussher	
Jeremiah	*First* captivity.	605	606	
Ezekiel	*Second* captivity.	597		
	Final captivity.	586	586	Nebuchadnezzar besieges Tyre, 585.
				Aesop.
Obadiah	Last of Ezekiel's prophecies.		571	Evil Merodach, Babylon, 562.
Daniel	Jehoiachin released.	561		Temple of Diana, Ephesus, 552.
				Public library at Athens, 544.
	Belshazzar's feast.	539	538	Babylon taken by Cyrus, 539.
	Daniel in den of lions.	538	538	First year of Cyrus, 538.
	The decree for the return.	538	536	
	End of first reckoning of 70 years.			Pythagoras, 540–510.
	First return. 50,000 under Zerubbabel.	538		Pisistratus, Athens, 560–527.
				Nabonidus, Babylon, 556.
Haggai	Foundation of Temple laid.	537–6		Darius in Babylon, 521.
Zechariah	Long delay.			
	Building of Temple resumed.	520		Beginning of Roman republic, 510.
	Temple dedicated.	516	516	Marathon, 490.
	End of second reckoning of 70 years.			Xerxes (Ahasuerus), 489.
	No knowledge of events until Feast of Ahasuerus (Xerxes).	483		Invasion of Greece, 480.
				Herodotus, Socrates.
	Esther becomes queen.	479		Xenophon, Plato.
	Haman's plot.	474		First decemvirate, Rome, 451.
Malachi	Second return under Ezra.	458		Pericles, Athens, 444.
	Return under NEHEMIAH.			Parthenon, Athens, 443–438.
	Wall of Jerusalem rebuilt.	444		First Peloponnesian war, 431.
	Reforms.			Xenophon's retreat, 401.
	Death of Nehemiah.	391		

NOTE : It will perhaps be easier to understand the double reckoning of the 70 years' captivity by the following diagram showing how it is reckoned as beginning at different points, and closing at equi-different points.

First Captivity began 605.	70 Years.	537–6	First Return.
Second Captivity began 597.	The Seventy Years of Exile foretold	516	
Third Captivity and Temple Destroyed, 586.	by Jeremiah.		Second Temple Completed.

IX. Period between the Testaments

B.C.	Jewish History	Contemporary History	B.C.	Jewish History (continued)	Contemporary History
350	Jaddua, High Priest.	Egypt a Persian Province.	165	Rededication of Temple.	
359		Philip II of Macedonia.	149		
336		Darius Codomannus king of Persia.	146		Third Punic War: Rome. Greece a Roman Province.
		Alexander the Great.	141	Deliverance of Judea complete.	
332	Alexander visits Jerusalem.	Alexandria in Egypt founded.	109	Pharisees and Sadducees first mentioned.	
331	Jews settle in Alexandria.	Battle of Arbela.	107	Aristobulus "king."	
330	Onias I, High Priest.	End of Persian Empire.	63	Pompey captures Jerusalem.	Judea annexed to Rome. Conspiracy
320	Ptolemy takes Jerusalem.	Ptolemy I, Soter.	58	Herod in Palestine.	of Catiline.
312	Seleucidae in Syria.	Seleucus I, Nicator.	54	Crassus plunders Temple.	Caesar in Gaul.
301	Palestine under Egypt.	Battle of Ipsus.	48		Battle of Pharsalia.
284	Septuagint.		47	Antipater procurator. Herod governor of Galilee.	Caesar dictator at Rome.
264		First Punic War: Rome.			
261		Mantho, in Egypt.	44		Caesar assassinated.
219	Beginning of War of Antiochus and Ptolemy.	Second Punic War: Rome.	40	Herod king of Judea.	Battle of Actium.
			37	Herod takes Jerusalem.	Egypt a Roman Province.
198	Antiochus the Great master of Palestine.		31	Earthquake in Judea.	Temple of Janus closed.
			30		
			29		
170	Tyranny of Antiochus Epiphanes.		27		Augustus made Emperor.
			19	Herod begins rebuilding the Temple.	
167	Revolt of Maccabees.				
166	Judas Maccabeus.		4	Herod dies at Jericho.	

8
Rome after Christ
(A.D. 100–500)

HIGHLIGHTS
Gospel of Christ • Persecution of Early Church
Constantine the Great • Fall of Rome

Rome and Christianity: Conflict

Jesus Christ

For about 33 years, **Jesus Christ,** the Son of God, lived on the earth as a human being. The facts of His life are among the best-recorded events of all time. God inspired Matthew, Mark, Luke, and John to record these events in a way that no writer working with merely human resources could ever do. The four gospels are the most important texts for the student of history to read and understand, for no single life has had as much influence on world history as the life of Jesus. It is doubtful that we could have found our way through the study of world history so far without following the thread that has led us to Christ. The calendar of history now begins to read years "A.D." As our study continues, continual reference must be made to Jesus; we have yet to see the last examples of His influence on history.

Around the age of 30, Jesus began to teach new things. Not rejecting the Old Testament but fulfilling it, Christ stressed love as the motive for all morality. He taught that we are to love all men, Jew or Gentile, friend or enemy, just as we love ourselves. He taught with the authority of God, and He performed miracles with the power of God. Jesus became so popular in Palestine that Jewish leaders, already envious of His teaching and miracles, began

to see him as a threat. By this time, the supreme ruler in Palestine was **Pontius Pilate** [pŏn′shŭs pī′lət], a Roman governor. Although Pilate had to admit Christ's total innocence of crime, the Jewish leaders persuaded him to have Roman soldiers crucify Jesus. The people who had only days before cheered Jesus now mocked Him. They had not expected a Savior who would not save Himself. Even His disciples—afraid, bewildered, dejected—deserted Jesus.

But three days later, Jesus arose from the dead. For the next 40 days, He walked, talked, and ate with friends. The disciples' faith was renewed and they were overjoyed to hear, see, even be able to touch Jesus in His glorified body. Even Thomas, who at first doubted that Jesus was really alive, was convinced that Jesus is God. *More than 500 eyewitnesses* saw the resurrected Jesus. When the 40 days had ended and it was time for Jesus to ascend into heaven, He instructed the disciples to carry the *gospel* to all men. The gospel is the good news that God had not simply canceled the death sentence for our sins, but that God Himself had died in our place to pay for our sins so that all who believe might have eternal life.

The disciples of Christ went out eagerly into all parts of the vast Roman Empire and beyond with the message of Christ's love. Before long, the followers of Christ became known as **Christians,** and their beliefs and way of life became known as Christianity.

114

Descent from the Cross: In this painting, Rembrandt shows the limp, lifeless body of the Son of God being lowered from the cross. By including his own picture (the figure in blue on the left) Rembrandt conveyed the idea that all men of all times are responsible for the death of Christ. It was for the sins of all men that He died, was buried, and rose again.

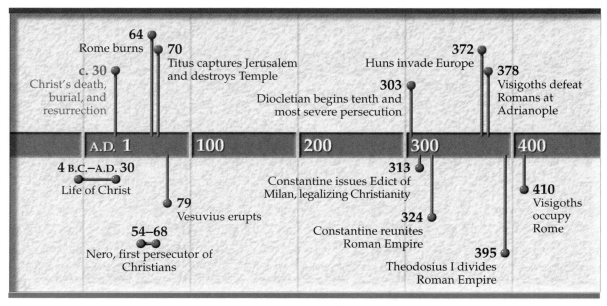

64 — Rome burns

70 — Titus captures Jerusalem and destroys Temple

c. 30 — Christ's death, burial, and resurrection

372 — Huns invade Europe

378 — Visigoths defeat Romans at Adrianople

303 — Diocletian begins tenth and most severe persecution

A.D. 1   **100**   **200**   **300**   **400**

4 B.C.–A.D. 30 — Life of Christ

79 — Vesuvius erupts

54–68 — Nero, first persecutor of Christians

313 — Constantine issues Edict of Milan, legalizing Christianity

324 — Constantine reunites Roman Empire

395 — Theodosius I divides Roman Empire

410 — Visigoths occupy Rome

115

Nero: The emperor Nero used a concavely ground emerald as a lens to correct his nearsightedness and watch the gladiators in the Roman arena.

Tiberius: The emperor Tiberius ruled at the time of Jesus' crucifixion, resurrection, and ascension.

During the first century after Christ, the number of people who trusted in Christ as their Savior grew rapidly. Although most of the very first Christians were Jews, the news of Christ was soon carried by Christian Jews like *Peter* and *Paul* to **Gentiles** (non-Jews) to places far away from Palestine. Paul, to whom Christ had made a special appearance, was writing to Christians living in the city of Rome by the middle of the century.

The Claudian Emperors

After Caesar Augustus died, four of his descendants, called the **Claudian** [klô′dǐ·ən] **emperors,** ruled from A.D. 14 to 68. After a year of turmoil, Vespasian [věs·pā′zhan] became emperor in A.D. 69. He and his descendants, called the **Flavian** [flā′vē·ən] **emperors,** ruled Rome for the rest of the first century A.D., from 69 to 96.

The first emperors after Christ. What the first three Claudian emperors learned of Christ, Christians, and Christianity is not known. Augustus' stepson **Tiberius** [tī·běr′ǐ·us], emperor from 14 to 37, was fair and capable as Roman emperors went, but he was not very popular. Tiberius was emperor during the time of Jesus' crucifix-

ion, resurrection, and ascension.

Tiberius's adopted son **Caligula** [kə·lǐg′ū·lə] ruled from A.D. 37 to 41. He is remembered for having gone mad to the point of selecting his favorite horse to be a member of the Roman Senate. His own bodyguards murdered him.

Caligula's uncle **Claudius** ruled from 41 to 54. During this time, the Romans occupied southern Britain, another part of the Roman Empire to which Christianity would soon spread. Claudius expelled Jews from Rome on the grounds that they were causing disorder; some of these Jews may have been Christians.

Nero and the first persecution. During the reign of Claudius's stepson **Nero,** who ruled from 54 to 68, Christianity became a crime in the Roman Empire. Nero was an extremely evil man who murdered his wife, adopted brother, and mother. He was also the first Roman emperor to persecute Christians.

In **A.D. 64,** *a fire destroyed over half the city of Rome.* Rumors spread that Nero had started it and that he even "fiddled" (played the lyre) while the city burned. To remove suspicion from himself, Nero blamed the Christians for the fire.

Arch of Titus: *This triumphal arch was begun by Vespasian to honor the victory of his son Titus over the Jews at Jerusalem in* A.D. *70. The close-up of the carving on the arch shows Titus's armies carrying spoil out of Jerusalem. Notice the seven-branched candlestick which the soldiers have removed from the destroyed and burned Temple in Jerusalem.*

Vesuvius: *This 18th-century oil painting depicts the eruption of Vesuvius that buried the cities of Pompeii and Herculaneum.*

Christians were easy targets for persecution. Most Christians were undoubtedly good, law-abiding citizens. Jesus, who had never disobeyed a Roman law, had said to "render unto Caesar the things that are Caesar's." Christianity would eventually be recognized as a foundation for good citizenship. But Christians lived godly lives, different from other Roman citizens. Many people were upset or angered because the Christians refused to take part in the immoral events sponsored by the Roman emperors. Thus, when Nero began to persecute Christians, many Romans supported him.

Christians suffered unbelievable tortures. Some were crucified, as Jesus had been, or torn apart by wild dogs. Others were covered with pitch and used as torches to light Nero's garden. According to tradition, Paul was beheaded by Nero in Rome. Yet, in spite of fierce persecution, the number of Christians increased.

Nero's persecution of Christians did not save him from his growing unpopularity. He ended life with a choice between assassination and suicide. After Nero killed himself, Rome fell into turmoil that no one could blame on Christians. No less than four men were proclaimed emperor by competing armies in the year that followed Nero's death. Force and violence continued to rule Rome as Roman armies made—and unmade—one Roman emperor after another.

The Flavian Emperors

Vespasian. Vespasian finally emerged victorious in the race for emperor that followed Nero's death. During Vespasian's reign as emperor (69 to 79), his son **Titus** [tī'təs] *captured Jerusalem* and *destroyed the Temple* in A.D. 70.

Titus. Titus succeeded his father as emperor and ruled from 79 to 81. At the beginning of his reign, in the summer of A.D. 79, **Mount Vesuvius** [vĕ·sū'vĭ·us] erupted and buried the city of *Pompeii* [pŏm·pā'ĕ] and two other southern Italian towns in lava and ash.

Domitian and the second persecution. Neither Vespasian nor Titus had persecuted Christians, but Vespasian's younger son **Domitian** [dŏ·mĭsh'an], who ruled

117

from 81 to 96, demanded to be worshiped as a god. While the early Christians acknowledged Caesar's authority, they refused to worship the emperor as a god and suffered the consequences with great courage. It was during this persecution that Domitian exiled the aged apostle John from the city of Ephesus to the island of Patmos (Rev. 1:9), where John received and recorded the words and visions of the book of the Revelation.

The Roman Empire generally tolerated differing religious views, as long as the people also recognized the emperor as a god. But Christians (and faithful Jews) acknowledged only one true God. If Roman emperors continued to insist that they were gods, then further conflict between Rome and Christianity could not be avoided.

CHECK UP

1. What Roman governor of Palestine authorized the crucifixion of Jesus?
2. How long did Christ stay on earth after His resurrection? How many people saw the resurrected Christ?
3. Who was emperor at the time of Jesus' crucifixion, resurrection, and ascension?
4. What insane emperor was murdered by his own bodyguards?
5. What emperor ordered the occupation of Britain and the expulsion of all Jews from Rome?
6. What emperor accused Christians of burning Rome and persecuted them?
7. Which two Flavian emperors did not persecute Christians? Which Flavian emperor demanded to be worshiped as a god?
8. Why could Rome not tolerate Christianity?

Identify: Jesus Christ, Christians, Claudian emperors, Flavian emperors, Peter, Paul, Gentiles, Claudius, Domitian

---

Two Centuries and More of Persecution

Christians in the Empire. By the end of the second century A.D., there were Christians in every province of the Roman Empire and beyond, perhaps as far away as central Asia. Rich and poor, educated and uneducated, noble and common—people from all walks of life found Christianity to be the truth they had been seeking. How many were converted we do not know, but it has been estimated that by the close of the third century, half the population of the Roman Empire were professing Christians.

"Good" emperors vs. Christ. From 96 to 180, the so-called **"five good emperors"** ruled Rome. Selected for their ability and specially trained to be emperors, these men are remembered as some of Rome's most intelligent rulers; yet at least three of them persecuted Christians. These men, Rome's best, dared to contest Christ for the title of Savior.

Trajan [trā′jăn] ruled as emperor from A.D. 98 to 117. He pushed the boundaries of the empire to their greatest extent, improved government in the provinces, and encouraged new roads and other public construction projects. During his days as emperor, it was against the law to be a Christian, and many Christians were killed. Some families died together. A widow who refused to sacrifice to false gods was whipped, hung by the hair of her head, and finally, with a large stone fastened about her neck, was thrown into a river to drown. Six of her sons were stabbed to death; her youngest son was sawn into pieces. The typical courage of Christians in the face of death convinced Trajan that anyone who denied his own personal faith in Christ was not truly a Christian. He allowed anyone accused of being a Christian to be pardoned upon denial of the charge.

Marcus Aurelius [mär′kŭs ô·rē′lĭ·ŭs] ruled from 161 to 180. A man of quiet thought who wrote books on philosophy, Marcus came to the throne after an extraor-

Marcus Aurelius: Marcus Aurelius was a hater and ardent persecutor of Christians.

Severus and vicious persecution. The general **Septimius Severus** [sĕp·tĭ′mĭ·us sĕ·vē′rus] emerged victorious and reigned as emperor from 193 to 211. Though at first friendly toward Christians, Severus commanded in 202 that no one could become a Christian, and a vicious persecution of Christians followed, concentrated in northern Africa and Egypt.

Descendants of Septimius Severus occupied the emperor's throne until 235. Throughout this period, the Senate was completely ignored while the army was enlarged. More than ever the Roman government rested on a foundation of force and violence. Soldiers murdered the last Severan emperor in 235. During the next 50 years of civil war, 26 different men claimed the emperor's title, and nearly all were murdered.

dinary training period. Yet this man, remembered as one of the most upright emperors, indeed as one of the greatest figures of ancient history, hated Christians. The persecution of Christians reached west into Gaul and across the Mediterranean into Africa. Cruelties made spectators shudder with horror. Some martyrs walked over nails, thorns, or sharp shells; others were beaten until their muscles and veins lay bare. After such torture, they were put to death by fire.

The mad emperor **Commodus** [kŏm′ə-dus] succeeded Marcus Aurelius and ruled from 180 to 193. With his assassination, Rome fell into civil war, and competing armies fought for the office of emperor. On one occasion, troops held the city of Rome and put the office of emperor up for sale. All pretenses were dropped; no one doubted that the armies controlled the emperors.

Persecution nearly ceases. From 235 to 250, except for one brief period, the persecution of Christians nearly ceased. The exception was under the emperor **Maximinus Thrax** [măk′si·mī′nus thrăks], who ruled for only four years (235–238).

Valerian's attack on Christian leaders. Persecution resumed around 250 and began to worsen. **Valerian** [va·lēr′ĭ·an], emperor from A.D. 253 to 260, believed that he could harm Christianity the most by attacking Christian leaders. But as they

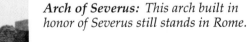

Arch of Severus: This arch built in honor of Severus still stands in Rome.

Temple of Diana at Ephesus: This bronze coin from the reign of Emperor Maximinus bears the image of the impressive temple in Ephesus dedicated to the goddess Diana.

119

bravely went to their death, refusing to deny Christ, these leaders inspired other Christians to be courageous and steadfast.

Rome at the end of the third century. As the end of the third century A.D. approached, Rome faced many problems. The army played a bigger role than ever before in the government, causing much disorder as it made and unmade emperors. Higher and higher pay for soldiers sent taxes soaring. Financial problems caused the government to reduce the amount of silver in the coins, and prices rose. People lost confidence in the coins, and the government eventually refused to accept its *own* money in payment for taxes.

At the same time the empire faced attacks from the outside. The western frontiers were attacked by German tribes such as the Franks, the Saxons, and the Goths. In the east, Persia, which had never been part of the Roman Empire, had new rulers called the **Sassanids** [săs′ə·nĭdz] who began to attack the Romans, sometimes successfully.

Diocletian and the Great Persecution

In 284, **Diocletian** [dī′ŏ·klē′shan] became emperor. He determined to reverse Rome's decline by strengthening the Roman government, which, of course, meant strengthening the Roman emperor. To accomplish this goal, Diocletian established government price controls and reorganized the army and the government of the provinces. Each province became a huge bureaucracy carefully organized to allow the emperor to control it from the top. New fortifications strengthened the empire's frontiers. Diocletian, recognizing that one man alone could not run the empire, divided the empire into two main parts, the East and the West. He took the East and gave the West to a co-emperor, **Maximian** [măks·ĭm′ĭ·an].

In 303, Diocletian began the *most severe persecution* that Christianity had yet experienced. No doubt this persecution, which extended throughout the empire and lasted more than ten years, was merely another part of his program to strengthen the Roman government. We do not know how many Christians died under Diocletian. Many were hunted down like animals and burned or thrown to wild beasts. Yet the number of Christians killed could not keep up with the number of people who chose to follow Christ rather than Caesar. Opposition by one of the most powerful governments the world has ever known was no match for the power of the gospel.

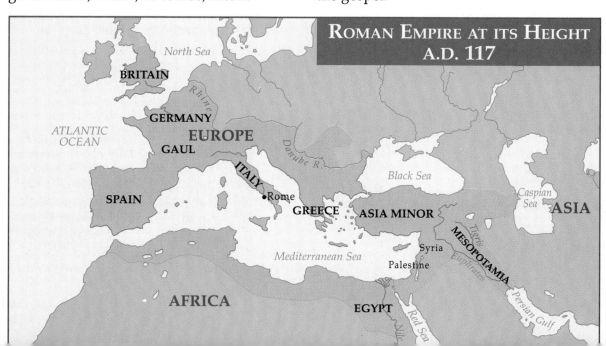

ROMAN EMPIRE AT ITS HEIGHT
A.D. 117

Rome and Christianity: Reconciliation—and Distortion

Constantine and Reconciliation to Christianity

Rise of Constantine. Diocletian voluntarily stepped down as emperor in 305, and persuaded his co-emperor to step down at the same time. Two new emperors had been trained; they were supposed to train two more, and so on. Diocletian hoped that this would become the method by which new emperors came to the throne, rather than by the force and violence of armies. After all, if an emperor is a god, he reasoned, should he not be the one to choose the next emperor?

In less than a year, however, civil war broke out again. Generals and soldiers were still determined that they would decide who the next emperor would be. By 311, there were four rival emperors. **Constantine** [kŏn′stạn·tēn] emerged victorious among the four, but it was not until 324 that he defeated all his rivals to become sole emperor of a reunited Roman Empire, west and east.

Constantine's vision. According to a story Constantine later told the church history writer **Eusebius** [ŭ·sē′bĭ·us], something very unusual happened during a critical battle in 312. Shortly after noon, Constantine claimed, he saw a cross in the sky on which was written, "Conquer by this." In a later dream, said Constantine, God appeared with the same sign and commanded him to carry a cross into battle for protection. Thus did Constantine describe his conversion to Christianity. He claimed that he won all of his victories because God sided with him.

Toleration of Christianity. Constantine is remembered in world history as the first Christian emperor of the Roman Empire. Whether or not Constantine truly knew Jesus as his personal Savior, the fact that he professed to be a Christian is of great impor-

tance. Abandoning the official policy of persecution, Constantine commanded that all people in the empire could worship any god they wished. This **policy of toleration** (encouraged by the **Edict of Milan** in 313) meant that it was no longer a crime to be a Christian.

What a wonderful moment this must have seemed to many Christians of the day! They could now publicly profess their faith in Jesus without having to die for it. The story of Jesus could now be told freely.

It appeared that Rome and Christianity had been reconciled. The emperor no longer demanded that the Christians call him a god. Christians could now obey Caesar *and* God.

Constantine and Distortion of Christianity

Persecution in the name of Christianity. Constantine did not completely understand true Christianity, however. He did not understand that God, Who freely gave His love to man, wants that love returned in a voluntary way, not by force. Slowly but surely, Constantine began to shift official Roman policy from toleration *back* to persecution. The new persecution would be in the *name* of Christianity, but it would be persecution nevertheless.

Constantine began to use his great power as emperor to "support," "defend," and "establish" Christianity in ways that Christianity does not need and Christians should not want. Christianity had prospered under difficult conditions in the three centuries since Christ had ascended into heaven, but Constantine began to *officially discourage* any religious beliefs except Christianity. He also took it upon himself, *as Roman emperor,* to settle disagreements among professing Christians about matters of belief. Later emperors went much further. Temples for false gods were closed, and sacrifices for such gods were forbidden.

121

Constantine: It is clear that Constantine did not completely understand what being a Christian involves. He took the first steps to persecute in the name of Christianity, but it was persecution nevertheless.

Arch of Constantine: Dedicated to Constantine, this arch still stands in Rome.

By the time of emperor **Theodosius I** [thē′ŏ·dō′shĭ·us: 379–395], a distorted form of Christianity was the official religion of the empire, and all other religions were persecuted.

Christianity now rested on the same foundation of force and violence as Rome!

Political use of Christianity. In our study of world history, we have seen that many times men have used religion for political purposes. This is an especially great temptation with the one true religion, Biblical Christianity. The true Christian is a good citizen. He knows the true principles of right and wrong. With his changed life, he strives to live by these principles. He is not overly attached to the things of this life that cause selfishness, corruption, and dishonesty. But government cannot *force* men to become Christians; it can only force them to *say* they are Christians. Government should never discourage Christianity. Neither should it "encourage" Christianity to the point of persecuting nonbelievers.

Perhaps Constantine thought that Christianity offered the solid foundation that the shaky Roman government had never possessed. Rome surely did need less force and violence, less selfishness, corruption, and dishonesty.

CHECK UP

1. What group of emperors ruled Rome from 96 to 180?
2. Who made it illegal to be a Christian in Rome? Why did he promise to free anyone who denied being a Christian?
3. What quiet, philosophical emperor spread persecution of Christians into Gaul and Africa?
4. What emperor tried to harm Christianity by attacking Christian leaders?
5. Name three of the German tribes that attacked Rome's western frontiers. What Persian rulers attacked from the east?
6. Who strengthened and enlarged the Roman government and divided the empire into two parts? Which part did he rule? Who ruled the other part?
7. How did Diocletian's reign end?
8. Who defeated three rivals to become emperor of Rome? What vision did this emperor have?
9. What edict encouraged toleration of Christianity?
10. How did the Roman Empire eventually go back to persecution?

Identify: Commodus, Septimius Severus, Maximinus Thrax, Eusebius, Theodosius I

A New Capital

The western part of the empire had been taxed so heavily that scarcely anything remained to be taxed. The eastern part of the empire, however, was in somewhat better shape. It was also in less danger of foreign invasion. Thus, Constantine decided to abandon the old city of Rome in the west and build a new capital in the east.

He chose to build his new city on the site of the old city of **Byzantium** [bǐ·zăn′-shǐ·əm] in Asia Minor, where the continents of Europe and Asia meet. The city could be reached only through a narrow, easily defended channel of water. Although Constantine wanted to call the city New Rome, people soon began calling it **Constantinople** [kŏn′stăn·t′n·ō′p′l]. For about 50 years after Constantine's death in 337, the unity of the old Roman Empire was more or less preserved, just as Constantine had hoped.

Fall of the Roman Empire

Division of the Roman Empire

In 395, the emperor Theodosius I—the same emperor who made Christianity the official religion of the Roman Empire—divided the empire between his two sons. This division turned out to be permanent.

Never again was the old Roman Empire governed as a single unit with one emperor. The **Eastern Roman Empire** (sometimes called **Byzantium**) lasted for more than a thousand years, following the patterns laid down by Diocletian and then Constantine. As we will see, the Eastern Roman Empire frequently played an important role in later world history, but the **Western Roman Empire** quickly fell.

The Germans

Many tribes. The greatest outside danger to the Western Roman Empire came from the **Germans,** people who were possibly descendants of Japheth's grandson **Ashkenaz** [ăsh′kĕ·năz]. These people lived in Europe on the frontiers of the Roman Empire beyond the Rhine River. The Germans were really not one people but many tribes, including the *Ostrogoths* [ŏs′trŏ·gŏths], *Visigoths* [vĭz′ĭ·gŏths], *Vandals, Franks, Angles, and Saxons* [săk′s′nz].

Admirable traits. Even though the Romans called these Germans "barbarians," the Romans soon learned to admire them in some ways. The Germans were very simple people. They enjoyed few of the luxuries that can make men soft. The Germans were courageous warriors who

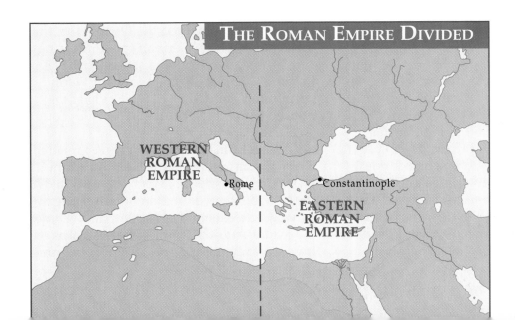

THE ROMAN EMPIRE DIVIDED

WESTERN ROMAN EMPIRE

•Rome

•Constantinople

EASTERN ROMAN EMPIRE

123

were very much concerned with honor. The best warriors led the tribes; followers remained loyal to their leader as long as he provided a good example of courage and honor. Perhaps the Romans saw in the Germans a reflection of their long-lost past in the "golden age" of the Republic.

Undesirable traits. But the Germans had many undesirable traits as well. They drank considerable amounts of alcohol and often killed one another in drunken sprees. They also had violent, uncontrolled tempers and many cruel customs. For example, they left unwanted babies and elderly people outdoors to die.

The Germans worshiped many false gods. It is hard to know which gods were purely German. At an early date German beliefs had been influenced by contacts with the Egyptians, Greeks, and Romans. The best-remembered German gods personified powers or objects in nature. Each day of the week had a corresponding god. *Sunna* [sun′ə], the god associated with the sun, was for Sunday. *Woden* [wō′dən], god of the wind, was for Wednesday. *Thor,* [thôr] god of thunder or the sky and the king of the gods for some Germans, was for Thursday. The Germans sometimes offered human sacrifices to their gods. Generally, the character of the Germans' gods blended well with their emphasis on war, courage, and honor, and with the cruelty characteristic of the German warrior.

German and Roman contact. German warriors fought Roman soldiers as early as the second century B.C., but the Romans won most of these early encounters. In A.D. 9, however, the Romans suffered a severe defeat by the Germans, forcing the Romans to give up any hope of extending their empire beyond the Rhine and Danube rivers. By the third century, the Germans posed a serious threat to Roman borders. Defense against German invaders became a major concern of emperors.

The Germans and Romans also had much friendly contact. They traded with one another, and many Germans entered the empire as workers. During the third century, Germans were invited to join the Roman army. By the end of the fourth century, the army and its leaders in the Western Roman Empire were almost completely German.

Although the Romans were influenced by the Germans (it was a fad among Romans for a while to imitate German hairstyles and clothing), the Romans had an even greater influence on the Germans. For example, the Germans organized into larger tribes with kings who imitated Roman emperors. The Germans learned Roman military methods and how to read and write. Christian missionaries began ministering to the Germans in the fourth century.

When the time came for the German "barbarians" to take over the Roman Empire, they had become like Romans in more ways than one. The fall of the Roman Empire to the Germans was a tremendous change, but in reality it was not as great a change as some people have thought.

German Invasions

In 372, a fierce people from Central Asia rode into eastern Europe. Known as the **Huns** [hŭnz], they had robbed and killed neighbors in Asia. Led by **Attila** [ə·tĭl′ə], they soon overpowered the Ostrogoths, the easternmost of the German tribes. Fearing a similar fate, the Visigoths asked permission to settle *within* the Roman Empire. With permission granted in A.D. 376, Visigoths poured across the Danube River in uncountable numbers seeking security.

When Roman officials began to mistreat them, the angry Visigoths went on a rampage. At **Adrianople** [ā′drē·ən·ō′p′l] in 378, the Visigoths gave the Roman army one of its worst defeats in nearly 400 years. Under the leader **Alaric** [ăl′ə·rĭk], the Visigoths invaded Italy, killing and looting along the way. In 410, Alaric occupied Rome for three days of pillage and plunder. What a great shock this was to people who had placed so much confidence in Rome! From Rome, the Visigoths moved on to invade southern Gaul and then Spain.

When Rome called its frontier troops home to protect the city, other German tribes began to invade the empire. The Vandals ravaged parts of Spain and northern Africa. The Angles, Saxons, and Jutes [joōts] began their invasion of Britain. The Franks seized northern Gaul, and the Ostrogoths overran what is now Romania.

Germans Rule Rome

Since the division of the Roman Empire in A.D. 395, the western emperors had become weaker and weaker. Military leaders held the real power in the Roman government, and the armies were made up mostly of Germans. In one 20-year period, there were nine Roman emperors; all but one were brought down by leading generals.

By about the middle of the fifth century, the Germans had pushed the boundaries of the Roman Empire back to the Italian peninsula. The Roman government itself was controlled by generals of German descent.

Why the Western Roman Empire Fell

Why did the Western Roman Empire fall? The most immediate reason for Rome's fall was the invasion of the German barbarians. Yet this cannot be the whole answer. Is it not surprising that a city that had managed to rule so much of the world for so long lost its empire so easily and so quickly? What had happened to Rome? By the time of the invasions, few people thought that Rome and its culture were worth making sacrifices to save.

End of the Empire: By A.D. 500, the Roman Empire had been reduced to ruin. But as the glory of the empire was fading, another institution was taking its place as the ruler of Europe. In the years to come, the Roman Catholic Church would dominate western Europe.

Force and violence were always the answer of the Roman government. From the beginning to the end, Rome never had any other foundation. Even when Constantine and later emperors tried to make a new foundation for Rome from Christianity, being a Christian ceased to be a matter of choice, and Roman force and violence distorted Christianity. No words better fit Rome than Jesus' warning to the disciple who violently resisted the men who came to arrest Him: "... they that take the sword shall perish with the sword" (Matt. 26:52).

For those who had thought of Rome as the savior of mankind, the fall of Rome was like the end of the world. The fall of Rome did indeed mark the end of ancient times. In a sense, Rome summed up world history before Christ. The fall of Rome marked the beginning of a new era in history.

Yet it was *during* the time of Rome that the one truly momentous event in world history occurred. The world has never been the same *since* Jesus Christ.

The new age after Rome was a time in which the world had to say yes or no to Jesus Christ.

Many major events of world history have, in one way or another, been a response to Jesus Christ.

CHECK UP

1. What ancient city was the site for Rome's new capital? What was the name of the new capital?
2. How long was the unity of the Roman Empire maintained after Constantine's death?
3. Who divided the Roman Empire for the last time?
4. Which lasted longer, the Eastern or the Western Roman Empire?
5. Who posed the greatest threat to the Western Empire?
6. Name three German gods. What days of the week are named for them?
7. How did the Germans influence the Romans? How did the Romans influence the Germans?
8. Why did the Visigoths ask permission to settle within the Roman Empire?
9. Where did the German army defeat the Roman army in 378? Who was the leader of the Germans? What city did he sack in 410?
10. What German tribes invaded Britain?
11. Why did the Western Roman Empire fall?
12. What most important historic event took place during the time of Rome?

Identify: Ashkenaz, Ostrogoths, Visigoths, Vandals, Franks, Angles, Saxons, Huns, Attila

CHAPTER 8 REVIEW

MULTIPLE CHOICE Write the answer of the letter that best completes the sentence.

1. The Roman governor of Palestine who authorized the crucifixion of Christ was ____.
   a Herod   *c* Caligula
   b Pontius Pilate *d* Vespasian

2. The Persian rulers who attacked Rome in the east were called the ____.
   a Goths   *c* Sassanids
   b Saxons   *d* Huns

3. While Diocletian ruled the eastern half of the Roman Empire, he appointed ____ to rule the western half.
   a Constantine   *c* Eusebius
   b Septimus Severus *d* Maximian

4. Constantine described his vision of the cross to the church history writer ____.
   a Augustine   *c* Theodosius
   b Eusebius   *d* Valerian

5. A policy of toleration toward Christianity in the Roman Empire was encouraged by the Edict of ____.
   a Rome   *c* Byzantium
   b Milan   *d* Constantine

6. The site of the old city of Byzantium became the site of the empire's new capital, which was called ____.
   a Constantinople *c* Adrianople
   b Ashkenaz   *d* Milan

7. The Germans possibly descended from Japheth's grandson ____.
   a Alaric   *c* Ashkenaz
   b Odavacer *d* Sunna

8. The barbaric Huns were led by ____.
   a Alaric   *c* Orestes
   b Attila   *d* Aëtius

9. In 378 the Visigoths defeated the Roman army at ____.
   a Adrianople *c* Constantinople
   b Aëtius   *d* Gaul

10. The Visigoths marched through Rome under the leadership of ____.
   a Romulus   *c* Odavacer
   b Aëtius   *d* Alaric

MATCHING Match the description with the correct name.

a Tiberius   *f* Trajan
b Claudius   *g* Valerian
c Nero   *h* Diocletian
d Vespasian *i* Constantine
e Domitian   *j* Theodosius I

____ 1. Emperor who spread the empire to its greatest limits; would not persecute anyone who denied being a Christian

____ 2. Emperor who expelled all Jews from Rome

____ 3. Emperor who ruled during the time of Christ's crucifixion, resurrection, and ascension

____ 4. The first Flavian emperor; did not persecute Christians

____ 5. First emperor to persecute Christians

____ 6. Emperor who claimed to have had a vision of the cross; encouraged tolerance of Christianity

____ 7. During this emperor's reign, Christianity became the official religion of the Roman Empire

____ 8. Emperor who divided the empire into two parts; began the severest persecution Christianity had ever known

CHAPTER 8 REVIEW (CONTINUED)

SHORT ANSWER Answer the following questions in the space provided.

1. How long did Christ stay on the earth after his resurrection?

2. How many people saw the resurrected Christ?

3. Who was emperor when Titus captured Jerusalem and destroyed the Temple?

4. Who was emperor when Rome burned? Who did he blame for the catastrophe?

5. Who was emperor when Vesuvius erupted? Name one of the towns buried in lava and ash.

6. Which lasted longer, the Eastern or the Western Roman Empire?

TIME LINE CHALLENGE Choose the letter of the correct date for each of the events listed below.

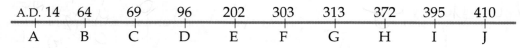

A.D. 14	64	69	96	202	303	313	372	395	410
A	B	C	D	E	F	G	H	I	J

_____ 1. Reign of the "five good emperors" begins

_____ 2. Half the city of Rome is destroyed in a fire

_____ 3. Septimus Severus declares it illegal to be a Christian

_____ 4. Reign of Flavian emperors begins

_____ 5. Reign of the Claudian emperors begins

_____ 6. Diocletian begins the most severe persecution that Christianity had yet experienced

_____ 7. Alaric and the Visigoths sack Rome

_____ 8. Attila and the Huns begin their invasion of eastern Europe

_____ 9. Constantine issues the Edict of Milan, encouraging toleration of Christianity

_____10. Theodosius I splits the Roman Empire into two parts, east and west

MAP SKILLS Use the map on p. 120 to answer the following questions.

1. What rivers in Europe marked the northern border of the Roman Empire?

2. How far did the empire extend into Asia?

CONCEPTS TO CONSIDER On a separate sheet of paper, answer the following questions using complete sentences.

1. What effect did persecution have on Christianity?

2. Briefly explain what caused the downfall of Rome.

Empires of Daniel's Prophecy

PERSIAN

BABYLONIAN

Gold

Silver

GREEK

Brass

ROMAN

Iron

"And the fourth kingdom shall be strong as iron. . . ."
—Daniel 2:40

So clear are these prophecies, and so definite even in their dates, that it is impossible for the boldest unbelief to deny the divine inspiration of the prophet, without at the same time asserting that the prophecies were written after the events to which they refer. But that they were not so, is demonstrable by the completest proof that ever was brought to bear on any historical or literary question; and for this reason, as well as from the circumstance that nearly all the events which form the subjects of predictions are the most conspicuous events in general history, and with the details of which we are amply informed by heathen or infidel historians, we have always been of opinion that the book of Daniel furnishes such powerful and unanswerable evidence of the divine authority of the sacred writers, that it is rather surprising that so powerful a weapon as this might be, in skillful and blessed hands, has not been wielded for the overthrow of unbelief.

—*From notes by John Kitto in The Illustrated Family Bible*

Kings and peoples who aspired to rule the world began to rise and fall in the 700s B.C. The main tendency of world history between about 800 B.C. and the birth of Christ was to build ever larger empires. As we follow the thread of God's plan for mankind, we come to the first of these empires, Assyria, which ruled the Middle East for about 100 years. Although the Assyrians worshiped false gods, God used them as instruments of His will to judge the Jews of the Northern Kingdom of Israel for their sin. When the Assyrian Empire had served its purpose, God judged the cruel Assyrians as well and raised up a new world power—the Chaldean Empire.

Like the Assyrians, the Chaldeans worshiped imaginary gods, but God used them to judge the Jews of the Southern Kingdom of Judah. One of the Jews carried away to Babylon, Daniel, rose to prominence and became an advisor to the king. Through a dream, God revealed the future to the Chaldean king. Daniel interpreted the dream, with God's help, as a prophetic vision of future world empires. Babylon would be the greatest, but the mighty Chaldean Empire would also be judged, and another empire would rise to take its place.

God raised up the Persian Empire to destroy the Chaldeans and free the Jews from the Babylonian captivity. Much larger and longer-lasting than its predecessors, the Persian Empire brought the entire Middle East into *one* unit ruled by *one* man for about two hundred years. Although the Persians contributed little that was new to world history, their methods of empire building and maintenance were copied by later empires.

Daniel continued to play an important role as an advisor to the Persian king. In fulfillment of Daniel's prophecies, a remnant of the Jews returned from captivity to the land where Christ would be born among them. Meanwhile, new peoples were arising in the West who, learning from the great empires of the ancient Middle East, would establish empires yet to be exceeded in splendor. Unknowingly, these western empires would help prepare the world for Christ.

In fulfillment of Daniel's prophecy, Alexander the Great conquered the Persian Empire. As Alexander conquered other lands, he spread the Greek culture and language throughout much of the known world. Soon Greece became the heart of a new world empire. Philosophers and other intelligent Greeks recognized that the many false gods of Greece and other cultures were creations of human imagination. The Greeks might have turned to the one true God, but pride caused them to turn instead toward a new extreme of humanism. Philosophers like Plato and Aristotle and great men of politics and war like Alexander began to think of themselves as gods. Alexander's conquests spread this new extreme of humanism throughout the Mediterranean world and beyond.

As Daniel foretold, Alexander's empire was short-lived, and Rome rose from an insignificant city in Italy to become the fourth empire of Daniel's prophecy. The mighty Roman Empire gathered much of the human race into "one world" as it had not been since God's dispersion of men from the tower of Babel. The people shared a common language once again, for Greek was widely spoken and read as a second language. Pirate-free seas and a vast network of roads made safe travel possible over several million square miles, and men with Roman citizenship could claim legal protection wherever they went. When the time came for Christ to be born, Rome had built a world in which good news could travel fast.

Rome had also built a world in which good news would be welcomed. History repeatedly demonstrated that Rome was built upon foundations of force and violence. Under the influence of Greek culture, many people had abandoned their faith in the old gods. With the beginning of the *Pax Romana*, people began to look upon the city of Rome and the Roman emperor as a new kind of god, as a kind of savior of the world. But these new "gods" offered nothing beyond this life. If Rome and its emperor were the only hope for mankind, then mankind had little hope for the future.

But Rome and its emperor were *not* the only hope. Unknowingly, they had made final preparations for Christ. For about 33 years, Jesus Christ, the Son of God, lived on the earth as a human being. Not rejecting the Old Testament but fulfilling it, Christ stressed love as the motive for all morality. He taught with the authority of God, and He performed miracles with the power of God. Jesus became so popular in Palestine that Jewish leaders, already envious of His teaching and miracles, persuaded the Roman governor to have Him crucified.

The gospel does not end there, however, for after three days in the grave, Christ arose from the dead. For 40 days, He walked, talked, and ate with his disciples and other friends. More than 500 eyewitnesses saw the resurrected Jesus. When the time had come for Christ to ascend into heaven, He instructed His disciples to carry the gospel to all men.

The message of Christ's love soon spread throughout the Roman Empire. By the end of the first century A.D., many people had trusted in Christ as Savior.

Before long these Christians, as they were called, began to face persecution at the hands of Roman emperors. Many were tortured and killed for their faith in Christ. Yet, in spite of fierce persecution, Christianity continued to flourish. In the early fourth century, Constantine the Great became emperor of Rome. Constantine issued the Edict of Milan, making Christianity legal throughout the Roman Empire. For the first time in over 200 years, believers could worship without fear.

Constantine used his power as emperor to "support," "defend," and "establish" Christianity. He even called and presided over church councils to settle disagreements among professing Christians about matters of belief. Soon, the Roman emperor began to officially discourage any religious beliefs other than Christianity. Later emperors went even further. By the end of the fourth century, a distorted form of Christianity had become the official religion of the empire, and all other religions were persecuted.

The fourth century also marked the end of the united Roman Empire. In 395, Theodosius I, the same emperor who made Christianity the official religion of the Roman Empire, divided the empire between his two sons. The old Roman Empire would never again be governed as a single unit under one emperor. The Eastern Roman Empire, Byzantium, lasted for more than a thousand years, but the Western Roman Empire soon fell to barbarian invaders. Thus, the mighty Roman Empire came to an end, and a new era of world history began.

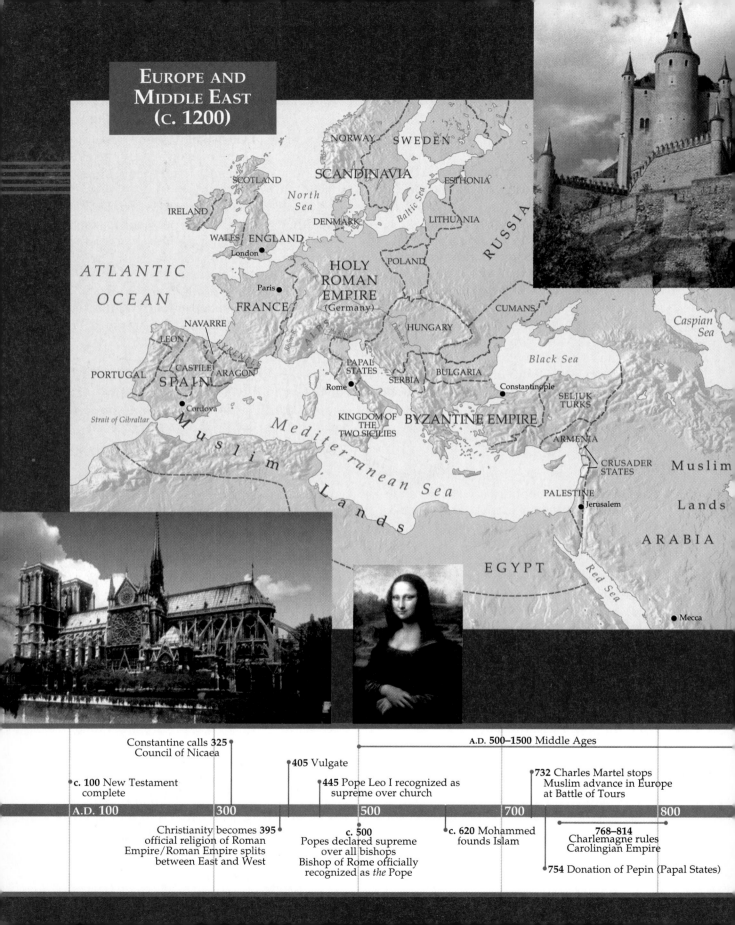

EUROPE AND MIDDLE EAST (C. 1200)

NORWAY
SWEDEN
SCOTLAND
SCANDINAVIA
ESTHONIA
North Sea
IRELAND
Baltic Sea
DENMARK
LITHUANIA
RUSSIA
WALES ENGLAND
London
POLAND
HOLY ROMAN EMPIRE (Germany)
ATLANTIC OCEAN
Paris
FRANCE
CUMANS
Caspian Sea
NAVARRE
PYRENEES
ALPS
HUNGARY
LEON
Black Sea
CASTILE ARAGON
PAPAL STATES
PORTUGAL SPAIN
Rome
SERBIA
BULGARIA
Constantinople
SELJUK TURKS
Cordova
KINGDOM OF THE TWO SICILIES
BYZANTINE EMPIRE
ARMENIA
Strait of Gibraltar
Muslim Lands
Mediterranean Sea
CRUSADER STATES
Muslim
PALESTINE
Jerusalem
Lands
EGYPT
ARABIA
Red Sea
Mecca

Constantine calls **325** Council of Nicaea

A.D. 500–1500 Middle Ages

405 Vulgate

c. 100 New Testament complete

445 Pope Leo I recognized as supreme over church

732 Charles Martel stops Muslim advance in Europe at Battle of Tours

| A.D. 100 | 300 | 500 | 700 | 800 |

Christianity becomes **395** official religion of Roman Empire/Roman Empire splits between East and West

c. 500 Popes declared supreme over all bishops Bishop of Rome officially recognized as *the* Pope

c. 620 Mohammed founds Islam

768–814 Charlemagne rules Carolingian Empire

754 Donation of Pepin (Papal States)

Unit 3

THE MIDDLE AGES AND THE DISTORTION OF CHRISTIANITY
(A.D. 100–1500)

Response to Christ

9 Early Church History
10 Islam versus Christendom
11 From Empire to Feudalism
12 An Age of Darkness

c. 1350–1600 Renaissance

843 Treaty of Verdun divides Carolingian Empire

1054 Roman Catholic Church splits between East and West

1231 Roman church begins the Inquisition

1415 Council of Constance condemns Huss to death

900	1100	1300	1500	1700

Holy Roman **962** Empire begins under Otto the Great

Council of Toulouse forbids **1229** laymen to own Bibles

1334–1351 Black Death in Europe

1453 Muslims conquer Constantinople—Eastern Roman Empire falls

c. 1100–1300 Crusades to Holy Land

1382 Wycliffe Bible completed

9
Early Church History
(A.D. 100–500)

The New Testament

Foundations for Christianity

In its last days, Rome had twisted Christianity into a political tool. The empire had fallen, but the consequences of Rome's vain response to Christ would echo throughout the next era of world history. This era, called the **Middle Ages** because it bridges the gap between ancient and modern history, lasted from about **A.D. 500 to 1500.**

The <u>distortion of Christianity</u> is *the most important characteristic of the Middle Ages,* but in order to see the distortion of Christianity for what it was, we must first go back to original Christianity. Let us return to the time of the very first Christians when the memory of Christ was fresh, when men who had seen Jesus Christ in the flesh still lived.

As long as the resurrected Christ remained with them, the first Christians enjoyed the visible presence of God. They had a sure basis for their beliefs. The very God of the universe was there to answer their questions and correct any mistakes.

When Christ ascended into heaven, He did not leave His followers without order

and direction. Jesus had given His disciples the right to speak and act for him (Matt. 18:18). The original disciples (minus Judas) plus **Paul** (to whom Christ made a special appearance) were called the **Apostles.** Specifically called out and sent by Christ to carry the gospel to all mankind, the Apostles differed from all other preachers or missionaries by their eyewitness or firsthand knowledge of Jesus.

The Apostle Paul: Paul and the other Apostles, inspired by the Holy Spirit, wrote the New Testament—the rule and measure for the faith and practices of Christians.

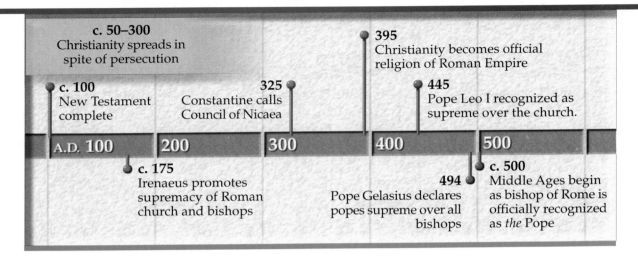

c. 50–300
Christianity spreads in
spite of persecution

395
Christianity becomes official
religion of Roman Empire

c. 100
New Testament
complete

325
Constantine calls
Council of Nicaea

445
Pope Leo I recognized as
supreme over the church.

A.D. 100 | 200 | 300 | 400 | 500

c. 175
Irenaeus promotes
supremacy of Roman
church and bishops

494
Pope Gelasius declares
popes supreme over all
bishops

c. 500
Middle Ages begin
as bishop of Rome is
officially recognized
as *the* Pope

But what would happen once the Apostles themselves had passed from this life? Soul winners of the future could not claim to be eyewitnesses of Christ, but they still had to be able to answer the inevitable question: How can we know these things about Jesus?

Believers in Jesus Christ had a continuing need for order and direction from God.

Early Christians and the Old Testament

Christ's example. Jesus frequently quoted from the **Old Testament** as the Word of God, even to the detail of every "jot or . . . tittle," every letter or stroke (Matt. 5:18). Jesus never disagreed with any part of the Holy Scripture, although He did take issue with some men's incorrect interpretations of it and additions to it. He always treated the Scripture word for word, never doubting, for example, that there was truly an Adam and an Eve or that God had destroyed Sodom and Gomorrah with fire and brimstone.

The first Christians followed Christ's example and used the Old Testament with reverence. The multiplying Christian churches continued to read and study the Scriptures just as the Jews in the synagogues did. The earliest Christians, of course, were Jews who had accepted Jesus' claim to be the Savior of whom the Old Testament spoke.

Need for a new witness. By itself, however, the Old Testament said only that the Savior *would* come, not that He *had* come. The world needed a permanent, completely trustworthy testament (witness) to the actual events of the birth, life, and resurrection of Jesus Christ, especially as the eyewitnesses passed from the scene.

Writing the Books of the New Testament

Date and author. By about A.D. 100, all 27 books of the **New Testament** had been written, thus meeting the need for a permanent record of the gospel. Either Apostles or men who had an extremely close relationship to an Apostle wrote the books of the New Testament under the inspiration of the Holy Spirit. The Holy Spirit fills all believers, but the Apostles received unique power to carry out their assignment from Jesus. The Holy Spirit taught them all things, and caused them to remember all that Jesus had taught them (John 16:12–15). Thus, books that measured up as works of

135

The Gospel of Matthew: *This papyrus fragment, dating from the third century, was discovered in Egypt. It is a fragment of a manuscript of the Gospel of Matthew. It contains a portion of Matthew chapter one.*

the Apostles were regarded as the very Word of God, for they established a permanent connection between Christians of all ages and the Apostles, setting a standard for Christian belief and practice. Many writings of men who lived during the time of the Apostles contain references or quotations from books of the New Testament.

The language used. The original books of the New Testament were most likely written in Greek. The New Testament employed **koine** [koi'nē], the <u>most common form of the Greek language</u>. Koine was spoken as a second language throughout most of the Roman Empire. Translations into other languages also appeared, but because so many people in the first century A.D. understood Greek, the New Testament books in their original language immediately enjoyed a vast circulation.

By the end of the second century, and possibly by A.D. 125 or even earlier, most Christians had accepted the books of the New Testament as the Word of God.

The New Testament as the Foundation for Christianity

With the New Testament, Christians had a sure and lasting link to Christ through the Apostles, a definite and solid basis for their beliefs and way of life. They had the written Word of God for order and direction in living and worshiping together. With the New Testament joined to the Old, Christians had the Bible, a book written by men inspired by the Holy Spirit in every word they wrote. Through the ages, true Christians have shared the conviction that the Bible is the inspired Word of God and is the rule of faith and practice for all believers.

— CHECK UP —

1. What period of history followed the fall of Rome? When did this period begin? When did it end?
2. What attitude did Christ and the first Christians have toward the Old Testament?
3. Why was a new record needed in addition to the Old Testament?
4. By what date was the New Testament completed?
5. Who wrote the New Testament? By whom was it inspired?
6. By what year had nearly all the books of the New Testament been accepted as the Word of God?

Identify: Paul, Apostles, Old Testament, New Testament, koine

The Rise of the Roman Church

Local Churches, Godly Leaders, Simplicity of Worship

The first church and Jews. Soon after Christ's ascension into Heaven, churches began to appear. In the New Testament, the word **church** means *an assembly or body of people.* Christian churches are assemblies or bodies of people who profess to believe that Christ is the Son of God who freely offers salvation from the punishment of sin.

The first Christian church was in *Jerusalem.* Undoubtedly most, if not all, of the members were Jews who accepted Jesus Christ as the Messiah. As Apostles and others spread the good news of salvation through Christ to other cities, the first to hear were generally the Jews. Believers in these other cities also assembled as local bodies or churches.

Judaism and Christianity. Soon, the Apostles and others began to carry the gospel of Christ to non-Jews, or **Gentiles,** just as Christ had commanded. Soon churches consisting of both Jews and Gentiles appeared around the Roman Empire. Some purely Gentile churches also appeared. The question of the precise relation of *Judaism* [jōōd′ē·ĭz′m: the religion of the Jews] to Christianity naturally arose. Some Jewish Christians believed that Gentile converts should practice all activities prescribed for Jews by the Law of the Old Testament. But Paul and others denied this.

A meeting in Jerusalem. Christian leaders held a meeting in **Jerusalem** to discuss the matter. Christians naturally respected the world's first Christian church, whose members were Apostles, and so looked to Jerusalem for guidance.

The Apostles and the elders of the Jerusalem church debated. *They reached an agreement after James quoted Scripture from the Old Testament.* A letter went out from the Jerusalem church to churches in Antioch, Syria, and Cilicia, summarizing the results of the debate. In brief, they said that Gentile Christians did not have to practice all the Jewish Laws of the Old Testament. But this letter was meant not so much as an *order* from the Jerusalem church to other churches as an effort to comfort Gentile Christians in the assurance of salvation (Acts 15:1–33).

Church independence. The first churches were independent and self-governing in that *no one church gave orders to the others.* Whatever special respect was paid to the Jerusalem church soon ended. Christians and unconverted Jews grew further and further apart after the Christians in Jerusalem refused to take part in violent revolts against Roman rule of Jerusalem. The Romans destroyed Jerusalem in A.D. 70, just as Christ had foretold (Luke 21:20–24). The Jewish people would not be independent in their homeland again until the 20th century.

Church leaders. Each early church had many leaders. Some were called **deacons** (from the Greek word meaning "servant"). Others were called **elders** (the Greek word for elder is *presbuteros,* which is also the source of the word *priest*), or **bishops** (from the Greek word meaning "overseer" or "superintendent"). Some churches had more than one bishop. Some, perhaps all, of the early churches used *elder* and *bishop* to refer to the same office (Titus 1:5–7).

The New Testament, while certainly not condoning the absence of leadership, order, and discipline in churches (1 Tim. 5:17–19; 1 Pet. 5:1–5; Heb. 13:7, 17), nowhere directs that any one man be all-powerful in any one church or group of churches. The Bible makes Christ the true Head of the Church. Of course, as long as the Apostles lived, the churches had the benefit of having special leaders appointed directly by Christ Himself, authorized to speak and act in His name. The churches recognized this *Apostolic* (ăp′ə·stŏl′ĭk) *authority,* but the Scriptures do not say that the Apostles passed on *their unique* authority to others. Instead the

137

The Catacombs: On the outskirts of Rome, the early Christians took refuge in underground passageways called catacombs. Unlike the Romans, who cremated their dead, the Christians buried theirs in the catacombs. Often, when persecution became especially intense, the Christians would gather in the catacombs for worship. Since the Romans held that any burial place was sacred, they would not molest Christians there. After Constantine, the catacombs were largely forgotten until 1578 when they were accidentally rediscovered.

Apostles wrote the New Testament, giving the churches the Word of God, their true authority.

Worship practices. Worship in the early churches was <u>simple</u>. Christians usually assembled in private homes, and, except for some remodeled houses, built no special buildings for worship prior to the fourth century. Scriptures were read—at first from the Old Testament, and then from parts of the New Testament as it was written. Leaders probably read aloud letters from the Apostles as well. Preachers delivered sermons based on the Scripture, and congregations prayed and sang songs from the book of Psalms as well as new hymns. Believers who had received salvation followed Christ in **baptism,** and churches frequently celebrated the **Lord's Supper** in remembrance of Christ.

Not everything that the first churches did was right and proper, however. More than once, Paul had to point out their mistakes, such as allowing more than one person to speak at a time. Some leaders domineered. **Diotrephes** (dī·ŏt′rə·fēz), for example, who loved "to have preeminence," placed himself above God's Word according to the Apostle John (3 John 9).

While no local church has ever been perfect, the New Testament, if read carefully, reveals clear guidelines for the ideal New Testament church. But,

> as time went by, many Christians moved away from the ideal of many churches, many leaders, and simple worship services.

One Church: Rome

The invisible catholic church. Of course, there are many local churches; but as God looks down from heaven He sees only one church made up of all true Christians. This one great "invisible" church that only God sees can never meet in the way that a local church does. The term *catholic,* which simply means "universal" or "one," may be used to describe this great "invisible" church of all believers.

A visible catholic church. The idea of a catholic church gradually separated from the New Testament idea of the "invisible" church and came to mean a single, visible, large, *organized* church for all Christians. Perhaps the motives were at first innocent— a desire to unite all believers (Christ had taught the goodness of unity) and to defend Christian beliefs against distortions. But the visible catholic church soon began to distort Christianity.

Such a large, organized church required official relationships between local churches. In all organizations, some give orders and others take them. The organization of the catholic church eventually led to the dominance of one local church over others.

Respect for the Church of Rome. Well before the end of the second century,

> many Christians began treating the **Church of Rome** with great respect, just as they had the church of Jerusalem earlier.

This was only natural, for the city of Rome was the most important city in the Roman Empire. Even Paul thought very highly of the Church of Rome, as his letter to the Romans in the New Testament states.

However, there is no record of Paul ever suggesting what **Irenaeus** (ī′rə·nē′*u*s), a church leader in Gaul, declared around 175—that every church *had* to agree with the Church of Rome. The Bible lends no support whatsoever to this opinion. Irenaeus claimed that the Roman church had been founded by Peter and Paul, but the New Testament does not say that Peter ever even visited Rome.

CHECK UP

1. What does the word *church* mean?
2. Where was the first Christian church located?
3. Where did church leaders meet to discuss the problem of Gentile believers and Jewish law? What was the decision of the meeting, and how was it communicated?
4. What were three names for early church leaders, and what do these names mean?
5. Who is the true head of the church?
6. Where did early Christians usually meet? Describe their worship services.
7. How did the Church of Rome come to be so respected?

Identify: Gentiles, baptism, the Lord's Supper, Apostolic authority, Diotrephes, Irenaeus

---

One Leader: The Pope

Bishops in the forefront. By the time of Irenaeus, the organization of many local churches had changed. Bishops had come to the forefront. By the early second century, a single bishop generally ruled each church. Exactly how and why this happened remains a mystery, but motives like that of Diotrephes undoubtedly played some role. Bishops of churches in cities became especially powerful. These metropolitan bishops, as they were called, took it upon themselves to govern the many new churches in the country (and the bishops of these churches).

Apostolic succession. Irenaeus, in addition to maintaining the supremacy of the Roman church, also tried to justify the supremacy of bishops by the idea of **"Apostolic succession."** The Apostles, said Irenaeus, were "guardians of the gospel." But instead of emphasizing the New Testament as the Christians' permanent link to the Apostles, Irenaeus claimed

- that the Apostles had appointed bishops as their successors,
- that these successors had in turn appointed successors of their own,
- and that much (if not all) of the authority of the Apostles had therefore been passed down in an unbroken line to the bishops of his day.

What about the "Apostolic Succession" in the Church of Rome? Since Irenaeus believed that Peter and Paul had founded this church, he naturally held that these two Apostles had appointed the first bishop of Rome.

The Petrine Theory. Peter's role in the "Apostolic Succession" eventually received great emphasis. Peter appears to some to have been the leader of the Apostles after Christ's ascension into heaven. The New Testament records that Jesus once said to Peter, whose name means "rock," that

---

... thou art Peter, and upon this rock I will build my church; and the gates of hell shall not prevail against it.

And I will give unto thee the keys of the kingdom of heaven: and whatsoever thou shalt bind on earth shall be bound in heaven: and whatsoever thou shalt loose on earth shall be loosed in heaven (Matt. 16:18–19).

During the fifth century, beginning with Leo I, bishops of Rome began using this Scripture to support the **Petrine** (pē′trĭn) **theory:** *that Christ made Peter the head of the catholic church and that Peter passed this power to the bishops of Rome, the first of whom (after himself) he appointed.* Yet the Bible never shows Peter acting as if he were "head" of *the* church." In referring to Peter as a church foundation, Christ meant Peter's kind of confession of faith in Him as the Son of God, for He, Christ, is the Rock of Ages. Peter himself warned against pastors lording over others rather than being good examples (1 Pet. 5:1–3).

The Petrine Theory permitted the ideas of the supremacy of the Church of Rome and of bishops to merge. The result was the idea of the *Roman Catholic Church* (or simply *Roman church*): *that the bishop of the Church of Rome is supreme over all churches.*

The bishop of the Church of Rome, eventually called the **Pope** (meaning "papa" or "father"), began to rule the Roman Catholic Church as supreme ruler or king. As in other human organizations, the quest for extreme unity in the church easily led to one-man rule—to kings—for the greatest degree of unity. Reminiscent of the old Israelite demand for a human king rather than God, many who called themselves Christians now sought a human king rather than Christ. Peter's great worry that the shepherds of Christian flocks would act as "lords over God's heritage" rather than "examples to the flock" came true (1 Pet. 5:3).

A Source for History

Philosophy

True philosophers love the truth. They are often among the first to see through the lies, deceit, and hypocrisy of an age. Their careful reasonings can be of utmost importance to the student of history, who must be cautious in what he accepts as true facts of the past.

During the Middle Ages, the unscriptural doctrines of the Roman church did not go completely unchallenged. **Marsilius** of Padua (mär·sĭl′ĭ-*us* of păd′ū·ə), born around 1275, could have had a successful career as a church official. But with a mind made razor-sharp by the study of philosophy, Marsilius would not blindly accept the teachings of the Roman church.

Marsilius knew that all beliefs must be measured against the absolute truth of God's Word, the one true authority for the Christian and the lover of truth. "For 'canon' means rule or standard," wrote Marsilius in his famous work *Defender of the Peace* (1324), "a standard because it is something certain, something that is peculiar to Holy Scripture alone as compared with other writings." When Marsilius examined religious opinions, he accepted "those which are in harmony with the canon of Scripture." On the other hand, declared Marsilius, "Those which are discordant with Scripture I will reverently reject, but never without the support of Scripture upon which I shall always rely." Relying upon the Bible, Marsilius rejected one Roman doctrine after another—including the opinion that without forgiveness by a priest, God's grace is insufficient to save a person from sin: "God alone absolves the truly penitent sinner without any action of the priest either preceding or accompanying."

Marsilius vehemently opposed the power of the popes as unscriptural. He realized how much the papal claims depended upon the Petrine theory, that Christ made Peter the head of the Roman church and that Peter passed this power to the bishops of Rome, the first of whom (after himself) he appointed. After demonstrating that the Bible does not support the claim that Christ gave Peter such power, Marsilius proved by Scripture that the Apostle Peter had not founded the Church of Rome, was not the first bishop of Rome, and therefore was not the first pope. As he slashed through the Petrine theory with his logic, Marsilius began with the fact that the Bible does not say Peter ever even visited Rome. "It can be proved by Scripture that Paul was two years at Rome, preached there and converted all Gentiles who were willing to be converted," said Marsilius,

> But, as to Peter, I say that it cannot be proved by Scripture that he was bishop of Rome or, what is more, that he was ever at Rome. For it seems most amazing if, according to some popular saint's legend, St. Peter came to Rome before St. Paul, preached there the word of God and was then taken prisoner, if then St. Paul after his arrival in Rome acting together with St. Peter had so many conflicts with Simon Magus and in defence of the faith fought against emperors and their agents, and if finally, according to the same story, both were beheaded at the same time for their confession of Christ, there fell asleep in the Lord, and thus consecrated the Roman Church of Christ—most amazing, I say, that St. Luke, who wrote the Acts of the Apostles and Paul himself make not the slightest mention of St. Peter.

Marsilius pointed out that, according to Acts 28:22, the Jews in Rome knew nothing of Christianity before Paul came to them, except that "everywhere it is spoken against." (Of course, there *were* some Gentile Christians already there to whom Paul wrote the book of Romans.) This proves, declared Marsilius, that Peter did not go to Rome before Paul, for surely Peter would have preached about Christ! Moreover, Marsilius continued,

> Can any one think that Paul was for two years with Peter at Rome and had no intimate relations with him, or, if he had, that the author of the Acts would not have mentioned it? For in other and less important places where Paul met Peter he mentions him, as at Corinth and at Antioch and many other places, and if he had met him at Rome, the most important city in the world, where, according to the above story St. Peter was in charge as bishop, how could he have failed to mention him? So that these things are practically (*quasi*) incredible, and that story or legend cannot with any probability be accepted as to this part of it, but must be reckoned among the apocryphal writings [fraudulent writings pretending to be part of the Bible].

Needless to say, Marsilius's ideas were not well received by the Roman church. The *Defender of the Peace* was condemned, and Marsilius was excommunicated. If he had not received protection from a German prince involved in a violent political fight with the pope, this philosopher might well have died for his stand on behalf of the Bible.

Marsilius's philosophy became fairly well known during his lifetime, but such Scriptural reasonings as his did not have their greatest impact on world history until about two centuries after his death.

From Simple to Complex:
Beginning with the reign of Constantine, many pagans professed Christianity. With this influx, many elements of pagan religion (including elaborate temples) were introduced into Christian worship. Eventually both the church building and the worship within it became very complex.

An Early Church: The early Christians met, not in church buildings, but in private homes. This house was built about A.D. 232 at Dura-Europas by the Euphrates River. It was remodeled so that it could hold about 100 people.

Romanesque Churches: At the beginning of the Middle Ages, architects developed a new architectural style called Romanesque. It was characterized by thick, massive walls and small windows with rounded arches. Churches built in this style often had towers, but few had steeples.

A Castle or a Cathedral? With its massive walls and small windows, this Romanesque German cathedral looks much like a fortress.

CHECK UP

1. Which church leaders became the rulers of the churches?
2. What theory states that the bishops were the successors of the Apostles?
3. What theory states that the bishop of Rome is Peter's successor as the head of the church? Would Peter have agreed with this theory?
4. What did the bishop of Rome come to be called?
5. Describe the attitude of Marsilius of Padua toward the Bible.
6. What did Marsilius think of the Scriptural basis for the necessity of priests?
7. Why is it important, in Marsilius's criticism of the Petrine theory, that the Bible never says Peter even visited Rome?
8. How does Acts 28:22 fit into Marsilius's argument?

Identify: Roman Catholic Church, pope, *Defender of the Peace*

Gothic Churches: *Toward the end of the Middle Ages, there developed, particularly in northern Europe, a new style known as Gothic. Unlike the Romanesque, it had tall walls with many pointed windows (often using stained glass). Gothic cathedrals were noted for their elaborate use of steeples and points, which seemed to give the churches a tall, light appearance, in contrast to massive Romanesque churches.*

Notre Dame: *The Cathedral of Notre Dame (French for "Our Lady," a reference to the virgin Mary) in Paris is perhaps the best example of Gothic architecture in the world.*

The Power of Popes

Constantine as church ruler. No doubt popes dreamed of ruling a visible, organized church of all Christians. But at first it was the Roman emperor who acted as if he ruled the church. Constantine the Great, as you will recall, tried during the early fourth century to use Christianity as a foundation for the shaky Roman government.

By this time, professing Christians were seriously divided over matters of belief. The most important division involved the core of Christianity: the relationship of God the Son to God the Father. **Arianism** [âr′ĭ·an·ĭz′m],

named for **Arius** [âr′ĭ·us], a church leader in Egypt, was *the belief that Jesus was not God but rather had been created by God the Father.* Arianism undermined the basis for salvation—that God through Christ took upon Himself man's punishment for sin. This could be true only if Christ as the Son of God *is* God, as the first chapter of the Gospel of John so obviously teaches. Yet Arianism gained many followers who found it easier to understand than the true Biblical teaching of the Trinity, that God is One God but also in three Persons—the Father, the Son, and the Holy Spirit.

143

The Emperor Constantine demonstrated his insufficient grasp of Christianity when he said that Arianism raised only a trifling issue. Constantine's only worry was the division Arianism was causing among professing Christians. The emperor saw Christianity as a way to unify his empire and to strengthen the foundation of his power. But now people who called themselves Christians were disagreeing and fighting among themselves!

Constantine took it upon himself in A.D. 325 to call a meeting of church bishops to resolve the disputes and acted as if he were head of the church. With the emperor presiding, the **Council of Nicaea** [nī·sē′ə] affirmed Christ's divinity in a statement of belief known as the **Nicene** [nī′sēn] **Creed** and placed Arians under "a curse." Constantine used his power as Roman emperor to enforce the decisions of the Council, commanding the death penalty for disobedience. All Arian books were to be burned and all Arians banished from the empire. Soon after the Council, the church history writer Eusebius, with the undoubted approval of Constantine, described the Roman emperor as God's representative on earth in *all* matters, obliterating Christ's distinction between the things that are Caesar's and the things that are God's.

Constantine's failure. Constantine's attempt to unify the empire through Christianity failed. As you have already learned, the empire permanently split into two parts after 395, and the western part of the empire was destroyed less than a century later. As late as the sixth century, professing Christians continued to disagree about the relationship between the Son and the Father, as well as the concept of Jesus' divinity and humanity. Especially in the east, first one opinion and then another would gain favor, and "official doctrine" changed almost as often as the emperors did.

Leo and the pope as church head. In the Eastern Roman Empire, the emperor remained the head of the church. But

in the West, where the empire and emperor steadily weakened, the pope was recognized as the head of the church.

In 445, the Western Roman emperor Valentinian III [văl′en·tĭn′ĭ·an] officially recognized Pope Leo I as supreme over the church. World history remembers **Leo I** as "the Great" because of his great power. It was Leo, not a Roman emperor, who went out to meet Attila (ă·tĭl′ə), leader of the Huns from Asia, to persuade the invaders not to attack Rome. Leo also urged that those who disagreed with the Roman church on matters of Christian belief should be put to death.

Leo and supremacy of popes. In 494, **Gelasius** [jĕ·lā′shĭ·us], a successor of Leo, went a step further than Leo, who had made the pope supreme over all bishops. Gelasius separated government and church power like "two swords." But in matters relating to God, said Gelasius, bishops are supreme over all human rulers.

After the Western Roman Empire crumbled and fell, Roman Catholic popes were for a time more powerful than any ordinary government in western Europe. The Middle Ages began about A.D. 500, around the time when the Bishop of Rome began to be officially called the Pope.

Christendom

New humanism. The Word of God is a permanent record of the gospel, providing the true basis for Christianity and for Christian churches. But when men, not the Scripture, became the foundation for a distorted Christianity that tried to rule the world in the name of Jesus Christ, humanism reappeared in a new form. Some men made themselves into gods by blocking the direct access of others to the Father through

St Peter's Cathedral: St. Peter's Cathedral in Rome is the largest church in the world.

and the Eucharist for a total of seven. The human rulers of the church alone administered the sacraments, and therefore appeared to hold the very keys to heaven. **Excommunication,** *being cut off from communication with the human rulers of the church* and, therefore, being denied the sacraments, seemed to mean nothing less than loss of salvation (or eternal damnation).

Such beliefs forced the people of the Middle Ages to obey men who dreamed that they themselves would build the very Kingdom of Christ on earth. These men hoped that **Christendom** (krĭs'′n·dum: *the portion of the world in which Christianity prevails*) would soon cover the entire planet. With Christ in Heaven and not yet returned to visibly govern an earthly kingdom, they took it upon themselves to rule the world for Him.

Jesus the Son. Men who said they were successors of the Apostles claimed, as no Apostle ever had, to be necessary for salvation.

Complicated worship. This new humanism manifested itself as worship services became more and more complicated. Each complication only increased the importance of the men who presided over the services, which came to be called **masses.** The congregation became more and more like spectators, having little hope of understanding what they saw and heard.

The most important part of the mass was the **sacrament** ("sacred act") of the Lord's Supper. Christ had commanded Christians to remember Him by celebrating the Lord's Supper, just as He had ordered believers to be baptized. But men had distorted baptism, making it an act necessary for salvation. The Lord's Supper—called the **Eucharist** (ū′kə·rĭst) from the Greek words for thanks, favor, and grace—also came to be regarded as having saving power. The Roman church later added five other sacraments in addition to baptism

CHECK UP

1. Who called the Council of Nicaea to discuss the controversy of Arianism? What was the result of the council?
2. Who remained the head of the church in the Eastern Roman Empire?
3. What pope was first recognized as the supreme ruler of the church? Which emperor recognized him?
4. Who said that popes are superior to all human rulers in matters relating to God?
5. When did the Middle Ages begin?
6. What were services in the Roman church called?
7. What word means "sacred act"? What sacred acts did Christ ordain?
8. What name did the Roman church give to the Lord's Supper?

Identify: Arianism, Arius, Leo I, Christendom, excommunication

145

CHAPTER 9 REVIEW

MULTIPLE CHOICE *Write the letter of the answer that best completes each sentence.*

1. The twelve men who had firsthand knowledge of Jesus and whom God sent out to preach the gospel were called _____.
   a presbyters   c missionaries
   b Apostles   d bishops

2. Which Apostle quoted Scripture that settled the issue being discussed by the church meeting at Jerusalem? _____
   a Peter   c James
   b Paul   d Philip

3. What word comes from the Greek word for "servant"? _____
   a elder   c priest
   b deacon   d bishop

4. What word is derived from the Greek word *presbuteros?* _____
   a minister   c bishop
   b elder   d deacon

5. What word comes from the Greek term meaning "overseer" or "super-intendent"? _____
   a priest   c bishop
   b elder   d deacon

6. The church leader who loved "to have preeminence" and who put himself above God's Word was _____.
   a Diotrephes   c Irenaeus
   b John   d Gelasius

7. Where was the first Christian church located? _____
   a Antioch   c Carthage
   b Jerusalem   d Rome

8. What church leader in Gaul said that every church must agree with the Church of Rome? _____
   a Gelasius   c Constantine
   b Irenaeus   d Diotrephes

9. According to the Roman church, who was appointed the head of the Catholic church by Christ? _____
   a Peter   c James
   b Paul   d Constantine

10. During the fifth century, _____ became the first bishop of Rome to support the Petrine theory.
    a Leo I   c Gelasius
    b Constantine   d Valentinian III

11. The bishop of Rome became known as the _____, a word that means "father."
    a elder   c presbyter
    b deacon   d pope

12. The Roman emperor _____ called a council to deal with the Arian controversy.
    a Leo I   c Constantine
    b Diotrephes   d Valentinian III

13. The council met in _____ in the year 325 A.D.
    a Jerusalem   c Rome
    b Nicaea   d Hippo Regis

14. In 445, the Western Roman emperor _____ recognized the pope as the supreme ruler of all the church.
    a Gelasius   c Valentinian III
    b Leo I   d Constantine

15. What pope was given the title "the Great" because of his great power? _____
    a Peter   c Valentinian III
    b Gelasius   d Leo I

16. What pope said that, in matters relating to God, leaders of the church are supreme over all human rulers? _____
    a Gelasius   c Constantine
    b Leo I   d Valentinian III

COMPLETION Choose the correct term to complete the sentence and write the letter in the blank.

- *a* Apostolic succession
- *b* Arianism
- *c* catholic
- *d* Christendom
- *e* church
- *f* Eucharist
- *g* excommunication
- *h* koine
- *i* masses
- *j* Middle Ages
- *k* Nicene Creed
- *l* Petrine theory
- *m* sacrament
- *n* canon

1. The period after collapse of the Roman Empire is called the _____.

2. The New Testament was written in _____, the most common type of Greek.

3. The word _____ means an assembly or body of people.

4. The word _____ means "universal" or "one."

5. The idea of _____ maintains that men like Peter and Paul handed down their power and authority from one generation of bishops to the next.

6. The _____ holds that Christ made Peter the head of the Catholic church and that Peter passed this power to the first bishop of Rome, whom he appointed.

7. _____ is the opinion that Jesus was not God but rather had been created by God the Father.

8. The statement of belief called the _____ affirmed Christ's divinity.

9. Services of the Roman church are called _____.

10. The word _____ means "sacred act."

11. The Catholic name for the Lord's Supper, _____, comes from the Greek words for thanks, favor, and grace.

12. _____ was being cut off from the rulers of the church and, therefore, from the sacraments.

13. The portion of the world in which Christianity prevails is called _____.

TIME LINE CHALLENGE Choose the letter of the correct date for each of the events listed below.

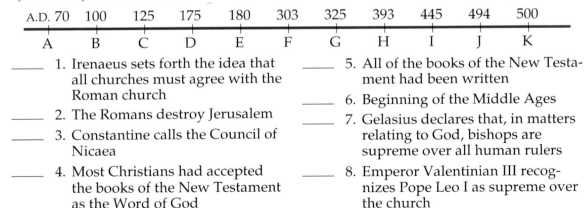

A.D. 70	100	125	175	180	303	325	393	445	494	500
A	B	C	D	E	F	G	H	I	J	K

_____ 1. Irenaeus sets forth the idea that all churches must agree with the Roman church

_____ 2. The Romans destroy Jerusalem

_____ 3. Constantine calls the Council of Nicaea

_____ 4. Most Christians had accepted the books of the New Testament as the Word of God

_____ 5. All of the books of the New Testament had been written

_____ 6. Beginning of the Middle Ages

_____ 7. Gelasius declares that, in matters relating to God, bishops are supreme over all human rulers

_____ 8. Emperor Valentinian III recognizes Pope Leo I as supreme over the church

CONCEPTS TO CONSIDER On a separate sheet of paper, answer the following questions using complete sentences.

1. How did Irenaeus help to bring about the rise of the pope and the Roman church?

2. How did worship services change from the days of the early church?

10
Islam versus Christendom
(A.D. 600–1300)

HIGHLIGHTS
Mohammed and Islam • Europe's Crusades

Mohammed and Islam

From Arabia

The building of Christendom had scarcely begun when Islam, a new religion, blew in from Arabia like a hot desert wind. **Arabia** is a huge peninsula in the Middle East. Approximately one million square miles in size, it lies directly southeast of the fertile crescent. Little rainfall, a lack of year-round rivers, and temperatures as high as 130˚F make most of Arabia a desert wasteland.

The Arabs inhabited this sea of sand. Divided into many tribes, they fought over the scarce feeding and watering spots for their camels, horses, sheep, and goats. For these superstitious *Bedouins* [bĕd′o͞o·inz], as Arab nomads are called, the bleak desert was alive with imaginary spirits in rocks, trees, and even little pieces of wood. Crude beliefs promoted idol worship and gross immorality.

But the Arabs, many of whom were descendants of **Ishmael,** Abraham's first son, were marked for a giant role in world history. While not heir to God's special promises to Abraham and his son Isaac, Ishmael did receive God's blessing to father "a great nation" (Gen. 17:20).

About 600 years after Christ's ascension into Heaven, many Arabs submitted to Islam and became Muslims. "There is no god but Allah, and Mohammed is his prophet," the Muslims cried as they charged into battle. United as never before, the Arabs in just over a hundred years established an empire that reached from southwestern Europe to the eastern border of India.

Islam's conquests confined Christendom—and distorted Christianity—to Europe. Several hundred years later, Europeans took the offensive to reclaim parts of the Middle East for Christendom, but their crusades were futile. The departure from Biblical Christianity grew greater and greater, and the crusades simply distorted Christianity even more with a mixture of politics and war, in much the same way that Mohammed had taught the Muslims to do.

Mohammed

Birth. **Mohammed,** whose name means "highly praised," was born about A.D. 570 in **Mecca,** one of three main cities in northern Arabia at that time. Mecca stood at the crossroads of trade routes. The many caravans of camels passing through Mecca made the merchants of the city rich. Mecca was also the home of the *Kaaba* [kä′bə], a religious building which housed a meteorite known as the *Black Stone.* Many Arabs visited Mecca to pay their respects to this rock they believed to be sacred.

Mohammed's claim. At the age of 40, Mohammed began to claim that he was receiving revelations from the angel Gabriel. Mohammed at first feared that he had lost his mind or become demon-possessed, but

148

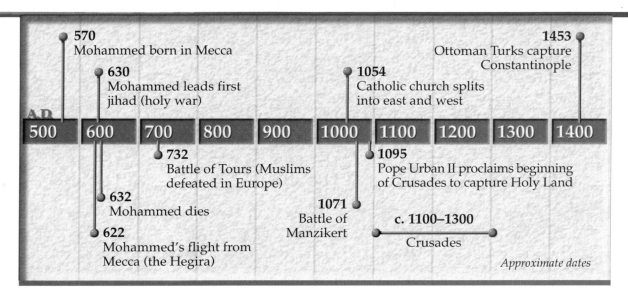

570
Mohammed born in Mecca

630
Mohammed leads first
jihad (holy war)

AD

500 **600** **700** **800** **900** **1000** **1100** **1200** **1300** **1400**

732
Battle of Tours (Muslims
defeated in Europe)

632
Mohammed dies

622
Mohammed's flight from
Mecca (the Hegira)

1054
Catholic church splits
into east and west

1453
Ottoman Turks capture
Constantinople

1095
Pope Urban II proclaims beginning
of Crusades to capture Holy Land

1071
Battle of
Manzikert

c. 1100–1300
Crusades

Approximate dates

he eventually became convinced that he was the specially appointed prophet of **Allah** [äl′ə], his name for the one and only god. Allah, said Mohammed, is the same as the One the Jews and Christians call God. I, said Mohammed, am Allah's choice to bring to men the perfect and complete truth. I, said Mohammed, am the last in a series of prophets that includes Adam, Noah, Abraham, Moses, *and Jesus.* All who believe in Allah *and me* and do all I teach, preached Mohammed, will spend eternity in Heaven.

Whereas over 500 people saw the resurrected Jesus Christ, no one witnessed Mohammed's supposed encounters with the angel. Only Mohammed saw the visions and heard the voices. People had to accept or reject his claim solely on the basis of his forceful personality or the appeal of his teaching.

Flight from Mecca. Mohammed's teachings alarmed the rich businessmen of Mecca. They feared that Mohammed's vehement opposition to the old Arabian religion of

Holy War vs. Crusade: *The holy wars of Islam and the crusades of Christendom both used religious zeal as a motive for violence.*

multiple gods, spirits, and idols threatened Mecca as the religious center of Arabia. By 622, Mohammed had decided that he and his few followers must leave Mecca. This "flight," called the **Hegira** [hĕ·jī′rə], from Mecca was the turning point for Mohammed and his new religion.

Acceptance in Medina. First his followers and then Mohammed himself fled several hundred miles north of Mecca to the city of **Yathrib** [yăth′rĭb], where many accepted Mohammed's claim. Soon the city was known as "the city of the Prophet," or simply **Medina** [me·dē′nə], "the city."

Mohammed quickly gained total power in Medina as both religious leader and head of the government. People who believed Mohammed's claims simply assumed that Mohammed should completely control them and all aspects of life. Mohammed did nothing to discourage such tendencies as he combined religion and politics.

Among the few in Medina who did not accept Mohammed's claim were the **Jews.** They discerned that Mohammed's teaching did not agree with the Old Testament and therefore rejected it as false. Mohammed denied that the Old Testament is the Word of God. Later, upon learning of the Jews' plans to help his old Meccan enemies who were attacking Medina, Mohammed beheaded all the Jewish men of Medina and enslaved the Jewish women and children.

Holy war. Having combined religion and politics, it was only natural that Mohammed would combine religion with war and empire.

Mohammed preached that Allah wanted everyone in the world to be Muslim or at least to be ruled by Muslims.

After successfully resisting a Meccan attack on Medina, Mohammed led about 10,000 of his followers on the first **jihad** [jĭ·häd′] or "holy war," in A.D. 630. They conquered Mecca, destroyed the idols in the Kaaba, and made the old city and its "purified" shrine the center of the new religion.

In the remaining two years of his life, tribe after tribe of Arabs submitted to Mohammed and his new religion. The new religion was called **Islam** and its followers **Muslims;** both names are derived from the Arabic word for *"surrender."*

Koran

Origin of the Koran. Mohammed claimed to have received revelations from Allah continually since the time of his first visions in the mountains near Mecca. Those around him wrote down or memorized what they heard Mohammed recite. These memories and writings became the basis of the **Koran** ("recitation"), the holy book of Islam.

The Koran's principal teaching is monotheism: "There is no god but Allah." The Koran presents this one god as the same one God of the Jews and Christians. But the Jews and Christians, according to

Muslim Shrine: Islam considers certain places as "holy places" or shrines and encourages (or requires) pilgrimages to them. The Dome of the Rock is a famous shrine located in Jerusalem.

A Prayer Rug: Five times a day a faithful Muslim must roll out his prayer rug and bow toward Mecca.

prevalent in Arabia. But because he rejected Jesus Christ as the Son of God, Mohammed could not avoid the trap of humanism. Though he never claimed to be a god or demanded worship, Mohammed elevated himself to the status of the "last prophet." In effect, Mohammed became the *only* "prophet," for he rejected the Bible record of earlier prophets as false. Thus Mohammed stood as one man between all other men and the supposed one true god, teaching that men could achieve salvation by what *they* did and not by Jesus Christ's finished work on the cross.

Conquests of Islam

Arabia's submission. By Mohammed's death in 632, nearly all Arabia had submitted to Islam as its religion and Mohammed as its ruler. Islam gave the Arabs a feeling of brotherhood that overcame tribal divisions. In holy wars, the Muslims believed they could not lose. Expecting either booty in this life or Heaven's pleasures in the afterlife, the Muslims were extremely fanatical, hard-fighting warriors.

Caliphs. Mohammed's successors, called **caliphs** [kā′lĭfs], led the Arab Muslims in holy wars to conquer much of the Middle East (except Asia Minor), part of the Far East, North Africa, and even Spain in Europe. Islam owed such victories to more than religious fanaticism. Muslim armies were not large and powerful, but they were led by able men. Islam's enemies were also divided against themselves. A long series of wars between the Eastern Roman (Byzantine) Empire and a revived Persia left both sides weak and open for conquest, and Syria and Egypt longed to be free from Byzantine rule.

the Koran, have misunderstood this one god. The Koran completely rejects the Bible, Old and New Testament alike. It holds that Allah disclosed the truth to Jews and Christians through prophets like Adam, Noah, Abraham, Moses, and Jesus, but that the Bible distorts the original revelations.

The Koran teaches that Allah has revealed his will through Mohammed, ". . . and Mohammed is his prophet." Mohammed was the last prophet, and the Koran has preserved his words correctly. Therefore, according to the Koran, submission to Allah's will demands submission to what Mohammed has said is Allah's will.

Islam and Christianity

The issue between Christianity and Islam could not be more clear-cut. Mohammed preached much about the power and mercy of the one god Allah, opposing the polytheism and idolatry

A Mosque: Muslim buildings for worship are called mosques. This mosque in present-day Iran is an excellent example of Islamic architecture.

After about 715, Arab victories ceased. The first failure came in Central Asia; by 715, Turkish forces had pushed the Arab Muslims out of Iran. Then a prolonged siege of Constantinople between 717 and 718 failed. Finally, the **Battle of Tours** (or Poitiers [pwä·tyā′]) in **732** spelled defeat in Europe.

The importance of the seven-day Battle of Tours and succeeding Muslim defeats in western Europe cannot be overemphasized. Muslim conquests seriously weakened Christianity in the Middle East, but the Battle of Tours checked Muslim advance into western Europe beyond Spain.

Christianity would survive at least in Europe. Whereas Islam had only the Koran, Christendom at least possessed the Word of God in the Bible. European Christianity, although seriously distorted because of its treatment of the Bible, at least had the possibility of someday returning to its original, true basis in the Bible.

By the end of the tenth century, the Muslim Arabs had ceased to control a single empire. Independent Muslim kings ruled in Spain; the North African countries of Morocco, Tunisia, and Egypt; Persia; Northern Mesopotamia; and Syria. Without Mohammed—or an agreed-upon successor—Islam had no unity. Mohammed's dream of a world conquered for Allah was shattered.

Islam lived on as a religion of separate peoples, with perhaps 500 million Muslims today in various parts of Asia and Africa. But the Muslim Arabs' great moment in world history seemed to have passed.

CHECK UP

1. In what year was Mohammed born? Where was he born?
2. What is the name of the religious building visited by many Arabs? What sacred treasure does this building contain?
3. What did Mohammed call his god?
4. Why were Meccan businessmen alarmed by the new religion?
5. To what city did Mohammed flee? What did the city come to be called?
6. What people had great discernment and therefore did not accept Mohammed's teachings?
7. What was the first city that Mohammed conquered?
8. What is the Koran?
9. Name five Biblical figures that the Koran names as prophets.
10. What is the main difference between Christianity and Islam?
11. When did Arab victories end? Where did the first defeat take place?
12. What vital defeat in 732 ended the Muslim march into Europe? Why was this defeat so important?

Identify: Arabia, Bedouins, Ishmael, Hegira, jihad, Muslims, caliph

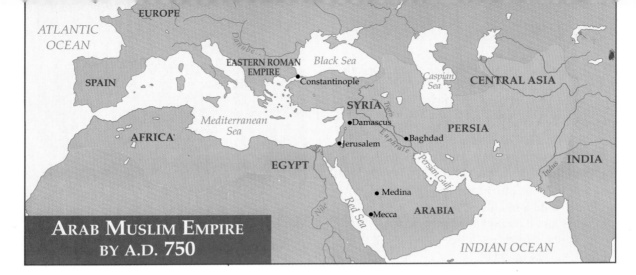

ARAB MUSLIM EMPIRE
BY A.D. 750

Europe's Crusades
(c. 1100–1300)

Origin of the Crusades

The **crusades** were Europe's version of "holy wars" during the Middle Ages. Named for the Latin *crux*, for "cross," these wars were *fought against Islam in the name of Christianity*. The Bible records the words of Christ to the one who thought to defend Him in Gethsemane: "Put up again thy sword into its place; for all they that take the sword shall perish with the sword" (Matt. 26:52). But the Bible had been so abused that many considered crusades a proper way to spread the gospel. The stated objective was to drive the Muslims from the Holy Land, where Christ had lived, and capture the city of Jerusalem for Christendom.

European pilgrims. For centuries people had traveled from Europe, in groups as large as 7,000, to worship in the Holy Land. These **pilgrimages** continued even after the Arab Muslims' conquest of the Holy Land in the seventh century.

Turkish conquerors. In the 11th century, however, **Seljuk** [sĕl·jōōk′] **Turks** from central Asia took much of the Middle East from the Arabs. The fierce Turks accepted Islam and became extremely fanatical. Stories of vicious persecution of European pilgrims to the Holy Land soon reached Europe. With a victory at the

Battle of Manzikert [män′tyĕ·kĕrt′] in *1071*, the Seljuk Turks conquered Asia Minor from the Eastern Roman Empire. Christendom lost control of another major land area, and more professing Christians lived under Muslim government. The Eastern Roman emperor began to plead with western Europe for help. In 1095, Pope **Urban II** responded enthusiastically by proclaiming the beginning of crusades for western European, Roman control of the Holy Land.

Popes and crusades. Popes hoped to increase their power and prestige with successful crusades. The church in Constantinople, to which many eastern Christians looked for leadership, had never accepted the claims of the popes to supremacy. Increasing bitterness between the churches in Rome and Constantinople had climaxed in *1054* when the one Catholic church officially split into western and eastern parts, just as the Roman Empire had. This schism [sĭz′m] has lasted to the present day as the Roman Catholic and Eastern Orthodox churches. But *the popes continued to dream of universal dominion*. They perceived the crusades as an opportunity to establish their control over the Eastern church and to enhance their leadership in Europe.

Pope Urban II eagerly preached the need to wrest the Holy Land away from the Turkish Muslims and to free eastern brethren from anti-Christian rulers. With gory

153

First Crusade: This old picture shows the four knights who led the First Crusade: Godfrey, Raymond, Bohemund, and Tancred.

detail, he recounted tales of Turkish torture and murder. The church even presented crusading as a way of ensuring one's salvation. Multitudes roared, "God wills it! God wills it!" Throughout western Europe, men put cloth crosses on their garments and prepared to battle Muslims.

The First Crusade

The Peasants' Crusade. Emotions were so high that before the official First Crusade had even begun, a group of 15,000 to 20,000 people, mostly simple farmers, embarked on the Peasants' Crusade. Militarily disciplined Turks destroyed this unruly mob of Europeans, leaving bones to bleach in the sun as a warning to future crusaders.

The official First Crusade. The official First Crusade (1096–1099), with great European nobles at the forefront, went forward nevertheless. By early 1097, 50,000 or more crusaders had converged on Constantinople from land and sea. The assembled force <u>recaptured Asia Minor</u> for the Eastern emperor **Alexius Comnenus** [ə·lĕk′sĭ·*us* kŏm·nē′n*us*] by the end of the year. After conquering other areas in the Middle East, the crusaders <u>took Jerusalem</u> on July 15, 1099.

The First Crusade conquered a strip of land along the eastern coast of the Mediterranean about 500 miles long and averaging 40 miles wide. This European foothold in the Middle East was divided into four little kingdoms ruled by the crusader knights. But the Muslims soon reorganized and began to reconquer this territory.

More Crusades

The Second Crusade. The Second Crusade (1147–1149) <u>accomplished nothing</u>. The French and German armies were defeated before they even reached the Holy Land, and an assault on the Muslim strong-

hold of Damascus (a city that was actually friendly to the crusader kingdoms) failed miserably.

Fall of Jerusalem. The Muslims grew stronger and more unified under their leader **Saladin** [săl′*a*·dĭn], the renowned sultan of Egypt. Jerusalem fell in 1187, and the Muslims again controlled most of the Holy Land. Only tiny remnants of the crusader kingdoms were left.

The Third Crusade. In the Third Crusade (1189–1192), the English king **Richard the Lion-Hearted** joined his French and German counterparts to lead what is remembered as the **"Crusade of Kings."** The Third Crusade <u>accomplished</u> so <u>little</u> that many people became disillusioned with the whole idea of crusades.

The Fourth Crusade. Crusades became more and more ridiculous. The Fourth Crusade (1202–1204) never even reached the Holy Land but instead <u>attacked and robbed the city of Constantinople</u>!

The pitiful Children's Crusades. The Children's Crusades occurred in 1212 when several thousand French and German children marched toward the Mediterranean Sea, expecting God to divide the waters so they could walk across to the Holy Land. Many never made it beyond the Alps; those who managed to reach the sea faced an even greater obstacle. Seamen offered to ferry the youngsters across the Mediterranean, but once on board, these foolish, pitiful children discovered that they had been tricked by slave traders, who sold them as slaves to North African Muslims.

The last crusades. Other crusades were attempted after the Children's Crusades, but they <u>achieved nothing</u>. By 1291, the Muslims controlled the Holy Land once again. The tragic crusades had <u>lasted some 200 years</u>, from about **1100** to **1300.**

Ottoman Turks end the Eastern Roman Empire. In the late 13th century, a new Muslim menace to Christendom arose. The **Ottoman** [ŏt′ŏ·mɑn] **Turks** became the most powerful force in the Muslim world of the Middle East. In <u>1453</u>, the Ottomans, led by a man who called himself **Mohammed II,** <u>captured Constantinople</u>. This event marked the *end of the Eastern Roman Empire.* The crusades had failed to permanently reclaim from Islam any part of the Middle East, and now Christendom lost even more territory. The Ottomans kept Europe on the defensive for about two centuries as they kept pushing into southeastern Europe.

Checked and balanced. Islam utterly rejected Christ, and Christendom distorted His gospel. Both combined religion, politics, conquest, and empire in a drive to rule the world. If Islam had won all its holy wars, Christianity might have disappeared altogether. If Christendom had succeeded with its crusades, distorted Christianity might have been imposed upon all man-

kind. Fortunately, each checked and balanced the aspirations of the other.

Christendom largely confined Islam to the Middle East and the farther reaches of Asia, while Islam restricted Christendom mainly to western Europe.

We now turn our attention to western Europe to learn more about the way of life that developed there during the Middle Ages, after the fall of Rome.

CHECK UP

1. What were Europe's "holy wars" called? What was the purpose of these "holy wars"?
2. What fierce tribe took much of the Middle East from the Arabs in the 11th century? What battle completed their conquest of Asia Minor?
3. Who proclaimed the beginning of the crusades?
4. When did the Roman church officially split?
5. In which crusade did Europeans reconquer Asia Minor and capture Jerusalem?
6. What did the Second Crusade accomplish?
7. What is another name for the Third Crusade? Was this crusade successful?
8. Why was the Fourth Crusade ridiculous?
9. What event marked the end of the Eastern Roman Empire? Give the date.
10. How did Islam and distorted Christianity "check and balance" each other?

Identify: pilgrimages, Peasants' Crusade, Alexius Comnenus, Saladin, Richard the Lion-Hearted, Children's Crusades, Ottoman Turks, Mohammed II

Crusader Ruins: By the end of the 14th century, it was obvious that the crusades were a dismal failure. The distorted Christianity of the Middle Ages remained confined to Western Europe, and Islam remained in control of many areas of the Middle East.

CHAPTER 10 REVIEW

MULTIPLE CHOICE Write the letter of the answer that best completes each sentence.

1. The one million square-mile peninsula that lies southeast of the fertile crescent is _____.
   a Arabia   c Iran
   b Mecca   d Jordan

2. The new religion that developed in Arabia about 600 years after Christ was _____.
   a Zoroastrianism   c Hinduism
   b Islam   d Judaism

3. Followers of this new religion were called _____.
   a Meccans   c Hegiras
   b Bedouins   d Muslims

4. Mohammed was born in _____.
   a Medina   c Yathrib
   b Mecca   d Antioch

5. Mohammed's name for the one he called the one and only god was _____.
   a Allah   c Yathrib
   b Jesus   d caliph

6. The city of Yathrib, which accepted Mohammed and his religion, was later called _____.
   a Medina   c Umayyad
   b Tripoli   d Baghdad

7. Mohammed's successors as leaders of the Arab nation were called _____.
   a Ottomans   c caliphs
   b Umayyads   d Seljuks

8. The _____ conquered the Middle East in the 11th century and became fanatical followers of Islam.
   a Meccans   c Ottoman Turks
   b Seljuk Turks d crusaders

9. The Turks' victory at the Battle of _____ in 1071 put Asia Minor under Muslim control.
   a Tours   c Poitiers
   b Manzikert   d Constantinople

10. The pope who started the crusades was _____.
    a Comnenus   c Innocent III
    b Eugenius III d Urban II

11. The Muslim leader who reconquered Jerusalem in 1187 was _____.
    a Seljuk   c Mohammed II
    b Saladin   d Ottoman

12. The powerful new tribe which swept over the Middle East and ended the Eastern Roman Empire in 1453 was the _____.
    a Ottoman Turks c Seljuk Turks
    b Abbasids   d Umayyads

COMPLETION Choose the correct term to complete each sentence and write the letter in the blank.

a Peasant's Crusade   g Bedouins
b First Crusade   h Hegira
c Second Crusade   i jihad
d Third Crusade   j Koran
e Fourth Crusade   k Ottomans
f Children's Crusade

1. The Muslims' term for "holy wars" is _____.

2. Mohammed's flight from Mecca in 622 is called the _____.

3. Arab nomads are called _____.

4. The holy book of Islam is called the _____.

5. The _____, made up mostly of simple farmers, met quick defeat at the hands of experienced Turkish warriors.

6. King Richard the Lion-Hearted of England helped lead the _____, also called the "Crusade of Kings."

7. The _____ never reached the Holy Land, but attacked the city of Constantinople instead.

8. The successful _____ captured Jerusalem in 1099.

TIME LINE CHALLENGE Choose the letter of the correct date for each of the events listed below.

GROUP A

A.D. 570   600   622   630   732   800   942   1054

A   B   C   D   E   F   G   H

_____ 1. The Hegira

_____ 2. Mohammed's first "jihad" (holy war)

_____ 3. Battle of Tours

_____ 4. Birth of Mohammed

_____ 5. Official split of the Roman and the Constantinople churches

GROUP B

1071   1099   1147   1189   1202   1212   1284   1321

A   B   C   D   E   F   G   H

_____ 1. Beginning of the Third Crusade

_____ 2. Children's Crusades

_____ 3. Beginning of the Second Crusade

_____ 4. First Crusade captures Jerusalem

_____ 5. Beginning of the Fourth Crusade

_____ 6. Battle of Manzikert

MAP SKILLS Use the map on p. 153 to answer the following questions.

1. How far did the Arab Muslim Empire extend eastward?

_____

2. What part of Europe did the Muslims control?

_____

3. Near what sea is Mecca located?

_____

CONCEPTS TO CONSIDER On a separate sheet of paper, answer the following questions using complete sentences.

1. What is the *main* difference between Islam and Christianity?

2. How did Islam and distorted Christianity "check and balance" each other?

157

11
From Empire to Feudalism
(A.D. 500–1000)

HIGHLIGHTS
Charlemagne and His Empire • Feudalism

A New Roman Empire for Europe

Dreams of Rome after Christ

While distorted Christianity and Islam battled in vain for the world, the work of building Christendom continued in Europe. Because so many events of history have, in one way or another, been a response to Christ, we now focus on the relatively small part of the world to which Christianity—in a very distorted form—was for a long time largely confined. The people of western Europe, though few in number compared to the rest of mankind, now become the main actors on the stage of world history.

Christendom, for all its grievous errors, did have the Bible. Though distorted, the simple but powerful truths of the Scriptures might someday be seen clearly again. With God's Word in its possession, Europe had tremendous potential for progress in politics, economics, philosophy, science, and all areas of life. Unfortunately, distorted Christianity held such a grip on western Europe that we can see little cause for optimism as the Middle Ages began around A.D. 500.

Invading German tribes had shattered the unity that western Europe had known under Rome, but the old Roman Empire still lived on as a dream. The combination of politics and distorted Christianity that Constantine had put together captured

imaginations. Men envisioned Christendom as an empire with basic Christian beliefs. Everyone knew that the old Roman Empire was dead, and we have already seen how Islam shattered the dream of Christendom as a world empire, but the goal of a Christian empire encompassing at least western Europe spurred many to action.

The Church as Heir to the Roman Empire

Filling a power vacuum. For a while, the Roman Catholic Church (Roman church) supplied almost the only unity in Europe after the massive Germanic invasions and the fall of Rome. Popes such as **Gregory the Great** (ruled 590–604) helped to fill the power vacuum in Europe, especially in the city of Rome and surrounding areas where there were no other rulers for a time. To many it seemed that the church had inherited the authority of the old Roman Empire.

Church organization. The church certainly resembled the old empire, for like Rome it had become a vast bureaucracy. Its territory was divided and subdivided into units with the same names as similar political units in the old empire, such as *diocese* and *parish.* One very powerful official headed each unit; this official was responsible to the next highest official and eventually to the pope. Just as the emperor had ruled the empire's bureaucracy, so the

158

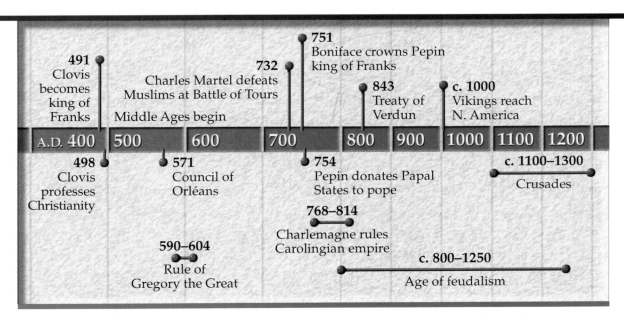

491 Clovis becomes king of Franks

Middle Ages begin

732 Charles Martel defeats Muslims at Battle of Tours

751 Boniface crowns Pepin king of Franks

843 Treaty of Verdun

c. 1000 Vikings reach N. America

A.D. 400 | 500 | 600 | 700 | 800 | 900 | 1000 | 1100 | 1200

498 Clovis professes Christianity

571 Council of Orléans

754 Pepin donates Papal States to pope

c. 1100–1300 Crusades

590–604 Rule of Gregory the Great

768–814 Charlemagne rules Carolingian empire

c. 800–1250 Age of feudalism

pope headed the *hierarchy* [hī′ẽr·är′kẽ: persons arranged in a series according to the degree of their power] of the Roman church. Popes even used the title **pontifex maximus** [pŏn′tĭ·fĕks măk′sĭ·mŭs: "high priest"], a title once used by Roman emperors.

But popes fell far short of the ancient emperors in power. Initially, they had to rely on supposed spiritual authority to enforce their will. It was not long, however, before they found a way to get armed might on their side. With the disintegration of the Western Roman Empire and the settlement of the German tribes, most of the armed might was in the hands of military strongmen called *lords* who controlled small dominions.

The Franks

The German tribe of the **Franks** settled in western Europe where *France* and *Germany* are today. The name *Frank* means "free." A Roman general had once oppressed the Franks, but they shook off the "cruel yoke of the Romans" and won their freedom. The Frank's love of freedom would be critically important for the future of the world. Although they had few powerful "lords" among them, the freedom-loving Franks established the first large empire in western Europe after the fall of Rome and helped popes acquire the worldly power they desired.

Gregory the Great

159

Order upon Disorder:
With force and violence, Charlemagne strove to erect a new empire in Europe.

Clovis

Ruthless and crafty. **Clovis** [klō′vĭs], the first great Frankish military and political leader, inherited the position of tribal king from his father in 481. Clovis began the *Merovingian* [mĕr′ō·vĭn′jĭ·an] series of kings, named for his grandfather Merovee [mā′rô′vā′]. As king, 15-year-old Clovis united the Franks as never before, not hesitating to double-cross, trick, or murder. He then led the Franks to victory over the Romans and fellow Germans in battles beginning in 486. Clovis's Frankish kingdom soon covered the area formerly known as *Gaul,* stretching from east of the Rhine River in the north to the Pyrenees [pĭr′e·nēz] Mountains in the south. Clovis was an extremely crafty warrior and ruler. He treated conquered people leniently and tried to connect his kingdom with the old Roman Empire, hoping to gain some of the respect with which people still remembered it.

Clovis and Christianity. By 498, Clovis was calling himself a Christian. Stories circulated that he had witnessed miracles. According to one story, God helped Clovis turn a losing military battle at *Tolbiac* [tŏl·bī′ak] in 496 into a great victory. Finally persuaded of his need for baptism, Clovis was baptized with 3,000 of his warriors on Christmas Day in 498.

Clovis soon began combining politics and religion—much like Constantine. He even called a church council, which met in the city of **Orléans** [ôr′lā′än′]. Clovis actively participated in the Council of Orléans in 511, much as Constantine had in the Council of Nicaea in 325.

The Roman church greatly benefited from having Clovis on its side, for wherever Clovis conquered, the church conquered. Thus, the church gained more and more land and became richer and richer from tithes and taxes the people were forced to pay. But Clovis also benefited from this relationship, for some people believed that God approved of everything Clovis did to increase his power and secure his position.

After his death in 511, Clovis's descendants ruled a sometimes-united, sometimes-divided kingdom until 751. They committed many savage and violent crimes as they fought over the throne. Even bishops participated in the lies and murders of the Merovingian family. The name *Christian* scarcely signified lives that were godly.

Charles Martel

Mayors of the Palace. The Merovingian kings' interest in private, immoral pleasures increased to the point that they had neither time nor energy to rule. Gradually, officials called **Mayors of the Palace** took over the kings' duties. One of the most famous of these mayors was **Charles Martel** [mär·tĕl']. Born about 688, Charles was the son of a powerful Frankish Mayor of the Palace. After his father's death in 714, Charles Martel became mayor and struggled to continue the work of holding the kingdom together. Charles quickly allied himself with the Roman church and supported the missionary work of **Bishop Boniface** [bŏn'i·fās] in northern Gaul. Charles thought his alliance with the church would help him hold on to his conquests. He also wanted the church's support against powerful new enemies to the south.

The "Hammer." When the Muslims pushed north from Spain in 732, Charles met and defeated them at the **Battle of Tours,** which was mentioned in the previous chapter. He continued to beat the Muslims back in a series of battles that lasted nearly a decade and earned him the name *Martel,* which means "Hammer." Charles Martel's victories prevented western Europe from being swallowed up by the Muslim empire. They also set the stage for Martel's son Pepin to take another step toward combining politics and religion and reviving the old Roman Empire.

CHECK UP

1. Describe the organization of the Roman church.
2. Where was Clovis's kingdom located? What were its boundaries?
3. How was Clovis like Constantine?
4. How did the Roman church benefit from having Clovis on its side? How did Clovis benefit from this relationship?
5. How did the Mayors of the Palace become so powerful?
6. How did Charles get the name Martel?
7. Name the great battle in which Charles Martel defeated the Muslims in 732. How did this and other victories benefit western Europe?

Identify: Gregory the Great, diocese, parish, pontifex maximus, Franks, Merovingian, Orléans, Bishop Boniface

Pepin the Short

King in fact, king in name. **Pepin the Short** became Mayor of the Palace upon his father's death in 741. Pepin felt that since he was doing the job of a king, he should have the title of king. But he needed a basis for this claim. From the earliest times, kings have claimed that they ought to be king either because they were gods or because the gods wanted them to be king. Pepin wanted to be able to say that God wished him to be king. He thought people would believe him if the pope, as the supposed spokesman for God, agreed.

Pope Zacharias replied to a letter from Pepin that ". . . it seemed better that he who has the power should be king rather than he who is falsely called so." Acting for the pope, the Bishop Boniface crowned Pepin king in 751. The next pope, **Stephen II,** crossed the Alps into France to crown Pepin king again and threatened excommunication for anyone who might try to overthrow Pepin or his descendants.

An amazing bargain. In return, the pope gained the support and defense of Pepin's military might. When the **Lombards,** a Germanic tribe that occupied northern Italy, showed interest in the pope's territory, Pope Stephen II requested Pepin's help. Pepin and his soldiers crossed the Alps into Italy in 754 and took from the Lombards a strip of land which Pepin donated to the pope. This *"Donation of Pepin"* became known as the **Papal States.**

Pepin and the pope had struck an amazing bargain. With the support of the Pope, Pepin was able to establish himself as king of the Franks and to enlarge and secure his kingdom. In return, the pope received the Papal States and, more importantly, assumed the enormous power of choosing kings. *The stage was set for a rebuilt Roman Empire jointly ruled by pope and emperor.* Pepin's rule was now connected with the old empire. The pope, taking a power only Roman emperors had previously used, gave Pepin the title, **"Patrician of the Romans."**

Carolingian kings. Pepin's kingship, backed by the pope, ended the Merovingian dynasty and commenced the *Carolingian* [kăr′ō·lĭn′jĭ·an] line of Frankish kings. The new dynasty took its name from either Pepin's father or Pepin's son, both of whom were named Charles.

Charlemagne

The "Great." When Pepin died in 768, his son Charles became king. Large and strong, with flashing eyes and a handsome face, Charles commanded respect and "looked" the part of a king. His accomplishments earned him the name **Charlemagne,** French for *"Charles the Great."*

Fifty years of war. Charlemagne inherited a kingdom threatened by enemies on north, south, and east. He spent nearly 50 years of ceaseless war and stopped short of no cruelty, once massacring 4,500 rebels *after they had surrendered.* In the name of security, he added substantial territory to

Charlemagne: By A.D. 800, Charlemagne ruled the largest area in the West since the Roman Empire.

his kingdom in western Europe. No important German tribe remained independent of the Carolingian kings. Frankish power extended across the Pyrenees Mountains into northern Spain. While helping the pope in Italy against the Lombards just as his father Pepin had done, Charlemagne made northern Italy part of his kingdom.

A "Christian" empire. Charlemagne was quick to recognize the political usefulness of religion. He made his wars seem like holy wars. New Roman churches sprang up wherever he conquered. Defeated peoples often received the choice of death or public profession of Romanism. Charlemagne never learned that forced statements of belief are of little value. He forced the conquered German Saxons to be baptized. The Saxons repeatedly rebelled and renounced Christianity; yet each time he reconquered them, Charlemagne forced the Saxons to say they were Christians. Charlemagne finally deported the Saxons into other areas of western Europe.

By the year 800, Charlemagne ruled the largest area in the West since the Roman emperors of the A.D. 300s. Charlemagne was called "leader of the Christian people" and "defender of the churches of Christ." His vast kingdom was called a "Christian empire."

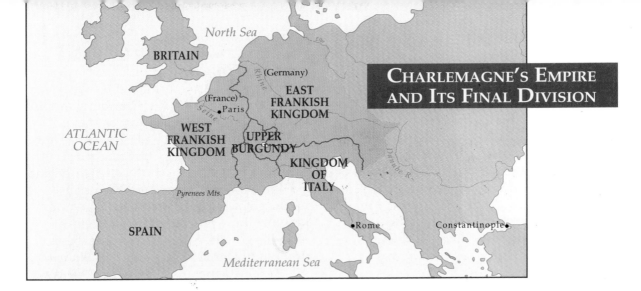

Emperor of the Romans. Charlemagne celebrated Christmas Day in Rome in A.D. 800. As the Frankish king knelt before a church altar, Pope **Leo III**—supposedly to Charlemagne's surprise—placed a crown of gold upon his head and called him **Charles Augustus, emperor of the Romans.** The crowd of people in the church shouted their approval. The old Roman Empire of Constantine seemed to have been reborn.

Yet there was one great difference between the empire of Charlemagne and that of Constantine the Great. Although a pope had crowned Charlemagne's father king and a pope had crowned Charlemagne emperor, no pope had crowned Constantine, for Constantine had ruled before the bishop of Rome was recognized as head of the church. Charlemagne's empire was erected by pope and emperor working together. Thus the seeds were sown for future conflict. Throughout the Middle Ages, popes and kings would struggle for power. They each needed the other, but their inability to get along made a revived Roman Empire difficult to maintain.

Charlemagne soon made it clear that he was second to no pope. He did not even invite the pope to the ceremony crowning his son Louis as co-emperor. *Charlemagne considered himself the ruler of both church and government,* and he often intervened in the affairs of the church, from appointment of bishops to matters of doctrine. Charlemagne thought very highly of himself. He considered himself "successor of the Caesars, heir to the power of David and Solomon, anointed of God." In 802, he forced all his subjects above 12 years of age to promise "fidelity to the lord emperor . . ." and, in the same breath, to vow "to live fully in the holy service of God in accordance with the precept (law) of God." Charlemagne was a strong ruler, and his government was very simple: Charlemagne simply had all power for himself.

Other Carolingians

Louis the Pious. Charlemagne's empire, though impressive, far from equaled the old Roman Empire in size, strength, or durability. As soon as Charlemagne died in 814, his empire began to crumble. Charlemagne's son **Louis** is remembered in history as "the Pious" because of the large role played by priests in his upbringing. Perhaps a better nickname for him would be "the Weak." Throughout most of his reign, his sons quarreled and fought civil wars over how the empire should be divided among them.

Treaty of Verdun. In 843, three years after their father's death, Louis's sons signed the **Treaty of Verdun** [vĕr·dûn'], which divided the empire into three parts. The middle kingdom, which consisted of north-

163

ern Italy and a strip of land from Italy to
the North Sea, was too diversified in
geography and nationality and soon
disintegrated. But the eastern and western
kingdoms were more permanent. The
western became the basis of modern
France, and the eastern became the basis of
modern *Germany.* Both were more geo-
graphically unified than the middle kingdom. The development of the French and
German languages encouraged the populations to begin thinking of themselves as
separate and distinct nations.

End of the Carolingians. The
Carolingians who ruled these kingdoms
did not measure up to Charles Martel and
Charlemagne. Rather than "the Hammer"
or "the Great," later Carolingians were
nicknamed "the Simple," "the Fat," "the
Stammerer," and "the Lazy." Except for a
brief period of three years, Charlemagne's
empire was never united again. The last
Carolingian died in the 900s.

CHECK UP

1. How did Pepin use Pope Zacharias to
   obtain the title of king? What did the
   pope receive from Pepin in return?
2. What does the name *Charlemagne*
   mean? By what other names was
   Charlemagne called?
3. How did Charlemagne use religion?
4. What important event occurred in
   Rome on Christmas Day in the year
   800?
5. How did the role of the pope make
   Charlemagne's empire different from
   Constantine's?
6. What happened to the new empire
   after Charlemagne's death? Why?
7. How did Louis compare with his
   father Charlemagne?
8. How did the Treaty of Verdun divide
   the empire? What happened to each
   division?

Identify: Stephen II, Lombards,
Carolingian, Gaul, Leo III

New Barbarians

Magyars. As Charlemagne's weak
successors quarreled, his crumbling empire
faced barbarian invaders just as the old
Roman Empire had in its last days. From
the east came the **Magyars** [măg′yärz],
penetrating deep into southern Europe and
even to Rome. They earned the name
"Scourge of Europe" for their fierce raids
in which they murdered, burned, and
plundered. The Magyars finally settled
down in the area known since as *Hungary.*

Moors. Muslims from North Africa,
known as **Moors,** attacked from the south.
Already firmly entrenched in *Spain,* the
Moors from time to time established
scattered outposts in other parts of Europe.
They also firmly controlled the Mediterranean Sea.

Norsemen. From the north came the
Norsemen, or **Vikings.** These blond-
haired, blue-eyed German barbarians had
been dwelling far to the north in
Scandinavia, where the countries of Sweden, Denmark, and Norway are located
today. Christianity had not yet reached
Scandinavia; to the Christians of the day,
the tall, big-boned Norsemen seemed
extremely fierce and wild. When in the
ninth century the Viking population
suddenly grew too large for Scandinavia to
support, the Norsemen took to the seas.
Some explored and settled faraway *Iceland*
and *Greenland,* large islands to the north
between Europe and America. By about
A.D. 1000, *Vikings had even reached the coasts
of North America,* although they failed to
establish any permanent settlements there.

Many Vikings descended upon western Europe. Some pursued trade, but the
best-remembered Vikings were pirates
who sacked and looted towns, monasteries, and churches. Eventually, many
Vikings settled down. Among the most
important Viking settlements was
Normandy, an area along the northern
coast of western Europe.

Feudalism

A New Way of Life

Fiefs, lords, and vassals. **Feudalism** is *a way of life based upon the ownership and use of land.* In a feudal society almost everything from politics and war to business and commerce is related to land. The feudal system of the Middle Ages centered on the **fief,** *a piece of land owned by one man who permitted another man to use it in return for certain promised services.* The <u>man who owned the land</u> was called a **lord,** and the <u>man who used the land</u> in exchange for his services was called a **vassal.**

Solemn vows. The relationship between lord and vassal was expressed in a promise. In the ceremony of **homage** [hŏm′ĭj], the vassal knelt and vowed to be his "lord's man." Next came an **oath of fealty** [fē′al·tĕ] in which the vassal swore, sometimes with his hand on a Bible, that he would be loyal to his lord. Finally, in the **act of investiture** [ĭn·věs′tĭ·t̯ūr], the lord gave the vassal some object—a lance or a spear, for example—as a symbol of the vassal's right to use the fief. People took the promises of feudalism very seriously. If a vassal failed to honor his promises to his lord, he forfeited his fief (called **forfeiture**).

Origins of Feudalism

In the Roman Empire. The origins of feudalism can be traced back to the last days of the old Roman Empire in the fifth century. In those unsettled times, Roman aristocrats left the cities and moved to the country. There, they offered military and police protection to other families in exchange for land and services.

Among the German barbarians. Feudalism can also be traced back to the German barbarians who invaded the Western Roman Empire. German warriors swore allegiance to their chieftains with solemn vows.

Vikings: The sight of a Viking warship was cause for alarm in medieval Europe, for the Norsemen were well known and greatly feared. The terror of the Vikings inspired the prayer, "From the fury of the Northmen, deliver us, Lord."

The End of the Empire

Quarrels from within and attacks from without reduced Charlemagne's western European empire to shambles. Soon hundreds of little kingdoms replaced the empire. In each kingdom, small groups of nobles elected kings. These kings were not very powerful, however. The scattered kingdoms of western Europe were held together not so much by their kings as by feudalism [fū′dəl·ĭz′m], the new way of life which became prevalent in western Europe during the ninth century.

After Charlemagne. The complicated system of feudalism known in the Middle Ages, however, did not come together until the ninth century. After the fall of Charlemagne's empire, disorder and insecurity ruled the day. The weak kings of Europe's scattered kingdoms provided little protection from barbarian invaders and criminals. The strong robbed the weak and went unpunished.

Knights. Men began to seek some sort of new government to protect their lives, families, and property. Gradually, here and there, certain landholders began to establish themselves as the strongest power in a given area or domain. Such a man might be a noble who could trace his ancestry all the way back to an old aristocratic Roman family, or he might merely be a retired bandit. But all were masters of medieval warfare. These **knights,** as they were called, wore heavy armor and fought on horseback with a variety of weapons. People in the various domains welcomed the knights as a source of security. They were glad to call a knight "lord" and perform services for him in return for protection. Kings were also glad to have the noble knights as warriors.

A Knight: Notice the coat of arms on his shield, banner, and horse. These symbols were used to identify knights in battle. Each noble family had its own coat of arms.

The Feudal System

At the top of the feudal system in each western European kingdom was a **king.** The king owned all the land in his kingdom, at least in theory. Part of his land he kept for personal use; this was called the royal or **crown land.** The rest he distributed as fiefs to high nobles such as dukes, counts, or earls. These nobles, in turn, promised to provide a specified number of knights for the king's service. By this time, knights provided the heart of the military force of the various kingdoms in western Europe. The feudal system enabled a king to call upon his knights for military service whenever a need arose.

Even the highest nobles themselves usually served as knights, but in order to fulfill their promises to the king they needed the support of other nobles. Therefore, these higher nobles distributed parts of their land holdings as fiefs to lower nobles. In return, these lower nobles agreed to help their lord fulfill his obligation to the king to provide a certain number of knights. Thus, another relationship of lord and vassal was created.

These lower nobles, in turn, made vassals of still lower nobles. The process continued down the ladder of nobility to the least knight, one whose fief could only support one mounted warrior.

1. Where did the Magyars come from? What name did they earn?
2. Where did the Moors come from? What sea did they control?
3. Describe the Norsemen. Where were they from?
4. Name one of the most important Viking settlements.
5. Describe western Europe after Charlemagne's empire disintegrated.
6. What is the basis of the feudal system?
7. Explain the origins of feudalism in the old Roman Empire and among the invading German barbarians.
8. When did feudalism appear in its complete form? What conditions helped develop this system?
9. Who were the knights, and how did they originate?
10. How were kings and nobles involved in the relationship of lord and vassal?

Identify: Hungary, Iceland and Greenland, fief, lord, vassal, homage, oath of fealty, act of investiture, forfeiture, crown land

War and Chivalry

The age of feudalism in western Europe (about 800 to 1250) was a time of almost continual warfare and strife. Thus fighting was the chief occupation of a noble. A man successful at warfare could expect to enlarge his territory. Even if he died in battle, he pursued the only life thought honorable for a gentleman.

The feudal period is also remembered as the age of chivalry. **Chivalry** [shĭv'al·rē] was *the code of conduct for the nobility and the knights.* This code stressed the good qualities of the warrior: strength, courage, and loyalty. Chivalry also emphasized other virtues. The chivalrous knight stood ready to defend the church and to aid the weak and feeble. He treated women with reverence and honor.

Chivalry had an important effect on the behavior of noble knights. But just as today, people of the Middle Ages did not always practice what they preached. Not every knight lived up to the code of chivalry. The Middle Ages were brutal times, and both men and women alike were brutal people. They rarely bathed, had terrible table manners, and drank considerable amounts of intoxicating beverages.

Knights and Castles

Knighthood. From earliest youth, a boy of noble birth aspired to learn the arts of war and become a brave knight. A boy began training for knighthood around the age of seven as a **page,** a household servant in the service of a lord. As a page, he learned to hunt and to uphold the ideals of chivalry. At the age of 15 or 16, he became a **squire,** a personal servant to his lord or to another knight in the lord's service. As a squire, his education in the art of war began. He learned to ride a horse in battle and to use a sword, a shield, and a long spear called a lance.

The typical squire officially became a knight around the age of 21. To begin the complicated ceremony, the squire placed his armor on the altar of the parish church, confessed his sins to a priest, and then spent the night in prayer. In the morning, he took a bath to symbolize his purity or worthiness and put on special clothes for the ceremony. At the knighting, the priest performed a mass and blessed the squire's sword, and the squire swore allegiance to the church, his lord, and the code of chivalry. To conclude the ceremony, he knelt before his lord who, tapping the squire's neck or shoulder with a sword, pronounced him a knight.

Armor and heraldry. Early knights wore simple leather coats. For greater protection, armorers developed the coat of mail, an intricate garment composed of

Castle: *The lack of windows and the thick stone walls combined to make castles dark, damp, and cold dwellings.*

thousands of metal links woven together. In the 1200s, they began to add pieces of metal plate to the coat of mail, especially at the joints and shoulders. By 1300, armorers were making heavy suits of plated armor.

Because knights often wore closed helmets that shielded the face, it was difficult to distinguish friend from foe in the midst of battle. Thus, each noble family had its own **coat of arms,** a group of emblems and figures usually displayed on a knight's armor for identification purposes. The study of these emblems and their designs is known as *heraldry* [hĕr′əl·drē].

Castles. With invasion and warfare so prevalent, nobles built heavily fortified dwellings called **castles** (from the Latin word *castra,* a military camp). Before 900, wooden castles were common, but later castles were made of stone. A protective trench of water called a *moat* surrounded many castles. Such castles could only be entered by way of a *drawbridge* (a bridge that could be raised or lowered). When raised, the drawbridge acted as a closed gate; when lowered, it provided access to the castle across the moat. From towers, or *turrets,* along the castle walls, watchmen surveyed the surrounding countryside, ready to warn of an approaching enemy. A castle's walls might enclose a space of several acres, with enough buildings and room for all the people of a domain to gather during an enemy attack.

Castles were difficult to attack. Devices had to be used that could hurl stones, arrows, and other missiles over the high walls. Soldiers scaled the walls with ladders or towers on wheels, used battering rams to break through the walls and gates, and sometimes even dug tunnels under walls in order to get inside. Meanwhile, a castle's defenders stood atop the walls and turrets, raining arrows, rocks, or even

boiling tar down upon the heads of the attackers. Whenever the need arose, the knights were ready to pour out of the castle and attack enemies. Clad from head to toe in iron armor and mounted upon armored horses, they charged into battle with sword, lance, and shield.

Medieval castles were not the bright, gleaming structures described in fairy tales. Designed for defense, they had no large windows. Rooms were dark, damp, and gloomy with but few decorations on the walls. The only warmth on a winter's night came from large fireplaces.

Medieval sports and pastimes. Nobles spent most of their day outside in sports. The main sport, of course, was war. Even in peacetime, the nobles preferred jousts and tournaments. In a **joust,** two knights fought to unseat or unhorse each other. In **tournaments,** two teams of knights fought a mock battle that lasted an entire day and ranged over the whole countryside. Naturally, people were often hurt in these fierce sports.

Nobles also liked to hunt. Sometimes they hunted on horseback, galloping through the fields with a crossbow. Another favorite method of hunting was **falconry.** Falcons were young hawks trained to hunt small game such as ducks or rabbits. Upon sighting his prey, the hunter released the falcon from his wrist, allowing the bird to pursue and kill the game and return it to his master.

At night, the nobles enjoyed indoor games, including backgammon and chess. Sometimes, clownlike jesters in long, pointed shoes with tinkling bells entertained with jokes and foolishness. Minstrels sang and played simple stringed instruments.

Manors and Serfs

Farmers. During the Middle Ages, however, *the vast majority of people did not live in castles and had no time or energy for games.* They worked as farmers on the **manors,** estates belonging to the nobles. These manors ranged in size from a few hundred to several thousand acres of land. The farmers of the manors, called **serfs,** lived in villages of 10 to 50 families. Each family had a little house with just enough land for a small garden and a few barnyard animals.

The serfs lived a life of hardship and knew nothing of freedom. In many ways, they were like slaves. They could not leave the land without the consent of their lord, and their serfdom was hereditary. The children of a serf were attached to the soil just as their parents were. *If born a serf, one died a serf.* Serfs did differ from slaves in that they possessed certain rights. As long as they performed their duties, their lords could not evict them from the land.

But the serfs paid a high price for their meager rights. They had to work two or three days each week in their lord's fields, the *demesne* [di·mān']. They might also have to do such work as repairing roads or building barns. In addition to paying taxes, the serfs paid fees to use the lord's mills for grinding grain or his ovens for baking bread.

Men and women worked sunup to sundown in the fields. Their life was hard, and they always lived on the brink of starvation. Their simple homes had walls made of mud and floors made of clay. A fire burned in the middle of the floor. As most serfs could not afford a chimney, the smoke escaped through a small hole in the roof. Windows were mere holes without glass. Furniture was sparse and purely functional. Pigs and chickens might wander in at any moment, for few homes had doors.

A Joust: In a joust, two knights fought with lances to unseat or unhorse each other. Men were often hurt in this fierce sport.

A Typical Manor

Paying taxes: *Besides working in their lord's fields, the serfs also paid annual taxes to their lord. As farmers, the serfs might pay with a goose, a lamb, or produce from their land.*

Churches. Each manor had its own little church, tying noble and serf alike to the Roman church. The last words a man heard might be from the same priest who had baptized him, fed him the bread of the Lord's Supper in the mass throughout life, and now uttered last rites over his death-bed. Men believed that the priests with their sacraments, not Christ with His grace, held the keys to Heaven. <u>Most people were unable to read, and few had access to Bibles</u>.

The men of the church generally fell right into step with feudalism. The church had become a great landholder as people willed property to the church in a last effort to secure their salvation. Many bishops even became lords and vassals.

As Europe disintegrated from an empire into feudalism, the light Christ had brought into the world remained dimmed. The truth of the Bible was hidden in darkness, and the people of the Middle Ages understood neither freedom in this life nor salvation in the next.

CHECK UP

1. What was the main occupation of nobles?
2. Describe the training of a knight. Describe the ceremony by which a squire became a knight.
3. What was the purpose of a coat of arms?
4. Describe the castles of the Middle Ages.
5. What outdoor sports did the nobles enjoy? What indoor activities did they enjoy?
6. How did most of the people of the Middle Ages spend their time?
7. How were the serfs almost like slaves? What were their homes like?
8. Describe the role of the Roman church in feudalism.

Identify: chivalry, page, squire, heraldry, moats, drawbridges, turrets, joust, tournaments, falconry, manors, demesne

---

CHAPTER 11 REVIEW

MULTIPLE CHOICE Choose the best answer.

1. After the fall of Rome, popes such as _____ filled the power vacuum in Italy and helped maintain unity in Europe.
   a Clovis
   b Gregory the Great
   c Pontifex Maximus
   d Leo III

2. The title used first by Roman emperors and later by popes was _____.
   a bishop
   b diocese
   c Mayor of the Palace
   d pontifex maximus

3. The freedom-loving Germanic people who settled in what is today called France and Germany were the _____.
   a Franks   c Moors
   b Lombards   d Magyars

4. The first great Frankish military and political leader was _____.
   a Pepin the Short
   b Clovis
   c Gregory the Great
   d Charles Martel

5. This Frankish ruler started the _____ line of kings.
   a Frankish   c Merovingian
   b Carolingian d Gregorian

CHAPTER 11 REVIEW (CONTINUED)

6. The church council called by Clovis met in the city of _____.
   a Nicaea   c Poitiers
   b Ravenna   d Orléans

7. As kings grew lazier and more wicked, the true power of government fell into the hands of officials called _____.
   a bishops   c Lombards
   b Magyars   d Mayors of the Palace

8. Charles Martel sought to win the favor of the church by supporting a missionary named _____.
   a Gregory of Tours
   b Bishop Boniface
   c Charles the Simple
   d Lothair

9. In 732, Charles Martel turned back a Muslim invasion of Europe at the Battle of _____.
   a Tolbiac   c Gaul
   b Tours   d Ravenna

10. Martel's son _____ felt that he should have the title of king since he performed the duties of a king.
    a Gregory the Great
    b Charlemagne
    c Leo III
    d Pepin the Short

11. Pope _____ permitted this Mayor of the Palace to be crowned king.
    a Gregory the Great   c Zacharias
    b Clovis   d Stephen II

12. Pope _____ crossed the Alps to crown Pepin and threatened excommunication to anyone who resisted the king's authority.
    a Zacharias   c Gregory the Great
    b Clovis   d Stephen II

13. The Papal States were also known as the _____.
    a Donation of Pepin
    b Carolingian States
    c Normandy District
    d Merovingian States

14. Pepin's title _____ connected his rule with the old Roman Empire.
    a Mayor of the Palace
    b Patrician of the Romans
    c Pontifex Maximus
    d Pope

15. Pepin started the _____ line of kings.
    a Carolingian   c Merovingian
    b Gregorian   d Patrician

16. Pope _____ crowned Charlemagne emperor of the Romans in A.D. 800.
    a Leo III
    b Louis the Pious
    c Gregory the Great
    d Zacharias

17. The Carolingian Empire was divided into three sections by the Treaty of _____.
    a Tours   c Verdun
    b Orléans   d Nicaea

18. The _____ were called the "Scourge of Europe."
    a Merovingians   c Moors
    b Franks   d Magyars

19. Muslims from northern Africa were called _____.
    a Moors   c Ottomans
    b Magyars   d Arabs

20. The Norsemen were also known as _____.
    a Goths   c Moors
    b Magyars   d Vikings

TIME LINE CHALLENGE *Choose the letter of the correct date for each of the events listed below.*

A.D. 481   498   511   732   751   754   800   843

A   B   C   D   E   F   G   H

_____ 1. Treaty of Verdun

_____ 2. Battle of Tours

_____ 3. Charlemagne is crowned "Emperor of the Romans"

_____ 4. Clovis professes Christianity and is baptized

_____ 5. Pepin invades Italy and creates the Papal States

_____ 6. Clovis becomes king of the Franks

_____ 7. Council of Orléans

_____ 8. Pepin becomes king

MATCHING *Match the term with its definition.*

a feudalism   f chivalry
b coat of arms   g crown land
c knights   h tournament
d fief   i joust
e serfs

_____ 1. Piece of land granted by a lord to a vassal

_____ 2. Great warriors who fought for kings and nobles

_____ 3. Land kept for the king's private use

_____ 4. A way of life based on the ownership and use of land

_____ 5. Code of conduct for nobles and knights

_____ 6. Emblems used to identify noble families

_____ 7. A contest between two knights who fought to unhorse each other

_____ 8. Mock "wars" in which two teams of knights battled

FILL IN THE BLANK *Write the word(s) that will best complete each statement.*

1. In the ceremony of _____, a vassal knelt and vowed to be his "lord's man."

2. With an oath of _____, a vassal swore that he would be loyal to his lord.

3. In the act of _____, the vassal received a token representing his right to use the land.

4. To train for knighthood, a boy first became a _____.

5. At the age of 15 or 16, a boy became a _____ and began to learn the art of war.

6. The noble knights lived in fortresses known as _____.

7. The large estates owned by the nobles were called _____.

8. The farmers who worked for the nobles and lived like slaves were called _____.

12
An Age of Darkness
(A.D. 500–1500)

HIGHLIGHTS
Distorted Christianity • Holy Roman Empire
Renaissance

Economic Depression

Spiritual and Material Poverty

During the Middle Ages, mankind fell into darkness. The true Light had come into the world, but the world had responded by distorting Christianity. The consequences of spiritual poverty were felt in every area of life.

By about the year 1000, it seemed that world history had taken a step backwards. Feudalism had descended upon Europe, and trade had all but ceased. Mankind had little hope for progress. It seemed unlikely that the people of Europe would ever again know the quality of life, for example, known in the cities of the ancient Roman Empire.

From Rome to the Middle Ages

Prosperity under Rome. When Rome ruled the world at the time of Christ, cities bustled and business boomed throughout the empire. Ancient cities thrived as never before, and from North Africa to Gaul, prosperous new cities arose. Many imitated the splendor of Roman architecture and life style. A network of trade routes connected the cities of the Roman Empire, allowing merchants to cross pirate-free seas and travel great highways across the continents. A shopper in Rome could find products to buy from all over the known world. The Pax Romana created conditions for the greatest prosperity the world had ever known.

Decline in the Middle Ages. Two centuries of Roman peace were followed by three centuries of confusion and violence, invasion and civil war, insecurity and uncertainty. By A.D. 500, prosperity had vanished along with the Empire. Towns shrank as people fled to the country. Rome shriveled from perhaps a million inhabitants to 50,000. Some cities on the frontiers of the empire were abandoned altogether. As Roman roads and bridges fell into disrepair and pirates reclaimed the seas, trade began to decline, dragging the economy down with it.

War and barbarians. The economy of western Europe continued to decline throughout the Middle Ages. Trade thrives in peace, but Europe was ravaged with war, disorder, and strife. Long-distance trade suffered another blow in the seventh and eighth centuries when the conquering Muslims stifled western European shipping in the Mediterranean. Then, with the new barbarian invasions of Norsemen and Magyars *in the ninth and tenth centuries, the western European depression reached its lowest point.*

A rural culture. By the tenth century, when feudalism descended upon Europe, many towns were little more than ruins with only a fraction of their former population. The urban (city) culture of the Roman Empire had been replaced by the mainly rural (country) culture of the Middle Ages. The average population of towns in Italy

174

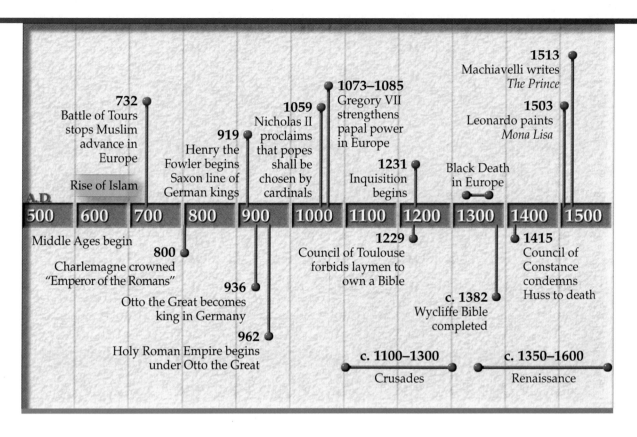

732
Battle of Tours
stops Muslim
advance in
Europe

Rise of Islam

919
Henry the
Fowler begins
Saxon line of
German kings

1059
Nicholas II
proclaims
that popes
shall be
chosen by
cardinals

1073–1085
Gregory VII
strengthens
papal power
in Europe

1231
Inquisition
begins

Black Death
in Europe

1513
Machiavelli writes
The Prince

1503
Leonardo paints
Mona Lisa

A.D.

500 | 600 | 700 | 800 | 900 | 1000 | 1100 | 1200 | 1300 | 1400 | 1500

Middle Ages begin

800
Charlemagne crowned
"Emperor of the Romans"

936
Otto the Great becomes
king in Germany

962
Holy Roman Empire begins
under Otto the Great

1229
Council of Toulouse
forbids laymen to
own a Bible

c. 1382
Wycliffe Bible
completed

1415
Council of
Constance
condemns
Huss to death

c. 1100–1300
Crusades

c. 1350–1600
Renaissance

was 1,000 to 1,500. The largest towns in the area of France and Germany numbered 7,000 to 8,000 in population. About 95% of the population of western Europe lived in the country. This population shift from the cities to the country combined with the general lack of trade resulted in a poor, backward society dependent on agriculture for survival. Thus, most of the people in medieval Europe were desperately poor, and even those considered "rich" by the standards of the day knew nothing of the wealth and splendor known in ancient Rome.

Spiritual Ignorance

Monasticism

During the Middle Ages, many people had a false notion of how Christians ought to live. *The first Christians lived separated lives, but they did not withdraw from the world.* In the late third and early fourth centuries, however, **monasticism** [mŏ·năs′-ti·sĭz′m: withdrawing from society and living in solitude] became the ideal of some who called themselves Christians. Men who practice monasticism are called **monks;** such women are called **nuns.** The Roman church encouraged monasticism among its people.

Hermits. The earliest monks (from the Greek word *monos,* meaning "alone") lived in the wilderness as **hermits.** These hermits sought to please God by torturing themselves. They prayed and prayed for hours on end, repeating short memorized prayers. They fasted and shunned sleep, sometimes bringing hallucinations upon themselves. Like other monks, they vowed **celibacy** [sĕl′i bə·sē: that they would never marry]. The hermits believed that the more they withdrew from the world, the more they would be alone with God.

Mont Saint-Michel: A medieval monastery overlooks the fortified village of Mont Saint-Michel on this rocky isle off the western coast of France. The cloister of the monastery is pictured below. The cloister was a place of quiet seclusion where the monks could study and pray.

Monasteries. Less extreme monks lived together in **monasteries,** *religious communities isolated from the rest of society.* Monasteries dotted the European landscape during the Middle Ages. Life in a monastery followed rigid rules (sometimes called *orders*). Most monks in Europe followed the rules of **Benedict** (c. 480–543), the founder of a monastery in Italy. Benedictine monks vowed life-long poverty, chastity, and obedience (obedience to the abbot, the head of the monastery). The Benedictine rules covered every part of a monk's daily activities, a never-ending cycle of work and prayer.

What was the purpose of it all? The monks thought that they were living as Christ had commanded, even though the Bible never says that marriage is wrong or directs Christians to live in isolation. In fact, the Bible says just the opposite. The monks fell into the trap prophesied by the Apostle Paul:

> . . . in the latter times some shall depart from the faith . . .
>
> Speaking lies in hypocrisy; having their conscience seared with a hot iron;
>
> Forbidding to marry, *and commanding* to abstain from meats which God hath created to be received with thanksgiving of them which believe and know the truth.
>
> For every creature of God *is* good, and nothing to be refused, if it be received with thanksgiving (1 Tim. 4:1–4).

Many monks spent much time copying the Bible, helping to preserve the Scriptures in the age before the printing press. *The monks thought their life of self-denial would please God so much that they would earn their salvation.*

Beginning in the 13th century, a new kind of monk called a **friar** appeared in Europe. Friars lived like other monks

176

except that they <u>preached and did missionary work outside the monasteries</u>.

Of course, not everyone became a monk, nun, or friar, but throughout the Middle Ages the monastic life remained the standard for those who were truly serious about their salvation.

Doctrines of the Roman Church

Baptism and the Eucharist. Even those who did not enter monasteries were taught that only by going through certain motions could they hope to be saved. The Roman church encouraged prayer, but the wrong kind of prayer, addressed to the wrong people. It preached the need for salvation, but the wrong way to obtain it.

Most people did everything that the church claimed a good Christian should do. Soon after birth, they were baptized. At mass, they received the sacrament of the **Eucharist** (the Lord's Supper). The people had been taught that when a priest said in Latin, "This is my body, this is my blood," the bread and wine really became Christ's blood and His body. This *belief that the elements of the Lord's Supper actually change their substance* (what they are made of) is called **transubstantiation** [trăn′sub·stăn′shĭ·ā′shun]. Of course, unless the people learned the Latin language, they could not understand anything that went on in the church services. Everything said and everything sung by the priests was in Latin.

The Virgin Mary, saints, and priests. The people followed many other false doctrines. They were taught to pray to Jesus' mother Mary (the Virgin Mary) and to believe that she could stand before God on behalf of sinners. They were even taught to pray to the long-departed Apostles and **saints** (*deceased persons officially recognized by the church as holy* because of martyrdom or other good deeds). But all was in vain without a priest. According to the church, only by confessing one's sins to a priest and obtaining his forgiveness could a man hope to escape punishment in Hell. <u>After going through all these motions, the people of the Middle Ages still agonized over their salvation</u>. They never experienced a sense of God's forgiveness in their souls, only guilt and condemnation.

St. Francis of Assisi: Born into the home of a cloth merchant in 1181, Francis was wealthy and very worldly. He became a soldier, but in a war with a neighboring city, he was taken prisoner and remained so for a year. After his release, his attitudes were changed. He gave himself to prayer to know what God wanted him to do. A certain church in Assisi had fallen into ruins, and Francis attempted to repair it. His father strenuously objected to his profligate spending on the church's reconstruction and, as a result, Francis left home. He rejected all material goods, dressed in a coarse brown robe, and traveled about Italy preaching. He and his followers became known as friars.

Indulgences, purgatory, and penance. People went to amazing lengths in vain efforts to earn salvation. Many bought **indulgences** [ĭn·dŭl′jen·ses], *certificates from the pope* that excused a person from doing penance and shortened the required stay in purgatory before going to Heaven. **Penance** [pĕn′ans] was the sacrament of *punishments in this life* which repentant sinners had to undergo to show that they were truly sorry for their sins. **Purgatory** [pûr′gə·tō′rē] was *the place where repentant sinners had to stay after death* until they had been properly punished for their sin and could enter Heaven. The sale of indulgences was one of the many ways the clergy (church leaders) enriched themselves by stealing what little money the people had. With this money, they erected many lavish church buildings to serve as their personal palaces.

The Roman church and the Bible. The Bible nowhere mentions penance, purgatory, or indulgences, but the Bible had fallen into such disuse that few ordinary people knew what it really taught. Over the years, the Roman church placed the writings of early church leaders and the pronouncements of popes and church councils on a level with the Bible. As a result, the Bible lost its place as the basis for true Christian beliefs. The church did not want people to have access to the Scripture. If people could read it for themselves, they would realize how much the church had departed from Scripture. The **Vulgate** [vŭl′gāt], a <u>Latin translation</u> that the church leader **Jerome** [je·rōm′] finished in 405, became *almost the only version of the Bible available in the Middle Ages.* As we have seen, not many ordinary people could read Latin. Furthermore, in 1229 the **Council of Toulouse** [tōō′lōōz′] *forbade* anyone except a church leader to possess a copy of the Bible (although not everyone heeded this dictate). The only exceptions were the Psalms and the passages of Scripture in the *breviary* [brē′vĭ·ăr·ē], a book with the official order of worship in church services. Even those who did have access to the Bible had to accept the church's "official" interpretation of it.

CHECK UP

1. Compare economic conditions during the Pax Romana with economic conditions during the Middle Ages.

2. When did the European depression reach its lowest point?

3. What is monasticism? What are men and women who practice monasticism called?

4. Briefly describe life in a Benedictine monastery.

5. What purpose did monks have for living as they did? Does the Bible agree?

6. Name two things good Christians were supposed to do according to the Roman church.

7. What language was used in the church services? What effect did this have on most people?

8. What did the church teach about Mary, the Apostles, and the saints? Why were priests thought to be important?

9. What things did the Roman church place on a level with the Bible?

10. Why did the people of the Middle Ages have limited access to the Scriptures? Who reserved the right to interpret the Bible for everyone?

Identify: hermits, friars, transubstantiation, indulgences, penance, purgatory, *Vulgate*, Jerome, Council of Toulouse, breviary

John Wycliffe: Perhaps Wycliffe's most outstanding work was his translation of the Bible from Latin to English. He did some of the translation work himself and encouraged others to help him in his work. The Wycliffe Bible was released about 1382.

Lollards: The Lollards (shown here being sent out by John Wycliffe) were poor priests or laymen who undertook to spread Wycliffe's teachings throughout England.

Early Challenges to the Roman Church

John Wycliffe. In the 14th century, **John Wycliffe** [wĭk'lĭf: c. 1329–1384], a teacher at Oxford University in England, challenged some of the central opinions of the Roman church. He did not believe that the elements of the Lord's Supper became Christ's body and blood upon the pronouncement of a priest. He saw that salvation did not depend upon church membership, and that Christians have no need for a priest to stand between them and God. The proper authority for a Christian, maintained Wycliffe, is the Bible—not a priest, not the church, and not the pope. Believing that ordinary people

can and should study the Scripture, Wycliffe had the entire Bible translated into English for the first time.

But although Wycliffe attracted many followers, called **Lollards** [lŏl'ĕrdz], the Roman church was too strong in England at that time to be successfully resisted. Wycliffe died in peace in 1384, but in 1409 a meeting of church leaders in London condemned Wycliffe's beliefs and his translation of the Bible. In 1415, the **Council of Constance** condemned Wycliffe of over 200 "crimes" and ordered his writings burned. In 1428, at the pope's command, Wycliffe's remains were dug up and burned as well.

179

John Huss. Wycliffe's writings found their way to Bohemia in central Europe, where the modern Czech Republic is located. **John Huss** (c. 1374–1415), a teacher and dean of the University of Prague, shared many of Wycliffe's views. He stressed the Bible as the only true authority for Christians. The Bible taught Huss that only God (not priests) can forgive sin and that salvation comes only through Christ.

In 1415, Huss attended the *Council of Constance* to defend his beliefs. There, he declared his willingness to be informed of any mistakes but made it known that he would not say anything that offended God. Although the Council had guaranteed his safety, it condemned Huss and burned him at the stake. As he was dying, Huss said, "Lord, into Thy hand I commend my spirit." His followers, called **Hussites,** suffered severe persecution in the years to follow.

Heresy and the Inquisition. John Huss was neither the first nor last to die for his beliefs at the hands of the Roman church. As early as the first centuries after Christ, such groups as the **Montanists** [mŏn′tə·nĭsts], **Novatians** [nŏ·vā′shɑnz], and **Dona-** tists [dŏn′ə·tĭsts], tried to withdraw from the church over moral issues. Groups called by such names as **Anabaptists** [ăn′ə·băp′tĭsts], **Waldensians** [wôl·děn′sĭ·ɑnz], and **Albigensians** [ăl′bĭ·jěn′sĭ·ɑnz] courageously made their disagreements with the Roman church known at various times and various places during the Middle Ages.

While we know that these groups challenged the doctrines of the church, it is hard to know everything that they believed. The Waldensians, for example, took a definite stand for the Bible, and some groups of Anabaptists understood the gospel very clearly, but the Albigensians departed from Biblical Christianity on certain matters of belief.

But the Roman church could not tolerate any disagreement. In the 12th century, popes began to declare crusades against **heretics** [hĕr′e·tĭks: baptized members of the Roman church *who disagreed with any official church opinion*]. By the middle of the 13th century, the Roman church had established the **Inquisition** [ĭn′kwi·zĭsh′un], a special church court with power *to inquire about and judge matters of heresy.*

John Huss: *Influenced greatly by the writings of John Wycliffe, John Huss tried to reform the church in Bohemia (now the Czech Republic). He emphasized the need for holy living and condemned such practices as worship of images and "superstitious pilgrimages."*

Death of Huss: *On July 6, 1415, the Council of Constance turned Huss over to the government to be burned at the stake. A paper crown proclaiming his alleged heresy was placed on his head, but he replied that to wear it was the least he could do for the One Who had worn a crown of thorns for him.*

When an inquisitor arrived in an area, he would call for reports of anyone suspected of heresy; those suspected were imprisoned to await trials. These trials were secret and might continue for years. At the trial, the inquisitor acted as judge, prosecutor, and jury, while the accused had no lawyer. It was often simpler to confess to heresy than to defend oneself, as torture might be continually employed until an individual repented. Possible punishments (penance) included attending a certain number of masses, wearing specially designed crosses as a symbol of heresy, and enduring whipping and imprisonment. Anyone who fell back into heresy was turned over by the Inquisition to the regular government to be burned at the stake. All this was done in the name of Christ.

In the Dark

Decline in Learning

Learning in Rome after Christ. In the first centuries after Christ, while the Roman Empire still stood in western Europe, many intelligent, well-educated men had accepted Christ as Savior. The truths of Christianity stirred new interest in subjects like philosophy which, without guidance from God's revelation, had failed to answer the basic questions of life. The truths of Christianity challenged the human mind as it had never been challenged before.

Such men as **Augustine** (354–430), bishop of the church at Hippo Regius in North Africa, discovered that his salvation through Christ stimulated him to think—and find answers—as never before. Augustine left the world a model of beautiful literature in *The Confessions,* a book of prayers, praises, and meditations addressed entirely to God. Few works of philosophy are more penetrating than *The City of God,* in which Augustine presented a Christian philosophy of history.

Decline of education. But as the Western Roman Empire fell into spiritual darkness, the "lamp of learning" also grew dim. During this era of violence and disorder, few people had the time or interest to think beyond the pressing needs of the moment. The invading German barbarians, of course, could not be expected to appreciate good books. Even Charlemagne, who valued learning and tried to revive it during the days of his empire, could read but not write. For centuries after Rome's fall, church officials and monks were almost the only educated men in western Europe. Even their education, most of it obtained in monasteries, compared poorly to that of the ancient Greeks and Romans.

Education fared better in the Eastern Roman Empire and under the Arab Muslims. For many centuries, learning thrived in Constantinople (also called Byzantium), the capital of the Eastern Roman Empire.

Scholasticism

"The Philosopher." Learning began to revive in western Europe between 1000 and 1300 with the growth of cities, the rise of commerce, and contact with Arab and Byzantine scholars who had preserved much of the classical learning of the Greeks and Romans. European scholars were most impressed with the works of the Greek philosopher **Aristotle.** In fact, they were so overwhelmed by his apparent wisdom that they were soon calling Aristotle "The Philosopher."

Schools and schoolmen. Under the sponsorship of the Roman church, teachers and pupils began to gather in organized groups. These institutions, the ancestors of modern universities, were often called simply **schools;** their teachers and pupils became known as **schoolmen.** By 1500, there may have been nearly 100 schools in Europe.

A tool of the church. These schools took an approach to learning known as

scholasticism [skŏ·lăs′tĭ·sĭz′m], which *tried to combine Greek philosophy and Romanism.* The church found scholasticism useful for making distorted Christianity seem reasonable, but it kept a watchful eye on the schools, lest curious minds break free of false religion and question ancient philosophy. The philosopher *William of Ockham* [ŏk′am: c. 1290–1349], for example, educated under scholastics at Oxford University, used logic to discredit the doctrine of the pope's absolute supremacy. For Ockham, the Scriptures were the only true authority. He did not hesitate to attack any Roman doctrine or pagan philosophy that contradicted the Bible. Ockham would probably have been killed for his reasoning if a German prince who was quarreling with the pope had not protected him.

Aquinas. By the time Aristotle's books came into the schools of the Middle Ages, the church had already so distorted Christianity that the ideas of "The Philosopher" were easily combined with Roman doctrine. The man who <u>combined Aristotle and Romanism</u> most successfully was **Thomas Aquinas** [ə·kwī′nas: 1225–1274]. Aquinas was known as the Dumb Ox because he spoke so slowly, but he had a brilliant mind. Greatly impressed by Aquinas's work, the Roman church gave it official approval and forbade anyone to disagree.

Progress in philosophy and science was virtually impossible under such conditions. Aristotle would have been surprised to find how his books were being used.

Literature. If Aquinas summed up the philosophy of the Middle Ages, **Dante** [dän′tā: 1265–1321] summed up the literature. Dante wrote *Divine Comedy,* one of the few pieces of medieval literature that is still widely read. Few poems have surpassed the beauty of his work. But just as Aquinas tried to mix the philosophies of

Aristotle with Christianity, so Dante tried to mix the ideas of the Roman poet Virgil with Christianity.

During the Middle Ages, the English poet **Chaucer** [chô′sĕr: c. 1340–1400], wrote *The Canterbury Tales,* one of the first great works of literature in the English language. Like Dante, he pointed out problems in the church. Chaucer was especially adept at depicting the hypocrisy that priests and monks often fell into. It is interesting that both Chaucer and Dante, the two major poets of the Middle Ages, were acutely aware of the religious hypocrisy of their age.

CHECK UP

1. What opinions of the Roman church did John Wycliffe challenge? What did he give the English people? What were his followers called?
2. What fate did Huss suffer for his beliefs? What were his followers called?
3. Name some early groups that tried to withdraw from the Roman church over moral issues.
4. How did the church respond to such groups and to others it regarded as heretics? Describe trials for heresy.
5. Why did learning decline when the Western Roman Empire declined?
6. Who were almost the only educated men for centuries in western Europe?
7. How did education fare in the Eastern Roman Empire and under the Arab Muslims?
8. Who became known as "*The* Philosopher"?
9. Describe the approach to learning that characterized the Middle Ages in western Europe.
10. Who wrote *Divine Comedy*? *The Canterbury Tales*?

Identify: Council of Constance, heretics, Inquisition, Augustine, *The Confessions, The City of God,* schools, schoolmen, William of Ockham, Thomas Aquinas

---

The Holy Roman Empire
(c. 900–1450)

Reviving the Empire

Decline of politics. As if economic depression, spiritual ignorance, and intellectual derangement were not enough, a sinister idea haunted the Middle Ages, possessing the minds of strong-willed, determined individuals, and wreaking war and disorder upon the people of Europe. The ghost of the Roman Empire lived on. The remains of Charlemagne's empire—itself an imitation of Constantine's combination of politics and distorted Christianity—rotted away under the feudal system. But would-be emperors and scheming popes would not let the dream of a Christian empire die. They fabricated a political monster called the Holy Roman Empire that kept a considerable part of Europe, especially Italy and Germany, in chaos.

Germany and Italy, like France, were parts of Charlemagne's empire that quickly disintegrated after the emperor's death. Germany crumbled into a number of small territories, each ruled by a powerful noble called a *duke.* The dukes of Germany had no desire for a powerful ruler over them. When the last Carolingian ruler of Germany died in 911, the dukes deliberately elected the weakest among themselves to be "king of Germany."

Otto the Great. After a series of weak kings, a powerful duke named **Henry the Fowler** came to the throne in Germany and set up the *Saxon* line of kings. Henry I ruled from 919 to 936, but Germany was still little more than a name.

Henry's son **Otto** became king in 936. Determined to succeed where his father had failed and subdue the unruly dukes, Otto joined forces with the pope. The first step in Otto's scheme was to stabilize his power in Germany. At that time, the king

Otto the Great: *In 962, the Holy Roman Empire began when Otto was crowned "Emperor of the Romans."*

had the power to appoint the Roman clergy (church officials) in Germany. This power enabled Otto to gain control of the wealth and power of the German clergy. So strengthened, Otto was able to restrain the dukes. Next, Otto defeated the Magyars and pushed Germany's borders further and further eastward, earning the title "the Great" from his victories. Having secured Germany, Otto invaded Italy. In 962, the **Holy Roman Empire** was born when the pope crowned Otto "Emperor of the Romans."

Popes and Politics

During the tenth century, the church (like Europe generally) had fallen into troubled times. Popes had little influence, for everyone knew that they were merely puppets of the Roman nobles. Italian dukes were continually threatening to take away the Papal States. By crowning Otto emperor, the pope hoped to gain a friend who would protect and strengthen him in Italy.

The independent pope. But popes would never be respected and powerful as long as they owed their position to Roman nobles. In order to appear to be independent of such influences, popes would have to be chosen within the church by other church officials. Thus, in 1059, Pope **Nicholas II** decreed that henceforth popes would be chosen only by *cardinals,* who at that time were *the priests of the churches in Rome or bishops of churches close to Rome.*

Gregory VII's vision. One of the first popes chosen in this way was **Gregory VII** (known also as Hildebrand [hĭl′də·brănd]), pope from 1073 to 1085. While Gregory favored the idea of the Holy Roman Empire, he wanted to be sure that popes were more powerful than emperors. He longed for a world dominated by the Roman church under the pope's absolute authority, demanding (1) that all princes shall kiss the feet of the pope alone, (2) that the pope be permitted to depose emperors, and (3) that the pope himself be judged by no one.

Pope versus Emperor

The "Holy Roman Empire" became a mockery of its name. "Holy?" What had started as cooperation between pope and emperor had become bitter opposition. Each needed the other, but pope and emperor inevitably envied one another's power and quarreled. "Roman?" The emperors, of course, had always been German, and after Frederick II few even interfered in Italy. "Empire?" The emperor scarcely governed his homeland, Germany. Emperors finally ceased even pretending to control the powerful German nobles. Germany (like Italy) was no more a united country at the end of the Middle Ages than it had been at the beginning.

The Holy Roman Empire presented a pitiful spectacle compared to the mighty Roman Empire of old, and the philosopher

Voltaire [vŏl·târ′] rightfully ridiculed it as *"neither Holy, nor Roman, nor an Empire."*

Turmoil in Europe

The plague. Between 1334 and 1351, the **Black Death,** a form of bubonic plague, swept across Europe. In less than 20 years, it killed from one third to one half the population of Europe. Infected rats and fleas carried the disease throughout the cities, because people did not understand basic sanitation. Everyone—from noble to peasant—lived in dread of the plague except for the Jews. Because they practiced the Biblical standards of cleanliness, many European Jews avoided the plague.

Worldly popes. People soon began to lose respect for the popes. The papacy had always distorted Christianity, but now it became corrupt in a way that was obvious to all. In pursuit of money and power, popes spent more and more time in politics. As popes became so worldly that they seemed more like ordinary governmental figures than church officials, they endangered the basis of their power. People looked up to the pope because they believed his false claim to be Christ's representative on earth as the successor of Peter. When popes appeared more interested in politics than the church, people were bound to lose respect for them.

Councils versus popes. By about 1400, many people in high positions—university teachers, advisers to kings, more thoughtful clergy—believed that something had to be done about the condition of the Roman church. During the next thirty years, popes and councils struggled against one another, and the popes gradually prevailed. By 1450, the popes declared a **Great Jubilee** (Holy Year) to celebrate their triumph over the councils.

Darkness. As history approached the year 1500 and the beginning of modern times, it seemed that the Middle Ages were ending just as they had begun. Politics and distorted Christianity remained as mixed as ever.

The Renaissance
(c. 1350–1600)

Europe in the 14th Century

Political and economic progress. The burden of distorted Christianity greatly hindered progress in Europe during the Middle Ages, but even that burden could not keep the Europeans from making some political and economic progress. Created free, men can to some extent rise above their circumstances. As we will study later, several powerful nation-states arose during the Middle Ages, including England, France, and Spain. This trend, compared to the vain efforts of some to rebuild the Roman Empire, bode well for the future political happiness of mankind.

Europe began to see some economic progress as a result of the *Crusades* (c. 1100 to 1300). The Crusades failed to capture the Holy Land for Christendom, but they did accomplish something: they revived interest in European trade with the Orient (Asia and the Middle East). As crusaders returned from the Middle East with spices, jewels, ivory, glassware, and silks, other Europeans began to desire these things.

Soon old trade routes came alive with merchant caravans and ships.

As trade with the Orient increased, a new social class arose in Europe—a **middle class** of merchants and businessmen who were neither extremely rich nor extremely poor. These hard-working merchants dared to take the first steps to lead mankind out of the economic misery of the Middle Ages.

Prosperity in Italy. The revival of trade with the Orient made the cities of **Italy** the largest and busiest in Europe. The spirit of liberty, individualism, and free-thinking that tends to thrive in the hustle and bustle of cities characterized Italy more than any other part of Europe. Their favorable location on the Mediterranean enabled the Italian cities to grow and prosper as centers of commerce. *Genoa* [jĕn′ō·ə], *Venice,* and other coastal cities imported goods from the Middle East and the Orient and then distributed these by land through such inland cities as *Milan* [mĭ·län′] and *Florence.*

Many businessmen made fortunes from manufacturing, banking, and trade, and their families grew fantastically wealthy and powerful. One good example was the family of Florentine **Giovanni de' Medici** [jō·vän′nē de mād′ē·chē], a 14th-century merchant and banker. The Medici family excelled in business and dominated the political scene in Florence for over 300 years with few interruptions.

A Revival of Learning

Beginnings in Italy. The wealth that poured into Italian cities from business and commerce gave men the time, money, and opportunity to pursue knowledge and support the arts. By the 14th century, many intelligent Italians were repulsed by the condition into which learning had fallen since ancient times. They looked back to the splendor of Rome and glory of Greece and longed for a rebirth of learning.

RENAISSANCE ITALY
A Puzzle of Political Disorder

This dream led to the **Renaissance** [rĕn'ə·säns: c. 1350–1600], a term which means "rebirth." At last, mankind began to emerge from the darkness of the Middle Ages.

Focus on the humanities. The Renaissance emphasized the **humanities,** subjects such as *history, grammar, rhetoric* [rĕt'ŏ·rĭk: the art of speaking], *and poetry.* The schoolmen of the Middle Ages typically had little interest in the humanities, for they assumed that the Roman church had all the answers to man's questions about himself. But the Renaissance Italians knew better; they wanted to pick up where the writers of Greece and Rome had left off on such subjects. But they first had to recover the ancient literature.

The writings of ancient Greeks and Romans suddenly became the rage in Italy. As Italian scholars hunted for old manuscripts, they found many collecting dust in church libraries, where they had been ignored for centuries. Many Greek manuscripts were brought to Italy as Byzantine scholars fled the crumbling Eastern Roman Empire, which finally fell into the hands of the Muslim Turks in 1473. By the middle of the 15th century, most of the important writings of ancient Greeks and Romans had been recovered.

Humanism. At first the word *humanism* meant only *intense interest in the subjects of the humanities.* As long as God is not left out of the picture, the classical books on the humanities should be studied. But if God is

Mona Lisa: one of Leonardo's most famous works.

The School of Athens: *Raphael depicted Plato and Aristotle walking together and discussing philosophy. The painting summed up in picture the Renaissance love for ancient learning.*

left out of such studies, man might be overemphasized to the point of neglecting God or even rebelling against Him. This kind of humanism, as you know, concludes by making man into a god.

The Renaissance humanists, at least at first, appeared to be hardly more than playful children imitating the past. Many refused to write in any language except the classical Latin of ancient Rome, and some Italians even began to dress like ancient Romans! *But what began as an interest in the humanities soon became an expression of human pride and vanity.* Nowhere was this expression more evident than in the art of the Italian Renaissance. Like the ancient Greek sculptors they admired, some Renaissance artists exaggerated the physical beauty of man, worshiping the creature rather than the Creator (Rom. 1:25).

Patrons. The word that gave the name to an age also gave the name to a new ideal of man—the **Renaissance man,** one who displays his talents in all fields. Successful Italian businessmen and politicians sought to fulfill the Renaissance ideal by reading books on humanities and supporting the arts. *People who use their own money to support the arts* are called *patrons.* The Medici family privately funded art and architecture in Florence. The powerful church leaders became the greatest patrons of all, using the great wealth of the church to fill their cathedrals and palaces with beautiful paintings and sculptures.

Renaissance Art

The Renaissance, particularly in Italy, produced some of the greatest art of all times. Renaissance art reached its peak of greatness in the work of three Florentines: **Leonardo da Vinci** [lä′ō·när′dō de vēn′chē: 1452–1519], **Raphael** [răf′å·ĕl: 1483–1520], and **Michelangelo** [mī′kel·ăn′je·lō: 1475–1564]. Many of the paintings and sculptures of these masters can still be seen today in museums around the world.

Leonardo. Often referred to simply as *Leonardo,* Leonardo da Vinci was a master painter, sculptor, inventor, and engineer who left notebooks filled with sketches of flying machines, tanks, parachutes, bicycles, and many other things that were centuries ahead of their time. Being left-handed, Leonardo found it easier to write backwards; for this reason, his notebooks must be read with a mirror. It is possible that he also did this to keep his ideas a secret. As a painter, he is best remembered for his *Mona*

The Last Supper, *by Leonardo da Vinci*

Lisa, a portrait of an unknown woman with a mysterious smile. In *The Last Supper,* Leonardo portrayed Christ and His disciples in the Upper Room.

Raphael. Raphael is known for his brilliant use of color. Among his famous paintings are the *Sistine* [sĭs′tēn] *Madonna* and the *School of Athens.* Although Raphael died at age 37, he managed in his short lifetime to paint several hundred pictures and to design St. Peter's Basilica in Rome.

Michelangelo. Michelangelo may have been the greatest artist of the Renaissance. His paintings often had Biblical themes and are noteworthy for their dramatic realism and sense of movement. In 1505, Pope Julius II hired him to paint the ceiling of the *Sistine Chapel* in the Vatican, the palace where the popes lived in Rome. Michelangelo spent two years on his back on top of high scaffolds (raised platforms) painting gigantic scenes from the Old Testament. Visitors to Rome today are awestruck by the color and almost three-dimensional quality of these paintings. Michelangelo is also known for his marble statues, including those of the Biblical leaders *David* and *Moses.*

Machiavelli and *The Prince*

The only book of lasting importance produced by the Italian Renaissance was

The Prince, a book on politics written in 1513 by a Florentine named **Niccolò Machiavelli** [mä′kyä·vĕl′lē]. Few men have been gifted with a more penetrating mind than Machiavelli's. Machiavelli saw through the hypocrisy of the age and looked in disgust at the mixture of distorted Christianity and politics that dominated 16th-century Italy. As he studied history, he dreamed of a rebirth of the political greatness of ancient Rome. Yet he realized that further political progress would not be possible until men's minds were freed from false religion. Here Machiavelli might have turned to God's Word and found "the truth that sets men free," but instead he turned to himself and man and advised the deliberate use of evil to achieve one's goals. He completely ignored the role of God in world events and exalted

Moses: one of Michelangelo's famous sculptures.

man in His place. Such thinking characterized the Italian Renaissance. Fortunately,
the Renaissance would follow a different
course in Northern Europe.

The End of the Middle Ages

From Italy, the Renaissance spread
northward to France and Germany, where
it sparked an interest in the original Greek
manuscripts of the Scriptures. As men
studied the Word of God, they discovered
such Scriptural truths as salvation by grace
through faith and the priesthood of the
believer. Thus, the Renaissance prepared
the way for a more important movement, a
movement that would lead Europe out of
the darkness of the Middle Ages and into
the light of the Modern Age.

CHECK UP

1. Define the term *Renaissance*. How was this term appropriate for the age?
2. Why had the schoolmen neglected the humanities?
3. Explain the ideal of the Renaissance man. How did it affect art?
4. What three Florentines brought Renaissance art to its peak of greatness?
5. What was the only book of lasting importance produced during the Renaissance?

Identify: middle class, Genoa and Venice, Milan and Florence, Giovanni de' Medici, humanities, humanism, patron

---

CHAPTER 12 REVIEW

TIME LINE CHALLENGE Choose the letter of the correct date for each of the events listed below.

405   c. 500   919   936   962   1059   1229   1334–1351 1415   1450
A   B   C   D   E   F   G   H   I   J

_____ 1. Jerome finishes translating the *Vulgate*
_____ 2. Middle Ages begin
_____ 3. Council of Toulouse forbids anyone except a church leader to possess a copy of the Bible
_____ 4. Council of Constance condemns John Huss and orders him burned at the stake

_____ 5. Nicholas II decrees that popes shall henceforth be chosen by cardinals
_____ 6. Henry the Fowler begins the Saxon line of kings
_____ 7. Otto comes to the throne
_____ 8. Holy Roman Empire is born
_____ 9. Popes declare a Great Jubilee (Holy Year)
_____ 10. Black Death hits Europe

MULTIPLE CHOICE Choose the best answer to complete the sentence.

1. The monk _____ founded a monastery in Italy and set a standard of rules or orders for other monks to follow.
   a Augustine   c Benedict
   b Thomas Aquinas d Chaucer

2. The Council of Constance burned _____ at the stake for his defense of the Bible as the true authority for Christians.
   a Peter Waldo   c Thomas Aquinas
   b John Huss   d John Wycliffe

189

3. The Englishman _____ had the Bible translated into the English language for the first time.
   a John Wycliffe
   b John Huss
   c Thomas Aquinas
   d William of Ockham

4. The English philosopher _____ used logic to disprove the doctrine of the supremacy of the pope.
   a William of Ockham
   b John Huss
   c Thomas Aquinas
   d John Wycliffe

5. The philosopher _____ wrote *Confessions* and *City of God*.
   a Dante   c Aristotle
   b Chaucer   d Augustine

6. The philosopher _____ combined the philosophy of Aristotle with Romanism so successfully that the church forbade anyone to disagree with him.
   a Augustine   c Aristotle
   b Thomas Aquinas   d John Huss

7. The Italian poet _____ wrote *Divine Comedy*.
   a Aristotle   c Dante
   b Thomas Aquinas   d John Huss

8. The English poet _____ wrote *The Canterbury Tales*.
   a Chaucer   c Dante
   b Thomas Aquinas   d John Wycliffe

9. The _____ condemned Wycliffe and Huss in 1415.
   a Lollards
   b schoolmen
   c Council of Toulouse
   d Council of Constance

10. The church set up a special court called the _____ to investigate and try cases of heresy.
    a Inquisition
    b Council of Orlèans
    c Holy Roman Empire
    d Renaissance

11. The attempt to combine Greek philosophy and Romanism was called _____.
    a monastery   c breviary
    b scholasticism   d penance

12. The _____ were powerful nobles in Germany.
    a monks   c dukes
    b lollards   d cardinals

13. The _____ were priests in Rome or bishops near Rome.
    a cardinals   c monks
    b dukes   d lollards

14. The practice of remaining unmarried is called _____.
    a Inquisition   c celibacy
    b scholasticism   d breviary

15. The Medici family was a wealthy and powerful family in the city of _____.
    a Genoa   c Florence
    b Rome   d Venice

16. The term Renaissance means _____.
    a prosperous   c religious
    b rebirth   d classical

17. All of the following men were great artists of the Renaissance except _____.
    a Machiavelli   c Leonardo da Vinci
    b Michelangelo   d Raphael

18. The Renaissance man was one who displayed his talents in _____.
    a art   c the humanities
    b science   d all fields

MODIFIED TRUE OR FALSE If the statement is true, write true in the blank. If it is false, replace the italicized term(s) with the term(s) that will make the statement true.

_____ 1. When Rome ruled the world at the time of Christ, cities and businesses *thrived*.

_____ 2. The *rural* culture of the Roman Empire was replaced by the *urban* culture of the Middle Ages.

_____ 3. The average population of towns in Italy during the tenth century was about 1,000 to 1,500.

_____ 4. A *monk* was a baptized member of the church who disagreed with any official church opinion.

_____ 5. Education fared *better* in Byzantium than in Rome.

_____ 6. Many educated men in the Middle Ages considered *Plato* to be "The Philosopher."

_____ 7. Otto the Great worked together with the pope to establish the *Holy Roman Empire*.

_____ 8. The pope's decision to be elected by other church officials greatly *weakened* his power.

_____ 9. The only book of lasting importance written during the Renaissance was <u>The Prince</u> by *Augustine*.

MATCHING Match the definition with the correct term.

a	saints	*g*	purgatory
b	transubstantiation	*h*	penance
c	Vulgate	*i*	indulgences
d	breviary	*j*	inquisition
e	monasticism	*k*	Black Death
f	friars	*l*	leprosy

____ 1. withdrawing from the world

____ 2. monks who preached and did missionary work outside the monasteries

____ 3. belief that the elements of the Lord's Supper actually change their substance

____ 4. deceased persons officially recognized by the Roman church as holy because of martyrdom or other good deeds

____ 5. certificates excusing a person from doing penance

____ 6. sacrament of punishments for repentant sinners

____ 7. killed one third to one half of the population of Europe

____ 8. place of temporary punishments after death

____ 9. Latin translation of the Bible

____10. book with the order of worship for Roman church services

CONCEPTS TO CONSIDER On a separate sheet of paper, answer the following questions using complete sentences.

1. How were the Middle Ages "Dark Ages" for western Europe?

2. Explain how the Crusades brought changes to Europe that indirectly helped to bring about the Renaissance.

God worked in history to prepare the world for His Son, and nothing has been the same since the Savior came. During the first century A.D., the New Testament was written. For all future generations of mankind, the most important facts of history—Christ's birth, life, death, resurrection, and ascension into Heaven—became the best documented facts as well.

At first, multitudes responded to Christ by accepting God's offer of salvation. With the Bible to rule their faith and practice, the early Christians assembled into local churches to worship with simple reverence. No single man or organization was allowed to dominate the multiplying churches. By A.D. 300, perhaps half the population of the Roman Empire had claimed the name *Christian,* an astounding fact considering the government's fierce, negative response to Christ during these centuries.

Persecution of Christians began during the first century and continued for more than 200 years. With a crumbling economy, invading barbarians, and rebellious armies, the Roman Empire faced a certain end as the *Pax Romana* drew to a close. In desperation, Roman emperors expanded their bureaucracies and intensified their claims to be gods. Because true Christians acknowledge only one true God and bow to no man or government as Savior, persecution was inevitable and severe.

The number of Christians killed, however, could not keep up with the number of new converts, and in the fourth century the Roman government suddenly reversed its response to Christ. In A.D. 313, Emperor Constantine made it legal to be a Christian. For a brief moment in history, Rome and Christianity seemed to be reconciled. But by the end of the fourth century, Christianity had become the *only* legal religion! Soon the Church of Rome and the Roman government were bound in a dangerous alliance, and Christianity became a tool of the state.

It was not the first time that religion had been used for political purposes. But when Rome responded to the one true religion as a political tool, the result was a monstrous distortion of Biblical Christianity. Many hoped that this false religion would at last give the Roman government a solid foundation, but the decline of Rome could not be reversed. By A.D. 500, the Western Roman Empire had fallen to German barbarians.

The Middle Ages began with the fall of Rome and the rise of the Roman Catholic Church. By A.D. 500, the bishop of Rome had been recognized as the pope, the official head of the church and the supreme authority for all Christians. As the Church of Rome gained acceptance, it began to build a vast religious empire with the pope as its emperor.

When men replaced the Bible as the ultimate authority, a new kind of humanism appeared *in the church.* Increasingly complicated worship services exalted the few who presided over them, while the congregation became more and more like spectators with little hope of understanding what they saw and heard. False beliefs about salvation led many to obey a few men who, with Christ in Heaven and not yet returned to visibly govern an earthly kingdom, took it upon themselves to rule the world in His name. Many hoped that Christendom would soon cover the entire planet.

Such hopes were soon shattered by the Arabs who in the A.D. 600s were united as never before by the religion of Islam. Mohammed, founder of this new religion, responded to Christ by utterly rejecting His claim to be God's Son. Refusing to believe the Bible, Mohammed claimed new revelations from the one he called Allah and offered yet another variety of humanism in place of Christianity. Men can earn their way to Heaven by doing the will of Allah, preached Mohammed, and Allah wants all men to be Muslims. Crying "There is no God but Allah, and Moham-med is his prophet," the Muslims charged out of Arabia to fight holy wars. In just over 100 years, they established an empire that stretched from Spain in Europe to India in Asia. But the Muslims were prevented from conquering the whole world (particularly in Europe at the Battle of Tours in 732) and by the 900s, the Muslim empire had crumbled into separate countries. Islam had failed to conquer the world, but it had succeeded in limiting Christianity to Western Europe.

Christendom did not easily accept its defeat by Islam. In the 11th century, after the Seljuk Turks accepted Islam and took most of the Middle East from the Arabs, western Europe launched the Crusades. These holy wars fought in the name of the cross were intended to recover the Holy Land, especially Jerusalem from Islam. But after seven major efforts accomplished nothing permanent, the Crusades ceased in the 13th century. In the 15th century, Ottoman Turks, who had come to dominate the Muslim world, finally destroyed the little that remained of the Eastern Roman Empire, which had remained for about 1,000 years after the fall of Rome. With the fall of Constantinople, Christendom lost even more ground. The Turks kept southeastern Europe on the defensive for about two centuries.

Looking back, we can see how Islam and Christendom checked and balanced one another during the Middle Ages. Islam utterly rejected Christ; Christendom distorted His gospel. Both were forms of humanism, and both combined religion, politics, and conquest in a drive to rule the world. If Islam had won all its holy wars, Christianity might have disappeared altogether. If Christendom had succeeded with its crusades, distorted Christianity might have been imposed upon all mankind. But Christendom largely confined Islam to the Middle East and farther reaches of Asia, while Islam restricted Christendom mainly to western Europe.

With so many events having, in one way or another, been a response to Christ, history's spotlight naturally falls on that small part of the world to which Christianity was restricted during the Middle Ages. Thus the people of western Europe, many of whom were descendants of the German barbarians who conquered Rome, enter as the main actors on the stage of world history. Christendom, for all its faults, still had the Bible. If the simple but powerful truths of the Bible were ever seen again, tremendous progress would be possible in all fields. Unfortunately, distorted Christianity gripped western Europe so tightly that there seemed to be little cause for optimism at the beginning of the Middle Ages.

The invading German tribes had shattered the unity that western Europe had known under Rome, but the old Roman Empire lived on as a dream. Many European leaders—especially popes and would-be emperors—longed for the combination of politics and distorted Christianity that Constantine had contrived. Islam did not let the dream go far in a geographic sense. But the goal of a "Christian" empire encompassing at least western Europe spurred many to action.

The Germanic Franks established the first large empire in western Europe after the fall of Rome. Efforts of the Frankish king Clovis to establish an empire bore considerable fruit during the fifth and sixth centuries. After a period of decline for the Frankish kingdom, the superior leadership of Charles Martel and Pepin the Short reversed the situation in the 700s. The climax came on Christmas Day in the year 800 when Charlemagne, ruler of the largest territory in the West since the Roman emperors of the A.D. 300s, was crowned emperor of the Romans by the pope, and his vast kingdom was called a Christian empire.

From Clovis to Charlemagne, the Frankish rulers had sought to connect their kingdom not only to the memory of the old Roman Empire but to distorted Christianity as well. Thus they struck a bargain with the pope and the Roman Church. With the support of false religious authority, their claims to be kings and emperors were more readily accepted, and their wars of conquest were portrayed as holy wars. Indeed, wherever the kings conquered, the Roman church conquered. From their part of the bargain, popes acquired the armed might to supplement their supposed spiritual authority and better enforce their will. Through this alliance of politics and distorted Christianity, much of western Europe became part of a rebuilt Roman Empire, jointly ruled by pope and emperor. Inevitably and immediately, however, signs of jealousy between pope and emperor appeared, for neither wanted to accept second place to the other in ruling Christendom.

The conflict between pope and emperor in Charlemagne's empire did not have much time to develop. After Charlemagne's death, quarrels from within and attacks from without reduced the new western European empire to shambles by the 900s. Many little kingdoms replaced the empire, and small groups of nobles in each kingdom elected kings. Gradually, a system of feudalism developed in western Europe.

Under the feudal system, everything from politics and war to making a living was tied to the land; people were so closely knit together that they could not live as individuals. Lord and vassal were bound by mutual promises based on the ownership and use of land. The vast majority of people were born and died as serfs, working like slaves from sunrise to sunset on the manors owned by the lords. The nobles, on the other hand, many of them knights who considered war a sport, often found pleasure in an age of violence and chivalry. But serf and lord alike lived under the tyranny of false religion. With the truths of the Bible hidden in darkness, the people of the Middle Ages understood neither freedom in this life nor salvation in the next.

The consequences of spiritual darkness were evident in every area of life. Economic depression impoverished the vast majority of people, feudalism enslaved them, and distorted Christianity controlled them. Some people withdrew into the shadows of monasteries in a desperate effort to please God. Even those who did not become monks, nuns, or friars went through a dreary round of religious motions in a vain effort to earn their salvation. In spite of the Roman church's desire to keep the Bible hidden from most people, some did see the Light. But these were very few, and generally the Church was quick to brand them heretics and through such means as the Inquisition tried to put out that Light. The lamp of learning was also dimmed. Even when it brightened somewhat in the last half of the Middle Ages, scholasticism clouded the mind with a mixture of distorted Christianity and Greek philosophy. In politics, while the remains of Charlemagne's empire rotted away under feudalism, would-be emperors and scheming popes refused to let the dream of a Christian empire stay buried. Though jealous and always quarreling, they fabricated a monster called the Holy Roman Empire that kept much of Europe, especially Germany and Italy, in political chaos during the long night of the Middle Ages.

Dawn first broke in Italy. By 1500, men had begun to recognize the Middle Ages as a time of darkness for the human spirit. Many longed for freedom in a new era. To guide the future, men might have looked to the Bible and to true Christianity. But through the mists of time, only one beacon seemed to shine for the Italians— ancient Greece and Rome. Thus, the *Renaissance*, a rebirth of learning, began in Italy.

Primarily interested in man, the Renaissance Italians naturally focused on the humanities (subjects such as poetry and rhetoric). At first, the term humanism meant only intense interest in such classical studies. But there was always the risk that this humanism would take a danger-ous turn, emphasizing man to the point of neglecting God or even rebelling against Him. There was a serious danger of this kind of humanism in Renaissance Italy, homeland of the Roman church. The Church had already distorted Christianity with humanism by daring to stand between Christ and other men. It would be easy to go one step further and deliberately remove Christ from the picture altogether.

The Renaissance produced some of the greatest art of all times. Renaissance artists succeeded in being far more than imitations of the past; their accomplishments in the arts exceeded those of ancient Greece and Rome. But as great as Renaissance art was, it contained ominous signs. The more they tried to return to the glory and splendor of Greece and Rome, the further Renaissance men went into extreme humanism. In paintings and statues, man began to take on the infinite power and majesty of the one true God Himself. How we respond to Christ determines our fate. As mankind stood on the brink of modern times and a new beginning, the distorted Christianity of the Middle Ages reached a climax with the extreme humanism of the Renaissance.

Fortunately, the Renaissance followed a different course in Northern Europe. There, interest in classical languages led men to study the Scriptures, sparking another, far more important movement. The simple but powerful truths of the Bible would dispel the darkness of the Middle Ages and usher in a new era of world history, the Modern Age.

PART 2

THE MODERN AGE AND THE TWENTIETH CENTURY

(A.D. 1500–THE PRESENT)

Overview of the Modern Age

The Meaning of the Modern Age

World history is divided into three periods: **Ancient History** (c. 4000 B.C.–A.D. 500), the **Middle Ages** (A.D. 500–1500), and the **Modern Age** (A.D. 1500–present). Our study of history has taken us from the ancient Middle East to Medieval Europe, and now we are about to enter the era in which we live, the Modern Age.

An Age of Individual Responsibility

The Modern Age is unique for its emphasis on liberty, individual responsibility, and human progress. In the Modern Age, people began to see and respect others as individuals created by God. This principle of mutual respect and responsibility has guided all that is good about the Modern Age. It has brought about more progress during the last 500 years than mankind had ever known before.

The modern ideas of individual liberty and responsibility under God encourage everyone to do his best, to go as far as his abilities will carry him. The Modern Age unleashed the energy of the individual. As we enter the Modern Age in our study of world history, we will learn this lesson again and again: *Give men who are right with God sufficient freedom and responsibility, and they will take steps that become leaps of progress for their countries and all mankind.*

But we will also learn that there have been many men and movements in the Modern Age that cried freedom but for selfishness, demanding liberty but for evil purposes. *The basis of individual freedom and responsibility is the **inner freedom** and responsibility of men **before God,** and that is the true spirit of the Modern Age.* Only when men are obedient to God are they able to use the freedom that He gives in a responsible, productive way. When a large number of people in a society have a right relationship with God, the entire society benefits and progresses.

An Age of Exploration, Science, and Invention

The world grows. One of the key discoveries of history was made on the very brink of the Modern Age, in *1492,* when **Christopher Columbus** <u>discovered America</u>. Since that time, our understanding of the world in which we live has increased tremendously. Men have sought out and mapped almost all parts of the earth and have even reached beyond the earth to explore the stars. The discoveries of the Modern Age remind us of Daniel's prophecy about the "time of the end," when *"many shall run to and fro, and knowledge shall be increased"* (Dan. 11:4).

Knowledge increases. Our understanding of the world and the universe has also been increased by modern science. Modern science, which began in the 1500s, has given us tremendous insights into the laws that God has established in the universe and how to use them in order to obey His command to master nature for the benefit of mankind (Gen. 1:28). The founders of modern science—magnificent individuals such as *Galileo, Kepler,* and *Newton*—were able to discover the secrets of nature because they rejected medieval philosophy and turned to God's Word for the answers.

Many inventions and discoveries that seem ancient to us today are actually products of the Modern Age. Not until the Modern Age did people know that the earth revolves around the sun and that the planets are held in their orbits because of the universal law of gravitation. During this age, the telescope and the microscope were invented, making it possible for man to look up into the stars and down into the smallest of creatures. Before the Modern Age, people did not know that blood circulates through the body, that the body burns food for energy, or that diseases are often caused by organisms too small for the unaided human eye to see.

Progress in the Modern Age has been so great that many important inventions of the age have already become obsolete. Such modern inventions as the steamboat, the cotton gin, the horseless carriage, and the talking machine have either been replaced or have been so greatly improved that we would hardly recognize the original inventions today. And many products of the Modern Age—telephones, radios, typewriters, automobiles, refrigerators, airplanes, synthetic fabrics, computers—have become so common in our daily lives that we barely notice them.

Books become available. The most important invention in the world actually came just before the Modern Age, and it did much to make the Modern Age possible. The *movable-type printing press*, invented by **Johann Gutenberg** [yǒ·hän gōō′ten·běrk] about *1440,* is the key invention of the Modern Age. Gutenberg's printing press allowed ordinary people to read and think for themselves, one of the greatest prerequisites of liberty. The first book that Gutenberg printed was the Bible, the key book of the Modern Age. **Modern history is really a record of how people have responded to the Bible.** It is no exaggeration to say that all the good in the Modern Age has come about through a correct understanding of the Bible and that all the evil of the age is the result of rejecting the truths of God's Word.

An Age of Great Art, Music, and Literature

The emphasis on individual freedom and responsibility in the Modern Age has made possible unprecedented achievements in art, music, and literature. Individuals with talents for the arts have been able to rise from all classes of people—rich and poor, noble and common—to leave the world a legacy of beauty.

A new world of art. There were some great artists before the Modern Age, such as the great sculptors of ancient Greece or the painters of the Italian Renaissance, but no era can match the Modern Age for quantity, variety, and excellence in all areas of the arts. Most of the greatest painters the world has known—men like Albrecht Dürer, Hans Holbein, Rembrandt van Rijn, Auguste Renoir—have lived in the past 500 years.

A new world of music and literature. Every great musician in the world has been a product of the Modern Age, including such musical giants as Bach, Handel, Haydn, and Beethoven, and the great hymn writers Isaac Watts, Charles Wesley, and Fanny Crosby. Before the Modern Age there were perhaps 25 great writers; the Modern Age has produced well over 200 men and women who are almost universally recognized as authors of great works of literature, including William Shakespeare, John Milton, John Bunyan, Charlotte Brontë, Jane Austen, and Alfred, Lord Tennyson.

The Key Movement of the Modern Age

Importance of religion. The most important factor in any age is the religion of the people. **Religion** determines how people think and, therefore, how they act. **History,** the record of what people have done with the time that God has given them, is therefore very much concerned with religion.

Medieval religion. During the Middle Ages, the majority of Europeans were ruled by a religion that still called itself Christianity, but it was a distorted Christianity that had largely departed from the teachings of the Bible. By A.D. 400, church and state had been united, and the result was that a few religious leaders were placed between God and the rest of the human race. The Bible was kept from the people, and the people were kept from the truth. For the Modern Age to begin, people had to be freed from the domination of the church of Rome.

The Italian Renaissance. Some men tried to throw off the power of the Roman church during the **Italian Renaissance** (c. 1300–1600). But these men looked back to the pagan ideas of Greece and Rome for their inspiration, ignoring the one Book that could give them true freedom. As the Renaissance spread northward to France and Germany, however, it sparked an interest in the study of the Scriptures.

Thus, the Renaissance prepared the way for a more important movement, the Reformation.

The Protestant Reformation. The key movement of the Modern Age was the **Protestant Reformation,** which was started in *1517* by **Martin Luther.** The Reformation was a movement which promoted the true faith of the Bible. *The Reformation marks the beginning of the Modern Age in Europe,* for it made men aware of the true principles of individual liberty and responsibility before God.

An Age of European Culture

As the curtain rises on the Modern Age about A.D. 1500, the spotlight of history falls on Europe. It was there that a *culture* (way of life) substantially influenced by Biblical Christianity began and went on to sweep much of the globe—a force of progress and advancement for the whole human race.

CHECK UP

1. Into what three periods is world history divided? Give the dates for each.
2. What three things does the Modern Age emphasize?
3. What is the true spirit of the Modern Age?
4. What was the first book printed on Gutenberg's press?
5. What is the key book of the Modern Age? Explain.
6. What is the most important factor in any age?
7. What does religion determine about people?
8. Define history.
9. What was the main religion in Europe during the Middle Ages?
10. What was the key movement of the Modern Age?

Identify: Christopher Columbus, 1492, Johann Gutenberg, movable-type printing press, modern science, Italian Renaissance, Martin Luther, 1517

Switzerland wins independence **1499**

Da Gama sails around Africa to India **1498**
European influence in Asia begins

Columbus discovers New World **1492**

Spanish Inquisition established **1480**

1516 Erasmus publishes first
printed N.T. in original Greek

1517 Luther posts Ninety-five Theses,
sparking Protestant Reformation

1529 English Reformation
begins under Henry VIII

1275 Marco Polo
reaches Peking,
China

Scandinavia **1397**
united under
Danish rule

1300

1400

1500

1280 Kublai Khan
establishes Yuan
dynasty in China

c. 1440
Gutenberg invents movable-
type printing press

Cortés conquers **1521**
Aztecs in Mexico

Peasants' Revolt **1524–25**
in Germany

1558 Elizabeth I becomes
Queen of England

1533 Pizarro conquers
Incas in Peru

1526 Mogul Empire
established in India

1337–1453
Hundred Years' War *(France vs. England)*

Unit 4

BEGINNING OF THE MODERN AGE
(A.D. 1500–1800)

The World Changes

13 The Protestant Reformation
14 Post-Reformation Europe
15 The English Nation
16 An Age of Exploration: Asia and the Americas
17 The United States—A New Kind of Nation
18 France in the Modern Age

588 England defeats Spanish Armada

1620 Pilgrims arrive in New England

1661 Louis XIV establishes absolute monarchy in France

U.S. Constitution ratified **1789**

American **1776** Declaration of Independence

1792 William Carey goes to India, beginning modern missions movement

1799 Napoleon comes to power in France

1814 Congress of Vienna

1600

1700

1800

1618–48 Thirty Years' War *(Protestants vs. Catholics)*

1688 Glorious Revolution in England

Great Awakening **1734** begins in America

1789–99 French Revolution

1775–83 American War for Independence *(American colonies vs. England)*

1804–1813 Napoleonic Wars

1850s Peak of Second Great Awakening in America

13
The Protestant Reformation
(c. 1400–1600)

HIGHLIGHTS

Forerunners of the Reformation • John Wycliffe • John Huss
Inquisition • Gutenberg and the Printing Press • Erasmus • Martin Luther

Preparation for the Modern Age

Lights in the Dark Ages

Medieval groups. During the Middle Ages, many groups rose up to protest the way the established Roman church was distorting the truth and denying people access to the Word of God.

One group that arose as glowing lights during the dark Middle Ages were the **Petrobrusians** [pĕt′rȯ·brōō′zhanz]. They were named for **Peter of Bruis** [brōō′ē], a Roman priest in the early 1100s. By reading the Bible for himself, Bruis was led to reject the Roman church in favor of God's Word. After preaching for 20 years in *Southern France,* he was burned at the stake for his faith. His life is a testimony to the fact that a man in any age can find truth if he has the Bible. Across the centuries, the light of the Petrobrusians continues to glow, undimmed by error.

Another group, the **Waldensians** [wŏl·dĕn′sĭ·anz], originated during the late 1100s in the Alps mountains of Europe. They were named for **Peter Waldo,** a prosperous French merchant. About 1170, Peter Waldo came to the conviction that Scripture is the sole authority for Christians. At his own expense, he had the Bible translated into the people's language. He and his followers, the Waldensians, rejected the Roman claim that ordinary people would be corrupted if they read the Bible for themselves. They struggled to get the Scriptures to as many people as possible and seized every opportunity to do so.

Some Waldensians traveled as peddlers, selling fabrics, jewelry, and other goods. When a customer asked if he had anything else, the peddler would reply, "Yes, great rarities; I have one precious stone through which you can see God, and another that kindles love to him in the heart." At that point, he would bring out the Bible.

The Waldensians were especially numerous in the Alps areas of *Italy, France,* and *Switzerland,* but they soon spread throughout Europe. At one time or another, they lived all over the continent and even in England.

In 1487, the pope announced a crusade against the Waldensians. But in 1500, as modern times were beginning, many Waldensians were still living in the French and Italian valleys of the Alps. In fact, there are still people today who call themselves Waldensians.

John Wycliffe in England. We have already been introduced to John Wycliffe (c. 1329–1384), who challenged the Roman church in 14th-century England. The clear teaching of Scripture convinced Wycliffe, a

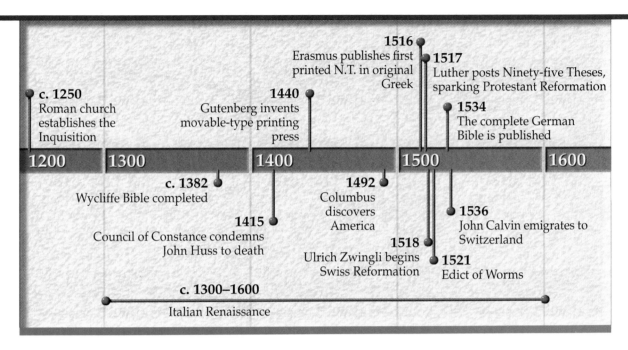

1516
Erasmus publishes first printed N.T. in original Greek

1517
Luther posts Ninety-five Theses, sparking Protestant Reformation

c. 1250
Roman church establishes the Inquisition

1440
Gutenberg invents movable-type printing press

1534
The complete German Bible is published

| 1200 | 1300 | 1400 | 1500 | 1600 |

c. 1382
Wycliffe Bible completed

1492
Columbus discovers America

1536
John Calvin emigrates to Switzerland

1415
Council of Constance condemns John Huss to death

1518
Ulrich Zwingli begins Swiss Reformation

1521
Edict of Worms

c. 1300–1600
Italian Renaissance

professor at *Oxford University*, that the church was greatly distorting true Christianity. Believing that ordinary people should read the Bible for themselves, he had the entire Bible translated into English for the first time. It was his hope that a Bible would someday be available to every man who could read. All copies of the Wycliffe translation were made by hand, because the printing press had not yet been invented.

At first, English authorities, including Oxford University, supported Wycliffe, and the pope's call for his arrest went unanswered. However, the Roman church was still strong in England. Under Wycliffe's leadership, what we would consider a "revival" today broke out among the people, and many joined Wycliffe in denouncing worldly, hypocritical, and repressive church officials. The authorities, fearful of what was happening, backed away from Wycliffe. His books were banned, and priests, monks, and friars harassed him until his death in 1384.

But the Roman church was not satisfied that Wycliffe was dead. In 1409, a meeting of church leaders in London condemned Wycliffe's beliefs and his translation of the Bible. After 1414, anyone who read the Bible in English could have his "land, cattle, life and goods" taken away from him. In 1415, the Council of Constance condemned Wycliffe for over 200 "crimes" and ordered his writings burned. In 1428, the pope commanded that Wycliffe's remains be dug up and burned as well.

The fruit of Wycliffe's work could not be destroyed, however. His followers, called **Lollards** [lŏl′ērdz], faced severe persecution for years. But as the Modern Age began in 1500, there were still Lollards and copies of the Wycliffe Bible in England. By putting the Word of God into the hands of the English people, Wycliffe did more to alter English history than any soldiers or kings of his day. For this, he is known as the *Morning Star of the Reformation.*

John Huss in Bohemia. We have also been introduced to John Huss (c. 1374–1415), who began a revival of Biblical Christianity in Bohemia (the modern Czech Republic).

203

Modern Men Before the Modern Age

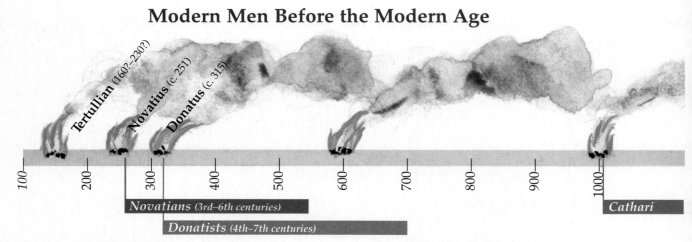

Tertullian (160?–230?)   Novatius (c. 251)   Donatus (c. 315)

100 — 200 — 300 — 400 — 500 — 600 — 700 — 800 — 900 — 1000

Novatians (3rd–6th centuries)

Donatists (4th–7th centuries)

Cathari

"... an uninterrupted succession of witnesses" The story of how the Bible illuminated believers during the Middle Ages brightens an otherwise dark age. Many Christians have been thrilled by the history of these people—persecuted and reviled by the established religious leaders, their martyrdom leaves a trail of blood leading across the centuries to the believers of today.

Huss studied philosophy and theology at the *University of Prague* [präg], where he eventually became dean of the philosophy department and headmaster of the university. As he read the writings of Wycliffe, Huss came to share many of that Englishman's views. Like Wycliffe, Huss considered the Bible to be the only true authority for Christians. Not priests but only God, he said, can forgive sin, and salvation comes only through Christ.

In addition to teaching and writing, Huss also preached at the large *Bethlehem Chapel* in Prague. He spoke not in Latin but in the native language of the people. Support for Huss came from all levels of society—from the common people to the wife of the king. Soon, a movement for true Christianity broke out in the country of Bohemia.

John Huss's message and the support he received from the people alarmed the Roman church. In 1415, church leaders summoned Huss to the Council of Constance in Switzerland to defend his beliefs. There he declared his willingness to be informed of any mistakes, but he also made it known that he would not say anything that offended God. "If anyone," said Huss, "can instruct me by the sacred Scriptures or

by good reasoning, I am willing to follow him. ... I have made it a rule to joyfully and humbly recede from a former opinion when in any matter I perceive a more rational opinion."

Though Huss had come to Constance with a safe-conduct guarantee, the Council condemned him to death. As he burned at the stake, Huss said, "Lord, into Thy hand I commend my spirit."

The burning of Huss did not accomplish its objectives. It only caused his doctrine to spread, and his followers, called **Hussites,** to increase. Through such groups as the **Bohemian Brethren** and the **Moravians** (famous for their missionary activities), the influence of the Hussites reaches even to the present day.

The Hussite movement was too strong to be stamped out. Hussite nobles and common people stood ready to defend themselves against any ruler—pope, emperor, or king—who would try to deprive them of their free exercise of religion. By 1500, in an age of powerful kings, Bohemia had achieved a surprising degree of political freedom. The Light of the gospel made Bohemia one of the few bright spots in Europe as the Modern Age began.

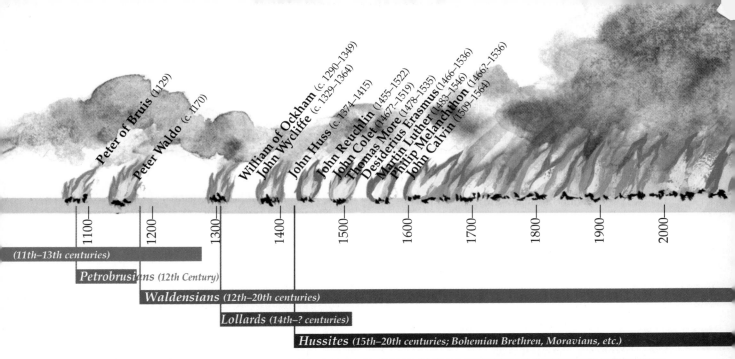

Peter of Bruis (1129)
Peter Waldo (c. 1170)
William of Ockham (c. 1290–1349)
John Wycliffe (c. 1329–1364)
John Huss (c. 1374–1415)
John Reuchlin (1455–1522)
John Colet (1467?–1519)
Thomas More (1478–1535)
Desiderius Erasmus (1466–1536)
Martin Luther (1483–1546)
Philip Melanchthon (1467–1536)
John Calvin (1509–1564)

(11th–13th centuries)
Petrobrusians (12th Century)
Waldensians (12th–20th centuries)
Lollards (14th–? centuries)
Hussites (15th–20th centuries; Bohemian Brethren, Moravians, etc.)

The Inquisition

In the mid-1200s the Roman church established a special church court known as the **Inquisition.** The job of the Inquisition was <u>to investigate matters of alleged heresy</u> and to mete out proper punishment for convicted heretics. Those classified as **heretics** were *any baptized members of the Roman church who disagreed with any official church opinion*.

Although the Inquisition was not officially established until the mid-1200s, its origins can be traced back to the merger of church and state around A.D. 400. With the power of the government at its service, the church could persecute all who opposed it.

When an **inquisitor** arrived in an area, he called for reports of anyone suspected of heresy. Sometimes he offered rewards to spies who would report suspected heretics. Those suspected were imprisoned to await trials. The trials were held in secret, and the inquisitor acted as judge, prosecutor, and jury. The accused had no lawyer. It was often simpler to confess to heresy than to defend oneself, especially since torture was often employed until a confession was made. Husbands, wives, and children were forced to testify against accused heretics. Even the testimony of criminals was acceptable evidence of guilt.

Possible punishments included attending a certain number of masses, wearing specially designed crosses as a symbol of heresy, being whipped, or being imprisoned. Anyone who fell back into heresy after repentance was turned over by the Inquisition to the regular government to be put to death. Most of those condemned to death were burned at the stake; others were beaten to death or drowned.

Although the Inquisition did its work throughout Europe, the main center of activity before 1480 was southern France. After 1480, most of the atrocities took place in Spain. The bloodshed continued throughout the 1400s and into the 1500s and 1600s.

The Inquisition was called the *sanctum officium* (Holy Office) because the church considered its work so praiseworthy.

205

CHECK UP

1. Name two groups in the Middle Ages that stood for the truth of the Scriptures.
2. For whom were the Petrobrusians named?
3. For whom were the Waldensians named? Where did they live?
4. When was the Inquisition established? What was its purpose?
5. What was Wycliffe's greatest contribution to the English people?
6. How did the people respond to Wycliffe's work? How did the church respond?
7. Name the Bohemian preacher who shared Wycliffe's beliefs. How did the people respond to his preaching? How was he punished?

Identify: heretics, "Morning Star of the Reformation," Lollards, Bohemian Brethren, Moravians

---

The Renaissance

Italian Renaissance. God used many men and movements to prepare the world for the Protestant Reformation. One such movement was the **Italian Renaissance,** which began about 1300 and lasted until about 1600. As we have learned, the Renaissance in Italy was a "rebirth" of learning that focused primarily on the classical books of ancient Greece and Rome and on the classical languages (Greek and Latin) in which those books were originally written. Attention centered on subjects such as history, grammar, rhetoric (the art of speaking), poetry, and philosophy, subjects collectively known as the *humanities* because they involve the study of man.

Northern Renaissance. By 1500, this rebirth of learning had spread from Italy north into other parts of Europe, and a

movement known as the **Northern Renaissance** had begun in such countries as Germany, France, the Netherlands, and England. Like their counterparts in Italy, the northern scholars avidly studied the classical books on the humanities as well as the classical languages.

But these northern scholars realized that there is no book about man or any other subject more important than the Bible.

Johann Gutenberg and the Printing Press

Most important invention in history. The revival of learning in Renaissance Italy was largely for the benefit of a select few. But in the north, the Renaissance was much more than merely an affair of scholars and college professors.

The Protestant Reformation grew out of the Northern Renaissance, partly because of the printing press.

Johann Gutenberg (1400?–1468) invented the *movable-type printing press* about **1440** in Mainz, Germany.

Fitted to European languages. The Chinese had developed printing methods centuries earlier, but the cumbersome picture language of China made printing

Johann Gutenberg with Movable-type Printing Press: the most important invention in the history of the world.

by movable type impractical because a different symbol would have to be made for every single word in the language. The alphabetical languages of Europe, however, seemed to have been especially prepared for Gutenberg's movable-type press. All the printer had to do was make a few metal characters for each letter of the alphabet. He could then arrange the letters in the right order, ink them, and print as many copies of the page as he needed. The same characters could be rearranged for the next page. This was much more practical than the old block printing method. In block printing, each page had to be carved of wood and then discarded when the printing was done.

Just when the world needed it. The timing of Gutenberg's invention is of great significance to the Modern Age. As one historian explained it,

---

Printing came when the world had need of it, when it could have value. It came in about 1440; in season for the grand events about to be unfolded. It had no relation to the present. The great mass of the people could not read; and if they had been able to read, there was nothing to print that would have been of value. The monasteries were in possession of many of the ancient manuscripts, but they contained nothing which was of interest to the masses. It might have been of some use in distributing the official papers of the higher religious authorities to their subordinates; there might, and probably would have been found for it, certain clerical uses, but nothing which would reach the body of the people. A little more than half a century later, Columbus was to discover the western continent; in three-quarters of a century, the Reformation was to make its appearance, and then there would be a use for the printing-press. The masses would begin to think, and when this should be the case, they would need books.

Gutenberg himself had a very special reason for all the work he put into inventing the printing press. "God suffers because there are such multitudes of souls to whom His sacred Word cannot be given."

In 1456, Gutenberg <u>produced the first printed edition of the Bible</u> (the Vulgate). It is called the **Gutenberg Bible** in his honor. By 1500, when the Modern Age began, printing presses were operating in nearly every country in Europe. In fact, by 1500 there were an estimated 9 million books in Europe in contrast to just a few thousand manuscripts before that time.

Scholars in northern Europe especially welcomed the printing press, for they wanted men in all walks of life to benefit from their scholarship. The printing press would make it possible for every person to have a Bible. And God was going to use these scholars, one in particular, to prepare a text of the New Testament in the original language, suitable for translating God's Word into languages the people could read.

Erasmus: Scholar of Scholars

By far, <u>the most famous figure of the Northern Renaissance</u> was **Desiderius Erasmus** [dĕs′ĭ·dēr′ĭ·*us* ĕ·răz′m*us*: 1466?–1536], a scholar from the Netherlands. Erasmus lived and studied all over Europe—in Germany, France, England, Italy, and Switzerland—and came to know (either in person or through letters) nearly every

Desiderius Erasmus: a portrait by Hans Holbein the Younger.

major scholar. They learned from him, he learned from them, and the admiration was mutual. He was the scholar of scholars.

Bible study convinced Erasmus that the Roman church had distorted Christianity. As he looked back over church history, Erasmus could see how the distortion of the faith by politics, force, and violence, with the confusion of church and state, was connected with neglect of the Bible. He hoped that if enough people saw this, things would change.

As Erasmus read the original Greek text of the New Testament, he discovered that the Latin Vulgate had many errors. Thus, in March 1516, he published the first printed edition of the New Testament in the original Greek. Erasmus hoped that other scholars would use his Greek text to translate the Scriptures into languages that the people could read. By the time Erasmus died in 1536, his wish had come true: scholars were translating the Bible into many different languages, and printing presses were making Bibles available to more and more people.

"Such a light has been shed abroad"

The Northern Renaissance, with Erasmus at the forefront, led straight to the Protestant Reformation. "Since the revival of learning," wrote Luther,

---

such a light has been shed abroad, and such important changes have taken place that the world is astonished, and must acknowledge that we have the Gospel . . . as pure and unadulterated as it was in time of the apostles.

As the Modern Age began, the Roman church had not changed its mind about the Bible. The command of the Council of Toulouse in 1229, forbidding ordinary people to own a Bible, was still in effect. But in the new era that was dawning, more people than ever would hear the truth that can make men free.

Martin Luther and the Protestant Reformation

The story of how the Protestant Reformation began is the story of individuals who searched for the truth about salvation and found it in God's Word. It is the story of one man in particular who knew that he was personally responsible to God—a man who was willing to step out and stand alone for what is right against the Church of Rome and the Holy Roman Empire. It is the story of a man who gave the Modern Age a model of spiritual freedom.

Search for Truth

Luther's crisis. **Martin Luther** (1483–1546) had reached a crisis. He had confessed that he hated God. Nothing he did seemed sufficient. Doubts about salvation gnawed at Luther. What were his good deeds in the sight of a Holy God? Luther despaired of loving a God Who, it seemed, was sending him to hell without a chance. Luther did everything that the Roman church told him a Christian ought to do, yet he never experienced a sense of forgiveness in his own soul, only guilt and condemnation.

Education at Erfurt. Luther graduated from the **University of Erfurt** [ĕr′fŏŏrt] in 1505, with his bachelor's and master's degrees in liberal arts. He had earned both degrees in the minimum amount of time required; only the most diligent students could do that. Fellow students called Luther an "erudite [learned] philosopher." In spiritual matters, however, Martin Luther had not yet found the answers.

After graduating from Erfurt, Luther planned to study law, but God had other plans for him. One hot summer day in 1505, lightning struck Luther down. As he fell from his horse, he cried out, "St. Anne, help me; I will become a monk."

Monastic life. Death's close call made eternity more vivid than ever to Luther.

Martin Luther Studying at Erfurt

Abandoning his plans to become a lawyer, Luther plunged into monasticism. He struggled to make himself acceptable to God and to earn the salvation of his soul. He went without food for days, stayed awake all night to say his prayers, and confessed his sins to a fellow monk over and over again. It was during this time Luther confessed that he hated God, for he knew that all that he did as a monk to justify himself before God was not enough.

"The just shall live by faith." Still searching for an answer, Martin Luther enrolled at *Wittenberg* [vĭt′en·bĕrk] *University* in 1508, and by 1512, he had received his doctorate. Soon he became a professor at the university. It was at Wittenberg that Luther, for the first time in his life, began a serious study of the Bible.

In 1515, Luther began a series of lectures on Romans. His studies climaxed when he finally understood Romans 1:16 and 17,

For I am not ashamed of the gospel of Christ; for it is the power of God unto salvation to every one that believeth . . . For therein is the right-

eousness of God revealed from faith to faith: as it is written, **The just shall live by faith.**

Thus Martin Luther came to realize that a man is saved not by his own works but by faith in the finished work of Christ on the cross. At last, Luther found assurance of his salvation.

Ninety-five Theses

Tetzel and indulgences. In 1517, a friar named **Tetzel** [tĕt′sel] traveled through Germany selling *indulgences,* certificates from the pope that excused a person from doing penance and shortened the required stay in purgatory before going to heaven. **Albert of Brandenburg** [brän′den·bŏŏrk], a German aristocrat, had just *purchased* the leading church office in Germany. (The practice of purchasing church offices [positions] is called *simony.*) To reimburse Albert, Pope **Leo X** (1513–1521) permitted the sale of indulgences in Germany. One half of the money would go to Albert, the other half to the pope for constructing a church building named for St. Peter in Rome. (This was the same St. Peter's Cathedral that stands in Rome today.)

Tetzel was clever; as he sold the indulgences he did not mention that Albert would receive any of the money. He also carried the idea of indulgences to new extremes. Any buyer, said Tetzel, would immediately be released from *all* punishment for his sins, and any friends in purgatory would be immediately freed to go to heaven. According to the slogan attributed to Tetzel, "As soon as the coin in the coffer rings, the soul from purgatory springs!"

Just a year before this, Luther had preached against indulgences. Thanks to his study of the Bible, Luther was now able to see through many of the false beliefs and practices of the Roman church. The pope had once offered indulgences to anyone who went to look at a famous collection of relics in Wittenberg—*and* made a required contribution in money. That was bad enough, but Tetzel's shameful selling tactics made Luther angry.

Luther's challenge. On October 31, 1517, Luther served notice that he was ready to debate about indulgences. It was the day before All Saints Day, when indulgences were again to be proclaimed in Wittenberg. Luther went to the church in Wittenberg and nailed a list of statements called the **Ninety-five Theses** [thē'sēz: statements, propositions] to the church door. (Church doors were commonly used to post public notices.) This act put into motion events that would change the course of world history.

The Protestant Reformation

The movement Luther began in **1517** is called the **Protestant Reformation** because Luther and others *protested* the corrupt practices of the Roman church and at first sought to *reform* it rather than to withdraw from it. The followers of this movement are called **Protestants.** Many brave men and women had challenged the Roman church over the centuries, preparing the way. By 1517, the world was ripe for the Reformation and ready for a man like Martin Luther.

At first, Luther did not intend to break with the pope or the church. His Ninety-five Theses merely attacked the way indulgences had been abused. Luther felt that people who believed that indulgences could save them had a false sense of security. He also felt that the pope should find another way to fund his building projects:

> The pope's riches at this day far exceed the wealth of the richest millionaires: cannot he therefore build one single basilica of St. Peter out of his own money, rather than out of the money of the faithful poor?

But Luther did not attack the office of the pope, or even the church's teaching on purgatory, at this time.

Luther had intended his Theses merely to start discussion among churchmen and scholars like himself. But within a few months the Theses had been translated into German from the Latin that Luther had originally used, and copies began to roll off the printing press. Distributed widely, the Theses struck many people favorably. Luther had skillfully said what many people were thinking. The controversy grew, but Luther was not one to back down. Gradually, the full extent of his disagreement with the Roman church became clear.

CHECK UP

1. Who invented the movable-type printing press? When?
2. Why was the timing just right for this invention? What reason did the inventor give for his invention?
3. What was the first printed edition of the Bible called? When was it printed?
4. What scholar published the first printed edition of the New Testament in the original Greek? How was his New Testament used?
5. When and why did Martin Luther decide to be a monk?
6. At what university was Luther a professor?
7. What passage in Romans led Luther to assurance of his salvation?
8. Who was Tetzel? What did he do that angered Luther?
9. What did Luther do on October 31, 1517 that sparked the Protestant Reformation?
10. Why is the movement that Luther began called the *Protestant Reformation?*

Identify: Northern Renaissance, Erfurt, Wittenberg, indulgences, purgatory, simony, Ninety-five Theses

Luther versus Pope and Church

The pope reacts. When Pope Leo X received a copy of Luther's Theses, he charged Luther with heresy and contempt of church authority. In the summer of 1518, the pope summoned Luther to Rome to answer these charges. Luther knew that to go to Rome charged with heresy meant either death or life imprisonment.

Meeting at Augsburg. Luther appealed to **Frederick the Wise,** the prince of Luther's part of Germany. Frederick decided that Luther should receive a hearing on German soil in connection with a meeting of the **diet,** an assembly of princes and high church officials in the Holy Roman Empire. Fortunately for Luther, the Diet of **Augsburg** [ouks'book] was at odds with papacy because popes had been taking much money from Germany to spend on crusades and other projects.

At Augsburg, the pope's representative tried to get Luther to retract (take back) some of his Theses, but Luther refused. Luther boldly told the cardinal that *popes can make mistakes.* He also said that the **papal bull** (official declaration by the pope) used by those who favored indulgences *was contrary to Scripture and should be rejected.* Finally, Luther appealed *above* the pope, saying that his case should be considered by a church council.

Debate at Leipzig. In July 1519, Luther debated **Johann Eck,** a Roman theologian and university professor at the *University of Leipzig* [līp'sĭk]. This debate forced Luther to clarify his views on the Roman church and the papacy. As a result of his study, he made these declarations:

(1) Neither the pope nor the church councils are infallible.
(2) The Church of Rome is not supreme over other churches.
(3) The Bible is the only authority for Christians.

Bible study and tracts. Luther plunged into more Bible study and, in 1520, wrote a series of tracts. These tracts written in ordinary German were printed and circulated widely. Returning to the Bible as the true basis for Christian beliefs, Luther rejected the teachings of the Roman church. In *To the Christian Nobility of the German Nation,* Luther attacked the "walls" that the Roman church had built. The first wall he described as the superiority of popes, bishops, priests, and monks over ordinary Christians. Against this wall he hurled the teaching that as far as God is concerned, all Christian believers are priests. The second wall Luther described was the pope's claim to sole right to interpret the Scripture. Luther used the "priesthood of all believers" to bring down this wall as well. Every true believer, said Luther, is competent to read the Bible for himself. "It belongs to each and every Christian," said Luther, "to know and judge of doctrine."

During the Modern Age, the doctrine of the priesthood of the believer affected not only the spiritual awakening but all other aspects of life and learning as well. Elevating the common man with dignity, responsibility, and spiritual freedom, this doctrine eventually bore fruit in academics, politics, and economics. Our freedom and responsibility under God is the basis for all human dignity and liberty.

In *The Freedom of the Christian Man,* Martin Luther addressed himself directly to the pope:

> One thing and one thing alone is necessary for life, justification, and Christian liberty: and that is the most holy Word of God, the Gospel of Christ.

Luther was rediscovering the true Christianity of the Bible.

Justification by faith
The priesthood of all believers
The authority of the Bible as God's Word
The right of each Christian to read the Bible for himself

Luther said nothing new; he simply revealed that the walls the Roman church had erected between man and Christ were a distortion of the Word of God. He only tried to restate the Bible. Many had died during the Middle Ages for the same thing, but now the world began to listen.

The pope responds. The pope heard Luther's message loud and clear. He compared Luther to a wild boar, condemned 41 of his "errors," and ordered his books to be burned. He then gave Luther 60 days to recant (renounce) his "heresies."

But Martin Luther did not recant. On the morning of December 10, 1520, when the 60 days had passed, Luther and his followers stood before a bonfire just outside Wittenberg. There, Luther threw into the flames a number of books that supported the pope, as well as the papal bull giving him 60 days to recant.

On January 3, 1521, the pope excommunicated Luther (cut him off from membership in the church). The pope had no power of his own by which to silence Luther, however. For that, he would have to depend upon rulers in Germany, particularly the new emperor of the Holy Roman Empire.

Luther versus Emperor

In March 1521, Emperor **Charles V** (ruled 1519–1556) of the powerful *Hapsburg* family, agreed that Luther should come to the diet that would meet in the city of **Worms** [vôrms]. The emperor promised to give Luther a fair hearing and guaranteed his safety to and from Worms. Luther had defied the pope; now he would have to face the emperor, the most powerful man in European politics. As a horse-drawn carriage carried Luther to Worms, people gathered along the side of the road to catch a glimpse of the courageous monk.

The Diet of Worms. At Worms, Luther boldly stood before the emperor and refused to recant. The time had come for Luther to take his stand. He spoke first in German, and then repeated his statement in Latin. The chains of the Middle Ages snapped as Luther said:

> Unless I am convicted by Scripture and plain reason—I do not accept the authority of popes and councils, for they have contradicted each other—my conscience is captive to the Word of God. I cannot and I will not recant anything, for to go against conscience is neither right nor safe. God help me. Amen.

The Edict of Worms. On May 26, 1521, the furious emperor issued the **Edict of Worms,** declaring Luther a heretic. No subject of the emperor was to give Luther any lodging, food, or drink. He was to be taken prisoner and turned over to the emperor so that both he and his books could be destroyed.

Having been excommunicated by the Roman church and outlawed by the Holy Roman Empire, Luther left Worms. He still had a few days of safe conduct guaranteed, but he knew better than to trust his adversaries. Years before, John Huss had received a safe conduct guarantee, and he had been burned at the stake. On the way back to Wittenberg, Luther and his party were intercepted by a band of masked men on horseback. Luther was spirited away, and the rumor spread through Germany that he had been killed.

Luther's Reforms

Contrary to rumor, Luther had not been killed. A sympathetic German nobleman, Frederick the Wise, had arranged a pretended kidnapping in order to protect Luther from harm. From April 1521 to March 1522, Luther, disguised as *"Knight George,"* hid in **Wartburg** [värt'bŏork] **Castle.**

A German Bible. The break with Rome was now complete. At Wartburg Castle, Luther began his first great task: to give the German people a substitute for papal authority—the Word of God in their own language. Using Erasmus's Greek New Testament, he translated the New Testament into German, completing his first draft in 11 weeks. The first edition rolled off the presses in 1522. At last, the German people had a Bible that they could read for themselves.

After returning to Wittenberg at the invitation of the town government, Luther began to translate the Old Testament from Hebrew into German. *The complete German Bible was finally published in 1534.*

Reforms in education. Of course, a German Bible was of little value if the people could not read. After Luther left Wartburg in April 1522 to return to Wittenberg, he worked diligently to promote **popular education** (the education of all people rather than just a privileged few).

With the Reformation, popular education became a major concern for the first time in world history. In 1524, Luther published his famous treatise, *To the Councilmen of All Cities in Germany that They Establish and Maintain Christian Schools.* He called upon the governing authorities in German cities and towns to set up schools for the education of their young people (including girls, who had been excluded from almost all formal education until this time in history). In addition, Luther called for the establish-

ment of public libraries. *This emphasis on popular education distinguishes the Modern Age from all previous eras,* and the Reformation made the difference.

Higher education also received much direction from the Reformation. When the **University of Wittenberg** was reorganized in the 1530s, it became the first Protestant university. It consisted of a liberal arts college with graduate schools in theology, law, and medicine. Biblical studies replaced the early study of scholastic philosophy and theology.

New church services. Luther perceived that, since all believers are priests, church services would have to change drastically.

- No longer could services be completely dominated by one man calling himself *the* priest.
- Services ought to be conducted in the language of the people rather than Latin, a language known only to the priest.
- Preachers are shepherds, and they should not wear elaborate ceremonial clothes that make them look more like kings than preachers. As for "priests and bishops":

. . . they are neither higher nor better than other Christians. Therefore they should not impose any law or decree on others without their will and consent. . . .

Luther with His Family: *Martin Luther eventually married Katharina, a former nun, and became the father of six children. Here they are pictured at Wittenberg on Christmas Eve, 1536.*

- In the Lord's Supper, all believers should participate, eating *and* drinking, as the Bible commands.
- Sermons should be given a prominent place in the services. Since all believers are priests, they should be instructed by men preaching the Bible.
- For instruction and worship, all believers—the whole congregation, not just a leader, not just a choir—ought to sing.

Hymns and spiritual songs. If the people were going to sing, they needed songs. Thus, Luther compiled a hymnbook. He wrote the words for 23 of the songs himself and even composed the music for some. Luther explained that he gave the German people their own Bible and their own hymnbook so that "God might speak directly to them in His Word, and that they might speak directly to Him in their songs." Luther's most famous hymn, **"A Mighty Fortress Is Our God,"** is still sung in many churches today.

Luther's ideas about the importance of music caused the whole Western world to "break forth into singing." Germany became the musical center of the world and produced the greatest musicians the world has ever known, beginning with the three leading German musicians of the post-Reformation period: *Heinrich Schütz* (1585–1672), *Johann Sebastian Bach* (1685–1750), and *George Friedrich Handel* (1685–1759).

The Reformation Spreads

Zwingli in Zurich (1518–1531)

In addition to the **Lutherans,** as those who followed Luther were called, many other kinds of Protestants soon appeared in Europe. Some of the most influential Protestant groups arose in *Switzerland,* the land of snowcapped mountains to the south of Germany. By the time of the Reformation, Switzerland had, after many years of struggle, won its independence from the Holy Roman Empire and the ruling Hapsburg family.

In the early 1500s, Switzerland consisted of several major cities (Zurich, Basel, Bern, Lausanne, and Geneva) and thirteen provinces called *cantons.* The cantons were united in the **Swiss Confederation,** but they were independent of one another, almost like separate countries. Some cantons enjoyed considerable political freedom, permitting the people a greater role in government than anywhere else in Europe at that time. It was in this atmosphere of freedom and diversity that a priest named **Ulrich Zwingli** [ŭl′rĭk tsvĭng′lē: 1484–1531] stepped forward in 1518 to attack the sale of indulgences.

When Zwingli was appointed to the post of "people's priest" in the city of **Zurich** [zōōr′ĭk], he announced that he would begin his duties by preaching through the book of Matthew in the New Testament. In Zwingli's day, priests customarily celebrated the mass in church services; the preaching of the Bible was virtually unheard of. Zwingli's bold action marked the beginning of the Reformation in Zurich. Returning to the Bible as the sole standard of faith and practice and to Christ as the only true Head of the church, Zwingli attacked one Roman doctrine after another. Under Zwingli's leadership, the Reformation spread throughout Switzerland.

Calvin in Geneva (1536–1564)

When King Francis I adopted a policy to halt the Reformation in France, **John Calvin** (1509–1564), like many other French Protestants, was forced to flee his native land. Calvin took refuge in the city of **Basel** [bä′zel], Switzerland, where he undertook a detailed study of the Bible, the writings of the early church fathers, and the works of Martin Luther. The French reformer gradually developed his under-

Ulrich Zwingli   *John Calvin*

standing of the Bible into an organized system of beliefs based on a few basic points of doctrine. The result was his famous work, *The Institutes of the Christian Religion,* which was probably the single most influential book of the Protestant Reformation apart from the Bible.

Calvin soon had the opportunity to put many of his ideas into practice in the city of **Geneva** [je·nē′və], Switzerland, where the Reformation had come earlier. Calvin spent most of the next 28 years in Geneva—writing, preaching, and influencing every aspect of the city's life.

Exiled Protestants from all over Europe found refuge in Geneva, and many Protestant leaders from other lands came to the city for training in the basics of faith and practice, so that Geneva soon became known as **"Protestant Rome."** The Scottish Reformer **John Knox,** who spent several years in exile in Geneva, called the city "the most perfect school of Christ."

By the time of his death in 1564, John Calvin's influence had spread far and wide. Today the Presbyterians and the churches that are called Reformed (the Dutch Reformed Church, the Christian Reformed Church, and the Reformed Church in America, for example) look back to Calvin as their founder. But over the centuries, many Christians of other denominations as well have considered themselves **"Calvinists."**

Anabaptists

Beginning about 1525, there arose in Switzerland a group of Protestants called **Anabaptists,** the spiritual descendants of groups who during the Middle Ages and even earlier had been called by that name. The name *Anabaptist* means "rebaptizer." Most of those who were called Anabaptists believed that only believers should be baptized. Often the Anabaptists would rebaptize people who had been baptized as infants. Anabaptist communities eventually sprang up throughout Switzerland, Germany, southern France, Holland, eastern Europe, and the British Isles.

Today, Protestants of many different denominations show the influence of Anabaptist ideas. The **Mennonites,** for example, trace their lineage directly back to **Menno Simons,** an Anabaptist preacher in Holland who, in April, 1535, "turned to the Lord in penitence and faith and was fully changed." By far, the largest group of Christians today who look back to the Anabaptists are **Baptists.** The name *Baptist* was applied to individuals and groups in England shortly after 1600, and a definite physical link can be established between these people and Reformation-era Anabaptists. But the historical connection is not as important as the similarity of doctrine.

The Future of Freedom

Although the truths of the gospel were not always perfectly understood or completely obeyed, they had a powerful influence on the Modern Age. The Protestant Reformation set loose the true spirit of individual spiritual liberty. It fostered respect for the dignity of every man and a sense of personal responsibility for all the activities of life. As a result, the Modern Age has been marked by tremendous progress, the fruit of freedom, in every field of human endeavor.

CHECK UP 🕊

1. How did Pope Leo X react to Luther's Theses?
2. What took place at the Diet of Augsburg?
3. What three things did Luther declare in his debate with Johann Eck?
4. What four important ideas did Luther defend in his writings?
5. What emperor summoned Luther to the Diet of Worms? What was the Edict of Worms?
6. Where did Luther hide for 11 months disguised as "Knight George"?
7. What kind of education did Luther promote?
8. How were church services changed?
9. What is Luther's most famous hymn? How did his teaching influence the world of music?
10. In what city did Ulrich Zwingli begin the Swiss Reformation?
11. To what country did John Calvin flee when Protestants were persecuted in France?
12. What was Calvin's most famous work?

Identify: Frederick the Wise, diet, papal bull, Leipzig, Lutherans, cantons, Swiss Confederation, Calvinists, Geneva, Anabaptists, Menno Simons

CHAPTER 13 REVIEW

(Chapter Review includes Overview on pp. 193–195.)

MULTIPLE CHOICE *Write the letter of the answer that best completes each sentence.*

1. Peter of Bruis preached for 20 years in southern ____.
   a Italy c England
   b Spain d France

2. The Waldensians originated in the ____ mountains of Europe.
   a Alps c Apennine
   b Caucasus d Pyrenees

3. The English scholar ____ had the entire Bible translated into English for the first time.
   a Peter of Bruis c John Wycliffe
   b John Huss d Martin Luther

4. The Bohemian preacher ____ led a revival of true Christianity in his homeland.
   a Peter of Bruis c John Wycliffe
   b John Huss d Martin Luther

5. ____ invented the movable-type printing press around 1440.
   a Johann Gutenberg
   b Desiderius Erasmus
   c John Huss
   d Martin Luther

6. The scholar of the Northern Renaissance known for his translation of the New Testament in the original Greek was ____.
   a Johann Gutenberg c John Huss
   b Desiderius Erasmus d Martin Luther

7. Modern history is a record of how people have responded to ____.
   a the church c the Bible
   b government d science

8. The key movement of the Modern Age was ____.
   a the Renaissance c the Inquisition
   b the Reformation d Modern Science

9. Martin Luther nailed his Ninety-five Theses to the door of the church in ____, Germany.
   a Zurich c Wittenberg
   b Geneva d Erfurt

10. Under the influence of John Calvin, the city of ____, Switzerland, became known as "Protestant Rome."
    a Geneva c Wittenberg
    b Zurich d Erfurt

MODIFIED TRUE/FALSE If the statement is true, write true *in the blank. If the statement is false, replace the italicized word with the word that will make the statement true.*

_____ 1. The Petrobrusians and Waldensians were two groups that *protested* the practices and doctrines of the Roman church.

_____ 2. The Council of *Prague* condemned John Huss and had him burned at the stake.

_____ 3. Any baptized member of the Roman church who disagreed with official church opinion was called a *heretic*.

_____ 4. The Roman church established a special court called the *Inquisition* to investigate matters of heresy.

_____ 5. The practice of purchasing church offices is called *simony*.

_____ 6. John Wycliffe's followers were called *Bohemians*.

_____ 7. The reformer John *Huss* is remembered as the "Morning Star of the Reformation."

_____ 8. One of the key discoveries of history was made in *1517* when Christopher Columbus discovered America.

_____ 9. The *Reformation* marks the beginning of the Modern Age in Europe.

_____10. The most important factor in any age is the *language* of the people.

_____11. The Edict of Worms declared Martin Luther a *saint*.

_____12. Luther hid for nearly a year as "Knight George" in *Wartburg* Castle.

MATCHING Match each description with the correct name.

a Charles V
b Frederick the Wise
c John Calvin
d John Huss
e John Wycliffe
f Martin Luther
g Pope Leo X
h Pope Alexander
i Tetzel
j Ulrich Zwingli

_____1. sold indulgences to raise money for the building of St. Peter's Cathedral

_____2. condemned Luther's Theses and excommunicated him

_____3. called Luther to the Diet of Worms

_____4. brought the Reformation to Zurich, Switzerland

_____5. wrote *The Institutes of the Christian Religion*

_____6. wrote the hymn "A Mighty Fortress Is Our God"

_____7. permitted Luther a hearing at the Diet of Augsburg

CONCEPTS TO CONSIDER On a separate sheet of paper, answer the following questions using complete sentences.

1. List the three periods of world history and give the dates for each. In which period do we live today? How is the current period of history unique?

2. Give one way in which the Northern Renaissance helped to bring about the Protestant Reformation. Explain.

3. What did Martin Luther do in 1517 that sparked the Protestant Reformation? Explain the name of this movement.

4. How did the Protestant Reformation open the door to the Modern Age?

217

14
Post-Reformation Europe
(c. 1500–1700)

The Peasants' Revolt

Feudalism in Germany

At the time of the Reformation, the people of Germany were held down by the system of feudalism. The German peasants labored from dawn until dusk for their lords with little reward. Often they were denied even the freedom to hunt and fish or to gather firewood in the forests. Peasants could be forced to perform almost any service, and they could be punished arbitrarily upon the whims of their lords. They had little that they could call their own, and what they did have (an orphan's inheritance, for example) might be taken away at any moment by the nobles.

The German peasants had revolted at least five times before the Reformation, and each revolt had failed in the face of superior forces. It could be safely predicted that future rebellions would also fail, but the people were desperate.

An Appeal to Luther

The "Twelve Articles." When Martin Luther preached salvation by faith, many peasants were converted. Spiritual freedom lifted their hopes for a better life. Naturally, they longed to be free from the tyranny of the church. They also hoped that the preaching of true, Scriptural Christianity in Germany would change lives and influence feudal lords to treat the peasants more justly. In a spirit of humility and restraint, certain moderate preachers drew up a list of the peasants' grievances, known as the **"Twelve Articles,"** and sent a copy to Luther.

Luther's response. Replying to the articles, Luther addressed remarks both to the peasants and to the nobles. He recognized that the peasants had many just grievances. To the nobles, he said: "Let down your stubbornness . . . and give up a little of your tyranny and oppression, so that the poor people get air and room to live." Unless the nobles repented, he warned, the common people would surely rise up. Luther was realistic about human nature; he realized that, rightly or wrongly, the people would not be able to restrain themselves if the injustices continued. To the common people, Luther advised patience. Violence and revenge would only make matters worse.

Response to Luther. However, neither the peasants nor the nobles took Luther's advice; the nobles would not change their ways, and the peasants would not be patient. The peasants were not at all satisfied with Luther's response; in fact, they felt he had betrayed them.

Luther's language had indeed been strong, but he was trying to make it clear that *Christianity must not be thought of as a revolutionary political movement.* Spiritual freedom does not always guarantee political or economic freedom.

218

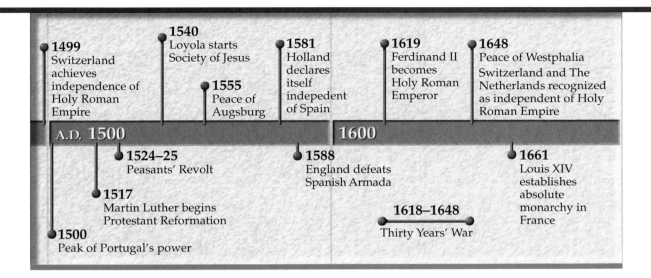

1499
Switzerland achieves independence of Holy Roman Empire

1540
Loyola starts Society of Jesus

1555
Peace of Augsburg

1581
Holland declares itself indepedent of Spain

1619
Ferdinand II becomes Holy Roman Emperor

1648
Peace of Westphalia Switzerland and The Netherlands recognized as independent of Holy Roman Empire

A.D. 1500   1600

1524–25
Peasants' Revolt

1517
Martin Luther begins Protestant Reformation

1500
Peak of Portugal's power

1588
England defeats Spanish Armada

1618–1648
Thirty Years' War

1661
Louis XIV establishes absolute monarchy in France

But the peasants did not understand. They felt more desperate than ever, especially since the nobles showed no signs of changing. Thus the peasants were ripe for leaders who wished to turn the Reformation into a political revolution. Fanatics led many peasants from moderate and simple requests to extreme and disorderly demands. Because the peasants took matters into their own hands rather than trusting God to let the gospel bring about change, they became the pawns of evil men—self-appointed prophets who twisted the Scriptures for their own purposes.

Rebellion among the Peasants

Rebels and tyrants. As a result of this unrest in Germany, the **Peasants' Revolt** broke out in 1524–1525. Peasants whose original goal had been to be treated like free men now rampaged like wild animals. Arson, robbery, and violence of every description became the order of the day. Throughout Germany, there arose such a breakdown of law and order "that hardly might a good man walk in the streets. Robbing and plundering . . . became so common that even pious men were tempted thereto."

The price of rebellion. Not *all* the peasants followed radical leaders. Many peasant communities were led by practical men. These wise leaders bargained with their feudal lords and helped advance the cause of freedom to a limited degree without bloodshed.

Unfortunately, the Peasants' Revolt gave the nobles the excuse they were looking for to crush *all* the peasants and take back *all* of what little freedom they had acquired. Thus, by the end of the Peasants' Revolt, the German people were worse off in every respect than they had been before they revolted. The tyranny over them was stronger and more severe than ever. Feudalism would continue in Germany for many years.

State Churches

Rejection of religious freedom. The Peasants' Revolt convinced Luther that government control of religion was necessary for law and order. He therefore urged the German princes to put a stop to all false teaching, improper worship, and heresy. Many Protestants agreed with Luther, but the resulting lack of religious freedom had some unfortunate consequences.

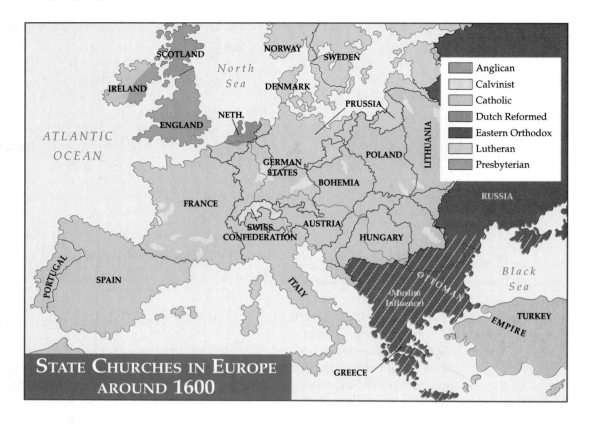

STATE CHURCHES IN EUROPE
AROUND 1600

Established churches. In accepting government control of religion, Protestants promoted the establishment of **territorial churches,** the idea that all inhabitants of a particular territory should be required by law to become members of a certain kind of church at birth. Such territorial churches were nothing less than **state** or **established churches,** *official government churches to which everyone had to belong.* Quite simply, the government of a particular territory or independent city in Germany could choose the church that its people would attend. Anyone who had different beliefs would either have to change his beliefs or move to a territory where the government held his particular beliefs. The territorial or state church concept, with each prince controlling religious life in his territory, soon became the general pattern in Germany.

The Peace of Augsburg. In 1555, an agreement known as the **Peace of Augsburg** gave official approval to the territorial, state-established church concept in Germany. Each prince would decide which religion, Romanism or Lutheranism, would be officially permitted and established in his territory. There were by now many other kinds of Protestant churches, but they were not acceptable choices. Once the government had decided upon the religion, the people were to either follow its dictates or move away.

In mixing church and state, the Peace of Augsburg produced cold, formal Protestant churches. Church membership became dependent upon birth—the fact that one happened to be born in a certain territory—rather than choice. Belief and practice were not the free choice of congregations but were instead the dictates of government. Thus, the spirit of the Protestant Reformation began to fade in Germany.

The Counter-Reformation

The Protestant Reformation so shook the Roman church that the pope soon responded with the **Counter-Reformation.** The Counter-Reformation attempted to produce certain limited changes (mostly in the morals of the clergy) within the Roman church. The main objectives were to prevent any more Catholics from becoming Protestants and to force as many Protestants as possible back into the Roman fold.

The Jesuits

While recuperating from a broken leg in 1521, a Spanish soldier named **Ignatius Loyola** [ĭg·nā′shᴜs loi·ō′lə: 1491–1556] read about the lives of pious Roman saints and the life of Christ. He began to feel that he came far short of perfection. After recuperating, he went to a shrine consecrated to the Virgin Mary where he confessed his sins for three days. Like Martin Luther, his conscience troubled him greatly. But unlike Luther, Loyola did not accept Christ's free offer of salvation. Instead, he decided to try to *earn* his salvation by obedient service to the Roman church and the pope.

In 1540, the pope gave Loyola and some companions approval to begin a religious organization called the **Society of Jesus,** or **Jesuits** [jĕz′o͞o·wĭts]. The Jesuits quickly grew in numbers. In 1541, the Society had only 10 members; by Loyola's death in 1556, there were over 1500 Jesuits. The Society of Jesus became the "spiritual arm" for the Counter-Reformation.

The goal of the Jesuits was to form a group of men absolutely dedicated to the pope and the Roman church. If that church "shall have defined anything to be black which to our eyes appears to be white," declared Loyola, "we ought in like manner to pronounce it to be black."

Before long, Jesuits had become teachers and professors in universities throughout Europe. Eventually, they started their own schools, colleges, and universities. Within 170 years of its founding, the Society of Jesus controlled 612 colleges, 24 universities, and 150 normal schools (schools for the training of teachers).

The Jesuits saw education as a way to serve the church by strengthening people who were already members and reclaiming those who had become Protestants. **"The end justifies the means"** became the hallmark of Jesuit philosophy.

Inquisition

The Counter-Reformation put new life into the **Inquisition.** Throughout Europe, particularly in Italy and Spain, the Inquisition used torture and terror to obtain confessions of heresy from its Protestant victims. The Inquisition virtually destroyed Protestantism in Spain and halted its growth in many other nations.

The Sides Line Up

The Counter-Reformation did not change Roman doctrine. The Roman church remained convinced that it was the Kingdom of God on earth, and it saw the Protestant Reformation as a threat to that kingdom. The church determined to regain what it had lost and to put the whole world under its religious domination once and for all. The pope and the political rulers who sided with the Roman church were prepared to use any means to promote the cause of Romanism.

The Protestants, on the other hand, considered the pope to be the *antichrist* of the last days. Many of them believed that when the forces of Romanism had been defeated (and they had no doubt that this would happen), *then* the Kingdom of God would be set up on earth in a political form.

As Europe entered the 1600s, devastating wars of religion and politics loomed on the horizon. Each side would claim to be fighting for nothing less than the Kingdom of God on earth.

The Hapsburgs

Over the centuries, certain families have risen to prominence in business, politics, and other areas of life, often influencing entire nations. One such family, the Hapsburgs, were prominent in European politics for almost 900 years.

The name *Hapsburg* is derived from a castle in Switzerland known as *Habichtsburg* ("Hawk's Castle"). The first member of the family to use the name Hapsburg was **Werner I,** who became known as the Count of Hapsburg. The Hapsburg family remained feudal rulers until 1273, when Rudolph I, a descendant of Werner I, was chosen to be Holy Roman Emperor. Upon his death, one of his sons, Rudolph II, inherited part of his father's domain. This inheritance eventually became known as **Austria,** a country bordering Switzerland, the Hapsburg homeland.

In 1452, Frederick III, another Hapsburg, was crowned Holy Roman Emperor. His election began a custom of Hapsburg emperors that would continue until 1711. For almost 300 years, the Holy Roman Emperors were Hapsburgs. Frederick III adopted as his motto *Austriae ets imperare orbi universo.* The *A.E.I.O.U.,* as it is sometimes called, means "Austria is destined to rule the world." The Hapsburgs took this motto very seriously.

Maximilian I, Frederick III's son, became emperor in 1493. Maximilian increased the Hapsburg holdings tremendously by instituting the custom of choosing wives who would bring various kingdoms and lands as their dowry. As a result of such marriages, the Hapsburgs gradually acquired the lands of other kingdoms. Maximilian I married Mary of Burgundy, and their son Philip I inherited the Netherlands and Luxembourg. To further increase Hapsburg property, Maximilian arranged for Philip to marry Joanna, the daughter of Ferdinand and Isabella of Spain. Through this marriage, the Hapsburgs acquired Spain, Naples, Sicily, and the island of Sardinia. Many Europeans began to say, "Let others wage wars: You, fortunate Austria, marry."

Because Philip I died prematurely in 1506, his son Charles succeeded Maximilian as archduke of Austria. In 1519, Charles V was elected Holy Roman Emperor. With his election, Charles controlled Germany, Austria, Spain, several Italian kingdoms (Naples and Sicily), the Netherlands, and Luxembourg.

But as the Modern Age continued, the Hapsburgs lost their domains one by one until only Austria remained. The Hapsburgs controlled Austria until the 20th century.

The Thirty Years' War

Only a Temporary Truce

The Peace of Augsburg (1555) was supposed to stabilize politics and religion in Germany by combining the two. According to the treaty, each ruler would decide whether his territory or city would be Roman or Lutheran. The people could either abide by the decision of their prince and attend the established church for the territory or move away.

But the Peace of Augsburg was only a temporary truce. The Reformation had set loose forces that no treaty could control, and the religious situation changed constantly. A change in religion meant a change in politics, and a change in politics meant a change in religion. As more territories formerly controlled by Roman officials became Lutheran, the balance between Lutherans and Romans was upset. In fact, by 1600 about $^9/_{10}$ of the population of the Holy Roman Empire professed to be Protestant.

As a further disturbance, **Calvinism,** although it had been excluded by the Peace of Augsburg, spread into Germany. Led by a Calvinist prince, the Protestant states formed a league in 1608 and prepared to fight if necessary. The Catholic states, strengthened by the Counter-Reformation, responded with a league of their own in 1609. As they prepared for war, each side appealed to foreign powers for help.

What followed was one of the most confusing and disastrous wars in the history of Europe. The **Thirty Years' War,** which occurred in phases between 1618–1648, was mainly a civil war in *Germany* and the *Holy Roman Empire* over religious and political issues (the two were so mixed that it is impossible to separate them). But many countries on the European continent, such as *Spain, France, Denmark,* and *Sweden,* also became involved.

Phases of the War

Bohemia (1618–1621). The Thirty Years' War began in Bohemia in 1618, one hundred one years after the beginning of the Protestant Reformation. Bohemia had experienced its own reformation under the great Christian martyr John Huss more than a century before the Protestant Reformation. By Luther's time, most Bohemians were members of Hussite churches. Throughout the 1500s, the Hussite Bohemians successfully defended themselves in wars against popes, emperors, and kings who wanted to put them back under Roman control.

But in 1619, **Ferdinand II** of the powerful Hapsburg family became Holy Roman Emperor. Ferdinand determined to return Bohemia to Romanism by force, if necessary. In spite of resistance among the people, the emperor began to wipe out political and religious liberty in Bohemia as he had done elsewhere. By 1621, this monstrous mixture of politics and religion had destroyed Bohemia.

Lands along the Rhine (1621–1625). The lands along the Rhine River were the next to suffer the ravages of war. By 1625, Spanish troops had conquered this region, as well.

The Danish Struggle (1625–1629). Denmark entered the war around 1625 under **Christian IV,** king of Denmark. With the support of England and Holland, Christian became the champion of Lutheran Protestantism. The Danish struggle lasted until 1629, when Denmark's forces were finally defeated.

The Swedish Struggle (1630–1632). It seemed as if Protestantism were on the verge of collapse in Germany, and that Romanism would again become the established religion of the empire. Then **Gustavus Adolphus** of Sweden, the great Lutheran warrior-king, landed in Germany with a well-trained army. Adolphus turned the tide of the war and, for a time, Protestant forces had the upper hand. But when Adolphus was killed in battle in 1632, Swedish hopes of a Protestant confederation in northern Europe were dashed. The Swedish army was destroyed in 1634.

The Peace of Westphalia. Alarmed by the growth of Hapsburg power, France allied herself with the Swedish, German, and Dutch Protestants. The combined armies won several victories against the Austrian and Spanish Hapsburg forces, and a peace conference convened in Westphalia to end the conflict. Finally, after several years of negotiation, the

Gustavus Adolphus: The Swedish warrior-king leads his forces into battle.

Peace of Westphalia [wĕst·fāl′yə] was signed in <u>1648</u>. Thirty years of war had been waged over religion, only to end with *a renewal of the same religious situation that had existed before the war.*

Throughout the Middle Ages, the goal of many religious and political leaders had been to make Europe into an empire with supposedly Christian beliefs. But the Thirty Years' War made the Holy Roman Empire even more ridiculous. The emperor lost territory in the north to Sweden and in the south to France. Holland and Switzerland were officially recognized as independent countries. In Germany, the emperor lost his power altogether, and the Protestant princes of Germany regained lost territory and authority. Calvinism acquired legal status in the empire along with Romanism and Lutheranism. As before, the ruler of each German territory would decide the official state church for his domain. The Hapsburgs retained their power only in Austria, Hungary, and Bohemia.

With the power of pope and emperor broken, **Christendom,** as Europe had been called, became a land of religious and political diversity. This diversity led to such extreme division that for the next two centuries Germany would remain a patchwork of territories.

CHECK UP

1. How did Luther counsel the nobles and the common people?
2. What were the consequences of the Peasants' Revolt?
3. What are territorial or state churches?
4. What was decided by the Peace of Augsburg?
5. What were the main objectives of the Counter-Reformation?
6. Who were the Jesuits? What were their goals? What phrase describes their philosophy?
7. What are the dates of the Thirty Years' War? In what land did it begin?
8. What did Ferdinand II want to do to Bohemia?
9. Who was the champion of Lutheran Protestantism in Denmark?
10. What king of Sweden won many victories for the Protestant forces before he was slain in battle?

Identify: Twelve Articles, Ignatius Loyola, Society of Jesus, Peace of Westphalia

EUROPE AFTER THE PEACE OF WESTPHALIA (1648)

Europe in the 17th Century

As we have seen, the situation in Europe changed drastically in the years following the Reformation. Thus far, we have concentrated mainly on Germany. Now we will briefly study some of the other European nations in the Post-Reformation era.

Switzerland: An Oasis of Peace

Helvetia. Nestled in the Alps mountains of central Europe, Switzerland has long been known for its political freedom and its long-standing policy of neutrality in war. Julius Caesar conquered the original inhabitants, a Celtic people, in 58 B.C. Under the Roman Empire, Switzerland became known as *Helvetia.* By the fifth century A.D., Germanic tribes had settled in Helvetia, but they were driven out in the early 500s by the Franks. When the Holy Roman Empire began in 962, Helvetia became a part of it, to be ruled either by the emperor himself or by appointed lords.

War with the Hapsburgs. When the Hapsburgs came to power, the Swiss cantons (states) of Schwyz and Uri resolved not to let Austrian power become too great in Helvetia. But the Hapsburgs already controlled much of Helvetia, and in 1273, the first Hapsburg Holy Roman Emperor, Rudolph I, began to rule over Schwyz and Uri. In 1291, Schwyz and Uri invited the region of Unterwalden to join them in their fight for independence. They jointly signed the Perpetual Covenant, a defense charter in which they agreed to defend each other against imposed foreign rule. This declaration of their freedom began the **Swiss Confederation,** which came to be called Switzerland, after the canton of Schwyz.

The Swiss fought many wars for independence from the Austrian Hapsburgs. In 1315, at the remarkable battle of Morgarten, 1,600 Swiss peasants defeated 20,000 Austrians. By 1353, five more cantons had joined the Swiss Confederation, and the Austrians continued to suffer defeat.

Swiss Alps

Independence and neutrality. During the 1400s, Switzerland proved to be a forceful military power, successfully entering wars to gain territory. In 1499, Switzerland won its complete independence from the Holy Roman Empire, although the empire did not acknowledge Swiss independence until almost 50 years later. In 1513, the Swiss defeated French armies in northern Italy. Two years later, however, the Swiss suffered a great number of casualties in a battle with the French; soon afterward, Switzerland decided upon a continuous policy of *national neutrality.*

By 1513, the number of cantons in the Swiss Confederation had reached 13. With no central government, the cantons governed themselves, meeting together occasionally in a national assembly with no real legislative authority.

Reformation and revolution. In the early 1500s, the Protestant Reformation split Switzerland into two armed religious camps, Protestant and Roman. The two groups engaged in four civil wars which did little to alter Switzerland in any way.

We have already studied the influence of the great Protestant reformers Ulrich Zwingli and John Calvin in Switzerland.

The Reformation bore much fruit in the Swiss cantons, though some cantons remained loyal to the Roman church. As the 17th century came to a close, Switzerland remained a land of political freedom and religious diversity.

The Netherlands

In the Netherlands, the Dutch have a saying, "God created the world, but the Dutch created Holland." As we will see, the saying does have some merit, for the history of the Netherlands is, in essence, the story of a brave people "creating" land where water once stood.

The Netherlands are appropriately named: *nether* means "low," and the Netherlands are indeed "low lands." In fact, much of the Netherlands lies below sea level, and some of the land once lay beneath the sea. The Netherlands is also sometimes called **Holland.** The people are called the *Dutch* or *Hollanders.*

There is much more to the history of Holland, however, than its struggle with the sea. The Dutch have also had to contend with more volatile enemies. Many times in history, the Dutch have shed blood to defend their political and religious freedoms.

226

Julius Caesar led the Roman conquest of the Low Countries (Holland, Belgium, and Luxembourg) in 58 B.C., the same year he conquered Switzerland. Later, in the fifth century A.D., Franks and Saxons drove out the Romans and settled in Holland. For several centuries, neither the French nor the Germans cared about this low, watery land which had no mountains, no great rivers, and seemingly no natural wealth of any kind. Thus, the noblemen of Holland grew accustomed to ruling themselves, and the Dutch people grew fond of their liberty.

Around A.D. 1000, the Dutch began to engage in shipping and trade. Towns sprang up throughout the Low Countries, and before long, Holland became quite prosperous.

Suddenly France and Germany saw Holland as a valuable prize to be won. During the 14th century, a French noble-man, the **duke of Burgundy,** gained control of the Netherlands. Burgundian control continued in Holland for centuries, but the freedom-loving Dutch did not resign themselves to it. The freedom of thought and action encouraged by the

Reformation caused the Dutch to rise up and fight for their independence. By the end of the Thirty Years' War, Holland was an independent nation.

France

Ancient Gaul. In ancient times, tribes of Celts and various other groups inhabited what is now France. The Romans, who began to invade French territory about 200 B.C., named the region Gallia, from which we have derived the name **Gaul.** Between 58 and 51 B.C., Julius Caesar's forces conquered the entire region of Gaul, and around 42 B.C., the area became an official province of Rome. Rome controlled Gaul until about A.D. 500.

The Franks. In the A.D. 400s, Germanic tribes, including the Franks and Visigoths, perceived that the Western Roman Empire was weak and invaded Gaul. Eventually, the strong Frankish king **Clovis** defeated the Romans, enlarged his conquered territory, and began the *Merovingian dynasty.*

The Merovingian Dynasty had declined by the mid-600s, having squandered the kingdom treasury on the court's own pleasures. Finally, **Pepin the Short** overthrew the last Merovingian in 751 and became the official king of the Franks, beginning the *Carolingian dynasty*. Under Pepin's son **Charlemagne,** the Frankish kingdom reached its greatest extent, including much of Europe. After Charlemagne died in 814, his huge empire was divided, and France arose as an individual kingdom.

France as a nation. By the late 900s, the French nobles had gained great power, and the Carolingian kings had fallen to a state of feudal lordship, in which their only distinguishing duty as king was leading the other feudal lords in times of war. The nobles had vast lands, great wealth, many

Castle in France

Events in Europe (c. 1400–1700)

British Isles	Germany and Scandinavia	France and Switzerland
1400s (15th Century)		
1455–85 The Wars of the Roses are fought between the Yorks and the Lancasters.	**1438** Austrian Hapsburgs begin their nearly continuous rule of the Holy Roman Empire.	**1499** Swiss independence from the Holy Roman Empire is established.
1485–1603 The Tudors rule England	**1438** Gutenberg introduces printing in Germany	
1500s (16th Century)		
1529 Beginning of the English Reformation.	**1517** Luther begins the Protestant Reformation in Germany.	**1515** Switzerland adopts a policy of neutrality.
1535 Henry VIII takes the title "Supreme Head of the Church of England."	**1524–25** Peasants' Revolt is crushed in Germany.	**1536** John Calvin makes Geneva, Switzerland, his home and the center of Protestantism.
1547 Knox begins the Scottish Reformation.	**1536** Lutheranism becomes the established religion of Norway and Denmark.	
1564 Shakespeare is born.	**c. 1540** Lutheranism becomes the established religion of Sweden.	
1587 Mary Stuart (Queen of Scots) is executed in England.	**1555** Peace of Augsburg divides Germany between Lutherans and Catholics.	
1588 The Spanish Armada is defeated by English fleets.		
1600s (17th Century)		
1603–1714 The Stuarts rule England.	**1618** Thirty Years' War begins.	**1648** Swiss independence is acknowledged by the Holy Roman Empire.
1688 The Glorious Revolution in England establishes government by consent.	**1648** Peace of Westphalia ends the Thirty Years' War; the Hapsburgs are defeated.	**1661** Louis XIV establishes an absolute monarchy.
1688–1702 William III and Mary II reign over England.		

vassals, and strong armies of their own; in peacetime, the king's only real domain was his personal estate.

In <u>987</u>, the nobles chose **Hugh Capet** to be king. Capet's coronation, which began the *Capetian dynasty,* is often marked by historians as <u>the birth of the French nation</u>.

France swiftly became a powerful nation, yet it failed to develop the political and religious freedoms known in Switzerland and the Netherlands. Instead, close ties developed between the crown and the Roman church. Together, church and state crushed the Reformation in France and either killed the Protestants or drove them out of the country. Further events in the history of France will be covered as we progress in our study of the Modern Age.

Spain, Portugal, and The Netherlands

1400s (15th Century)

1479 The kingdoms of Aragon and Castile are united.

1480 The Spanish Inquisition is established.

1488 Portuguese explorer Bartholomeu Dias sails to the Cape of Good Hope.

1492 Moorish dominion in Spain ends when Spanish forces conquer Granada.

1492 Columbus discovers the New World and claims it for Spain.

1497–98 Portuguese navigator Vasco da Gama makes his voyage to India.

1500s (16th Century)

1500 Pedro Cabral discovers Brazil for Portugal.

1513 Balboa discovers the Pacific and claims possession of all regions bounding it for Spain.

1516 Spain's Ferdinand V dies; Charles I (afterward Emperor Charles V) succeeds him.

1519 Magellan—a Portuguese in the employ of Spain—begins the first expedition to circumnavigate the globe.

1521 The Spaniard Cortés captures the city of Mexico.

1542 Portugal becomes the first European nation to open official trade relations with Japan.

1550 Spain brings the Inquisition to Holland.

1554 Philip II of Spain marries Mary Tudor of England.

1555 Charles V abdicates his throne in Spain; Philip II succeeds him.

1556–98 The Spanish Empire reaches its peak and then begins its decline under Philip II.

1566 The Netherlands revolts against Philip II and the Inquisition.

1567 Spain institutes the Council of Blood in the Netherlands; many Dutch are executed.

1579 Most of the provinces in the Netherlands unite to form the Union of Utrecht, which vows to continue the fight against Spain.

1580 King Philip II makes Portugal a part of Spain.

1581 Holland declares itself independent of Spain; the Dutch Republic is formed.

1588 Defeat of the Spanish Armada.

1600s (17th Century)

1640 A nationalist revolution reestablishes Portugal as an independent country.

1648 Spain finally recognizes Holland's independence.

1668 Spain officially recognizes Portugal's independence.

1686 The League of Augsburg is formed.

Scandinavia

Three kindred kingdoms. The region known as Scandinavia includes the countries of **Norway, Sweden, and Denmark.** When **Finland** and **Iceland** are included in this group, the five countries are collectively called *Norden* (though the people of each country may be referred to as *Scandinavians*).

Vikings. The **Vikings** (or **Norsemen**) inhabited Scandinavia long before the Middle Ages; however, we have no written record of them in their own language before the ninth century A.D. In fact, the Vikings left very few written records of their history, partly due to their limited alphabet. Most of what we know about them has been gleaned from uncovered artifacts, including those recovered from the wreckage of Viking ships. Roman coins discovered in Scandinavia indicate that the Vikings had trade relations with Rome before the birth of Christ.

While other Europeans were slowly advancing, the Vikings retained primitive ways throughout the Middle Ages. The Scandinavians did not practice the feudal system like the rest of Europe; the division of land among descendants from generation to generation ruled out any such system. Nevertheless, tyranny found its stronghold in the land: heads of tribes became despotic and levied heavy taxes on the people. Many Scandinavians fled to the sea to escape the heavy hand of their tribal chieftain and to make their own living apart from their tribe.

These independent Scandinavians became proficient seamen—sailors, navigators, and fishermen—sailing throughout the North Atlantic and Mediterranean. They also gained expertise in trade and pirateering. Many coastal towns and monasteries in Europe were plundered by Viking raiders. The Vikings were also great explorers. They discovered and colonized both Iceland and Greenland, and they even reached the New World (although they failed to successfully colonize there).

By 842, the Vikings controlled half of Ireland, and by the end of the century they controlled three-fourths of England. About 900, the Vikings attacked the northern coast of France, and in 911, the French king ceded the region of **Normandy** to a Viking chieftain who promised to protect France from other Norsemen. In England, however, the Vikings continued their raids; by 1013, all of England had submitted, and Denmark and England were united. This union lasted until 1042, when the Danish Empire dissolved.

By the 11th century, Catholic missionaries were working in Scandinavia. As a result, many Scandinavians embraced Romanism.

Another Danish Empire. From the 11th to the 14th centuries, no central government of lasting consequence arose in Scandinavia. The centuries were instead marked by civil wars and short dominations. When the kings of Norway and Sweden died in the late 14th century, the nobles of these two countries petitioned **Margrete of Denmark** (1387–1412), the "lady king," to rule them. Margrete's empire eventually extended from Finland to Greenland, making it *the largest kingdom in Europe at that time.* Sweden and Norway were allowed to maintain their own laws while acknowledging Denmark as their constitutional head. In the early 16th century, Sweden won its independence, but Norway remained under Danish rule for over three more centuries.

Reformation in Scandinavia. The truths of the Protestant Reformation were welcomed in Scandinavia and, within a few years, **Lutheranism** had become the established religion of Norway, Sweden, and Denmark. During the Thirty Years' War, Sweden and Denmark fought the Hapsburgs in behalf of the Lutheran Protestants. Both the Swedes and Danes were defeated, but when the war was finally over, Sweden gained territory in northern Europe. Denmark realized little from her participation in the Thirty Years' War, and hostilities with Sweden continued throughout much of the 17th century.

Spain

Ancient Iberia. About 1000 B.C., **Phoenicians** arrived to trade and colonize Spain's southern coast. They founded **Cádiz** [kə·diz'], which became a large, prosperous city in the ancient world. About 400 years later, Spain saw the arrival of Greek merchants and colonists who called the natives of the peninsula **Iberians** and the land **Iberia.** The *Greeks* fought with the Phoenicians for trade. Next *Celts* came down from the Pyrenees Mountains northwest of Spain and built forts and walled cities in the north and west. Further disputes about land and trade brought *Carthaginians* from North Africa to help the Phoenicians.

Hispania. The **Romans** came next and conquered Iberia after a century and a half of struggle. The Romans called their new territory **Hispania** (Spain). Spain became very Romanized and rich during the six centuries of Roman rule. (The Spanish language is derived from the Roman Latin; the fundamental laws of Spain are based on Roman law; and Spanish culture and religion are essentially Roman.)

Goths and Moors. In the fifth century, Germanic tribes swept over the Pyrenees into Spain, and the *Goths* set up a kingdom that lasted almost three centuries. In the early eighth century, *Moors* (Muslims) from North Africa crossed the Strait of Gibraltar and invaded Spain. After conquering the Goths, the Moors marched over the Pyrenees into France, where they were defeated by Charles Martel (732). Because they could not push forward into Europe, they settled in Spain, where their Moorish state lasted almost 800 years.

Rich Moorish culture. Moorish influence placed Spain's progress far ahead of the other European countries. **Cordova,**

Spain's capital at the time, flourished with a population of more than a million people. Cordova also provided such rare pleasures as clothing made of silk, cotton, and linen; lighted streets; and 900 bathhouses. The Moors, masters of mosaic art, built a palace for their Caliph (Moorish ruler) that exceeded the finery and comfort of medieval castles, with such luxuries as Persian rugs on the cold floors in winter and hot and cold piped water.

Moorish economy was based on agriculture, trade, and silk. They had no shortage of silks, brocades, velvet, leather, and jewels. The Moors also introduced rice, cotton, peaches, lemons, and oranges to Spain.

In medieval Europe, the scholarship of Greece and the ancient Near East was all but forgotten, except in Spain. The Moors founded hundreds of schools and universities, many of which could be attended without charge. In the 10th century, the Caliph collected 500,000 volumes from all over the world for his library. Moorish learning engaged the interest of western Europe, and, in the 11th century, Spain further enriched medieval scholarship as non-Moors hastened to the peninsula to benefit from studies in philosophy, medicine, math, chemistry, astronomy, botany, and other fields.

The Reconquista. Back in the eighth century, when the Moors had driven the Goths from power, some of the Goths had escaped to establish small kingdoms in northern Spain. Gradually, the kingdom of **Castile** became the most powerful. By the late 11th century, the Castilians extended their power over Toledo. Soon most of the northern half of the country had fallen into non-Moorish hands. In the 13th century, the Castilians conquered the Moorish cities of Cordova and Seville. Soon feudal

The Alhambra: *The pool pictured here is part of the Alhambra, a Moorish palace in Spain.*

warriors from all over Europe poured into Spain to fight the Moors. Gradually, the Moors were driven south to Granada in southern Spain.

Ferdinand and Isabella. Over the next two centuries, government and scholarship prospered under Castilian leadership, and church and state became more and more mixed. By the mid-1400s, Castile controlled most of Spain, and the kingdom of **Aragon** ruled the eastern part of the peninsula. *Castile and Aragon were united* through the marriage of **Isabella** of Castile and **King Ferdinand** of Aragon, who became joint rulers of the two kingdoms in 1479.

Ferdinand and Isabella extended their kingdom, spread Romanism (in an effort to wipe out Islamic beliefs in Spain), and revived the Spanish Inquisition to further religious and political unity. In <u>1492</u>, the year Columbus discovered the New World, <u>Jews who refused to embrace Romanism were exiled from Spain</u>. Upon the emigration of the Jews, there was a marked decline in Spanish prosperity, for many Jews were prosperous craftsmen and businessmen.

Spain's wealth bolstered its power. The Moorish rulers of Granada had to pay an annual tribute to the Spanish government. When the Moors rebelled, war ensued (1492), and Granada surrendered. As with the Jews, <u>Moors who refused to profess Romanism were driven from Spain</u>. During the next century, North Africa received back about 3 million of its Muslim descendants. The emigration of the Moors slowed progress in Spain, but the nation's fight against the Moors stirred a stong feeling of nationalism among the people.

Spain's golden age. Spain took the lead in exploring the New World and claimed much foreign land for the Spanish crown. Throughout the 16th century, gold from Spanish colonies in America fattened the national treasury, and Spain became Europe's wealthiest nation. It was during this period of prosperity that the Protestant Reformation took Europe by storm. Unfortunately, the Roman church had such a powerful influence in the Spanish court that the Reformation was quickly snuffed out before it could make a lasting impact on the people.

For the most part, the 1500s were Spain's Golden Age. But *with England's destruction of the Spanish Armada in 1588, Spain began to decline.* As the country grew weaker, she lost her colonies and influence abroad. As a result, the leadership in Spain tightened its grip at home. By the 17th century, the powerful union of church and state smothered political, religious, and economic liberties in Spain.

Portugal

Lusitania. Some of the Phoenicians and Greeks who came to the Iberian Peninsula settled in what is today **Portugal.** When the Romans conquered Spain, they also conquered Portugal, which they called **Lusitania.** In the A.D. 400s, a Germanic tribe conquered the Romans; these Germans stayed in Portugal until they in turn were conquered by the Moors in the 700s.

The Moors ruled Portugal until the 11th century, when the Castilian kings began to reclaim the peninsula for Christendom. Soon Portugal fell under Spanish control. In 1143, Spain recognized Portugal's independence.

Age of discovery. In 1385, **John I** became king of Portugal. His reign marked the beginning of Portugal's greatest days of glory. King John had a son, **Prince Henry the Navigator,** who was an avid sailor and explorer. Prince Henry urged Portuguese explorers to sail into uncharted waters and establish new trade routes; he even offered rewards to navigators who discovered new lands. Thus, <u>Portugal led the way in the great age of exploration</u>.

Explorers eventually claimed numerous islands for the Portuguese empire. In 1488, **Bartholomeu Dias** sailed all the way to the tip of Africa, the Cape of Good Hope, a feat many Europeans had said was impossible. This encouraged other explorers to sail even farther. In 1498, **Vasco da Gama** became the first European to reach India by sailing around Africa. With access to the fabulous wealth of the Orient, Portugal grew in wealth and power. **Pedro Cabral's** discovery of Brazil in 1500 marked the beginning of Portugal's empire in the New World.

Portugal's power peaked in 1500, but it began to decline in the following century. As in Spain, the Protestant Reformation had little impact in Portugal, where the Roman church held sway. By 1580, Portugal had once again come under Spanish domination. The nation regained its independence 60 years later, but it never again knew the greatness it had achieved during the age of exploration.

State Churches

As we study Post-Reformation Europe, we see that in the major countries on the European continent, the Reformation either failed or else brought established Protestant churches controlled by the government with little or no toleration for dissenters. The state church concept eventually produced cold, formal Protestant churches in which belief and practice stemmed from the dictates of government rather than the free choice of congregations in the light of their understanding of the Bible. There were a few somewhat brighter spots, such as the Netherlands, where the people achieved a level of religious freedom. But for a more complete fulfillment of the Reformation, we must look away from the Continent and study in detail the history of England.

CHECK UP

1. When did Switzerland win its independence from the Holy Roman Empire? What caused the nation to establish a policy of neutrality in 1515?

2. What does the name "Netherlands" mean? How is this name appropriate for the region?

3. What name did the Romans give to the region of France? When did Julius Caesar conquer the region?

4. Under what king did the Frankish kingdom reach its greatest extent?

5. Whose coronation marks the birth of the French nation?

6. What countries does the region of Scandinavia include? What were the inhabitants of ancient Scandinavia called?

7. What reputation did the Scandinavians have in medieval Europe?

8. Who united the countries of Scandinavia under one empire in the 14th century?

9. What name did the Greeks give to Spain? What did the Romans call this region?

10. What effect did Moorish influence have on Spain? How did the Moors further education?

11. Who became the joint rulers of Castile and Aragon in 1479? What groups did they drive out of Spain?

12. Under what king did Portugal begin its rise to glory in the 14th century? Why was his son called Prince Henry the *Navigator?*

Identify: Helvetia, Swiss Confederation, Holland, Dutch, Clovis, Pepin the Short, Normandy, Cádiz, Cordova, Spanish Armada, Bartholomeu Dias, Vasco da Gama, Pedro Cabral

CHAPTER 14 REVIEW

MULTIPLE CHOICE Write the letter of the answer that best completes each sentence.

1. A Spanish soldier named ____ began the Society of Jesus.
   a Charlemagne   *c* Hugh Capet
   b Loyola   *d* Pedro Cabral

2. The first family member to use the name Hapsburg was ____.
   a Rudolph I   *c* Maximilian I
   b Frederick III   *d* Werner I

3. The Holy Roman Emperor ____ determined to return Bohemia to Romanism by force if necessary.
   a Christian IV   *c* Ferdinand II
   b Rudolph I   *d* Werner I

4. ____ became the champion of Lutheran Protestantism in Denmark.
   a John I   *c* Werner I
   b Christian IV   *d* Rudolph I

5. Gustavus Adolphus the great Lutheran warrior-king of ____.
   a Sweden   *c* Norway
   b Denmark   *d* Bavaria

6. The French Duke of ____ gained control of the Netherlands in the 14th century.
   a Schwyz   *c* Burgundy
   b Normandy   *d* Uri

7. ____ defeated the Romans and began the Merovingan Dynasty.
   a Clovis   *c* Pepin the Short
   b Hugh Capet   *d* Charlemagne

8. ____ overthrew the last Merovingian king and began the Carolingian Dynasty.
   a Clovis   *c* Pepin the Short
   b Hugh Capet   *d* Charlemagne

9. Under ____ the Frankish kingdom reached its greatest extent.
   a Clovis   *c* Pepin
   b Hugh Capet   *d* Charlemagne

10. The coronation of ____ is often marked by historians as the birth of the French nation.
    a Clovis   *c* Pepin
    b Hugh Capet   *d* Charlemagne

11. The empire of ____ in the 14th century was the largest kingdom in Europe at that time.
    a Clovis   *b* Pepin the Short
    c Charlemagne   *d* Margrete of Denmark

12. The reign of ____ marked the beginning of Portugal's greatest days of glory.
    a Werner I   *c* Pedro Cabral
    b John I   *d* Philip II

13. ____ urged Portuguese explorers to sail into uncharted waters and establish new trade routes.
    a Prince Henry the Navigator
    b Bartholomeu Dias
    c Vasco da Gama
    d Pedro Cabral

14. ____ sailed to the Cape of Good Hope.
    a Pedro Cabral   *c* Vasco da Gama
    b Hugh Capet   *d* Bartholomeu Dias

15. ____ discovered Brazil in 1500.
    a Hugh Capet   *c* Bartholomeu Dias
    b Pedro Cabral   *d* Vasco da Gama

MATCHING Match each description with the correct term.

a Romans   *f* Holland
b Helvetia   *g* Scandinavia
c Phoenicians   *h* Franks
d Normandy   *i* Hispania
e Gaul

____ 1. Spain

____ 2. The Netherlands

____ 3. Norway, Sweden, Denmark

____ 4. ceded to a Viking chieftain

____ 5. Switzerland

____ 6. France

____ 7. Germanic tribe

____ 8. colonized Spain's southern coast

COMPLETION *Choose the correct term to complete each sentence and write the letter in the blank.*

- *a* Peasants' Revolt
- *b* Twelve Articles
- *c* State churches
- *d* Peace of Augsburg
- *e* Jesuits
- *f* Inquisition
- *g* Peace of Westphalia
- *h* Christendom
- *i* Vikings

1. The _____ a list of the peasants' grievances sent to Martin Luther.
2. The _____ broke out as a result of the unrest in Germany.
3. Those who belonged to the Society of Jesus were known as _____.
4. The _____ were inhabitants of Scandinavia who terrorized Europe during the Middle Ages.
5. The _____ used torture and terror to obtain confessions of heresy from its Protestant victims.
6. The _____ gave official approval to the territorial, state-established church concept in Germany.
7. _____ were official government churches to which everyone had to belong.
8. The _____ was merely a renewal of the same religious situation that had existed before the Thirty Years' War.

TIME LINE CHALLENGE *Choose the letter of the correct date for each of the events listed below.*

1385	1498	1499	1524	1540	1555	1588	1618	1619	1648
A	B	C	D	E	F	G	H	I	J

_____ 1. Peasants' Revolt breaks out
_____ 2. Peace of Augsburg is signed
_____ 3. Loyola begins the Society of Jesus
_____ 4. Thirty Years' War begins
_____ 5. Peace of Westphalia is signed
_____ 6. England defeats the Spanish Armada
_____ 7. Vasco da Gama reaches India by sailing around Africa
_____ 8. Switzerland wins complete independence from Holy Roman Empire

MAP SKILLS *Use the maps on pp. 216 and 221 to answer the following questions.*

1. Which two churches controlled the most territory in Europe around 1600?

2. Name the two great empires that controlled much of Europe in the 17th century.

CONCEPT TO CONSIDER *On a separate sheet of paper, answer the following question using complete sentences.*

Explain the consequences of mixing church and state in Germany.

15
The English Nation
(c. 55 B.C.–A.D. 1689)

HIGHLIGHTS

Alfred the Great • Norman Conquest • Magna Carta • Parliament
Hundred Years' War • Wars of the Roses • Henry VIII • English Reformation
Elizabeth I • Defeat of the Spanish Armada • Great English Civil War
Restoration of the Monarchy • Glorious Revolution

The Modern Age has been the **Age of Nations,** but that fact alone does not account for the progress and freedom of modern times. Those nations that have been deeply affected by Biblical Christianity have enjoyed by far the greatest progress and freedom.

The history of one European nation in particular, **England,** has become an inspiration to all freedom-loving people, particularly Americans, for the heritage of the United States is deeply rooted in English soil. English colonists brought to America their rights, their language, their common law, their representative form of government, and their belief in self-government. They also brought Biblical Christianity and a deep love of religious and political freedom. This heritage has been a blessing to people throughout the world in the Modern Age.

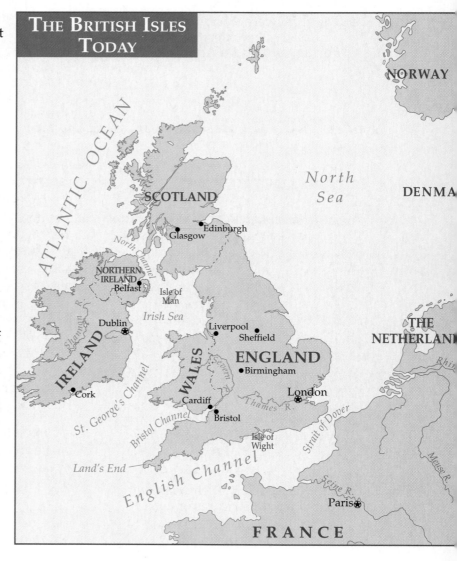

THE BRITISH ISLES TODAY

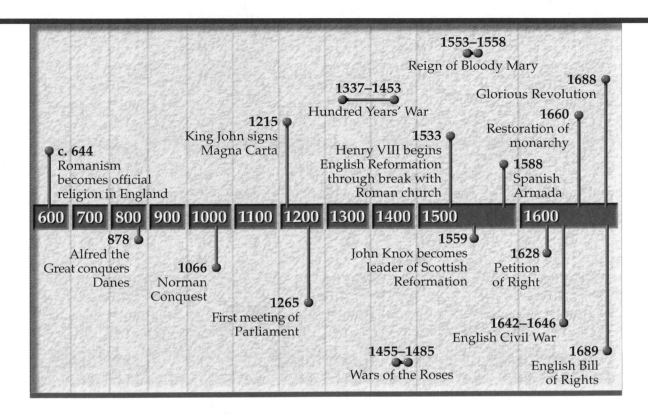

1553–1558
Reign of Bloody Mary

1337–1453
Hundred Years' War

1688
Glorious Revolution

1215
King John signs
Magna Carta

1533
Henry VIII begins
English Reformation
through break with
Roman church

1660
Restoration of
monarchy

c. 644
Romanism
becomes official
religion in England

1588
Spanish
Armada

| 600 | 700 | 800 | 900 | 1000 | 1100 | 1200 | 1300 | 1400 | 1500 | | 1600 |

878
Alfred the
Great conquers
Danes

1066
Norman
Conquest

1559
John Knox becomes
leader of Scottish
Reformation

1628
Petition
of Right

1265
First meeting of
Parliament

1642–1646
English Civil War

1455–1485
Wars of the Roses

1689
English Bill
of Rights

Early History

Ancient Britain

Among the earliest known inhabitants of the British Isles were the **Celts,** descendants of people from the European mainland. The ancient Celts were known for their wild appearance in battle (they dyed their bodies blue to terrify their enemies) and for their pagan religion. The *Druids,* a special group of Celtic men who acted as teachers, judges, and priests, conducted religious ceremonies which included human sacrifice.

Julius Caesar conquered the Celts about 50 years before the birth of Christ, around 55 B.C., and Britain became the westernmost province of the Roman Empire. Christianity reached Britain during the Roman occupation, and many Celts became Christians. In the 5th century A.D., waves of *Jutes, Angles,* and *Saxons,* Germanic tribes, sailed across the North Sea

from the region south of Denmark. The Romans had left Britain by this time, and the Celts had little means of protection. By the time the invaders had finished their attack, only a few ruins remained as evidence that Rome had ever ruled Britain. Most of the Celts were either killed, enslaved, or pushed out of Britain.

The Celts have never been forgotten, however. Some of them remained in Ireland, Wales, and Scotland, where the people are sometimes called Celts even today, and the musical Celtic language still survives to some extent. Some Celtic heroes, such as *King Arthur,* live on in imaginative legends.

England Enters the Middle Ages

The Anglo-Saxons. The Jutes, Angles, and Saxons who conquered Britain were collectively called **Anglo-Saxons.** These pagan people worshiped many gods, but they had a deep love of freedom and independence and a firm sense of justice. They

237

all spoke the same Germanic language. The Angles would give their name to the southern part of the island of Britain—"*Angleland*," or **England**—and also to the English language that developed over the centuries.

The early Saxons were renowned for their wandering poets, or **scops.** The greatest Saxon poem that still remains, *Beowulf,* gives us a good idea of the warlike, barbaric manners of the ancient Saxons.

The triumphant Anglo-Saxons carved England into dozens of small, hostile kingdoms, but as early as the seventh century, some steps toward unity had been taken. **Augustine** [ô'gŭs·tēn], a missionary appointed by Pope Gregory the Great in 597, began the great task of converting the Anglo-Saxons to Roman Catholicism. He eventually became <u>the first archbishop of Canterbury</u>. *All of England officially accepted Romanism around 664.* This gave the English people religious unity, encouraging them to think of England as one country in spite of its many little kingdoms.

New invasions. In the mid-800s, Vikings (particularly **Danes**) began to invade England. By 870, Danes controlled most of England outside of Wessex, the leading Saxon kingdom.

Alfred the Great

A young conqueror. In 871, a new king came to the throne in Wessex. At the age of 24, **Alfred** was already renowned for his love of wisdom and for his proficiency as a hunter. Over the years, he bravely led his people against the Danes, and by 878, he had achieved complete victory over the Viking invaders.

A wise king. Alfred's accomplishments earned him the title **"Alfred the Great."** As <u>the first great king of England</u>, he helped in many ways to make England a nation-state. He obliged *all* able-bodied men to serve in the national army and laid the foundations

Alfred the Great

of the great English navy. He promoted learning by having important books, including the four gospels, translated into the Anglo-Saxon language. Alfred made Englishmen aware of their common history through a running account of current events, the *Anglo-Saxon Chronicle,* which continued to be written for hundreds of years.

Soon after Alfred's death in 899, the Danes and English began fighting once again. But Alfred's descendants defeated the Danes, and by the late 10th century all of England was a single kingdom.

Canute the Dane

England had come a long way as a nation, but it was only as strong as its king. Under less competent leadership, England fell to new Viking invaders, and in 1016 **Canute the Dane** became king of England. Canute *ruled England, Denmark, and Norway as a great empire.* His careful treatment of the English people, the internal peace he provided, and the increased foreign trade his empire brought to England made this Danish king surprisingly popular with most Englishmen.

Norman Conquest

William the Conqueror. In 1042, a Saxon king returned to the throne of England. When he died in 1066, leaving no sons to inherit the throne, his kinsman **William, the duke of Normandy,** a vassal

William the Conqueror

of the king of France, stepped forward to claim the throne. (You will remember that Normandy was a region in northwestern France settled by Vikings or Norsemen [called *Normans* by the French] in the 800s.) Ignoring William's claims, the English nobles made the most powerful among them, **Harold Godwin,** king of England.

William sailed to England with an army of 10,000 or more men and met Harold's forces at the **Battle of Hastings** in *1066.* There, William defeated Harold's infantry, and Harold himself was killed. Victorious, William marched to London to be crowned king of England. William became known as *William the Conqueror,* and his victory at the Battle of Hastings became known as the *Norman Conquest.*

William's goal as king of England was to increase his own power. As he ruthlessly pursued his objective, he transformed England into one of Europe's strongest nation-states.

Feudalism. William the Conqueror brought feudalism to England in full force. As king, he claimed ownership of all the land. He kept some for his royal domain and granted the rest as fiefs to vassals (mostly fellow Normans). He also required all vassals, from the greatest to the least, to

swear allegiance to him, and made it illegal for a lord to build a fortified castle without a license.

Domesday Book. King William acted as if *everything* in England truly did belong to him. He directed his assistants to take a **census** (*a count of the people and property*). The results were entered in the *Domesday Book* [dōōmz'dā: from "doomsday" or "day of judgment"]. Not a person or piece of land, not "a solitary ox nor cow nor pig was left out." When the *Domesday Book* was completed in 1086, William could be sure of collecting every penny of taxes or feudal fees due him as king.

A powerful monarch. William abolished the old assembly of powerful nobles, the **Witan,** and replaced it with the **Great Council,** a body composed only of his chief vassals. He also took control of the Roman church in England. As king, he appointed England's church officials, including the *archbishop of Canterbury,* the most influential church official in England. No representative of the pope could enter England without William's approval, and no papal decrees could be published in England without his permission.

Norman influence. The Norman Conquest changed England greatly. One change that remains evident even today is the influence that the Normans had on the language and culture of England. Many of the Normans spoke French; as they settled in England, their language and culture mixed with that of the Anglo-Saxons. In fact, French was England's official language for a time. As a result, hundreds of French words became a permanent part of the English language.

The most immediate results of the Norman Conquest were political. The Normans occupied all positions of power and importance in England. Gradually, most English farmers lost their freedom and became serfs like their counterparts on the European continent.

The Plantagenet Kings of England

Powerful Henry II

In 1154, **Henry II,** a descendant of William the Conqueror, became king and began the **Plantagenet** [plăn·tăj′*e*·nět] line of kings (so named for the sprig of broom *plante genêt* that his father Geoffrey, count of Anjou [än′zhōō′], wore in his hat). Henry II was very powerful on the European mainland. In addition to Normandy, he held the territories of Anjou and Aquitaine [ăk′wǐ·tān] in France. Though he was a vassal to the French king, he actually held more land in France than the king did!

Henry II labored tirelessly to reestablish royal authority. He suppressed unruly nobles and even tore down castles that had been built without a license. He also strengthened the national army and improved the royal courts. It was during his reign that the *common law* began to develop, laws common to all Englishmen, from case-by-case decisions of judges based upon long-accepted customs. Henry also instituted *trial by jury.* The impartiality and speediness of the king's courts made Henry II very popular with the English people.

Richard the Lion-Hearted

When Henry II died in 1189, he was succeeded by his son **Richard I**, the English king known for his love of Crusades to the Holy Land. Richard's exploits earned him the name **Lion-Hearted.** Richard actually spent only six months in England out of his ten years as king. In his absence, the nobles grew in power, but thanks to the stable government that Henry II had established, England fared well even without her crusading king. Some of the legends of *Robin Hood,* the infamous outlaw of Sherwood Forest, are set in the reigns of Richard I and his brother John.

John: A Hated King

Richard's brother John became king in 1199. To the regret of his countrymen, **John,** unlike his brother Richard, spent most of his time in England. Already well-known for his treachery, selfishness, and cruelty, John succeeded in becoming the most hated king of English history.

King *Philip II* of France used John's bad behavior as an excuse to take more than half the English king's land in mainland Europe, including Normandy. This and other failures of King John convinced the English people that something must be done.

The Magna Carta

The principle that "No man is above the law" is one of the keys to political liberty. King John considered himself above the law. But the English had grown accustomed to the just courts and laws

240

King John at Runnymede

(1) It forbade the king to levy new taxes without the agreement of the Great Council of nobles. Later ages would conclude: **No taxation without representation!**

(2) The king promised not to sell, deny, or delay justice to *anyone,* noble or not. Soon Englishmen would claim the right of *habeas corpus* [hā′bĕ·*a*s kôr′p*u*s], the right of an arrested person to appear before a court to determine if his imprisonment is legal.

(3) The king promised not to imprison a man "except by the legal judgment of his peers or by the law of the land," setting a precedent for the right to **trial by jury** and **due process of law.**

Under the Magna Carta, England would have the **rule of law.** The Magna Carta would become an important part of the English **constitution** (*rules for exercise and restraint of governmental power*). England would lead the world in *constitutional government* which, through effective rules, <u>restrains rulers from violating their subjects' freedoms</u>.

Parliament

Seeds of representative government. John's son **Henry III** became king of England in 1216. Although he was a better man than his father, Henry was a weak king and made many mistakes. Before long, the nobles rebelled, led by Earl **Simon de Montfort** [sĕ·mân′ *de* môn′fôr′]. De Monfort took control of the government and <u>called what is remembered as the first meeting of Parliament in 1265</u>. The king's Great Council of nobles had sometimes been called a Parliament, from the French *parler* [pär′lā′], "to speak." But Simon de Montfort invited representatives from shires (counties) and towns as well as nobles. Though de Montfort soon fell from power, his idea of Parliament planted the seed that would grow into English *representative government.*

established by Henry II. The time had come to place the king himself under the common law of England.

Early in the morning on the 15th of June **1215,** a group of English noblemen and clergy met King John on the meadow of **Runnymede** [rŭn′ĭ·mĕd], near London, and forced him to sign one of the most important documents in the history of the world—the **Magna Carta (Great Charter).** In the Magna Carta, *the ancient rights and privileges of the people were clearly defined.*

To the people of 1215, the Magna Carta was mainly an agreement between the king and the nobles. But people soon recognized that it had far greater implications. The Magna Carta made it clear that not even the king is above the law. "Now for the first time the King himself is bound by the law." If the king violated the law, he could rightfully be forced to obey.

The Magna Carta established many precedents of freedom.

241

Model Parliament. Henry III's son **Edward I** came to the throne in 1272. Edward longed to unite the whole island of Great Britain in one kingdom. (*Wales* to the west and *Scotland* to the north were independent of England.) He managed to subdue Wales after five years but was less successful with Scotland. Edward also warred with France over English possessions on the Continent.

These wars cost the king much money, but because of the Magna Carta, he could not impose new taxes without the approval of his Great Council, now routinely called Parliament. King Edward saw more clearly than did English kings before him the importance of considering the needs of *all* the people, including the ever-growing middle class. Following Simon de Montfort's example, Edward I included two representatives from each shire and town in Parliament. Beginning with Edward's **"Model Parliament"** of 1295, <u>representative government became a regular feature of English government.</u>

Wars Bring Unity to England

The Hundred Years' War (1337–1453)

The kings of France frequently clashed with the kings of England. English kings longed for the lands in France that King John had lost, while French kings determined to keep what they had taken and take more of the French lands claimed by the English kings. A dispute over the French throne provided an excuse for war, and the **Hundred Years' War** (which actually lasted, with a few interruptions, from 1337 to 1453) began.

The English win battles. At the outset of the war, French knights could not match English soldiers armed with **longbows**— six-foot-long wooden bows capable of shooting deadly steel-tipped arrows hundreds of yards. England won several famous battles in this war fought on French soil—at **Crécy** [krā·sē′] in 1346, **Poitiers** [pwä·tyā′] in 1356, and **Agincourt** [ăj′ĭn·kôrt] in 1415. Such victories encouraged English patriotism. Resistance to foreign invasion had previously encouraged the people of England to think of themselves as a nation; now war with France inspired a new spirit of nationalism in England.

English victories were made easier by the fact that the kings of France, with few exceptions, were very weak. One of the weakest French kings allowed **Joan of Arc,** a peasant girl who claimed to hear "heavenly voices," to lead the French army into battle. Surprisingly, the "Maid of Orleans" did win a few victories, but they proved to be temporary, and Joan was captured and executed by the English.

The French win the war. Joan of Arc's example, however, had stirred up the patriotism of the French people. The French war effort revived, and a reorganized army and strong artillery forces with gunpowder weapons hit the field. Stronger French

The Battle of Crécy: *This illustration is from a 15th-century manuscipt.*

Joan of Arc: This painting by Ingres shows Joan of Arc in her armor.

kings came to the throne. After more than a hundred years of fighting, <u>England lost the war and all its land in France</u> except the port of **Calais** [kə·lā′].

Wars of the Roses (1455–1485)

England's defeat in the Hundred Years' War was a blessing in disguise. With no significant amount of land on the European mainland, England could now concentrate on its internal development as a nation-state.

Lancastrian kings. The last Plantagenet king, Richard II (1377–1399), lost the throne during the Hundred Years' War. The war was going badly for England, the royal treasury was empty, and discontent spread from noble to peasant. It was no time for an English king to play the tyrant, but Richard II did. When he seized the property of his powerful opponent, **Henry, duke of Lancaster,** Henry rallied his discontented countrymen to his side and deposed Richard. In his place, Henry of Lancaster became **Henry IV,** king of England, and the **Lancastrian** [lăng·kăs′trĭ·an] dynasty began.

The last Lancastrian king, Henry VI, went insane in 1453. **Richard, duke of York,** now the most powerful man in England, began ruling on Henry's behalf. But other members of the Lancaster family resented this new power for the House of York. In 1455, the Yorks and the Lancasters began what later became known as the

Wars of the Roses (so-named because the Yorks used a white rose as their emblem and the Lancasters used a red rose as theirs).

The wars were essentially struggles between different groups of English nobles. The English people, especially the growing middle class, favored stability and order. They grew weary of selfish nobles who stopped at nothing to satisfy ambition and vengeance. England was ready for a strong king. The Wars of the Roses ended in 1485 with the **Battle of Bosworth Field,** when **Henry Tudor** (Lancaster) defeated Richard III (York) and became **Henry VII,** the first Tudor king of England. Henry VII united the Houses of York and Lancaster through marriage in 1486.

CHECK UP

1. Who was the first Plantagenet king? What territories did he control in Europe? How did he improve the legal system in England?
2. Why was Richard I known as "Lion-Hearted"?
3. Who became king after Richard I? Why was he hated?
4. Describe the events at Runnymede on June 15, 1215. What precedents of freedom were contained in the Magna Carta?
5. What was the immediate cause of the Hundred Years' War?
6. Name some famous battles that the English won.
7. How was the English defeat in the Hundred Years' War a blessing in disguise?
8. What two houses fought the Wars of the Roses? How did the name originate?
9. What was the outcome of the Battle of Bosworth Field?

Identify: common law, *habeas corpus,* constitution, Hundred Years' War, Joan of Arc, Calais, Henry Tudor

The Accomplishments of Tudor England (1485–1603)

The Tudor period in English history was an eventful time for the people of England, marked by great progress in art, literature, science, and trade. But the greatest event of the period was the *English Reformation.* During the reign of the Tudors, England was severed from the spiritual empire of Rome, and Protestantism was firmly established on the island.

Tudor Rulers of England
(1485–1603)

Henry VII (1485–1509)
Henry VIII (1509–1547)
Edward VI (1547–1553)
Mary I (1553–1558)
Elizabeth I (1558–1603)

The First Tudor Monarch

Henry VII became the first Tudor king of England in 1485 and reigned until 1509. During his reign, the great geographical discoveries that opened the world for the Modern Age began. *Columbus* discovered America in *1492, Vasco da Gama* found a sea route to the West Indies in *1497,* and in the same year *John Cabot* claimed territory in North America for England.

Henry VIII (reigned 1509–1547)

Tudor absolutism. By the time Henry VII's son, **Henry VIII,** had ascended to the throne, England was gripped by *Tudor absolutism* (the absolute, unlimited rule of the Tudor monarchs). It could safely be predicted that, sooner or later, such strong monarchs would run into conflict with the popes and the Roman church.

"Defender of the Faith." Henry VIII became king of England in 1509 at the age of 18 and ruled until 1547. Eight years after Henry's ascent to the throne, Martin Luther nailed his Ninety-five Theses to the door of the Wittenberg church. Henry, a devout member of the Roman church, attacked Luther's doctrines in 1520 by writing a book called **Defense of the Seven Sacraments.** Pope Leo X rewarded him with the title "Defender of the Faith."

Desire for a son. Circumstances in Henry's personal life, however, caused him to turn away from the faith he had so ardently defended. Henry's first wife, **Catherine of Aragon,** the daughter of Ferdinand and Isabella of Spain, had been married to Henry's brother Arthur. In that day and time, whole countries could be allied with one another through marriages between the royal families that ruled them. The first Tudor, Henry VII, freely arranged marriages for his children in order to link England with kings and queens of foreign countries. When Arthur died, Henry VII obtained permission from the pope for the future King Henry VIII to marry Catherine, who was about five years older than the young prince. Special permission was needed because it was against the rules of the church for a man to marry his brother's widow. Since Henry was only 13 at that time, the marriage did not take place until after he became king at the age of 18.

By the time Henry was in his mid-30s, Catherine was already 40. All their children but one had died, and the surviving child was just what Henry did not want—a girl (**Mary**). Thus Henry determined to get rid of Catherine and marry 24-year-old **Anne Boleyn** [bo͞ol'ĭn].

Conflict with the pope. The pope— who at the time was under the firm control of Hapsburg Emperor Charles V, Catherine's nephew—refused Henry's request for permission to divorce Catherine. Thus the pope and the church became obstacles in the path of Henry VIII. To get around them, Henry broke England's ties with the church, sparking the **English Reformation.**

The Beginnings of the English Nation

ANCIENT HISTORY

(c. 4000 B.C.–A.D. 500)

	55–54 B.C.	**Julius Caesar** conquers Britain, defeating the **Celts.**
Birth of Christ	4 B.C.	
	A.D. 449	**Anglo-Saxons** invade Britain and give England its name and language.

THE MIDDLE AGES

(A.D. 500–1500)

	664	**Romanism** becomes the official religion.
	835–870	The **Danes** conquer Britain.
	878	**Alfred the Great** conquers the Danes.
	1016	**Canute the Dane** rules England, Denmark, and Norway.
	1066	**The Norman Conquest: William the Conqueror,** from Normandy, in France, wins the Battle of Hastings and becomes king of England.
	1086	The *Domesday Book,* an official census of all the people and property of England, is completed by William the Conqueror.
	1215	The **Magna Carta** is signed by King John at **Runnymede.**
	1265	**Simon de Montfort** calls what is remembered as the first meeting of **Parliament.**
	1295	Edward I's **Model Parliament** makes representative government a regular feature of the English government.
	1329	Birth of **John Wycliffe,** first translator of the entire Bible into English.
	1337–1453	England and France fight the **Hundred Years' War.**
	1346	**Battle of Crécy** is won by English in France.
	1356	**Battle of Poitiers** is won by English in France.
	1415	**Battle of Agincourt** is won by English in France; Council of Constance condemns **Wycliffe** and orders his writings burned.
	1428	Wycliffe's remains are dug up and burned.
Seige of Orleans: **Joan of Arc** delivers France.	1429	
Johann Gutenberg invents the printing press.	1450	
	1455–1485	**Wars of Roses** are fought between the House of Lancaster and the House of York.
	1485	**Battle of Bosworth Field** makes Henry VII the first Tudor king of England.
Columbus discovers America.	1492	

THE MODERN AGE

(A.D. 1500–present)

Martin Luther begins the Protestant Reformation.	1517	

Henry VIII

Ripe for reformation. England was ripe for reformation. During the Middle Ages, two of the most important voices raised against the church had been English voices—**John Wycliffe** and **William of Ockham.** Luther's works were studied with interest by some at **Cambridge University** (one of England's oldest universities). An English translation of the Bible by **William Tyndale** circulated widely. Many Englishmen who were otherwise strong members of the Roman church had become disgusted by the popes' love of luxury, and they wanted reform.

The English Reformation. Men never see themselves right unless they see God right. Man was created in the image of God; all have equal access to the King of the universe through Jesus Christ. The priesthood of believers makes it obvious that all men are created equal in value and moral responsibility to God. Not before the Reformation came to England and men understood this truth would the freedom and dignity of Englishmen have a solid foundation.

The English Reformation, at least the end of official ties with Rome, proceeded with breathtaking speed. In 1531, Henry forced the English clergy assembled in the **Convocation** to recognize him as "the single protector, the only supreme lord, and as far as is permitted by the law of Christ even supreme head" of the English church. By 1534, the *Parliament had declared the king to be "supreme head of the Church."* What the pope was to the Roman church, Henry VIII now became to the Church of England.

The break with Rome was a necessary first step in the English Reformation, and only a strong king like Henry VIII could take such drastic measures. Soon the English monasteries were closed, and the <u>Bible</u>, in translations that the people could read (or at least understand when read aloud to them), <u>became accessible to all Englishmen.</u>

Henry VIII: king and pope. Despite the progress made under Henry VIII, the fact remains that for England, the king had simply replaced the pope. In a sense, the English people were worse off than before. *Now one man had both absolute political power and absolute religious power.* Henry's political power made his religious power stronger, and his religious power made his political power stronger.

Henry VIII ruthlessly suppressed pro-Catholic farmers who rebelled ("destroy their goods, wives, and children with all extremity," he said). On the other hand, he basically agreed with the Roman church on doctrine and practice. In 1539, Henry had Parliament pass the *Six Articles*, making much Roman doctrine, including transubstantiation, the official belief of the Church of England.

In a letter, Henry described himself as "King and Sovereign, recognizing no superior in earth but only God, and not subject to the laws of any earthly creature." No one could preach unless he had a government license (unless he agreed with the king's religious beliefs), and ". . . to publish or pronounce maliciously by express words that the King was a tyrant or heretic was made high treason. As the brutality of the reign increased many hundreds were to be hanged, disembowelled, and quartered on these grounds."

The wives of Henry VIII perhaps suffered most from his rages. He humiliated

246

his first wife, Catherine of Aragon, by having it declared that she was never really his wife at all. This cleared the way for him to marry Anne Boleyn. Anne, however, gave Henry VIII not a son but rather another daughter (**Elizabeth**). The outraged king had Anne executed on charges of adultery and married a third wife, who gave him the son he desired.

Incomplete reformation. At the death of Henry VIII, the future of freedom in England was very much in doubt. England would learn a hard lesson: without religious freedom there cannot be political freedom, and without political freedom there cannot be religious freedom. The English Reformation had stopped short because the king had simply substituted himself for the pope. Henry had taken a necessary first step in freeing England from Rome, but nothing *guaranteed* that the country could hold onto even this limited gain.

Edward VI. Henry's male heir, **Edward VI,** was only a child of nine when he came to the throne. Because his mother was a Protestant, the regents who ruled for him were Protestants. **Thomas Cranmer,** archbishop of Canterbury, had been restrained from going as far with the Reformation as he wanted. Now, with the help of scholar **Nicholas Ridley** and preacher **Hugh Latimer,** Cranmer led England in more drastic Reformation. He invited reformers from Germany and Switzerland to teach Protestant ideas at English universities. Parliament repealed the Six Articles of Religion, replacing them with the more Protestant *Forty-two Articles* (1553). Worship services became much more Protestant as a result of the *Book of Common Prayer* (first issued in 1549, with a revised version in 1552), which was made up of prayers to be spoken or even sung. But progress in Protestantism was not necessarily progress in freedom. Roman Catholics and Protestants who wanted to conduct church services in a different way were punished.

CHECK UP

1. What explorations took place during the reign of Henry VII?
2. What was the first response of Henry VIII to the Protestant Reformation?
3. What circumstances caused Henry VIII to begin the English Reformation?
4. What men in the Middle Ages had prepared England for the Reformation?
5. Whose English translation of the Bible circulated widely during the Middle Ages?
6. Who became the head of the Church of England in 1534?
7. Why were the English people worse off after Henry broke with Rome?
8. What contributions did Thomas Cranmer, Nicholas Ridley, and Hugh Latimer make to the English Reformation?

Identify: Tudor absolutism, *Defense of the Seven Sacraments,* Catherine of Aragon, Anne Boleyn, Six Articles, Edward VI, Forty-two Articles, *Book of Common Prayer*

Mary I (reigned 1553–1558)

Upon the death of Edward VI in 1553, **Mary,** the first daughter of Henry VIII, became queen of England. Catholic like her mother Catherine of Aragon, Queen Mary firmly resolved to return the English nation to the Roman church.

We who are accustomed to freedom can scarcely imagine being forced, on penalty of death, to suddenly change our religion. About 300 persons who refused to obey **"Bloody Mary,"** as this queen of England is remembered, died for their convictions. Two thirds of the martyrs were Protestant clergymen—among them Cranmer, Ridley, and Latimer. As he burned at the stake, Latimer said: *"We shall this day light such a candle, by God's grace, in England as I trust shall never be put out."* As is usually the case with martyrdom, however, Mary only strengthened the cause of her opponents when she persecuted them. Such scenes eventually became an eternal flame in the pages of the *Book of Martyrs,* written by the English historian **John Foxe** in 1563. Persecution helped to burn Protestant beliefs deeper and deeper into the English nation.

Queen of a people that hated her, Bloody Mary died in 1558, having accomplished just the opposite of what she had set out to do. "The tragic interlude of her reign was over. It had sealed the conversion of the English people in the Reformed faith."

Elizabeth I (reigned 1558–1603)

Good Queen Bess. When Bloody Mary died in 1558, **Elizabeth,** another of Henry VIII's daughters, became queen of England at age 25. Her mother was Anne Boleyn, but her qualities left

> . . . no doubt who her father was. A commanding carriage [posture], auburn hair, eloquence of speech, and natural dignity proclaimed her King Henry's daughter. Other similarities were soon observed: high courage in moments of crisis, a fiery and imperious resolution when defied, and an almost inexhaustible fund of physical energy. She enjoyed many of the same pastimes and accomplishments as the King had done—a passion for the chase, skill in archery and hawking, and in dancing and music. She could speak six lan-

guages, and was well read in Latin and Greek. As with her father and grandfather, a restless vitality led her. . . .

She had a difficult, dangerous childhood (her half sister Queen Mary had been urged to have her killed), but she learned from hard times, "when to keep silence, how to bide her time," how to be cunning, as rulers sometimes must be. But she also knew how to get the best out of men for their country. "She had . . . a high gift for picking able men to do the country's work." Few men *or* women surpassed her in intelligence.

People will look up to and admire excellence in their rulers, and the queen

> . . . had a capacity for inspiring devotion that is perhaps unparalleled among British sovereigns . . . with her people she never went wrong. By instinct she knew how to earn popular acclaim. . . . She gave to her country the love that she never entirely reposed in any one man [never marrying, she acquired the name **The Virgin Queen**], and her people responded with a loyalty that almost amounted to worship.

For her remarkable character and extraordinary performance as ruler of England, **Elizabeth I** won the acclaim of her country and earned the affectionate nickname of **"Good Queen Bess."**

Queen Elizabeth I: painting of a procession by Robert Peake the elder, c. 1600.

Elizabeth faced many problems, but in one way or another, they all had their roots in the religious problems of England. Her own religious views are not known; according to one rumor she had none. But she was brought up a Protestant, and among her close associates she counted many Protestant scholars, clergymen, and statesmen.

The experience under Queen Mary had confirmed England as a Protestant country, but English Catholics had the encouragement and support of foreign powers—especially **Philip II,** king of Spain. They were determined to overthrow Elizabeth and make the Catholic queen of Scotland queen of England as well.

Mary, Queen of Scots. **Mary Stuart** was only a week old when her father's death made her queen of Scotland in 1542. She was destined to be **Queen of the Scots** when the Reformation began to influence Scotland.

It had been agreed that Mary Stuart would marry the son of Henry VIII, making the future **Edward VI** of England also the future king of Scotland. But the infant queen's French mother, Mary of Guise, and her close associate **Cardinal David Beaton,** had other ideas. They wanted to keep the country Catholic, and they wanted it closely allied with France. So they sent Mary to France to be brought up in the court of the king and there be prepared for marriage to Francis, the king's eldest son and heir to the throne.

The Scottish Reformation. The **Scottish Reformation** opened violently with the execution of preachers who urged reform. **John Knox** (c. 1505–1572), the outstanding <u>leader of the Scottish Reformation</u>, was captured at the castle of St. Andrews by Scottish and French troops and forced to serve as a slave on French ships for 19 months. King **Edward VI** of England finally secured his release and brought him to England, where Knox promoted the

Knox and the Queen: *John Knox opposing the plan of Mary Queen of Scots, to marry Catholic Spanish Prince Don Carlos.*

Protestant cause. But when Edward died and Mary Tudor (Bloody Mary) came to the throne, Knox and other Protestant leaders were forced to leave. Knox traveled to Geneva, Switzerland, where John Calvin made him minister of the growing congregation of English Protestants living in exile there.

In 1559, the Scottish Protestants called Knox home to lead them. By now, Mary Queen of Scots was married to Francis II, who had become king of France. As Queen Regent, Mary of Guise planned to depose Elizabeth and make her daughter Mary Stuart, who was next in line to the English throne, queen of England. Knox and his followers, under heavy attack by French mercenaries, appealed to Queen Elizabeth, urging that she intervene for herself and England, if not for the Scottish Protestants. Elizabeth responded by sending 10,000 troops to Scotland. This act—plus the death of Mary of Guise—caused the French to give up. By treaty, the French agreed to withdraw their troops, and the English did likewise. *The Scottish Protestants were left in control,* and the Scottish Parliament set up an independent Church of Scotland (the **Scottish Presbyterian Church**).

When Mary Queen of Scots returned to Scotland in 1561 (after the death of her husband Francis II), she found herself the Catholic queen of a Protestant country. Over the years, she and John Knox locked horns on a number of occasions, particularly when she attempted to marry the son of King Philip II of Spain. The Scots, having had enough of Mary's mischief, finally imprisoned her and forced her to abdicate (give up the throne) in favor of her infant son **James VI.** The typical turbulence of Scottish politics continued, but supporters of the young king managed to keep him on the throne until he was old enough to rule in his own right. Meanwhile, James's mother, Mary Queen of Scots, escaped and fled to England, hoping to find refuge with her cousin Queen Elizabeth.

The Netherlands. King Philip II of Spain was determined to rule the world on behalf of the Roman church, but Protestant England stood in his way. If the world were to be reconquered for Rome, England would have to be dealt with sooner or later.

Events in the **Netherlands** soon made it clear how much of an obstacle England really was. When Philip inherited the Netherlands from his father, **Charles V,** friction sparked immediately. To the people of the Netherlands, Philip II was first and foremost a Spaniard, the king of Spain. Adding to the friction, there were many Protestants in the Netherlands. The Protestant Reformation had arrived there at an early date, and the Netherlands had also become a place of refuge for Protestants from other lands (including many from England who were unable to practice their religious beliefs in their own country).

In 1566, two hundred nobles formed a league to suppress Spanish influence in the Netherlands. This league (which included both Catholics and Protestants) asked Philip not to use the Spanish Inquisition in their regions. When Philip refused the request, the Dutch people decided to de-

William the Silent of Orange

fend themselves against Spain and the Roman church.

Philip II responded by sending in more Spanish troops led by the Spanish **Duke of Alva.** Alva set up a council which came to be known as the **Council of Blood** because of the brutal way it treated the people of the Netherlands. About 8,000 people were executed; 30,000 had their property taken away. One noble who lost his estate, **William the Silent,** Prince of Orange, became the leader of the repressed Dutch patriots in 1568. The Dutch Protestants formed the **Dutch Reformed Church** in 1571, and William, a former Catholic, joined it in 1573.

On land and on sea, though vastly outmanned and outgunned, the Dutch fought on. Dutch self-defense reached its height in 1579, when the 10 northern provinces joined to form the **United Provinces of the Netherlands,** or the **Dutch Republic.** Two years later (1581), the United Provinces *declared the Netherlands to be independent of Spain.* The Dutch declaration of independence, however, only hardened the tyrant's heart, and the fighting continued.

In 1584, the Dutch suffered a severe blow when a Spanish agent assassinated William of Orange. The **"father of his country,"** as he was known, reflected the desperate situation of his people in his dying words: "God hath pity on this poor people." The Dutch had, by 1585, but one hope, that God would permit Queen Elizabeth of England to help them.

CHECK UP

1. What was "Bloody Mary" determined to accomplish? How many people were martyred during her reign?
2. What book tells of the people killed for their faith during the reign of Mary and at other times in history? Who wrote it?
3. Describe the character of Queen Elizabeth.
4. Who became queen of Scotland in 1542? Why did her mother send her to France?
5. Who was the outstanding leader of the Scottish Reformation?
6. Why did Queen Elizabeth intervene in the affairs of Scotland? What was the result?
7. Why did the people of the Netherlands decide to defend themselves against Spain? Who became their leader in 1568? By what title was he known?
8. What one hope did the Dutch have by 1585?

Identify: Philip II, Scottish Presbyterian Church, Charles V, Duke of Alva, Council of Blood, Dutch Reformed Church

England prepares for war. In 1586, Elizabeth sent about 6,000 troops to the Netherlands. For quite some time she had realized that if Spain subdued the Netherlands, England would be next. Philip II would use the Netherlands as a base from which to invade England. War with Spain was therefore inevitable, and in preparation for it Elizabeth had long been taking measures to strengthen England and weaken Spain.

Spain's greatest strength was on the seas. To match it, the queen employed **John Hawkins** to build up the English fleet. He designed the English ships to be very fast, weather any seas in any wind, and deliver crushing shots with heavy long-distance guns. With these ships, **Sir Francis Drake**— at first "unofficially," but in fact with

Elizabeth's full knowledge and approval— attacked and raided Spanish ships. Needless to say, such unofficial piracy made Spain very bitter toward England.

Protecting the queen and England. Perhaps the most important measure was taken in 1587. The assassination of William of Orange had reminded many Englishmen of how vulnerable their queen was. If Elizabeth were killed, Mary Stuart would become queen of England. Elizabeth and most of her countrymen were convinced that Mary could no longer be permitted to live. When Mary was caught in a conspiracy to assassinate the queen, she was tried and convicted for treason. With the greatest reluctance—Parliament had to send her a petition—Elizabeth finally signed the death warrant for her cousin. The English Protestants were glad to be rid of Mary, but Elizabeth found no cause for joy in her cousin's death. Even though the act had been necessary for the cause of justice and England's security, the queen "sat alone in her room, weeping."

Spain prepares for war. By May **1588,** Philip had prepared a fleet. Called the **Armada** in Spanish, it consisted of 130 ships, 2,500 guns, and more than 30,000 men, including 180 friars and priests. Per-

Sir Francis Drake

251

haps the greatest naval force the world had seen, this *Invincible Armada,* as it was soon known, sailed forth.

Defeat of the Spanish Armada. The plan was for the Armada to sail up the English Channel, pick up more troops from the Netherlands, and invade and conquer England.

Philip's design was to overthrow the government of Queen Elizabeth and to restore popery throughout Great Britain. If he had succeeded, the whole subsequent history of England and Scotland would have been changed; there would have been no Protestant North America, and no Anglo-Saxon civilization [culture]. It would have made Spain the mistress of the world, and that nation would have set the type for civilization in the ages which have followed.[1]

The promise of freedom and the further history of the whole world hinged on the outcome of Philip's plan.

Fortunately, the plan failed, for Elizabeth, too, had been preparing. Her fleet was smaller, but much better designed. Her men were fewer, but they were abler seamen. The country was united as never before, and Elizabeth reassured those who might worry about being led by a woman in the man's business of war:

I know I have the body of a weak and feeble woman, but I have the heart and stomach of a king, and of a king of England too, and think foul scorn that . . . Spain or any prince of Europe should dare to invade the borders of my realm; to which, rather than any dishonour shall grow by me, I myself will take up arms, I myself will be your general, judge and rewarder of every one of your virtues in the field.

The Armada missed a golden opportunity to trap the English fleet in the vicinity of **Plymouth harbor** on July 19 and 20. The adverse winds made it quite difficult for the English to clear the land. But the Spanish commander, following his instructions, continued to sail up the channel to pick up the troops from the Netherlands. Those troops, however, were never picked up. Through excellent seamanship, the English got the wind on their side. After 10 days of fighting, the English completely defeated the Armada and destroyed many of the Spanish ships. As the remaining Spanish ships sought to escape by sailing northward around the British Isles, a terrible tempest arose. Many of the fleeing ships were dashed to pieces on the rocky shores of Scotland and Ireland. Only half of the ships of the Armada returned to harbor.

According to one story, when he received the news of the Armada's disaster, the Spanish king calmly and simply said: "I sent my ships to fight against men and not against the winds and waves of God."

Spain recovered in a material sense, but its morale was destroyed. Its glory gone, Spain began to decline in nearly every matter that determines the greatness of a nation.

The Elizabethan Age. As for England, the country was naturally grateful to God for the victory. The English had secured their independence and their Protestant Reformation by defeating the most powerful country in the world. Furthermore, they "had not lost a single ship, and scarcely a hundred men." To commemorate the event, a special medal was issued which read "God blew and they were scattered." Other medals, and many, many poems expressed the same thought.

Until 1603, England basked in the sunlight of glory under Good Queen Bess. Greatness radiated from the throne, light-

---

[1] Robert Pollock Kerr, 19th-century scholar: author of *The Voice of God in History, Presbyterianism for the People,* and *The People's History of Presbyterianism.*

William Shakespeare

ing up the whole culture. From politics to poetry, whether in the real drama of war or the make-believe drama of a theater stage, the **Elizabethan Age** shines in English history, and in the history of the world. In a sense, England had its own Renaissance. During this time, **William Shakespeare,** *perhaps the greatest writer the world has ever known,* began his 20-year career as a playwright. He wrote 38 plays, containing more than a million words of beautiful poetry that have been recited over and over by great actors through the centuries. Rich and poor alike crowded into the open-air **Globe Theater** in London to see Shakespeare's plays.

Elizabeth symbolized England in its moment of pride. When Englishmen bowed to her, they bowed to England. In their minds, Elizabeth *was* England.

End of an Age

Elizabeth was such a good queen that the people of England did not at first realize the consequences of the dreamlike allegory in which they lived. Elizabeth was a strong monarch, but she was no tyrant.

She seems to have truly loved her people and governed with their best interests in mind. After 45 years as queen of England, Elizabeth made this last speech: "Though God hath raised me high, yet I count this the glory of my crown, that I have reigned with your loves. I have cause to wish nothing more than to content the subject, which is a duty that I owe."

The English Reformation started by Henry VIII had stopped short of a complete return to Biblical Christianity; an all-powerful pope had been exchanged for an absolute monarch. But it was a step in the right direction. England's defeat of the Spanish Armada in 1588 assured her independence of Rome once and for all. As one historian has said, "England's victory was the final turning point in the great duel between Protestantism and Romanism; it not only assured England and Scotland, but Holland, North Germany, Denmark, Sweden, and Norway, to the Protestant cause." By the end of the Elizabethan Age, England's struggle for freedom was well under way.

CHECK UP

1. Why did Elizabeth send troops to the Netherlands?
2. Describe the English ships.
3. Who attacked and raided Spanish ships?
4. What was Elizabeth's reaction to the execution of Mary?
5. Describe the Spanish Armada.
6. How would the history of the world have been different if Philip had succeeded with his plans?
7. Describe the battle between England and the Spanish Armada.
8. What other European countries were affected by England's victory? What did the victory secure for England?

Identify: John Hawkins, Invincible Armada, Elizabethan Age, William Shakespeare

The Struggle for Freedom in England

James I (reigned 1603–1625)

The end of the Tudor dynasty. The Tudors were some of the strongest rulers in English history. They claimed to be *absolute* rulers, having no responsibility to Parliament or anyone else for their decisions. In actual practice, however, they usually worked through Parliament to obtain the country's consent for new laws and taxes. Thus the absolutism of the Tudors was more of a theory than a practice.

The first Stuart monarch. When Elizabeth I, the last of the Tudors, died in 1603 without an heir, it was decided that King James VI of Scotland, the only son of Mary, Queen of Scots, would unite the crowns of Scotland and England as **James I.** James had very definite ideas about the divine right of kings. "As it is atheism and blasphemy to dispute what God can do," he said, "so it is high contempt in a subject to dispute what a king can do, or to say that a king cannot do this or that."

Contempt for Parliament. For Parliament, James had only contempt, and he made no secret of the fact. Because Parliament was a representative assembly, a variety of opinions were expressed there. To this king who cared only for his own opinion, meetings of Parliament seemed but "cries, shouts, and confusion."

However, James had no choice but to deal with Parliament. Spending freely to maintain a large and lavish court, he constantly had to ask Parliament for more money. When Parliament proved unreceptive, James lectured them on their duty under God to provide him with whatever money he felt he needed as king. But Parliament, determined to uphold traditional English liberties, refused to yield.

Ignorance of the law. James also came into conflict with the English courts of law. Shortly after his arrival in England he

Rulers of England (1603–1714)

Stuarts
James I (1603–1625)
Charles I (1625–1649)

Republican Interregnum (period of English republic, without a king)
The Commonwealth (1649–1653)
The Protectorate
  Oliver Cromwell, Lord Protector (1653–1658)
  Richard Cromwell (1658–1659)

Restored Stuart Line
Charles II (1660–1685)
James II (1685–1688)
William III* (1689–1702) and Mary II (1689–1694)
Anne (1702–1714)

---

*William was not a Stuart, but his wife Mary was. He was the great-grandson of William the Silent, Prince of Orange, the "founder of Dutch Liberties."

displayed his ignorance of England's traditional law by ordering a thief to be hanged without trial, merely upon royal command. James believed that divine right placed him above both the common law and the enactments of Parliament, and that he had the prerogative to do as he thought best regardless of any laws. Thus James insisted that the English judges obey him without question, and he fired those who would not. One of those dismissed, **Chief Justice Edward Coke,** one of England's greatest lawyers, maintained that no man, not even the king, is above the law. King James angrily replied, "The King maketh judges and bishops."

James saw a vital connection between his roles as head of the Church of England and as king of England. Unless he controlled both religion and the church, his divine right would be limited. He knew that if he admitted this one limitation, he would have to admit more. King James was wise enough to see that religious and political freedom go hand in hand, and he wanted neither one for England.

Even though England had broken its ties with the Roman church, it retained the *episcopal form of church government* in which bishops ruled. It also retained the idea of *apostolic succession,* that the bishops' power had been passed down to them from the apostles in an unbroken line. The major change in church government was the severing of connection with the bishop of Rome—the pope. But just as the pope controlled the Church of Rome by controlling the bishops, so the king of England effectively controlled the Church of England by controlling its bishops.

The Puritans. By now many English Protestants were dissatisfied with the Church of England. The **Puritans,** as some of these dissatisfied Protestants were called, wanted to "purify" the Church of England to make it less like the Roman church. By the 1580s, some Puritans had rejected the bishops altogether, advocating a *presbyterian form of church government* in which ministers and elders (presbyters) rule the church through a series of representative bodies. Other Puritans rejected both episcopal and presbyterian church government. These **Independents** or **Separatists** wanted each local church to be independent and separate from other churches, particularly from the Church of England.

James versus the Puritans. There had been an attempt under Elizabeth to suppress the Puritans, but by the early 17th century, the Puritans were stronger than ever. It was during the reign of James I that one group of Separatists, the Pilgrims, sailed first to Holland and then to America.

The king subjected the Puritans to greater repression than ever before, vowing to "harry [them] out of the land." James did agree with the Puritans on one issue, however: a new English translation of the Bible was needed. By **1611,** scholars had completed the **King James** or **Authorized Version** of the Bible, the best-loved and most widely used translation of God's Word ever produced.

Rejected and suppressed by the king, the Puritans turned to Parliament. It was in this way that the cause of Parliament and the cause of the Puritans began to come together.

James versus Parliament. James found it impossible to work with a Parliament increasingly protective of its traditional rights and increasingly dominated by Puritans. Because Parliament continually refused to provide the money James wanted, the exasperated king dissolved the assembly in 1610. Except for a short, confusing session called in 1614, Parliament did not meet for 11 years. After James had used every device he could think of to get money, he had no choice but to call Parliament into session in 1621. The king dissolved Parliament once more before the end of his reign, but by then England was at war with Spain, and her new king, James's son Charles, found himself in desperate need of money from Parliament.

Charles I (reigned 1625–1649)

In need of Parliament. **Charles I** inherited from his father a contempt for Parliament and a stubborn belief in divine right of kings, but wars with Spain and later France made him very dependent upon that assembly he so despised. Charles needed money, and for that he needed Parliament. But Parliament would give him little.

Charles tried for a while to get by without asking Parliament for money. He forced citizens to give him "loans," imprisoning or drafting for military service those who refused to pay. Troops were billeted (lodged and fed) for free in private homes; citizens who objected were tried in military court martials, a practice illegal under traditional English law. In further violation of customary legal procedure, many people were imprisoned without trial.

The country was in an uproar, and the newly elected Parliament shared the sentiments of the English people. Parliament decried the way the king had trampled down traditional English liberties established in the common law and described Charles as a lawbreaker and a rebel. The *Magna Carta*, that rule of law which had been won from an overbearing king centuries before, was dusted off. No taxation without representation, *habeas corpus*, due process of law, trial by jury—these and many more vital principles of representative government under law were brought forth to challenge the king.

Charles had to face the facts. He was not going to get the money he needed unless he bowed to traditional English liberties.

Petition of Right. In 1628, Parliament, the legal representative of the people of England, drew up the **Petition of Right,** and Charles, though evasive at first, grudgingly assented.

The Petition stated nothing new; it merely <u>reaffirmed the liberties and rights which Englishmen had won in the past</u>. But now custom and tradition were embodied in a formal declaration, written down officially, for all to read and heed.

The Petition of Right should have ended the struggle between king and Parliament, but instead it simply marked the beginning of greater conflict. Charles had no intention of respecting it; in his opinion there was *nothing, no law,* not even the Petition of Right, that he did not have the prerogative to override. On the other hand, this *declaration* of rights made Parliament even more aware of the principles of English liberty and more determined than ever to make the king respect those rights and obey the law.

Puritans in Parliament. The Puritans, increasingly dominant in Parliament, were still determined to purify the Church of England. However, they were not defend-

*Charles I
of England*

ing religious freedom for everyone in the way that Parliament was defending everyone's rights and liberties with the Petition of Right. Though Independents or Separatists tended to be tolerant of some people who held different opinions from their own, they were not tolerant of Catholics or Protestant episcopalians, and most did not favor separation of church and state.

The Eleven Years' Tyranny. Charles dissolved Parliament in 1629. Defying the trends of English traditions and customs, Charles openly proclaimed that he would rule England without Parliament or the people's consent. Thus began the 11 years that stand out in English history as the **"Eleven Years' Tyranny."** During this time, the government of England was changed from a government by monarchs, lords, and commons, to what was in effect an absolute and irrepressible monarchy, like that of France or Spain.

Under Charles I, the Puritans suffered severe persecution, including imprisonment, branding on the cheek, and other abuses. Many Puritans left England at this time (some went to America, as we will see). But many stayed—embittered but increasingly determined to deal with their tyrannical king.

─── CHECK UP ───

1. Who was the first Stuart king of England? How did this king feel about Parliament?
2. Why did James I want to control religion in England?
3. How did the Puritans get their name?
4. What famous Separatist group lived at the time of James I?
5. What was James's attitude toward the Puritans?
6. When was the King James Version of the Bible completed?
7. How did James respond when Parliament refused to give him money?
8. What was new about the Petition of Right? How did Charles respond to it?

Identify: Edward Coke, Presbyterians, Independents, Separatists, Eleven Years' Tyranny

The English Civil War (1642–1646)

Issues of the War

The war begins. As the conflict between king and Parliament continued to grow, each side prepared for civil war. Those against the king were called *Roundheads* because many of them wore their hair short, cut in the shape of a bowl. Those for the king were called *Cavaliers* [kăv′ə·lērz′] because many of them wore their hair in long ringlets after the French fashion. The **English Civil War** began officially on August 22, 1642, when the king raised his banner in the town of Nottingham.

Divine right versus government by consent. The Cavaliers fought for the principle of **divine right.** They believed that Charles was king of England because God wanted him to be; therefore, the consent of the people is not necessary nor does it limit his power. They also extended the idea to religious matters. As

head of the Church of England, Charles had the right to determine the government, doctrines, and practices of the Church of England.

Many of the Roundheads fought for the principle of **government by consent.** Rejecting divine right, they believed that a government, whether by a king or some other form, is *legitimate* (lawful) only if it is based upon the consent of the governed.

The Puritans, who wanted to "purify" the Church of England, opposed the king because, as head of that church, he would not make desired religious changes. Many of the Puritans also stood for government by consent, but as the war continued, they became increasingly interested in the religious question.

Civil War—Part One

The English Civil War began as a battle between the king and Parliament, but as in all wars, armies did the actual fighting. Very early in the war, **Oliver Cromwell** built a reputation as a military genius. Soon people were saying that Cromwell's successes proved that he was, in some special way, God's chosen instrument.

Cromwell imposed the strictest possible discipline on his troops. On occasion, with sword in hand, he rode alone through

Oliver Cromwell

mutinous groups, quelling rebellion by the very example of his courage. His army chaplains preached constantly to the troops, inspiring them with sermons on the Providence of God and on prophecy. Most Puritans believed that prophecy about the end times was being fulfilled right before their eyes. Confident that they knew the mind and purpose of God, the Puritans plunged into action under Cromwell's leadership.

Hardened by military discipline, stiffened by religious zeal, and armed with steel—Cromwell's 22,000 troops (known as the **New Model Army**) were aptly called **Ironsides.**

By June 1646, the last of the king's forces had surrendered and the king had fled the country. The first stage of the English Civil War was over, and Parliament, or rather <u>Cromwell's army, had won</u>.

Civil War—Part Two

In the first part of the English Civil War, it had been roughly one half the country against the other half, but in the second half of the war, the sides lined up differently. On one side stood Cromwell and his Ironsides; on the other side stood the Scots who invaded England in 1648 and the Englishmen who had been royalists before, as well as many people who opposed Cromwell for other reasons.

Some fought Cromwell because they were Presbyterians, but others opposed him because they believed in traditional rights and liberties of Englishmen and felt that Cromwell was more of a threat to the rule of law in England than King Charles had been. But whatever their motives, Cromwell's opponents, in the second round of the Civil War, included, significantly, one half the British navy plus the multitudes of London, the city which had previously been a center of anti-royalist feeling. To the great majority of English-

men, the prospect of a new tyranny was more threatening than the memory of a past one.

But Cromwell's Ironsides, facing their greatest foes, swept the field. <u>By the end of 1648, the New Model Army had become master of England</u>.

Death of the King

Most of the soldiers in the army had long ago made up their minds that the king—the **"Man of Blood"** they called him—must die. Parliament created a special court to try King Charles, but the court faced several problems. There was no specific established English law under which the king could be tried. Furthermore, the tide of sentiment in the country, even among Puritans, was now running in the king's favor. On January 18, 1649, for example, 47 prominent Puritan preachers in London spoke up against the actions of Cromwell and his army.

Nevertheless, *King Charles I was declared guilty and beheaded* before thousands of horrified Englishmen.

The Lord Protector

England's new government was called the **Commonwealth,** and the country was proclaimed a *republic,* a government ruled by elected representatives of the people. But England's supposedly republican Commonwealth actually turned out to be a <u>military dictatorship under Cromwell</u>.

The Commonwealth lasted from 1649 through 1653. Though Parliament continued to meet for about four years, the real power of government resided in the *Council of State*, of which Cromwell was chairman. In 1653, Cromwell finally dissolved Parliament altogether and set up a new government called the **Protectorate.** As **Lord Protector,** Oliver Cromwell divided the country into districts, each with a Major-General, cavalry, and militia ruling over it.

Disasters in 17th-century London

The Plague

Beginning in the East and spreading rapidly over the continent of Europe, the Plague (an incurable, infectious disease transmitted by the rat flea) left in its wake the burden of grief and the stench of infection and death. As devastating as it proved to be on the Continent, the disease raged nowhere else worse than in London where, in **1665,** it killed more than half of the city's population. Whole families were wiped out in a matter of days. The rich fled into the country in hopes of escaping the Plague, while the poor were forced to remain in the city, where many who did not die of the disease perished from hunger.

Trade ceased, and travel declined so drastically that grass grew in the streets. Nearly every plague-stricken home bore in red chalk a cross and the words "Lord have mercy on us." All night long, carts rattled through the streets, with tolling bells and the buriers' dismal cry, "Bring out your dead!" No mourners followed the processions, and no coffins cradled the lifeless bodies. Instead, the victims were lowered en masse into deep trenches which served as collective graves.

About 100,000 people perished in London alone. Not until winter came did the Plague subside, leaving the city laden with filth, contagion, and the menace of perhaps yet another outbreak of the deadly, indomitable disease.

The Great Fire of London

The Plague had hardly ceased when, in **1666,** a great fire broke out in London. For three days the flames raged uncontrollably. Thousands of people, homeless and destitute, were driven to the open fields; so swift was the blaze that they barely escaped with their lives. Despite the efforts of King Charles II and his brother to quench the ravaging flames, the city of London was reduced to ruins.

As severe as the calamity was, however, nothing could have proved more beneficial for London's recovery from its bout with the Plague. The purging fire cleansed the foul London of that day by sweeping away miles of narrow streets crowded with wretched buildings and filthy, plague-infested dwellings. The rebuilding of London, engineered by the famous English architect **Sir Christopher Wren,** led to outstanding metropolitan improvements.

Most of the capital's structures had been made of wood; now they were refabricated of superior brick and stone. Streets were made wider, and more comfortable houses were

The Great Fire of London

259

built without the overhanging second story that had kept the air in the old, narrow streets stale and close. St. Paul's, an ancient Gothic cathedral which had been burned to its foundation, was redesigned by Wren and reconstructed on the old site. Under the dome of St. Paul's where Wren is buried is a tablet bearing the inscription in Latin: "Reader, if you seek his monument, look around."

After reconstruction, London was never again seized by the Plague. The Great Fire of London, the flaming holocaust whose origin remains a mystery, ultimately proved invaluable to the prosperity of English health and life.

The Restoration (1660)

Return of the Monarchy

Richard Cromwell succeeded his father as Lord Protector in 1658, but he quickly fell from power. Most Englishmen now favored a restoration of the old monarchy; thus Parliament opened negotiations with **Charles II,** son of the deposed Charles I, who had been living in France. In May 1660, Charles II stepped ashore at Dover as the new king of England. By 1662, the monarchy was fully restored, and the nation rejoiced, at first.

Unfortunately, Charles II created new problems for England. Without Parliament's knowledge, he secretly signed the **Treaty of Dover** with *King Louis XIV* of France in 1670. In order to get money from the French king to carry on his foreign policy, Charles *agreed to obtain toleration for English Catholics and to join the Roman church himself!* England was by now a solidly Protestant nation. The fear that Romanism might be reimposed was enough to bring Englishmen together. As Charles became increasingly pro-Catholic, a group known as the **Whigs** arose in Parliament to oppose him. When Charles II died in 1685, his brother **James II,** a Catholic, became the new king of England and head of the Church of England. Over the next three years, James tried unsuccessfully to reimpose Romanism on England.

The Glorious Revolution

By 1688, England seemed destined for another civil war. In June, seven leaders of Parliament wrote a letter to **William of Orange,** the ruler of the United Provinces of the Netherlands and great-grandson of William the Silent, offering him the throne of England. When William arrived with his army, James tried to protect his throne, but finding little support among his subjects, he fled England for France, never to return.

Thus **William III** and his wife **Mary II** (the Protestant daughter of James II) became King and Queen of England and ruled, as all English monarchs after them, under the strict limitations of the **English Bill of Rights.** The **Glorious Revolution** of **1688,** also known as the *Bloodless Revolution,* established once and for all in England the principle of government by consent. Future English kings and queens would be chosen in accordance with rules set by Parliament.

Foundations of Freedom

Since the Glorious Revolution in 1688, England has enjoyed the blessings of civil peace and freedom as few other nations have. Why? Because the English people learned that political freedom and religious freedom are inseparable. The Englishmen established their liberties on the solid foundation of Biblical truths revealed by the Protestant Reformation. Of course, not everyone in England accepted the gospel, but the truths of the Bible influenced many.

A New World

The Biblical truths set loose by the Protestant Reformation gave the Modern Age more potential for progress than any previous era. The magnitude of that potential for progress first became evident in England, where the Protestant Reformation had a tremendous impact on the thought and behavior of the people. By the end of the 17th century, a whole new way of thinking had appeared. Based on eternal principles, these self-evident truths opened a New World of ideas in the minds of men, sparking progress in politics, philosophy, art, science, economics, and other areas of life.

By the 1600s, Europeans had realized that Europe and the Middle East occupy only a small part of the earth's surface. They began traveling the oceans, exploring the coasts of Africa, pursuing with trade and commerce in Asia, and colonizing America. Wherever Europeans went—especially Englishmen—they took with them this new way of thinking, a whole culture influenced by the Bible. And the day would come when missionaries would strive to carry the pure truths of the gospel to the four corners of the world, proclaiming that

> . . . God is no respecter of persons . . . in every nation he that feareth him, and worketh righteousness, is accepted with him (Acts 10:34–35).

The entire globe became a New World!

CHECK UP

1. When did the English Civil War begin? What were the two opposing parties called?
2. Who was the Puritan leader in the war? What were the troops in his New Model Army called?
3. Why did some people who had supported Cromwell change sides?
4. How did most of the people feel about the execution of the king?
5. Was Cromwell's commonwealth really a republic? Explain.
6. Who became king through the restoration of the monarchy?
7. What did Charles II promise France in the Treaty of Dover?
8. Whom did the people of England ask to rule England in place of James II?
9. What did the Glorious Revolution establish in England? Who became the new king and queen?
10. How did later monarchies differ from previous monarchies?

Identify: republic, Lord Protector, Whigs, Richard Cromwell, English Bill of Rights, Bloodless Revolution

---

CHAPTER 15 REVIEW

MULTIPLE CHOICE Write the letter of the answer that best completes each sentence.

1. Among the earliest known inhabitants of the British Isles were the _____.
   a Greeks   c Angles
   b Celts   d Romans
2. _____ conquered the Celts around 55 B.C.
   a Canute the Dane   c Julius Caesar
   b Augustine   d King Arthur
3. King Alfred the Great was responsible for _____.
   a *Beowulf*
   b *The Canterbury Tales*
   c *The Domesday Book*
   d *The Anglo-Saxon Chronicle*
4. The first Plantagenet king was _____.
   a Henry II   c John
   b Henry VIII   d Richard I

CHAPTER 15 REVIEW (CONTINUED)

5. _____ was forced to sign the Magna Carta in 1215.
   a Canute the Dane   c Richard I
   b Henry II   d John

6. _____ called the first meeting of Parliament in 1265.
   a Simon de Montfort c Henry Tudor
   b Edward I   d Henry VIII

7. The Wars of the Roses ended in 1485 with the Battle of _____.
   a Agincourt   c Bosworth Field
   b Calais   d Orleans

8. _____ was the first Tudor king of England.
   a Edward I   c Edward VI
   b Henry V   d Henry VII

9. Parliament declared _____ to be the supreme head of the English church.
   a Henry VIII   c James I
   b John Wycliffe d Charles V

10. _____ led Dutch patriots in defense against Spanish attacks.
    a Philip II
    b William the Silent
    c Queen Elizabeth I
    d Mary Stuart

11. _____ was the first Stuart ruler of England.
    a Elizabeth I   c James I
    b Mary Stuart   d Charles I

12. Those who supported the king in the Civil War were called _____.
    a Roundheads   c Cavaliers
    b Puritans   d Ironsides

13. King _____ was tried and executed by Cromwell's army.
    a Charles I   c Charles II
    b James I   d James II

14. _____ became Lord Protector of England after the Civil War.
    a Edward Coke   c Oliver Cromwell
    b Charles II   d Richard Cromwell

15. Charles II secretly signed the Treaty of _____ with Louis XIV.
    a Bosworth Field   c Agincourt
    b London   d Dover

16. _____ took England's throne in the Glorious Revolution.
    a William III and Mary II
    b Sir Christopher Wren
    c Charles II
    d James II

MATCHING _Match each description with the correct term._

a King Arthur   f John Foxe   k Roundheads
b _Domesday Book_   g William of Orange   l Oliver Cromwell
c Catherine of Aragon h John Hawkins   m Whigs
d Elizabeth   i Edward Coke   n _Beowulf_
e _Book of Common Prayer_ j Ironsides

_____ 1. built up the English fleet
_____ 2. made worship services more Protestant
_____ 3. Henry VIII's first wife
_____ 4. called the "Father of his country"
_____ 5. one of England's greatest lawyers
_____ 6. Cromwell's troops
_____ 7. opposed Charles II
_____ 8. called the "man of blood"
_____ 9. daughter of Anne Boleyn
_____ 10. greatest Saxon poem that still remains
_____ 11. Celtic hero
_____ 12. contained the results of the census
_____ 13. those who fought against Charles I
_____ 14. wrote the _Book of Martyrs_

COMPLETION *Choose the correct term to complete each sentence and write the letter in the blank.*

a John Knox
b William Shakespeare
c Mary, Queen of Scots
d Petition of Right
e Augustine
f Spanish Armada
g Puritans
h Druids
i William the Conqueror
j Richard the Lion-Hearted
k Edward I
l Hundred Years' War
m Sir Christopher Wren

1. The _____ were a special group of Celtic men who acted as teachers, judges, and priests.
2. _____ was the first archbishop of Canterbury.
3. _____ became the king of England after winning the Battle of Hastings.
4. The king known for his crusades to the Holy Land was _____.
5. _____ established the Model Parliament in 1295.
6. The _____ stemmed from a dispute over the French throne.
7. _____ was sent to France to be brought up in the court of the king.
8. The outstanding leader of the Scottish Reformation was _____.
9. The _____ was the greatest naval force the world had ever seen.
10. Perhaps the greatest writer of all times was _____.
11. Protestants who wanted to make the Church of England less like the Roman church were called _____.
12. The _____ merely reaffirmed the liberties and rights which Englishmen had won in the past.
13. _____ engineered the rebuilding of London after the Great Fire.

TIME LINE CHALLENGE *Choose the letter of the correct date for each of the events listed below.*

55 B.C.	878	1066	1215	1265	1485	1588	1642	1666	1688
A	B	C	D	E	F	G	H	I	J

_____ 1. Great Fire of London
_____ 2. First meeting of Parliament
_____ 3. Glorious Revolution
_____ 4. Julius Caesar conquers the Celts
_____ 5. King John signs the *Magna Carta*
_____ 6. William the Conqueror invades England
_____ 7. England's defeat of the Spanish Armada
_____ 8. Beginning of the English Civil War

CONCEPTS TO CONSIDER *On a separate sheet of paper, answer the following questions using complete sentences.*

1. What precedents for freedom were set by the Magna Carta and the Model Parliament?
2. Explain the significance of England's defeat of the Spanish Armada.

The Age of Exploration:
Asia and the Americas

HIGHLIGHTS

Prince Henry the Navigator • Marco Polo
Christopher Columbus • America • India • China • Japan, Korea, Indonesia

A Time of Discovery

Influence of Western Civilization

Throughout the Modern Age, Europe has had a tremendous impact on the rest of the world. In fact, **modern European civilization** (sometimes called **Western civilization**) has so profoundly influenced the world that the Modern Age is some-times called the *European Age.* There is scarcely a person in the world today who has not been affected by Western culture and its benefits, particularly the influence of Biblical Christianity. This spread of European influence across the globe began with the **Age of Exploration,** when the people of Europe began in earnest to explore all the oceans and continents of the world.

America and the Modern Age

World history, of course, would have been quite different if God had permitted European civilization, while still in medie-val darkness, to establish dominion over the rest of the world, especially in America. Some historians believe that a *Viking* explorer named **Leif Ericson** sailed to America around A.D. 1000, but Viking activity in the New World remained unknown to most Europeans and had no lasting consequences. The most important discovery of the age did not occur until 1492, when **Christopher Columbus,** an Italian explorer sailing on behalf of Spain, came to the New World. In the words of Alexis de Tocqueville [dĕ tôk′vēl′], one of the most profound thinkers of the Modern Age, it was "just then" that America was discovered, "as if it had been kept in reserve by the Deity and had just risen from beneath the waters of the Deluge."

America was not settled by Europeans on any great scale until the Modern Age began, and in North America the colonies of England eventually prevailed. After the Protestant Reformation, Biblical Christi-anity exerted more influence upon Eng-land than upon any other major country of Europe. As we have seen, this influence had, by the end of the 17th century, pro-duced a distinctively modern way of thinking in that country. This influence spread westward to the New World through the English colonies.

Christopher Columbus

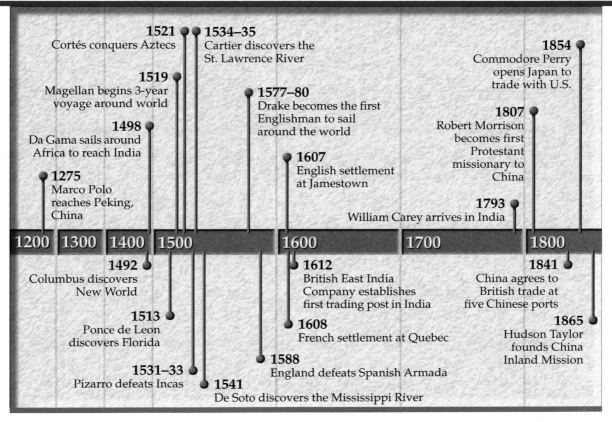

In 1588, England defeated the Spanish Armada in one of the most important battles in the history of the world. If God had permitted that fateful battle to end otherwise, England might have ceased to exist as an independent country. Perhaps there would have been no English Protestant colonies in America—and no United States of America as we know it today.

Eventually, England's American colonies became the independent country of the United States of America, where the true spirit of the Modern Age has received its most complete expression. We will study the United States in greater detail in the next chapter, but first we must broaden our focus beyond Europe and learn of other peoples and lands.

New Horizons

Effect of the Crusades. The Age of Exploration actually began as an outgrowth of the Crusades of the 11th, 12th, and 13th centuries. Europe's crusades failed in their stated objective: to reclaim the Holy Land from the Muslims. But they did accomplish something; they revived European interest in trade with the East, or **Orient,** as many Europeans called Asia. As crusaders returned from the East with silks, cotton, muslin, sugar, spices, and glassware, they kindled in other Europeans a desire for such goods, encouraging the growth of trade and commerce. In addition to these new goods, the Orient offered exciting ideas and inventions—algebra, arabic numerals, the mariner's compass, and paper—that captivated the minds of Western scholars.

Portugal and Henry the Navigator. It was in Portugal, Spain's western neighbor, that the "Age of Crusades" merged with the Age of Exploration. The crusading spirit remained strong in Portugal, and nowhere was it stronger than in the mind of **Prince**

Henry the Navigator (1394–1460), third son of King John I of Portugal.

Henry acquired his unusual name because of his one consuming interest: navigation. He set up a special school for sea captains, employed skilled mapmakers, and built an observatory to study the position of the sun and stars. He also developed a new kind of ship, the *caravel*, able to sail against the wind because of its triangular sail, and made use of all available navigational instruments, including the compass and *astrolabe* [ăs′trȯ·lāb: a device for determining navigational location by measuring the angles of celestial bodies above the horizon]. Henry sent out ship after ship—to the islands of the **Azores** [ə·zōrz′], the **Madeiras** [mə·dēr′əz], and the **Canaries** in the Atlantic, and further south down the coast of Africa until, in 1445, one reached **Cape Verde** [vār′dē], the westernmost point of the African continent.

Toward the Far East. As early as the 1200s, medieval Europeans were traveling by land to the **Far East.** They brought back glowing reports of wealth and splendor. The most important of these travelers was **Marco Polo** (c. 1254–1324), the son of an Italian merchant, who accompanied his father and his uncle on a trip to **China.** Marco Polo became *the first European to travel the whole length of Asia.* Upon his return in 1295, he wrote a book describing "the Kingdoms and Marvels of the East," especially China, with its swarming populations, its huge wealthy cities like Peking (modern Beijing), and its mighty ruler the Great Kublai Khan [kū′blī kän′]. Polo's colorful descriptions of the Orient spurred in many Europeans a keen interest in Asia.

By the 1300s, a brisk trade between Europe and Asia had developed, with Arab merchants of the Middle East acting as middle men. But when Europeans learned that Asia was bounded by an eastern ocean (they had previously considered Asia an indefinite land mass), they began to think

Marco Polo

that those middle men might be avoided if the Far East could be reached by water. <u>Finding a sea route to the Far East was thus a major objective of the Age of Exploration.</u>

In search of this route, Portuguese navigator **Bartholomeu Dias** [dē′əsh: 1450?–1500] sailed around the southern end of Africa (the **Cape of Good Hope**) in 1487. A mutiny prevented Dias from sailing on to Asia, but his voyage was nevertheless a trailblazing event in the Age of Exploration.

America: A New World to Explore

Christopher Columbus

A man with a vision. In 1488, when Bartholomeu Dias returned from his voyage, **Christopher Columbus** (1451–1506), an Italian-born adventurer, was waiting to greet the daring explorer. By that time, Columbus had his own plan for a voyage to the **"Indies,"** as the Far East was sometimes called. Columbus believed that Asia could be reached from Europe by sailing westward across the Atlantic Ocean.

Religion played a large role in Columbus's motives and plans. Columbus, who made much of the fact that his first

Columbus Landing in the New World

name means "Christ-bearer," was a devout Roman Catholic; it is said that he went through the daily prayers and chants of the Roman church more than the average priest did!

One word describes the kind of man Columbus was: *crusader*. He was very much a child of the age, and the same mixed motives that motivated Henry the Navigator (and the crusaders of the Middle Ages) also inspired Columbus. He wanted to sail across the Atlantic Ocean directly to Asia, conquer that continent, and use the wealth to finance one more crusade to capture the Holy Land from the Moslems—a crusade Columbus hoped to lead personally!

Naturally, Columbus took his plan to Portugal, which so far had been the leading country in the Age of Exploration. But King John II had determined to try to reach Asia by sailing around Africa, and in 1484 he rejected Columbus's proposal. Columbus then went to *Spain*, where he worked for *nine* years altogether to obtain support for his plan. His perseverance finally paid off in 1492 when **King Ferdinand** and **Queen Isabella,** overruling their advisers (who were actually better geographers than Columbus), agreed to sponsor Columbus's voyage.

The first voyage to America. After setting sail from Spain on August 3, 1492, Columbus and his men reached the Canary Islands on August 12. From there, they

sailed westward across the Atlantic. The journey started off well enough, for favorable winds kept the tiny ships—the *Niña* [nē′nyǎ], the *Pinta* [pēn′tǎ], and the *Santa Maria* [sän′tä mä·rē′ə]—moving quickly across the water. But the crew's fear increased each day as they sailed further and further from home.

After three weeks of sailing without sight of land, it became difficult to calm the fearful crew. But Columbus had not come this far in the fulfillment of his dreams to turn back now, and the indomitable explorer displayed the courage, determination, and iron will that have made him one of the great heroes of world history. He declared that he "had sailed to go to the Indies and would continue until he found them," and the cry was heard, "Sail on! Sail on!" In legend and story, in song and poem, those words—and the heroic character traits they represent—ring out in the history of the world, giving heart to all explorers to persevere, whether it be in the world of seas and continents or in the world of ideas.

By October 10, however, the sailors had begun to talk of mutiny. In desperation, Columbus agreed that if land were not sighted in three days the ships would turn around and head for home. On **October 12, 1492,** the third day, they finally reached land. Columbus had discovered America!

Asia or the New World? Columbus had discovered the New World—he had landed on the island of **San Salvador** [sǎn sǎl′və·dôr: "Holy Savior"] in the **Bahamas,** but he refused to believe it. Nothing, it seems, could shake his opinion of his destiny.

He refused to accept the plain evidence, which everywhere confronted him, that this was an entirely new world. All about were strange plants, known neither to Europe nor Asia. The copper-colored natives who paddled out to inspect his fleet could no more follow the Arabic widely understood in the east than they could Spanish. Yet Columbus, consulting his charts, convinced himself that he was in the Indies and called the natives "Indians."[1]

Continuing his search, Columbus discovered the islands of **Cuba** and **Hispaniola** [hĭs′pɑn·yō′lə: modern Haiti and the Dominican Republic]. After several weeks of exploring, he returned to Spain, still confident that he had reached the outskirts of Asia.

From adulation to frustration. King Ferdinand and Queen Isabella gave Columbus a hero's welcome upon his return. They thought that they had beaten Portugal to the Far East. (The Portuguese explorer **Vasco da Gama** [də gă′mə] did not sail around Africa and across the Indian Ocean to reach India until *1498*. Da Gama was actually the first European to reach the Far East by sea.)

But the tide soon turned against Columbus. In 1500, he returned from his third voyage to the New World—*in chains!* Columbus, like a typical crusader, could in one breath speak of himself as a kind of missionary while in the next breath demand wealth and glory as his reward. When he had made his proposal to the Spanish monarch for his first voyage, Columbus had demanded, in addition to three ships, that he be given the title *Admiral of the Ocean Sea,* that he be ruler of all the lands he might discover, and that he receive 10 percent of all the gold he brought home.

Columbus proved himself a harsh and cruel taskmaster in governing the Spanish colony he had started on the island of **Hispaniola.** A government agent sent to investigate put Columbus in chains and shipped him back to Spain to stand trial. The king and queen released him, but they decided that Columbus was not the man to govern the lands under their control.

Vasco da Gama

Columbus persuaded Ferdinand and Isabella to sponsor a fourth voyage to the "Indies" in 1502 by presenting the Spanish sovereigns with his *Book of Prophecies.* Supposedly interpreting the Bible, Columbus prophesied that the world would end in 1650 but that before that time, he would lead a crusade to liberate Jerusalem. To the end, Columbus seems to have been obsessed with the idea of finding gold in the Far East to finance a crusade to the Middle East.

But Columbus never found the gold, never found Asia, and, of course, never liberated Jerusalem. In 1504, he returned to Spain. Sick and frustrated, he died in 1506—certainly a man of destiny, but not as he had expected.

The Naming of America

On his third voyage to the New World, Christopher Columbus had stepped ashore on the continent of South America, on the coast of **Venezuela.** He called the continent an "Other World" (*otro mundo*). By this he meant not the New World, not the continents of North and South America, as we think of them, but rather some new land mass in south Asia trailing off from the Malay Peninsula. Columbus's main purpose on his fourth voyage was to find a strait (narrow passage connecting two large bodies of water) through this land mass, believing that Asia would be just on the other side.

The first man to realize that Columbus had discovered a new continent and not

---

[1]John A. Garraty, *The American Nation: A History of the United States* (New York: Harper-American Heritage, 1966) p. 18.

merely a part of Asia was **Amerigo Vespucci** [ä′mȧ·rē′gō vĕs·pōō′chĕ: 1451–1512], an Italian seaman who claimed to have made four voyages to the New World and allegedly wrote letters about his exploits. In one of these letters, he supposedly made this statement:

> These regions we may rightly call *Mundus Novus*, a New World, because our ancestors had no knowledge of them....[2]

In 1507, a German cartographer (mapmaker) suggested that the New World be named for Amerigo Vespucci, and by 1530 it had become common practice in Europe (except in Spain and Portugal) to call the New World *America.*

CHECK UP

1. Why is the Modern Age sometimes called the European Age?
2. Who may have made the first discovery of America? When?
3. Explain the significance of England's defeat of the Spanish Armada to American history.
4. How did the crusades lead to the Age of Exploration?
5. In what nation did the Age of Crusades merge with the Age of Exploration?
6. Name the first European to travel the length of Asia.
7. What was Christopher Columbus's plan for reaching the Far East?
8. Describe the religious motives of Christopher Columbus.
9. Who agreed to assist Columbus?
10. Who actually *did* become the first European to reach the Far East by sea? When?
11. For whom was America named?

Identify: Prince Henry the Navigator, caravel, astrolabe, Bartholomeu Dias, San Salvador, Hispaniola, Admiral of the Ocean Sea, *Book of Prophecies*

---

[2]Quoted in Morison, *The Oxford History of the American People*, p. 31.

Spain in the New World

Spain's crusade in America. Moving out from the colony Columbus had established on Hispaniola, Spain began to eagerly explore and conquer the New World.

(1) The islands of the Caribbean Sea were quickly and easily subdued.

(2) In 1513, **Ponce de León** [dā lā·ôn′] *made the first Spanish landing on the North American mainland* when he discovered Florida while searching for a mythical "fountain of youth."

(3) Also in 1513, **Vasco de Balboa** [bäl·bō′ȧ] *crossed the Isthmus of Panama and discovered the Pacific Ocean.* Europeans now realized that, contrary to what Columbus had thought, a vast ocean lay between the New World and the Far East.

(4) In 1519, **Ferdinand Magellan** [mȧ·jĕl′ȧn], a Portuguese sailor working for Spain, embarked on a *three-year voyage around the world.* (Magellan died in the Philippines, but his crew finished the voyage.) Of the five ships that began the expedition, only one ship with 18 men made it home safely. Magellan's epic voyage proved once and for all that the world *is* round. It also demonstrated the size of South America and the vast distance between the New World and the Orient.

(5) Also in 1519, the Spanish conquest of the American mainland began when **Hernando Cortés** [kôr·tĕz′] landed in Mexico. By 1521, he had *conquered the Aztec Indians.* The Aztecs, ruled at the time by a rich and powerful chieftain named *Montezuma,* had developed a remarkably advanced culture that included a calendar, writing, and beautiful architecture. It was their rich gold and silver mines, however, that impressed Cortés.

(6) Between 1531 and 1533, **Francisco Pizarro** [pĭ·zär′ō] *conquered the Inca Indians of Peru.* The Incas had also developed an impressive civilization. Advanced in engineering and architecture, they developed an excellent

system of roads and built amazing structures with stones cut so precisely that they fit together without mortar. Like Cortés and other *conquistadores* [kŏn·kēs′tə·dôrz: conquerors], Pizarro confiscated the Indians' wealth and then enslaved them, forcing them to work in gold and silver mines for Spain.

(7) In 1540–1542, **Francisco Coronado** [kŏr′ō·nä′dō] explored the southwestern United States—marching through parts of Arizona, New Mexico, Texas, Oklahoma, and Kansas. One party of his men *discovered the Grand Canyon.*

(8) Around the same time, **Hernando de Soto** [dĕ sō′tō] explored the southern United States, including parts of Florida, Georgia, the Carolinas, Tennessee, Alabama, Mississippi, Arkansas, and Louisiana. De Soto *discovered the Mississippi River* in 1541.

(9) In 1542, **Juan Cabrillo** [kä·brē′lyō], a Portuguese employed by Spain, *explored the coast of California.*

Vasco de Balboa

Francisco Coronado

Ferdinand Magellan

Hernando Cortés   *Hernando de Soto*   *Ponce de Leon*

THE NEW WORLD TODAY

160°   140°   120°   100°   80°   60°   40°   20°   0°

80°

ARCTIC
OCEAN

Ellesmere
Island

GREENLAND

Victoria
Island

Baffin
Bay

Baffin Island

ICELAND

ARCTIC CIRCLE

Alaska
(U.S.)

60°

Gulf of Alaska

Labrador
Sea

Hudson
Bay

UNITED
KINGDOM

IRELAND

CANADA

NORTH
AMERICA

FRANCE

Ottawa

40°

UNITED STATES

PORTUGAL   SPAIN

Washington, D.C.

ATLANTIC OCEAN

PACIFIC

MEXICO

Gulf of
Mexico

MOROCCO

ALGERIA

TROPIC OF CANCER

OCEAN

Hawaii
(U.S.)

20°

Havana

WEST INDIES

MAURITANIA

Mexico City

Caribbean Sea

MALI

CENTRAL

AMERICA

Caracas

VENEZUELA   GUYANA   SURINAME

Bogotá

COLOMBIA

FRENCH
GUIANA

0° EQUATOR

ECUADOR

SOUTH

PERU

BRAZIL

AMERICA

THE WEST INDIES
AND CENTRAL AMERICA

Lima

Brasília

BOLIVIA

Florida

BAHAMAS

PUERTO
RICO

PARAGUAY

Havana

CUBA

JAMAICA   HAITI

DOMINICAN
RUPUBLIC

20°

TROPIC OF
CAPRICORN

GUATEMALA

Caribbean Sea

BELIZE

HONDURAS

CHILE

URUGUAY

EL SALVADOR

NICARAGUA

PANAMA

VENEZUELA

ARGENTINA

Buenos
Aires

COSTA
RICA

COLOMBIA

40°

Falkland Islands
(U.K.)

Strait of
Magellan

Tierra del Fuego

Cape Horn

160°   140°   120°   100°   80°   60°   40°   20°

Many Africans accompanied the Spanish as they explored the New World, some as slaves or hired servants and some as freemen. One of the best-known Africans to join the Spanish explorers was **Estevanico** [ås·tå·vä·nē′kŏ], who accompanied expeditions through Florida, Texas, New Mexico, Arizona, and Mexico.

Within 50 years of Columbus's discovery, Spain controlled a vast empire in the New World that included South America (except Brazil), Central America, Florida, California, and the southwestern United States. Still claiming exclusive rights to the rest of the North American continent, Spain set out to build a "New Spain" on American soil. The Spanish remade the New World in the image of the "Old World," complete with medieval cities, universities, and churches typical of the homeland. They even established a feudal arrangement for the Indians, forcing them to work as slaves in gold and silver mines and in the fields of Spanish plantations. The huge quantities of gold and silver that poured into Spain from the New World soon made her the most powerful country in the world.

Spain's crusade against Protestantism. Meanwhile, the Protestant Reformation had shattered the religious unity of the Old World. When the Roman church responded with the *Counter-Reformation,* Spain dedicated its wealth and power to the defeat of Protestantism. This new crusade was led by King **Philip II,** who came to the Spanish throne in 1556. With his claimed or actual possessions in the New World, Philip probably <u>controlled more of the surface of the earth than any other human being in history</u>. In 1580, he succeeded to the throne of Portugal, acquiring Portugal's claims in Asia and South America. But all of this was not enough: Philip wanted to rule the world.

Like the crusaders before him, however, Philip had plans that clashed with the Divine Will. God used little England to sink Philip's ships and Philip's hopes. *Along with Columbus's discovery in 1492, England's defeat of the Spanish Armada in 1588 ranks as a key event in the Modern Age.*

Other Nations in the New World

Portugal. Shortly after Columbus discovered America, a dispute arose between Portugal and Spain over the new lands. As a result, the two nations agreed in 1494 to divide the New World. All lands west of a certain point were reserved for Spain, and all lands east of that point were reserved for Portugal. Although Spain gained the most land by this agreement, Portugal gained the rich territory of **Brazil.** Portuguese navigator **Pedro Cabral** [kə·bräl′: 1460?–1526?] *discovered Brazil* and claimed it for Portugal in 1500. By the 1530s, the Portuguese had begun to colonize the region.

France. While Spain and Portugal concentrated on the southern half of the New World, France began to explore the northern half, hoping to find the *Northwest Passage,* a supposed water route through North America to the Pacific.

(1) In 1524, **Giovanni de Verrazano** [dä vär′rä·tsä′nŏ], an Italian, *explored the eastern coast of North America* for France, from North Carolina to Nova Scotia.

(2) Between 1534 and 1535, **Jacques Cartier** [kår′tyā′] led an expedition that *discovered the St. Lawrence River.*

(3) In 1608, **Samuel de Champlain** [de shăm·plān′], known as the "<u>Father of New France</u>," *founded the first permanent French colony in the New World, Quebec.*

(4) In 1673, **Jacques Marquette** [mår′kĕt′] and **Louis Joliet** [zhô′lyĕ′], a Jesuit missionary and a fur trader respectively, *explored the central Mississippi River.*

(5) In 1682, **Robert Cavalier de la Salle** [kå′vĕ·ĭyā de lə săl′] sailed down the Mississippi to the Gulf of Mexico. La Salle *claimed the entire Mississippi Valley for France* and named it *Louisiana* in honor of King Louis XIV.

Jacques Cartier

Sir Francis Drake

France eventually claimed Canada, the Great Lakes region, and the Mississippi Valley as **"New France."** The French established a thriving fur trade in North America, but they never fully settled "New France." France would eventually give up, by war or by sale, her New World possessions.

Holland. In 1609, **Henry Hudson,** an English navigator sailing for the Dutch, *discovered Delaware Bay and the Hudson River* and claimed the area for Holland. But by 1664, **"New Netherland"** had been absorbed by the one European country which more than any other would leave her mark on the North American continent—England.

England. In 1497, **John Cabot,** an Italian navigator in the service of King Henry VII of England, explored the eastern coast of North America from *Labrador* to *Virginia.* Cabot was the <u>first explorer</u> (for any country) <u>to reach the North American mainland</u>; he staked England's claim to territory in the New World **("New-found land"**—later Newfoundland of eastern Canada). These English activities in America were naturally quite disturbing to Spain.

Between 1577 and 1580, the explorer **Sir Francis Drake** became *the first Englishman to sail around the world.* As he followed Magellan's route around South America, Drake looted Spanish ships of their cargoes of silver and gold and raided Spanish settlements on the Pacific Coast of North America. He even explored the western coastline, California in particular, and claimed the region for England, calling it **Nova Albian—**"New England."

It was the destiny of England, however, to build *New England* not on the Pacific Coast of North America but rather on the Atlantic Coast, and after the defeat of the Armada in 1588, there was absolutely nothing that Spain could do to prevent it. Indeed, by that time, Englishman **Sir Walter Raleigh** had already founded a colony on *Roanoke Island,* off the coast of North Carolina. Sometime before 1590, the Roanoke colony disappeared without a trace. But in **1607,** more English settlers came to America and established the <u>first permanent English settlement in the New World</u> at **Jamestown, Virginia.**

Meanwhile, another spirit stirred England during the Elizabethan Age—the

273

spirit of individual freedom and responsibility, which grew as more and more Englishmen read the Bible for themselves. Within a century of the defeat of the Spanish Armada, an untold number of lives would be changed in England as men recognized that God holds them personally accountable for their beliefs and actions. A flood of blessings came to 17th-century England as the true spirit of individual freedom and responsibility spilled over into the affairs of this life—in politics, economics, philosophy, science, art, and literature.

America's Destiny

Midst such momentous events, bold individuals, thinking the possibilities of immediate freedom to be brighter in the wilderness of America, set out for the New World. If it is true that "America" is in a sense as much an idea as a land—as much an ideal, a vision, or a dream, as an actuality—these freedom-loving, 17th-century Englishmen were the true discoverers of America. They, more than anyone who came to America before, correctly sensed God's true purpose, as subsequent events would reveal, for setting aside the New World from the Old and permitting it to remain hidden for so long.

"It was there," as Alexis de Tocqueville wrote, "that civilized man was destined to build society on new foundations, and for the first time applying theories till then unknown or deemed unworkable, to present the world with a spectacle for which past history had not prepared it." It was there that the blessings of religious and civil liberty flowed most fully, watered by the blood of patriots who died for the privilege of shouldering the responsibilities of freedom, and this not only for themselves but for their posterity and indeed for all mankind. It was there that the leading country of the Modern Age arose—a country destined to become the hiding place of the world from tyranny. Contemplating the

providence of God in the history of America, we stand amazed; we can only ask in wonder, as did Roger Williams, one of many 17th-century Englishmen who sought refuge for their consciences in America,

How unsearchable are the depths of the wisdom and power of God in separating from Europe, Asia, and Africa such a mighty vast continent as America is? And that for so many ages? As also, by such a western ocean of about three thousand English miles' breadth in passage over?

CHECK UP

1. Name three Spanish explorers and conquerors and describe their accomplishments.
2. What Spanish king probably controlled more of the surface of the earth than any other human being in history? What do you remember about him from your study of England?
3. What are two key events of the Modern Age?
4. What part of the New World did France concentrate on exploring? Did she keep her New World possessions?
5. Name three French explorers and describe their accomplishments.
6. Who was the first explorer to reach the North American mainland? For whom did he explore? What area did he explore?
7. Who became the first Englishman to sail around the world? What name did he give to California?
8. Name the colony founded by Sir Walter Raleigh. What happened to it?
9. What spirit stirred England during the Elizabethan Age? How would this affect the destiny of America?

Identify: conquistadores, Estevanico, "Father of New France," Quebec, Louisiana, New France, Henry Hudson, New Netherland, Newfoundland, Jamestown

Asia: Mysterious Lands of the East

With the opening of the Modern Age, the people of Europe "rediscovered" the countries of **Asia,** *the largest continent.* The resulting impact of East upon West and West upon East would be inestimable.

General Early History of the Far East

Early cultures and inventions. History indicates that people came to Asia shortly after the dispersion. River valleys in Southwest, South, and East Asia became sites of organized cultures very early in history. By the time these cultures developed, Asians knew the fundamentals of cookery, ore smelting, pottery, irrigation, crop rotation, animal domestication, wood carving, stone cutting, monument making, and calculation (including the decimal system and measurement). They had invented the *wheel,* the *saddle,* the *harness,* the *chariot,* and a form of *paper.* They had also made advances in medicine and law.

Religions. All major world religions had their beginnings in Asia. The ones we will focus on here are **Buddhism, Confucianism, Hinduism, Islam, Shinto,** and **Taoism.** As you will see, all of these non-Biblical religions are basically the same and lead to the same spiritual, social, and economic results. Each rejects the one, true God of the Bible, and embraces the worship of false gods—whether spirits, men, or idols— espousing rebellion against the Creator. Under the tyranny of these false religions that glorify, even deify, men, countless souls are forced to try to work out their own salvation. The darkness of pagan religions and traditions has impeded economic and social progress in Asia for centuries, robbing the people of their individual freedoms and keeping them in spiritual darkness.

Dynasties and empires. The ancient history of Asia is mainly a story of dynasties and empires. Some early city-states developed, but the tendency was to build ever-larger empires. In spite of early cultural advances, Asian civilizations brought forth the idea that their rulers were god-kings with total power over everyone and everything.

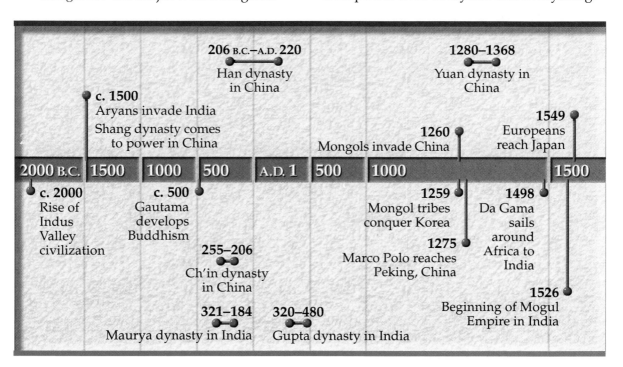

Timeline (2000 B.C.–1500):

- **206 B.C.–A.D. 220** Han dynasty in China
- **1280–1368** Yuan dynasty in China
- **c. 1500** Aryans invade India; Shang dynasty comes to power in China
- **1260** Mongols invade China
- **1549** Europeans reach Japan
- **c. 2000** Rise of Indus Valley civilization
- **c. 500** Gautama develops Buddhism
- **1259** Mongol tribes conquer Korea
- **1498** Da Gama sails around Africa to India
- **255–206** Ch'in dynasty in China
- **1275** Marco Polo reaches Peking, China
- **1526** Beginning of Mogul Empire in India
- **321–184** Maurya dynasty in India
- **320–480** Gupta dynasty in India

ASIA TODAY

ARCTIC OCEAN

Bering Sea

RUSSIA

Moscow

Ural Mountains

Arctic Circle

Lena R.

Sea of Okhotsk

PACIFIC OCEAN

KAZAKHSTAN

Aral Sea

MONGOLIA

Ulan Bator

Sea of Japan

JAPAN

Tokyo

Black Sea

TURKEY

Ankara

Caspian Sea

Tashkent

Bishkek

Alma-Ata

KYRGYZSTAN

N. KOREA

CYPRUS
Nicosia
LEBANON
Beirut
ISRAEL
Jerusalem
JORDAN
Amman

SYRIA
Damascus

IRAQ

Baghdad

Tehran

UZBEKISTAN

TURKMENISTAN

TAJIKISTAN

AshKhabad

Dushanbe

P'yŏngyang

Beijing

S. KOREA
Seoul

KUWAIT
Al Kuwait

IRAN

AFGHANISTAN

Kabul

CHINA

Hoang Ho R.

Yellow Sea

SAUDI

BAHRAIN

Riyadh

QATAR

UNITED ARAB EMIRATES

Abu Dhabi

Islamabad

Indus R.

Yangtze R.

East China Sea

ARABIA

PAKISTAN

NEPAL

Himalayas

Taipei

Muscat

Gulf of Oman

New Delhi

Kathmandu

BHUTAN
Thimphu

TAIWAN

San'a
YEMEN

OMAN

BANGLA-DESH
Dhaka

Hong Kong
(U.K.)

Gulf of Aden

Red Sea

Persian Gulf

INDIA

Ganges R.

BURMA

Hanoi

Philippine Sea

Arabian Sea

Vientiane

LAOS

VIETNAM

Manila

Bay of Bengal

Rangoon

THAILAND

PHILIPPINES

Bangkok

CAMBODIA

Phnom Penh

SRI LANKA

South China Sea

Colombo

Gulf of Thailand

Equator

MALDIVES

BRUNEI
Bandar Seri Begawan

New G

INDIAN OCEAN

Kuala Lumpur

MALAYSIA

Singapore
SINGAPORE

Borneo

Celebes

Sumatra

INDONESIA

Java

Jakarta

Mediterranean Sea

Asian feudalism. The common man in the ancient Asian world was subject to forced labor or forced relocation; it was the practice during those times to move large groups of people whether or not they desired the change. Feudalism tied people so closely together that it was hard for them to live as individuals. Plagued by *feudal wars,* in which professional soldiers of the noble class fought in horse-drawn chariots, the scattered states of Asia were governed by little more than anarchy.

India: Ancient Subcontinent

Indus Valley civilization. Separated from most of Asia by the **Himalayan Mountains,** the nation of India (named for the **Indus River**) is called a *subcontinent* because of its size and relative isolation. Indian civilization first arose about 2000 B.C. in the **Indus River Valley** (in northwestern India and Pakistan). The Indus Valley people, possibly descendants of Ham, built great cities such as **Harappa** [hə·răp′ə] and **Mohenjo-Daro** [mō·hĕn′jō·dä′rō: "Mound of the Dead"]. These ancient cities were both prosperous and advanced, with populations as large as 35,000. The streets were carefully planned and contained extensive drainage systems. The houses were con-

structed of bricks, and some consisted of two stories built around an open courtyard. Some homes even had indoor plumbing! The Indus Valley people developed an industry of cotton spinning and weaving and produced fine pottery. The growth of agricultural and commercial economy through irrigation and trade allowed for the swift spread of India's population to other parts of the country, such as the fertile **Ganges River Valley** (in northern India).

Aryan conquests. About 1500 B.C., fierce nomadic tribes called **Aryans** entered India from the northwest mountain passes and overwhelmed the native population. The Aryans, descendants of Japheth, brought a new language (Sanskrit), new gods, and a new social structure (priests, warriors, and commoners) to India. The social and religious customs that the Aryans developed laid the groundwork for India's two distinctive cultural features: **Hinduism** and the **caste system.**

Caste system. To better understand the religion of Hinduism, one must first examine the caste system. To control the native Indian population, the Aryans devised a strict social structure known as the caste system. The four traditional castes were the **Brahmans** *(priests and scholars),* the **Kshatriyas** *(warriors and rulers),* the **Vaisyas** *(skilled workers and merchants),* and the **Sudras** *(unskilled workers).* Each caste was hereditary and had its own distinctive rules of behavior. A person born into a particular caste could never hope to work his way to a higher caste, in spite of all his aspirations and achievements. He had to marry within his caste, follow its rules religiously, and pass his caste on to his children. Gradually, the four traditional castes were subdivided into thousands of subcastes, creating a very complicated society.

India: Countryside in Rajasthan during dry season (top) and during monsoon season (below).

277

Buddha

Hinduism. The caste system became a major component of Hinduism. Hinduism is not based on the teaching of any one man. It is polytheistic (involving worship of many gods) and includes animal worship (mainly sacred bulls and cows); for this reason, some sects prohibit the consumption of meat. Hindus believe that the soul of every being in the universe, including the many gods they worship, is part of one absolute, impersonal, universal spirit they call **Brahma.** The ultimate goal of the Hindu is to identify so closely with nature that he loses all consciousness of his individual spirit and will—his personal identity—and becomes one with this universal spirit. This union involves a continuous process of rebirth called *reincarnation,* the supposed appearance of a soul after death in another body. Hindus believe that a person's deeds in this life determine his station in the next: a good man may be reincarnated as a person of higher caste, whereas an evil man may be reincarnated as a person of lower caste or even as an animal.

Buddhism. The religion of Buddhism also originated in India. About 500 B.C., Siddhartha **Gautama** (563–483 B.C.), an upper-caste Hindu nobleman, became dissatisfied with Hinduism and developed his own religious philosophy. Gautama renamed himself **Buddha** ("Enlightened One"), abandoned his wife and infant son, and became a monk, exchanging a life of luxury for one of self-denial. Concluding that desire is the cause of all suffering, Buddha said that man's righteousness, or self-discipline, is the path to perfect peace and happiness. The belief in reincarnation prompted Buddha and his followers to work toward that perfect peace, a paradise of escape called *nirvana,* by breaking any attachment they had to worldly, material things. Before Buddha's death his disciples virtually worshiped him, praying to him and revering any articles associated with him.

The Maurya Empire. Between 521 and 367 B.C., much of northwestern India was part of the mighty Persian Empire. Alexander the Great conquered the Persian Empire and invaded India in 326 to establish a short-lived Greek rule over the Indus Valley. After Alexander's death, a native Indian family, the Mauryas [mä′o͞or·yəz], drove out the Greeks, conquered the entire northern plain, and established the **Maurya Empire** (321–184 B.C.). Its greatest ruler, **Asoka** (273–232 B.C.), extended his dominion southward until he *controlled over two thirds of the Indian subcontinent.* Asoka then converted from Hinduism to *Buddhism,* renounced war and conquest, and devoted the remainder of his life to spreading Buddhism throughout southeastern Asia. In keeping with Buddhism's reverence for animals, he set up animal hospitals and made laws to prevent cruelty to animals. He also had hospitals built for his subjects. During Asoka's reign, wells were dug, roadways were beautified with trees, and Indian art and literature flourished.

Gupta, Mogul, and British rule. The collapse of the Maurya Empire was followed by centuries of foreign invasion, internal disorder, and civil strife. Between A.D. 320 and 480, the **Guptas,** another native Indian dynasty, established rule over northern India and *inaugurated a "golden age" of peace and prosperity.* During this time, the Indians made great advances in art, literature, mathematics, and science. Under the Guptas, *Hinduism* again became the chief religion of India, and Buddhism declined in the region.

India was subject to foreign invasions throughout the Middle Ages. *Islam* came to India during this time, and large numbers of Indians became Muslims. In 1526, Muslim invaders founded the mighty **Mogul Empire.** The beautiful *Taj Mahal* at Agra was built by a Mogul emperor as a tomb for his favorite wife. Under Mogul rule, 20 percent of India's people became Muslims. The Mogul Empire ruled India until the 1700s, when the **British East India Company** came to power.

Consequences of pagan religion. Although the Indians made many cultural advancements over the centuries, their <u>pagan religions hindered progress</u>. The results of the Hindu social structure and religious system on education are not hard to understand. The majority of the people were of the lower castes and were therefore deemed unworthy of education. Consequently, most of the Indian population was illiterate.

The Hindus failed to recognize the value of each man as a human being. Instead, men were respected or despised according to their level in society. If a man belonged to an exalted level, such as the Brahmans, he was almost venerated; if he belonged to a lower level, such as the Sudras, he was overlooked, or leaned upon, or trodden underfoot. There was no recog-

nition of a man's inherent right to be educated for the best of which he is capable. *The primary educational law was that each person be taught his place in life.*

Thus, the only hope of the lower-caste Hindu was that at the end of his life his soul might reappear in a personality of higher caste. His dread was that it might reappear in some still lower form of existence.

As a result, the Indian people generally became patient, docile, peaceable, resigned, and polite. They developed almost none of that ambition for high personal achievement which makes men energetic in character and effective in life. They learned little of that self-reliance and sense of personal responsibility that are necessary to the performance of duty.

It is not surprising, then, that in India, as one scholar has pointed out:

. . . we find the department of *history* altogether neglected, or rather nonexistent. For history requires understanding—the power of looking at an object in an independent objective light, and comprehending it in its rational connection with other objects. Those peoples therefore are alone capable of history, and of prose generally, who have arrived at that period of development (and can make that their starting point) at which individuals comprehend their own existence as independent, i.e. possess self-consciousness.

. . . the Hindus . . . are by birth given over to an unyielding destiny, while at the same time their spirit is exalted to ideality. This makes them incapable of writing history. All that happens is dissipated in their minds into confused dreams. What we call historical truth and veracity—intelligent, thoughtful comprehension of events, and fidelity in representing them—nothing of this sort can be looked for among the Hindus.

Taj Mahal

Bathing in the Ganges: *Hindu pilgrims come to the city of Varanasi to bathe in the sacred Ganges River, believing its waters can wash away their sins.*

CHECK UP

1. List some inventions of early Asian people.
2. Name six religions that began in Asia. How are they similar? What have been the results of these false religions?
3. Why is India called a subcontinent?
4. Where did the first Indian civilization develop? Name and describe two ancient cities located there.
5. Why was the caste system formed? Name the four traditional castes.
6. Name some basic Hindu beliefs. What is the goal of Hinduism?
7. Describe some of the teachings of Buddha.
8. Who was the greatest ruler of the Mauryan Empire? What religion did he promote?
9. Which dynasty began a golden age of Indian culture? What religion became prevalent during this dynasty?
10. What religion did the Mogul Empire promote?

Identify: Aryans, Brahma, reincarnation, nirvana, Taj Mahal, British East India Company

China

Geographical features. With a written history extending over 35 centuries, China is the world's oldest living civilization. Mainland China is today the *world's largest country in population* and the *third largest in area.* Ancient China was bounded by the Gobi Desert to the north, the Pacific Ocean to the east, and the Tibetan mountain systems to the south and west. One of these mountain systems, the Himalayas, separates China from India. Two great river systems—the **Hwang Ho** [hwäng' hō'] and the **Yangtze** [yăng'[t]sē]—begin in the Tibetan highlands and drain the fertile, heavily populated plains of eastern China before emptying into the Pacific Ocean. The Hwang Ho is called the "Yellow River" because of its yellowish-brown color; it is also called "China's sorrow" because of frequent flooding.

Early dynasties. The first known Chinese civilization arose in the **Hwang Ho Valley** shortly after the dispersion from the Tower of Babel. The ancient Chinese called their land *Chung-kuo* ("Middle Country") because they believed that China stood at the geographic and cultural center of the earth. Because China is surrounded by towering mountains, vast deserts, and great seas, the ancient Chinese developed a culture distinctly different from that of Mesopotamia, Egypt, or even India. For centuries, the Chinese lived in virtual isolation from the rest of the world.

China's history revolves around ten dynasties. Around 1500 B.C., the **Shang dynasty** (1766–1122 B.C.) came to power. During the Shang dynasty, the Chinese began casting bronze, building horse-drawn chariots, and cultivating silkworms. Most important, they developed a system of writing. The priests of this dynasty used pictographs to record events and keep records, laying the foundation of the intricate written Chinese language.

After about 500 years, the Shang dynasty was replaced by the **Ch'ou dynasty**

Imperial Palace in Beijing (Peking): Built for the Ming emperors in the 15th century, the Imperial Palace still stands in Beijing. It contains 9,000 rooms and covers 250 acres.

Confucius

(1122–255 B.C.). During this time, the arts and scholarship flourished, Chinese laws were written down for the first time, and the basis of oriental thought was formulated by Confucius and Lao-tse.

Confucianism. Confucianism had its beginnings in China about the time that Buddhism arose in India. **Confucius** (c. 551–479 B.C.) did not teach worship or life after death; he saw high standards of morality to be the savior of society. *From the 100s B.C. to the mid-20th century, Confucian thought was the most influential force in Chinese education, government, and attitudes.* As the official state "philosophy," Confucianism, which held the past as sacred, also held back Chinese progress.

Confucius was born in a time of great degeneracy and disorder. The country then had a feudal system. A succession of weak monarchs had so strengthened the nobles that they were almost independent of imperial authority. Confucius endeavored to improve the state of society by reviving interest in the ideas and customs of the past. He tried to do this in a practical way as an official in his own province. He at first met with some success, but was soon obliged to give up his office and depart from the capital. With persistent devotion to the interests of his country, he wandered from court to court, offering his services and instructing disciples. Most rulers were unwilling to adopt his measures, and in his old age he returned disappointed to his native province to die.

Confucius's books set forth a comprehensive natural system of morals recognizing five human relations: **sovereign and subject, parent and child, husband and wife, brother and brother, friend and friend.** These relationships require the exercise of five fundamental virtues: **benevolence, justice, wisdom, politeness,** and **good faith.**

The books abound in excellent precepts. The following are a few of the best:

Pity the widow and the fatherless, and give succor to brute animals.

When you see the right, do it; when you know your fault, correct it.

Kindness must be repaid, but not injury.

Do not to others what you would not have done to you.

One important relationship omitted by Confucius was the relation of man to his Maker. Confucianism fails to recognize the living God, who is the source of all goodness, justice, and judgment.

Taoism. **Lao-tse** (c. 604–531 B.C.) emphasized harmony with nature. His teachings became known as Taoism. Its polytheistic beliefs, based on Chinese folk religion, rejected Confucianism's emphasis on society, teaching instead that people should avoid worldly affairs and live close to nature. In Taoism, a priest acts as a mediator between the people and the gods. In group meetings, Taoists seek elimination of sins by means of incantations, penance, fasting, and extremely loud music. Desperate for assurance of future life, some Taoist groups have in vain sought immortality by means of special diets, meditation, and magic.

Ch'in dynasty. Weakened by feudal strife and warfare, the Ch'ou dynasty crumbled, and in its stead arose the remarkable **Ch'in dynasty** (255–206 B.C.). The name *China* comes from the Ch'in dynasty. Led by Ch'in *Shih Huang Ti* [shǐr′ hwäng′ tē′: *Shih* meaning "first" and *Huang Ti* meaning "sovereign emperor" or "imperial ruler"], this new dynasty abolished the trouble-ridden ancient feudal system and established a centralized monarchy. Emperor Ch'in joined the feudal states and built <u>the first united Chinese empire</u>.

The Ch'in dynasty made great strides of progress. A new method of irrigation was introduced, and a vast inland communication system spread across the empire. Rivers were joined by a series of canals, and a network of roads further aided travel and communication. The **Great Wall of China**—built during the Ch'in dynasty primarily for protection against the nomadic, barbarous *Huns*—remains <u>the world's longest fortification</u>. Constructed partly of masonry and partly of packed earth, the Great Wall connected already existing feudal walls and finally stretched 1,500 miles. The wall itself is 30 feet high and is garrisoned by 40-foot-high watchtowers. So many lives were lost in its construction that the Great Wall of China has been called "the longest cemetery in the world."

The Ch'in dynasty became a relentless military government. Ch'in felt the retrospective, conservative ideas of Confucius were a threat to the advancement of his power and would not stand for any oppo-

The Great Wall of China

sition from Confucian scholars. He ordered that 460 of them be buried alive and that most Confucian books be burned.

Han dynasty. The **Han dynasty** (206 B.C.–A.D. 220) marked the height of ancient China's power and glory. The **Great Silk Road** linked China with the Roman world, and it is possible that the first Christian missionaries came to China over this road during the Han Empire. *Buddhism* also entered China from India under the Han rulers, joining Confucianism and Taoism as a cultural force in Chinese life. During this dynasty, Chinese astrologers devised a calendar of 365 ¼ days, like our own, and Chinese artisans wove silk cloth and made glazed pottery plates (chinaware). About A.D. 105, **T'sai Lun** [tsī′ lo͞on′] <u>invented paper</u>.

Printing in China. Printing began in China over 1000 years ago (when Europeans were still laboriously producing handwritten books). In 1045, **Pi Sheng,** a Chinese printer and alchemist (practitioner of the medieval form of trial-and-error chemistry), <u>developed the first movable type</u>. However, because of the thousands of characters (symbols) in the Chinese language, printing from wood blocks was more practical for their language. In 1313, **Wang Chen,** a magistrate interested in publishing a treatise on the history of technology, had over 60,000 Chinese characters carved and also <u>developed a system for the easier handling</u>

<u>of type</u>. The complicated written Chinese language greatly hindered scientific development, and the spoken language had no distinct, individual sounds to be represented by individual letters or symbols. Therefore, a great number of characters had to be employed singly and in combinations to represent things and ideas.

Science and anthropomorphism. Though the Chinese made great advances over the centuries, the cultural boons of the dynasties were near-sighted conceptions meant to suit the needs of the moment. Progressive measures were not founded upon scientific principles but were based solely upon observation and trial-and-error experimentation. This unscientific approach to nature is the product of Asiatic paganism, which stresses the "oneness" of nature—complete unity of everything— and assigns human characteristics to gods, animals, and even inanimate objects, a practice called *anthropomorphism.*

When man projects his own characteristics on nature, man is, in effect, worshiping himself, worshiping the creature rather than the Creator (Rom. 1:21–25). While striving for this unity with nature, man deliberately relinquishes his individuality. Paradoxically, rather than satisfying or exalting man, *this humanistic view of nature actually stifles man's achievement* because he is overly awed by nature and does not strive to subdue it as Scripture commands. Thus, instead of conquering and mastering nature, he becomes a slave to its tyranny.

Since the main motive of science is the mastery of nature, the Asians were left without the motivating force for more substantial, consequential levels of cultural and economic activity. Their shifting sands of technology lacked the basic, solid foundation of theoretical, natural science.

Mongolian rule. Medieval China was beset by civil wars and a succession of dynasties. Finally, in the 1200s, the **Mongols,** fierce nomads from northern Asia, swept into China. Under **Genghis Khan** [jěng′gĭs kän′], they conquered northern China and Korea and plundered northern India and Persia (modern Iran). His empire, which extended from China and Korea to Europe's Danube River, was <u>the largest empire in history</u>. The Mongol empire reached its peak in the mid-1200s under Genghis Khan's grandson, **Kublai Khan,** who established the **Yuan dynasty** (1280–1368). It was during the Yuan dynasty that Europeans once more became aware of China, which they called Cathay. Italian *Marco Polo* traveled to China with his father and uncle in the 1200s and spent nearly 20 years in the kingdom of Kublai Khan.

Ming dynasty and British rule. The Mongols were succeeded by the emperors of the **Ming dynasty** (1368–1644) and the Manchu **Ch'ing dynasty** (1644–1912). During this time, Europeans attempted to open up China to the West, but the Chinese emperors did all in their power to hinder European trade and influence in China. Finally, in the mid-1800s, the Chinese were forced to sign treaties which guaranteed trading rights and special privileges to Westerners. Soon many European nations had carved out colonies along the Chinese coast. Great Britain established a colony at **Hong Kong** in 1841.

Chinese Farmer: Some farmers still plow by hand with water buffaloes.

Pagan Religion and the State

The religions and systems of thought founded in both India and China are of great consequence to Asian progress and freedom. Because there was no distinction between religion and politics, the lack of personal freedom in the pagan religions necessarily had its effect in the government. In India and China, the ways of thinking, mainly Hinduism in India and Confucianism in China, dictated the outcome: tyranny. *Whenever men are set up in the place of God, there will be a smothering of freedom and a subsequent rise of tyranny.* Thus, in both countries, the people were enslaved to false religions and despotic rulers.

Mount Fujiyama: *This beautiful mountain southwest of Tokyo is the highest peak in Japan.*

CHECK UP

1. Where did the first known Chinese civilization develop?
2. What are the five fundamental virtues of Confucianism? What relationship did Confucius leave out?
3. What does Taoism teach?
4. Who built the first united Chinese empire? What dynasty did he establish?
5. Which dynasty marked the height of Chinese power and glory? What religion became a strong cultural force in China during this dynasty?
6. Who invented paper and when?
7. Who developed the first movable type? When? Why was it not practical?
8. Who established the Yuan dynasty?
9. Name the two dynasties that fought to hinder European influence and trade in China between the 1300s and the 1800s.
10. Which European nation established a colony at Hong Kong? When?

Identify: Hwang Ho, Yangtze, Shang dynasty, Ch'ou dynasty, Great Wall of China, Great Silk Road, anthropomorphism, Wang Chen, Genghis Khan, Marco Polo

---

Japan, Korea, and Indonesia

Besides India and China, three other countries of Asia are especially worthy of attention as we advance toward the Modern Age. These countries are Japan, Korea, and Indonesia.

Japan. The islands of Japan lie east of China in the northern Pacific Ocean. Japan's early history was not well documented, and much remains unknown. Basically, warring clans ruled the country until about the 6th century A.D. One of these clans, the **Yamato,** established a loose rule over the other clans around the 4th century and eventually became *the clan of Japan's emperors.*

Shinto, influenced by Buddhism and Confucianism, is the oldest surviving religion of Japan. The religion is polytheistic and holds that **Kami,** the basic forces of nature, created the world and established customs and laws. Followers of Shinto offer gifts to the forces of nature to appease them, and the people enshrine men and natural objects alike as gods. Shinto puts no emphasis on life after death, but rather encourages the satisfaction of nature, which Shinto teaches is not controlled by the mind of God but by attitudes of its own. Thus, nature has complete mastery over the followers of Shinto.

Buddhism, which was <u>introduced to Japan in the 500s</u> by a Korean kingdom, also had great cultural consequences in Japan. The Japanese people were extremely impressed by Buddhist temples, images, and paintings. They were also deeply interested in the mystical powers of a religion which sought for temporal benefits in the present world.

The *"founder of Japanese civilization,"* **Prince Shotoku,** ruled from A.D. 593 to 622. Shotoku promoted Buddhism and other Chinese influences (such as Confucianism) in the Japanese culture and government. His greatest accomplishment was the establishment of a "constitution," which laid the groundwork for a centralized government. After Shotoku's death, the **Taika** (Great Reform) period began in which <u>a central government was formed</u>, the emperor became the owner of the land, and a tax system was set up.

Gradually, however, the **Mikado** (emperor) lost his ruling power, though he

Prince Shotoku

still remained on the throne. For about 700 years (c. 1200–1900), Japan was a feudal, aristocratic society dominated by **shoguns** (feudal lords), **daimios** (local landlords), and **samurai** (warriors or knights). The majority of the Japanese were mere peasants, much like the serfs of medieval Europe.

Europeans (Portuguese, Spanish, Dutch, and English) reached Japan during the 1500s; many Jesuit priests were sent there to promote Romanism. By the 1630s, the Japanese, fearful that Jesuit activity would destroy traditional Japanese culture and that extensive trade with foreigners would result in foreign domination, expelled the Europeans and withdrew into over two centuries of isolation from the rest of the world.

Korea. The Korean Peninsula extends southward from northeastern China between the Yellow Sea and the Sea of Japan. The recorded history of Korea does not begin until 108 B.C., when the Han Empire of China conquered the peninsula. China controlled the northwestern territory of **Lolang** until A.D. 313, when the Koreans won it back. Chinese culture strongly

Shirasagi Castle: A 17th-century feudal castle in Himeji, Japan.

Korean Women Planting Rice:
Rice is the staple food of many Asian countries.

Korea: *The Korean landscape varies from rugged mountain ranges to fertile river valleys.*

influenced Korea's art, government, and sciences. *Buddhism* (also learned from the Chinese) became Korea's chief religion.

In the 660s, the Korean kingdom of **Silla** gained control of the peninsula. Silla maintained close ties with China and was strongly influenced by Chinese *Confucianism.* Silla divided in the 800s, but Korean General **Wang Kon** mended the kingdom in 936 and named it *Koryo,* from which the name "Korea" is derived. Interest in printing increased, and schools were built to further education.

In 1259, Mongol tribes under Kublai Khan conquered Korea. Korea broke free from Mongol domination in 1368, but then split into warring factions. General **Yi** won, renamed the country *Choson,* and founded a new dynasty. This dynasty ended official government support of Buddhism, and the religion became less and less important to Korean life. *Buddhism was replaced by Confucianism* shortly before the arrival of the Europeans in the mid-1600s.

Indonesia. Indonesia, in Southeast Asia, is made up of more than 13,600 islands, including parts of the second and third largest islands in the world, **New Guinea** and **Borneo.** Other important Indonesian islands are **Sumatra, Java,** and **Bali.** The temperatures of Indonesia's hot, rainy climate vary little; the different seasons are gauged by rainfall and monsoons.

The first inhabitants of Indonesia came from the Asian mainland. By the 400s, small kingdoms were developing in Indonesia. Like other Asians, the Indonesians believed their kings to be either descendants of gods or gods themselves. During this time, *Hindu* and *Buddhist* influence was strong, and for hundreds of years, kingdoms of the two religious groups rivaled one another for power.

The islands of Indonesia became important international crossroads for trade after the Italian explorer **Marco Polo** visited them in 1292. In the 1400s Muslim traders from Arabia and India brought *Islam* to the islands. Known to European explorers and traders as part of the fabled *Spice Islands* or *East Indies,* Indonesia was

Indonesia: Bamboo rafts are used for transportation on this small lake on the island of Java.

visited first by the Portuguese and later by the English and the Dutch. By the 1700s, however, the Dutch had forced their Portuguese and English competitors out of the islands and had made Indonesia into a Dutch colony—the **Netherlands East Indies.**

The Far East and European Contact
Beginnings of European influence.
With a few exceptions, the Far East's relationship with Europe before the Modern Age was one of isolation and separation. At the end of the 15th century, desire for the treasures and exotic goods of mysterious Asia enticed European merchants into journeying to the Orient. Portuguese navigator *Vasco da Gama's* voyage to India marked the <u>beginning of European influence in Asia</u>.

At the time of Europe's move eastward much of Asia was in a constant state of change. Central Asia was involved with the militant spread of Islam. Both Southeast and Southwest Asia were experiencing political changes. In South Asia, the Mogul Empire was expanding its power over India. In the wilderness of North Asia, no political states had been formally established. Only East Asia's established systems maintained any stability.

Competition for trade. By 1700, the Europeans had established trade posts along the coasts of South and Southeast Asia. Europeans had not yet touched all of Asia at this time: European trade interest did not include some of the smaller Asian countries (Burma, Vietnam, Thailand), and the Europeans ran into closed doors in some of the larger countries (China, Korea, and Japan).

Wars in the East between the Dutch, French, and English were often reflections of conflicts taking place in the West. These wars determined the trade boundaries of each country. The East Indies (now Indonesia) came under Dutch control, and the Philippines fell to Spain, which had begun its commercial adventures in Asia about 1565. The British eventually controlled most of India, a feat begun by the British East India Company in the early 1600s.

During the 1800s, most of Asia was controlled by the economic and military might of Western nations. France, Great Britain, The Netherlands, Portugal, and

287

Spain dominated about one third of the Asian expanse and controlled trade between the East and the West. By 1842, China had agreed to British trade at five Chinese ports. By 1854, Japan had agreed to trade with the United States. As the East became even more open to Western commerce and influence, increasingly intense competition ensued among the Western powers for colonial expansion and trade rights.

Opposition to missions. At the beginning of the 19th century, Christian missions in Asia were almost non-existent. In **India,** as Kenneth Scott Latourette, the great historian of missions explains, "The English East India company had long opposed missions within its territories from the fear that by stirring up religious animosities among non-Christians they would make its rule more difficult and cut into its profits."

> In many cases the policy of the British was oppressive and cruel, and they were by no means favorable to Christian missions. But the character of British rule changed, and when the missionaries had an opportunity to show the fruits of religion in making the Indians better subjects, the government came to encourage the efforts of those who were endeavoring to lead the people out of darkness into the lifegiving light of the Gospel [Latourette].

Modern Missions in the Far East

India. In 1793, missionary **William Carey** (1761–1834), called the "Father of Modern Missions," sailed for India from England. As usual, Biblical Christianity and scholarship went together. Carey's goal was to translate the Bible into all the languages of Asia. He also wrote grammar books in six different Asian languages, and he and his associates translated great

works of Western literature into the Asian languages and also translated some of the Asian classics into English. **Henry Martyn,** (1781–1812) arrived in India in 1806 as a chaplain for the East India Company. Martyn also preached to Hindus and Muslims, began educational institutions for Indians, and translated the New Testament into three languages.

In 1874, an Indian prince spoke with gratitude about the English missionaries and their Bible:

> Where did the English-speaking people get all their intelligence, and energy, and cleverness, and power? It is their Bible that gives it to them. And now they bring it to us and say, "This is what raised us. Take it and raise yourselves." They do not force it upon us, as the Mohammedans did the Koran, but they bring it in love, and translate it into our languages, and lay it before us and say, "Look at it, read it, examine it, and see if it is not good."

Indonesia and the Philippines. The Dutch introduced Protestantism to **Indonesia** in the 17th century. As the Dutch East Indies expanded in the 19th century, missions activity grew with the territory. "The results of Christianity were striking, not only numerically, but also in other ways. Scores of languages were reduced to

William Carey in India

Robert Morrison in China

They pioneered in the introduction of Western medicine, in public health education, and in the creation of medical and nursing professions which would apply the rapidly advancing medical skills of the Occident [the Western world]. They led in the care of the insane and the blind. They engaged in famine relief. They sought to prevent famines by introducing or developing improved methods of agriculture and forestry, ways of fighting plant and animal diseases, and increasing the yields of grains and fruits. Largely under the leadership of Timothy Richard (1832–1919) through the Christian Literature Society, in the 1890s and early 1900s they provided literature by which the Chinese could learn of the history and institutions of the Occident. In other words, through many channels they were striving to prepare the Chinese for the vast changes which were inevitable and to make the impact of the Occident a blessing and not a curse to the millions of that great realm [Latourette].

In the 1880s, Korea finally opened up trade with Western merchants, giving up its history of seclusion like China. Presbyterian and Methodist missionaries from the United States began establishing mission outposts in Korea at this time.

Japan. Isolated from the Western world since the 1600s, Japan began to open up in the 1800s. First, Commodore **Matthew Perry** persuaded the country to open its harbors for trade (**1854**). Then, Ambassador **Townsend Harris** negotiated the treaty which bears his name, opening Japan to Christian missionaries (**1858**). By the 1860s, Japan began to assimilate much of Western civilization. Yet, some age-old traditions were also strengthened at this time, including Shinto, Buddhism, and homage to the emperor.

Despite the undergirding of these pagan ideas, "great innovations were made. The

writing and the beginnings of a Christian literature were made in them. Hundreds of schools were founded, medical care was given, and the status of women was improved. More significant still, churches were growing with an increasing number of indigenous leaders" [Latourette].

In the Spanish **Philippines,** Romanism became the dominant religion. It would not be until the end of the 19th century that the United States would occupy the Philippines and introduce Protestantism as well as democratic political institutions.

China and Korea. Early 19th-century **China** seemed a gloomy prospect for the spreading of the gospel; the empire with a larger population than any other in Asia remained isolated from the West. In 1807, **Robert Morrison** (1782–1834) of Scotland became the first Protestant missionary to China. Morrison compiled a Chinese dictionary and translated the Bible into the Chinese language. Christian missions in China remained limited, however, until the mid-1800s, when European powers forced the Chinese to open their borders for Western trade. In 1865, Englishman **J. Hudson Taylor** (1832–1905) founded the *China Inland Mission.* His testimony and work had a great influence on missions in China and the rest of the world.

According to Latourette, most of the best high schools and colleges in China before 1914 were founded by missionaries and Chinese Christians.

prevailing feudalism was abolished, telegraph lines, railways, and a commercial marine were built, industrialism was introduced, an army and navy were created on Western models, codes of law and law courts inspired by the Occident were brought into being, a constitution with a diet or parliament and a cabinet was framed and put into force, and an educational system of a Western type was developed based upon universal, compulsory primary education and culminating in universities. Population was mounting and the standard of living was rising. Hard work, intelligence, and intense national pride and ambition were outstanding characteristics. By 1914, Japan was on the way to becoming one of the major world powers" [Latourette].

The success of missions in Asia. At the opening of the 1860s, Asia had been an inhospitable mission field. But

---

at the beginning of the last decade of the century, what change do we see? The whole of Protestant Christendom arousing to the great work of missions; the Bible circulated in over two hundred and fifty languages and dialects, and a network of mission stations spreading over the whole earth, while here and there thousands of congregations of native converts from heathenism shine like stars in the darkness. There is hardly a country on earth where Christians are not free to preach the gospel, and to worship God [Robert Pollack Kerr].

By 1914, Christianity had circled the globe. With few exceptions, the countries of South, Southeast, and East Asia and the surrounding islands had small Christian minorities, but Christianity had indeed triumphed in these areas as never before.

By the 20th century, great changes had been effected throughout Asia. Colonial rule by the various Western nations had fostered economic growth and had introduced modern political administration. As the century progressed, nationalistic movements, based upon independent political and cultural ideas with an emphasis on tradition, gradually ended European colonialism in Asia.

CHECK UP

1. Name the clan of Japan's emperors.
2. What does Shinto teach?
3. Name the three groups that dominated feudal Japan.
4. How many islands make up Indonesia? Name five of them.
5. What was the effect of Marco Polo's visit to Indonesia?
6. What marked the beginning of European influence in Asia?
7. Name two early missionaries to India. Which is remembered as the "Father of Modern Missions"?
8. What country sent missionaries to Indonesia? What were the results of Christianity there?
9. Who was the first missionary to China? Who founded the China Inland Mission?
10. What did Christian missionaries and Chinese Christians do for China?

Identify: Kami, Prince Shotoku, Taika period, Mikado, Silla, General Wang Kon, General Yi, Commodore Matthew Perry, Townsend Harris

CHAPTER 16 REVIEW

MULTIPLE CHOICE Write the letter of the answer that best completes each sentence.

1. _____ discovered Florida.
   a Vasco da Gama   *c* John Cabot
   b Ponce de Leon   *d* Pedro Cabral

2. _____ discovered the Pacific Ocean.
   a Ferdinand Magellan
   b Ponce de Leon
   c Vasco de Balboa
   d Hernando Cortes

3. The three-year voyage begun by _____
   proved that the world is round.
   a Vasco de Balboa
   b Ferdinand Magellan
   c Ponce de Leon
   d Hernando de Soto

4. _____ conquered the Inca Indians of
   Peru.
   a Juan Cabrillo
   b Francisco Pizarro
   c Samuel de Champlain
   d Pedro Cabral

5. _____ probably controlled more of the
   surface of the earth than any other
   human being in history.
   a Philip II   *c* Ferdinand
   b John I   *d* Elizabeth I

6. _____ discovered Brazil and claimed it
   for Portugal.
   a Samuel de Champlain
   b Hernando Cortes
   c Pedro Cabral
   d John Cabot

7. _____ discovered the St. Lawrence River.
   a Jacques Cartier
   b Samuel de Champlain
   c Pedro Cabral
   d Giovanni de Verrazano

8. _____ founded Quebec, the first permanent French settlement in the New
   World.
   a John Cabot
   b Pedro Cabral
   c Samuel de Champlain
   d Jacques Cartier

9. The first explorer to reach the North
   American mainland was _____.
   a Jacques Cartier   *c* Pedro Cabral
   b John Cabot   *d* Henry Hudson

10. The first Englishman to sail around the
    world was _____.
    a John Cabot
    b Sir Francis Drake
    c Ferdinand Magellan
    d Vasco de Balboa

11. _____ founded a colony at Roanoke
    Island, off the coast of North Carolina.
    a Sir Walter Raleigh
    b Henry Hudson
    c John Cabot
    d Sir Francis Drake

12. The _____ developed the caste system
    in India.
    a Aryans   *c* Buddhists
    b Mongols   *d* British

13. The belief in a continuous process of
    rebirth is called _____.
    a reincarnation   *c* Buddism
    b nirvana   *d* monotheism

14. _____ is the world's oldest living civili-
    zation.
    a India   *c* Japan
    b China   *d* Korea

15. _____ built the first united Chinese
    empire.
    a Wang Chen   *c* T'sai Lun
    b Pi Sheng   *d* Ch'in

16. In 1841, Great Britain established a
    colony at _____.
    a Indonesia   *c* Lolang
    b Silla   *d* Hong Kong

17. The _____ became the clan of Japan's
    emperors.
    a Silla   *c* Yamato
    b Kami   *d* Mikado

CHAPTER 16 REVIEW (CONTINUED)

COMPLETION *Choose the correct term to complete each sentence and write the letter in the blank.*

a movable type
b Robert Morrison
c Townsend Harris
d J. Hudson Taylor
e Great Wall of China
f William Carey
g Prince Shotoku
h Commodore
   Matthew Perry
i Hwang Ho River
j paper
k Indus River
l Great Silk Road

1. The river called "China's Sorrow" is the _____.
2. Pi Sheng invented the first _____.
3. The _____, built during the Ch'in dynasty, is the world's longest fortification.
4. _____ negotiated the treaty that opened Japan to Christian missions.
5. T'sai Lun invented _____.
6. The "founder of Japanese civilization,"_____, promoted Buddhism and other Chinese influences in Japan.
7. _____ led an American naval mission to open Japan to trade with the United States.
8. _____ is called the "Father of Modern Missions."
9. _____ translated the Bible into the Chinese language.
10. The _____ Valley was the site of the first Indian civilization.

MATCHING *Match each description with the correct name.*

a Leif Ericson
b Bartholomeu Dias
c Christopher Columbus
d Ponce de Leon
e Francisco Coronado
f Prince Henry the Navigator
g Hernando Cortes
h Amerigo Vespucci
i Marco Polo
j Hernando de Soto
k Sir Francis Drake

_____ 1. first European to travel the length of Asia
_____ 2. first to realize that Columbus had discovered a new continent
_____ 3. promoted exploration in the early 15th century
_____ 4. made the first Spanish landing on the North American mainland
_____ 5. Viking who may have sailed to America around A.D. 1000.
_____ 6. conquered the Aztec Indians
_____ 7. discovered the Grand Canyon
_____ 8. sponsored by King Ferdinand and Queen Isabella of Spain
_____ 9. sailed around the Cape of Good Hope in 1487
_____10. discovered the Mississippi River

CONCEPT TO CONSIDER *On a separate sheet of paper, answer the following question using complete sentences.*

List five major religions that originated in Asia and indicate the geographic source of each. How are they all similar? How has religion hindered progress and freedom in Asia?

TIME LINE CHALLENGE **Choose the letter of the correct date for each of the events listed below.**

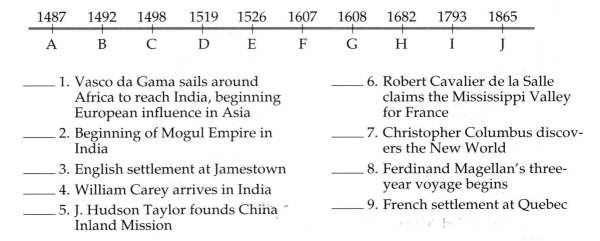

```
1487    1492    1498    1519    1526    1607    1608    1682    1793    1865
  A       B       C       D       E       F       G       H       I       J
```

_____ 1. Vasco da Gama sails around Africa to reach India, beginning European influence in Asia

_____ 2. Beginning of Mogul Empire in India

_____ 3. English settlement at Jamestown

_____ 4. William Carey arrives in India

_____ 5. J. Hudson Taylor founds China Inland Mission

_____ 6. Robert Cavalier de la Salle claims the Mississippi Valley for France

_____ 7. Christopher Columbus discovers the New World

_____ 8. Ferdinand Magellan's three-year voyage begins

_____ 9. French settlement at Quebec

MAP SKILLS **Use the maps on pp. 270 and 271 to answer the following questions.**

1. Name the three largest nations in North America with their capitals.

2. Which South American countries border the Pacific Ocean?

3. What is the largest nation in North America? in South America?

4. Name the sea that lies between Central America and the West Indies.

5. Which Central American nation connects North America to South America?

6. What sea separates Japan from the Asian mainland?

7. Name the nations that border India.

8. What mountain range separates China from India? Which range divides Russia?

9. Which Asian nation extends north of the Arctic Circle? What is its capital?

10. Into what body of water does the Hwang Ho River empty? the Yangtze? the Indus? the Ganges?

11. Name the capital of the largest nation located entirely within Asia.

12. Which Asian nation extends south of the equator? What is its capital?

17
The United States—
A New Kind of Nation

HIGHLIGHTS
Pilgrims • Great Awakening
War for Independence • Constitution of the United States
Expansion and Progress • Rise as a World Power • Revival and Missions

The Spiritual Foundations of America

Toward the beginning of the 17th century, when the outcome of the struggle for freedom in England still seemed very much in doubt, some Englishmen sought better conditions in the New World. One of the first groups to make the journey was the **Pilgrims,** who came to America in 1620. The story of the Pilgrims reads like an allegory of a nation that dedicated itself to truth and freedom. The United States would become the leading country of the Modern Age. It would be a new kind of nation unique in the history of the world— **one nation under God, indivisible, with liberty and justice for all.**

Persecution in England
The political and religious authority in England were so closely tied together that the one depended upon the other. English sovereigns understood that any move toward religious liberty was a threat to their political power. For this reason, King **James I** wanted all Englishmen to conform to the established Church of England and vowed to "harry out of the land" all those who refused to conform. Among these *Dissenters,* as such nonconformists were called, was that group known as the **Puritans,** who *wished to purify the Church of England.* King James found the Puritans

especially threatening because they believed strongly in republican government. As Alexis de Tocqueville [tôk′vēl′], a Frenchman who visited the United States in 1831, would later write:

> Puritanism was not merely a religious doctrine, but corresponded in many points with the most absolute democratic and republican theories. It was this tendency that . . . aroused its most dangerous adversaries.

(You will remember from our study of the English nation that the Puritans eventually waged a civil war against James's successor, Charles I, and deposed him.)

The Separatists. Most Puritans remained in England despite the persecution, but some Puritans, particularly certain Separatists, left the country. While many Puritans remained members of the Church of England, the Separatists would have no part of it. They insisted on having their own "separate" churches. Indeed, the Separatists *believed that every local church congregation should be independent,* free from any religious hierarchy, and entirely self-governing.

The Scrooby Congregation. One group of Separatists "whose hearts the Lord had touched with heavenly zeal for his truth" formed an independent church in 1606 at **Scrooby,** England. These people resolved,

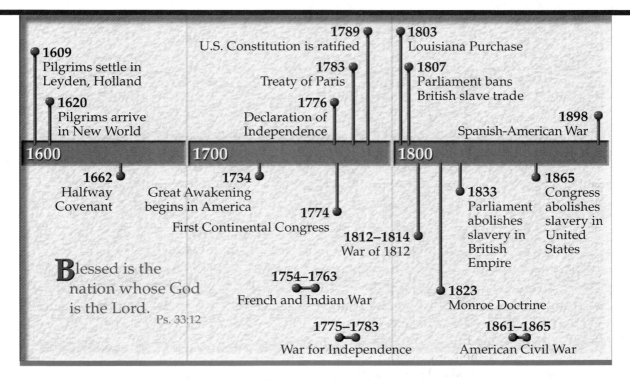

1609
Pilgrims settle in
Leyden, Holland

1620
Pilgrims arrive
in New World

1789
U.S. Constitution is ratified

1783
Treaty of Paris

1776
Declaration of
Independence

1803
Louisiana Purchase

1807
Parliament bans
British slave trade

1898
Spanish-American War

1600

1700

1800

1662
Halfway
Covenant

1734
Great Awakening
begins in America

First Continental Congress

1774

1812–1814
War of 1812

1833
Parliament
abolishes
slavery in
British
Empire

1865
Congress
abolishes
slavery in
United
States

Blessed is the
nation whose God
is the Lord.
Ps. 33:12

1754–1763
French and Indian War

1823
Monroe Doctrine

1775–1783
War for Independence

1861–1865
American Civil War

"whatever it might cost them, to shake off the anti-Christian bondage, and, as the Lord's free people, to join themselves by a covenant into a church . . . in the fellowship of the gospel." There were many in that congregation whom history would elevate from obscurity to fame, including John Robinson (1576?–1625), pastor of the church at Scrooby, the Elder William Brewster (1567–1644), postmaster at Scrooby, and especially **William Bradford** (1590–1657), then only a teenager. In future years, Bradford would rise to a position of prominent leadership in the New World. His writing, *History of Plymouth Plantation,* from which we have just quoted, would become the first American history book. Bradford is known as the **"Father of American History."** We cannot do better than cite Bradford's eloquent words in telling the story of the Scrooby congregation, known in history as the *Pilgrims,* who "knew they were PILGRIMS, and looked not much on those things, but lifted up their eyes to heaven, their dearest country. . . ."

Refuge in Holland

Persecution became so severe in England that the Pilgrims resolved to flee to Holland, "where, they heard, was freedom of religion for all men." In 1609, they arrived in the city of **Leyden,** where they found religious liberty. There was then more freedom of religion among the Dutch than anywhere else in the world. In 11 years, the Pilgrims grew in number from about 300 to more than a thousand. But in coming to Leyden, these brave people had scarcely begun their pilgrimage. Life in Holland was difficult for the Pilgrims. Dutch authorities placed work restrictions on English immigrants, forcing children to work long hours and often neglect schooling. Furthermore, Holland was a very worldly place, full of undesirable influences that could lead children astray. Concerned for their children, the Pilgrims resolved not to stay in Holland permanently. More and more they sensed a calling to the New World, where they might rear their children in freedom and where they had "great hope and inward zeal of laying some good foundation for the propagating and advancing of the Gospel of the Kingdom of Christ in these remote parts of the world, yea, though they should be as stepping-stones to others for performing of so great a work."

The Voyage to America

Preparing for the voyage. The Pilgrims needed a patent for settlement in the New World. With the help of **Sir Edwin Sandys,** a Puritan nobleman, they obtained permission from the **London Company** in 1620 to settle in *Virginia,* a long and indefinite section of North America's Atlantic coast. The Pilgrims also requested an official guarantee of religious toleration from James, but the king refused. They were promised, however, that the king would "not molest them, provided they conducted themselves peaceably."

The Pilgrims also needed money for the voyage and for the founding of a colony once they arrived in the New World. Such an undertaking required a great deal of money. A group of London businessmen, known in history as **"the Adventurers,"** agreed to finance the venture in return for a share in the Pilgrims' profits during the first seven years.

On September 6, 1620, the Pilgrims boarded the *Mayflower* in Plymouth, England, and set sail for the New World. Besides officers and crew, the ship carried "about a hundred souls." Only 35 of the passengers aboard the *Mayflower* were from the Leyden congregation. The rest of the congregation were forced by various circumstances to remain in Leyden, hoping to join their brethren in America before long. The other 66 passengers on board the *Mayflower* were almost all non-Separatists, whom the Pilgrims called

Pilgrims Going to Church *by George H. Boughton from the Collection of The New-York Historical Society.*

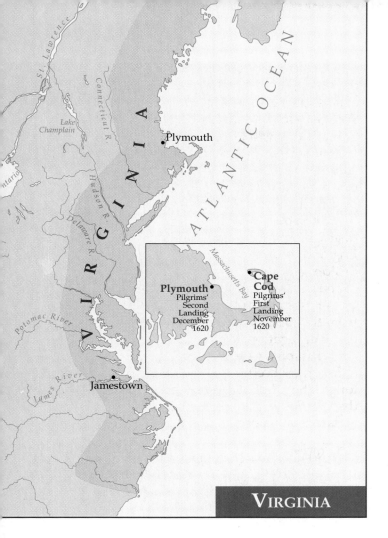

VIRGINIA

because no one group could physically dominate the other, but out of *principle*, because beliefs are matters of the heart and soul that cannot be forced. For the Separatists in particular, toleration was a matter of conviction; as Bradford wrote, "they were willing and desirous that any honest men may live with them, that will carry themselves peaceably and seek the common good," and "they had many [non-Separatists] amongst them." Later historians, when listing the passengers of the *Mayflower*, made two groups, Separatists and Strangers, but it is interesting that Bradford in his list intermingled the two without distinction. Bradford expressed the essence of religious toleration as understood by the Separatists when he acknowledged that it would be arrogant of any man or church to think that they could force their beliefs on other Christians.

The voyage of the Mayflower. After more than two months at sea, the *Mayflower* finally reached the shores of North America. However, a storm had blown the ship off course, far to the north of the territory where the Pilgrims had permission to settle. With winter fast approaching, they decided to remain where they had landed, in a region called **New England.** On November 11, 1620, they maneuvered the ship into Cape Cod harbor. William Bradford later wrote:

> Being thus arrived in a good harbor and brought safe to land, they fell upon their knees and blessed the God of heaven who had brought them over the vast and furious ocean. . . .

The Mayflower Compact

Before they could go ashore, the Pilgrims had to address a matter of utmost importance. Having landed outside the territory of the London Company, they had no basis for civil government. They wisely recognized the importance of

"Strangers." Most of the Strangers were headed to the New World for better economic opportunities, but in spite of their differences the Separatists and Strangers got along well together.

The *Mayflower* well-represented the nation that America would later become: it contained a variety of people with a variety of ideas, backgrounds, goals, and beliefs, but all were able to live and work together because they respected one another's rights and did not demand that everyone be the same. Above all, there was a healthy spirit of **toleration,** recognizing and respecting the beliefs of others even though they are different from one's own beliefs. The toleration practiced by the Pilgrims was not just out of *necessity*,

297

government, and decided that one must be established for the colony to succeed.

Therefore, the Pilgrim leaders retired to the cabin of the *Mayflower* and drew up what has become known as the **Mayflower Compact.** Since the Pilgrims were followers of the Bible, they *stressed individual civic responsibility even more than individual liberty.* They knew that they had a responsibility to obey their leaders, to pay taxes, to be loyal citizens, and to pray for their civic leaders (1 Tim. 2:1–4). Forty-one of the men aboard the *Mayflower,* including many of the Strangers, signed the compact, promising all due submission and obedience to "such just and equal laws, ordinances, acts, constitutions, and offices, from time to time, as shall be thought most meet and convenient for the general good of the colony."

Before leaving the *Mayflower,* the Pilgrims crossed another great milestone of republican self-government, the establishment of daily, practical institutions of a democratic republic. They elected one of their number, **John Carver,** as governor. In the early years of the colony, the people continued to exercise a high degree of authority, and the government was in part a direct democracy.

On December 21, **1620,** the Pilgrims finally stepped ashore at a place they named **Plymouth** (after Plymouth, England). Their first winter in the cold North American wilderness was difficult, but by the fall of 1621, the Pilgrims could thank God for a bountiful harvest.

Cradle of a Nation

Of course, the Pilgrims were still under the ultimate authority of the king of England, but he rarely interfered and sent no royal officials to represent him. Thus *the Plymouth colony was virtually independent.* The political accomplishments of the Pilgrims at Plymouth colony would inspire future generations with a prime example of

Signing the Mayflower Compact
by Edward Percy Moran

free republican government, a realistic alternative to the tyranny and despotism that have been the usual lot of men in the history of the world.

Plymouth Colony became the cradle of a nation. The year **1620** points straight to **1776** (War for Independence) to **1789** (ratification of the Constitution) and to **1791** (adoption of the Bill of Rights). In 1620, we can see the essential connection between religious and political freedom.

As the Pilgrims sought to practice the pure precepts of Biblical Christianity and to follow the key doctrines of the Protestant Reformation, they seem to have been led—naturally, unconsciously, but logically—to separation of church and state and to republican self-government. The Pilgrims' landing at Plymouth Rock in 1620 inaugurated not only the history of New England but the history of the distinctively modern nation that would grow from the seeds planted in colonial America.

CHECK UP

1. What did the Separatists believe about church government?
2. By what name did the Scrooby congregation become known to history?
3. What was the first American history book? Who wrote it?
4. The Pilgrims fled to what city in Holland to escape persecution? Why were they dissatisfied in Holland?
5. What Puritan nobleman helped the Pilgrims obtain a patent from the London Company?
6. How many passengers on the *Mayflower* were from the Leyden congregation? How many passengers were there in all?
7. What civic responsibilities did the Pilgrims recognize?
8. Who was the first governor of Plymouth?

Identify: James I, Dissenters, "Adventurers," 1620, "Strangers," toleration, Virginia, New England, Mayflower Compact

---

The Great Awakening

During the 18th century, Europe, England, and America were visited by a remarkable series of spiritual revivals which changed the lives of many people and eventually affected the entire world. These revivals probably had their beginning in Europe at the end of the 17th century. After the Thirty Years' War (1617–1648), Europe had been divided into Protestant and Catholic territories, and each country had established an official **state church.** People often attended the state church only because it was "the thing to do." The churches were cold and formal, and Europe greatly needed a moving of the Spirit of God.

Pietism in Germany

Philipp Spener [shpā′nĕr: 1635–1705], a German Lutheran pastor, became con-

Philipp Spener

cerned about the spiritual coldness and the lack of moral consciousness in Germany. He felt that the state interfered too much in the affairs of the church and that the people were not being taught the necessity of genuine conversion and obedience to the standards of the Scriptures. Spener gathered a group of interested people from his congregation into his home each week for serious Bible study, prayer, and discussion of the Sunday sermons. The idea spread rapidly throughout Germany. Groups such as Spener's became known as *assemblies of piety*, and those who attended them were called **Pietists.** The increased Bible study in Germany <u>led to increased evangelism, increased missionary work, and increased Christian influence</u> on the daily lives of hundreds of thousands of Germans. The movement spread to Scandinavia, where it had much influence for good, especially among the people of Norway.

Many Pietists remained in their state church, but some (either because they could no longer feel comfortable in it, or because they had never been a part of it) started new churches. The **Brethren,** or German Baptists, were one group that broke with the state church. In the 1700s, most German Brethren emigrated to America, where they settled in Pennsylvania. The Brethren set up one of the first printing presses in America near Ephrata, Pennsylvania.

Another group revived by Pietism was the *Unitas Fratrum* (United Brethren), better known as the **Moravians.** Dating back to the 1400s when they were founded by John Huss, the Moravians were actually forerunners of the Protestant Reformation. During the Pietist revival, the Moravians became a vital force for the spread of the Gospel.

The Wesleyan Revival in England

John Wesley. The great English revivalist, **John Wesley** (1703–1791), was born in England at a time when that country, once known for its goodness and love for the Bible, had fallen into terrible moral decadence. Thousands of England's finest Puritans had migrated to America. Persecution had ceased, and those who remained in England had lost much of their zeal and influence for good.

The English people had more freedom in the 1700s than they had known at any time before in their history, but they had left the teachings of the Bible and had become slaves to their own passions. Gambling was the favorite indoor sport; gin the favorite drink. Immorality was rampant among the rich and poor alike. The political leaders were known for their loose living, love of liquor, and weakness to bribery. The popular literature of the period was coarse and immoral, and very little of it is read today.

England in 1700 "seemed barren of all that is good," wrote J. C. Ryle, a bishop in the Anglican church nearly two centuries later (1885). "How such a state of things can have arisen in a land of free Bibles and professing Protestantism is almost past comprehension. Christianity seemed to lie as one dead. . . . Morality, however much exalted in pulpits, was thoroughly trampled under foot in the streets."

People from all walks of life had forsaken the churches of the land, and with

John Wesley

good reason, for the vast majority of churches had forsaken the plain truth of the gospel. Many Anglican churches had turned to the philosophy of *Deism,* the false teaching that after God created the world and its natural laws He left things to run on their own. Many people rejected this barren philosophy and completely turned away from all religion.

It seems that the Anglican clergy were "determined to know everything except Jesus Christ and him crucified," and "when they assembled it was generally to toast 'Church and King,' and to build one another up in earthly-mindedness, prejudice, ignorance, and formality." They preached "as seldom as possible," but "when they did preach, their sermons were so unspeakably and indescribably bad, that . . . they were generally preached to empty benches" [Ryle].

As students, John Wesley, his brother **Charles Wesley** (1707–1788), and their friend **George Whitefield** (1714–1770) met regularly with several other young men to study the Bible and the classics and to encourage each other in their spiritual development. Other students laughed at this group and nicknamed them the **"Methodists"** because of the regularity of their meetings and their well-ordered methods of conduct. Little did they know that this term of ridicule was destined to become a title of respect and honor.

Whitefield and the Wesleys "began vehemently to 'call sinners to repentence,' " wrote John Wesley. "In two or three years they had sounded the claim to the utmost borders of the land," and "many thousands gathered together to hear them. . . ." For the next 65 years, John Wesley traveled the length and breadth of England on horse-back, sharing the gospel of Christ with his sin-hardened countrymen. Thousands responded to the message of salvation by faith alone, and in the power of Christ their lives were transformed. England became a changed country. Woodrow Wilson, an American president of the 20th century, wrote that John Wesley's place in history prepared England for peaceful reform and saved it from a political revolution such as the one that convulsed France:

> No doubt he [Wesley] played no small part in saving England from the mad-ness which fell upon France ere the century ended. The English poor bore no such intolerable burdens as the poor of France had to endure. There was no such insensate preservation of old abuses in England as maddened the unhappy country across the Channel. But society was in sharp transition in England; one industrial age was giving place to another, and the poor particu-larly were sadly at a loss to find their places in the new. . . . It might have gone hard with order and government in a nation so upset, transformed, distracted, had not the hopeful lessons of religion been taught broadcast and the people made to feel that once more pity and salvation had sought them out.

George Whitefield. Perhaps the most powerful figure in the English revivals and, as we shall see, in America was **George Whitefield** (1714–1770). Whitefield began his preaching when he was just 23 and immediately became England's most popu-lar preacher. He later became the best-known man in America. For 34 years, until his death, Whitefield's aim in life was to preach the gospel.

George Whitefield did not leave a denomination or books to perpetuate his ministry, as Wesley did, and thus he is not as well known to historians as Wesley. But wherever he spoke, the power of the Spirit of God was obviously upon him. "Of all the spiritual heroes of a hundred years ago," wrote J. C. Ryle in 1885, "none saw so soon as Whitefield what the times demanded, and none were so forward in the great work of spiritual aggression."

The extent of revival. When the churches of England closed their doors to Whitefield and Wesley, the great revivalists began to hold meetings outdoors in the open air. Such great crowds attended that the churches could not have held them even if they had wanted to. In these great **out-door meetings**, the English people not only heard the mighty preaching of George Whitefield and John Wesley but also sang the mighty hymns of Charles Wesley. The results were such, as John Wesley put it, that no "reasonable man can deny . . . that God is now visiting this nation, in a far other manner than we had cause to expect. Instead of pouring out his fierce displeasure upon us, he hath made us yet another tender of mercy: So that even when sin did abound, grace hath much more abounded."

Many Anglican and Dissenter churches were greatly revived, and the **Methodist** church was founded by John Wesley. The Methodist church became a leading denomi-nation in England as well as America's largest denomination for part of the 19th century. The revival of religion brought great moral and social changes in England, illustrating the Scriptural truth that Chris-tians are the salt of the earth.

The "reformation of manners." The work of God that began in the great masses of the people during the Wesleyan Revival spread to the upper classes where it touched **William Wilberforce** (1759–1833), one of the great Christian statesmen of English history. Wilberforce was converted from what he

William Wilberforce

considered "nominal Christianity" (in name only) to what he called "real Christianity." He wrote a book reminding England's upper classes that true Christianity will show in a changed life and that precisely because they were rich, they had even greater duties to their neighbors and to all men.

As a result of Wilberforce and other influences, a "reformation of manners" took place in English society. Immorality and drunkenness declined, for example, and kindness, generosity, and a sense of duty characterized the upper classes in their attitude toward others.

End of slavery. As a member of Parliament for more than 50 years, Wilberforce led the movement in England to abolish slavery. In *1807,* Parliament banned the British slave trade, and in *1833,* Parliament finally abolished slavery altogether throughout the British Empire.

Beginning of popular education. In 1780, **Robert Raikes** started a Sunday school for poor street children. He gathered the children together each Sunday and hired four women to teach them Bible, manners, right living, and the basics of reading, writing, and arithmetic, which they would not have received in any other way. Classes lasted from 8:00 A.M. until 5:00 P.M. with a break for lunch and were followed by attendance at the evening church service. Raikes's efforts inspired people throughout England, Ireland, Scotland, Wales, and America to start similar schools. Historians see the Sunday school movement as the beginning of popular education (education for all children) in Great Britain. Raikes is remembered as the *"Father of the Sunday School Movement."*

The rise of modern missions. Perhaps the greatest effect of the English Evangelical Revival was the rise of modern missions. The Moravians and others had done some missionary work earlier, but **1792** marks the official beginning of modern missions, for it

was then that **William Carey** (1761–1834), an English shoemaker saved during the Wesleyan Revival, began his historic ministry in India. Carey will always be remembered as the *"Father of Modern Missions."*

Soon missionary societies were formed in England, Scotland, and America, and thousands of men and women were sailing to foreign lands with the gospel. Some of the best-known English missionaries were **David Livingstone, J. Hudson Taylor,** and **Robert Moffat.** Thus the Wesleyan revival begun in the little country of England eventually had an effect upon the entire world. The effect was so great that the next century, the 19th century, was called "The Great Century of Missions."

CHECK UP

1. What Lutheran pastor started the Pietist movement in Germany?
2. What was England like in John Wesley's day? Describe the churches of the time.
3. For how many years did John Wesley preach? What did President Woodrow Wilson say that John Wesley's preaching did for England?
4. When did Parliament ban the British slave trade? When did it abolish slavery throughout the British Empire?
5. Historians see the Sunday School movement as the beginning of what in Great Britain?
6. Who is the "Father of Modern Missions"? In what year did modern missions begin?

Identify: Pietists, Brethren, Moravians, Diesm, Methodists, William Wilberforce, Robert Raikes

The Great Awakening in America

Jonathan Edwards. The Wesleyan revival in England had its counterpart in America, where it was called the **"Great Awakening."** The Great Awakening <u>began in 1734</u>, a few years earlier than the English revival, under the preaching of **Jonathan Edwards** (1703–1758), one of America's greatest thinkers.

Edwards was born in Connecticut, New England, the same year that Wesley was born in England. New England's problems at the time were very different from England's—at least on the outside. New England did not share England's problem of moral decadence. Many of England's most devout Christians had left for America in the 1600s, and their high moral standards were still influencing New England for good in the 1700s.

New England was different from England in other ways as well. The Puritans saw work as a way of exalting God, and they did not look down on poor working people. In fact, because of the Puritan attitude toward work, New England did not *have* any poor people!

The Puritan emphasis on education also meant that no children were going unschooled like the children in England. The New Englanders of Jonathan Edwards's day were intelligent, well-educated, hard-working, and fairly well-to-do; on the outside, they seemed very good and moral. Though well prepared for success in this life, however, many of them gave little thought to the next life.

True faith in Christ had declined sharply from the original Puritan begin-

nings, and the New Englanders were beginning to lose interest in religion. By the 1660s, church rolls were dwindling, for very few people could give evidence of salvation. Because most New England colonies did not keep church and state separate, only church members could have political rights. Very soon there were not enough church members to keep the government going.

In order to remedy this situation, the Puritans passed the **Half-Way Covenant** in 1662, which <u>allowed unconverted relatives of church members to join the churches</u>. This was a move away from the earlier Puritan teaching that churches ought to be bodies of true, converted believers. By the time of the Great Awakening, it was well known that even some ministers in the New England churches were unconverted!

The great institutions of higher learning in New England—**Harvard** (founded in 1636 in Massachusetts) and **Yale** (founded in 1701 in Connecticut)—which were originally supposed to guard future piety by educating good ministers, had by now become a main cause for the decline of piety in the pulpit. In these schools, Christianity had been turned into a mere intellectual exercise.

This was the New England that Jonathan Edwards faced when he became the pastor of the Congregational church in Northampton, Massachusetts, in 1729. As Edwards preached the powerful truths of the gospel, revival began to stir among his people. By the end of the year 1734, "the Spirit of God began extraordinarily to set in," and as Edwards wrote in his *Faithful Narrative of the Surprising Work of God,*

Jonathan Edwards

This work of God, as it was carried on, and the number of true saints multiplied, soon made a glorious alteration in the town; so that in the spring and summer following, anno 1735, the town seemed to be full of the presence of God; it was never so full of love, nor of joy, and yet so full of distress, as it was then. There were remarkable tokens of

God's presence in almost every house. It was a time of joy in families on account of salvation being brought unto them; parents rejoicing over their children as new born, and husbands over their wives, and wives over their husbands.

As the revival spread, Edwards continued to preach. His sermons made the realities of heaven and hell clear and distinct to all who listened. In his most famous sermon of all, **"Sinners in the Hands of an Angry God,"** delivered in 1741 at Enfield, Connecticut, Jonathan Edwards described the dreadful way of the sinner who, but for the grace of God, has no more than a spider's web to keep him from falling into Hell. By this time, what had started in Northampton had spread all over colonial America and was affecting the middle and southern colonies just as much as New England.

Whitefield in America. The great English revivalist *George Whitefield* arrived in America in 1739 for the first of seven evangelistic tours throughout the colonies. He had begun preaching outdoors in England because the ministers of the established church disliked his evangelistic messages and closed the churches to him. Finding similar opposition in America, he preached outdoors there, too. Benjamin Franklin, the great American statesman and scientist, knew Whitefield personally and summarized the results of his ministry:

He was at first permitted to preach in some of the churches; but the clergy, taking a dislike to him, soon refused him their pulpits and he was obliged to preach in the fields. The multitudes of all sects and denominations that attended his sermons were enormous. . . .

It was wonderful to see the change soon made in the manners of our inhabitants. From being thoughtless or indifferent about religion, it seemed as if all the world were growing religious, so that

one could not walk through the town in an evening without hearing psalms sung in different families of every street.

The best-known Great Awakening evangelist and probably the best-known man in America at the time, George Whitefield is estimated to have preached over 18,000 sermons to over 10 million people in the 34 years of his ministry. On some occasions, Whitefield preached to crowds of 20,000 people.

Spiritual impact. No merely localized event, the Great Awakening affected the masses of the American people. The best estimate is that between the years 1740 and 1743 alone, there were 30,000 to 40,000 conversions in the colonies.

Reckoning the purely spiritual consequences alone, the Great Awakening must be deemed incredibly important. Here was the beginning of the Methodist movement in America, which had already begun in England. Many existing churches of various denominations experienced revival, with a new emphasis on evangelism. The Presbyterians and the Baptists also experienced great growth during the Great Awakening era.

The leaders of the Great Awakening may be considered the **"spiritual Founding Fathers"** of America, for their teaching did much to shape the spiritual heritage of America. God used them to lay the foundation, in Biblical Christianity, for the basic beliefs that would see America through the War for Independence, through the adoption of the Constitution and the Bill of Rights, throughout her history.

Political impact. The Great Awakening was stongly opposed by the majority of established churches in America, just as the Wesleyan Revival was opposed by the established Church of England. Whitefield, for example, experienced intense opposition from established religious leaders in both England and America. In 1742, Connecticut passed a law providing for the punishment of anyone who preached in a given area

George Whitefield

without the permission of the official, government preacher! But as we have seen, God was able to use such human opposition for His glory by leading the revival evangelists to preach outdoors, where they reached more people than they ever could have in church buildings. This opposition was also important for moving the American people as a whole to recognize the principle of *separation of church and state*.

It is in no small measure due to the Great Awakening that, on the eve of the War for Independence, America was a land in favor of both true religion and true religious freedom. By 1776, when the American people faced the crisis of an actual break with the mother country, their basic beliefs were settled in their minds and hearts. When the time had come for America to fight for her independence, she was, in a sense, already independent, for as Calvin Coolidge, an American president of the 20th century, put it, "America was born in a revival of religion."

The preaching that Americans heard during the Great Awakening helped the colonists to see more than ever that all men are equal in worth to God. This revival perhaps did more than anything else to draw the colonists together into one nation under God. President Coolidge explained:

> The American Revolution was preceded by the great religious revival of the middle of the eighteenth century, which had its effect both in England and in the colonies. When the common people turned to the reading of the Bible, . . . when they were stirred by a great revival, . . . the way was prepared. . . . It was because religion gave the people a new importance and a new glory that they demanded a new freedom and a new government. We cannot in our generation reject the cause and retain the result.
>
> If the institutions they adopted are to survive, if the governments which they founded are to endure, it will be because the people continue to have similar religious beliefs. It is idle to discuss freedom and equality on any other basis. It is useless to expect substantial reforms from any other motive. They cannot be administered from without. They must come from within. That is why laws alone are so impotent. To enact or to repeal laws is not to secure real reform. It is necessary to take these problems directly to the individual. There will be a proper use of our material prosperity when the individual feels a divine responsibility. There will be a broadening scholarship when the individual feels that science, literature, and history are the revelation of divine truths. There will be obedience to law when the individual feels that government represents a divine authority.
>
> It is these beliefs, these religious convictions, that represent the strength of America, the strength of all civilized society. . . . It is righteousness alone which exalteth the nation. . . .

One nation under God, indivisible, with liberty and justice for all—nourished from the beginning with Puritan piety and fed with the Word of God in national revival, colonial America was the cradle for the first country in the history of the world *born* with the knowledge of the true principles of individual liberty and able, as a mere infant on the stage of world history, to walk and talk in the true Spirit of the Modern Age.

---CHECK UP---

1. What name was given to the nation-wide revival in 18th-century England? In America?
2. Why did New England not share England's problem of moral decadence?
3. How did the Puritan attitude toward work benefit New England?
4. What was Jonathan Edwards's most famous sermon?
5. What famous American described George Whitefield's preaching? What change did he say it brought?
6. How many times did George Whitefield come to America? To how many people did Whitefield preach in his lifetime?
7. Who are the "spiritual founding fathers" of America?
8. The opposition of the government churches to the Great Awakening helped Americans to recognize what principle?

Identify: Half-Way Covenant, Jonathan Edwards, George Whitefield

The Birth of the Nation

Colonial America

With a godly foundation laid by the Pilgrim fathers and the Great Awakening, America was ready for the responsibilities of nationhood. But first, America had to win her independence. The story of the birth of the United States as a nation begins in the early 18th century, when a storm began to brew between the American colonies and Great Britain.

Mercantilism. By 1733, the Atlantic coast of North America had been divided into 13 colonies and, though not all founded by Englishmen, all 13 colonies had come under English rule. England's early colonial policy as a whole revolved around commerce. The government followed a policy of **mercantilism,** an economic theory which measured a nation's wealth by the amount of gold and silver it possessed. As long as colonial trade benefited England, the English were content to let the colonies prosper. When colonial manufacturing interfered with English manufacturing, however, England stepped in to protect her industries. After all, according to the theory of mercantilism, the colonies existed solely for the good of the mother country. But the colonies saw things differently; they existed for their own good, not England's.

Colonial governments. With time, many Americans were native-born, and many non-English settlers came to America as well. America remained English in many ways, but it also developed a **uniquely American** way of life, including institutions of self-government which, though they bore the image of the English political tradition, had American peculiarities.

By the middle of the 18th century, all the colonies had **written charters** which functioned as comprehensive written constitutions. Americans developed an early preference for having every detail of governmental institutions spelled out in black and white, and they had a habit of holding their governments to the letter of the law.

In every colony, important legislative bodies developed—bicameral (two houses) in all except Pennsylvania. These **legislatures** consisted of elected representatives. While many colonies had some property qualifications for voters, a relatively high percentage of adult males held the right to vote.

Each colony also had a **governor** who served as its chief executive officer. Although this governor had great power, the legislature held the power to appropriate finances. If the governor refused to cooperate, the legislature could withhold funds, including his salary.

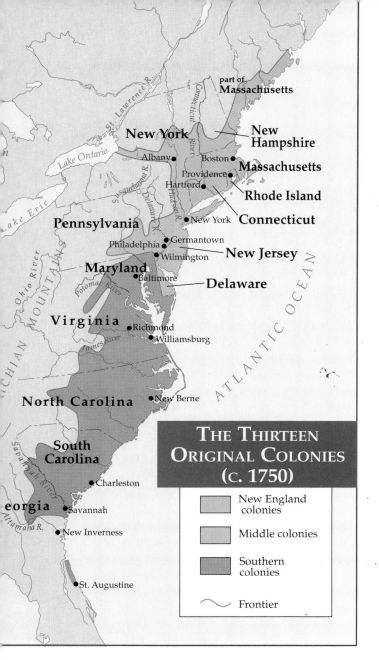

**THE THIRTEEN
ORIGINAL COLONIES
(C. 1750)**

New England colonies

Middle colonies

Southern colonies

Frontier

*King
George III*

over 50 years old when he ascended to the throne in 1714. He never learned to speak English, and he was not a very strong king. The next Hanoverian, **George II** (ruled 1727–1760), was even weaker. The real power in government fell to the king's chief minister, **Robert Walpole** (1676–1745). Robert Walpole is considered <u>the first true prime minister of England</u>, a position he held from 1721 to 1742.

George III (ruled 1760–1820) hoped to reverse the trend of the declining power of the English monarchy that had begun in 1688. He removed all effective opposition to himself and greatly reduced Parliament's power in England. He also clamped down drastically on the English colonists. *After about 1760, British interference in America became the rule rather than the exception.*

Wars between France and England

Three European wars. Like the Great Awakening, the struggle between England and France for empires in the New World helped prepare the colonists for independence. The rival nations fought four wars between 1689 and 1763. The first three wars began in Europe but spread to America, where they were fought under different names.

The Hanoverian Kings

While the colonies were developing in relative freedom across the Atlantic, England was busy with other interests. In **1707**, <u>England and Scotland were united</u> under Queen Anne (ruled 1702–1714) into a single kingdom called **Great Britain.** After Queen Anne died, it was decided that the Hanoverian dynasty from Germany would provide England with its monarchs. **George I** (ruled 1714–1727) was

Wars Between France and England (1689–1763)

In Europe	In America
War of the League of Augsburg (1689–1697)	King William's War (1689–1697)
War of Spanish Succession (1702–1713)	Queen Anne's War (1702–1713)
War of Austrian Succession (1740–1748)	King George's War (1744–1748)
Seven Years' War (1756–1763)	French and Indian War (1754–1763)

The French and Indian War. The fourth war, which lasted from 1754 to 1763, started in America and spread to Europe, where it became known as the **Seven Years' War** (1756–1763). Because the French and Indians banded together in this war against the British, it was called the **French and Indian War** in America. The French and Indian War had great significance for America as well as for England. It not only removed the threat of French interference in eastern North America, but it *united the colonists against a common enemy* and *gave them valuable military experience,* preparing them for the coming conflict with England.

In the *Peace of Paris* of 1763, France surrendered Canada and all other possessions east of the Mississippi (except New Orleans) to England. (Spain ceded Florida to England, but received New Orleans and French territory west of the Mississippi, later known as the Louisiana territory.)

The Growing Conflict between England and America

Grenville's reforms. George III came to the throne in the middle of the French and Indian War (1760), and in 1763, the year the war ended, he appointed a new prime minister, **George Grenville** (1712–1770). Faced with a huge national debt from the recent war with France, Grenville convinced the king and Parliament to raise taxes both in Britain and the colonies. With the king's approval, Grenville pushed a program of "reforms" through Parliament, including rigid enforcement of trade laws and new taxes in the colonies. Of all the parts of Grenville's program, the most repulsive to the colonists was the **Stamp Act of 1765,** which required the colonists to buy special stamps which had to be affixed to legal documents (wills, bills of sale, licenses), pamphlets, and even newspapers. The colonists' reaction to the Stamp Act was adverse and widespread. Merchants determined that they would not import any more British goods, and the people said that they would not buy any more British products until the tax was repealed.

Faced with boycotts, petitions from English merchants who were losing money, and serious outbreaks of violence in American cities, Parliament repealed the Stamp Act. But on the same day, it adopted the **Declaratory Act of 1766,** declaring that it had full power to make laws for America "in all cases whatever."

A few men in Parliament such as **Edmund Burke** (1729–1797), one of Britain's greatest statesmen and political thinkers, defended the colonies. Burke argued that the colonies had grown strong and that, whether Parliament liked it or not, they must be dealt with on the principle of freedom for they would refuse to be dealt with any other way.

The Townshend Acts. In 1767, just a year after the repeal of the Stamp Act, Parliament enacted the Townshend Acts, named for King George's Chancellor of the Exchequer, **Charles Townshend** (1725–1767). The acts <u>imposed duties on several types of imports</u> into the colonies—paper, paint, lead, glass, and tea—and the bill specifically stated that it was a revenue measure. The acts also *established a board of customs* in Boston to oversee customs collection and *created special courts* to try customs dodgers without a jury. Documents called <u>writs of assistance</u> permitted British officials to search American ships and buildings for smuggled goods. The reaction in America was swift and predictable. The colonists insisted that by English law, they should be protected from *taxation without representation.* Pamphlets and letters began to circulate, voicing opposition to the Townshend Acts, and when Parliament failed to respond to the outcry, the colonists resorted to boycotts once again, refusing to buy British goods.

The uproar in the colonies and the pleas of British merchants finally resulted in the repeal of the Townshend duties *except the tax on tea* in 1770. From 1771–1773, there was a "lull in political affairs" which proved to be only the calm before the storm.

Committees of Correspondence. During these years of calm, **Samuel Adams** filled the newspapers with warnings that the calm and peace were temporary. Adams made the issues very simple for the people: "No free people," he wrote, "ever existed, or ever can exist without . . . keeping the purse-strings in their hands."

Adams also initiated the formation of the **Committees of Correspondence** to keep neighboring towns informed of the conflict with England and to make America's position known to the world. Soon Committees of Correspondence were organized throughout the colonies. When the American War for Independence, or "Revolution" came, it would not be the disorganized rioting we usually think of

when we hear the word "revolution." It would be the calm, deliberate, organized act of a free people. America experienced not a moment of anarchy.

The Boston Tea Party. In 1773, the calm ended and the storm began when Parliament authorized the faltering East India Company to sell an enormous surplus of tea in America *exempt from regular trade duties.* In effect, this exemption gave the East India Company a monopoly on tea in the colonies. The colonists were outraged.

Some of the colonies ordered the tea-laden ships to turn around and return to England; others simply left the tea to spoil on the docks. But in Boston, the royal governor refused a citizen request to send the tea back to England. On the night of December 16, 1773, a group of American patriots disguised as Indians boarded the tea-laden vessels and dumped 340 chests of tea into the harbor. Although the men harmed nothing but the tea, the **Boston Tea Party,** as it was called, outraged British authorities.

Intolerable Acts. Determined to punish the Massachusetts colony, Parliament enacted a series of measures which Americans named the "Intolerable Acts" of 1774. The British <u>suspended the Massachusetts legislature</u> and <u>appointed a military governor</u> to rule the colony. The *Boston Port Bill* closed the port of Boston—one of the main ports in the colonies—to all commerce. The *Quartering Act,* which applied to all the colonies, declared that troops would be quartered in every colony to preserve order. Other laws restricted the colonists' freedom to govern themselves and infringed on their traditional rights as Englishmen.

The First Continental Congress. The First Continental Congress convened in Philadelphia on <u>September 5, 1774</u>. All the colonies except Georgia sent delegates. William Pitt the Elder, a great British

Lexington and Concord by Henry Sandham

statesmen and member of Parliament, later called it "the most honorable assembly of statesmen since those of the ancient Greeks and Romans." The Congress approved an association to stop all trade with England until the Intolerable Acts were repealed, and directed the Committee of Correspondence to carry out the plan.

The pleas of the colonists, however, were refused. Parliament and George III were determined to govern America by force, if necessary. As King George put it: "Blows must decide whether they are to be subjects of this country or independent."

The War for Independence

The shot heard 'round the world. On the morning of <u>April 19, 1775</u>, the first shots of the **War for Independence** (sometimes called the *Revolutionary War*) were fired at Lexington, Massachusetts. It is not known for sure who fired the first shot, but it was a shot heard 'round the world, for it was to change the course of human history.

After killing eight Americans and wounding ten others at Lexington, the British marched on to Concord, destroying the military supplies stored there. The **Battle of Lexington and Concord** was not quite over, however. As the British troops headed back to Boston, patriots fired on them from behind trees, shrubs, and barns. Although 93 Americans died that day, the British lost 273 men. For a brief moment in history, little Massachusetts stood alone against one of the great empires of the world.

The Second Continental Congress. Less than a month after the Battle of Lexington and Concord, on <u>May 10, 1775</u>, the Second Continental Congress convened in Philadelphia. John Hancock was elected president. The assembled representatives of the American people decided emphatically that they would fight. The *Continental Army* was established, a call was issued to the colonies to raise troops and funds, and **George Washington** (1732–1799), who had distinguished himself as a lieutenant colonel in the French and Indian War, was <u>appointed commander-in-chief</u>.

Attempt at Reconciliation

On July 6, 1775, the Second Continental Congress adopted a *Declaration of the Causes and Necessity of Taking Up Arms*, which reviewed the history of America leading up to the present conflict and listed the specific injuries done by the mother country to the

The Spirit of '76 by Archibald Willard

colonies. The Declaration also stated the resolve of the colonists to take up arms to preserve American liberty, if necessary. But the Americans were not yet ready to declare independence; the *Declaration of the Causes and Necessity of Taking Up Arms* ended on a note of reconciliation and moderation.

Nevertheless, on August 23, 1775, George III issued *Proclamation of Rebellion,* declaring that the Americans were in "open and avowed rebellion," and calling upon all officers and subjects to aid and assist "in the suppression of such rebellion."

Declaration of Independence

By this time, the point of reconciliation had passed, and war was well under way. The tide of opinion in America was moving toward formal separation from Britain. On **July 4, 1776,** the Continental Congress unanimously adopted the **Declaration of Independence,** the most important human statement of political principles in the history of the world.

The Treaty of Paris. In 1781, five years after the Declaration of Independence, the last major battle of the War for Independence was over—an American victory, a British surrender! Early in 1782, Parliament voted to stop fighting and negotiate peace. In September 1783, Britain and America signed the **Treaty of Paris.** A new nation, dedicated to the principles of freedom and justice, had been born. The United States of America would become the envy of all peoples who cherish freedom.

CHECK UP

1. Briefly describe the typical colonial government.
2. In what year did England and Scotland unite to form Great Britain?
3. Name the Hanoverian king that ruled England when America won her independence.
4. How was the French and Indian War significant for America? What treaty ended the war?
5. What part of Grenville's reforms did the colonists hate most?
6. What effect did the Townshend Acts have on the colonies? How did the colonists respond?
7. What groups were formed to keep Americans informed of the conflict with England?
8. What happened at the "Boston Tea Party"? How did Britain respond?
9. Where were the first shots of the War for Independence fired? When?
10. Who was chosen to lead the Continental Army?
11. What document has been described as the most important human statement of political principles in the history of the world? When was it adopted?

Identify: mercantilism, Robert Walpole, Declaratory Act, Edmund Burke, Samuel Adams, Continental Congress, Treaty of Paris

A New Government

The Articles of Confederation. Even before the War for Independence had ended, the Continental Congress moved toward establishing an official, permanent American union, with permanent institutions of government for the country as a whole. In March 1779, after all the states had given their approval, the **Articles of Confederation,** the first basis for a national government of the United States, went into effect. However, because the Articles could not protect free trade or individual property, they left the nation weak and divided.

The Constitutional Convention. Convinced that the Articles of Confederation must be amended, the states agreed to send delegates to a <u>Constitutional Convention</u> at *Independence Hall* in Philadelphia in <u>1787</u>. As James Madison said from the floor of the convention, "They were now to decide the fate of the republican government."

The Constitutional Convention has been called "the most distinguished assembly which America had ever seen." As one historian explained, the men present represented "the conservative elements of the nation, who were dismayed by the appearance of discord and lawlessness, and who appreciated the national danger." The first order of business was to elect a president to preside over the convention. On this issue, the delegates unanimously agreed: George Washington would lead the convention.

In the Declaration of Independence, the American people had proclaimed their commitment to the leading political ideas of the Modern Age. The War for Independence gave birth to a new kind of nation in the history of the world—a nation founded on the principles of individual liberty. It is one thing, however, to *proclaim* principles, and quite another to embody them in a stable government. But the American people achieved this as well in **1789,** with the ratification of the **United States Constitution.** A new bicameral

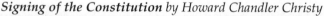

Signing of the Constitution *by Howard Chandler Christy*

*George
Washington*

century is a story of continual growth and expansion. In 1783, the United States consisted of all the land from the Atlantic to the Mississippi between British Canada and Spanish Florida. Despite this huge holding, however, the New World, including North America, was still divided among half a dozen colonial powers.

Beginning in the early 19th century, the United States began to expand her borders. First, she purchased the **Louisiana** Territory from France in 1803; then she acquired **Florida** from Spain in 1819. **Texas** joined the Union in 1845, and in 1846 the United States acquired the **Oregon** Territory by treaty with Britain. After a brief war with Mexico, the United States gained most of the **Southwest** (what is now California, Nevada, Utah, and Arizona) in 1848. By the middle of the 19th century, the United States spanned the continent, making it one of the largest nations in the world.

Congress of elected representatives was soon established, and George Washington, commander-in-chief of the Continental Army and president of the Constitutional Convention, was unanimously elected the first President of the United States.

The Growing United States
Territorial expansion. The history of America from the end of the War for Independence to the beginning of the 20th

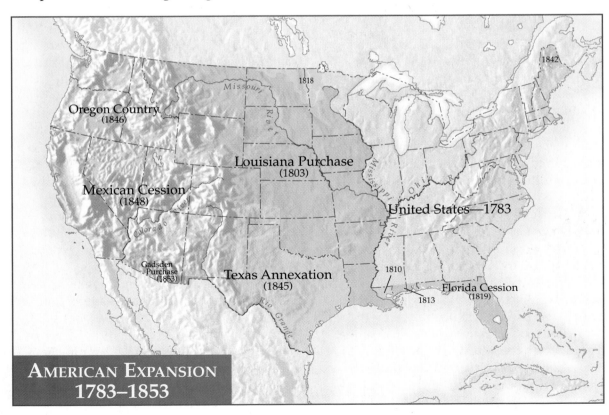

Oregon Country
(1846)

Louisiana Purchase
(1803)

Mexican Cession
(1848)

United States—1783

Gadsden
Purchase
(1853)

Texas Annexation
(1845)

Florida Cession
(1819)

**AMERICAN EXPANSION
1783–1853**

The Oregon Trail
by Albert Bierstadt

Immigration and growth of cities. Not only did the territory of the new nation expand, but its population grew as well due to a tremendous influx of immigrants. Events such as famine in **Ireland** and political turmoil in **Germany** prompted thousands to leave their ancestral homes and become aliens in the new world. Many of these immigrants obtained work in the growing factories. Their numbers swelled the populations of the cities, which, until then, had been quite small in comparison. **New York City** more than doubled in size from 1850 to 1870, becoming a metropolis of almost one and a half million people. By 1890, **Chicago,** the metropolis of the Midwest, had reached over a million inhabitants.

The United States Becomes a World Power

The adoption of the United States Constitution in 1789 gave America a stable, efficient, and democratic system of government, capable of governing a great nation of free men. America began to emerge as a world power, equal with Britain, France, Spain, and other European powers. This firm footing was acquired through both delicate diplomacy and occasional displays of armed might.

The War of 1812. As early as 1812, the United States again fought a war with Great Britain—this time not for its independence but for its rights as a free nation. Britain was seizing American merchant and naval vessels and forcing the American seamen to serve on British ships. The young American nation refused to tolerate such behavior and declared war. The War of 1812 (1812–1815) accomplished few tangible results, but it <u>proved</u> to Britain and to the world <u>that the young United States was well able to defend its interests</u>.

The Monroe Doctrine. The United States also began to look out for the interests of its neighbors. Many Spanish colonies in South America had recently won independence from Spain and were still quite weak. It was noised about in diplomatic circles that France, and perhaps other powers which manipulated Spain, would seek to regain the former colonies. In 1823, President **James Monroe,** realizing that such action would endanger American liberty and trade relations, issued what became known as the Monroe Doctrine. Monroe <u>warned Europe that the Western Hemisphere nations were off-limits for European interference</u> and "henceforth not to be considered as subjects for future colonization by any European powers."

314

James Monroe

Abraham Lincoln

The Mexican War. In 1846, the United States and Mexico went to War over Texas, which had been annexed a year earlier. Though President **James Polk** attempted to avoid open conflict and preserve peace, the Mexican government stubbornly claimed all of Texas and refused to negotiate. From the beginning, the outcome of the war seemed to be a foregone conclusion, for the Mexican forces were poorly equipped and poorly led. By September 1847, the American flag flew over the Mexican capital, and California and New Mexico had fallen into American hands. In the Treaty of Guadalupe Hidalgo (1848), Mexico recognized the Rio Grande as the southern boundary of Texas and ceded California and New Mexico to the United States. In return, the United States agreed to pay Mexico $15 million and to assume the claims of American citizens against the Mexican government.

The American Civil War. Between 1861 and 1865, a civil war interrupted America's progress. Brought on by sectional differences between North and South, this war threatened the very survival of the United States as a nation. The Civil War began when 11 Southern states seceded (withdrew from the Union) and formed a confederacy. Determined to preserve the Union, President **Abraham Lincoln** led the nation to war with the Confederate States. For four years, brother fought against brother in a bitter conflict that devastated the South. The Civil War finally ended in April 1865 when Confederate General Robert E. Lee surren-

dered to Union General Ulysses S. Grant at Appomattox, Virginia. With her Union intact, the United States could continue her progress as a nation. One of the first steps of progress made after the war was the *13th Amendment* to the Constitution, which outlawed slavery in the United States.

Spanish-American War. In 1895, a revolution broke out in Cuba against the Spanish. The Spaniards cruelly subdued the revolutionists, burning villages, treating the populace like captured prisoners, and inciting more anti-Spanish spirit. Many Americans had business interests in Cuba and were concerned by the problems there. The entire nation became interested in Cuban developments when, in February 1898, the **U.S.S.** *Maine* suddenly exploded in the harbor at Havana, Cuba, killing 260 American soldiers. Although the Spanish government of Cuba denied any responsibility, the American people were outraged. This and other circumstances led the United States to declare war on Spain in April 1898. "Remember the *Maine!*" became the battle cry of the Spanish-American War.

After a brief war, the United States defeated Spain and won control of Cuba and **Puerto Rico** as well as **Guam** and the **Philippines** (Spanish possessions in the Pacific). As soon as the people of Cuba were able to govern themselves, the United States granted Cuba her independence. The Philippines would be granted their independence later, in the 20th century, but Guam and Puerto Rico would remain U.S. territories.

As the 20th century began, the United States, once a handful of former colonies, had become one of the five major world powers along with England, France, Germany, and Russia.

A Spectator from France

In 1831, the great French political philosopher and historian **Alexis de Tocqueville,** one of the most profound

Alexis de Tocqueville

thinkers of the Modern Age, arrived in America for a nine-month visit. His famous *Democracy in America*, perhaps the greatest book ever written about America, was published in 1833—the same year that the last feeble remnant of established religion was eradicated from the statute books of Massachusetts. Thus, about the time that the unfolding drama of the Modern Age reached its climax in America, a suitable spectator was on hand, one able to appreciate the magnitude of the achievement of representative democracy in America, to see it in the perspective of the known past and prospective future history of the world.

De Tocqueville came to America from France to study democratic political institutions, but what immediately caught his attention was the religion of the nation:

> On my arrival in the United States the religious aspect of the country was the first thing that struck my attention; and the longer I stayed there, the more I perceived the great political consequences resulting from this new state of things.

In America, de Tocqueville found that "the spirit of religion and the spirit of freedom" were not "marching in opposite directions" but rather "were intimately united and . . . reigned in common over the same country."

One would naturally think that reli-

gion would be stronger where church and state are mixed and religion is officially established in the laws. But as de Tocqueville asked the opinion of men from different groups in America, he was struck by this paradox:

> . . . they all attributed the peaceful dominion of religion in their country mainly to the separation of church and state. I do not hesitate to confirm that during my stay in America I did not meet a single individual, of the clergy or the laity, who was not of the same opinion on this point.

Education and Civil Liberty

In 1832, while de Tocqueville was touring America, the nation's greatest educator, **Noah Webster,** published his *History of the United States.* God's timing is breathtaking! Could any reasonable man doubt that history is a story written by the finger of God? Webster's "little volume, intended for the use of American youth," reads like a deliberate confirmation of de Tocqueville's assertions about American beliefs at that time.

Generations of 19th-century American schoolchildren would learn from Webster the origin of civil liberty:

> Almost all the civil liberty now enjoyed in the world owes its origin to the principles of the Christian religion. Men began to understand their natural rights, as soon as the reformation from popery began to dawn in the sixteenth century; and civil liberty has been gradually advancing and improving, as genuine Christianity has prevailed. By the principles of the Christian religion we are not to understand the decisions of ecclesiastical councils, for these are the opinions of mere men; nor are we to suppose that religion to be any particular church established by law,

with numerous dignitaries, living in stately palaces, arrayed in gorgeous attire, and rioting in luxury and wealth, squeezed from the scanty earnings of the laboring poor; nor is it a religion which consists in a round of forms, and in pompous rites and ceremonies. No; the religion which has introduced civil liberty, is the religion of Christ and his apostles which enjoins humility, piety, and benevolence; which acknowledges in every person a brother, or a sister, and a citizen with equal rights. This is a genuine Christianity, and to this we owe our free constitutions of government.

CHECK UP

1. When was the U.S. Constitution ratified? Who became the first President of the United States?

2. Name some of the territories the United States acquired in the 19th century. In what other way did the nation grow?

3. In what war did the United States prove that it was able to defend its interests?

4. What warning did America issue to Europe regarding colonization in the Western Hemisphere?

5. What war interrupted the nation's progress and threatened its very survival? What was the outcome?

6. What territories did the United States gain after the Spanish-American War?

7. Why did Alexis de Tocqueville come to America? What immediately caught his attention? To what did the people with whom he talked attribute the religious strength of America?

8. How did Noah Webster explain the origin of civil liberty?

Identify: Articles of Confederation, U.S.S. *Maine*, James Monroe, James Polk, Treaty of Guadalupe Hidalgo, Abraham Lincoln, 13th Amendment

The Second Great Awakening

Nationwide Revival

In the first half of the 19th century, a series of widespread revivals swept the nation. Peaking in the 1850s, this time of nationwide revival became known as the **Second Great Awakening.** Few were unaffected by this surge of Christianity. The truths of the Bible thoroughly permeated the nation, producing a zeal for evangelism and a motivation for social reform. Just as reverence for the Bible played a key role in the founding of America, it played a key role in the maturing of the nation.

Need for revival. The first Great Awakening (1730s) had sustained our nation through the Revolutionary War, but, as often happened, spiritual concern declined during the peace and prosperity that followed the war. By 1790, America was in desperate need of spiritual revival.

Revival in New England. The revivals that led to the Second Great Awakening began quietly in New England. Gradually churches began to increase, and new churches were founded by various denominations. The Methodists experienced such dramatic growth that the 19th century has been called the **"Age of Methodism."** The growth of Methodism came about through the preaching of **Methodist circuit-riders,** evangelists who rode regular routes, or circuits, on horseback, preaching at various points along the way.

Circuit-riding Preacher

317

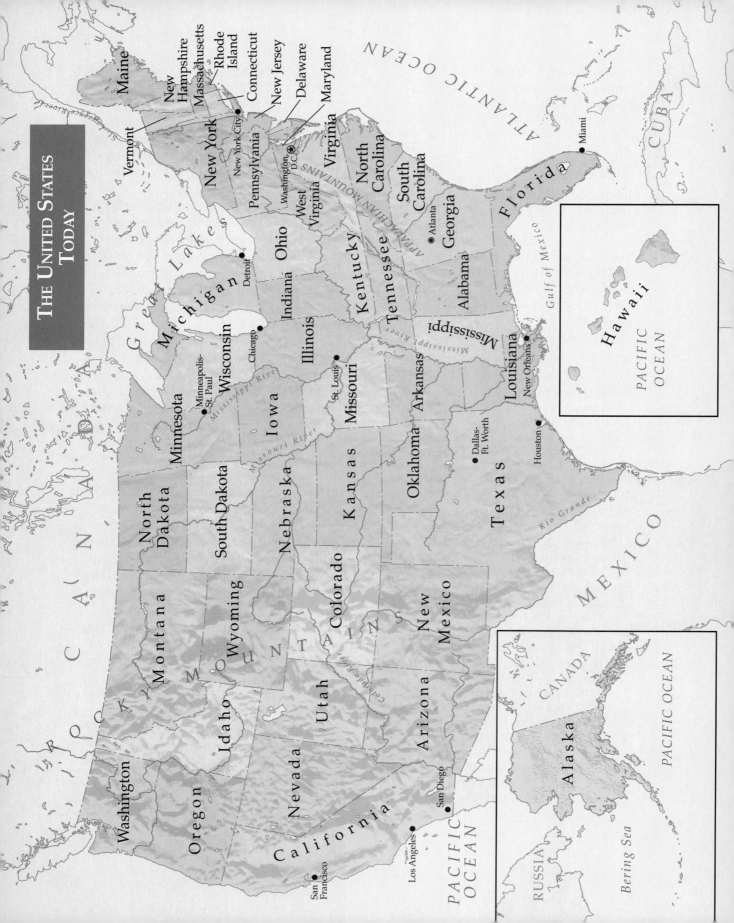

THE UNITED STATES TODAY

ATLANTIC OCEAN

CUBA

Maine

New Hampshire
Massachusetts
Rhode Island
Connecticut
New Jersey
Delaware
Maryland

Vermont

New York

New York City

Pennsylvania

Washington, D.C.

West Virginia

Virginia

North Carolina

South Carolina

Miami

Florida

Gulf of Mexico

Hawaii

PACIFIC OCEAN

Great Lakes

Michigan

Detroit

Ohio

Indiana

Illinois

Chicago

Wisconsin

Minneapolis-St. Paul

Minnesota

Kentucky

Tennessee

APPALACHIAN MOUNTAINS

Atlanta

Georgia

Alabama

Mississippi

Mississippi River

Louisiana

New Orleans

Iowa

Missouri

St. Louis

Missouri River

Arkansas

Oklahoma

Kansas

Nebraska

North Dakota

South Dakota

Montana

Wyoming

Idaho

Colorado

New Mexico

Arizona

Utah

Nevada

Texas

Dallas-Ft. Worth

Houston

Rio Grande

MEXICO

Colorado River

Washington

Oregon

California

San Francisco

Los Angeles

San Diego

PACIFIC OCEAN

CANADA

ROCKY MOUNTAINS

Alaska

CANADA

PACIFIC OCEAN

RUSSIA

Bering Sea

Methodists began circuit riding in New England in 1789 under the leadership of **Francis Asbury** (1745–1816), whom John Wesley had sent to America from England. In less than a decade, there were Methodist circuits throughout New England. The horseback circuit-riding preacher was a welcome visitor each time he reappeared at the lonely pioneer villages or homesteads on his circuit.

Revival on the frontier. By 1799, revival had spread to parts of Kentucky, largely through the work of a Presbyterian minister from North Carolina. Soon revival was breaking out across the frontier under the preaching of Presbyterian, Methodist, and Baptist evangelists. The Second Great Awakening brought revival to all parts of the West, especially to **Indiana, Ohio, Kentucky,** and **Tennessee.**

Charles G. Finney and the Second Great Awakening

Revival surged from the western frontier to the cities of the East, reaching its peak in the 1850s. The man most responsible for the nationwide revival that came to be known as the *Second Great Awakening* was **Charles G. Finney** (1792–1875). Finney came to know Christ as a young lawyer in New York. "In studying elementary law," he recalled in his autobiography, "I found the old authors frequently quoting the Scriptures . . . as authority for many of the great principles of common law. This excited my curiosity so much that I went and purchased a Bible, the first I had ever owned; and whenever I found a reference by the law authors to the Bible, I turned to the passage and consulted it in its connection. This soon led to my taking a new interest in the Bible, and I read and meditated on it much more than I had ever done before in my life."

Through the grace of God, Finney was saved, called to preach, and so anointed by God's Spirit that he *became one of the most*

Charles G. Finney

powerful revivalists America has ever known. He held meetings in many large Northern cities, including New York City, Syracuse, and Buffalo, New York; Boston, Massachusetts; and Hartford, Connecticut. He also went to the British Isles twice to preach revival. God used Finney's keen, analytical, legal mind to present to his listeners so clear a case of their guilt that many, burdened down with the weight of sin, cried out for a Savior. Then he presented to his audience the legal transaction that had taken place in the courtroom of heaven when the blood of Christ paid for our sins.

Through Finney's ministry, entire cities were affected by the gospel, and changes were seen even among those who did not accept the gospel message. Public interest in the revivals was so great that newspapers in New York and other cities would devote entire issues to revival news. Many of Finney's meetings lasted for months at a time. In Rochester, New York, he once preached revival for six months. It is estimated that some 500,000 people were converted under Finney's ministry.

D. L. Moody

In the second half of the 19th century, the great American revivalist **D. L. Moody** (1837–1899) brought the gospel to great crowds of people in America and Great Britain. **New York, Philadelphia, Baltimore, St. Louis, Cincinnati, Chicago, Boston**, and many other cities were stirred by his dynamic ministry. Quickened by the Spirit of God, D. L. Moody reached out to America's masses, and the whole country felt the purifying fires of revival. His work was greatly used of God to bring America back to the position of "one nation under God."

America and Missions

The Second Great Awakening stirred in many Christians a burden for the needs of people in other parts of the world to be evangelized. Many churches and Christian groups started mission boards, and Americans became leaders in foreign missions.

Great numbers of American missionaries sailed to distant shores where countless souls had never heard the gospel message. The *Hawaiian Islands* became the first great center of American missions activity. The first American missionaries arrived in Hawaii in 1820. By the 1850s, Christianity had transformed the islands; countless souls were converted, schools and churches were established, and Hawaii became a constitutional monarchy with just laws and a representative form of government.

Adoniram Judson (1788–1850), one of the first foreign missionaries to be sent out from the United States, served in *Burma* (Myanmar), a nation in Southeast Asia. Judson is remembered as the "Father of American Missions." **Lott Carey** (?–1828),

D. L. Moody

an African-American preacher, ministered in *Liberia*, Africa's first black republic. Carey became known as the "Father of West African Missions."

By 1914, the United States was sending more missionaries to foreign fields than any other country, and Christians in America were the greatest financial supporters of foreign missions. The missionary efforts of the American people did much to keep Americans thinking of others and therefore better able to handle true freedom. Some people think that America's missionary vision has been one great reason why God has blessed America.

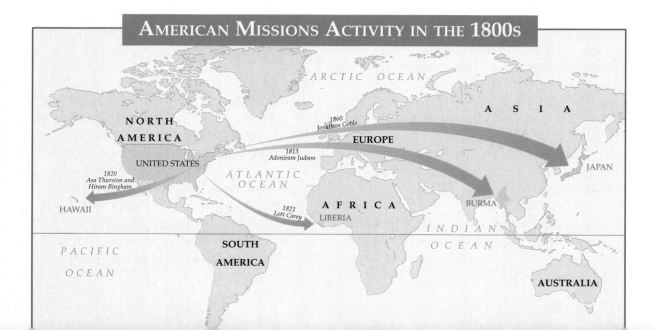

AMERICAN MISSIONS ACTIVITY IN THE 1800s

--- CHECK UP ---

1. When did the Second Great Awakening begin? Where did it begin?
2. Who organized the Methodist circuit-riders?
3. What three denominations were prominent in the revivals on the frontier?
4. What caused Charles Finney to take an interest in the Bible?
5. Name the "Father of American Missions." Where did he serve as a missionary?
6. What country led the world in foreign missions efforts by 1914?

Identify: circuit-riders, D. L. Moody, Hawaiian Islands, Lott Carey

CHAPTER 17 REVIEW

MULTIPLE CHOICE Write the letter of the answer that best completes each sentence.

1. _____ began the Pietist movement.
   a Adoniram Judson *c* Robert Raikes
   b Philipp Spener *d* William Carey

2. The _____ church was founded by John Wesley.
   a Methodist *c* Baptist
   b Presbyterian *d* Anglican

3. _____ led the movement in England to abolish slavery.
   a Robert Raikes *c* William Wilberforce
   b William Carey *d* Adoniram Judson

4. _____ was the first true prime minister of England.
   a Edmund Burke *c* George Grenville
   b Robert Walpole *d* Charles Townshend

5. In America, the Seven Years' War was called the _____ war.
   a French and Indian *c* Queen Anne's
   b King William's *d* King George's

6. George III appointed _____ to be prime minister in 1763.
   a Robert Walpole *c* George Grenville
   b Edmund Burke *d* Charles Townshend

7. To the colonists, the most repulsive of Grenville's reforms was the _____ Act.
   a Quartering *c* Tea
   b Sugar *d* Stamp

8. _____ was a member of Parliament who defended the colonies.
   a Edmund Burke *c* Charles Townshend
   b George Grenville *d* Robert Walpole

9. The _____ taxed colonial imports.
   a Intolerable Acts *c* Townshend Acts
   b Quartering Act *d* Stamp Act

10. Parliament enacted the _____ to punish the colonists for the Boston Tea Party.
    a Stamp Act *c* Townshend Acts
    b Quartering Act *d* Intolerable Acts

11. The first shots of the War for Independence were fired at _____, Massachusetts.
    a Boston *c* Springfield
    b Lexington *d* Concord

12. The _____ ended the War for Independence.
    a Treaty of Paris
    b Declaration of Independence
    c Proclamation of Rebellion
    d Articles of Confederation

13. The _____ Amendment outlawed slavery in the U.S.
    a 12th *c* 14th
    b 13th *d* 15th

14. The _____ was destroyed by an explosion while anchored in the harbor at Havana, Cuba.
    a U.S.S. Connecticut *c* U.S.S. Maine
    b U.S.S. Alabama *d* U.S.S. Vermont

15. _____ wrote *Democracy in America*.
    a Teddy Roosevelt *c* Charles Finney
    b Noah Webster *d* Alexis de Tocqueville

16. _____ led the circuit riders in New England.
    a Adoniram Judson *c* Francis Asbury
    b Charles Finney *d* Lott Carey

CHAPTER 17 REVIEW (CONTINUED)

17. The first great center of American missions activity was _____.
   a Burma   c India
   b South Africa   d Hawaii

18. _____ was one of the first foreign missionaries to be sent out from the United States.
   a Billy Sunday   c William Carey
   b Adoniram Judson   d Jonathan Edwards

COMPLETION *Choose the correct term to complete each sentence and write the letter in the blank.*

- a John Carver
- b Adventurers
- c Leyden
- d *Democracy in America*
- e Sir Edwin Sandys
- f John Robinson
- g Mayflower Compact
- h Separatists
- i Philipp Spener
- j London
- k Plymouth
- l New England
- m Strangers
- n William Bradford
- o Pilgrims
- p *History of Plymouth Plantation*
- q Puritans

1. The _____ desired to "purify" the church of England.
2. The _____ insisted on having independent, self-governing churches.
3. _____ was the first American history book.
4. The Scrooby congregation is remembered in history as the _____.
5. When the Pilgrims left England, they settled in the city of _____, Holland.
6. _____ helped the Pilgrims secure a patent to settle in Virginia.
7. A group of London businessmen known as the _____ provided the financial backing for the Pilgrims' journey.
8. The Pilgrims called their non-Separatist friends _____.
9. The Pilgrims landed in _____ instead of Virginia.
10. Before leaving the ship, the Pilgrims signed the _____.
11. When they arrived in the New World, the Pilgrims settled at _____.
12. The Pilgrims elected _____ to be their first governor.

TIME LINE CHALLENGE *Choose the letter of the correct date for each of the events listed below.*

1620	1707	1754–63	1775–83	1789	1791	1823	1833	1861–65	1898
A	B	C	D	E	F	G	H	I	J

_____ 1. French and Indian War
_____ 2. Spanish-American War
_____ 3. Monroe Doctrine
_____ 4. Pilgrims land at Plymouth Rock
_____ 5. Bill of Rights
_____ 6. American Civil War
_____ 7. American War for Independence
_____ 8. Slavery outlawed in British Empire
_____ 9. Constitution of the United States
_____ 10. England and Scotland unite to form Great Britain

MATCHING Match each description with the correct term.

- *a* War of 1812
- *b* George III
- *c* George Whitefield
- *d* Adoniram Judson
- *e* Charles Finney
- *f* Samuel Adams
- *g* Robert Raikes
- *h* William Bradford
- *i* George Washington
- *j* Jonathan Edwards
- *k* William Carey
- *l* Lott Carey
- *m* Monroe Doctrine
- *n* Alexis de Tocqueville
- *o* Abraham Lincoln

____ 1. "Father of the Sunday School Movement"

____ 2. "Father of Modern Missions"

____ 3. began the Great Awakening

____ 4. the best known Great Awakening evangelist

____ 5. King of England during American War for Independence

____ 6. started the Committees of Correspondence

____ 7. Commander-in-chief of the Continental Army and first President of the United States

____ 8. proved that America was capable of defending itself

____ 9. warned against European interference in the the Western Hemisphere

____ 10. President during the Civil War

____ 11. Frenchman who studied American democracy

____ 12. revivalist most responsible for Second Great Awakening

____ 13. "Father of American Missions"

____ 14. "Father of West African Missions"

____ 15. "Father of American History"

MAP SKILLS Use the maps on pp. 307, 313, and 318 to answer the following questions.

1. List the thirteen original colonies by region.

2. What territory did the United States acquire in 1803?

3. What purchase completed the continental United States? When?

4. What states border the Pacific Ocean?

5. What river separates Texas from Mexico?

6. Which state is composed entirely of islands? What ocean surrounds it?

7. Into what body of water does the Mississippi River empty?

8. What tributary of the Mississippi begins in western Montana?

9. Name the largest mountain range in the eastern United States.

CONCEPTS TO CONSIDER On a separate sheet of paper, answer the following questions using complete sentences.

1. How did the *Mayflower* represent the nation that America would later become?

2. Describe England's moral condition in the 1700s.

3. Explain how the Great Awakening prepared America for independence.

18
France in the Modern Age
(c. 1500–1850)

HIGHLIGHTS
Huguenots • Age of Enlightenment
French Revolution • Reign of Terror • Napoleon Bonaparte
Congress of Vienna • July Revolution

France during the Reformation

Political Power

France emerged from the Middle Ages a powerful nation-state, destined to play a major role in the history of the world in the Modern Age. But unlike England, France exhibited no trends toward political freedom and individual rights. The French had no established rights, as the English had, to provide purpose, direction, and limitation for government. Furthermore, France had nothing to compare with the English Parliament to give it limited, representative government.

During the *Hundred Years' War* (1337–1453) with England, while the French king's power grew greater, the **Estates-General,** the French version of a parliament, grew weaker. The king controlled France's purse strings, and the Estates-General simply approved the laws he wanted. In the late 1400s, during the reign of **Louis XI** [loo'ē: 1461–1483], the Estates-General met only once, and at that time it specifically requested that the king govern in the future without it. As the Modern Age began, there seemed to be no obstacles to the growing power of the French monarchy.

Religious Power

In addition to his political power, the king of France also exercised considerable religious power. French kings had never been as strongly controlled by medieval popes as other European monarchs had been. In 1516, the king of France acquired the power to appoint the bishops of the Roman church in France. This gave the French king such power over the Roman church in France that he was practically a national pope. On the eve of the Protestant Reformation, the idea was taking hold in France that the king was the same as the state (the government), and that the state was the same as the church.

The Reformation in France

Rejection by the kings. Protestant leaders repeatedly declared that the Reformation was not a political revolution and that Protestants were not rebels. But the king of France saw the Reformation as a threat to his authority over church and state. Church and state had become so closely tied together in France, and religion had been viewed from a political vantage point for so long, that any change in religion foreshadowed a change in politics as well. Whether the king of France liked it or not, many Frenchmen would soon be leaving the Church of Rome. Great religious turmoil and therefore political instability loomed on the horizon for France.

Acceptance by the Huguenots. The king had political motives for rejecting the Reformation, but many French people

324

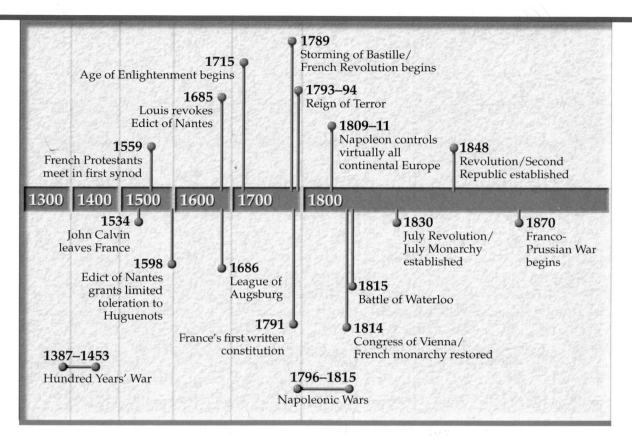

1789
Storming of Bastille/
French Revolution begins

1715
Age of Enlightenment begins

1793–94
Reign of Terror

1685
Louis revokes
Edict of Nantes

1809–11
Napoleon controls
virtually all
continental Europe

1848
Revolution/Second
Republic established

1559
French Protestants
meet in first synod

| 1300 | 1400 | 1500 | 1600 | 1700 | 1800 |

1534
John Calvin
leaves France

1830
July Revolution/
July Monarchy
established

1870
Franco-
Prussian War
begins

1598
Edict of Nantes
grants limited
toleration to
Huguenots

1686
League of
Augsburg

1815
Battle of Waterloo

1791
France's first written
constitution

1814
Congress of Vienna/
French monarchy restored

1387–1453
Hundred Years' War

1796–1815
Napoleonic Wars

welcomed it. A large number of French-men became **Huguenots** [hū′gē·nŏts], or French Calvinist Protestants.

Protestant leader **John Calvin** remained in France until 1534, when he was forced to flee from persecution. Calvin's *Institutes*, though originally published in Latin, was very early translated into French. After leaving France, Calvin carried on his work in nearby *Geneva, Switzerland.*

In spite of the political hostility toward them, the number of Huguenots continued to increase until they became an important

Huguenots: a protestant pastor addressing a secret assembly of Huguenots.

325

minority. Protestants came from all classes, from peasants to lords, but Protestantism was especially strong in the noble class. *By the mid-1500s, nearly half of the nobles in France had become Protestants.*

From its very beginning, the Protestant movement in France was suppressed by the kings; both **Francis I** (ruled 1515–1547) and **Henry II** (ruled 1547–1559) took actions against the Huguenots. By the 1550s, the prisons were filled with Huguenots. But as persecution intensified, the Huguenots increased in number.

Appeal from the Huguenots. In the early 1550s, most of the Huguenots met in secret. But in some areas their numbers increased so rapidly that they soon took over old Roman church buildings (which their tithes had built) and used them for public worship.

In 1559, French Protestants met in their first **synod** [sĭn′ud: an assembly of representatives] and drew up a confession of faith and rules of discipline. They also composed an address to the king, asking for official permission to hold meetings for public worship. The Huguenot assembly very carefully pledged loyalty to the king and raised no purely political points. However, the very fact that the Protestants were organized in an assembly was taken as a threat by the king.

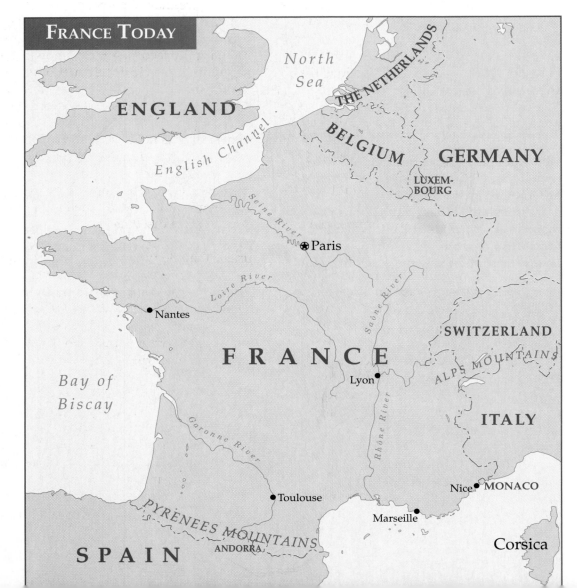

FRANCE TODAY

Civil and Religious Wars

Three weak kings. In 1559, the year of the Huguenot synod, King Henry II was mortally wounded in a jousting tournament. The king left three sons, each of whom served as king during the course of the next 30 years: **Francis II** (ruled 1559–1560), **Charles IX** (ruled 1560–1574), and **Henry III** (ruled 1574–1589). During this 30-year period, the mother of these kings, **Catherine de Médicis** [kà′trēn′ dĕ mā′dē′sēs′: 1519–1589], attempted to rule for her young sons. She proved ruthless and unscrupulous in her scheming to control the country for her own selfish interests.

Meanwhile, behind the scenes, various factions (small groups), with their own political ends to serve, tried to control these weak kings and their powerful mother. The two chief rival factions that tried to control the monarchy identified themselves with the basic religious divisions in France: Catholics and Protestants.

Nine civil wars. In the last four decades of the 16th century (1562–1598), nine civil wars were fought in France, all in the name of religion (though political issues and religious matters had become so thoroughly mixed that it is impossible to separate the two). The Protestants were led by such men as **Admiral Gaspard de Coligny** [gäs·pär′ də kô′lē′nyē′], who had previously won fame as a military leader, and **Henry of Bourbon,** king of Navarre, a small independent kingdom in the area of the Pyrenees Mountains between Spain and France. The Catholic forces were led by the prominent **Guise** [gēz] family.

Catherine de Médicis was more or less caught in the middle. Realizing that both Catholics and Protestants desired to supplant her power, Catherine shrewdly calculated her defense and tried to play one side against the other. She wanted peace in France simply for her own security: civil peace would certainly do more

Catherine de Médicis

to ensure her leadership position than would civil war.

Because Catherine feared the Protestants more than she feared the Catholics, she contrived a feeble, futile effort at peace in January 1562. The so-called **Edict of January** decreed that Huguenots could worship in public if they met outside town limits and if they admitted royal officials to inspect their services. Like later attempts at toleration in France, this one had tragic flaws. It was not based on the acceptance of toleration as a matter of principle but as a matter of convenience. What is "convenient," however, can change from one moment to the next, as the Huguenots would soon discover.

Outbreak of war. Beginning in 1562, more than 30 years of religious wars tore France to pieces. These wars wreaked havoc on the countryside and in the towns, causing massive destruction of property and people. Neither side was able to subdue the other completely, and therefore many temporary truces were negotiated.

St. Bartholomew's Day Massacre. During one of these unstable truces, in 1572, the most infamous episode of the French religious wars occurred—the St. Bartholomew's Day Massacre. Hundreds of Huguenots had gathered in Paris to attend the marriage of Henry of Navarre, one of the Protestant leaders, to the king's sister. It now seemed in the interest of the king's mother to crush the Huguenots, so Catherine convinced her weak son that Protestant leader Admiral Coligny, with whom he had struck up a close relation, was now plotting against him. It is said that Catherine whispered in Charles's ear: "Perhaps, sir, you are afraid." King Charles, raving like a madman, burst out: "Kill the admiral, if you like, but kill all the Huguenots with him—all—all—all—all. . . . See to it at once—at once; do you hear?"

At dawn on August 24, Catholic forces attacked their Protestant rivals while they were still in their beds. The violence lasted for three days. It started in Paris, where nearly all the Huguenots were killed. Admiral Coligny was one of the first murdered. Henry of Navarre escaped death only by vowing to change his religion! The massacre spread from Paris throughout France; perhaps as many as 100,000 Huguenots were murdered. In Rome, a medal was struck to commemorate the massacre, and rousing songs of thanksgiving were sung. Pope Gregory XIII praised the king of France and expressed the hope that the massacre was the beginning of a final solution to the Protestant problem. The massacre, however, only aroused the surviving Huguenots to furious resistance, and the warring resumed.

The politiques. As the religious wars dragged on, a new group called the *politiques* [pŏ′lē′tēks′: "politicals"] developed in France. Some were Catholics, and some were Protestants, but all agreed that religious unity in France was hopeless and persistent bloodshed was futile. The politiques were willing to overlook a man's religious persuasion if he would obey the law and live at peace with the rest of society.

The politiques believed that the citizens of a country may have religious differences and still maintain law and order. Some of the politiques even understood that the key to living peaceably in spite of religious differences is to understand that *true* religion cannot be forced. But few Frenchmen really understood religious freedom. The best that could be hoped for in France was purely religious toleration as a practical necessity.

CHECK UP

1. What was the French Estates-General? How powerful was it? Who had the real political power in France as the Modern Age began?
2. How much power did the popes have over medieval French kings?
3. What idea was taking hold in France on the eve of the Protestant Reformation?
4. Who were the Huguenots? How were they treated? About how many nobles in France were Huguenots by the mid-1500s?
5. What queen mother attempted to rule for her young sons from 1559 to 1589? What kind of ruler was she?
6. How many civil wars were fought in France in the last 40 years of the 16th century? Name two Protestant leaders. What family led the Catholic forces?
7. How many Huguenots were killed in the St. Bartholomew's Day Massacre? How did Henry of Navarre escape death?

Identify: John Calvin, synod, Edict of January, politiques

Henry of Navarre

First Protestant king of France. In 1589, reigning King Henry III and Henry of Guise, a Catholic leader who had been trying to dethrone the king, were both assassinated, each by a supporter of the other. By the rules of succession, the crown passed to Henry of Navarre, who became **Henry IV** (ruled 1589–1610)—the first of the Bourbon line of French kings and the first Protestant king of France.

Henry IV

In reality, Henry IV was much more a politique than he was a Huguenot. During the St. Bartholomew's Day Massacre, he had been confronted by the French king personally with the choice of renunciation of Protestantism or immediate death, whereupon Henry had declared himself a Catholic. Shortly after that renunciation, Henry had become an avowed Protestant again. But now, as a Protestant king of France, Henry faced a great dilemma. The majority of Frenchmen were still Catholics, and the leaders of the Catholic forces in France refused to accept a Protestant king. It seemed that bloodshed over religion would continue. Even after his coronation as King Henry IV, the people of Paris would not admit him to his own capital city!

Henry's most intimate Huguenot adviser, **Rosny** [rō′nē′], advised him to declare himself a Catholic for the good of France. "The Huguenots will not desert you," said Rosny to Henry, "as long as you treat them well." Henry officially renounced Protestantism on July 25, 1593. Pondering that as a Protestant he could not enter the city of his throne, Henry is said to have concluded, "Paris is worth a mass." His professed conversion effectively ended the religious wars in France.

The Edict of Nantes. Outraged with Henry's latest change of religion, the Huguenots perceived Henry to be a traitor. In 1598, however, Henry eased their displeasure with what is known as the **Edict of Nantes** [nänt]. The Edict stipulated that Huguenots could live in any towns or districts of France they chose, but could practice their worship only in specifically designated towns where Protestantism had previously been the prevailing form of worship. Huguenots were forbidden to practice or teach their religion or to publicly instruct children in it anywhere outside the designated territories; specifically forbidden was practice of the Huguenot religion at the king's court, or anywhere in Paris or in a zone surrounding the city. On the other hand, Huguenots were not to be discriminated against in admission to colleges and universities, use of public health facilities, or holding of public office. For their protection, the Edict also gave the Huguenots 100 fortified towns to be held by Protestant military garrisons.

The Edict eased tensions for the moment. The Huguenots basically wanted toleration and seemed to be satisfied with the Edict. Like earlier efforts at limited toleration in France, the Edict of Nantes *followed the principle of territorial toleration, allowing the Huguenots freedom of worship only in certain territories.* Thus it was in reality only a political compromise. The Edict would shortly prove to be unworkable and would lead to more religious problems in France.

From Henry IV to Louis XIII

After settling the religious question, Henry proceeded to build a monarchy that was stronger than ever. Though he made many changes in the government and laws of France, Henry never called the Estates-General for approval or advice. He laid the foundation for the later period of French history (c. 1650–1789) known as the Age of Absolutism, which hurt France even more than the wars of religion had.

329

Marie de Médicis. When Henry IV was assassinated in 1610, his wife, **Marie de Médicis** [má′rē′ dĕ mā′dē′sēs′], attempted to rule in his stead. The clergy forced her to call the Estates-General, but there were so many conflicting interests in the assembly that she soon dismissed it. The Estates-General was not called again in France until 1789.

Cardinal Richelieu. The control of the government gradually fell into the hands of (**Cardinal Richelieu** [rē′shĕ·lyû′: 1585–1642], who ruled for Marie de Médicis and her young son, King **Louis XIII** (1610–1643). Cardinal Richelieu worked tirelessly and ruthlessly for his own political advancement and for the increased power of the monarchy.)

As France moved closer and closer to political absolutism, the limited religious liberty established by the Edict of Nantes was slowly chipped away. Richelieu seemed content to leave the Huguenots alone until some of them showed signs of trying to regain political power in France. When he took steps to subdue their action, they rebelled. Richelieu crushed the rebellion and then amended the Edict of Nantes with the **Peace of Alais** [á·lĕs′] of 1629. For the moment, the <u>Huguenots</u> retained their civil and religious rights, but they <u>lost their fortified towns and armies</u>.

Cardinal Richelieu

The Reign of Louis XIV

Louis XIV Comes to Power

Cardinal Mazarin. Louis XIII died in 1643 when his son Louis XIV was less than five years of age. Cardinal Richelieu, who died in 1642, had groomed a young cardinal, **Mazarin** [má′zá′răn′: 1602–1661], to rule for the new child-king. During Mazarin's reign, royal authority was challenged by an outbreak of civil war (1648–1653), but after six years the rebellion was put down and royal authority went unquestioned, at least for several generations.

France in the 17th century. During the reign of **Louis XIV** (1643–1715), France was among the most important nations of Europe and, therefore, the world. Its population of 21,000,000 was four times larger than that of England and twice as large as that of Spain. The industrious French people, working the country's rich soil and managing its considerable international commerce, made France a prosperous nation. France was also a flourishing center of philosophy, science, and art. Whatever happened in France would therefore have important repercussions far beyond its own borders. And important things indeed were to happen in the reign of Louis XIV.

The Absolutism of Louis XIV

When Cardinal Mazarin died in 1661, Louis XIV, then 23 years old, announced that he would take personal control of the affairs of state. After living under Mazarin, the French people were well prepared for a strong monarch, and few seemed to seriously question the unlimited authority with which Louis ruled. Louis's reign of over <u>70 years</u> was *one of the longest reigns of any king in history.*

Louis XIV became known for his display of pomp and splendor. He surrounded his life with such ceremony that it literally took an army of servants to oblige

The Palace of Versailles

The Hall of Mirrors at Versailles

Politics and War

Government policy and organization. Louis XIV's absolutism was demonstrated by the fact that he called no Estates-General during his long reign. As king, he established one of the first modern **bureaucratic** governments. (The term bureau is the French word for "desk." *Bureaucracy* literally means "government by men who sit at desks.") Louis destroyed the independence of local and town governments by setting up various councils of state. Each council was headed by an **intendant,** who represented Louis. In this way, *all local matters were handled by agents of the centralized government.*

To fill his various bureaucratic offices, Louis preferred to appoint men of the **bourgeoisie** [boor'zhwä'zē': the French term for middle class]. Louis kept the nobility occupied with less important but more pleasurable and pacifying positions. By granting prestige and material favors, Louis convinced many important members of the nobility to live at court, where he could keep an eye on them. About 10 miles from Paris, Louis had the famous **Palace of Versailles** built. One of the great

him. Six different groups of persons took part in the ceremony of the king's rising each morning. A certain servant had the task of holding the right sleeve of the king's nightshirt just as the king removed it.

Because Louis XIV chose the sun as the symbol of his reign, he became known as **"the Sun King."** Embodying the doctrine of *absolutism* (unlimited rule by one man) in its purest form, Louis XIV was the epitome of absolutist rulers. In fact, he once said **"L'état, c'est moi"** [lā·tä' sā mwä']—"I am the state." He put his government on a religious foundation and claimed that his absolute power was by **divine right.**

works of architecture in the Modern Age, Versailles housed many government offices (bureaus), but with its Hall of Mirrors, tapestry, chandeliers, and frequent formal occasions, it also offered much to keep the **aristocracy** (nobles) occupied.)

Military conquest. In Europe, armed forces were traditionally run not by governments but by private military leaders. Military leaders recruited, trained, and supplied their own troops, and then these armies hired themselves out to governments as they chose. However, such independent armies presented a threat to ordered government.

Recognizing this threat, Louis set up a definite military organization in France with himself at the top. Armed persons in France fought only for the king. The French government took charge of recruiting and training troops, and it increased the size of the French army from 100,000 to 400,000 men. Louis's highly organized military became an important instrument to ensure order and regimentation throughout France. It also gave him confidence to engage in several wars with neighboring countries. In 1667 and 1672, Louis XIV fought two unsuccessful wars for Spanish territory,

and in 1679 he invaded *Alsace* [ăl'sās] and *Lorraine* (territories on the border of France and Germany) to secure holdings there.

Realizing that Louis had plans to conquer Spain and perhaps more, the nations of Europe joined together against France in the **League of Augsburg** in 1686. The league consisted of the Holy Roman Empire and Spain; Sweden; Bavaria, Saxony, and the Palatinate (parts of Germany); the Dutch Republic; and eventually England. The War of the League of Augsburg broke out in 1688. The French won battles but could not defeat so many enemies at once. In 1697, Louis signed the **Treaty of Ryswick** [rīs'vĭk], which established the *status quo ante bellum* (the existing state of things before the war).

Louis XIV

CHECK UP

1. Who was the first Protestant king of France?
2. What were the provisions of the Edict of Nantes?
3. Who attempted to rule France after the assassination of Henry IV? Who really controlled the government?
4. What did the Huguenots lose in the Peace of Alais?
5. How old was Louis XIV when his father died? Who ruled for him while he was a child?
6. Describe the importance of France during the reign of Louis XIV.
7. For what was Louis XIV known? What was he called?
8. What is absolutism? What saying of Louis XIV expressed his belief in absolutism? How did he demonstrate this belief?
9. Describe the Palace of Versailles. What was the purpose of all its splendor?
10. How did Louis XIV change the military system in France?

Identify: Rosny, bureaucracy, intendant, bourgeoisie, aristocracy, Alsace and Lorraine, League of Augsburg, Treaty of Ryswick

Economics and Finance

Economic independence. In order to increase the wealth and power of the country, Louis XIV wanted to make France economically independent of other nations. To this end, he instituted policies to encourage industry. The underlying purpose of such policies was to create a broader base of wealth in the country from which to collect taxes.

Taxation. In the area of taxation, Louis was less fortunate than in some of his other endeavors. Traditionally in France, methods of tax collecting were costly and inefficient. The main problem arose from an old agreement with the nobility that the king could raise taxes without consent but that the nobility did not have to pay. The bourgeoisie (middle) class was often able to escape taxation, too, by certain exemptions. So the tax burden fell upon the peasants, who could not afford to bear it. Louis had only limited success in changing this impractical situation.

Religion

Toward one religion. At Louis XIV's ascension to the French throne, the Huguenots still enjoyed a fair degree of toleration. They had not been viewed as a threat in France for quite some time. Because many Huguenots were well educated and skilled in crafts and commerce, they held more than their proportionate share of the nation's wealth and were important assets to the country. It was inevitable that Louis XIV would eventually see the religious freedom of the Huguenots as a threat.

Revocation of the Edict of Nantes. Beginning in 1679, Louis issued a series of over 125 documents limiting the liberties of the Huguenots. The Huguenots pleaded with the king and, in 1685, submitted a special appeal, in which they tried to convince Louis XIV that

Religion has its seat in the soul and cannot penetrate there except by way of persuasion and prayer. Methods of force only make atheists and hypocrites and rouse in those of good faith a courage and a perseverance which makes them despise punishment.

Nevertheless, Louis officially revoked the Edict of Nantes that same year. According to his new policies,

(1) All Huguenot church buildings were to be destroyed.

(2) No public or private Huguenot worship services were to be allowed.

(3) Ministers who would not convert to Catholicism had to leave the country within 10 days or be put to death.

(4) Children born to Huguenot parents were to be baptized by Catholic priests and raised as Catholics.

(5) Huguenots (except ministers) were forbidden to leave the country.

Despite the prohibition on Huguenots leaving the country, thousands of them fled to other parts of Europe and even to America. Perhaps half a million Protestants fled France before and after the revocation of the Edict. All these skilled Huguenot craftsmen, sailors, soldiers, and officers who fled France were then gained by her neighbors and rivals. Thousands fled to the city of Berlin, Germany; some scholars attribute the beginning of this city's greatness to the Huguenots' arrival. Many Huguenots also went to America and contributed to the greatness of that land.

Age of Enlightenment

As Louis XIV's reign drew to a close in 1715, France entered what is known as the **Age of Enlightenment.** In reality, the Age of Enlightenment proved to be almost a new Dark Age for France. A blatant anti-Christianity, openly boasting of its rejection of the Bible and disbelief in the deity of Christ, emerged for the first time in the Modern Age on a grand scale.

Through the work of such French Enlightenment thinkers as **Voltaire** [vôl′târ′: 1694–1778], **Montesquieu** [môn′tĕs′kyû′: 1689–1755], and **Jean-Jacques Rousseau** [zhän zhäk roo′sō′: 1712–1778], modern political ideas became known in France. (The British trend toward freedom and the American political achievement were much discussed and much admired.) But in England and America, modern political ideas such as the rights of man, government by consent, and representative democracy were both strengthened and restrained by the Christian heritage of the people. In France, however, Biblical Christianity, the one thing that can make modern political ideas workable in any country, had been driven out of the country with the Huguenots. *The persecution of the Huguenots laid the foundation for the French Revolution* and all the horrors that it brought to the French people.

In France, modern political ideas and religion were disconnected. In fact, the official position of the **"old regime"** (the system of government and way of life in pre-Revolutionary France) was that religion (identified with the Roman church) justified the right of kings to rule as selfish tyrants. Thus, in the hearts and minds of many Frenchmen, a great tension existed between their religion and political freedom.

Louis XIV's actions in the name of religion set the stage for an attack on Christianity that would serve as a model for later anti-Christian movements of the Modern Age. In fact, Louis XIV opened the door to one of the great political catastrophes of all times. Because in France modern political ideas had been disconnected from the Christian heritage, they would go to extremes, leading to new forms of tyranny, trampling down, in new and terrible ways, both individual rights and political freedom.

The French Revolution

Louis XV

Louis XV (ruled 1715–1774) inherited the throne of France in 1715 when his father died. A weak ruler, Louis XV showed more interest in personal pleasure than he did in governing the country. Conditions, especially the financial plight of the government, steadily worsened as the treasury was drained. Despite his lack of leadership, Louis XV did recognize that the "old regime" was in deep trouble. On his deathbed in 1774, he said **"Après moi le déluge"** [à·prĕ mwä lə dā·lūj′]—"After me the deluge." His prophecy of doom would be fulfilled before the end of the century.

Louis XVI

When **Louis XVI** (ruled 1774–1792) came to the throne in 1774, France had yet another ruler who was grossly unfit for the

Louis XVI

task of leading a great nation. He had neither the education nor the character for the job. If ever a country needed a qualified leader, it was France in 1774. From religion to politics, the "old regime" was in turmoil.

Religious turmoil. Many Frenchmen were disturbed about religious conditions in their country. The Roman church, the only legal church in France, which had been so closely tied to the absolute monarchy, was being questioned as never before. Some who were considered France's best thinkers, such as Voltaire, became active atheists. They equated Christianity with Romanism, and

> . . . a corrupt ecclesiasticism, especially when united with the state, breeds atheism and atheism breeds restlessness and torment. It looses the tiger. . . . Given the ecclesiastical corruption in France—then comes Voltaire. . . . Given Voltaire and then the tiger is loosed. . . . Infidelity in France, voiced by Voltaire . . . is a rebound from corrupt ecclesiasticism. . . .[1]

Economic and social turmoil. France was also gripped by economic and social turmoil. The France of the "old regime" was highly aristocratic, or even feudalistic, with a rigid class structure. Everyone belonged to one of three estates or orders. The **First Estate** was the clergy, the **Second Estate** was the nobility, and the **Third Estate** was everyone else in France—from prosperous merchant to poor peasant.

The burden of taxation fell upon those of the Third Estate least able to bear it—**the peasants,** who comprised over 80% of the population but owned only about 30% of the land. The peasants had to pay a forced tithe to the church, an income tax called the taille [tä′y′], and a tax on salt called the gobelle [gə·bĕl′]. The peasants were not, strictly speaking, serfs; they were not tied to the land as in true feudalism. But they still had to pay many feudal-like fees to their landlords. The average peasant usually paid about half of his annual income in taxes of one sort or another.

But since they had always been poor and uneducated, the peasants had, for the most part, resigned themselves to poverty as a way of life. They did not think of poverty as a "problem," because they had no idea that there might be a solution to the problem. But if the French masses were ever to be awakened, 80% of a 24.5 million population would represent a mighty force indeed.

One part of the Third Estate was already very much awake in the old regime—the bourgeoisie, the rising middle class. Unlike the peasants, the middle class managed to get itself exempted from most taxes. The bourgeoisie wanted political power to match its growing economic power, and if it ever got the chance to change things in France, it would.

[1]B. H. Carroll, *An Interpretation of the English Bible,* Vol. 6 (Grand Rapids, Mich.: Baker Book House, 1948), pp. 112–113.

CHECK UP

1. Upon whom did the tax burden in France fall? Why?
2. What were the terms of the revocation of the Edict of Nantes?
3. When did the Age of Enlightenment begin in France? What was it like? Who were some of its chief thinkers?
4. Why have modern political ideas worked in England and America? Why could they not work in France? What laid the foundation for the horrors of the French Revolution?
5. What kind of king was Louis XV? What was his death-bed prophecy?
6. Name the three estates of France and tell who belonged to each. Which estate included the largest percentage of the population?

Identify: Louis XVI, "old regime"

Calling of the Estates-General

The financial problems of the French government increased as Louis XVI's reign continued. By 1789, the government had a huge debt. But as long as the clergy, the nobility, and the rising middle class refused to pay taxes, there was little that the government could do to lift the heavy load of debt.

With the government nearly bankrupt, Louis XVI asked the nobility to accept a tax that all landowners, including the nobles, would have to pay. But they balked. Determined to regain some of the power they had lost, the French nobility told the king that he would have to call the Estates-General, which *had not met for over 170 years* (since 1615).

Louis XVI did not want to call the Estates-General into session. To do so would at best call into question his absolute authority; at worst, it would be an outright admission that he had lost it. But the king had little choice; in July 1788, Louis XVI agreed to have the Estates-General meet the following May, in 1789.

By forcing the king to summon the Estates-General, the nobility initiated the French Revolution. They expected to control the Estates-General and to regain the power they had lost to the king. But the French nobility greatly miscalculated. The meeting of the Estates-General would unleash forces for change that would radically alter France and all of Europe, but not in the way that the nobles wanted.

The Revolution Begins

First stage. The French Revolution began as an aristocratic revolution—a revolt of the nobility against the king— when they forced him to call a meeting of the Estates-General in 1789. But the Third Estate, that of the middle class and peasants, soon became the most powerful force in the assembly. *By 1789, the Third Estate included 98% of the French population.* The middle class parties within the Third Estate had grown large and powerful.

Second stage. When the Estates-General met at Versailles in May 1789, the Third Estate refused to vote by estates. (In the past, each estate had voted as a unit.) Instead, they insisted that the representatives of each estate vote as individuals in one big assembly. With twice as many representatives as the other two estates, plus supporters they expected to gain from the clergy and nobility, the middle class leaders of the Third Estate hoped to control the Estates-General. But after five weeks of quarreling, the assembly came to a deadlock.

Finally, after a few priests from the First Estate joined its ranks, the Third Estate took drastic action. On June 17, it declared itself to be the **National Assembly,** the official representative body of all the people of France!

Thus what had begun as an aristocratic revolution became a bourgeoisie revolution, for though the representatives of the Third Estate supposedly spoke for 98% of the people of France—everyone but the nobility and clergy—they were overwhelmingly middle class.

Under pressure from the nobles, Louis XVI ordered the members of the Estates-General out of their meeting hall, but the Third Estate defiantly reassembled on a nearby indoor tennis court. On June 20, the National Assembly took the so-called **Tennis Court Oath,** vowing to continue meeting until a national constitution had been written. Soon most of the clergy, as well as a few nobles, had joined the National Assembly.

Third stage. Louis XVI's beautiful but haughty wife, **Marie Antoinette** [än′twȧ′-nĕt′], his brothers, and some nobles who lived at court told the king that the National Assembly threatened his dignity and authority. At the end of June, the king summoned about 18,000 troops to

The Oath of the Tennis Court, by Jacques Louis David, a French painter who lived through the Revolution.

Marie Antoinette and Her Children

Versailles. Quite likely he intended to disband the National Assembly by force. But the revolution now entered its third stage—mass revolution—when the great mass of the common people below the bourgeoisie began to rise.

As it progressed, the revolution gave the French people their first real hope of improving their conditions; but with the rumor spreading that the king was going to use force against the people's representatives at Versailles, panic was added to that hope. Economic conditions drastically worsened: the price of bread, for example, doubled. In Paris there were demonstrations, and the people began to arm themselves.

On July 14, 1789, to secure more arms and also free people imprisoned for opposing the "old regime," the people of Paris stormed the **Bastille** [bâs·tēl′], an old castle stronghold, then used primarily as a prison. In the ensuing events, troops killed 98 people, and in retaliation, several government officials were murdered, their heads cut off, put on poles, and paraded through the city.

It is reported that when a messenger told Louis XVI of the storming of the Bastille, the king said, "This is a revolt," whereupon the messenger replied, "No Sire, it is a revolution." The Bastille was unimportant in itself, for there were only seven prisoners inside at the time; but it was

337

Capture of the Bastille: a painting by Claude Cholat, an eyewitness.

important as a symbol. July 14, **Bastille Day,** became the national holiday of France, where it is celebrated as July 4, Independence Day, is in the United States.

In effect, though not in intention, the storming of the Bastille saved the National Assembly and the revolution itself. Not knowing what else to do, Louis XVI accepted the situation in Paris (where a citizen committee formed a new municipal government), sent away the troops from Versailles, and told the nobles and clergy who had not already done so to join in the National Assembly.

Reforms of the French National Assembly

The countryside was now in turmoil as the peasants armed themselves, at first primarily for protection. Then, in fear and anger, they began to attack the homes of the lords of the manors, burning the records of their debts and fees owed to nobles. The last vestiges of feudalism in France were being destroyed by force.

In order to restore order, the National Assembly had to meet the demands of the peasants. On the night of August 4, some noblemen, sympathetic to the Revolution, arose in a symbolic act to renounce their feudal rights. The so-called **"August 4 Decrees"** followed, by which the National Assembly <u>ended the lords' privileges</u> of collecting land taxes from the peasants, hunting on peasants' lands, and taking special privileges over peasants in courts of law. From that time, forced tithes ceased, everyone had to pay taxes, and all citizens became eligible for public office. The National Assembly aptly summed up its decrees with this statement: **"Feudalism was abolished."**

With the "old regime" seemingly finished, the National Assembly laid, so it hoped, the foundations for the future. On August 26, 1789, the French National Assembly adopted the *Declaration of the Rights of Man and Citizen,* which was soon translated into other languages and printed in thousands of copies, proclaiming to the world **"Liberty, Equality, Fraternity,"** the slogan for the new regime in France and eventually all of Western Europe. With America's Declaration of Independence in mind, the representatives of the French people thus declared the principles to justify their revolution and to guide the work of building a new society. With breathtaking speed, so it seemed, France had finally left the Middle Ages and entered the Modern Age.

But as events would show, declaring modern political principles on paper is one thing, and embodying them in permanent institutions of civil government is quite another.

From Revolution to War

Revolution vs. Counter-Revolution

In September 1789, the National Assembly, having proclaimed the principles of the new regime in France, set about to establish a new government. The conditions in France, however, were not conducive to the spirit of calm and deliberation needed to draw up a good constitution. The classes of French society, in fact, were now more hostile than ever toward one another, and Frenchmen were deeply divided over matters of fundamental principles. The revolution had scarcely started when forces of Counter-Revolution arose.

Many clergy and nobility were not reconciled to their loss of wealth and special privileges. Emigrating to other countries, they plotted as *émigrés* [ȧ′mē′grāz′] and traitors, aiding and abetting foreign regimes to attack France and counter the Revolution.

As for the king, he said, "I will never consent to the spoliation of my clergy or of my nobility." The king's hostility made the people very suspicious of him. On October 4, a hungry mob of women and revolutionary agitators raided bread stores in Paris and then marched off, along with the Paris National guard, to besiege and invade the royal residence at Versailles. Louis and his family bowed to the pressure and moved to Paris, where he could be more closely watched.

Such mob action deeply disturbed men of more conservative persuasion who had previously favored the Revolution. They began to drop out of the National Assembly and into the ranks of the Counter-Revolution. But on the other side were many who wanted the revolution to go to extremes. It was around this time that the radical **Jacobin** club, so named because it met in an old Jacobin monastery in France, was organized.

The Constitution of 1791

From October 1789 to September 1791, the National Assembly, now known as the **Constituent Assembly,** devised France's first written constitution, known as the **Constitution of 1791.** The main institution of government was to be a popularly elected, one-house *Legislative Assembly.* The constitution gave the king only the very limited power of a suspensive veto: he could slow down action by the Legislative Assembly, but not block it indefinitely. The king could no longer say "I am the State"; instead, he had to say "Louis by the grace of God and the Constitution, King of the State." <u>France was to be a constitutional monarchy with a very weak king</u>.

In June 1791, Louis attempted to flee France, join the *émigré* nobles, and get help from foreign powers to restore the old monarchy. However, he and his family were intercepted in the town of **Varennes** [vä′rĕn′] and promptly returned to Paris. The *"flight of Varennes"* had failed.

The Civil Constitution of the Clergy

Many more people in France besides the king were dissatisfied with the new order of things. A major cause of dissatisfaction was the **Civil Constitution of the Clergy,** adopted by the Constituent Assembly in 1790. Essentially, the Civil Constitution of the Clergy set up a Church of France. It reduced the authority of the pope in France and made the church more subservient to the government than ever. When the pope denounced the Civil Constitution and condemned the Revolution, the Assembly required the clergy to take an oath of loyalty to the new regime and to the Civil Constitution of the Clergy. Half the clergy took the oath, but the other half refused, and the French church split down the middle. Most Frenchmen who were serious about their religion favored the unofficial clergy. Thus, in addition to economic problems, religion became a source of discontent as well.

Right, Center, and Left

The National Assembly that convened under the Constitution of 1791 reflected a badly divided country. The divisions in the Assembly originated the now common political distinctions between Right, Center, and Left.

About one third of the representatives were conservatives who supported the king and wanted the Revolution to go no further. They were satisfied with the Constitution of 1791. This group became known as the **Right** because they sat on the right side of the Assembly.

In the center sat a group without any particular program or principles. They became known as the **Center.**

To the left sat young radicals who distrusted the king and were displeased with the Constitution of 1791. Led by such prominent Jacobins as **Jean Paul Marat** [zhän päl mà′rà′], **Georges Jacques Danton** [zhôrz zhäk dän′tôn′], and

Maximilien Robespierre [mȧk′sē′mē′lyan′ rô′bĕs′pyâr′], the **Left,** as this group came to be known, wanted the Revolution to go much further in France. In fact, they were soon urging "a crusade for universal liberty."

On April 20, 1792, with very little opposition, the French National Assembly declared war on Austria, and Prussia soon entered the conflict as an ally of Austria. Europe was thus plunged into the beginning of what would be one of the most important series of wars in the history of the world, the **Napoleonic Wars** (1796–1815).

The Execution of Louis XVI

The National Assembly was replaced by a **National Convention,** which was to rule temporarily and write another new constitution. The first thing the Convention did was execute Louis XVI. The king was convicted as a traitor because he had tried to flee the country and because he had attempted to influence foreign powers to stop the revolution. Louis was executed on the *guillotine,* a machine devised for chopping off human heads. Named for Dr. Guillotin, who perfected the device, the guillotine would become a symbol of the French Revolution.

Robespierre and the Reign of Terror

By 1793, the National Convention was losing support within France, largely because of worsening inflation and defeat of French armies on foreign battlefields. There was much protest and popular uprising against the government. To suppress anarchy at home, the Convention set up the **Committee of Public Safety,** composed of 12 men holding extensive police and judicial powers. One member of the Committee of Public Safety, **Maximilien Robespierre** (1758–1794), soon became the most influential man in the French government.

France's Reign of Terror: *victims being carted to the guillotine.*

Maximilien Robespierre

To suppress anti-revolutionary movements, the Committee of Public Safety, under Robespierre's leadership, instituted what was soon called the **"Reign of Terror."** Thousands of known and suspected "enemies of the republic" were suppressed, and many politically influential people were guillotined, including the queen, Marie Antoinette. Altogether, some 40,000 people died, and hundreds of thousands were arrested.

Atheism. At this point, atheism reached its height in France. It is no coincidence that *the Terror was bloodiest at the same time that atheism was at its peak.* Convinced that all religion was counter-revolutionary, one extreme group of revolutionaries promoted a program of de-Christianization in France. To remove any remnant of religion from government, the Convention introduced a new calendar, which removed Sundays, Easter, Christmas, and all other religious holidays. To avoid dating history by the birth of Christ, they declared the year 1792 to be the year I (beginning of the Republic). Months were renamed, and weeks were declared to be ten days long rather than seven. (They were renamed "decades," and the tenth day of each dec-

ade took the place of Sunday). It is said that people and even horses were physically unable to cope with ignoring God's law of one day of rest in every seven. The system was shortly abandoned as unworkable.

The Reign of Terror illustrates how the French Revolution led to its own failure by embracing atheism. What had started as a political revolution to overthrow a tyrant became a social revolution to bring about social equality in France. In the early stages of the revolution, the aim had been to establish a government in the hands of the upper or middle classes, instead of the hands of Louis XVI. But by the time of the Terror, when the masses rose up, it had become a move to eliminate social class and make all Frenchmen equal, in a sense to make them all rulers of the country. There seems to have been an idea that if enough dissenters were eliminated by the guillotine, those left alive would be free, equal, prosperous, and happy. In stark contrast to this bloody failure, the American War of Independence (often called a revolution) was a success because it was not a social movement, of rights without acceptance of responsibility, and because it was firmly grounded in principles, not merely selfish desires. Most

Americans in 1776 were reasonably well off; there were no "peasants" on our shores. The purpose for declaring independence was not equality but freedom. There was no need for a social revolution. And if the American War of Independence had become a social revolution, the whole thing could only have been a bloody failure, as it was in France. War can make people politically free, but it cannot make people intellectually, materially, or socially equal. Many nations have attempted to repeat the French Revolution. At best these revolutions have been failures; at worst they have created their own "terrors."

Fall of Robespierre. Within a year, Robespierre's Committee of Public Safety had antagonized every political faction in France. Denouncing Robespierre as a tyrant, the National Convention arrested him on July 27, 1794, and the next day he and some of his associates were guillotined. The Reign of Terror was over.

CHECK UP

1. What was France's first written constitution called? What kind of monarchy did it give France?
2. Describe the "flight of Varennes."
3. What group sat on the right of the National Assembly? On the left?
4. Name three prominent Jacobins.
5. What member of the Committee of Public Safety was the most influential man in government between 1793–1794?
6. What was the Reign of Terror? How many people were killed during this time?
7. Describe how the revolutionaries tried to de-Christianize France.
8. What lesson about war can the French Revolution teach us?

Identify: Constituent Assembly, Legislative Assembly, Civil Constitution of the Clergy, Napoleonic Wars, National Convention, guillotine

---

The Tyranny of Napoleon

The Rise of Napoleon

Military hero. In 1799, **Napoleon Bonaparte** (1769–1821) returned to Paris from a military campaign in Egypt. Bonaparte, born in Corsica in 1769, had been trained in the French military schools. During the French Revolution, he had been chosen to command an invasion of England. Deciding that a direct invasion was premature, he chose to strike indirectly at England by threatening India (a British possession) through an invasion of Egypt. As a result of this invasion, England, Austria, and Russia formed a coalition against France. Upon his return to Paris, Napoleon learned that a few revolutionary leaders were planning a change in the government. He intended to be a part of that change.

Political success. Napoleon, still only 30 years old, was the man this group needed to take control of the government. On November 9, 1799, Napoleon and his followers drove the legislators from their chambers and proclaimed a new republic—the **Consulate.** It was headed by three consuls, with Napoleon as First Consul.

Napoleon Bonaparte

The Consulate

Napoleon drew up a new constitution and submitted it to the people in a *plebiscite* (an election in which the people express their will). In reality, they had little choice but to accept it. The constitution established a kind of make-believe parliamentary system, but the real power lay with the Council of State, under the leadership of the First Consul, Napoleon.

Napoleon Bonaparte, like many dictators who have come to power in time of turmoil, firmly established himself by promising and obtaining peace. In 1799, Russia withdrew from the coalition against France. In 1801, Austria made peace, and in 1802 Britain did the same. Internal reforms, too, helped to make Napoleon popular. Taxes were collected by professional collectors, so that there was a minimum of corruption. Napoleon established law codes; of all the law codes since those of the Romans, Napoleon's are the most famous. Frenchmen felt secure in peace and enjoyed a type of "justice" under their new ruler.

Perhaps the most significant accomplishment of Napoleon in internal affairs was that he made peace with the Catholic church. To him, religion was a tool. It was his practice to claim to be a follower of the religion of whomever he was dealing with at a given time.

In 1804, at Napoleon's own request, Pope Pius VII went to Paris to bestow upon him the seal of religious consecration. In the church of Notre Dame, accompanied by his wife, **Josephine,** and in the presence of the great dignitaries of the French government and the Church of Rome, *Napoleon was declared emperor of the French by the pope himself.* Napoleon now had the official sanction of the church upon his dictatorship. To disobey the dictates of Emperor Napoleon would be to disobey God. Napoleon demonstrated his arrogance, even at this religious ceremony,

by taking the crown from the altar and placing it on his own head. Thus <u>Napoleon crowned himself Emperor</u>.

The French Empire

Failure in the New World. Like all ambitious tyrants, Napoleon intended to rule not only his own country but as much of the world as possible. He had plans for an empire in the New World, but these plans failed after a slave revolt in Haiti, and in 1803 he was forced to sell the Louisiana Territory to the United States.

Battle of Trafalgar. Napoleon also met with failure on the high seas of Europe. On October 21, <u>1805</u>, the *British navy defeated the combined French and Spanish navies* at the famous **Battle of Trafalgar,** one of the greatest sea battles in history. (Trafalgar is located on the southern coast of Spain at the entrance to the Strait of Gibraltar.) The commander of the British navy at Trafalgar was the renowned **Lord Nelson,** considered by some to be *the greatest naval hero the world has ever known.* Mortally wounded during the battle, Nelson was carried below deck, where he continued to issue the appropriate orders to ensure a victory. As he lay dying, the English completed their victory over the French. Lord Nelson's last words still ring through history: "Thank God, I have done my duty!"

Success on the continent. Napoleon had more success with continental Europe. Two years after Trafalgar, **Austria, Russia,** and **Prussia** (Germany) made peace with Napoleon and were essentially under his control. <u>From 1809 to 1811, Napoleon controlled virtually all of continental Europe</u>. Most of the conquered peoples of Europe seemed satisfied to live under the French imperial system. In 1809, the 40-year-old Napoleon divorced his wife Josephine, who had remained childless. The next year he married **Marie Louise,** the 18-year-old daughter of the Austrian emperor. His new wife was a niece to Marie Antoinette (Louis XVI's queen), and so by marriage Napoleon became a nephew of Louis XVI. Marie Louise soon bore him a son, giving him an heir to his throne. Napoleon's main misfortune of this period was that in 1809 he had a quarrel with the Roman church and was excommunicated by Pope Pius VII, the same pope who had proclaimed him emperor.

The Continental System. Having failed to defeat England on the high seas, Napoleon decided to bring England to its knees by destroying its trade. In 1806, he established the **"Continental System,"** which forbade the importation of British goods into any European country which was under French influence. The trade war that ensued between England and France, combined with the trickery of Napoleon, drew the United States into the **War of 1812** against England.

The Continental System was doomed to eventual failure. Europe could not get along without British imports. Smuggling abounded, and Napoleon even made legal exceptions. Ironically, the French troops wore coats made in Great Britain. The most significant result of the Continental System was that it turned many Europeans against Napoleon's regime.

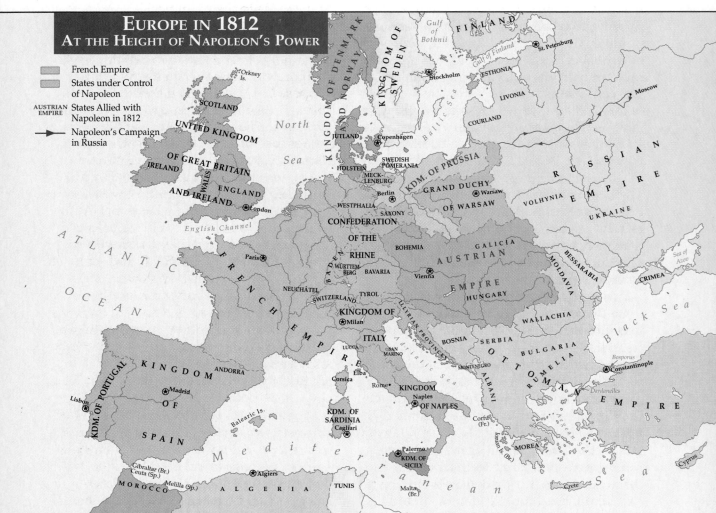

EUROPE IN 1812
AT THE HEIGHT OF NAPOLEON'S POWER

French Empire

States under Control of Napoleon

AUSTRIAN EMPIRE — States Allied with Napoleon in 1812

→ Napoleon's Campaign in Russia

The Fall of Napoleon

Reaction against tyranny. For a time, Napoleon's conquest of Europe seemed to be welcomed by many European peoples. By instituting his famous law codes throughout Europe and by doing away with the last remnants of feudalism, he seemed to be establishing what had come to be called "the rights of man" throughout the continent. National monarchs were overpowered and a form of "equality" prevailed throughout the empire.

But his subjects soon began to realize they had exchanged national monarchy for a new kind of tyranny—an international tyranny. People became even more attached to their own nations than they had been before. This growing spirit of *nationalism* played a large part in the fall of Napoleon. More and more people desired their nations to be independent of the French Empire.

A fatal mistake. In spite of smuggling, the Continental System had hurt the trade of European nations, and discontent increased. In 1810, **Czar Alexander I withdrew Russia from the Continental System** and began to trade with England. In retaliation, Napoleon marched his Grand Army into Russia, intending to conquer the czar and make Russia a part of his empire. The decision to invade Russia proved to be a grave mistake.

It has been said that the Russian winter was Napoleon's worst enemy. He began the invasion in June and took few provisions, hoping to live off the land, but that was nearly impossible in the cold climate, even at this time of year. The march to Moscow took much longer than Napoleon anticipated. Russian troops kept refusing to fight. They retreated, leading the French army further into the cold country. Finally, early in September, Napoleon's troops arrived in Moscow and drove out its inhabitants. But the French had no sooner won the city than the Russians set it on fire. Within several days, Napoleon found himself living in charred ruins. Czar Alexander refused to discuss a treaty. After more than a month in the remains of Russia's capital, Napoleon ordered a retreat. But it was too late; winter had set in.

Across the vast, frozen plains of Russia marched the French, as the temperatures dropped far below zero. Exhausted, starving, and half-frozen men dropped by the wayside as the army marched. One colonel who survived recounted: "Each bivouac [over-night camp] seemed next day like a battle-field, and men found dead at their side those beside whom they had gone to sleep the night before." Napoleon lost about 300,000 men in the Russian campaign.

Collapse of the empire. With Napoleon's defeat in Russia, forces that opposed his empire saw their chance to bring it to an end. Russians attacked from the East. Prussia, Austria, and the German states rose up against Napoleon in the North. British troops marched through Spain to attack France from the South. Napoleon left his army in Russia and by sleigh and coach made it back to Paris in a record 13 days. Meanwhile, Napoleon's second-in-command over the French army deserted and fled, and the Grand Army fell apart. Back in Paris, Napoleon raised a new army, but it was untrained. In October 1813, *the combined forces of Europe defeated Napoleon's new army* at the **Battle of Leipzig,** sometimes called the **Battle of Nations.** More troops engaged in the Battle of Leipzig than in any other battle of history until the 20th century.

Finally, in April 1814, Napoleon was forced to abdicate (give up his throne). The forces of Europe exiled Napoleon to the island of *Elba,* on the Italian coast, where he was sentenced to live out his days as the sovereign of the island, his own little kingdom. The coalition of

Waterloo: the retreat of a humiliated Napoleon and his staff after Warterloo.

European nations restored the Bourbon monarchy to the throne of France, and Louis XVI's brother was crowned **Louis XVIII.**

The Hundred Days. But the determined Napoleon was not finished. He escaped from Elba and landed on the coast of France on March 1, 1815. Since the restoration of the Bourbon monarchy, Louis XVIII had received much criticism, and so Napoleon easily regained a large following. He again proclaimed the French Empire and headed for Paris to raise an army. Napoleon's triumphant return from exile perhaps reveals his leadership appeal better than any other part of his life. As Napoleon marched toward Paris, troops were sent to repel him. Napoleon appealed to the men, and they began to cry out over and over again, "Vive l'empereum!"—"Long live the Emperor!" The troops joined Napoleon and marched on to Paris with him.

Napoleon reached Paris, raised an army, and marched toward Belgium, where he intended to break up the Congress of Vienna. On June 18, 1815, *Napoleon met his final defeat* at the **Battle of Waterloo** in Belgium by allied troops under the command of the British **Duke of Wellington.** The "Hundred Days" of Napoleon's final reign were over.

Napoleon was again exiled, this time to the distant island of *St. Helena,* in the south Atlantic, where he lived out the remaining six years of his life.

The Little Corporal. Perhaps no man has had a greater influence on modern European history than Napoleon Bonaparte. Early in his military career, his small stature and outstanding accomplishments won him the title of "the Little Corporal." Napoleon was the first of several modern tyrants to attempt—and almost succeed—to conquer Europe and the world by military force. His abilities and accomplishments won him respect and hatred at the same time. The Duke of Wellington, who defeated Napoleon at Waterloo, called him the "grand disturber of Europe."

1. How did Napoleon Bonaparte distinguish himself during the French Revolution?
2. Who declared Napoleon emperor? Who crowned him?
3. What took place at the Battle of Trafalgar? Name the commander of the British navy who died there.
4. When Napoleon's empire was at its height, how much of Europe did he control?
5. What was the Continental System? Why did it fail?
6. What czar withdrew Russia from the Continental system? How did Napoleon retaliate?
7. What has been called Napoleon's worst enemy? Why? How many men did Napoleon lose in his Russian campaign?
8. What battle is called the Battle of Nations? What is distinctive about it?
9. Who became king of France after Napoleon was exiled?

Identify: Josephine, Marie Louise, War of 1812, nationalism, Elba, Battle of Waterloo, Duke of Wellington, St. Helena

France after Napoleon

The Congress of Vienna

New governments needed. As Napoleon's empire had spread, it had destroyed the political systems of most of the countries of Europe. Now that he had been defeated, national boundaries needed to be redrawn and new governments needed to be established. The upset was not easily or quickly rectified.

Key diplomats. In 1814, while Napoleon was still in exile on the island of Elba, the leading diplomats of Europe met in Vienna, Austria, to redraw the map of Europe. Although every European country was represented at the **Congress of Vienna,** the key diplomats were **Czar Alexander I** of Prussia, Lord **Castlereagh** [kås′′l·rā] of Great Britain, **Talleyrand** [tà′lā′rän′] of France, and **Prince von Metternich** [mĕt′ẽr·nĭk] of Austria. Metternich, the *"Prince of Diplomats,"* was to be the most influential spokesman.

Decisions at Vienna. Socially, the Congress of Vienna was a raving success. For 10 months the kings, diplomats, and their ladies participated in festivals, balls, and hunts. It was for this exalted group that Beethoven conducted the premiere of his Seventh Symphony.

Politically, however, the Congress would prove to be less of a success. Prince von Metternich so dominated the decision-making at Vienna that the first half of the 19th century is often called the **Age of Metternich.** Metternich's basic plan was to reestablish the political structure of Europe as it had existed *before* Napoleon.

The Congress of Vienna adopted Metternich's plans virtually without question, and the old monarchies were reestablished, with one major exception. The Holy Roman Empire was to remain as Napoleon had organized it, as a confederation of 38 states called the **German Confederation.** In an attempt to surround France by strong nations and keep her from expanding in the future, certain geographical changes were made. The **Austrian Netherlands (Belgium)** became part of Holland, creating a strong barrier on the North of France. **Savoy,** in northwest Italy, was enlarged and **Prussia,** in Germany, was given territory along the Rhine. These two moves created a strong eastern barrier for France. Each nation that gave up territory was compensated by being granted other territory.

The new balance of power created at Vienna gave each of the four major powers of the day—Prussia, Russia, Austria, and Great Britain—confidence that it could produce enough allies to protect itself from aggression by any of the others. This **balance of power** would not break down completely until World War I.

France in the 19th Century

After the Congress of Vienna. The Congress of Vienna wisely restored France to its status before the war, leaving its national sovereignty intact. France was fortunate that the Congress did not choose to crush it politically. But France faced a long, hard road to stable government. The old French proverb, "The more we change, the more we stay the same" was to prove true again and again.

Restoration of the monarchy. With the fall of Napoleon, the old French monarchy was reestablished under **Louis XVIII** (ruled 1814–1824), brother of the guillotined Louis XVI. Louis XVIII maintained many of the democratic reforms introduced by Napoleon. The lower house of the legislature was elected by the voters, citizens enjoyed considerable civil rights, and all citizens were equal before the law.

Louis XVIII tried to take a moderate course between a strong monarchy and a democracy. By doing so he maintained peace within France, but pleased no one

with his reign. Staunch monarchists thought his policies were too weak, and advocates of democracy criticized him for being too *autocratic* (absolute or dictatorial). Even those whose political beliefs fell somewhere between monarchy and democracy seemed to disagree with many of Louis's policies. Out of this dissension over the proper type of political system grew a tradition still evident in France, the tradition of a **multiparty system.** Instead of having two major political parties like England or America had, France developed a tradition of numerous parties, each holding political doctrines slightly different from any other. In the long run, this system necessitated difficult compromises between parties and contributed to a tradition of rather unstable government in France.

Charles X and the July Revolution. Louis XVIII was succeeded by his brother **Charles X** (ruled 1824–1830), who favored a strong monarchy. Once Charles became king, the government quickly became more

EUROPE IN 1815
AFTER THE CONGRESS OF VIENNA

July Revolution: a barricade in the Boulevard Montmartre, Paris.

autocratic, making his reign unpopular with many Frenchmen. In July of 1830, the French legislature refused to support Charles X's autocratic program. In protest, he dissolved the legislature and took matters into his own hands. Citizens of Paris revolted. Barricades went up in the streets and blood began to flow. As a result of this **July Revolution,** as it was called, Charles X was forced to flee to England, and France soon had a new king.

Louis Philippe and the July Monarchy. The July Revolution brought **Louis Philippe** (ruled 1830–1848) to the French throne. His 18-year reign was known as the **July Monarchy.** Louis repudiated the theory of divine right and replaced it with the principle of sovereignty of the people. He identified with the upper middle class, the business interests of the country. Louis liked to present himself as a true representative of the people, but in reality, only those of wealth were represented by his government. Consequently, Louis's unpopularity with the common people grew steadily. By 1848, France was *again* ready for change.

The 1848 Revolution. All of Europe was wracked by revolution in 1848. There were uprisings in *Austria, Italy, Switzerland, Holland, Belgium,* and *Poland,* and *France* was no exception. In February 1848, a Paris insurrection (uprising) turned into a major revolution. Louis Philippe fled to England and a new government, known as the **Second Republic,** was proclaimed. The new republic immediately adopted universal manhood suffrage (right to vote). The new, struggling government could not control the political unrest. In June 1848 another insurrection, known as the **June Days,** broke out among the common workers. This revolt was finally crushed, but not before confidence in the new republic was badly shaken. The people of France wanted a republic, but they also wanted a strong leader.

Louis Napoleon. When the election for the president of the Second Republic was held, the winner was none of the leading candidates that one would have expected to be chosen. Instead he was a rather obscure political radical. In this time of turmoil and need for strong leadership, it was his *name* that won him the election. He was **Louis Napoleon,** nephew of the late emperor of the French empire. Louis Napoleon (ruled 1848–1871) became extremely popular with the people—so popular, in fact, that he was able to dissolve the legislature *with the people's approval* and rule as a dictator. In 1852, he proclaimed himself **Emperor Napoleon III.**

Napoleon III

349

Events in Europe (c. 1700–1900)

British Isles	Germany and Scandinavia	Italy and Switzerland
1700s (18th Century)		
1700s Evangelical Revival takes place with the preaching of John Wesley and George Whitefield.	**1740–1786** Prussia becomes a great power.	**1796** Italy is conquered for France by Napoleon Bonaparte.
1707 England and Scotland are united as Great Britain.		**1798** Switzerland is invaded by the French; the Helvetic Republic is established and ruled by France.
1756–1763 Great Britain wins Seven Years' War with France.		
1760–1820 George III is king of England.		
1760–1830 Modern industry has its beginnings during the Industrial Revolution.		
1775–1783 Britain fights the Revolutionary War with America and loses American colonies.		
1800s (19th Century)		
1793–1815 Britain defeats France in the Napoleonic Wars.	**1806** Prussia is defeated; the Holy Roman Empire is ended by Napoleon's armies.	**1803** Napoleon gives Switzerland a new constitution, returning much governing power to Swiss cantons.
1801 Ireland and Great Britain form the United Kingdom of Great Britain and Ireland.	**1809** Sweden loses Finland to Russia.	**1815** Napoleon is defeated at Waterloo.
1812–1814 Britain battles the United States in the War of 1812.	**1814** Denmark loses to Sweden in the Napoleonic Wars and gives up all of Norway except its island colonies. Norway's union with Sweden is established.	**1815** The independence and neutrality of Switzerland are guaranteed by the Congress of Vienna.
1837–1901 The Victorian Age; the British Empire reaches its height during this golden age of British capitalism.	**1815** Congress of Vienna creates the German Confederation.	**1848** Switzerland becomes a representative democracy.
1845–1847 Ireland's potato famine kills about 750,000 persons.	**1849** Denmark adopts its first democratic constitution.	**1861** Kingdom of Italy is established.
	1866 War between Prussia and Austria; Austria is defeated.	**1863** The International Red Cross is founded in Geneva by Jean Henri Dunant, a Swiss banker and author.
	1867 North German Confederation is established by Prussia.	**1870** Rome is added to the Italian kingdom; national unity is completed.
	1870–1871 Franco-Prussian War; France is defeated; German states are united, and the German Empire begins.	**1871** Rome is made Italy's capital.

France, Spain, Portugal, and The Netherlands

1701 Holland joins the "Grand Alliance," a league of countries who tried to stop French expansion in Europe.

1701–1713 The war of Spanish Succession; Portugal sides with England against France.

1702–1712 The Dutch wage a losing war against France. During the war England becomes the world's chief naval power.

1762–1763 Portugal, with England's help, withstands a Spanish/French invasion.

1774 Louis XVI succeeds to the French throne.

1780–1783 The English, angered by Holland's support of America in the Revolutionary War, wage a naval war against Holland, and the Dutch are defeated.

1789–1799 The French Revolution takes place, ending absolute rule by French kings.

1792 France's first Republic is set up.

1793 Louis XVI of France is executed.

1793–1794 The Reign of Terror is carried out by French revolutionists determined to rid France of all aristocrats and "traitors."

1795 A weakened Holland is conquered by France.

1804 Napoleon is coronated, and France's First Empire is established.

1805 The Battle of Trafalgar is fought between Nelson's British fleet and Napoleon's fleet on the southwest coast of Spain; Nelson is victorious.

1805 Napoleon sets up a puppet ruler in Holland.

1810 Holland is annexed to France and becomes part of Napoleon's empire.

1813 The French are finally driven from Spain by British, Portuguese, and Spanish forces.

1814 Napoleon is exiled; Louis XVIII comes to the French throne.

1815 Holland and Belgium are united into one country.

1815 Napoleon returns to rule France but is defeated at Waterloo; Louis XVIII returns to power.

1815 Portugal and Brazil are officially united.

1822 Brazil becomes independent.

1825 The Spanish Empire by this time has lost almost all its landholdings.

1826 The Spanish Inquisition stages its last execution.

1830 Belgium declares itself independent of Holland.

1831–1834 Civil war breaks out in Portugal.

1848 The Second Republic in France is established by Revolutionists.

1852 The Second Empire in France is set up by Napoleon III.

1854 Portugal frees its slaves.

1870–1871 France surrenders to Prussia in the Franco-Prussian War. The Third Republic in France is begun.

1890 Luxembourg severs its ties with Holland.

1890 Portugal and Britain quarrel about boundaries of African possessions; Britain wins out.

1898 Spain is defeated in the Spanish-American War and loses Cuba, the Philippines, and Puerto Rico.

Otto von Bismarck

The Franco-Prussian War. For a decade, Napoleon III was very popular and his foreign policy met with great success. He brought new territory within the boundaries of France and gained new colonial holdings for France. But it was eventually his foreign policy which led to his demise. In 1863, while the United States was involved in its own civil war, Napoleon III supplied troops to support **Archduke Maximilian of Austria** in a takeover of Mexico. When the American Civil War was over, the United States forced the French troops out of Mexico and Maximilian was executed by the Mexican people. The fiasco cost France a great deal of money and Napoleon III a great deal of prestige.

Later in the 1860s, Napoleon III tried to gain more territory for France by involving himself in several political intrigues with **Otto von Bismarck, the Chancellor of Prussia.** In the end, Napoleon and Bismarck came to odds with one another. France declared war on Prussia in July 1870. The immediate cause of the **Franco-Prussian War** (1870–1871) was the question of who would succeed to the Spanish throne. The Spanish queen had been exiled and her throne offered to Leopold, a Prussian prince. France was opposed to having Prussian influence so close to its own border. Bismarck, the chancellor of Prussia, saw an advantage in a war with France, so he made it to appear that the French ambassador to Prussia and the Prussian king, William I, had insulted each other. As a result, the people of both countries were ready for war.

France declared war first, but the French troops were no match for the highly trained Prussian forces. Eventually the French army and Napoleon III were forced to surrender to the Prussians. Once more the French Empire was a thing of the past.

The Third Republic. The Third Republic, France's third attempt at a republican form of government, was born in hard times. It would be many years before it became a relatively stable government. There were too many factions with too many different ideas about what kind of government France should have.

Finally, by the opening of World War I in 1914, the Third Republic had become a relatively stable government. Most Frenchmen enjoyed the right to vote, freedom of the press, and equality before the law. The majority of the people had become supportive of the government. There were still a great number of political parties, which complicated French politics, but France was one of the most democratic and most powerful nations in the world.

CHECK UP

1. What was the purpose of the Congress of Vienna? Who were the key diplomats there?
2. Who was the most influential man at the Congress of Vienna? What was he called?
3. What geographical changes were made in Europe by the Congress of Vienna?
4. Name the three monarchs who came to the throne after Napoleon and tell what kind of ruler each was.
5. What was the immediate cause of the Franco-Prussian War? When was it fought? Who was Chancellor of Prussia at the time?

Identify: Age of Metternich, autocratic, multiparty system, July Revolution, July Monarchy, Second Republic, June Days, Archduke Maximilian of Austria, Third Republic

CHAPTER 18 REVIEW

MULTIPLE CHOICE *Write the letter of the answer that best completes the sentence.*

1. The ruthless queen who attempted to rule for her young sons was ____.
   a Josephine
   b Marie Antoinette
   c Marie de Médicis
   d Catherine de Médicis

2. ____ escaped death only by changing his religion.
   a Henry of Navarre *c* Louis XIII
   b Henry of Guise   *d* Louis XIV

3. The first in the Bourbon line of French kings was ____.
   a Henry I   *c* Henry III
   b Henry II   *d* Henry IV

4. Cardinal ____ ruled for Marie de Médicis and her son.
   a Mazarin   *c* Robespierre
   b Richelieu   *d* Calvin

5. Cardinal ____ ruled for the young Louis XIV.
   a Mazarin   *c* Robespierre
   b Richelieu   *d* Calvin

6. During the reign of ____, France was among the most important nations of Europe.
   a Louis XI   *c* Louis XIII
   b Louis XII   *d* Louis XIV

7. Louis XIV reigned ____ years, one of the longest reigns of any king in history.
   a 80   *c* 60
   b 70   *d* 50

8. On his deathbed, ____ said "after me the deluge."
   a Louis XIII   *c* Louis XV
   b Louis XIV   *d* Louis XVI

9. ____ called for a meeting of the Estates-General for the first time in over 170 years.
   c Louis XVI   *a* Louis XIV
   b Louis XV   *d* Louis XIII

10. ____ was the beautiful but haughty wife of Louis XVI.
    a Josephine
    b Marie Antoinette
    c Marie de Médicis
    d Catherine de Médicis

11. The first act of the National Convention was to execute ____.
    a Louis XVI   *c* Louis XIV
    b Louis XV   *d* Louis XIII

12. ____ was the most influential man in the French government between 1793 and 1794.
    a Cardinal Mazarin
    b Cardinal Richelieu
    c Maximilien Robespierre
    d John Calvin

13. ____ crowned himself emperor.
    a Alexander I
    b Napoleon Bonaparte
    c Louis XVIII
    d Charles X

14. The most influential spokesman at the Congress of Vienna was ____.
    a Maximilien Robespierre
    b Prince von Metternich
    c Cardinal Mazarin
    d Cardinal Richelieu

15. ____ was so popular with the French people that he was able to dissolve the legislature and rule as a dictator.
    a Louis XVIII   *c* Louis Napoleon
    b Louis Philippe   *d* Charles X

CHAPTER 18 REVIEW (CONTINUED)

COMPLETION *Choose the correct term to complete each sentence and write the letter in the blank.*

a Franco-Prussian War	*d* Reign of Terror	*h* "old regime"	*l* Hundred Years' War
b Continental System	*e* League of Augsburg	*i* July Monarchy	*m* Treaty of Ryswick
c Tennis Court Oath	*f* Third Republic	*j* Bastille	*n* Age of Enlightenment
	g Second Republic	*k* Vikings	

1. During the _____, the French King became more powerful than the Estates-General.

2. The nations of Europe joined together against France in the _____.

3. The _____ ended the War of the League of Augsburg.

4. The _____ was actually almost a new Dark Age for France.

5. The _____ was a vow made by the National Assembly to continue meeting until a new constitution had been written.

6. _____ was an old castle stronghold stormed by the people of Paris.

7. Under the _____, many politically influential people were arrested and executed.

8. The _____ forbade the importation of British goods into any European country which was under French influence.

9. The 18-year reign of Louis Philippe was known as the _____.

10. The new government proclaimed in France after Louis Philippe fled the country was known as the _____.

11. The immediate cause of the _____ was the question of who would succeed to the Spanish throne.

12. By 1914, the _____ had become a relatively stable government in France.

MATCHING *Match the description with the correct term.*

a Edict of January	*d* Estates-General	*g* bureaucracy	*i* absolutism
b synod	*e* bourgeoisie	*h* St. Bartholomew's Day Massacre	*j* Edict of Nantes
c *politiques*	*f* Huguenots		

_____ 1. French version of a parliament

_____ 2. French Calvinist Protestants

_____ 3. an assembly of representatives

_____ 4. decreed that Huguenots could worship in public

_____ 5. most infamous episode of the French religious wars

_____ 6. believed that people can have religious differences and still maintainlaw and order

_____ 7. gave Huguenots the freedom to live where they chose

_____ 8. unlimited rule by one man

_____ 9. "government by men who sit at desks"

_____ 10. French term for middle class

*TIME LINE CHALLENGE Choose the letter of the correct date
for each of the events listed below.*

1453	1598	1685	1686	1715	1789	1791	1796	1804	1805	1815
A	B	C	D	E	F	G	H	I	J	K

_____ 1. Napoleonic Wars begin

_____ 2. Age of Enlightenment begins

_____ 3. Battle of Waterloo

_____ 4. Battle of Trafalgar

_____ 5. Napoleon becomes emperor

_____ 6. League of Augsburg

_____ 7. Louis revokes Edict of Nantes

_____ 8. Storming of the Bastille

_____ 9. France's first written constitution

_____ 10. Edict of Nantes

*MAP SKILLS Use the maps on pp. 326 and
348 to answer the following questions.*

1. What nations border France on the European Continent?

2. What body of water separates France from England?

3. On what river is the city of Paris located?

4. What lands did Russia gain from the Congress of Vienna?

5. What three nations bordered the German Confederation on the west?

6. Which Scandinavian countries were united in 1815?

7. What three empires lay east of the German Confederation?

*CONCEPTS TO CONSIDER On a separate
sheet of paper, answer the following
questions using complete sentences.*

1. Explain why modern political ideas succeeded in England and in America but failed in France.

2. How did the French revolutionaries try to de-Christianize France? How do you suppose atheism might have contributed to the Reign of Terror?

3. Compare the American War for Independence with the French Revolution. What are some key differences?

Throughout the Middle Ages (c. 500–1500), the majority of Europeans followed a distorted form of Christianity that had largely departed from the Bible. By A.D. 500, a few religious leaders had placed themselves between God and the rest of mankind. In keeping the Bible from the people, they kept the people from the truth. For the Modern Age to begin, people had to be freed from the domination of the Church of Rome.

God raised up several lights in the Dark Ages—such as John Wycliffe, John Huss, and the Waldensians—to protest the false teachings of the Roman church and to proclaim the truths of the Bible. These faithful believers faced great opposition and persecution for their faith (Huss was martyred), but their stand for the truth prepared the way for still greater revival in the years ahead.

While Wycliffe was preaching in England and Huss in Bohemia, the Renaissance was gaining momentum in Italy. The Italian Renaissance (c. 1300–1600) was a "rebirth" of learning that focused mainly on the classical books of ancient Greece and Rome and on the classical languages (Greek and Latin) in which those books were originally written. By 1500, this rebirth of learning had spread northward from Italy into other parts of Europe, and a movement known as the Northern Renaissance had begun in such countries as Germany, France, the Netherlands, and England.

The revival of learning in Renaissance Italy was largely for the benefit of a select few, but in the north the Renaissance was much more than merely an affair of scholars and college professors. The northern scholars wanted men in all walks of life to benefit from their scholarship. In God's perfect timing, Johann Gutenberg invented the movable-type printing press in 1440. With the printing press, the works of the northern scholars, particularly their translations of the Scriptures, could be spread abroad for the benefit of all mankind. By 1500, printing presses were operating in nearly every country in Europe.

The stage was set for the Protestant Reformation, and God had prepared just the man to lead the movement—a German monk named Martin Luther. On October 31, 1517, Martin Luther began the Protestant Reformation when he posted a list of statements called the Ninety-five Theses on the church door in Wittenberg.

The Modern Age began with the Protestant Reformation, when the light of the Scriptures dispelled the darkness of the Middle Ages. The Reformation in Germany quickly gained momentum under Luther's leadership. Though excommunicated by the pope and banned by the Holy Roman emperor, he continued to speak out against the false teachings of the Roman church, calling for a return to Biblical Christianity. Soon, the movement spread beyond Germany, bearing fruit in Switzerland, Scandinavia, the Netherlands, and the British Isles. By 1600, about $^9/_{10}$ of the population of the Holy Roman Empire professed to be Protestant.

The Protestant Reformation so shook the Roman church that the pope soon responded with a Counter-Reformation to prevent any more Catholics from becoming Protestants and to force as many Protestants as possible back into the Roman fold. As Europe entered the 17th century, devastating wars of religion and politics loomed on the horizon. Between 1618 and 1648, the Thirty Years' War devastated Europe as Catholic and Protestant forces fought for territory across the continent. By the end of the war, Europe had become a land of religious and political diversity.

In the major countries of the European continent, the Reformation either failed (as in France, Spain, and Portugal) or else brought established Protestant churches (as in Scandinavia and parts of Germany). The state church concept eventually produced cold, formal churches in which belief and practice stemmed from the dictates of government rather than the free choice of congregations in the light of their understanding of the Bible. There were a few somewhat brighter spots (such as the Netherlands and parts of Switzerland) where the people achieved a level of religious freedom. But for a more complete fulfillment of the Reformation, one must look away from the Continent to the island nation of England.

By the 16th century, England had become a powerful nation. Many important precedents of freedom had been set by the Magna Carta and the Model Parliament. A system of representative, constitutional government had been established, unlike any other in Europe. England still had a long road ahead to political freedom, but first she needed spiritual freedom. The English Reformation began in 1533 when King Henry VIII broke England's ties with the Roman church and established the Church of England. Though Henry made the break with Rome for selfish reasons, he had unwittingly set into motion a movement that would transform England and lead her to greatness.

When Elizabeth I came to the throne in 1558, England was a thoroughly Protestant nation. For her remarkable character and extraordinary performance as Queen of England, "Good Queen Bess" won the acclaim of her country. In 1588, Elizabeth's fortitude was put to the test when Philip II of Spain sent his "Invincible Armada" to conquer England for the Roman church. As God willed, the English navy defeated the Spanish Armada, securing England's independence from Rome once and for all. Spain began to decline, and England basked in the glory of the Elizabethan Age. The English would face many trials in the years ahead, but their struggle for freedom would continue until, in 1688, the Glorious Revolution established the principle of government by consent.

During the Protestant Reformation and the Post-Reformation Era, some Europeans began to explore the world, sparking an Age of Exploration. Gradually European influence spread across the globe, leaving its mark particularly in Asia and the Americas. River valleys in Southwest, South, and East Asia became sites of organized cultures very early in history. For example, impressive civilizations developed in India and China long before the birth of Christ. The Asians made many cultural advances in such areas as architecture, medicine, mathematics, and law, but they failed to develop any true freedom. Politically, the vast majority of people were enslaved by feudalism; economically, they were desperately poor; and spiritually, they were dominated by pagan religions such as Buddhism, Hinduism, and Islam.

European influence in Asia began in 1498, when Portuguese navigator Vasco da Gama sailed around Africa to reach India. By 1700, the Europeans had established trading posts along the coasts of South and Southeast Asia. During the 1800s, most of Asia was controlled by the economic and military might of Western nations. France, Great Britain, the Netherlands, Portugal, and Spain dominated about ⅓ of Asia and controlled trade between the East and West. Eventually, China, Japan, and Korea opened up to trade with the West. By the middle of the 19th century, the countries of Asia had opened their doors to Christian missionaries. Christianity had a tremendous influence for good in the countries of Asia, although pagan religions continue to control many Asians to this day.

The most important discovery of the Age of Exploration was made in 1492, when Christopher Columbus, an Italian navigator sailing for Spain, discovered the New World. By the 18th century, the Spanish had established a vast empire including much of Central and South America, the West Indies, and the southwestern United States; the Portuguese had colonized Brazil; the French had settled in Canada and controlled a vast territory in the heart of North America; and the English had colonized the Atlantic coast of North America.

Toward the beginning of the 17th century, when the outcome of the struggle for freedom in England still seemed doubtful, some Englishmen sought better conditions in the New World. One of the first groups to make the journey was the Pilgrims, who came to America in 1620. The foundation of political and religious freedom laid by these and other Christian immigrants would make the future United States of America the leading nation of the Modern Age. The Great Awakening reinforced this foundation in the early 1700s, bringing revival to the American colonies. By 1776, when they faced the crisis of a break with the mother country, the American people knew what they believed and why they believed it.

In the Declaration of Independence,

the Americans had proclaimed their commitment to the leading political ideas of the Modern Age. The War for Independence gave birth to a new kind of nation in the history of the world—a nation founded on the principles of individual liberty. It is one thing, however, to *proclaim* principles, and quite another to embody them in a stable government, but the American people achieved this as well in 1789 with the ratification of the United States Constitution. The Constitution gave America a stable, efficient, democratic system of government, capable of governing a great nation. By the 20th century, the United States had emerged as a world power, equal with Britain, France, Spain, and other European powers. Yet, America's strength lay not in her democratic political institutions, but in the spiritual character of her people. America was great because America was good.

France emerged from the Middle Ages as a powerful nation-state, destined to play a major role in the history of the world in the Modern Age. But unlike England, France exhibited no trends toward political freedom and individual rights. By the 16th century, the French monarch had considerable power over both church and state in France.

French kings considered the Protestant Reformation a political threat to their authority, so they suppressed the Reformation in France, persecuting and imprisoning Huguenots by the hundreds. Nevertheless, the Huguenots continued to increase in number until they became an important minority. By the mid-1500s, nearly half of the nobles in France had become Protestants. The tension between Catholics and Protestants mounted until 1562, when the first of nine civil wars began in France.

Finally, in 1598, Henry IV, the first Protestant king of France, issued the Edict of Nantes, granting limited toleration to the Huguenots. This eased tensions for the moment, but the conflict was far from over.

In 1685, Louis XIV revoked the Edict of Nantes, and thousands of Huguenots fled France for other parts Europe and even America. Louis, the epitome of absolute rulers, ruled for 70 years. Toward the end of his reign, the Age of Enlightenment began in France. A blatant anti-Christianity, openly boasting of its rejection of the Bible and disbelief in the deity of Christ, emerged for the first time in the Modern Age on a grand scale.

The British trend toward freedom and the American political achievement were much admired in France. In England and America, however, modern political ideas such as the rights of man, government by consent, and representative democracy were both strengthened and restrained by the Christian heritage of the people. In France, Biblical Christianity, the one thing that can make modern political ideas workable in any country, had been driven out with the Huguenots. The persecution of the Huguenots laid the foundation for the French Revolution and all the horrors that it brought the French people.

Beginning in 1789, the French Revolution transformed France from an absolute monarchy to a near anarchy. By 1793, the king had been beheaded, and the Reign of Terror had begun. Under Maximilien Robespierre, thousands of known or suspected enemies of the Revolution were executed, and thousands more imprisoned. Atheism reached its height in France at the time the Terror was the bloodiest.

After a year of terrible bloodshed, the Reign of Terror came to an end with the execution of Robespierre. Five years later, in 1799, Napoleon Bonaparte came to power, and France experienced a new kind of tyranny. After bringing peace to France, Napoleon began to conquer her neighbors. By 1809, he controlled virtually all of continental Europe. But Napoleon, too, was destined to fall, and in 1815, he was defeated at the Battle of Waterloo. The Congress of Vienna, under the leadership of Prince von Metternich of Austria, restored most of Europe to its pre-war status and established a balance of power on the continent. France retained her national sovereignty, but she faced a long, hard road to stable government.

The Modern Age brought many changes to the world. It gave rise to powerful nations; it unveiled new continents; it renewed trade between the East and the West; and it brought new political ideas of individual freedom and responsibility. But most important, the Modern Age brought spiritual freedom through the Protestant Reformation and the resulting influence of the Bible in Europe and America. Throughout history, man's response to Christ has determined his fate.

We have seen the consequences of distorted Christianity and atheism in France, where men rejected the Bible, and the results of pagan religions and traditions in Asia, where men worshiped creation rather than the Creator. But we have also seen the blessings of Biblical Christianity in England and America, where men embraced the principles of God's Word and put them into practice. As we continue our study of the Modern Age, we will see this truth illustrated again and again: "righteousness exalteth a nation, but sin is a reproach to any people" (Prov. 14:34).

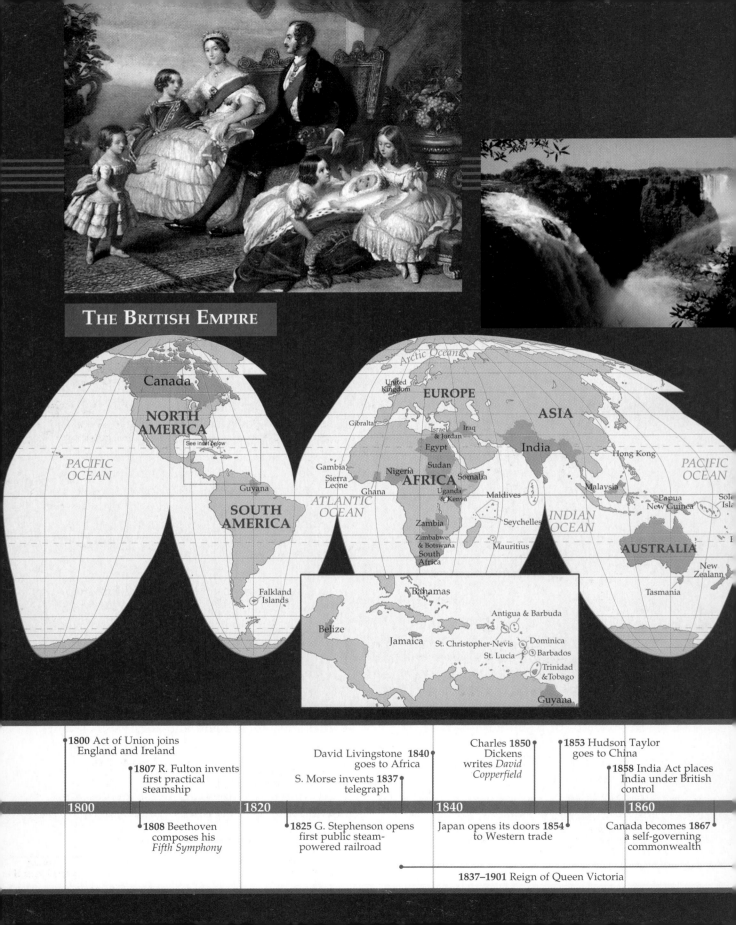

THE BRITISH EMPIRE

Canada

NORTH
AMERICA

PACIFIC
OCEAN

Guyana

SOUTH
AMERICA

ATLANTIC
OCEAN

Falkland
Islands

Arctic Ocean

United
Kingdom

EUROPE

ASIA

Gibraltar

Israel
& Jordan   Iraq

Egypt

India

Hong Kong

PACIFIC
OCEAN

Gambia
Sierra
Leone
Ghana

Nigeria

Sudan

AFRICA   Somalia

Uganda
& Kenya

Zambia

Zimbabwe
& Botswana
South
Africa

Maldives

Seychelles

Mauritius

Malaysia

INDIAN
OCEAN

Papua
New Guinea

Solo
Isla

AUSTRALIA

New
Zealand

Tasmania

Bahamas

Belize

Jamaica

Antigua & Barbuda

St. Christopher-Nevis

St. Lucia

Dominica

Barbados

Trinidad
&Tobago

Guyana

See inset below

1800 Act of Union joins
England and Ireland

1807 R. Fulton invents
first practical
steamship

1808 Beethoven
composes his
Fifth Symphony

David Livingstone 1840
goes to Africa

S. Morse invents 1837
telegraph

1825 G. Stephenson opens
first public steam-
powered railroad

Charles 1850
Dickens
writes *David
Copperfield*

Japan opens its doors 1854
to Western trade

1853 Hudson Taylor
goes to China

1858 India Act places
India under British
control

Canada becomes 1867
a self-governing
commonwealth

1800   1820   1840   1860

1837–1901 Reign of Queen Victoria

Unit 5

PROGRESS IN THE MODERN AGE
(C. 1800–1900)

Mankind Advances

19 Science and Industry in the Modern Age
20 The New World of Classics: Music, Art, and Literature
21 The British Empire: Asia, Africa, and Australia

1876 A. Bell invents
telephone

Australia becomes **1901**
an independent
commonwealth

1903 Wright Brothers
make first successful
airplane flight

1930–1940
Great Depression

1907 New Zealand becomes
an independent dominion

1880

1900

1920

1940

1879 T. Edison invents
light bulb

1899–1902 Boer War

1908 H. Ford invents
Model T

1921 Ireland partitioned

1914–17
World War I

1939–45
World War II

19
Science and Industry in the Modern Age
(c. 1500–1900)

HIGHLIGHTS

Founders of Modern Science • Darwin and Evolution
Agricultural Advancement • Industrial Revolution
Inventors and Captains of Industry • Triumph of Capitalism

The New World of Science

The Modern Age is the age of science. Man has lived on the earth for several thousand years, but only in the Modern Age—the past 500 years—has he begun to earnestly fulfill God's command to subdue the earth and exercise dominion "over every living thing that moveth upon the earth" (Gen. 1:28). Modern science (science since 1500) has changed the world by changing the way people think about the world. A study of world history would not be complete without a study of the rise of modern science.

Why Ancient Science Failed

No foundation. From the dawn of history, men have looked up at the stars in wonder. Many ancient peoples studied the heavens and even developed calendars based on their observations. They should have seen the workings of the universe as the creation of the all-wise, all-powerful God, for "The heavens declare the glory of God; and the firmament sheweth his handiwork" (Ps. 19:1). They should have understood the origin of the universe, but because they turned away from God, their understanding was darkened (Rom. 1:21). Thus they became slaves to **superstitions,** *false beliefs based on fear and ignorance,* which drove many to follow the whims of witch doctors, pagan priests, and rulers who claimed to represent the gods.

No general principles. Occasionally, ancient people did accomplish some magnificent feats of engineering and invention—consider the pyramids of Egypt and the Great Wall of China. But most people believed in **astrology,** *the confused idea that the stars, rather than the Creator of the stars, rule the destinies of men.* They never understood that the stars are controlled by natural forces and rational laws of nature established by God, Who can intervene for His purposes whenever He sees fit. Instead, they worshiped nature itself as a god. This nature worship prevented them from discovering the general principles that have made science possible, and thus their "science" was merely a series of trial and error discoveries. The Asian people, with their emphasis on harmony with nature and with their own system of astrology, were likewise unable to discover scientific principles, although they developed some valuable technology, such as printing and papermaking. Only God's direct revelation, the Bible, could show man the true nature of the universe and give him the foundational truths necessary for science.

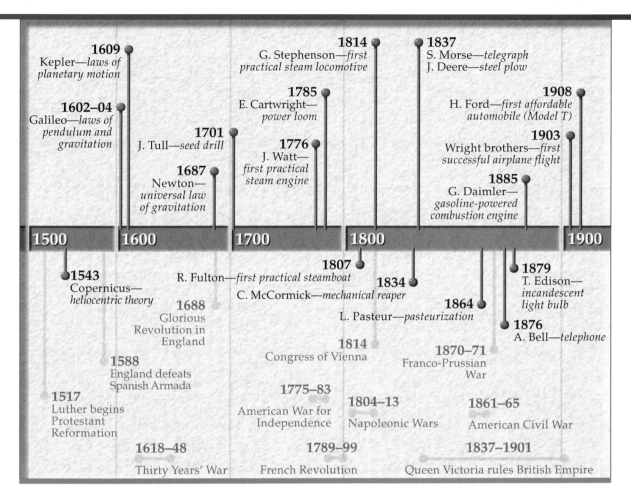

1609
Kepler—*laws of planetary motion*

1602–04
Galileo—*laws of pendulum and gravitation*

1701
J. Tull—*seed drill*

1687
Newton—*universal law of gravitation*

1814
G. Stephenson—*first practical steam locomotive*

1785
E. Cartwright—*power loom*

1776
J. Watt—*first practical steam engine*

1837
S. Morse—*telegraph*
J. Deere—*steel plow*

1908
H. Ford—*first affordable automobile (Model T)*

1903
Wright brothers—*first successful airplane flight*

1885
G. Daimler—*gasoline-powered combustion engine*

1500   **1600**   **1700**   **1800**   **1900**

1543
Copernicus—*heliocentric theory*

1688
Glorious Revolution in England

R. Fulton—*first practical steamboat*

C. McCormick—*mechanical reaper*

1807

1834

L. Pasteur—*pasteurization*

1864

1879
T. Edison—*incandescent light bulb*

1876
A. Bell—*telephone*

1588
England defeats Spanish Armada

1814
Congress of Vienna

1870–71
Franco-Prussian War

1517
Luther begins Protestant Reformation

1775–83
American War for Independence

1804–13
Napoleonic Wars

1861–65
American Civil War

1618–48
Thirty Years' War

1789–99
French Revolution

1837–1901
Queen Victoria rules British Empire

Why Medieval Science Failed

Age of darkness. By A.D. 500, the Western Roman Empire had fallen to barbarian invaders, and Europe had entered an age of spiritual and intellectual darkness. For centuries after Rome's fall, church officials and monks were almost the only educated men in Western Europe. Even their education, most of it obtained in monasteries, compared poorly to that of the ancient Greeks and Romans.

Scholasticism. Although the entire Middle Ages may be considered an age of darkness, learning did revive somewhat in the last half of the era. Under the sponsorship of the Roman church, teachers and pupils began coming together in organized groups. These institutions, the ancestors of modern universities, were often called simply *schools;* their pupils and teachers became known as *schoolmen.* In the 1200s, important schools arose in Paris, France; Padua, Italy; and Oxford and Cambridge, England. By the year 1500, there may have been nearly 100 of these institutions in Europe. The schools of the Middle Ages took an approach to learning called *scholasticism,* which *tried to combine Greek philosophy and Roman Catholicism.*

Aristotle and Aquinas. Through contacts with Muslims in Spain and elsewhere, educated men in Western Europe discovered the writings of the Greek philosopher **Aristotle.** They were so overwhelmed by his apparent wisdom that they were soon calling Aristotle *"The* Philosopher."

The scholastic **Thomas Aquinas** [ə·kwī′nas: 1225–1274] was perhaps the most successful at combining Aristotle's ideas with Roman Catholic teachings. Greatly impressed by Aquinas's work, the Roman church gave it official approval and forbade anyone to disagree with it. The almost sacred regard with which Aristotle's ideas on **physics,** *the basic science of matter and energy,* were held put a serious block in the road to new scientific knowledge. Anyone who did not accept Aristotle's ideas about physics and the movement of the heavenly bodies was suspected of heresy.

Aristotle's physics. The basic problem with Aristotle's ideas about physics stemmed from his confusion of the Creator with His creation. Aristotle talked about a single god, but his god was not the personal, loving Creator of the universe described in the Bible. Having failed to recognize God as Creator, Aristotle, like the other Greeks, attributed characteristics to the physical universe that only God possesses. Only God is eternal, but Aristotle believed that matter of some sort has always existed. He attributed purposes and goals to material things themselves rather than to God Who created all things for His purposes. When Aristotle spoke of "motion," he often implied that material things have a "desire" to move. He so emphasized purpose that he seldom dealt with *what things are made of* and *how they work.* His emphasis on material things having purposes within themselves led to a kind of physics that did not match up with the real universe that God created. Aristotle's physics produced nothing to help man fulfill God's command to subdue the earth.

The Rise of Modern Science

God's truth is stronger than error. At the same time that the light of the true gospel broke through with the Reformation, the long night of the Middle Ages drew to a close with the dawning of modern science. During this time, the ancient books of philosophy, which the church had venerated for so long, were proven false, and the greatest of the ancient books, the Bible, was returned to the people and found to be true. This was a very important discovery for science as well as for all other areas of life. Without the Bible, men would have never discovered the foundational truths upon which modern science is based. **Francis Bacon** (1561–1626), the English philosopher who played an important role in formulating the principles of the <u>modern scientific method</u>, explained the connection between the Protestant Reformation and modern science in this way:

> . . . When it pleased God to call the Church of Rome to account for their degenerate manners and ceremonies, and sundry doctrines obnoxious and framed to uphold the same abuses; at one and the same time it was ordained by the Divine Providence that there should attend withal a renovation and a new spring of all other knowledges.

People learned to search for truth for themselves, both in the Scriptures and in nature, rather than to depend on the pagan authorities and the church leaders. As they turned to the Scriptures, they learned that God created the Universe, that He is separate from the universe, and that He established reasonable, orderly laws which nature obeys.

Scientists began to search for the laws that God had established so they could understand nature and control it for the good of mankind, as God commanded in Genesis 1:28. Once countries such as Holland and England became Protestant, scientists had a place where they could carry on their work free from persecution. Most of the early scientists were Protestants; others were Catholics who dared to question the official church dogma on scientific issues. Many were devout Christians. Because they believed the Bible, they had a good under-

Nicolaus Copernicus   *Johannes Kepler*   *Galileo Galilei*

standing of basic truths about the universe, for the Author of the Bible is the Creator of the universe. People taught by the Bible felt a responsibility to use their God-given talents to find ways to help other people. Science gave them a very important tool for benefiting mankind.

Founders of Modern Science

Copernicus. One of the first important breakthroughs in modern science came in 1543 when **Nicolaus Copernicus** [nĭk′ō·lā′*u*s kō·pûr′nĭ·k*u*s: 1473–1543], a Polish astronomer, proposed a new way of understanding the universe. Copernicus said that the planets, including the earth, revolve around the sun, and that the earth is not a motionless body about which everything else in the universe moves. Today we accept this **heliocentric** [hē′lĭ·ō·sĕn′trĭk: *sun-centered*] approach without question, but in Copernicus's day, the universe was believed to be **geocentric** [jē′ō·sĕn′trĭk: *earth-centered*]. Copernicus's heliocentric theory sparked a scientific revolution. A whole new approach would be required in physics.

Kepler. The German Lutheran astronomer **Johannes Kepler** (1571–1630) took modern science another great step forward. Kepler dedicated his life to "finding the mathematical harmonies in the mind of the Creator." Copernicus had followed Aristotle in one respect: he retained the idea that the orbits of the planets are circular. Using facts that his teacher *Tycho Brahe* (1546–1601) had collected through careful observation of the skies, Kepler calculated that the orbits of the planets could *not* be perfect circles.

Taking "pleasure in the exalted contemplation of the divine mechanism" and straining to imitate in his human mind the divine mathematics "derived by the most wise Creator," Kepler discovered the three **laws of planetary motion.** The first law states that planets orbit the sun in oval-shaped paths called *ellipses*. The second law explains why a planet moves faster when it is closer to the sun, and the third explains the relation between the time it takes a planet to orbit the sun and its distance from the sun.

In three simple propositions, Kepler had mathematically described the orbits of the planets about the sun. It was a monumental scientific feat, and he humbly gave the glory to God: "I give thee thanks, O Lord and Creator, that thou hast gladdened me by thy creation when I was enraptured by the work of thy hands. . . ."

Galileo. God had already permitted another man to look up to His glorious heavens and observe His handiwork. The great Italian philosopher and scientist **Galileo Galilei** [gä′lē·lâ′ō gä′lē·lâ′ē: 1564–1642] lived about the same time as Kepler, but Catholic Italy was not as receptive to new scientific ideas as Protestant Germany. Around 1610, Galileo built a **telescope** and turned it to the skies. (The telescope had only recently been invented by a Dutchman.) As he beheld stars "so numerous as to be almost beyond belief," his eyes and his reason told him that Aristotle had been wrong. Galileo's observations convinced him that Copernicus and Kepler were correct in their heliocentric view.

But together with its immensity, Galileo also discovered the basic uniformity of the

The History of Scientific Progress

Prior to A.D. 1500

c. 350 B.C. Aristotle formulated geocentric view of the universe

c. 300 B.C. Aristotle wrote *Physics*

c. 300 B.C. Euclid wrote *The Elements*, on geometry

c. 200 B.C. Archimedes discovered laws of levers and liquids

c. A.D. 150 Ptolemy further developed geocentric view

1500s

1520 Philippus Paracelsus discovered hydrogen

1543 Nicolaus Copernicus presented heliocentric view of the universe

1543 Andreas Vesalius published book on human anatomy

1600s

1600 William Gilbert mentioned "electricity" in book on magnetism

1602–1604 Galileo Galilei formulated laws of pendulum and gravitation

1609 Johann Kepler developed laws of planetary motion

1616 William Harvey described circulation of blood

1662 Robert Boyle formulated Boyle's law of gases

1665 Robert Hooke discovered live cells in plants

1665 Isaac Newton developed binomial theory and calculus

1668 Isaac Newton invented refracting telescope

1675 Anton van Leeuwenhoek discovered one-celled animals

1682 Edmund Halley made observation of comet

1687 Isaac Newton formulated the law of gravitation

1700s

1704 Isaac Newton published *Opticks*

1714 Gabriel Fahrenheit developed mercury thermometer

1742 Anders Celsius developed temperature scale

1758 Carl Linnaeus began modern taxonomy

1767 Joseph Priestley wrote about electricity

1772 Daniel Rutherford discovered nitrogen

1774 Antoine Lavoisier proved water and carbon dioxide are produced in breathing

1775 Joseph Priestley discovered hydrochloric acid and sulfuric acid

1781 F. W. Herschel discovered planet Uranus

1800s

1801 John Dalton formulated law on gas pressures

1802 John Dalton made atomic weight tables

1810 John Dalton explained atomic theory

1819 Hans Christian Oersted founded the science of electromagnetism

1820 André Ampère formulated laws of electromagnetism

1825 Hans Christian Oersted produced aluminum

1827 G. S. Ohm formulated law of electric currents

---

physical universe. Aristotle had said that the moon is perfectly smooth, but Galileo declared that "the moon is a body like the earth," consisting of the same basic kind of material. By this statement, he directly contradicted Aristotle's opinion that the earth is made of different material than the rest of the universe. With Galileo's observations, mankind was well on the way to recognizing a single physical universe, unified by the same basic components and laws. (The Latin prefix *uni* means "one." The universe is unified because it is the creation of one God, the God of the Scriptures.)

Galileo looked upon the physical universe as if it were a machine, stripping the material world of attributes which it does not have and distinguishing the Creator from His creation. But at the same time, Galileo approached the physical universe as the "Book of Nature . . . written in mathematical characters." "A hundred passages of holy Scripture," he said, "teach us that the glory and greatness of Almighty God are marvelously displayed in all His works and divinely read in the open book of Heaven." "That book," he said, "cannot be read until we have learned the language." The language of science is *mathematics*.

Through experiments and mathematical reasoning, Galileo discovered that gravity (the attraction all bodies have for each other) causes heavy and light bodies of the same substance to fall at the same speed. The only reason a feather will fall more slowly than a brick is that the feather is subject to greater resistance from the air. According to

1828 Friedrich Wohler founded organic chemistry

1831 Michael Faraday discovered the principle of electromagnetic induction

1838 Justus von Liebig founded biochemistry

1842 John Benet Lawes produced artificial fertilizers

1845 John Couch Adams discovered planet Neptune

1858 Joseph Lister observed coagulation of the blood

1858 Louis Pasteur showed milk fermentation due to bacteria

1859 Charles Darwin published *Origin of Species*

1864 Louis Pasteur invented pasteurization

1866 Gregor Mendel established principles of heredity

1867 Alfred Nobel invented dynamite

1869 Dmitri Mendeleev formulated periodic table of chemical elements

1887 Heinrich Hertz discovered electromagnetic waves

1895 Wilhelm Roentgen discovered X-rays

1896 Henry Becquerel first detected radiation from uranium

1898 Marie and **Pierre Curie** discovered radium

1900s

1900 Max Planck formulated quantum theory

1905 Albert Einstein formulated theory of relativity

1906 Joseph Thomson discovered gamma rays

1911 Ernest Rutherford formulated theory of atomic structure

1913 Niels Bohr established structure of atom

1930 Clyde W. Tombaugh discovered the planet Pluto

1938 Nylon invented

1939 Otto Hahn and **Fritz Strassman** discovered nuclear fusion

1941 Manhattan Project (atomic research)

1945 Atomic bomb perfected and used

1947 First supersonic flight

1951 Electricity first produced from atomic energy

1952 First hydrogen bomb exploded

1953 Structure of DNA

1957 U.S.S.R. launched *Sputnik I*

1958 James Van Allen discovered belt of radiation around the earth

1960 Laser beams developed

1961 Alan Shepard became first American in space

1961 Francis Crick and **James Watson** made model of DNA

1961 Yuri Gagarin became first man to orbit the earth

1962 John Glenn became the first American to orbit the earth

1962 U.S. launched *Telstar*, a communications satellite

1962 U.S. unmanned spacecraft reached the moon

1964 Quark model

1969 Neil Armstrong became first man to walk on the moon

1971 U.S.S.R. unmanned spacecraft reached Mars

1980 U.S. *Voyager I* explored rings of Saturn

1985 Human Genome Project

1990 Hubble Space Telescope

Galileo's *law of uniform acceleration*, the speed of a body falling in a vacuum—any body, regardless of weight—accelerates (increases) uniformly with time.

Aristotle's physics had produced little or no knowledge of practical value. But by studying the physical universe as a machine governed by exact, precise mathematical laws, Galileo found principles by which man could build new and wonderful machines. Galileo's discovery of the *laws of the pendulum* provided the kind of precise knowledge needed to construct a pendulum clock, imitating the precision with which the heavenly bodies God created move through space "to divide the day from the night . . . and for days, and years" (Gen. 1:14).

Scientists during this era were called **natural philosophers;** in fact, the name *scientist* was not coined until 1840. *Philosopher* is a Greek word that means "lover of truth." If any men ever deserved to be called true philosophers, they were the early modern scientists like Galileo. But the greatest scientific discoveries were yet to come.

Newton. The English philosopher **Isaac Newton** (1642–1727) contributed more to the scientific progress of mankind than any other individual before or since. Standing upon the shoulders of Galileo, Kepler, and Copernicus, Newton reached with his brilliant mind for an understanding of God's most basic laws of the physical universe.

Copernicus had determined that the planets orbit the sun, and Kepler had described the elliptical paths they follow.

But what causes the planets to stay in their orbits? What keeps them from flying off into space? These were questions that remained unanswered.

For Newton, a devout Christian, the problem was not what causes the planets to move—he knew that God had put the planets into motion—but what force God had created to make them move in elliptical orbits, and what force causes the moon to orbit the earth in like manner. And is there a connection between the movements of the heavenly bodies and the force of gravity on earthly objects?

In 1666, Newton observed an apple fall from a tree. That same year he "began to think of gravity extending to the orb of the Moon. . . ." Trying to imitate in his mind the divine simplicity by which God governs the universe, Newton reasoned that the force of gravity which brought the apple down extends beyond the top of the tallest apple tree, all the way to the moon and even beyond the sun. He further reasoned that the earth's force of gravity would be less for objects farther away.

In 1687, twenty years after he had first compared the orbiting moon to a falling apple, Newton published his *Mathematical Principles of Natural Philosophy* (known as *Principia*). God had permitted Newton to discover the **universal law of gravitation,** which states that every particle of matter in the universe attracts every other particle of matter with a force directly proportional to its quantity of matter, decreasing as the square of the distance increases.

With this single mathematical law, Newton stated a truth about every particle of matter in the physical universe. One formula explained the motion of a falling apple, the orbit of the moon, the revolution of the earth and other planets around the sun, the eccentric orbits of comets, and even the tides of the earth's oceans (which are affected by the *moon's* gravitational force). One formula demonstrated that the physical universe is *one* universe.

Newton searched for a truth about God's universe, and the world has ever since marveled at the great scientific discovery he made. Newton's *Principia* is considered by authorities on the history of science to be "the foundation stone of modern thought." It has been said that "our conception of the world was utterly changed by it."

Isaac Newton

Check Up

1. How did nature worship keep ancient people from developing science?
2. What did Thomas Aquinas do? How did the Roman church support his work?
3. Why were Aristotle's ideas about physics wrong? Did his physics help man to subdue the earth?
4. How did Francis Bacon explain the connection between the Protestant Reformation and modern science?
5. Describe Copernicus's view of the universe. How did it differ from the accepted view of his day?
6. What laws did Kepler discover?
7. What convinced Galileo that Copernicus and Kepler were right? What laws did Galileo develop?
8. What is the language of science?
9. When was the name "scientist" coined? What were scientists called before that time?
10. Who contributed more to scientific progress than any other individual? What famous law did he discover?

Identify: superstition, astrology, scholasticism, Aristotle, physics, Tycho Brahe, *Principia*

The Scientific Societies

The universities did not support the new sciences right away. Most of them clung to the old scholasticism until the end of the 17th century. The people who took the greatest interest in the work of the scientists, especially in England, were the *Puritans.* In 1645, **John Wilkins** (1614–1672), a Puritan clergyman, led in the formation of the **Philosophical College,** which met regularly in London to conduct experiments and discuss scientific theories. Most of its members were Puritans.

Wilkins had already done much work to popularize the heliocentric view of the universe in England, and he had been encouraging Englishmen to apply science to industry—to develop new machines to speed things up in mining and the manufacture of goods. In 1662, the **Royal Society** for the Improvement of Natural Knowledge was formed in London under John Wilkins. The Royal Society was <u>the first permanent scientific society of the Modern Age</u>. Its early members included the great English scientists Isaac Newton, Robert Hooke, and Robert Boyle, as well as the renowned English architect Christopher Wren.

Several groups of scientists had tried to start academies in Italy, but the opposition of the pope was too great for most of them to last. The **French Academy of Science** was founded in Paris in 1666. It was supported largely by *Huguenots* (French Protestants) and *Jansenists,* a group of French Catholics who believed in salvation by God's grace. ***Blaise Pascal*** [blâz păs′kȧl′: 1623–1662], a brilliant French mathematician and philosopher, was a prominent Jansenist. By 1800, there were scientific societies in many parts of Europe, including Germany, Denmark, Italy, and Russia. America also had a scientific society, which began in Philadelphia in the 1740s. All the great scientists of the day belonged to these societies, and by sharing their findings, they did much to further the progress of science and prepare the way for future scientists.

Toward More Truth

Other forces. Besides gravity, other forces and laws of God are at work in the universe. Magnetism and electricity, for example, remained for later scientists to discover.

More truth about gravity. Even Newton had not discovered the whole truth about gravity. Careful observations eventually disclosed that the planet Mercury does not move in precisely the way it should, according to the universal law of gravitation. The disagreement is very slight, but physics is an exact science. In the 20th century, the American Jewish physicist **Albert Einstein** (1879–1955), "obliged by the facts," as he said, discovered new principles of order and reality which dramatically increased our understanding of gravity. "A conviction, akin to a religious feeling, of the rationality or intelligibility of the world," Einstein believed, "lies behind all scientific work of a high order." Mankind has only glimpsed the benefits that may be reaped from the work of Einstein, who was certainly the greatest scientist since Newton. Einstein is especially remembered for stating the <u>theories of relativity</u>.

Albert Einstein

Limitations of science. Newton, who spent much of his life studying the Bible, realized that there are profound facts about God's creation and governance of the world that will forever escape the efforts of scientists to explain with their discoveries of laws. "Gravity may put the planets into motion," Newton wrote, "but without the divine power, it could never put them into such a circulating motion as they have about the sun; and therefore, for this, as well as other reasons, I am compelled to ascribe the frame of this system to an intelligent Agent." No scientist will succeed in explaining *how* "God created the heaven and the earth" (Gen. 1:1). But if God had not established general laws for the physical universe He created, man's science would be vain and foolish.

Blessings to Mankind

Food. Dedicated to the mastery of nature, modern science has had a tremendous impact on daily life. Thanks to modern science, farming has changed from a backbreaking struggle to a prosperous and rewarding employment. The work of scientists has allowed farmers to subdue the earth with machines rather than with their own limited muscle power. It has also given them the ability to control and subdue weeds and insects, to fertilize and water crops, and to develop new and better foods. The earth now yields food in quantities that would have staggered the imagination of our ancestors 500 years ago.

Medicine. Progress in medicine since 1500 has also been astounding. **Andreas Vesalius** [ăn′drē·as vē·sā′lĭ·us: 1514–1564],

Important Events in the History of Agriculture

Before A.D. 1500

c. 450 B.C. Herodotus described Egyptian agricultural methods

c. 100 B.C. Romans introduced planting legumes to enrich the soil

c. A.D. 1 Romans added iron blades to plow

1500s

c. 1550 Potatoes first taken to Europe from South America

1600s

1613 John Rolfe introduced tobacco as a cash crop in Virginia

1620 Indians taught settlers in New England to plant corn

1700s

c. 1700 Charles Townshend demonstrated the benefits of fertilization and fencing

c. 1700 Moldboard added to plow

c. 1701 Jethro Tull invented seed drill

c. 1750 Robert Bakewell introduced systematic breeding of sheep and cattle

1793 Eli Whitney invented the cotton gin

1800s

1819 Jethro Wood invented the cast-iron plow

1831 Cyrus McCormick invented mechanical reaper

1834 John and **Hiram Pitts** invented threshing machine

1837 John Deere developed steel plow with replaceable parts

1847 Mormans in Utah began irrigation in Western U.S.

1849–1926 Luther Burbank developed many new varieties of plants

1864–1943 George Washington Carver discovered numerous industrial uses for the peanut and other plants

1865 Gregor Mendel published his discovery of laws of inheritance of plants and animals

c. 1870 Mennonite immigrants from Russia introduced winter wheat to Kansas

1877 Carl Gustaf de Laval invented the cream separator

c. 1880 Chemical fertilizers were developed

1890 Stephen Babcock developed a test to measure butterfat in milk

1892 John Froehlich built first gasoline-powered tractor

1894 Carl Gustaf de Laval invented the milking machine

1900s

1917 Combination reaper-thresher ("combine") came into general use

1936 Lord Boyd Orr published *Food, Health, and Income*

1939 Paul Mueller developed the insecticide DDT

c. 1950 Liquid fertilizers were developed

1970 Norman E. Borlaug won Nobel peace prize for development of new varieties of wheat

1972 Use of DDT prohibited in U.S.

Important Events in the History of Medicine

Before A.D. 1500

460–370 B.C. Hippocrates, the "Father of Medicine," showed that disease has natural causes

A.D. 131–201 Galen, Greek physician, wrote on various medical practices

c. A.D. 1000 Avicenna, Arab physician, wrote a medical encyclopedia, *The Canon of Medicine*

c. A.D. 1000 First medical school founded, in Salerno, Italy

1500s

1537 Michael Servetus discovered circulation of blood in the lungs

1543 Andreas Vesalius published *On the Fabric of the Human Body*

1552 Bartolommeo Eustachio discovered Eustachian tubes

1563 Ambroise Paré improved surgical techniques

1600s

1603 Geronimo Fabrizio described valves in veins

1604 Johann Kepler described lens principle of eye

1616 William Harvey described circulation of blood

1658 Jan Swammerdam observed red corpuscles

1675 Anton van Leeuwenhoek discovered protozoa

1677 Anton van Leeuwenhoek observed spermatoza

1700s

1796 Edward Jenner developed vaccination against smallpox

1800s

1812 Jean Larrey developed local analgesia (pain killer)

1816 R. T. Laënnec invented stethoscope

1834 Louis Braille developed reading method for the blind

1842 Crawford Long first used anesthetic

1844 Nitrous oxide first used in dentistry

1846 Ether used as an anesthetic

1847 Chloroform used as an anesthetic

1851 Hermann von Helmholtz invented opthalmoscope

1867 Joseph Lister developed antiseptic surgery

1874 Armauer Hansen discovered leprosy bacillus

1874 Andrew Taylor Still developed osteopathy

1880 Charles Laveran discovered malaria protozoa

1880 Louis Pasteur developed immunization against anthrax

1882 Robert Koch discovered tuberculosis bacillus

1885 Louis Pasteur developed treatment for rabies

1890 Emil von Behring discovered antitoxin for tetanus

1894 Shibasabuso Kitasoto discovered bubonic plague germ

1896 Ronald Ross discovered cause of malaria

1899 Aspirin first used as medicine

1900s

1900 Walter Reed discovered cause of yellow fever

1901 Jokichi Takamine isolated adrenalin

1903 Willem Einthoven developed electrocardiograph

1906 Frederick G. Hopkins discovered vitamins

1922 Frederick Banting and **Charles Best** discovered insulin

1925 Joseph Goldberger identified Vitamin B

1928 Alexander Fleming discovered penicillin

1930 Max Theiler developed vaccine against yellow fever

1931 Paul Karrer identified Vitamin A

1933 Influenza virus isolated

1934 Tadeus Reichstein synthesized Vitamin C

1938 Paul Karrer synthesized Vitamin E

1940 Blood plasma used in transfusion

1943 Selman A. Waksman discovered streptomycin

1949 Philip Hunch and **Edward Kendall** used cortisone as treatment for rheumatism

1950 Kidney transplant

1952 Ultrasound

1955 Jonas Salk developed polio vaccine

1963 Anti-measles vaccine developed

1964 Soft contact lens

1967 Christiaan Barnard performed heart transplant

1969 Dorothy Hodgkin discovered structure of insulin

1972 Magnetic resonance scanner

1974 Soviet doctors invented ultrasonic vibration scalpel

1979 Laser surgery

---

known as "the Father of Anatomy," pioneered the scientific study of the human body in the 1540s when he published the first complete description of the human body. In 1616, **William Harvey** described the circulation of the blood in the human body. Harvey's work was crucial to the advance of medical science; for, as the Bible proclaimed more than two thousand years before Christ, the life of the flesh is in the blood.

Since Harvey's time, medical scientists have studied in great detail the cells and organs of the human body; they have discovered ways to cure, prevent, or relieve scores of diseases. There were doctors long before the 16th century, but so little was known about the human body,

Important Historical Inventions

Before A.D. 1500

c. 2000 B.C. potter's wheel
c. A.D. 1 paper
c. A.D. 600 gunpowder
c. 1200 firearms
1439 **Johann Gutenberg**—movable-type printing press

1500s

1590 **Zacharias Janssen**—microscope

1600s

1610 **Hans Lippershey**—telescope
1644 **Evangelista Torricelli**—barometer
1650 **Otto von Guericke**—air pump
1656 **Christian Huygens**—pendulum clock

1700s

1705 **Thomas Newcomen**—steam engine
1711 **Thomas Newcomen**—steam pump
1733 **John Kay**—flying shuttle loom
1740 **Benjamin Huntsman**—crucible steel
1742 **Jean Malouin**—galvanized iron
1752 **Benjamin Franklin**—lightning rod
1764 **James Hargreaves**—cotton spinning jenny
1769 **Richard Arkwright**—water powered cotton spinning mill
1776 **James Watt**—first commercial steam engine
1779 **Samuel Crompton**—hydraulic spinning mule
1780 circular saw
1783 **J. M.** and **J. E. Montgolfier**—manned balloon
1785 **Edmund Cartwright**—power spinning loom
1792 gas lighting in England
1793 **Eli Whitney**—cotton gin
1797 **Charles Newbold**—singlecast iron plow

1800s

1800 **Alessandro Volta**—electric battery
1800 **Joseph Jacquard**—loom for patterned fabric
1807 **Robert Fulton**—steamboat
1809 **Humphry Davy**—arc lamp
1814 **George Stephenson**—first successful steam locomotive
1821 **Michael Faraday**—electric motor
1823 **Charles Macintosh**—waterproof fabric
1824 Portland cement
1829 **Josef Ressel**—ship's screw propeller
1834 **Cyrus McCormick**—mechanical reaper
1835 **Samuel Colt**—revolver
1837 **Samuel Morse**—telegraph
1838 **Louis Daguerre**—daguerreotype
1839 **Charles Goodyear**—vulcanization of rubber
1846 **Elias Howe**—sewing machine
1846 rotary printing press
1848 safety matches
1849 **Joseph Monier**—reinforced concrete
1850 **R. W. Bunsen**—gas burner
1852 **Samuel Morse**—Morse telegraphic code
1852 **Jean Foucault**—gyroscope
1859 First oil well in U.S.
1860 **Etienne Lenoir**—internal combustion engine
1862 **Richard Gatling**—machine gun
1867 **P. D. Armour**—meat packing
1868 **George Westinghouse**—railroad air brake
1868 **C. L. Sholes**—typewriter
1872 **Thomas Edison**—"duplex" telegraph
1876 **Alexander Graham Bell**—telephone
1877 **Carl Gustaf de Laval**—cream separator
1877 **Thomas Edison**—phonograph
1878 **David Hughes**—microphone
1879 **Thomas Edison**—incandescent electric light
1879 **Constantin Fahlberg** and **Ira Ramsen**—saccharin
1879 **William Crookes**—cathode ray tube
1884 **Ottmar Mergenthaler**—linotype machine
1885 **Gottlieb Daimler**—gasoline engine
1885 **William Burroughs**—adding machine
1886 **Gottlieb Daimler**—motorcycle
1888 **John Boyd Dunlop**—pneumatic tire
1888 **George Eastman**—Kodak box camera
1889 first skyscraper
1889 **Thomas Edison**—motion pictures
1893 **Rudolf Diesel**—diesel internal combustion engine
1895 **Guglielmo Marconi**—radio
1896 **Henry Ford**—automobile

1900s

1903 **Orville** and **Wilbur Wright**—airplane
1907 **Lee de Forest**—triode vacuum tube for radio
1908 **Henry Ford**—Model T Ford
1913 **Hans Geiger**—geiger counter
1913 household refrigerator
1915 armored tank
1926 **John Baird**—television
1926 **Robert Goddard**—liquid-fuel rocket
1927 **John Baird**—color television
1928 "Talkie" movies
1935 **Robert Watson-Watt**—radar
1937 **Frank Whittle**—jet engine
1938 Teflon
1939 **Igor Sikorsky**—helicopter
1944 V-1 guided missile
1946 electronic computer
1948 transistor
1949 fax machine
1954 solar battery
1954 nuclear submarine
1958 integrated circuit ("chip")
1958 stereo phonograph records
1960 weather satellite
1960 **Theodore H. Maiman**—laser
1961 industrial robot
1972 maglev train
1974 ultrasonic vibration scalpel
1974 personal computer
1979 compact disc (CD)
1979 cellular phone
1981 space shuttle
1986 ceramic superconductors

germs, and the chemistry of medicine that they could only isolate the sick, bind broken bones, and dispense herbs and a few medicinal drugs. Not until after the rise of modern science did medical men earnestly try to find the *cause* for illnesses so that they might find a *cure* for them. It has taken many dedicated men and women over three centuries to bring medicine to a place where it can prevent many diseases in a safe, relatively painless way.

Modern inventions. Through technology, modern science has produced "an infinity of devices." Thousands of inventions that are now commonplace would have seemed like magic to the men of A.D. 1500. Since the invention of the telescope and the microscope, people's lives have been enriched by devices for telling time, spinning cloth, transporting people, capturing and transmitting sights and sounds, heating and cooling homes, making life more comfortable, and generally extending man's power over nature in ways undreamed of during the Middle Ages.

Darwinism:
A Threat to Modern Science

Foolish errors. Around the middle of the 19th century, a number of foolish errors arose from the failure of scientists and other men to keep their thinking in line with God's Word. The error that was destined to affect the thought of great masses of people by the dawn of the 20th century and to detour many scientists from their true work was **Charles Darwin's** *theory of evolution.*

Charles Darwin

Studies. Charles Darwin did not possess the intellectual gifts that helped to make the great founders of modern science remarkable. "I believe that I was considered by all my masters and by my father as a very ordinary boy," he wrote, "rather below the common standard in intellect." His father sent him to Edinburgh University in Scotland to study medicine, but it soon became clear that he would not make a good physician. He was then sent to Cambridge University to prepare for the Anglican ministry, but there he spent more time on sports than with his studies. "I attempted mathematics, . . . but I got on very slowly. The work was repugnant to me, chiefly from my not being able to see any meaning in the early steps of algebra." *Without ability in mathematics, Darwin lacked the chief tool of the great scientists.* As a naturalist, however, he was well equipped, for he had a passion for collecting and a keen sense of observation.

Voyage of the **Beagle.** Darwin's first great opportunity as a naturalist came in 1831–1836 when he sailed with a surveying expedition on the H.M.S. *Beagle* around South America and to islands in the Pacific Ocean. It was evidently during this voyage that he learned the habit of diligence in work that marked the rest of his career. He spent his time on the voyage observing rain forests, unusual land formations, and other natural wonders; collecting strange animals from oceans, shores, and rivers; and taking careful notes on all his observations.

The Origin of Species. Darwin took with him a copy of *Principles of Geology* by **Charles Lyell** (1797–1875), who is regarded as the "Father of Modern Geology." From this book, Darwin learned Lyell's false *principle of uniformity,* the idea that <u>the present is the key to the past</u>, that we can only explain what happened in the past on the basis of observations that we can make in the present. (The great founders of modern science believed just the opposite:

373

that *the past*—God's account of the Creation—*is the key to the present.*) As he considered the many varieties of plants and animals that he saw on his voyage, Darwin applied the false idea of uniformitarianism to the origin of life on the earth and formulated a theory of evolution.

In **1859,** Charles Darwin published his book *The Origin of Species,* in which he rejected the Biblical record of creation and proposed that "probably all the organic beings which have ever lived on the earth have descended from some one primordial [existing from the beginning] form, into which life was first breathed." This idea was not new to the world. Many pagan people without the benefit of the Scriptures, including the ancient Greeks, had expressed similar ideas; and during Darwin's time and for about a century before him a number of Europeans who did not wish to accept the Bible had been quietly bringing it up again. But Darwin presented his theory of evolution in scientific language that made it sound reasonable. *The Origin of Species* was joyfully received by many people who preferred to keep the Bible from controlling their lives.

Survival of the fittest. In his book, Darwin suggested that the fittest and strongest of each species, those best adapted to their environment, were the most likely to survive and reproduce. He said that this method of **natural selection,** which he called *"survival of the fittest,"* was the means by which one species slowly evolved into a new species.

Darwin's reasoning had some serious flaws, however. It is true that some characteristics make a species more fit to survive under certain conditions than others, but natural selection is not evolution—it produces no new characteristics. It merely brings out the variety created within a kind.

Darwin rejected the Bible because he misunderstood God's holiness, love, and justice. He believed that the God of the Bible was a cruel tyrant because He allowed people to suffer. This is not true, of course, but that was how Darwin perceived things. Darwin's idea of "survival of the fittest," however, was perhaps the cruelest idea ever imagined. Not only does it offer no hope for the present or the future, but it expresses a complete lack of compassion for the physically and mentally impaired. In the 20th century, Darwin's theory of evolution and the survival of the fittest would bring untold suffering to millions of people around the world. Like all men who choose to leave God out of their thoughts, Darwin ended up doing the very thing that he erroneously accused God of doing!

No missing links. Interestingly, Darwin, the great collector, could never find the "missing links," the transitional forms between evolving species, that his theory required. If evolution were true—if species gradually changed into other species over time—there would be evidence of intermediate forms. But this is not the case; there are actually great gaps between each kind of animal. The fact that no missing links have ever been found is the greatest evidence against evolution. Darwin himself recognized this problem:

> The number of intermediate varieties, which have formerly existed on the earth, [must] be truly enormous. Why then is not every geological formation and every stratum [layer of earth] full of such intermediate links? Geology assuredly does not reveal any such finely graduated organic chain; and this, perhaps, is the most obvious and gravest objection which can be urged against my theory.

The evidence was sketchy and incomplete when Darwin wrote *The Origin of Species,* but since then over 100 million fossils, representing a quarter of a million species, have been excavated, cataloged, and placed in museums. Still not one transitional form has been found. Though various "missing links" are occasionally proclaimed to be found, closer examination invariably reveals them to be imaginative "reconstructions" based on tiny fragments of bone, or different kinds altogether. Yet evolutionists continue to assume that these missing links must exist because they assume evolution to be true.

Evolution of man. In a later book, the **Descent of Man** (1871), Darwin stated his idea of the evolution of man: "Man is descended from a hairy quadruped, furnished with a tail and pointed ears, probably arboreal [living in trees] in its habits, and an inhabitant of the Old World." Many people strongly rejected evolution during Darwin's lifetime, and a great controversy arose over his ideas. Soon, however, because Darwin the naturalist was called a scientist and because science was so highly respected in the 19th century, many people began to accept his views.

Threat to science. Many scientists were detoured from their true calling of mastering nature for the benefit of mankind to the task of trying to prove Darwin's ideas, which they soon realized he had not really proved at all. The harder scientists tried to prove Darwin's theory of evolution, however, the more they realized that it had serious problems. Rather than rejecting the idea altogether and returning to the Scriptures as the starting point for science, however, some scientists chose to look for new theories of evolution, even though mathematicians say that the chance of just *one* creature changing into another, even over a period of billions of years, is zero. This search for an explanation for the origin of living things other than that offered in the Bible has threatened the very existence of modern science.

Evolution is an attempt to separate science from its Christian heritage. It denies the role of God as Creator and Sustainer of the universe. As many scien-

tists begin to realize the implications of this, they see that their work has no reasonable foundation.

The deadening effect of this kind of thinking is well illustrated by Darwin's own life. He lost all interest in the higher things of life—the things about man that can only be explained if he is a creature made in the image of God. He lost his love for poetry, music, and literature. In Darwin's own words, his mind had been reduced to "a kind of machine for grinding general laws out of large collections of facts."

Possibly the saddest effect of evolution is what it has done to many scientists. These men, dedicated to a task and generally very honest and open-minded in their work, are unable to be honest, objective, and open-minded about evolution without being severely ridiculed and shunned by their colleagues. In the 20th century, evolution has become a cult in which scientists are expected to believe despite all evidence against it.

Science, God's Truth, and Human Freedom

God wrote "two great books—nature and Scripture," declared Charles Spurgeon, the great 19th century "Prince of Preachers."

How foolish and wicked are those who instead of accepting the two sacred tomes, and delighting to behold the same divine hand in each, spend all their wits in endeavoring to find discrepancies and contradictions. We may rest assured that the true "Vestiges of Creation" will never contradict Genesis, nor will a correct "cosmos" [world as a whole] be found at variances with the narrative of Moses. He is wisest who reads both the world-book and the Word-book as two volumes of the same work, and feels concerning them "My Father wrote them both."

This is the spirit with which modern science began, and only as scientists and the general public continue to believe the foundational truths about the creation of man and the universe proclaimed in the Bible can modern science continue to bless mankind. Men developed modern science when they turned to the Bible and found it to be true. Scientists and all men still need God's Word today to guide them in their search for further truths about God's world as well as in their daily living. The Bible is not a science book, but whatever it says about science is true. Wise scientists will always check their ideas about God's world by God's Word, and thus avoid foolish errors that could darken man's understanding and destroy his freedom.

CHECK UP

1. During the 17th century, what group of people took the greatest interest in the work of the scientists?
2. What was the first permanent scientific society in the Modern Age? When was it founded? Where?
3. For what is Albert Einstein especially remembered?
4. Who is known as "the Father of Anatomy"? What did William Harvey describe?
5. What is a scientist's most important guidebook?
6. What kind of student was Charles Darwin? In what subject was he notably deficient?
7. What does the principle of uniformity say? What opposite principle did the founders of modern science believe?
8. What did Darwin say in *Descent of Man*?
9. Why did many people begin to accept Darwin's ideas?
10. How does evolution threaten the quality of science?

Identify: John Wilkins, Philosophical College, French Academy of Science, Huguenots, Jansenists, Blaise Pascal, Charles Lyell, H.M.S. *Beagle, The Origin of Species,* "survival of the fittest"

The New World of Industry

A New Age of Technology

The rise of modern science in the 16th and 17th centuries and the revival of Biblical Christianity in England, America, and some European countries in the 18th century set the stage for the **"Industrial Revolution,"** a time of profound changes in agriculture, industry, and technology. (The word *revolution* means a complete change or turning around.) The 19th century, or more specifically the period from about 1760 to 1900, is often called the **Age of Industry.** The Industrial Revolution and the Age of Industry it began brought major advances in food production, health care, manufacturing, transportation, communication, and living standards.

The emphasis on the Bible freed men's minds and souls, encouraging free and original thought about God's universe. It also gave men a renewed sense of responsibility and a desire to help others. The rise of modern science led to the discovery of many of God's natural laws of the universe—how things work. All of this led to new *technology—the practical application of science to industry.* The technology of the Industrial Age revolutionized life for civilized man.

Improvements in Agriculture

Poverty. Throughout most of world history (and in undeveloped nations even today), the vast majority of people have engaged in *"subsistence farming"—growing just enough food to feed their own families.* People working under such conditions have no provision against drought, disease, or other natural conditions, and are doomed to a life of poverty. <u>Mastery of the food supply is the most critical material factor in determining how far a nation may advance.</u>

Superstition. Before there could be an improvement in agricultural productivity, there had to be a change among the people. This change was most obvious among the people of England. During the first part of the 18th century, the masses of lower-class Englishmen, both in towns and in the country, were known for their crime, immorality, ignorance, and poverty. Many depended on "charms" and astrology to produce food crops. Such superstition always produces fear, and many people feared the forces of nature rather than following God's command to harness nature for the good of man (Gen. 1:28).

Revival and economic freedom. The **Wesleyan revival** changed the way people thought by changing their hearts. Englishmen began to depend less on charms and astrology to make their crops grow and more on principles (God's laws) of agriculture. As farmers gained a greater sense of responsibility, and as inventors gained a new desire to help others, the stage was set for greater productivity. ***Work was given a new sense of nobility.*** People began to take seriously the injunction of Colossians 3:23: "And whatsoever ye do, do it **heartily** as unto the Lord, and not unto men." The effect of Ephesians 4:28 must have been profound upon newly awakened men who now heard it for the first time: "Let him that stole steal no more: but rather let him *labour*, working with his hands the thing which is good, that he may have to give to him that needeth."

The **Protestant work ethic,** *the Biblical teaching that God expects all men to work and that all work is a noble duty to be performed toward God,* paid off in more food production, more technology, and a generally more advanced civilization—a better world for mankind. It brought the greatest good, physically and spiritually, to those individuals who obeyed God's command to use part of the profits of their industry to help others.

Drastic changes in agriculture became evident first in England, where revival had made the greatest overall changes in society. The movement soon spread to America, which had also been visited with spiritual revival. Eventually, it spread to other parts of Europe, where freedom, based on a Biblical understanding of man, was on the rise. The lands most profoundly affected by the Protestant work ethic were England, America, Germany, Holland, Switzerland, and Scandinavia.

Better use of land. The Protestant work ethic encouraged farmers to seek ways to use their land more efficiently, and the rise of modern science provided them with the means of meeting this goal. They began by using more land for food production and by finding ways to increase the yield of each acre of land they cultivated.

Men drained swamps and reclaimed land in other ways to make more land available for tilling. They found that animal manure could be used to increase soil fertility and crop production. They also discovered that if crops were *rotated* (a different crop planted in a field each year) it was not necessary to let ground lie *fallow* (plowed up but not used) as often as when the same crop is planted year after year.

Better tools. New inventions made even greater agricultural production possible. Most of the earlier inventions, such as **Jethro Tull's** *seed drill,* introduced about 1701, were developed by the English. But the practical-thinking Americans soon took the lead in applying scientific knowledge for useful purposes.

In 1837, **John Deere** patented his famous *steel plow.* Before long, the gang plow, which could be used to plow several furrows at once, became popular in America. In 1831, **Cyrus McCormick** introduced his *reaper* to American farmers. The introduction of the *thresher* made it possible to more efficiently separate grain from its chaff. By 1900, the reaper and the thresher had been combined in one ma-

Cyrus McCormick's Reaper

chine appropriately dubbed the *combine.* These valuable inventions, all products of American ingenuity, revolutionized agriculture in Europe and America, making greater production possible with fewer workers.

Fewer farmers feed more people. While Europe's total population was increasing, the percentage of the population engaged in agriculture was decreasing. In other words, because of agricultural advancements, fewer and fewer farmers were able to feed an ever-increasing number of people. In England, for example, agriculture employed nearly 50% of the population in 1760. In 1800, it employed 35%, and by 1830, it employed only 25%. In other European countries, the change was considerably less dramatic, but the trend was the same: some food was being imported to help feed the factory workers, but to a large extent the countries were able to feed themselves, thanks to major agricultural improvements.

Agriculture and industry. The agricultural advances of the 18th century comple-mented the Industrial Revolution. If some were to be free to work in industrial facto-ries, others must be able to produce enough food not only for themselves but also for those who would move to the cities to work in the factories. As **Adam Smith** (1723–1790), a famous 18th century Scottish economist, said, "The cultivation and improvement of the country . . . must necessarily be prior to the increase of the town." The increased agricultural produc-tion brought about by more efficient farm-ing methods and new farming implements prepared the way for the Industrial Revolu-tion.

The Industrial Revolution

England takes the lead. England, perhaps more than any other nation, stood poised at the end of the 18th century to spark an industrial revolution. She had an excellent system of rivers and harbors for transportation and waterpower, ample supplies of coal and iron, the world's largest non-farming labor supply, a govern-ment that rewarded private initiative and protected private property, capital (surplus money) to invest in new technology, and the world's largest navy and merchant marine. Most important, England had a population inspired by the Protestant work ethic to work and improve its economic lot.

A new manufacturing system. Before the Age of Industry, manufacturing was carried out under a process known as the **domestic system.** Under the domestic system, *work was done in small private shops,* usually within a craftsman's home. Often the entire family participated in the manufacturing process, spending long hours of hard labor to earn a living.

Increased food production in the 18th century freed more people to leave the farms and take employment in the newly developing industrial cities. Slowly, through technology, the domestic system of manufacturing was replaced by the **factory system,** in which ever-increasing numbers of *people were employed to produce manufactured goods in a systematic way for wages.* By 1800, the Industrial Revolution was well under way.

Spread of industrialism. The industrial advancement began in England and soon spread to America. By the mid-19th century, both nations abounded in railroads and factories. Western Europe experienced industrial growth to a lesser extent than England or America for two important reasons. **(1)** Some European countries had experienced a degree of revival during the Pietist movement of the late 17th century, but the English Wesleyan Revival and the American Great Awakening had more far-reaching effects, having been kept alive by subsequent religious revivals. **(2)** In England and America, where spiritual fires and political freedom prevailed, industrial growth was spontaneous. In most other countries, monarchal governments undertook various projects to promote industry for national advancement, but government-promoted technology did not work as effectively as the private business enterprises of England and the United States.

Growth of cities. As industrialism increased, the rapidly growing populations of industrial countries moved to the cities to find employment in the new factories. Old cities expanded rapidly, and new cities sprang up in locations where transportation and waterpower were available. In 1785, England and Scotland had only four cities with over 50,000 people; 75 years later there were 31 such cities.

Blessings and curses. Much has been written about the evils of life in the industrial cities of the 18th and 19th centuries. Indeed there were bad living conditions (low wages and poor housing) and bad working conditions (long hours, air and water pollution created by factory waste, dangerous working areas, and child labor). But many Europeans had faced even worse conditions on the farms they left behind. In the United States, most farmers owned their own land, but in Europe, many farmers rented their land and worked like slaves in the fields of their landlords. These people found it profitable to leave the farms and work in the cities, where they could improve their standard of living.

In 1843 a London woman, Mrs. Cooke Taylor, visited Lancashire, the industrial heart of England. Before describing what she saw there, she first described the average Londoner's opinion of factory cities:

> I need not remind you of the statements put forward in the newspapers, relative to the miserable conditions of the operatives, and the tyranny of their masters, for they made such an impression on me that it was with reluctance that I consented to go to Lancashire; indeed these misrepresentations are quite

general, and people believe them without knowing why or wherefore. As an instance: just before starting I was at a large dinner party, at the west end of the town, and seated next to a gentleman who is considered a very clever and intelligent man. In the course of the conversation I mentioned that I was going to Lancashire. He stared and asked, "What on earth could take me there? That he would as soon think of going to St. Giles's; that it was a horrid place—factories all over; that the people, from starvation, oppression, and over-work, had almost lost the form of humanity; and that the millowners were a bloated, pampered race, feeding on the very vitals of the people." I answered that this was a dreadful state of things; and asked "In what part he had seen such misery?" He replied, that "he had never *seen* it, but had been *told* that it existed; and that for his part he never *had been* in the manufacturing districts, and that he *never would*." This gentleman was one of the very numerous body of people who spread reports without ever taking the trouble of inquiring if they be true or false.[1]

After visiting the industrial area herself, Mrs. Taylor concluded:

Now that I have seen the factory people at their work, in their cottages and in their schools, I am totally at a loss to account for the outcry that has been made against them. They are better clothed, better fed, and better conducted than many other classes of working people.[2]

Better living conditions. Industrialism ushered in a great age of wealth and luxury for all civilized mankind, and not just the rich. Modern scholarship shows that **"real wages"** *(wages as compared to the cost of living)* increased in England during the Age of Industry. Between 1800 and 1825 real wages increased 25 percent, and between 1825 and 1850 they increased by 40 percent. This means that people could afford to buy more and better things than they ever had before.

Industrialism helped to alleviate the problems that come with expanding populations. One of the best-known modern-day historians of the Industrial Revolution, T. S. Ashton, reminds us of what happens to an expanding population that does not industrialize:

The central problem of the age was how to feed and clothe and employ generations of children outnumbering by far those of any earlier time. Ireland was faced by the same problem. Failing to solve it, she lost in the 'forties about a fifth of her people by emigration or starvation and disease. If England had remained a nation of cultivators and craftsmen, she could hardly have escaped the same fate, and, at best, the weight of a growing population must have pressed down the spring of her spirit. She was delivered, not by her rulers, but by those who, seeking no doubt their own narrow ends, had the wit and resource to devise new instruments of production and new methods of administering industry. There are today on the plains of India and China men and women, plague-ridden and hungry, living lives little better, to outward appearance, than those of the cattle that toil with them by day and share their places of sleep by night. Such Asiatic standards, and such unmechanized horrors, are the lot of those who increase their numbers without passing through an industrial revolution.[3]

[1]F. A. Hayek, ed., *Capitalism and the Historians* (Chicago: University of Chicago Press, 1954), p. 20.
[2]*Ibid.*, p. 21.
[3]T. S. Ashton, *The Industrial Revolution: 1760–1830* (New York: Oxford University Press, 1948), p. 111.

CHECK UP

1. What set the stage for the Industrial Revolution? What years are called the "Age of Industry"?
2. What is subsistence farming? What is the most critical material factor in determining how far a nation may advance?
3. List some of the inventions that increased agricultural production.
4. Why did England take the lead in the Industrial Revolution in the 18th century?
5. Compare the domestic system of manufacturing with the factory system.
6. How did industrialism affect the size of cities?
7. What happens in countries that grow in size and do not industrialize?

Identify: Industrial Revolution, technology, Protestant work ethic, Jethro Tull, John Deere, Cyrus McCormick, real wages

Advancing Industries

Textiles. The Industrial Revolution began in England's textile factories. In 1738, **John Kay** invented the *flying shuttle,* which allowed one person to weave bolts of cloth; before, two had been needed. This meant that cloth could be woven faster than thread could be spun. In 1764, **James Hargreaves** solved this problem by inventing the *spinning jenny,* which automatically spun fiber into thread. The shortcoming of the spinning jenny was that flax had to be mixed with cotton in order to get the thread to spin properly. Cotton alone was too coarse. In 1769, **Richard Arkwright** invented the *water frame,* on which cotton alone could be spun into thread. In 1779, **Samuel Crompton** made a major advancement by combining the spinning jenny and the water frame into the *spinning mule.* In 1785, **Edmund Cartwright** patented a *power loom* to replace hand weaving.

The Enclosure Movement. As the textile industry began to grow in England, more sheep were needed for the wool market. Landowners began to enclose their land with fences or hedges in order to raise sheep. Although it often put peasant crop tillers out of employment, this **Enclosure Movement** made it possible for landholders to control breeding of livestock and thereby to increase the size and quality of livestock as well as milk production.

"King" cotton. English textile mills also needed a source of plentiful and inexpensive cotton. The fields of the southern United States provided a source, and **Eli Whitney** (1765–1825) made it inexpensive. As a young New Englander just out of Yale College, Whitney visited a cotton plantation in Georgia while he was on his

Spinning Thread: the old and the new way.

381

Henry Bessemer: The Bessemer process was the chief method of making steel in the late 1800s.

way to take his first job as a schoolteacher. It was his first trip to the South, and he had never seen cotton before. As he heard about the tedious, time-consuming process of removing the seeds from the cotton fibers by hand, his brilliant mind began to work. In 1793, he introduced the *cotton gin,* making it possible for one plantation slave to do the work that had previously required 50 slaves. The cotton gin revolutionized agriculture in the South and made cotton "king" in the southern states.

Steam power. The growth of the textile industry created a need for better power sources. Waterpower was too limited and inaccessible to meet the needs of the new factories. **James Watt,** a Scotsman, developed an efficient, coal-burning *steam engine* in 1776. Before long, steam engines were powering factories throughout England.

Coal mining. The British Isles possessed vast quantities of coal to power the new steam engines. The chief problem in coal mining was the water which seeped into the mine shafts, but now steam engines could be used to pump the water out. Thus, the same technology that consumed the coal also made more coal available. *Improvements in technology always improve upon or add to our natural resources to make life better for all.*

Other advances in the coal mining industry increased production and made the work somewhat safer than it had been before. The most important invention for the safety of coal miners was the *miner's safety lamp,* invented by **Sir Humphry Davy,** an English chemist, in 1815.

From iron to steel. With more coal available, men began to experiment with ways to smelt (heat to remove impurities) iron ore using coal rather than charcoal. Charcoal is made from wood, which was in short supply in England. Raw coal contains sulphur, which makes iron brittle, but **Abraham Darby** and his son Abraham Darby, Jr., discovered that they could burn raw coal to produce coke, which could be used to smelt high-quality iron. Gradually, iron replaced wood in machinery.

Iron was still too brittle for more strenuous uses, but it could be made stronger by adding carbon in the smelting process to produce steel. The process for converting raw iron (pig iron) into steel was too expensive to be practiced on a large scale until the 1850s, when **Henry Bessemer,** an Englishman, discovered a cheap process for converting iron into steel by using currents of air. Although **William Kelly,** an American working independently of Bessemer, discovered essentially the same process in the same decade, the process is called the *Bessemer process.*

THE NEW WORLD OF INDUSTRY

Better Transportation

The growth of manufacturing created a need for better means of transportation. Improved roads were built in both England and America in the 18th century, but the technology was limited and travel by road remained slow and difficult.

Canals. One solution to the transportation problem was canals. Canals were dug in various countries of Western Europe but became especially popular in America, where hundreds of miles of canals were dug in the 18th century. The most famous was the **Erie Canal,** completed in 1825, connecting Lake Erie to the Hudson River. International trade was boosted by the opening of the **Suez Canal** in 1869, joining the Mediterranean Sea and the Indian Ocean by way of the Red Sea. A glance at a world map will show how much travel time by ship the Suez Canal saved seafaring merchants.

Ships. New **steamships** also aided industrial trade. The American inventor **Robert Fulton** (1765–1815) built the first practical steamship, the *Clermont,* which sailed 150 miles up the Hudson River in 1807. Soon, large ocean-going vessels were propelled by steam engines. Throughout the 19th century, American shipbuilders outdid their English rivals by constructing the best **clipper ships,** long, lean sailing vessels known for their speed on the high seas.

Railroads. Another new form of transportation in the 19th century was the railroad. **George Stephenson,** an Englishman, opened the world's first public steam-powered railroad in 1825. By 1840, there were major rail systems crossing Europe and the United States. In 1869, the **transcontinental railroad** joined America's midwest to her west coast.

Automobiles. By the late 1800s, inventors in Europe and America were tinkering with new kinds of engines and dreaming of new modes of transportation. In Germany,

Robert Fulton's **Clermont**

Steam Locomotive

A Clipper Ship

383

Gottlieb Daimler developed the gas-fueled *internal combustion engine* in 1886. Another German, **Rudolf Diesel,** soon unveiled his *diesel engine,* which was powerful enough for larger vehicles such as locomotives and even ships. **Karl Benz** in Germany, **Louis Renault** in France, and **Henry Ford** in the United States took the internal combustion engine, mounted it on a carriage, and founded automobile companies in their respective countries.

Improved Communications

Communication facilities also improved considerably in the mid-19th century. In 1840, England introduced the **penny post,** which made mail significantly less expensive. In 1844, in America, **Samuel Morse** (1791–1872), perfected the *electric telegraph.* Another American, **Cyrus Field,** finally succeeded in 1866, after years of effort, in laying the first successful *transatlantic telegraph cable.*

Inventors in the Age of Industry

In the late 19th century, several American inventors made outstanding contributions to the communications and transportation industries. Their work laid the foundation for many of the conveniences that we enjoy today.

Alexander Graham Bell. Because of his life-long interest in the problems of the deaf, Alexander Graham Bell (1847–1922) carefully studied the principles of sound transmission. In 1876, he patented his first *telephone.* Bell's first successful transmission of intelligible speech over a telephone was by accident. As he prepared to test a new transmitter, he spilled battery acid on his clothes and called to his assistant in the next room, "Mr. Watson, come here. I want you!" His assistant failed to hear Bell directly, but he heard the voice over the transmitter!

Also in 1876, America celebrated its 100th birthday with a large Centennial

Alexander Graham Bell with His Telephone: making the first long distance call (from New York to Chicago) in 1892.

Exposition in Philadelphia. The exposition featured demonstrations of America's amazing technological advances in its first 100 years. When Bell demonstrated his telephone at the Centennial Exposition, the English scientist Lord Kelvin called it "the most wonderful thing in America."

Thomas Edison. Thomas Alva Edison (1847–1931) has been called *the greatest inventor in history.* His contributions to modern living are numerous. In Menlo Park, New Jersey, he established the first modern scientific laboratory. For that feat and others he won the title "the Wizard of Menlo Park." He patented 1,093 inventions, including the *phonograph,* the *motion picture projector,* the *mimeograph machine,* and an *improved telephone system.* Although Edison always considered the phonograph his favorite invention, there is no doubt that his *incandescent electric light bulb* has had the most profound effect upon the 20th century. In 1882, the Edison Illuminating Company began supplying electricity to provide lighting for 85 customers. At the turn of the century, electricity was in common use in many parts of the country; by the 1940s, few Americans were without electricity.

Thomas Edison with His Phonograph: *the exhausted inventor after spending five days and nights to perfect his invention.*

Edison was always deeply involved in his work, declaring that "genius is one percent inspiration and ninety-nine percent perspiration."

The Wright Brothers. Wilbur (1867–1921) and Orville (1871–1948) Wright <u>made the first successful airplane flight</u> at Kitty Hawk, North Carolina, on December 17, 1903. These brothers, the owners of a bicycle shop, had experimented for about six years in their study of flight. Through their experiments they added to and corrected scientific knowledge about aeronautics. Few people took the airplane seriously in 1903, but through experiments and later flights by the Wrights and others, its significance soon became apparent. Today the basic principles discovered by the Wright brothers provide us with the fastest means of transportation available. Airplanes eventually replaced trains as a major means of public transportation. The airplane has revolutionized public transportation in the 20th century.

Henry Ford. Henry Ford (1863–1947) built his first automobile in 1896 and organized the Ford Motor Company in 1903. At first he followed the example of his competitors, building an expensive automobile that only the wealthy could afford. Then he decided to build a car that was affordable for all Americans. By engineering an inexpensive model, the **Model T,** and by employing the *assembly line* process to increase speed and cut cost of production, <u>Ford was able to produce a low-cost, dependable automobile for the average American.</u>

Ford not only introduced Americans to a revolutionary method of manufacturing and employed many people at wages well above average for the time, but he also gave America a car that thousands could

Henry Ford in 1896
with His First Automobile

Wilbur and Orville Wright: *testing their airplane at Kitty Hawk, North Carolina.*

385

afford to drive. In the first year of production, he sold 11,000 Model T's. Sales continued to soar and prices for the Model T continued to drop, until by 1925, a Model T cost under $300. In addition to mobilizing Americans, Ford stimulated road building, the rubber industry, the steel industry, and the oil industry, all of which created thousands of jobs to help make Americans the most prosperous people in the world.

Assembly Line: the final assembly line at the Ford Motor Company's Highland Park plant in 1913.

Captains of Industry

Big business as America knows it today began to develop during the industrial boom between the Civil War and 1900. The 20th century brought new forms of business organization, geared to the development of giant manufacturing concerns. Some Americans were able to accumulate enough wealth to build their own "super-size" businesses and thus control certain areas of industry. Industrial giants like **John D. Rockefeller** (1839–1937) in the <u>oil industry</u>, and **Andrew Carnegie** (1835–1919) in the <u>steel industry</u>, became famous and immensely rich. Such business tycoons have been called "robber barons" and have been criticized for their relentless drive to eliminate competition, expand their businesses, and increase profits. But their critics often forget the manifold benefits these men brought to mankind. In their drive to increase their own wealth they brought untold benefits to others.

Through their businesses, Rockefeller and Carnegie not only provided thousands of jobs but also stimulated other industries. Each also helped to provide America with a much-needed commodity to help create better, safer, and more enjoyable living conditions for everyone.

In addition to the primary benefits they brought to America through their

---

CHECK UP

1. Where did the Industrial Revolution begin?
2. Name the inventor of each of the following inventions: *flying shuttle, spinning jenny, water frame, spinning mule, power loom.*
3. What device did Eli Whitney invent? What crop did it make "king" in the southern states?
4. What is the Bessemer process? What two men developed it?
5. Name two famous canals that were dug in the 19th century.
6. Who invented the first practical steamship? What was it called?
7. Who opened the world's first public steam-powered railroad? When?
8. How did Gottlieb Daimler and Rudolf Diesel improve transportation?
9. Who invented the electric telegraph? Who laid the first successful transatlantic telegraph cable?
10. Who has been called the greatest inventor in history? Name five of his inventions.
11. When did the Wright brothers make their first successful flight? Where?
12. Who made the automobile affordable for most Americans?

Identify: Enclosure Movement, James Watt, Sir Humphry Davy, clipper ships, transcontinental railroad, penny post, Alexander Graham Bell, Model T

John D. Rockefeller   *Andrew Carnegie*

The Triumph of Capitalism

Rise of industrial trade. We have discussed four major causes of the industrialism in the 19th century. **Spiritual revival** in England, America, and parts of Europe gave a new incentive, a new sense of responsibility, and a new understanding of the dignity of labor that established the *Protestant work ethic.* The **rise of modern science** gave men a clearer understanding of the workings of the universe and an ability to harness nature for the good of mankind. These two forces led to major **advances in agriculture** and to new **technological developments.**

A fifth factor which helped to expand industry to even greater lengths was the **rise of international trade.** Prior to the late 1700s, European countries had operated under a **mercantile** system (tight government control) of foreign trade. When European governments began to see the advantages of **free trade**—*trade without government regulations or tariffs*—they began to practice a policy of **"laissez faire"** *("hands off" or letting business alone).*

The mind largely responsible for the laissez faire policies of England and America was that of **Adam Smith** (1723–1790), a Scottish professor of philosophy. In 1776, (significantly the same year as the American Declaration of Independence) Smith published his famous work *An Inquiry into the Nature and Causes of the Wealth of Nations* (usually referred to simply as *Wealth of Nations*). In his book, Smith espoused a philosophy that *individual freedom in economics leads to the greatest good not only for the individual but for society as a whole.*

On the international scale, Smith called for free trade, which would allow for individual investors within each country to put their capital (money) to the wisest use. Each investor in manufacturing would produce what he could produce cheapest and best, depending on materials and labor available to him. Adam Smith was one of the earliest

business enterprises, these men also used their accumulated wealth for **philanthropy.** (*Philanthropy* comes from two Greek words meaning "love of mankind.") Rockefeller granted funds to make possible the creation of the University of Chicago in 1891. After 1897, he completely devoted himself to philanthropy. One of his endeavors that Americans and visitors from other countries still enjoy today is the restoration of Williamsburg, Virginia, to its 18th century appearance. He and his sons made philanthropic contributions amounting to $3 billion.

In 1889, Andrew Carnegie wrote *The Gospel of Wealth*, in which he stated his principles of good stewardship. Many wealthy Americans followed his example by distributing their surplus wealth to build and maintain public institutions such as hospitals, libraries, and schools. Carnegies' own philanthropic endeavors were numerous. He funded the Carnegie Institute of Technology and the Carnegie Institution of Washington. He was also a major benefactor of Booker T. Washington's Tuskegee Institute in Alabama. He is perhaps best remembered for helping to finance the foundation of public libraries in the United States and in England.

advocates of **capitalism,** or the *free market.* In an age when men were learning that political freedom is the best system of government, Smith realized that economic freedom was the best system of manufacturing and trade. He also saw that political freedom and economic freedom are inseparable; if a man is not free to use his financial resources as he chooses, he is not free. **Adam Smith was largely responsible for the rise and triumph of capitalism.**

Adam Smith

The blessings of a free market. In the late 19th and early 20th centuries, **capitalism,** or the **free market system,** brought to the western world the greatest wealth and luxury for the greatest number of people that the world has ever known. Since America had the greatest degree of political freedom and the greatest supply of labor and natural resources, *the blessings of capitalism were most abundant in America.*

Economic freedom and prosperity. The Industrial Revolution had reached America by about 1800, but it was not until after the Civil War that the industrial boom really took place. During the Civil War (1861–1865), the United States lagged behind Europe in manufacturing, but by 1900 she was in the lead. Between 1850 and 1900, America's national wealth increased from $7 billion to $88 billion. It is estimated that the GNP (**Gross National Product,** *or the total output of goods and services*) increased 44% between 1814 and 1883 and then continued to expand more slowly.

With the arrival of the modern era, cities continued to grow as industry expanded. Because of their transportation facilities and natural resources, certain American cities came to be known for certain products. **Pittsburgh** became the steel center; oil-refining cities sprang up in **Ohio** and **Pennsylvania; Minneapolis** and **St. Paul** became known for their flour mills. **Chicago** and **Cincinnati** became the meat packing centers. Breweries became the center of industry for **Milwaukee** and **St. Louis.**

Benefits of Technology and Capitalism

The development of capitalism in the 19th century made the 20th century the greatest financial age mankind has ever known. Andrew Carnegie expressed the situation well in 1889. Praising the benefits of capitalism, he said:

> To-day the world obtains commodities of excellent quality at prices which even the generation preceding this would have deemed incredible. . . . The poor enjoy what the rich could not before afford. What were the luxuries have become the necessities of life. The laborer has now more comforts than the farmer had a few generations ago. The farmer has more luxuries than the landlord had, and is more richly clad and better housed. The landlord has books and pictures rarer, and appointments more artistic, than the King could then obtain.

He reminded us that:

> The "good old times" were not good old times. Neither master nor servant was as well situated then as to-day. A relapse to old conditions would be disastrous to both—not the least so to him who serves—and would sweep away civilization with it.

Once men of any culture cease to be good, of course, they cease to be great, and their riches tend to degrade character rather than build it. Once men begin to love money rather than God, they begin a course that leads to all kinds of evil (1 Tim. 6:10). This is why John Wesley gave this oft-repeated advice to his followers:

Gain all you can; save all you can; give all you can.

Riches yielded to God bring great blessings; the person under God's control will see every possession as a gift of God and will obey God by giving part of his wealth back to Him in tithes, offerings, and charity.

─── CHECK UP ───

1. Who was the leader in the oil industry? The steel industry? Describe the philanthropic endeavors of these men.
2. List five major causes of industrialism in the 19th century.
3. What philosophy did Adam Smith advocate in *Wealth of Nations?* What did he call for on the international scale?
4. What country has enjoyed the greatest blessings of capitalism?
5. For what industry is each of the following cities noted: *Pittsburgh, Minneapolis, St. Paul, Chicago, Cincinnati?*
6. When did modern big business begin?

Identify: mercantilism, free trade, laissez faire, GNP, philanthropy, *The Gospel of Wealth*

CHAPTER 19 REVIEW

MULTIPLE CHOICE   Write the letter of the answer that best completes the sentence.

1. Because of his apparent wisdom, _____ came to be called "The Philosopher."
   a Johannes Kepler   c Thomas Aquinas
   b Francis Bacon   d Aristotle

2. _____ is known for combining Aristotle's philosophy with Roman Catholicism.
   a Thomas Aquinas   c Isaac Newton
   b Johannes Kepler   d Francis Bacon

3. _____ played an important role in formulating the principles of the modern scientific method.
   a Johannes Kepler   c Aristotle
   b Thomas Aquinas   d Francis Bacon

4. The three laws of planetary motion were discovered by _____.
   a Galileo Galilei   c Johannes Kepler
   b Isaac Newton   d Nicolaus Copernicus

5. _____ formulated the laws of the pendulum as well as the law of uniform acceleration.
   a Galileo Galilei   c Johannes Kepler
   b Isaac Newton   d Nicolaus Copernicus

6. The scientist who discovered the universal law of gravitation was _____.
   a Galileo Galilei   c Isaac Newton
   b Johannes Kepler   d Nicolaus Copernicus

7. _____ founded the Philosophical College in London.
   a John Wilkins   c Blaise Pascal
   b Christopher Wren   d William Harvey

8. The American Jewish physicist known for his theories of relativity was _____.
   a John Wilkins   c Blaise Pascal
   b Albert Einstein   d Andreas Vesalius

9. _____ is known as the "Father of Anatomy."
   a Andreas Vesalius   c Blaise Pascal
   b William Harvey   d Charles Lyell

10. The first man to describe the circulation of blood in the human body was _____.
    a Andreas Vesalius   c William Harvey
    b Charles Lyell   d Blaise Pascal

11. _____ popularized the theory of evolution with his book *Origin of Species.*
    a Charles Lyell   c Albert Einstein
    b Charles Darwin   d William Harvey

12. _____ is known as "the Father of Modern Geology."
    a William Harvey   c Andreas Vesalius
    b Charles Lyell   d Albert Einstein

CHAPTER 19 REVIEW (CONTINUED)

13. _____ discovered a cheap process for converting iron into steel.
    a John D. Rockefeller c Henry Bessemer
    b Andrew Carnegie   d Samuel Crompton

14. The Scottish professor who was largely responsible for the rise and triumph of capitalism was _____.
    a Henry Bessemer   c John D. Rockefeller
    b Adam Smith   d Andrew Carnegie

15. _____ was a giant in the oil industry who was known for his philanthropy.
    a Andrew Carnegie   c Adam Smith
    b John D. Rockefeller d Henry Bessemer

16. _____ was a giant in the steel industry who wrote a book entitled *The Gospel of Wealth*.
    a John D. Rockefeller c Adam Smith
    b Andrew Carnegie   d Henry Bessemer

MATCHING *Match the description with the correct name.*

Section A

a power loom   f flying shuttle
b steam engine   g steel plow
c cotton gin   h spinning jenny
d seed drill   i water frame
e reaper   j spinning mule

_____ 1. Jethro Tull
_____ 2. John Deere
_____ 3. Cyrus McCormick
_____ 4. John Kay
_____ 5. James Hargreaves
_____ 6. Richard Arkwright
_____ 7. Samuel Crompton
_____ 8. Edmund Cartwright
_____ 9. Eli Whitney
_____10. James Watt

Section B

a steamship   g airplane
b phonograph   h miner's safety lamp
c Model T   i steam locomotive
d transatlantic cable j internal combustion
e electric telegraph   engine
f telephone

_____ 1. Sir Humphry Davy
_____ 2. Robert Fulton
_____ 3. George Stephenson
_____ 4. Gottlieb Daimler
_____ 5. Samuel Morse
_____ 6. Cyrus Field
_____ 7. Alexander Graham Bell
_____ 8. Thomas Edison
_____ 9. Wilbur and Orville Wright
_____10. Henry Ford

TIME LINE CHALLENGE *Choose the letter of the correct date for each of the events listed below. Answers may be used more than once.*

1543	1645	1662	1666	1687	1760	1776	1825	1859	1869	1903
A	B	C	D	E	F	G	H	I	J	K

_____ 1. transcontinental railroad completed
_____ 2. Erie Canal completed
_____ 3. Darwin publishes *Origin of Species*
_____ 4. Royal Society founded
_____ 5. Copernicus presents heliocentric view

_____ 6. Newton publishes *Principia*
_____ 7. Suez Canal completed
_____ 8. first successful airplane flight
_____ 9. Age of Industry begins
_____10. Adam Smith publishes *Wealth of Nations*

COMPLETION *Choose the correct term to complete each sentence and write the letter in the blank.*

- a Enclosure Movement
- b factory sytem
- c "subsistence farming"
- d Protestant work ethic
- e principle of uniformity
- f Huguenots
- g natural philosophers
- h geocentric
- i physics
- j domestic system
- k scholasticism
- l heliocentric
- m Puritans
- n technology

1. The idea that the universe is sun-centered is called the _____ view.
2. The idea that the universe is earth-centered is called the _____ view.
3. The attempt to combine Greek philosophy and Roman Catholicism was called _____.
4. The basic science of matter and energy is _____.
5. Before 1840, scientists were called _____.
6. French Protestants called _____ supported the French Academy of Science.
7. The _____ is the idea that the present is the key to the past.
8. The practical application of science to industry is called _____.
9. Growing just enough food to support one's own family is known as _____.
10. Under the _____, work was done in small private shops, usually within a craftsman's home.
11. Under the _____, ever-increasing numbers of people were employed to produce manufactured goods in a systematic way for wages.
12. The _____ is the Biblical teaching that God expects all men to work and that work is a noble duty to be performed toward God.
13. The _____ enabled landholders to control breeding of livestock and thereby to increase the size and quality of livestock as well as milk production.

CONCEPTS TO CONSIDER *On a separate sheet of paper, answer the following questions using complete sentences.*

1. Why did mankind make little progress in science before the Modern Age? What brought about the rise of modern science in the 16th century?
2. How did the Protestant work ethic help to bring about the Age of Industry?
3. Why did the Industrial Revolution begin in England and not in France or another European country?
4. How is the idea of evolution a threat to scientific progress?
5. Discuss the advantages of capitalism, or the free market system.

20
The New World of Classics

What Is a Classic?

The Modern Age, with its emphasis on individual responsibility and achievement, has witnessed the production of an amazing number of classics in music, art, and literature. A **classic** is *a work of superior excellence that has stood the test of time—a work for all people of all ages.* Classics have reflected the thinking of men throughout history and have also helped to shape men's thinking. We can better understand history if we understand the works that men have produced throughout history.

The **ancient classics** are the books and works of art produced during ancient times, especially in Greece and Rome. The ancients produced well-known works of philosophy, poetry, drama, and sculpture that showed just how much man, created in God's image, could achieve without acknowledging his Creator. Many of the ancient classics are worth studying today because they help us to understand ancient history and human nature. They must be handled very carefully, however, because they are the works of people who worshiped many gods or who did not believe in God.

During the Middle Ages, few classics were produced and most ancient classics were forgotten. The *Italian Renaissance* revived interest in the works of the ancient Greeks and Romans, whose many pagan ideas led many scholars and artists into the trap of humanism, emphasizing man and ignoring God. With the exception of some great artistic geniuses like Michelangelo, Raphael, and Leonardo da Vinci, the Renaissance Italians did not produce many lasting works.

The great **modern classics** began with the *Northern Renaissance* and the *Protestant Reformation.* The return to the Bible gave men a new sense of responsibility and brought forth an outburst of individual creativity such as the world had never known. All of the great music in the world, with the exception of a few traditional songs, has been written in the past 500 years. At least 90% of the world's great books have been written since 1500, and many of the world's great works of painting and architecture are unique products of the Modern Age.

Evaluating Works of Art

Not every work of art, music, and literature produced in the Modern Age is good, of course. Many are tainted with ideas that reveal man's continued rebellion against God. Because of the variety and wide availability of art, music, and reading material in the Modern Age, we are responsible to carefully choose which works we allow to influence us.

In general, the modern classics possess a greater purity than the ancient classics and modern "popular" works. **Popular works** are *works created for the pleasure of the moment rather than for the ages.* They are usually created by people who do not have the sense of responsibility for the future that classical artists had. In literature, they include sensational, poorly written novels. Popular music includes rock music, modern "folk" music, "easy listening" music, and

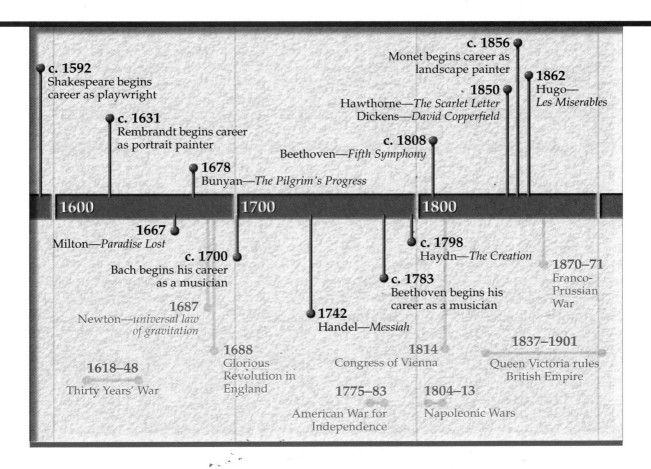

c. 1592
Shakespeare begins
career as playwright

c. 1631
Rembrandt begins career
as portrait painter

1678
Bunyan—*The Pilgrim's Progress*

c. 1856
Monet begins career as
landscape painter

1850
Hawthorne—*The Scarlet Letter*
Dickens—*David Copperfield*

1862
Hugo—
Les Miserables

c. 1808
Beethoven—*Fifth Symphony*

1600 **1700** **1800**

1667
Milton—*Paradise Lost*

c. 1700
Bach begins his career
as a musician

1687
Newton—*universal law
of gravitation*

1742
Handel—*Messiah*

c. 1798
Haydn—*The Creation*

c. 1783
Beethoven begins his
career as a musician

1870–71
Franco-
Prussian
War

1688
Glorious
Revolution in
England

1814
Congress of Vienna

1837–1901
Queen Victoria rules
British Empire

1618–48
Thirty Years' War

1775–83
American War for
Independence

1804–13
Napoleonic Wars

country music. <u>The classics are also popular, of course, but their popularity lasts through the ages, not just for the moment.</u>

Choosing the Best
Even the modern classics should be chosen with care; some of them should be handled the way a chemist handles poison—to evaluate their contents but not to let them get into one's blood. All human works should be evaluated in light of *the greatest classic of all,* the **Word of God,** which is *the* book for all people of all times, the *one* source of truth untainted by error. When we evaluate man's work according to the Scriptures, we will be able to choose things that are true, honest, just, pure, lovely, and of good report, works full of virtue and worthy of praise, and we will want to "think on these things" (Phil. 4:8).

Music in the Modern Age

Medieval Music
The greatest music in the history of the world has been written in the Modern Age. Much of the music of the Modern Age has been decisively influenced by Biblical Christianity, particularly by the Protestant Reformation, which brought the Bible to the people.

In the churches. In the Middle Ages, the established church controlled the music, allowing only the priests, professional musicians, and choirs to sing in the services. Church music was meant to give the people a "religious experience" by creating a mystical mood. Early Roman church music was based on the **Gregorian chant,** which was originally an unaccompanied line of melody with no harmony.

Because the lyrics of the chants were in Latin, they were unintelligible to the congregation. The droning of the monks created an eerie, other-worldly effect, keeping the congregation from personal worship in the church. The chant became the most important musical form used by the Catholic church.

Throughout the week. For pleasure, the men of the Middle Ages turned to secular songs written for them in their own languages. **Minstrels,** professional musicians who wandered from town to town and castle to castle, sang ballads and poems recounting the deeds of national heroes. In southern France, these minstrels were called *troubadours* [trōō′ba·dŏōrz]; in Germany, they were called *meistersingers* [mīs′tĕr·sĭng′ĕrz].

Reformation Music

Martin Luther, the leader of the Protestant Reformation, was himself a singer and composer who highly valued the educational and moral power of music. "Music is a gift of God, not a gift of men," he said. ". . . After theology, I accord to music the highest place and greatest honor." Luther strongly believed that the congregation should take an active part in the music of the church services. He knew that in order to do this, the people needed music they could sing and understand. To meet this need, Luther began writing hymns. He explained,

I wish to make German psalms for the people, that is to say sacred hymns, so that the Word of God may swell among the people also by means of song.

Luther adopted much of the traditional music of the church, changing words and ideas to conform to his understanding of Scripture. But by far his most original and lasting musical achievements were his hymns or **chorales** [kō′ralz]. Luther wrote

23 original hymns and a number of translations and adaptations. He also encouraged the German people to develop a skill for poetry in order to write hymns to the glory of God. The Germans rose to the challenge, and in 1546 the preface to a hymnal said that in the Protestant part of Germany "there is scarcely a pastor or shoemaker who lacks the skill to make a little song or tune to sing at church with his neighbors."

Seventeenth-Century Music

Germany, the birthplace of the Reformation, became the musical center of the world and produced the world's greatest musicians. Germany's musicians were greatly influenced by the Italian musicians **Monteverdi** [mōn′tâ·vär′dê: 1567–1643], who created the *opera* form; **Vivaldi** [vê·väl′dê: 1675?–1741], who developed instrumental music; and **Corelli** [kô·rĕl′lê: 1653–1713], who founded the classical technique of violin playing.

The three leading German musicians of the Post-Reformation period were Heinrich Schütz, Johann Sebastian Bach, and George Frederick Handel. **Heinrich Schütz** [shüts: 1585–1672], the most important composer before Bach, wrote a collection of **madrigals** (songs). His greatest contribution, however, is his church music, for which he used the Bible as his text.

Johann Sebastian Bach [bäk: 1735–1782] became one of history's greatest composers. Bach believed that everything

Johann Sebastian Bach

George Frederick Handel

Isaac Watts

should be done *"to the glory of God."* He said that the aim of music is "to produce a well-sounding harmony to the glory of God and the permissible delight of the spirit." Bach composed in almost all the musical forms of his day, bringing together German, Italian, and French styles and raising them to an unprecedented level of perfection.

Early in his musical career, **George Frederick Handel** (1685–1759) became interested in opera. After studying in Hamburg, the center of opera in Germany, he wrote his first opera at the age of 19. It was not until he was in his mid-50s and living in England that he discovered the *oratorio,* a sacred choral (choir) work often using a Biblical text. Handel perfected the form and wrote several oratorios. By far, his best-loved oratorio is the *Messiah,* a masterpiece which he wrote in 24 days. The **"Hallelujah Chorus"** in the *Messiah* is perhaps the best-known choir piece in the world. When King George II first heard the *Messiah,* he rose to his feet in deep respect during the "Hallelujah Chorus," beginning a tradition still followed today.

Isaac Watts: Father of the English Hymn

The English churches had no hymnals and no Martin Luther to give them songs in their own language. Englishmen had only the old Latin songs (which were banned in England for a period of time) and the psalters (versions of the Psalms set to music.)

Isaac Watts (1674–1748), the "Father of the English Hymn," revived the music of the church. Watts grew up in a noncon-formist (Dissenter) church where the psalter was used. As a young man, he criticized the psalters for their lack of depth and beauty. One such psalm read,

Ye monsters of the bubbling deep,
Your maker's praise spout out
Up from the sands ye codlings peep,
And wag your tails about.

Watts determined to give the people something better, and the next Sunday evening the congregation sang his first hymn. He continued to supply the congre-gation with a new hymn every Sunday night thereafter, until he had produced over 200 hymns. Of the more than *600 hymns* Watts wrote in his lifetime, many are still favorites today, including **"When I Survey the Wondrous Cross," "Joy to the World," "O God Our Help in Ages Past,"** and **"Alas, and Did My Savior Bleed."**

Eighteenth-Century Classical Music

The two leading musicians of the late 18th century, Franz Joseph Haydn and Wolfgang Amadeus Mozart, established what is called the **classical style.** **Franz Joseph Haydn** [hī'd'n: 1732–1809], an Austrian, wrote about a hundred symphonies and two notable oratorios, *The Creation* and *The Seasons.* He is *best known for writing cheerful music for the church.* When criticized for his cheerfulness, Haydn explained that at the thought of God his heart "leaped for joy." One familiar hymn sung to Haydn's music is "Glorious Things of Thee Are Spoken." (The words are by the English hymn writer John Newton, famous for "Amazing Grace.")

Wolfgang Amadeus Mozart [mō'tsärt: 1756–1791], another Austrian, was a *child prodigy* (a child of highly unusual talent or genius). At three, he amused himself at the piano; at four he began music lessons; at five he composed his first pieces; at seven he made a grand tour of Europe, performing in the musical centers of the day; at nine he wrote his first symphony; and at 11 he wrote his first opera. By the time he was 13, Mozart had mastered all musical forms. In addition to piano **concertos** and **sonatas,** Mozart wrote between 40 and 50 symphonies and several famous operas including *The Magic Flute* and *The Marriage of Figaro.*

Franz Joseph Haydn

Nineteenth-Century Music

The climax of modern music came in the 19th century with the work of German composer **Ludwig van Beethoven** [bā'tōv'en: 1770–1827], who perfected the symphony form in his masterpieces. While still a young musician, Beethoven realized that he was developing the most serious handicap that could befall a musician—he was becoming deaf. But he did not give up; his deafness made him all the more determined to excel as a musician. Because Beethoven did overcome the obstacles against him, he is still remembered today for his great works.

Beethoven's **symphonies** mark the highest point in the development of the symphony form. The **Fifth Symphony** is perhaps best known of all, especially its four opening notes—three short and one long—which have become symbolic of victory.

Young Mozart at Vienna

Ludwig van Beethoven

Beethoven's **Ninth Symphony,** his last and most unusual, employs a chorus and soloists in the finale (ending). The choral setting is from the German writer Friedrich von Schiller's poem "Ode to Joy," which expresses the idea of the common nature of all men and the joy in which all men can participate. This theme particularly appealed to Beethoven, whose deafness made it difficult for him to participate in joy and fellowship with others. When the Ninth

Symphony was first performed, the audience applauded enthusiastically and waved their hats and handkerchiefs, but Beethoven had his back to them and could not hear. A soloist took him by the sleeve and turned him around so he could see the audience's response; then he bowed.

Before Beethoven, music which had a written message (an opera, a cantata, or a song) was considered superior to purely instrumental music (a sonata, concerto, or symphony). But during Beethoven's time, instrumental music became as important as vocal music for the first time in history, and people learned to enjoy the music itself, independent of words.

An explosion of individual effort and creativity in music followed Beethoven. Musical instruments were improved, and with the rise in music schools, musicians became more skillful. There was a shift in music from the courts and churches to the concert hall. Greater emphasis was placed on expression of emotion and on individuals

Great Musicians of the 19th and 20th Centuries

Ludwig van Beethoven (1770–1827)	Germany	famous for his Fifth Symphony and many others
Franz Schubert (1797–1828)	Germany	famous for his symphonies
Felix Mendelssohn (1809–1847)	Germany	famous for his oratorio *Elijah* and many symphonies
Robert Schumann (1810–1856)	Germany	famous for his piano music
Frederic Chopin (1810–1849)	Poland	famous for his piano music
Franz Liszt (1811–1886)	Hungary	famous for his Hungarian Rhapsodies
Johannes Brahms (1833–1897)	Germany	famous for his "Lullaby" and *A German Requiem*
Peter Ilich Tchaikovsky (1840–1893)	Russia	famous for his *1812 Overture* and the ballets *Swan Lake*, *Sleeping Beauty*, and *The Nutcracker*
Edward Grieg (1843–1907)	Norway	famous for his *Peer Gynt Suite*, an orchestral composition
Claude Debussy (1862–1918)	France	famous for "Clair de Lune" and other orchestral works
Sergei Rachmaninoff (1873–1943)	Russia	famous for his Second Piano Concerto and his second symphony

and soloists rather than the chorus. Songs and piano pieces with melodies that were easy to sing and play became increasingly popular.

Twentieth-Century Music

There are many 20th-century musicians whose works enjoy wide appreciation. Which works will become classics we do not know for sure yet, for a classic is a work that has stood the test of time. The 20th century has also brought forward much "popular" music, particularly rock music, which, with its anti-intellectual emphasis on sensuality, has become a symbol of the times.

CHECK UP

1. What is a classic? With what two movements did the modern classics begin?
2. What are popular works? How do they differ from the classics?
3. How should all human works be evaluated?
4. What was the Gregorian chant? Why could the people not understand the lyrics?
5. What was Martin Luther's most lasting contribution to music?
6. What country produced the world's greatest musicians?
7. Name three influential Italian musicians and the contributions of each.
8. Name the three leading German musicians of the Post-Reformation Period and briefly state what each man was known for.
9. Name the two leading musicians who established the classical style and briefly state what each man was known for.
10. What musician's work marked the climax of modern music in the 19th century? What physical condition did he overcome?

Identify: minstrel, troubadour, meistersinger, madrigal, oratorio, Isaac Watts

---

Art in the Modern Age

Through the ages, men have created paintings, sculptures, and works of architecture to please the eye and to reflect their understanding of the world. With its emphasis on the importance of the individual and on a greater awareness of the physical universe, the Modern Age has produced some of the greatest art the world has ever known.

The 16th Century

Dürer. Art in the Modern Age began in 16th-century Germany with **Albrecht Dürer** [dü′rẽr: 1471–1528]. Dürer was born in Nuremberg, Germany, and was first trained as a goldsmith like his father. After he mastered the goldsmith's art of engraving, he was apprenticed to a painter and woodcutter from whom he learned to use the pen and brush, to work with watercolor and oils, and to develop the art of **woodcutting** (making prints by engraving designs on wooden blocks).

Dürer's paintings show his concern with accurately portraying nature. Many, however, believe that Dürer's engravings such as *The Prodigal Son* are his greatest achieve-

The Prodigal Son by Dürer

Dürer and the Praying Hands

According to an interesting legend, when Dürer was young and unknown, he lived with another struggling artist. Both men were trying to become great artists and keep food on the table at the same time. Finally, Dürer's partner said, "One of us should work full time to earn money for rent and food while the other concentrates on developing his skill as an artist. I will work while you produce art; then, when your art becomes famous and you become wealthy, you will be able to support me." So Dürer trained as an artist while his partner worked in a restaurant. And Dürer *did* become famous; soon he was making enough money to allow his partner to quit the hard manual labor. But the hard work had made the artist's hands rough and calloused. No longer could he hold a brush and make it do wonderful things on a canvas. His career as an artist was over. Dürer felt responsible

Praying Hands by Dürer

for his friend's loss and promised to provide his friend with food and shelter for the rest of his life. One day when Dürer came home, he found his friend praying. As Dürer saw his friend's rugged hands folded in prayer, he was moved by the beauty and dignity of the scene. He drew a picture of the praying hands, and that picture has become Dürer's most famous work.

ment. He was able to make prints from his woodcuts and engraved etchings and make them available to the public. For the first time in history, men and women of ordinary means could own art in the form of prints; this was art for the people. Dürer made art realistic and human. Even today people who know very little about art are probably familiar with Dürer's most popular work, *Hands of an Apostle* (sometimes called *Praying Hands*).

Holbein. One of the greatest <u>portrait painters</u> of all times was German artist **Hans Holbein the Younger** [hōl′bīn: 1497–1543]. Holbein spent much of his life at the court of King Henry VIII of England. There he painted portraits of Henry and his wives

and even designed court fashions. (See page 246 for Holbein's portrait of Henry VIII.) Holbein painted his greatest works while at Henry's court. He was the last of the German Renaissance painters and certainly one of the best.

Edward VI of England by Holbein

The Supper at Emmaus
by Rembrandt

Rembrandt
van Rijn
(self-portrait)

The 17th Century

Rembrandt. Some of the most famous artists of the Modern Age have come from Holland. *The greatest of the many Dutch masters,* **Rembrandt van Rijn** [rĕm′brănt vän rīn′: 1606–1669], was one of the greatest painters of all times. Rembrandt, known for his paintings, drawings, and etchings, used his art to probe into the soul of man. His use of light and shadow and color in his works was unparalleled in his time. Rembrandt's greatest achievements were his realistic illustrations of <u>Biblical scenes</u>. In one of his paintings of the crucifixion, Rembrandt included himself in the scene, making Christ's death on the cross personal (see page 115).

Vermeer. While Rembrandt was painting in Amsterdam, another accomplished Dutch master was painting in Delft, Holland—**Jan Vermeer** [vĕr•mār: 1632–1675]. Vermeer produced only a few paintings, but they are excellent. His best works were his <u>landscapes</u>, but he is also known for painting <u>interiors</u> of middle-class Dutch homes. Vermeer presented pictures of tranquil domestic scenes enhanced by subtle lighting from an open window, usually placed at the far left of the composition.

Young Woman with a
Water Jug by Vermeer

The Grace by Chardin

Industry and Idleness *by Hogarth*

The 18th Century

Hogarth. Influenced by the Dutch painters of the 17th century as well as his French contemporaries, **William Hogarth** [hō'gärth: 1697–1764] became one of the most important artists in England in the 18th century. Living in the great age of satirical writing, Hogarth became a master of satirical painting. Many of his works portray the manners and morals of the English middle class of his day, showing why England was in need of spiritual revival in the days of Wesley and Whitefield. It was actually his engravings, and not his paintings, that brought Hogarth popularity in his lifetime. Hogarth was the first artist to secure a copyright to protect his engravings from being copied by others.

Chardin. In the tradition of the Dutch masters of the preceding century, **Jean-Baptiste-Siméon Chardin** [shär'dăn': 1699–1779] chose subjects from his daily world and, using his acute powers of observation, rendered them in a peaceful, controlled manner. His paintings capture the simple, natural beauty of common scenes.

The 19th Century

Neoclassicism. The 19th century is characterized by a revolutionary series of movements in art, all of which were mainly centered in France. The first great artist of the late 18th and early 19th century was the Frenchman **Jacques Louis David** [dä'vēd': 1748–1825], who lived during the French Revolution. Perhaps his most famous painting is *The Oath of the Tennis Court,* which shows the members of the National Assembly swearing to establish a constitution (see page 337). Those who followed David and believed that France should use classical Rome as a model were called **Neoclassicists.** Neoclassic paintings were clear and balanced and used simple forms and bright colors.

Romanticism. Another important French painter was **Eugène Delacroix** [dĕ·là'krwä': 1798–1863] who depicted the great individuals of his age as romantic heroes. With Delacroix, the emphasis of art shifted from reason to passion and imagination. Delacroix is considered to be the major leader of the Romantic tradition of painting, which began in the 1830s. **Romanticism** is characterized by a reaction against the balanced, orderly, Neoclassical style, the expression of emotion for its own sake, and the representation of exotic locations.

Realism. The next great painter to contribute significantly to the history of art was **Gustave Courbet** [koor'bě': 1819–1877], who developed a new philosophy of painting. Courbet believed that the artist should paint the things around him as they really are. He became the leader of a movement known as **Realism**. Realistic art is concerned with the incidental and the momentary as opposed to classical art which deals with the universal and the typical.

Impressionists. Toward the end of the 19th century, the **Impressionist** school became prominent. The Impressionists attempted to show the ever-changing reality of a particular moment by emphasizing the minute details of the effect of changing light. They used light colors, predominantly white, and they avoided black altogether, creating a sensation of freshness. Some of the best known Impressionists are Frenchmen *Pierre Auguste Renoir* [rě·nwår': 1841–1919] and *Claude Monet* [mô'ně': 1840–1926], and the Dutch painter *Vincent van Gogh* [văn·gō': 1853–1890].

The 20th Century

Artists in the 20th century have continued to produce a wide variety of beautiful works. However, many modern artists have expressed a disturbing attempt to escape from reason, order, and reality. In their works, they express the rebellion, immorality, pride, and delusion that God said would characterize the last days (2 Tim. 3:1–7).

Great Artists of the 19th and 20th Centuries

Jacques Louis David (1748–1825)	France	famous for *The Oath of the Tennis Court* and other Neoclassical paintings
J. M. W. Turner (1775–1851)	England	famous for his paintings of seascapes
John Constable (1776–1837)	England	famous for his paintings of English countryside
Eugène Delacroix (1798–1863)	France	famous for *The Lion Hunt* and other Romantic paintings
Honoré Daumier (1808–1875)	France	famous for his political cartoons
Gustave Courbet (1819–1877)	France	famous for *The Stone Breakers* and other Realistic paintings
Paul Cézanne (1839–1906)	France	famous for his emphasis of the geometrical forms of everyday objects
Claude Monet (1840–1926)	France	famous for Impressionistic paintings of outdoor scenes
Pierre Auguste Renoir (1841–1919)	France	famous for Impressionistic paintings of happy scenes
Vincent van Gogh (1853–1890)	Holland	famous for his Impressionistic paintings of common, everyday scenes

*The Bridge
at Argenteuil
by Monet*

CHECK UP

1. With whom did art in the Modern Age begin? What is his most popular work?
2. Who was the greatest of the Dutch masters? What were this artist's greatest achievements?
3. Who was one of the most important artists in England in the 18th century? What was he known for?
4. Describe the paintings of Jean-Baptiste-Siméon Chardin.
5. Who were the Neoclassicists? Name a leader of the Neoclassical movement.
6. What was Romanticism? Name a leader of the Romantic movement.
7. What was Gustave Courbet's philosophy of painting?
8. Who were the Impressionists? What type of colors did they use in their paintings? Name three of the best-known Impressionists.

Identify: Hans Holbein the Younger, woodcutting, Jan Vermeer

Literature in the Modern Age

An Age of Classics

The Modern Age has been a time of great advances in literature. Until Gutenberg's invention of the printing press about 1440, books as we know them today were not available. The only reading material consisted of ancient manuscripts copied by monks and kept in the monasteries. The average man, even if he had been able to read, had no interest in such manuscripts.

Almost all the great classics of world literature have been written during the Modern Age. Books from many nations and cultures teach us that human nature is the same the world over. They help bridge the gap between people of different races, religions, and backgrounds, expanding our knowledge and developing our appreciation for the God Who created all mankind.

Since Gutenberg's time, great literature has rolled from the presses of the world. Although some of what has been printed has been bad, much of it has been good. The first book produced on Gutenberg's press was the Bible, the only source of truth unmixed with error. The great classics of world literature should be judged according to their relationship to that one Book. Some have been produced in defiance of the Scriptures, but those that have stood the test of time and are still read by great numbers of people today are for the most part the products of people and nations that have honored the Scriptures.

The 17th Century

After the Reformation, the English people had access to the Bible and enjoyed freedom as never before. For this reason, some of the greatest classics of modern literature have come from England.

Shakespeare. During the Elizabethan Age, **William Shakespeare** (1564–1635) began his 20-year career as a playwright. Shakespeare has been called <u>the greatest writer the world has ever known</u>. With the exception of the Bible, Shakespeare's plays have surpassed all other works in molding modern thought. Even those who have never read his plays cannot escape his

Great Writers of the 19th and 20th Centuries

Johann von Goethe (1749–1832)	Germany	famous for *Faust* and other plays and poems
Johann von Schiller (1759–1805)	Germany	famous for *William Tell* and other plays and poems
William Wordsworth (1770–1850)	England	famous for *Lyrical Ballads* and other poems
Jacob and Wilhelm Grimm (1785–1863) and (1786–1859)	Germany	famous for "Cinderella" and other fairy tales
Victor Hugo (1802–1885)	France	famous for *Les Miserables* and other novels
Ralph Waldo Emerson (1803–1882)	America	famous for "Concord Hymn" and other poems
Nathaniel Hawthorne (1804–1864)	America	famous for *The Scarlet Letter* and other stories
Hans Christian Andersen (1805–1875)	Denmark	famous for "The Ugly Duckling" and other fairy tales
Henry Wadsworth Longfellow (1807–1882)	America	famous for *The Song of Hiawatha* and other poems
Edgar Allan Poe (1809–1849)	America	famous for "The Raven" and other poems as well as short stories
Alfred, Lord Tennyson (1809–1892)	England	famous for *In Memoriam* and other poems
Robert Browning (1812–1889)	England	famous for *Pippa Passes* and other poems
Charles Dickens (1812–1870)	England	famous for *David Copperfield* and other stories
Herman Melville (1819–1891)	America	famous for *Moby Dick* and other stories
George Eliot (1819–1880)	England	famous for *Silas Marner* and other stories
Fyodor Dostoevsky (1821–1881)	Russia	famous for *Crime and Punishment* and other novels
Leo Tolstoy (1828–1910)	Russia	famous for *War and Peace* and other novels
Rudyard Kipling (1865–1936)	England	famous for *The Jungle Book* and other stories and poems

influence, for he has affected the English language. Everyone has heard the familiar lines "What's in a name" and "To be or not to be—that is the question." Shakespeare's plays and poems are great because he understood human nature and was able to show the feelings and thoughts of men in general.

Milton. After Shakespeare, the next greatest English writer of modern times was **John Milton** (1608–1674). In his prose, Milton became a great champion for freedom of the press and for liberty in the church and state. However, he is best-known for his literary masterpiece *Paradise Lost, the greatest poem in the English language.* Like Shakespeare's plays, *Paradise Lost* has deeply influenced thought in the Modern Age.

Bunyan. Though poor, uneducated, and from a humble family, **John Bunyan** (1628–1688) produced the world's most popular and beloved allegory, *Pilgrim's Progress.* Bunyan wrote the book while in jail for preaching without a license from the Church of England. *Pilgrim's Progress* has been read more than any other book in the English language apart from the Bible itself.

The 18th Century

With the decline of religion in 18th-century England came a decline in literature. As the English people discarded the Biblical ideas of the Puritans, moral degradation, ignorance, and crime became the rule rather than the exception. In this period before the great revivals of Wesley and Whitefield, many English writers began to imitate French authors who found their inspiration in the ancient works of Greece and Rome. Thus, many of their works are tainted with Deism, humanism, and atheism. Poetry in rhymed couplets, plays following strict rules, and satire became favorite forms. *Alexander Pope*

(1688–1744), the greatest poet of the 18th century, is known for perfecting satirical verse. *Daniel Defoe* (1667–1745), one of the first English novelists, also wrote during the 18th century. Defoe is probably best known for his *Adventures of Robinson Crusoe,* which reflects his Puritan upbringing.

The 19th and 20th Centuries

The 19th century was an era of great development and expansion in literature. A new interest in nature led to the development of **Romantic Poetry,** which was characterized by a concern for the beauty and power of nature, an emphasis on feeling, and the use of rich, vivid imagery and figurative language. The 19th century also produced many classic novels and short stories. The proliferation of literature continued into the 20th century and then began to decline as evolution, modernism (religious liberalism), and other false philosophies took root in Europe and America.

CHECK UP

1. What was the first book printed on Gutenberg's printing press?
2. Who has been called the greatest writer the world has ever known? What makes his plays and poems great?
3. What poem is considered by many to be the greatest poem in the English language? Who wrote it?
4. Who produced the world's most popular and beloved allegory? Name the allegory.
5. Describe literature in the 18th century.
6. What caused the decline of modern literature in the 20th century?

Identify: Alexander Pope, Daniel Defoe, Romantic poetry

CHAPTER 20 REVIEW

MULTIPLE CHOICE   Write the letter of the answer that best completes the sentence.

1. Martin Luther was known for his
   _____.
   - a chants
   - b chorales
   - c operas
   - d oratorios

2. _____ created the opera form.
   - a Vivaldi
   - b Corelli
   - c Schütz
   - d Monteverdi

3. The musician who believed that everything should be done "to the glory of God" was _____.
   - a Johann Sebastian Bach
   - b George Frederick Handel
   - c Monteverdi
   - d Corelli

4. _____ wrote the *Messiah* oratorio in 24 days.
   - a Johann Sebastian Bach
   - b George Frederick Handel
   - c Monteverdi
   - d Corelli

5. _____ was the "Father of the English hymn."
   - a Franz Joseph Haydn
   - b Wolfgang Amadeus Mozart
   - c Isaac Watts
   - d Martin Luther

6. The musician who was a child prodigy was _____.
   - a Franz Joseph Haydn
   - b Wolfgang Amadeus Mozart
   - c Isaac Watts
   - d Martin Luther

7. The climax of modern music came in the 19th century with the work of German composer _____.
   - a Ludwig van Beethoven
   - b Franz Joseph Haydn
   - c Wolfgang Amadeus Mozart
   - d Isaac Watts

8. Art in the Modern Age began in 16th-century Germany with _____.
   - a Hans Holbein the Younger
   - b Albrecht Dürer
   - c Rembrandt van Rijn
   - d Jan Vermeer

9. _____ was the greatest of the Dutch masters in the 17th century.
   - a Hans Holbein the Younger
   - b Albrecht Dürer
   - c Rembrandt van Rijn
   - d Jan Vermeer

10. _____ was the greatest writer the world has ever known.
    - a John Bunyan
    - b William Shakespeare
    - c John Milton
    - d Alexander Pope

11. _____ wrote *Paradise Lost,* the greatest poem in the English language.
    - a John Bunyan
    - b William Shakespeare
    - c John Milton
    - d Alexander Pope

12. _____ produced the world's most popular and beloved allegory, *Pilgrim's Progress.*
    - a John Bunyan
    - b William Shakespeare
    - c John Milton
    - d Alexander Pope

13. _____ was the greatest poet of the 18th century.
    - a John Bunyan
    - b William Shakespeare
    - c John Milton
    - d Alexander Pope

COMPLETION *Choose the correct term to complete each sentence and write the letter in the blank.*

a Bible
b Impressionists
c classic
d oratorio

e Realistic art
f woodcutting
g Romanticism
h popular works

i minstrels
j Neoclassicists
k Protestant Reformation
l Gregorian chant

1. A ____ is a work of superior excellence that has stood the test of time.

2. Modern classics began with the Northern Renaissance and the ____.

3. ____ are works created for the pleasure of the moment rather than for the ages.

4. The greatest classic of all is the ____.

5. The ____ became the most common form of music in the Roman church during the Middle Ages.

6. ____ were professional musicians who wandered from town to town and castle to castle, singing ballads and poems recounting the deeds of national heroes.

7. A(n)____ is a sacred choral work often using a Biblical text.

8. ____ is the art of making prints by engraving designs on wooden blocks.

9. Those who believed that France should use classical Rome as a model were called ____.

10. ____ is characterized by a reaction against the balanced, orderly, Neoclassical style, the expression of emotion for its own sake, and the representation of exotic locations.

11. ____ is concerned with the incidental and the momentary as opposed to classical art which deals with the universal and the typical.

12. The ____ attempted to show the ever-changing reality of a particular moment by emphasizing the minute details of the effect of changing light.

CONCEPT TO CONSIDER *On a separate sheet of paper, answer the following question using complete sentences.*

Why have more classics been produced in the Modern Age than during any other time in history?

21
The British Empire:
Asia, Africa, and Australia

HIGHLIGHTS

Queen Victoria • The British Empire • India and the Far East
Africa • Australia and New Zealand • Canada
Christianity in Victorian England

England's Age of Progress

England Enters the 19th Century

By the 19th century, England was rapidly becoming the leading nation of the world, largely because the Industrial Revolution of the late 18th century had made her the wealthiest country in Europe. As England spread her dominion to many lands, she shared her representative form of government with them as well as her Christian heritage.

The great Wesleyan Revival of the 18th century had stirred the hearts of many Christians in England to spread the gospel by means of widespread missionary efforts. As Englishmen came to understand the worth of all men, regardless of their family background and economic status, they also became concerned about their less-fortunate countrymen. The "reformation of morals" that came in the wake of the revival led many upper class Englishmen to voluntarily help the poor and needy.

Thus, while most of Europe was wracked by violent revolutions during the 19th century, England was able to bring about peaceful reforms through the benevolence of her people and the workings of her Parliament. Nineteenth-century England was noted for its progress toward more **representative government,** the establishment of **religious toleration,** and the growth of the **British Empire.** It is also known for the reign of **Queen Victoria,** the *longest-ruling monarch in English history.*

Rulers of England (1714–1910)

George I (1714–1727)
George II (1727–1760)
George III (1760–1820)
George IV (1820–1830)
William IV (1830–1837)
Victoria (1837–1901)
Edward VII (1901–1910)

The Victorian Age (1837–1901)

Victoria's resolution. King William IV's niece Victoria (1819–1901) was just 11 years old when she learned that she would probably be England's next ruler. Knowing the sad state of the English monarchy under the Georges and her immoral uncle William, Victoria resolved that her reign would be different. *"I will be good,"* she declared. When Victoria was 18 years old, William IV died and the responsibilities of the crown fell to her. Throughout the 64 years of her reign she kept her childhood resolution, changing the people's view of the monarchy from one of disdain to one of respect and pride.

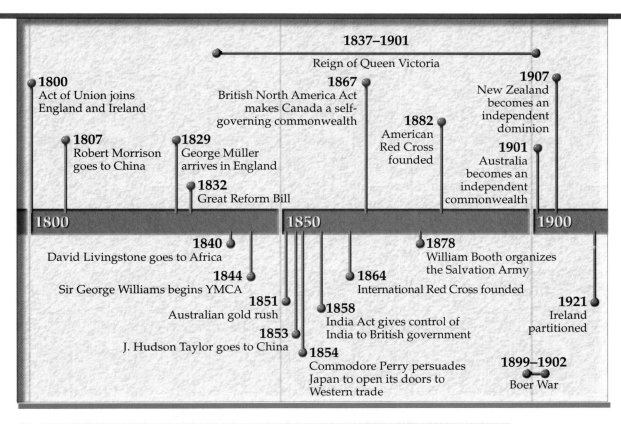

1837–1901
Reign of Queen Victoria

1800
Act of Union joins
England and Ireland

1807
Robert Morrison
goes to China

1829
George Müller
arrives in England

1832
Great Reform Bill

1867
British North America Act
makes Canada a self-
governing commonwealth

1882
American
Red Cross
founded

1907
New Zealand
becomes an
independent
dominion

1901
Australia
becomes an
independent
commonwealth

1800

1850

1900

1840
David Livingstone goes to Africa

1844
Sir George Williams begins YMCA

1851
Australian gold rush

1853
J. Hudson Taylor goes to China

1854
Commodore Perry persuades
Japan to open its doors to
Western trade

1858
India Act gives control of
India to British government

1864
International Red Cross founded

1878
William Booth organizes
the Salvation Army

1921
Ireland
partitioned

1899–1902
Boer War

Queen Victoria, answering the question of a visiting African prince, presented him a Bible and said, "Here is the secret of England's greatness."

409

The greatness of Victorian England. Under the wise leadership of Queen Victoria (ruled 1837–1901), Great Britain reached the height of its glory and became the leading country of the world. The British Empire covered a quarter of the globe and included about a quarter of the world's people, so that it could be said, ***"The sun never sets on the British Empire."*** Canada, Australia, New Zealand, India, South Africa, and many other parts of Africa and Asia belonged to the British Empire.

A policy of free trade and a worldwide reputation for honesty made England the world's leading manufacturing country, the wealthiest nation in the world, and the world's banker. The English pound sterling was the standard of international trade, and British merchant ships carried almost half the trade of the entire world. Victorian England has often been compared with the age of England's other great queen, Elizabeth I, for its expansion of knowledge and geographical dominion and for its high cultural achievements. So beloved was Queen Victoria by her sub-jects that British people still speak of the **Victorian Age** with respect and pride.

Victoria and Albert. In 1839, Queen Victoria married **Prince Albert** of Germany, who was called the *prince consort.* Their model marriage was an inspiration to the English people. Together, they had nine children—four sons and five daughters. Albert helped Victoria develop as queen by introducing her to leaders in the arts and sciences and encouraging her to do the "right thing." In 1861, Queen Victoria was severely shaken by the death of her beloved husband. The "Widow of Windsor" retreated to her castle and was seldom seen in either Parliament or London society. It remained for another man, much like Albert, to help her face her new life. **Benjamin Disraeli** [dĭz·rā′lē], perhaps more than any other prime minister, was especially regarded by Victoria. She was flattered by "Dizzy's" praise, cajoled by his humor, and influenced by his politics. He succeeded in returning her once again to London and the national limelight.

The secret of England's greatness. Queen Victoria and the people of Victorian

Queen Victoria and her family

England were not deluded into thinking that it was merely their own intelligence and diligence that had made their country great. Victoria spoke for the nation in her reply to a visiting African chief who asked her the secret of England's greatness. The queen did not take him to the Tower of London to see the glittering crown jewels or to hear the brilliant orators who debated in Parliament. Instead, she presented the chief with a Bible, and said, "Here is the secret of England's greatness."

Victoria—symbol of the nation. Victoria, perhaps more than any other individual, characterized the thoughts, beliefs, and attitudes of the majority of Englishmen in the 19th century. The rising middle class had taken over the nation, including the throne. They disapproved of the **Oxford Movement** (*the movement within the Church of England to reintroduce many Roman Catholic practices*); so did Victoria. They disliked the Irish and refused to allow them to rule themselves; so did Victoria. They experienced doubt when confronted with the rise of evolution and attacks on the Bible; so did Victoria. They loved the overly ornate style so abundant in their homes; Victoria redecorated her palaces in the new style. They were decidedly moral and domestic; Victoria and her husband Albert raised the level of morality at court and delighted in their "domestic home" and "the good example" it presented to the nation. Many of her subjects participated in charitable and philanthropic activities; Victoria out-did them all. In general, both the vices and virtues of the English middle class were hers as well. The life of the queen simply magnified the lives of millions of her subjects.

Progress toward Democracy

Gladstone and Disraeli. In the 1850s, Parliament was divided into two parties, called the Liberals and the Conservatives. The **Liberals** represented the middle class

of the Industrial Age. They sponsored reform to grant more rights to more people. The **Conservatives** represented the nobility and other wealthy people. They tended to oppose change and were hesitant to grant new political powers to the masses. Ironically, the most famous leaders of these two parties—William Gladstone and Benjamin Disraeli—both switched party affiliation before coming to their places of leadership. Disraeli and Gladstone alternated with one another as prime minister from 1867 to 1880.

Born to wealth and luxury, **William Gladstone** (1809–1898) was for a time a Conservative before joining the ranks of the Liberal party and fervently espousing the rights of the common man. Gladstone, who has been called *"The Grand Old Man,"* was known as a deeply religious man and a great orator. He was responsible for much political and social reform during his several terms as prime minister. It was said of him that during his lifetime "he was the one statesman to whom oppressed peoples turned in hope."

Benjamin Disraeli (1804–1881), of Jewish descent and lowly birth, swung from liberalism to become the renowned leader of the Conservative party. In spite of their hesitancy to change the political status quo, Disraeli and his Conservative party did sponsor certain reforms for the benefit of the masses.

Benjamin Disraeli   *William Gladstone*

Gladstone and Christianity

The leadership abilities of Prime Minister William Gladstone—his power of oratory, his desire to benefit the masses of his countrymen, and the sway he held over English politics for many years—can largely be attributed to his great respect for the Scriptures and the power of Christianity. "I have known 95 of the world's great men in my time," he once said, "and of these, 87 were followers of the Bible. The Bible is stamped with a specialty of origin, and an immeasurable distance separates it from all competitors."

The following tribute to Gladstone ends with Gladstone's tribute to Christianity.

The greatest modern statesman in Great Britain was, as everyone knows, William E. Gladstone. Gladstone was a classicist, a churchman, Christian, statesman, brilliant speaker, gentleman, gifted writer, intellectual giant, a man of great vision and flawless character, as men go. There was not a greater man in Europe during his premiership than Gladstone. He was emphatically a believer in every fundamental truth of the Christian faith, from the time of his youth to the time of his death. He spoke lovingly, humbly, and boldly, concerning Jesus Christ, and His salvation, and the truthfulness of the Word of God. Now there is one thing that Gladstone understood, and in which he played an enormous part, namely the affairs of state of a great empire.

Gladstone certainly knew what was for the welfare of men, and what worked for their hurt and harm. A man of his vast knowledge, and his place in a great government, has a right to speak with authority on the value of any powerful influence playing upon his nation. Let us then carefully consider Gladstone's own verdict concerning the influence of Christianity upon men. A verdict like this coming from a statesman who knew the problems of government and who always sought the welfare of the greatest number is worth ten verdicts of skeptical philosophers, who have never had to wrestle with the intricate problems of modern government:

"I say, then, choosing points of the most definitive character, that Christianity abolished (1) gladiatorial shows, and other spectacles of horrid cruelty to men; (2) human sacrifices; (3) polygamy; (4) exposure of children; (5) slavery (in its old form, and has nearly accomplished the work in its new); (6) cannibalism. Next, Christianity drove into the shade all unnatural lusts, and, indeed, all irregular passions. But the former it effectually stamped as infamous. Next, Christianity established (1) generally speaking, the moral and social equality of women; (2) the duty of relieving the poor, the sick and the afflicted; (3) peace, instead of war, as the ordinary, normal presumptive relation between nations. Here is a goodly list. I speak not of what it taught. It taught the law of mutual love." [1]

[1] Wilbur M. Smith, *Therefore Stand*, Grand Rapids: Baker Book House, 1945, 1974.

A model for the world. By the turn of the 20th century, England and America had become models for the world. Many nations aspired to copy the United States' political system, but many others aspired to copy the British system. British colonies, on the road to independence, had no thought of abandoning the mother country's system of government and longed to become "little Britains." Many of these colonies succeeded, and in the process came to enjoy the Christian influence that made Britain great.

Britain at the beginning of the 20th century was an example of a pure representative democracy. After the 1780s, the power of the British government lay with Parliament rather than with the monarch, and after 1911, it lay with the House of Commons, whose members were directly elected by the people.

CHECK UP

1. How was England different from most of Europe in the 19th century? For what four things was England noted in the 19th century?
2. Who was the longest-ruling monarch in English history? What did she resolve when she discovered she might become queen?
3. Who was her husband? Which prime minister had the greatest influence on her?
4. What was the secret of Victorian England's greatness?
5. Whom did the Liberals represent in 1850? the Conservatives? Who was the leader of the Liberals? of the Conservatives?

Identify: Victorian Age, Oxford Movement

England and Ireland

Religious issue. During the 19th century, the "Irish question" caused many debates in England. *The key issue preventing peace between England and Ireland has always been religion.* England has been Protestant since the days of Henry VIII, and Ireland has remained predominantly Catholic. Much of the bloodshed over the centuries has been the result of religious conflict. The greatest atrocity of England against the Catholic Irish came in 1649 under Oliver Cromwell's Puritan regime. With his passionate hatred of Catholicism running high, Cromwell determined to take revenge for the 1641 massacre of Protestant landlords by Irish Catholic peasants.

Cromwell himself led 10,000 troops upon the Irish Catholic strongholds of Drogheda and Wexford. He believed the complete slaughter of the garrisons would so frighten the Irish as to prevent any further bloodshed. Cromwell recorded that 2,000 men were put to death. Unfortunately, none of those killed had any connection with the past massacre. This atrocity more than any other incident seemed to make peaceful relations between Ireland and England in future generations next to impossible.

Attempts at reform. The 19th century brought great attempts on the part of certain Englishmen to pacify the Irish. In 1800, Parliament passed the **Act of Union,** which finally and officially joined England and Ireland. The Irish Parliament was abolished and Ireland was permitted to send

Protestant representatives to the British Parliament in London. Catholics could now hold land and had some religious freedom, but they still had no political representation. Anti-British feelings in Ireland were eased somewhat when Parliament passed the **Catholic Emancipation Act** in 1829, which, among other things, allowed Catholics to vote and to sit in Parliament. Irish representation in Parliament was expanded even further by the **Great Reform Bill** of 1832.

Gladstone's attempts. In the course of the 19th century, as England itself became more democratic, Englishmen became more concerned about correcting the grievances of Ireland. During his years as prime minister, William Gladstone worked endlessly to aid the Irish. When he first became prime minister in the late l860s, one of his first measures was to secure the disestablishment of the Anglican church in Ireland, so that Irish Catholics would no longer have to pay taxes to support an organization to which they did not belong. Gladstone also made several valiant attempts to get Parliament to establish home rule for Ireland, even at the expense of splitting his own party over the issue. But home rule was not to be obtained in his lifetime.

Ireland divided. In the 20th century, when the British Parliament finally consented to grant Ireland home rule, the six predominately Protestant counties of northeast Ulster were not interested in obtaining it. They preferred to remain a part of Protestant England. So in 1921, Ireland was partitioned. The bulk of

Ireland became the **Irish Free State,** with membership in the Commonwealth of Nations, and the six counties of **northeast Ulster** remained a part of the United Kingdom.

Independence. But even Commonwealth status did not satisfy many in the Irish Free State. Finally, in 1949, after a long, hard struggle, the Irish Free State became completely independent of the Commonwealth of Nations. Today it prefers to be called just **Ireland**. The six counties of Ulster are known as **Northern Ireland.**

Today Ireland and Northern Ireland continue to differ on certain issues, and both have shaky relations with England. Many Catholics in Northern Ireland are calling for its union with Ireland. In recent decades, violence in Northern Ireland has been a common occurrence.

The Growth of the British Empire

The British Empire expanded throughout the 19th century until it included territory in every region of the globe. Between 1880 and 1900 alone, *the great age of British imperialism,* nearly a million square miles of territory were added to the British Empire. The empire was a great benefit to Britain, and Britain was in many ways a great benefit to the lands in her dominion. While the colonies gave Britain wealth and power, Britain shared with her colonies its traditions of Christianity, technology, representative government, and reform.

Reasons for Expansion

Someone has said that Britain expanded her empire throughout the world for three reasons: **gold, God,** and **glory.** The *economic factors* were important from the very beginning. This was the golden age of British capitalism, and businessmen wanted raw materials to fuel their industries. They also wanted the open markets and the investment opportunities which the empire afforded them. The *religious factors* came next. At first, missionaries were denied access to the new territories for fear they would hurt business. Before long, however, the sincere Christian convictions of many Englishmen led them to promote missions in such a way that the 19th century became the **"Great Century of Missions."** The *patriotic factors* grew with the empire. Britons were intensely proud of their queen, their flag, their fleet, and their empire. The British people eagerly followed the growth of the empire. They were fascinated by stories of strange people, fantastic animals, and unusual geography and architecture, and by the exotic clothing and other goods that explorers brought back with them. The great expansion of their empire only increased their patriotic love of country.

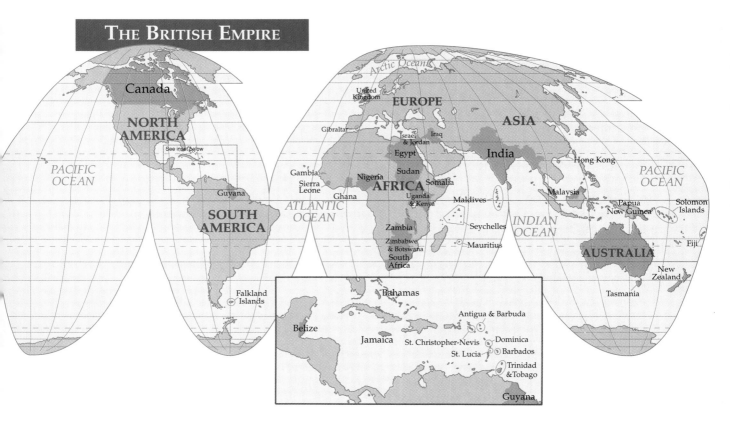

THE BRITISH EMPIRE

Asia: Colonization and Missions

India

The East India Company. The vast subcontinent of India was plagued by political unrest during the 18th century as the once great Mogul empire began to crumble. Both England and France took advantage of this unrest to stake claims in India. The *tool of British settlement* was the **East India Company,** a powerful trading company. The East India Company fought France to protect its territories in the 1750s (about this same time England and France were fighting the French and Indian War in North America). The British government aided the East India Company liberally but did not involve itself directly in the conflict. Government aid proved valuable: by 1760, England was the only European power left in India.

Sepoy Rebellion. But the people of India were not resigned to British rule, and various tribes caused problems for the East India Company. The government gradually acknowledged that the company was not capable of controlling India. By acts of Parliament in 1813, 1833, and 1853, the British government progressively reduced the power of the East India Company and assumed control of India itself. But the British government did not take complete control until a serious uprising called the **Sepoy Rebellion,** precipitated drastic action. The rebellion started among native soldiers in the British army and involved the age-old religious traditions of India. Believing that the British had little or no respect for their religious beliefs, they rebelled rather than violate their religion. The revolt soon spread beyond the bounds of the military. Many civilians shared the fears of the soldiers that British influences would weaken and finally destroy India's traditions and political autonomy. The British government quelled the rebellion and took measures to ensure that such an incident never happened again. In <u>1858</u>, the **India Act** wrested away the last vestiges of political authority from the East India Company and <u>gave full political control of India to the British government</u>.

Blending of East and West. England usually tried to respect the religious customs and traditions of India. Sometimes, however, a custom was so barbaric that it had to be stopped. A good example would be *suttee,* the practice of burning a widow alive along with her dead husband's body. Such cruelty shocked the British, and rightly so. The British ended such practices while preserving most traditions. Thus the culture of India was a blending of East and West, a mixing together of the time-hallowed old and the civilized new.

Missions in India. When **William Carey,** the *"Father of Modern Missions,"* went to India in 1793, he had to settle in Danish territory because of the hostility of the East India Company toward missions. Gradually, however, more and more British missionaries were able to settle in India and share the gospel with the Indian people. Another famous missionary to India, **Amy Carmichael** (1867–1951) of Ireland, worked for years to rescue young Indian girls from a life of prostitution in the pagan temples and to bring them to Christ and teach Indians the way of salvation. With the Bible came a written language, education, literature, and a more humane treatment of individuals.

The Far East

Both China and Japan were suspicious of any foreign influences. These countries, with their reverential love of the past and of tradition, were not eager to welcome the modern, totally alien cultures of Europe. Therefore, British colonization in the Orient was limited. One of the chief British possessions was **Hong Kong,** which occupies a tiny corner of the Asian continent.

Amy Carmichael

J. Hudson Taylor

China. China remained largely isolated from the West until the mid-1800s, when Britain forced the Chinese to open their ports to trade. China, with its tremendous population, was an obvious mission field. In 1807, a young Presbyterian minister, **Robert Morrison**, supported by the London Missionary Society, became the *first Protestant missionary in China.* The Chinese, steeped in pagan religion and resistant to anything that seemed to be "Western" or "non-Chinese," were unmoved by Morrison. In his 27 years in China, Morrison made only 10 converts! But he saw to it that a Chinese Bible was prepared and that schools were set up. Although he saw little increase himself, Morrison had prepared the way for future missions.

J. Hudson Taylor (1832–1905) of Yorkshire, England, went to China as a missionary in 1853. In 1865, he founded the *China Inland Mission.* Taylor was known for his complete dependence upon God for needed money and supplies. He appealed to others for prayer and new missionaries to aid the work, but never for money. He is often called the **"Father of Faith Missions."** By the beginning of the 20th century, Taylor and other missionaries had spread the gospel throughout China, and hundreds of thousands of Chinese had become Christians.

Japan. Like China, the island nation of Japan isolated itself from the West until the middle of the 19th century. Japan was opened to trade and missions not by British but by American efforts. In 1854, Commodore **Matthew Perry** persuaded Japan to open its doors to western trade, and in 1858, American ambassador **Townsend Harris** negotiated the treaty which bears his name, opening Japan to Christian missionaries. Thus, despite the fact that there was no open colonization of China and Japan, England enjoyed a vigorous trade with these nations, and many missionaries were able to labor there.

CHECK UP

1. What key issue has always prevented peace between England and Ireland? Explain.
2. Into what two sections was Ireland divided in the 20th century? What are they called today?
3. Explain the economic, religious, and patriotic factors of the expansion of the British Empire. What three words sum up these factors?
4. What influence did Christian missionaries have in India?
5. What Indian uprising led the British government to take over control of India? What act established this control?
6. Explain how East and West were blended in India.
7. Who was the first Protestant missionary to China? How did he prepare the way for future missionaries?
8. Who was the "Father of Faith Missions"? What mission did he found?
9. Describe how Japan was opened to trade and missions.

Identify: Act of Union, Catholic Emancipation Act, East India Company, William Carey, Amy Carmichael, Hong Kong

Africa in the Modern Age

Sahara Desert

At the dawn of the 19th century, Africa, the **Dark Continent,** remained by and large an unexplored mystery. But it was no mystery that Africa possessed a wealth of natural resources. The nations of Europe saw Africa as a vast treasure chest waiting to be opened. Though it is the <u>second largest continent</u> (second only to Asia), Africa has only recently begun to play a role in international affairs.

Physical Geography

The physical geography of Africa is dynamic, with magnificent contrasts of terrain and climate. Deserts and rain forests, towering mountains and humid valleys, steep plateaus, and active volcanoes can all be found in Africa.

Deserts. Most of Africa falls into one of three descriptive categories: desert, forest, or grassland. About ²/₅ of the continent is covered with **desert.** Few humans, animals, or plants are found in this wilderness. The **Sahara,** <u>the world's largest desert</u>, covers most of northern Africa. The **Kalahari** desert covers much of southern Africa.

Forests. A dense **forest** or jungle stretches across the center of the continent. Although frequent rainfall and high temperatures make this forest region of Africa very uncomfortable, it is a highly populated part of the continent.

Savannas. Between the deserts and forests are **savannas,** *vast tracts of grasses and small shrubs.* Here, there is enough rainfall to support bushes, shrubs, and tall grasses (some 12 feet tall), yet there is not enough to enable large trees to grow. Eastern central Africa is made up mostly of this type of terrain.

Rivers. Africa's rivers generally begin in the highlands and flow down to the sea. The **Nile River,** *the world's longest river,* begins in the tropical forest and flows

Savanna

northward to the **Mediterranean Sea.** The **Congo River** and the **Niger River** flow into the **Atlantic Ocean.** The **Limpopo River** and the **Zambezi River** drain eastern Africa and flow into the **Indian Ocean.** Most of these rivers begin in large freshwater lakes. **Lake Victoria** is *the source of the mighty Nile.* **Lake Tanganyika,** almost a mile deep, is a source of water for the Congo.

Mountains. In the northwest are the **Atlas Mountains,** Africa's longest mountain range. At the opposite end of the continent, the extreme southeast, are the rolling **Drakensberg Mountains.** Throughout Africa are other large peaks, such as **Mount Kilimanjaro** and **Mount Kenya,** both in central eastern Africa. These mountains have always proven to be barriers in the conquering of the African continent.

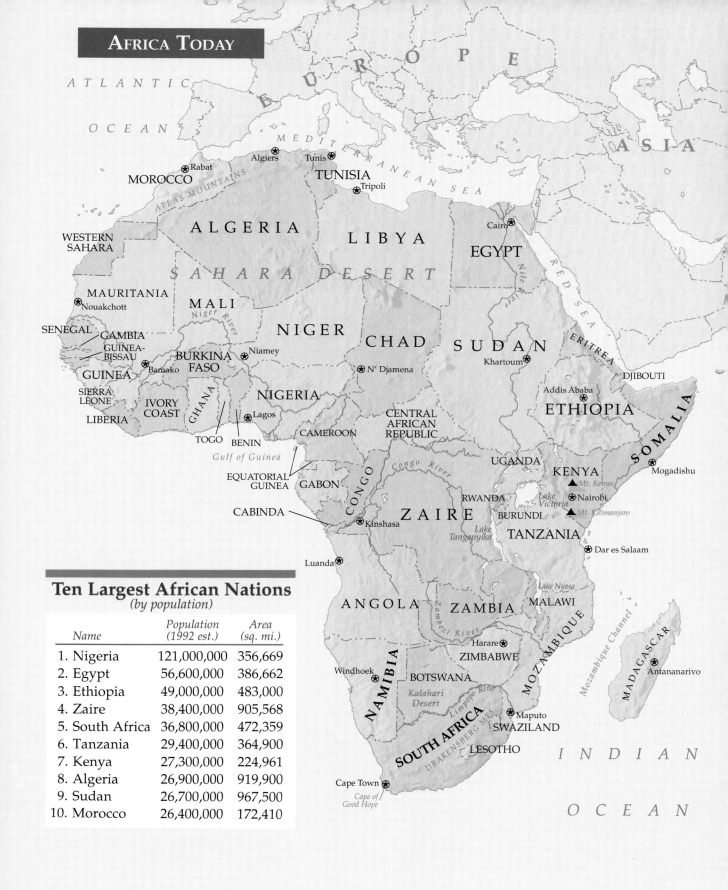

AFRICA TODAY

ATLANTIC

OCEAN

EUROPE

ASIA

MEDITERRANEAN SEA

⊛ Rabat
MOROCCO
⊛ Algiers
Tunis ⊛
TUNISIA
⊛ Tripoli

ATLAS MOUNTAINS

WESTERN
SAHARA

ALGERIA

LIBYA

EGYPT

⊛ Cairo

RED SEA

SAHARA DESERT

Nile River

MAURITANIA
⊛ Nouakchott

MALI

Niger River

NIGER

CHAD

SUDAN

⊛ Khartoum

ERITREA

SENEGAL
GAMBIA
GUINEA-
BISSAU
GUINEA

⊛ Bamako

BURKINA
FASO

⊛ Niamey

⊛ N' Djamena

DJIBOUTI

Addis Ababa ⊛

ETHIOPIA

SOMALIA

SIERRA
LEONE

IVORY
COAST

GHANA

NIGERIA

LIBERIA

TOGO   BENIN

⊛ Lagos

CAMEROON

CENTRAL
AFRICAN
REPUBLIC

⊛ Mogadishu

Gulf of Guinea

UGANDA

KENYA

▲ Mt. Kenya

EQUATORIAL
GUINEA

GABON

CONGO

Congo River

ZAIRE

RWANDA

BURUNDI

Lake
Victoria

⊛ Nairobi

▲ Mt. Kilimanjaro

CABINDA

⊛ Kinshasa

Lake
Tanganyika

TANZANIA

⊛ Dar es Salaam

Luanda ⊛

Lake Nyasa

MADAGASCAR

Ten Largest African Nations
(by population)

Name	Population (1992 est.)	Area (sq. mi.)
1. Nigeria	121,000,000	356,669
2. Egypt	56,600,000	386,662
3. Ethiopia	49,000,000	483,000
4. Zaire	38,400,000	905,568
5. South Africa	36,800,000	472,359
6. Tanzania	29,400,000	364,900
7. Kenya	27,300,000	224,961
8. Algeria	26,900,000	919,900
9. Sudan	26,700,000	967,500
10. Morocco	26,400,000	172,410

ANGOLA

ZAMBIA

MALAWI

Zambezi River

MOZAMBIQUE

Mozambique Channel

⊛ Antananarivo

⊛ Harare
ZIMBABWE

Windhoek ⊛

NAMIBIA

BOTSWANA

Kalahari
Desert

Limpopo River

⊛ Maputo

SWAZILAND

SOUTH AFRICA

DRAKENSBERG MTS.

LESOTHO

INDIAN

Cape Town ⊛

Cape of
Good Hope

OCEAN

Plant life. Plant life in the Dark Continent is varied and extensive. Swaying date palms cluster around desert oases. Gnarled olive and oak trees grow in the warm Northwest and Southeast. The valuable ebony and mahogany trees, from which beautiful furniture is made, are only two of the many species which grow in the tropical forests. The plant life of Africa is varied because the terrain is so varied.

Animals. Lions, elephants, crocodiles, apes, antelopes—perhaps these are what first come to mind when one thinks of Africa. Certainly Africa is rich in animal life: no other continent has so many different species. Huge herds once roamed the continent, but since men began inhabiting the land, these large numbers have decreased somewhat. Today, many African nations set aside large tracts of government-owned land as game preserves.

History

People. After seeing all these bountiful gifts of God in the natural world, the people of Africa might have joined with the Psalmist in saying "O Lord, how manifold are thy works! In wisdom hast thou made them all" (Ps. 104:24). The Africans *might* have done so; yet, by and large, they did not. Rather, like the early Celtic and Anglo-Saxon inhabitants of Britain, the Vikings of Scandinavia, and all other people who have not received the gospel, "they glorified him not as God, neither were thankful; but became vain in their imaginations, and their foolish heart was darkened." The history of mankind in Africa has been sad. Like the rest of mankind, the Africans turned from the truth of God and began to "make unto themselves idols." Even today many inhabitants of this continent "bow down to wood and stone."

Early Christianity. The gospel came early to Africa. Right after Christ's resurrection, the treasurer of the nation of Ethiopia became a Christian and took the truth back with him to his homeland. As a result, Christianity spread into Ethiopia and other North African countries. In **Ethiopia** today there are some (members of the **Coptic Church**) who trace their church back to the first century A.D.

About the middle of the fourth century, two young Christians were shipwrecked in the Red Sea. They were taken as slaves to Ethiopia, where they served in the royal court. They preached the gospel in the court, even though they were slaves, and so many people came to Christ that one of the young men was allowed to return to Egypt to ask other Christians to come and help with the church work in Ethiopia. This young man, **Frumentius,** became a leader of the church in Ethiopia.

Alexandria, in Egypt, had a strong Christian church and a famous Christian training school by A.D. 200. We do not know for sure how this work began, but tradition says that **John Mark,** the young associate of the Apostle Paul, took the gospel there. One famous church leader in Alexandria was *Clement.*

Northern Africa, along the Mediterranean Sea, was one of the strongest centers of the early Christian church. Well-known early Christians in northern Africa were *Tertullian, Cyprian,* and *Augustine of Hippo.*

One of the leaders of the African church, **Athanasius the Great,** boldly stood for the truth of the deity of Christ when some people were doubting it. He was one of the greatest leaders in all of church history.

The Age of Discovery. In the 15th century A.D., Africa began to attract the attention of some Europeans. In 1498, *Vasco da Gama,* the Portuguese explorer, sailed around the **Cape of Good Hope** (the extreme southern tip of Africa) and on to India. Other Portuguese adventurers tried to establish trading posts along the western

Slave Trade: A slaver's canoe in the Congo Basin of Africa (c. 1880).

began around 1500. They were not the first—the Arabs had been buying and selling African slaves for centuries—but the Portuguese brought the slave trade to Europe and the New World, giving the trade a much larger market. The Africans themselves bought and sold each other with a readiness that was shocking. Native African chiefs often raided other tribes, abducting men, women, and children to sell to Arab and Portuguese slave traders. Some chiefs even sold their own people to the slave traders. Yet, while many Africans owned slaves themselves and even caught them for the traders, they despised the slave traders, and suspected any white men, including European explorers and missionaries, of engaging in that despicable trade.

coast of the continent, but the Africans were not hospitable to strangers. Few explorers returned to tell about their adventures.

Slave trade. One reason for the Africans' hostility toward strangers was the slave trade. The Portuguese slave trade

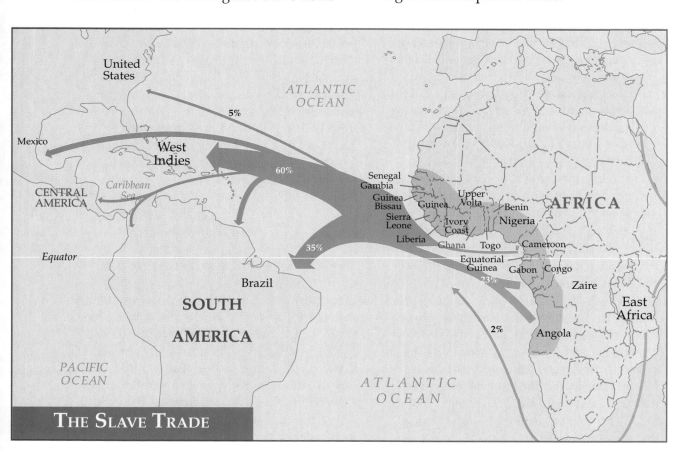

THE SLAVE TRADE

David Livingstone:
Missionary Explorer of Africa

Victoria Falls:
Named by David Livingstone in honor of his queen.

Perhaps the most famous missionary of the 19th century was David Livingstone (1813–1873). Born into a devout but poor Scottish family, Livingstone began work in a cotton mill when he was 10 years old. Greatly desiring to receive an education, he purchased a Latin grammar book with his first wages. He was eventually able to study medicine and theology. Hearing of the success of other missionaries, Livingstone was eager to devote his life, too, as a missionary. In 1840, he went to Africa, and there joined a handful of Christians already at work.

In 1853, he began an expedition to explore the Zambezi River, God's highway into the interior, as he called it. In 1855, he became the first white man to lay eyes on the beautiful falls which he named **Victoria Falls,** in honor of his queen. Livingstone spent 30 years in Africa, part of them as an official missionary and part as a representative of the British government.

Livingstone believed that Africa needed three things: *Christianity,* to end paganism and superstition; *commerce,* to end the slave trade; and *civilization,* to end the despicable tyranny and oppression on every hand in the "Dark Continent." Yet no Europeans had ever gone into the interior of the continent. Livingstone, as good at sailing and surveying as at teaching, proceeded inland. "I shall open up a path into the interior," he said, "or perish." Though mauled by a lion, deserted by native

---

The discovery of the New World greatly increased the market for slaves. As the Spanish settled in the West Indies and Central America and the Portuguese in Brazil, they established vast plantations, creating a need for a large supply of cheap labor. At first, they enslaved the native Indians, but as the Indian population fell prey to disease and began to dwindle, plantation owners looked to Africa for a new source of slaves. Thousands of black slaves were sold to Brazilian plantation owners between the 1500s and the 1800s—in fact, more than $1/3$ of the slaves brought from Africa to the New World were sold in Brazil (most of the other $2/3$ were sold in the West Indies and Central America). By the 1800s, slavery had spread to the English colonies of North America, though on a smaller scale than in the Spanish and Portuguese colonies. There it became entrenched as a way of life, particularly in the South.

"Dr. Livingstone, I presume?" The meeting of Livingstone (right) and Stanley in central Africa.

now-famous words, *"Dr. Livingstone, I presume?"* Stanley greeted the pioneer missionary of Africa. After a time of exploring with Livingstone, Stanley departed to give the world the latest news about the famous missionary.

For another two years, Livingstone continued his explorations. The years of hardship had borne heavily on him. One morning in May 1873, Livingstone's servants found him dead; he had died while kneeling beside his bed in prayer. Though they loved Livingstone, the Africans knew that others must be told of his death. After burying his heart in a jungle clearing, they carried his body to the coast; from there it was taken to England, where Livingstone was buried with honor in Westminster Abbey.

A man of dedication and resolve, David Livingstone succeeded in stirring the consciences of English and American Christians. As a result of his work, Africa was opened up to Christianity, the barbarous slave trade was abolished, and the blessings of civilization became possibilities for millions of Africans.

helpers, and separated from his family, David Livingstone persevered and, as a result, opened up a continent to the gospel.

Livingstone's activities were followed with great interest by Englishmen and Americans. After 1866, however, as he went further into the interior of Africa, Livingstone was unable to communicate with the outside world. Some reports said that he was dead. The *New York Herald,* a major American newspaper, sent the young reporter **Henry Stanley** to find Livingstone. After searching for months, Stanley found Livingstone alive near Lake Tanganyika. With the

Missionary activity. Eventually, there arose some Europeans who saw Africa as more than a source of ready labor. By the late 1780s, Protestants of many countries began to see the need of sending the gospel to the masses of Africa. A stream of missionaries began to open up the interior of Africa to Christianity, and, ultimately, to civilization as well. **Robert Moffat** (1795–1883), **David Livingstone** (1813–1873), and other pioneers in the first half of the 19th

century laid a foundation upon which hundreds of others would build before the century came to a close. The light was beginning to shine in the Dark Continent.

Commerce. Following the missionaries were merchants who introduced legitimate commerce to Africa, purchasing palm oil, ivory, and beautiful woods to sell in Europe and America. With their growing industries, the Western European countries also saw Africa as a market for their

423

THE BRITISH EMPIRE: ASIA, AFRICA, AND AUSTRALIA

manufactured goods. Soon many African women wore dresses of cloth identical to those worn by women on the streets of London.

Colonization. With the merchants came the need for organized government. Tribal governments were too small and limited in scope to handle the complex problems of an intertribal society based on trade with Europe. European governments began to carve out for themselves areas of control and to colonize these areas with civil servants and army officers. By 1914, only two nations in Africa were independent—**Ethiopia** (an ancient nation, independent for centuries) and **Liberia** (a republic founded by freed American slaves). The mad scramble for colonies had resulted in almost total ownership of Africa by non-Africans. In fact, virtually every European power established colonies in Africa: Germany, France, Italy, Portugal, Spain, The Netherlands, and Great Britain. The **French** established colonies in northern Africa; the **Belgians** colonized in the region of the Congo River; and both the **Dutch** and the **English** set up colonies in South Africa. Africa's wealth—particularly its gold, ivory, and diamonds—made colonization a profitable venture.

The Europeans generally exhibited one of two attitudes toward native Africans. Some regarded Africa as a place to be exploited, and the African people as nothing more than a source of cheap labor. Others saw Africa as a country needing the light of the gospel and the civilizing influence of Western culture.

South Africa. The history of South Africa provides an interesting example of European colonization on the continent and the many struggles the Europeans faced with each other and with the native Africans. The Dutch had colonized the Cape of Good Hope during the 17th century under the Dutch East India Company. Most of the Dutch settlers, called **Boers** (a Dutch word

Robert Moffat

meaning "farmers"), farmed and raised cattle. As the Boers advanced northward, they encountered black African tribes, and a struggle for territory began.

After the Napoleonic Wars, the Cape Colony became a British possession. The Boers resented the British and resisted the changes they brought. In 1835, hundreds of Boers packed up and left the Cape, beginning the *"Great Trek."* North of the Cape Colony, they established two new republics, the **Transvaal** and the **Orange Free State.**

As the Boers claimed more and more land, they frequently clashed with African tribes. The British felt it necessary to step in and restore order because many British settlers were being slain along with the Dutch, but the Dutch resented Britain's determination to interfere in Dutch affairs.

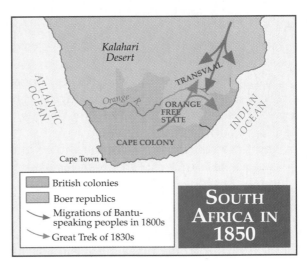

Kalahari Desert

ATLANTIC OCEAN

Orange R.

TRANSVAAL

ORANGE FREE STATE

INDIAN OCEAN

CAPE COLONY

Cape Town

☐ British colonies
☐ Boer republics
→ Migrations of Bantu-speaking peoples in 1800s
→ Great Trek of 1830s

SOUTH AFRICA IN 1850

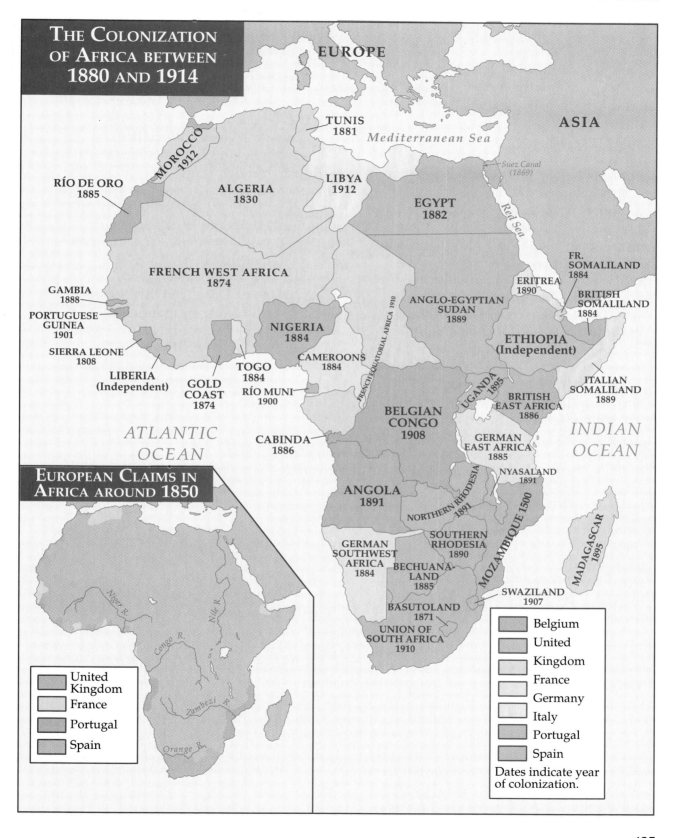

THE COLONIZATION OF AFRICA BETWEEN 1880 AND 1914

EUROPE

ASIA

Mediterranean Sea

TUNIS 1881

Suez Canal (1869)

MOROCCO 1912

RÍO DE ORO 1885

ALGERIA 1830

LIBYA 1912

EGYPT 1882

Red Sea

FR. SOMALILAND 1884

ERITREA 1890

FRENCH WEST AFRICA 1874

ANGLO-EGYPTIAN SUDAN 1889

BRITISH SOMALILAND 1884

GAMBIA 1888

PORTUGUESE GUINEA 1901

SIERRA LEONE 1808

LIBERIA (Independent)

GOLD COAST 1874

NIGERIA 1884

CAMEROONS 1884

TOGO 1884

RÍO MUNI 1900

FRENCH EQUATORIAL AFRICA 1910

ETHIOPIA (Independent)

UGANDA 1895

BRITISH EAST AFRICA 1886

ITALIAN SOMALILAND 1889

ATLANTIC OCEAN

CABINDA 1886

BELGIAN CONGO 1908

GERMAN EAST AFRICA 1885

INDIAN OCEAN

NYASALAND 1891

EUROPEAN CLAIMS IN AFRICA AROUND 1850

ANGOLA 1891

NORTHERN RHODESIA 1891

MOZAMBIQUE 1500

MADAGASCAR 1895

Niger R.

Nile R.

Congo R.

GERMAN SOUTHWEST AFRICA 1884

SOUTHERN RHODESIA 1890

BECHUANA- LAND 1885

SWAZILAND 1907

Zambezi R.

BASUTOLAND 1871

Orange R.

UNION OF SOUTH AFRICA 1910

	United Kingdom
	France
	Portugal
	Spain

	Belgium
	United Kingdom
	France
	Germany
	Italy
	Portugal
	Spain

Dates indicate year of colonization.

To make matters worse, gold was discovered in Transvaal in 1885, and British settlers rushed into the Dutch republics with hopes of striking it rich. The Dutch detested the British settlers and went out of their way to make the British feel unwelcome. Britons were discriminated against in many ways: they were taxed more heavily than their Dutch neighbors, and their children did not receive the same educational opportunities as Dutch children. As the British settlers cried out to their government for help, the relationship between the British and Dutch colonies, already quite weak, fell apart entirely. The **Boer War** broke out in **1899.**

At first the Boers were successful; their skilled soldiers out-shot and out-maneuvered the British. But as the war progressed, Britain sent in a flood of soldiers under the leadership of Lord Roberts and Lord Kitchener. After suffering several defeats by the British, the Boers surrendered in 1902. The terms of surrender were generous; both the Transvaal and the Orange Free State were quickly restored to independence. Later, the British ideals of self-government once again took root and grew on foreign soil: in *1910,* the Boers and the British joined together to form the **Union of South Africa,** a dominion with a representative government in the tradition of Great Britain. Thus European government came to Africa.

Egypt. In addition to its colonies in South Africa, Britain was able to exert strong influence on (and eventually control) Egypt. Britain had a strong interest in Egypt because of the **Suez Canal** (completed in 1859). The Suez Canal connects the Red Sea with the Mediterranean Sea; trade ships from India and the Far East use the canal as a short cut to Europe without going all the way around Africa. Thus the Suez Canal was vitally important to all countries, but especially to England—a small nation, short on natural resources, which depended upon goods from its colonies to support its economy. To survive, England had to insure that the canal remain open. When the leader of Egypt ran into financial difficulties and was forced to sell his shares in the canal, the British Prime Minister **Disraeli** bought them, thereby securing British control of the canal by 1875. After showing further signs of instability, the Egyptian leader was forced to accept Anglo-French control of Egypt's financial affairs. In 1882, a native uprising precipitated France's withdrawal from Egypt, but the British stayed on to protect their interests, although they never fully controlled Egypt. Thus, Egypt was a troubled spot in the empire. British involvement in Egypt did not end until the 20th century.

Civilization. Africa progressed greatly during the 19th century. Bloody tribal wars ceased, slavery was abolished, men realized the sanctity (sacred worth) of human life, and Christianity was given an open door to evangelism. With Christianity came written languages, education, books, and hospitals. The spiritual darkness which had so long held Africa in its grip was beginning to be expelled.

The influence of African Christians. African Christians have done much to bring the gospel and its fruits to their own people. Some brilliant African linguists have worked with missionaries for years to translate the Bible accurately into the languages of the African people. African Christians have raised the literacy level in their countries by teaching their countrymen to read and write and by giving them the Bible and Christian books to read. Many leaders of the various African nations were educated in mission schools by missionaries and African Christians.

Samuel Adjai Crowther

many have since given up democracy and returned to various forms of dictatorial government.

The spiritual darkness of Africa has not been completely dispelled. Only about 8% of all Africans profess Christianity—most practice Islam or a tribal religion. Commerce and manufacturing are limited. Governments are often dictatorial, and Communism is spreading rapidly. Yet the light has dawned in Africa, and its effects remain to be seen.

One outstanding African, **Samuel Adjai Crowther,** who was rescued from a slave ship as a young boy and later became a Christian, was <u>the first black bishop of the Church of England</u>. He started the first mission in Niger to be completely staffed by African nationals. He and his staff established churches, elementary schools, high schools, and a college in Africa.

Desire for self-government. After World War I and especially after World War II, Africans began to demand more voice in their government. Particularly in British-held colonies, the natives had for a long time been given some measure of self-government. In other colonies, such as Belgium's **Congo,** Portugal's **Mozambique,** and France's **Algeria,** the people were little trained for self-government. Gradually, through wars and threatened wars, the countries of Africa were given their independence. For most countries, independence brought new problems. Differences in tribal loyalties, varied religions, and outside revolutionary influences threatened virtually every nation in Africa. For many of them the strain proved too much, and

---

CHECK UP

1. What is the largest continent? the second largest?
2. In what African country was the gospel preached in the first century A.D.? Who brought the gospel to this country in the fourth century A.D.?
3. What area was one of the strongest centers of the early Christian church?
4. What discovery greatly increased the slave trade in Africa? Where were most of the slaves sold?
5. Who was the most famous missionary in the 19th century? How many years did he spend in Africa? What three things did he believe Africa needed?
6. What European countries established colonies in Africa? What two differing opinions did Europeans have about Africa?
7. What two countries fought the Boer War? Where and when did it take place? What dominion was finally established in 1910?
8. Why was Britain interested in Egypt?
9. What changes came to Africa during the 19th century?
10. How have African Christians influenced Africa? Name one outstanding African Christian and describe his work.

Identify: Sahara Desert, Savannah, Nile River, Cape of Good Hope, Victoria Falls, Boers, Liberia, Ethiopia

AUSTRALIA AND NEW ZEALAND

Captain James Cook

Australia, New Zealand, and Canada

Australia and New Zealand

Much about **Australia**—including its very existence—was in doubt until **Captain James Cook's** (1728–1779) explorations in the 1770s. Cook discovered that Australia was a huge land mass, big enough to be considered a continent. Cook also explored **New Zealand,** a group of islands southeast of Australia.

Britain began colonizing Australia in 1788 by sending convicts and debtors to settle the land (the same plan had been used to colonize Georgia). As the convicts settled into a life of idleness, drunkenness, thievery, and immorality, however, it became apparent that the colonies could not survive under these conditions. To remedy the problem, colonial authorities encouraged free settlers to colonize Australia. Christian groups in England and Scotland saw to it that strong churches were established in Australia, and mission-

aries were sent to the **Aborigines** [ăb′o·rĭj′i·nēz], the original inhabitants of the land. As Biblical standards of morality were established and observed under Britain's watchful eye, Australian society grew more stable. By the middle of the 19th century, the colonies were prospering. The **Australian Gold Rush** (1851) greatly escalated the rate of colonization. In the decade following the gold rush, Australia's population increased by nearly 800%. Parliament granted Australia self-government in 1850, and in *1901,* Australia became an <u>independent commonwealth</u> (federation of states) with its own parliamentary government.

New Zealand's first exposure to British colonization was not a happy one. The British whalers and sealers who settled in New Zealand were a rowdy crew who exposed native **Maoris** [mä′ŏ·rēz] to disease, alcoholism, violence, and modern weaponry. As settlement increased, land disputes between the Maoris and the white settlers often led to bloodshed. Christian missionaries tried to overcome the bad influence of the early settlers and to keep the peace, but they were only partially successful. Finally, the Maori's themselves cried out for official British action to maintain order and sanity. In 1840, more than 500 Maori chiefs signed a treaty acknowledging Queen Victoria as their sovereign in return for her promise of protection. (Unable to write, they "signed" the document by drawing the patterns tattoed on their faces.) Thus New Zealand became a British colony. New Zealand prospered under British rule, and by 1852, she was largely self-governing. In *1907*, New Zealand became <u>independent</u>, like Australia, with a parliamentary government of its own.

Thus both New Zealand and Australia acquired forms of government similar to England's own, and political reforms adopted in England were quickly accepted in Australia and New Zealand.

Canada

After the **French and Indian War** (1756–1763), British seniority in North America was unquestioned. But the American War for Independence diminished Britain's empire substantially, and *Canada became England's chief North American possession.* There were still many French settlers in Canada, however, and they did not get along very well with the British. In 1791, **William Pitt,** the British prime minister, <u>divided Canada</u> into two sections (British and French) to ease tensions. But by the middle of the 19th century, Canada was again in turmoil. Queen Victoria sent **Lord Durham** to investigate conditions in Canada, and he made these suggestions for settling the Canadian problem:

(1) Reunite the two sectors of Canada into one country.
(2) Give the Canadians a representative government.
(3) Follow a plan for settlement of unoccupied territories.

Durham's plan was gradually enacted, and in *1867,* the **British North America Act** made Canada a <u>self-governing commonwealth</u>.

Apparently England had learned the lessons of the American Revolution. The focus of attention in the British empire shifted from North America, but England's treatment of Canada set a good example. Canada and England benefited from each other. England prepared Canada for and eventually granted self-government. This process repeated itself throughout the history of the empire.

"The Sun Never Sets on the British Empire"

With uncanny skill, and with a remarkable absence of violence and armed force, the British in the 19th century acquired an empire unparalleled since Roman times. Indeed, the British flag flew over every imaginable terrain in every conceivable climate over the entire earth. And British administrative efficiency kept the empire together for well over a century. Britain developed the governments of her colonies as carefully as she developed their industries. Britain greatly profited from the empire, but the countries of the empire greatly profited from Britain as well, for she shared two most important gifts with them: her Christian faith and her representative form of government. By the 1920s, Canada, Australia, and New Zealand had become independent members of the *British Commonwealth of Nations,* an association of nations acknowledging the British monarch as their *symbolic* head. Eventually, most of the former colonies of the British Empire would follow their example. Other Commonwealth nations include India, Malaysia, Nigeria, Kenya, Zimbabwe, Jamaica, the Bahamas, and Belize.

Christianity in Victorian England

Christianity and Charity

The world has probably never seen such selfless charity as burst forth in the 19th century in the wake of England's Wesleyan Revival and the subsequent preaching of the gospel. Never before in history had so many people done so much for others. Their acts of benevolence were freely performed, compelled only by the inner sense of duty and the love for mankind that come from obedience to Scriptural truth.

George Müller's orphans. One of England's most famous humanitarians was actually a German missionary, **George Müller** (1805–1898), the *"Father of Homeless Waifs."* In 1829, Müller came to England as a missionary to the Jews. He soon began the work for which he is best known, the founding of orphanages for the forsaken children of Bristol, England. Every day for years God miraculously provided the physical needs of up to 2,000 orphans in answer to George Müller's prayers. Over the years, thousands of children were clothed, fed, educated, and won to Christ in Müller's orphanages.

The Salvation Army. In 1865, **William Booth** (1829–1912), a young Methodist evangelist, began a mission in the darkest slums of London. Believing that the main problem of London's "down and outers" was not their poor environment but rather their sinful hearts, Booth dedicated his life to winning the poor to Christ and helping them with their physical needs. In 1878, his work became known as the **Salvation Army.** Booth organized his converts in military fashion and led them in a grand campaign to reach other needy people for Christ. The Salvation Army spread rapidly throughout England, the United States, the British colonies, and India.

George Müller *William Booth*

The YMCA. The **Young Men's Christian Association** (YMCA) was just one of many organizations formed in the 19th century to do benevolent work. Many young men had moved to the cities from rural areas to work in the new industries. There they faced many temptations that they had not known at home, and they needed a place where they could stay temporarily, get meals, and enjoy Bible study, recreation, and good Christian fellowship. After reading *Lectures on Revivals of Religion* by American evangelist Charles Finney, **Sir George Williams** (1821–1905), an Englishman, helped begin in 1844 an organization to aid "the improvement of the spiritual condition of young men." This organization brought boys and young men involved in trade together for Bible study and recreation. Soon the YMCA, as it came to be called, became well respected as a means of improving the lives of thousands of young men on both sides of the Atlantic.

Christianity and Medical Care

Modern medical care has generally ebbed or waned with Christianity. As a result of Christianity, medicine became a respected profession in the Roman world in the first century. Until then it had been practiced mostly by Greek slaves. The early Christians built hospitals, hospices, and other medical facilities, and Christian women nursed the sick. With the fall of the

Jean-Henri Dunant

Clara Barton

Roman Empire and the rise of feudalism, caring for the sick became the work of monks, particularly one group known as the Knights Hospitaller. Although the Reformation brought about some change in medical practice, it was not until the 19th century that the major medical break-throughs came about. One innovation which wrought particular change in medicine was the birth of the modern nursing profession.

Florence Nightingale. In 1850, **Florence Nightingale** (1820–1910), the daughter of a wealthy Christian family in England, chose to become a nurse, then an occupation practiced by the uneducated and, often, the intemperate. After training in Germany, she returned to Britain, where *she singlehandedly created the modern nursing profession.* During the Crimean War in 1854, she and her nurses became widely respected for their devotion to caring for the injured. In 1860, "The Lady with the Lamp," as she was known, succeeded in opening the first school for nurses in England.

Dunant and the Red Cross. Others also saw the need for higher quality in medical facilities, especially for soldiers, who often died in agony on the battlefield. **Jean-Henri Dunant** (1828–1910) led in an effort to bring doctors and nurses to the front to attend the wounded. Reared in a pious Swiss home, Dunant realized something must be done to alleviate some of the suffering taking place on the battlefields of Europe. Finally, in 1864, he persuaded the governments of several European countries to unite at the *Geneva Convention.* At this meeting the governments agreed to care for the wounded during times of war, without regard to nationality. This agreement led to the establishment of the **Red Cross,** an international relief organization.

Clara Barton. The United States did not join the Red Cross at first. After the Civil War, however, **Clara Barton** (1821–1912) succeeded in establishing the **American National Red Cross,** and in 1882 the United States signed the Geneva Agreement. Barton is remembered in history as the founder of the American Red Cross.

Florence Nightingale: nursing wounded soldiers in the Crimean War.

Age of Great Preachers

The England of the Victorian Age was known for its great preachers. Many people today still read the printed versions of sermons that thundered from London pulpits during the 19th century. These men followed in the footsteps of Whitefield, Wesley, and Finney to help keep England filled with the kind of righteousness that exalts a nation.

C. H. Spurgeon. One of the wonders of Victorian London was **Charles Haddon Spurgeon** (1834–1892), pastor of that great city's largest church. Spurgeon has been universally acclaimed as the *"Prince of Preachers";* many consider him to be the greatest preacher of modern times. Spurgeon ministered to the same congregation for almost 40 years, regularly speaking to crowds of five or six thousand. When he could find a hall large enough, he spoke to 10,000 people at a time, and on one occasion he spoke in the Crystal Palace to a crowd of 23,654 people. His regular ministry was carried on in the huge **Metropolitan Tabernacle.** Besides ministering faithfully week after week to his own huge congregation, Spurgeon ran almshouses for the poor, founded two orphanages, administered a Bible college, wrote a number of books, and published a monthly magazine. Spurgeon used the profits of his publications to promote evangelism, education, and Christian charity.

"Gypsy" Smith. "Gypsy" Smith (1860–1947) was no doubt one of the most interesting evangelists of the Victorian era. His real name was Rodney. He got his nickname because he was born in a gypsy wagon near London. While Rodney was still a young child, his mother died of smallpox, leaving his traveling father to care for Rodney and his four sisters and one brother. Before long his father attended an evangelistic service at a mission and was converted. At about the same time, two of Rodney's uncles were converted. They

Charles Haddon Spurgeon

teamed up with Rodney's father and started a traveling evangelistic team. Although they could not read, the three brothers sang, played, and preached from large portions of Scripture which they memorized.

The life of a poor, illiterate, motherless, traveling gypsy family was hard, but Rodney did have the benefit of a Christian family and a father who, although poorly trained, was determined to do right. When Rodney was 16 years old, he attended a Primitive Methodist Chapel and was converted. Almost immediately he answered God's call to preach. At 17 he preached his first sermon, beginning a ministry of <u>70 years</u>. Although Rodney had no chance to get a formal education, he determined to educate himself. The Lord so anointed this humble servant that he became <u>one of the best-known revivalists</u> of his day.

Rodney began his ministry as a mission evangelist for the *Salvation Army.* Soon he became a full-time traveling evangelist. By 1881, he was known as "Gypsy" Smith. He preached in many parts of England, and in 1889, he launched a world-wide ministry.

The Beginning of Britain's Decline

Queen Victoria's 64-year reign had restored dignity and prosperity to the British empire, but when she passed from the scene, the glory faded. After Victoria's death in 1901, her son **Edward VII** (1841–1910) ascended the throne. Edward did not share his mother's resolution to "be good," and when the morality of the monarchy fell, so did that of the nation. As the Victorian

Age came to an end, Britain began a period of decline both at home and abroad. By the turn of the 20th century, the faith, energy, and morality of the British people were under attack by the false philosophies of Darwinism, socialism, and modernism. As these ideas took root in Europe, particularly in Germany, they would lay the groundwork for the terrible bloodshed and destruction of the first world war.

CHECK UP

1. Who explored Australia and New Zealand?
2. How did Britain first attempt to colonize Australia?
3. How did New Zealand come to be under British authority?
4. What did the British North America Act do?
5. Who was called the "Father of Homeless Waifs"? Why?
6. Who founded the Salvation Army? What was its purpose?

7. Why was the YMCA founded? What do the initials stand for?
8. Who led in the founding of the International Red Cross? The American National Red Cross?
9. Who is called the "Prince of Preachers"? What was the name of his church?
10. When did Queen Victoria die? Who succeeded her to the throne?

Identify: Aborigines, Maoris, Sir George Williams, Florence Nightingale, Gypsy Smith

---

CHAPTER 21 REVIEW

MULTIPLE CHOICE   Write the letter of the answer that best completes the sentence.

1. The longest-reigning monarch in English history was _____.
   a Queen Victoria   c Edward VI
   b Prince Albert   d Benjamin Disraeli

2. _____ was a famous leader of the Liberal Party in England.
   a William Pitt   c William Gladstone
   b William Carey   d William Booth

3. The "Father of Modern Missions" was

   _____.
   a William Pitt   c William Gladstone
   b William Carey   d William Booth

4. The first Protestant missionary to China was _____.
   a J. Hudson Taylor
   b William Carey
   c Samuel Adjai Crowther
   d Robert Morrison

5. _____ was the "Father of Faith Missions."
   a J. Hudson Taylor
   b William Carey
   c Samuel Adjai Crowther
   d Robert Morrison

6. The first black bishop of the Church of England was _____.
   a William Carey
   b Samuel Adjai Crowther
   c Robert Morrison
   d William Gladstone

7. _____ explored Australia in the 1770s.
   a J. Hudson Taylor   c James Cook
   b George Müller   d Robert Morrison

8. _____ became known as the "Father of Homeless Waifs."
   a J. Hudson Taylor c James Cook
   b George Müller   d Robert Morrison

9. The Salvation Army was founded by _____ in 1865.
   a William Pitt   c William Gladstone
   b William Carey   d William Booth

10. The YMCA was founded by _____ in 1844.
   a Sir George Williams
   b George Müller
   c William Booth
   d Robert Morrison

433

CHAPTER 21 REVIEW (CONTINUED)

11. _____ came to be known as the "Lady with the Lamp" because of her care for the injured during the Crimean War.
   a Florence Nightingale
   b Clara Barton
   c Victoria
   d Amy Carmichael

12. The American Red Cross was founded by _____.
   a Florence Nightingale
   b Clara Barton
   c Victoria
   d Amy Carmichael

13. _____ was called the "Prince of Preachers."
   a J. Hudson Taylor
   b Robert Morrison
   c William Carey
   d Charles Haddon Spurgeon

14. Queen Victoria's son _____ became king after she died.
   a Charles Haddon Spurgeon
   b Prince Albert
   c Edward VII
   d Benjamin Disraeli

TIME LINE CHALLENGE Choose the letter of the correct date for each of the events listed below.

1498	1791	1837	1840	1858	1865	1880–1900	1902	1929
A	B	C	D	E	F	G	H	I

_____ 1. Vasco da Gama sails around Cape of Good Hope

_____ 2. Boer War ends

_____ 3. Victorian Age begins

_____ 4. Canada divided into two sections—British and French

_____ 5. Japan opened to missions

_____ 6. Great Age of British imperialism

_____ 7. David Livingstone goes to Africa

_____ 8. J. Hudson Taylor founds China Inland Mission

MAP SKILLS Use the maps on pp. 415 and 419 to answer the following questions.

1. What was the largest British colony in North America? In Asia?

2. Name the mountain range located in Morocco and Algeria. In South Africa.

3. What body of water separates Madagascar from the African continent?

4. Which African nations border the Red Sea?

5. Name the lake that lies between Tanzania and Zaire.

6. Which African nations border the Mediterranean Sea?

MATCHING *Match the description with the correct term.*

- *a* British North America Act
- *b* Oxford Movement
- *c* India Act
- *d* Sepoy Rebellion
- *e* Victorian Age
- *f* Liberals
- *g* Conservatives
- *h* Ireland
- *i* Northern Ireland
- *j* Act of Union

_____ 1. the 64-year reign of Queen Victoria

_____ 2. the movement within the Church of England to reintroduce many Roman Catholic practices

_____ 3. represented the middle class of the Industrial Age

_____ 4. represented the wealthy class of the Industrial Age

_____ 5. officially joined England and Ireland

_____ 6. Irish Free State

_____ 7. the six counties of Ulster Parliament

_____ 8. uprising in India against the British East India Company

_____ 9. gave political control of India to the British government

_____ 10. made Canada a self-governing commonwealth

CONCEPTS TO CONSIDER *On a separate sheet of paper, answer the following questions using complete sentences.*

1. How did Great Britain benefit from her empire? How did the colonies benefit from Great Britain?

2. How did the reign of Queen Victoria illustrate Proverbs 29:2? How did Victorian England illustrate Proverbs 14:34 and Psalms 33:12?

COMPLETION *Choose the correct term to complete each sentence and write the letter in the blank.*

- *a* Geneva Convention
- *b* Suez Canal
- *c* East India Company
- *d* Liberia
- *e* Aborigines
- *f* suttee
- *g* Nile
- *h* Sahara
- *i* Lake Victoria
- *j* Ethiopia
- *k* Boers
- *l* Africa
- *m* Maoris
- *n* savannas

1. The _____ was a powerful trading company that was used as a tool of the British government to settle in India.

2. _____ was the Indian practice of burning a widow alive with her dead husband's body.

3. The second largest continent is _____.

4. The _____ is the world's largest desert.

5. _____ are vast tracts of grasses and small shrubs.

6. The _____ is the world's longest river.

7. The source of the Nile is _____.

8. _____ is an ancient African nation which has been independent for centuries.

9. The African republic founded by freed American slaves is _____.

10. _____ is a Dutch word meaning "farmers."

11. The _____ connects the Red Sea with the Mediterranean.

12. The _____ were the original inhabitants of Australia.

13. The _____ was the meeting at which the governments of Europe agreed to care for the wounded during times of war.

The Modern Age has truly been an age of progress for all mankind. As men rediscovered the Scriptures through the Reformation and opened their minds to truth, they began to advance in the arts and sciences as never before. Modern science began in the 16th century when the ancient books of philosophy, which the church had venerated for so long, were proven false, and the greatest of ancient books, the Bible, was returned to the people and found to be true. Without the Bible, men would never have discovered the foundational truths upon which modern science is based.

Rather than depend on pagan philosophers and church leaders, people learned to search for truth themselves, both in the Scriptures and in nature. As they turned to the Scriptures, they learned that God created the universe, that He is separate from the universe, and that He established reasonable, orderly laws which nature obeys. Scientists began to search for the laws that God established so they could understand nature and learn to control it for the good of mankind, as God commanded in Genesis 1:28. Copernicus, Kepler, Galileo, Newton, and other founders of modern science led the way, and countless others followed. From agriculture to medicine, they gradually transformed the world and improved life for all mankind.

Since the mid-19th century, Charles Darwin and other proponents of evolution have threatened modern science by denying the role of God as Creator and Sustainer of the universe. Evolution attacks the very foundation of modern science—the source of all scientific laws and principles that make science possible—and detours scientists from their true calling of mastering nature for the benefit of mankind. Fortunately, not all scientists believe in evolution, and many acknowledge it only in theory and ignore it in practice. As a result, scientists continue to make important discoveries and to develop new technology.

In the 18th century, the development of new technology gave rise to the Industrial Revolution, sparking the Age of Industry (1760–1900), a time of great advances in agriculture, manufacturing, transportation, communication, and other areas. The Industrial Revolution began in England, where the Wesleyan revivals established the Protestant work ethic among the people and gave them a desire to work, save, and give. Advances in agriculture paved the way for the rise of industry by increasing crop production while decreasing the number of laborers required on the farm. This freed many to work in the factories that were springing up across England. The growth of manufacturing created a demand for new and better means of transportation and communication. Soon inventors in England and America were producing such wonders as the telephone, the steamship, the train, the automobile, and the airplane. England and America made the greatest advances during the Age of Industry, largely because both nations embraced capitalism, or the free market system, in which businesses and industries are privately owned and managed without government interference. In the late 19th and early 20th century, capitalism brought to the western world the greatest wealth and luxury for the greatest number of people that the world has ever known.

The Modern Age also opened a new world of classics in music, art, and literature. The great modern classics began with the Northern Renaissance and the Protestant Reformation. The return to the Bible gave men a new sense of responsibility and brought forth an unprecedented outburst of individual creativity. All of the great music of the world, with the exception of a few traditional songs, has been written in the past 500 years. At least 90% of the world's great literary works have been written since 1500, and many of the world's great works of art are products of the Modern Age.

No nation exemplified the progress of the Modern Age more than Great Britain. By the 19th century, England was noted for its progress toward representative democracy, the establishment of religious toleration, and the growth of the British Empire. It is best-remembered today for the reign of Queen Victoria, the longest-ruling monarch in English history. Under Victoria's wise leadership, Great Britain reached the height of its glory and became the wealthiest, most powerful nation in the world. The British Empire covered a quarter of the globe and included about a quarter of the world's people, so that it could be said, "The sun never sets on the British Empire."

As the British spread their dominion to many lands, they shared their representative form of government as well as their Christian heritage. The great Wesleyan Revival of the 18th century had stirred the hearts of many Christians in England to spread the gospel by means of widespread missionary efforts, making the 19th century the "Great Century of Missions." As Englishmen came to understand the worth of all men, regardless of their family background and economic status, they also became concerned about their less-fortunate countrymen. The "reformation of morals" that came in the wake of the revival led many upper class Englishmen to voluntarily help the poor and needy. Thus, while most of Europe was wracked by violent revolutions during the 19th century, England was able to bring about peaceful reforms through the benevolence of her people and the workings of her Parliament.

By the turn of the 20th century, the false philosophies of Modernism, Darwinism, and socialism had begun to take root in Europe. In England, the result would be a decline in morality, power, and influence. On the Continent, particularly in Germany, the result would be more devastating. As people rejected the Word of God and embraced the vain philosophies of men, they set the stage for the death and destruction of the world wars.

Bolshevik Revolution **1917**
Lenin establishes Communist
state in Russia

1922 Mussolini comes
to power in Italy
U.S.S.R. created

Israel becomes a nation **1948**

1930–40
Great Depression

1941 Japan attacks
Pearl Harbor

1933 Hitler comes to
power in Germany

1944 D-Day
invasion

1910

1920

1930

1940

1914–18
World War I

1919 Conference of
Versailles
League of
Nations formed

1927 Charles Lindbergh
makes first non-stop
transatlantic flight

1939–45
World War II

Yalta Conference/UN organized **1945**

NATO organized **1949**
Communist revolution in China

Unit 6

THE TWENTIETH CENTURY
(1900–1995)

Philosophies Clash

22 World War I and the Rise of Communism
23 Before and During World War II
24 The Cold War Era
25 Era of Change

1969 Neil Armstrong
lands on the moon

Western Europe forms **1958**
the Common Market

Cultural Revolution **1966**
in China

Ronald Reagan **1980**
becomes President of the U.S.

Persian Gulf War **1991**
Collapse of Soviet Union

| 1960 | | 1970 | | 1980 | | 1990 |

Berlin Wall built **1961**

1950–53
Korean War

1965–73
Vietnam War

Israel and Egypt **1979**
sign a peace treaty

Communists lose **1989**
control of Eastern Europe
Berlin Wall opened

1962 Cuban Missile Crisis

22
World War I and the Rise of Communism
(c. 1900–1930)

HIGHLIGHTS

World War I • Czarist Russia
Karl Marx and Communism • Bolshevik Revolution
Nikolai Lenin • Joseph Stalin • Soviet Union

Europe in the Late 19th Century

Civilization had progressed so far by the beginning of the 20th century (1900) that it seemed the world could only get better and better. Little did people realize that on the horizon loomed two of the greatest wars the world had ever known.

Spiritual Coldness

By the late 19th century, the seeds of **Modernism,** or *religious liberalism,* had taken root in Germany, the Land of the Reformation. Theologians in German universities denied the authority of the Bible, exalting their own reason above God's Word and teaching that the Bible was a collection of myths and legends with a few historical facts. They *denied the basic doctrines of Christianity*, including Christ's deity, man's sin nature, and the reality of heaven and hell. The state churches of Germany were cold and formal; they no longer preached the gospel. Like much of Europe, Germany was spiritually dead. The Bible was not read, and few people had a personal knowledge of God. When the people turned from faith in God, they fell prey to political revolutionaries and ultimately to tyranny. England and America were spared from these anti-Christian influences because of the preaching of evangelists and Bible teachers.

Discontent and Revolution

The chaos of French politics inspired a spirit of *revolutionary nationalism* in many European nations. Many people longed to break loose from their established governments and rule themselves, based on what they saw as the "natural" boundaries of national origin. Consequently, the continent was plagued by revolts and discontent. In 1830 and 1848, revolutions erupted in France, setting off explosions all over Europe.

Italian Unification

Beginning in 1831, several attempts were made to free Italy from Austrian rule and unify the Italian states as one independ-ent nation. Italy's first parliament met in 1861, proclaiming **Victor Emmanuel II** of Sardinia the first king of Italy. In 1870, when the Franco-Prussian War broke out, French troops were withdrawn from Rome, where they had been protecting the pope. Italian troops quickly took over the **Eternal City.** Pope Pius IX retreated to the *Vatican,* and *for the first time in over a thousand years, the pope had no temporal power.* **Rome** became the capital of a united Italy in 1871.

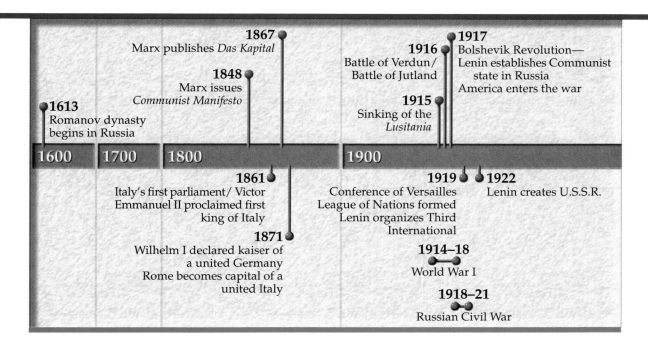

1867 Marx publishes *Das Kapital*

1848 Marx issues *Communist Manifesto*

1613 Romanov dynasty begins in Russia

1916 Battle of Verdun/ Battle of Jutland

1917 Bolshevik Revolution— Lenin establishes Communist state in Russia America enters the war

1915 Sinking of the *Lusitania*

1600 | 1700 | 1800 | 1900

1861 Italy's first parliament/ Victor Emmanuel II proclaimed first king of Italy

1871 Wilhelm I declared kaiser of a united Germany Rome becomes capital of a united Italy

1919 Conference of Versailles League of Nations formed Lenin organizes Third International

1922 Lenin creates U.S.S.R.

1914–18 World War I

1918–21 Russian Civil War

German Unification

In the mid-19th century, Germany was still a conglomerate of states, heavily influenced by the political strength of Austria. Among the states of the German Confederation, Prussia was dominant, making it the logical state to take the lead in German unification. **Otto von Bismarck** (1815–1898), chancellor (prime minister) of Prussia, set out to build a strong, unified German empire with Prussia at the helm. Through wars with neighboring nations, he expanded German boundaries and united the German states. In 1871, King **Wilhelm I** of Prussia was declared **kaiser** (emperor) of a united Germany.

Major Wars of History

Before the Modern Age	The Modern Age	
499–478 B.C. Greco-Persian Wars	**1618–1648** Thirty Years' War	**1870–1871** Franco-Prussian War
431–404 B.C. Peloponnesian War	**1701–1714** War of the Spanish Succession	**1898** Spanish-American War
264–241 B.C. First Punic War	**1740–1748** War of the Austrian Succession	**1899–1902** Boer War
218–201 B.C. Second Punic War	**1755–1763** French and Indian War	**1904–1905** Russo-Japanese War
149–146 B.C. Third Punic War	**1756–1763** Seven Years' War	**1914–1918** World War I
830–19th C. Islamic Invasion of Europe	**1775–1783** American War for Independence	**1936–1939** Civil War (Spanish)
1066 Norman Conquest	**1796–1815** Napoleonic Wars	**1939–1945** World War II
1096–1291 Crusades	**1812–1815** War of 1812	**1950–1952** Korean War
1338–1453 Hundred Years' War	**1846–1848** Mexican War	**1948–1973** Vietnam War
1455–1485 Wars of the Roses	**1861–1865** Civil War (United States)	**1948–1949, 1955–1967, 1973** Israeli Border Wars
		1991 Persian Gulf War

PRUSSIA

Otto Von Bismark   *Wilhelm II*

Bismarck determined to maintain peace in Europe and give Germany a chance to develop as a powerful nation. He accomplished this goal by keeping Germany closely allied with powerful nations. In the process, he was careful to keep France diplomatically isolated (without allies) and therefore harmless. During the **"Era of Bismarck"** (1871–1890), Germany became a strong industrial and military power.

Steps toward War

German aggresssion. In 1890, the young Kaiser **Wilhelm II** dismissed Bismarck and took foreign policy into his own hands. Wilhelm II began a program to build a naval fleet to rival the British navy, and by 1914, Germany's navy was second only to Britain's.

Under the leadership of Wilhelm II, Germany was eager to flex its muscles, expand, and demonstrate its strength to the older established nations of Europe. Most of the German people had by this time rejected all but an empty form of their Christian heritage and had accepted Modernism almost without question. The vacuum left by this rejection of true Christianity was destined to bring terror and destruction to Germany.

Opposing alliances. By 1914, the major European powers were divided into two hostile camps. On the one side was the **Triple Alliance,** including *Germany, Austria-Hungary,* and *Italy.* On the other side was the **Triple Entente,** consisting of *England, France,* and *Russia.* Smaller nations allied themselves with whichever power bloc they feared less. Europe was divided and ready for war.

World War I (1914–1918)

The Archduke's assassination. On June 28, 1914, the nations of Europe found an excuse for war when **Archduke Francis Ferdinand,** heir to the Austrian throne, and his wife were assassinated by a Serbian revolutionist in the town of Sarajevo [sä′rä·yĕ·vô] in Bosnia. Convinced that anti-Austrian propaganda coming out of Serbia had led to the assassination, Austria decided to take aggressive action. On July 28, *1914,* Austria declared war on Serbia. **World War I (1914–1918),** known in its day as *the Great War,* had begun.

Global conflict. Within months, all the major powers of Europe and their worldwide colonies were at war. First, Russia agreed to help Serbia, and Germany, an ally of Austria, declared war on Russia. Then France agreed to help Russia, and Germany declared war on France. The next day, Germany, putting into effect a long-planned scheme to conquer France, sent troops through neutral Belgium to attack Paris. England insisted that Belgium's neutral rights be respected, but the German chancellor said the 1839 treaty guaranteeing Belgian neutrality was "a scrap of paper." So England came to the aid of Belgium by declaring war on Germany. World War I would be the first war to be fought on a global scale.

Winston Churchill (1874–1965), one of the few men in Britain who had seen war with Germany coming years ahead of the first shots, had done what he could to build friendly relations with Germany. But as First Lord of the Admiralty, Churchill had also modernized and expanded the British navy and had developed the navy's first air force. Thanks to Churchill, when England declared war on Germany, the British fleet was ready.

Opposing sides. As the nations of Europe took sides in the conflict, the Triple Entente (England, France, and Russia) and

The Assasination of Archduke Francis Ferdinand and His Wife, 1914

EUROPE DURING WWI

- Allied Powers, 1918
- Central Powers, 1918
- Neutral nations, 1918
- Farthest advance by Central Powers
- ✳ Battle sites

its allies became known as the **Allies,** and the Triple Alliance (Austria-Hungary, Germany, and Italy) and its allies became known as the **Central Powers.** Because Germany and Austria were not fighting a *defensive* war, Italy refused to fulfill her treaty obligations to aid them. Instead, Italy remained neutral and eventually joined the Allies, quite confident she had joined the winning side.

The Western Front, 1914–1916

The Battle of the Marne. Within three months, the Germans had conquered Belgium and had overrun much of France. By September, they were only 15 miles from Paris. Finally, French forces stopped the German advance and miraculously drove the Germans back across the *Marne River.* Paris and the French army were saved.

The "Race to the Sea." Between October and November, the Allies and Germans raced each other to ports on the English Channel and the North Sea. At *Ypres* [ē′pr'], Belgium, the small but gallant British Expeditionary Force lost 50,000 men in its courageous defense against the German onslaught. The Germans were finally stopped, and both sides settled down to dig *trenches* (deep ditches used in battle for cover against enemy gunfire).

By Christmas of 1914, the **western front** stretched for 600 miles from the English Channel to the Swiss Alps. The number of casualties (soldiers killed or wounded in battle) mounted as trenches, machine guns, and barbed wire came to dominate the battlefield. New "secret" weapons—the Germans introduced poisonous gas and the flamethrower and the Allies developed the military tank—made local gains possible but failed to achieve a breakthrough.

The Battle of Verdun. In 1916, the Germans tried to break through the French line with a massive assault (attack) on the fortress-city of *Verdun.* After 24 hours of heavy artillery, the Germans stormed the city's fortifications. French opposition was so great, however, that in six months the Germans advanced only about four miles at the staggering cost of 540,000 French and 430,000 German casualties.

The Battle of the Somme. In an attempt to relieve the pressure at Verdun, British forces launched an intense offensive against the Germans at the *Somme River.* For a solid week, British guns pounded the German lines day and night. When the barrage lifted, long rows of British infantrymen charged the German lines. Instead of being crushed, however, the Germans emerged from their trenches and raked the British troops with intense machine-gun fire. The British suffered over 600,000 casualties to gain just seven miles of land! The German army likewise suffered the loss of more than 500,000 officers and men. In disgust, Kaiser Wilhelm II dismissed the

The Rock of the Marne by Mal Thompson

*General
Paul von
Hindenburg*

chief of the German General Staff and replaced him with General Paul von **Hindenburg** (1847–1934), who became supreme commander of all Central Powers forces. Hindenberg would be the virtual dictator of Germany during the last two years of the war.

The Battle of Jutland. It was also in 1916 that the most important naval battle of the war took place. At the Battle of Jutland, in the *North Sea* west of Denmark, the British navy defeated the German fleet, forcing it to remain in home port throughout most of the rest of the war.

Other Fronts

The eastern front. Throughout the war, the Central Powers had been fighting French, British, and other Allied troops on the western front and Russian troops on the eastern front. Although the Russian army lacked armaments (military equipment) and discipline, it was large enough to inflict heavy casualties on the Austrians and the Germans. Russia was not prepared for a prolonged struggle, however, and by the winter of 1917 she had suffered 1 million casualties. *The unpopularity of the war led to the* **Russian Revolution** in **February 1917,** when the people overthrew the czar and established a Provisional Government modeled after Western representative democracies. With the collapse of the czarist government, the Russian army soon began to fall apart.

In **October 1917,** Communist revolutionaries, led by **Nikolai Lenin** (1870–1924) overthrew the Provisional Government in the **Bolshevik Revolution** and established a *Communist state* in Russia. Lenin quickly signed an armistice (cease-fire) with Germany, allowing the Germans to concentrate all of their strength on the Western Front. With the Treaty of Brest-Litovsk (1918), Russia was forced to give up much land and many people, but Lenin was willing to pay the price for peace.

War in Africa and Asia. Germany's African colonies were quickly subdued by French and British forces. In Asia and the Pacific, the German colonies fell to the Japanese. British Colonel T. E. **Lawrence** ("Lawrence of Arabia") led Arab revolts against Turkish rule in the Arabian Peninsula, and British troops under General **Allenby** captured Jerusalem in December of 1917. (The British would remain in the Holy Land until Israel achieved independence in 1948.)

The Gallipoli Campaign. By far the greatest British offensive in the east was the Gallipoli [gȧ·lĭp'ŏ·lĕ] Campaign, the strategy of the First Lord of the British Admiralty, **Winston Churchill.** Realizing that it was useless to hurl men and equipment against the well-entrenched German fortifications in France, Churchill proposed instead to strike at the Central Powers through the "back door" of the much weaker Ottoman Empire (Turkey), which had sided with the Central Powers. The plan called for the landing of British troops at Gallipoli, in Turkey, and the swift capture of Istanbul (Constantinople), the Turkish capital. The few Australians and New Zealanders who landed at Gallipoli fought bravely but were greatly outnumbered. The Allies were compelled to withdraw after suffering heavy casualties. As a result of the tragedy at Gallipoli, Churchill was forced to resign his post.

— Check Up —

1. Who led Prussia in the unification of Germany?
2. Describe Germany under Kaiser Wilhelm II.
3. Which three nations formed the Triple Entente? What three nations formed the Triple Alliance?
4. What event sparked the beginning of World War I in 1914?
5. When and why did England declare war on Germany?
6. What did Winston Churchill do to prepare the British fleet for war?
7. Why did Italy refuse to aid the Triple Alliance? What role did Italy end up playing in the war?
8. What group became known as the Central Powers? The Allied Powers?
9. Name some important battles on the western front. What was the most important naval battle of the war?
10. What took place in Russia in February 1917? In October 1917?
11. What did the armistice on the eastern front allow Germany to do?
12. Who captured Jerusalem for the Allies? When? Who was "Lawrence of Arabia"?

Identify: Modernism, revolutionary nationalism, Victor Emmanuel II, Rome, Prussia, kaiser, Era of Bismarck, trenches, western front, Paul von Hindenburg, Bolsheviks, Nikolai Lenin

America Enters the War

American interest in Allied cause. Hoping to avoid involvement in the conflict, *the United States had declared her neutrality at the beginning of the war.* However, as the war progressed, America became increasingly drawn to the Allied cause. Between 1914 and 1916, her exports to the Allies quadrupled. Much of what the Allies purchased from America was bought on credit. If the Allies were to pay the debt, they must win the war. But more important than America's financial involvement with the Allies was the growing pro-English and anti-German sentiment. England had been the bulwark of freedom through the 19th century. The tyranny of the German government over its own people and other people of Western Europe was incompatible with American ideals. America's basic belief in the dignity and rights of mankind would not allow it to remain genuinely neutral in the European conflict.

Submarine warfare. This growing belief that America must support the Allies was reinforced when Germany provoked the U.S. in two important ways. At the start of the war, Great Britain had set up a naval blockade of Germany's ports. To get around the British blockade, Germany resorted to a new weapon of war—the **U-boat** (undersea boat) or **submarine.** With its deadly torpedoes, the submarine would prove to be a very effective weapon. In early 1915, the Germans declared all waters surrounding the British Isles to be a war zone and threatened to sink without warning any ship that passed through these waters.

One of the first victims of submarine warfare was the British luxury liner *Lusitania.* Before the *Lusitania* sailed from New York, the German embassy in the U.S. warned people not to board the ship, claiming that it carried war supplies for the British army. But the *Lusitania* embarked with passengers and crew despite the warning, and on May 7, 1915, the vessel sank off the coast of Ireland after being hit by torpedoes from a German submarine. Some 1,198 passengers, including 128 Americans, were killed.

The U.S. government sent Germany an ultimatum, demanding the termination of unrestricted submarine warfare. Germany replied that in the future merchant ships would *not* be sunk without warning and that provision would be made for the safety of those on board. For a time, it seemed

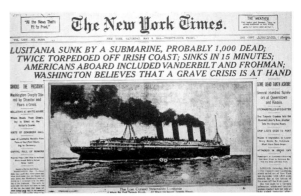

New York Times *Headline May 7, 1915*

Unrestricted Submarine (U-boat) Warfare:
A German submarine sinks an American freighter.

that the U.S. might avoid the war after all. But then, in January 1917, Germany announced the resumption of unrestricted submarine warfare. The Germans hoped to win the war by cutting off British sup-plies and defeating the Allies before the U.S. had time to mobilize (prepare for war) and join the Allied forces. In February, the U.S. broke off diplomatic relations with Germany.

Air Warfare Makes Its Debut

In addition to military tanks and submarines, World War I also witnessed the debut of *airplanes* and other aircraft in the military. At first, airplanes were used mainly for scouting purposes. In the earliest air combat encounters, pilots fought with pistols or rifles. Later, planes were used to drop bombs and were equipped with machine guns. Many daring pilots called "aces" flew on both sides, engaging in colorful "dogfights" in the skies over France and Belgium.

The Germans also used giant *Zeppelins* (similar to blimp air balloons) to bomb targets in England. Containing highly flammable hydrogen gas, these airships had to fly so high to avoid anti-aircraft fire that their diesel engines froze up and their crews developed frostbite.

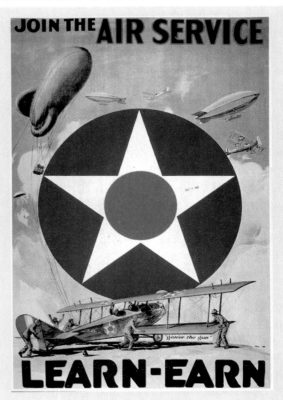

447

The Zimmerman Note. Meanwhile, British agents intercepted a message from German Foreign Minister Arthur **Zimmerman** to the German delegate in Mexico. The Zimmerman Note instructed the delegate to offer Mexico its lost land in the American Southwest in return for Mexico's help if the U.S. should enter the war. The British released this message to America, and in March the Zimmerman Note appeared in newspapers across the country. This news was shortly followed by news of renewed submarine attacks on American vessels.

America declares war. Americans now demanded retaliation. President **Woodrow Wilson** addressed Congress, declaring that "The world must be made safe for democracy," and <u>Congress declared war on Germany</u> on April 6, **1917.**

America's entrance quickly turned the tide of the war. As soon as Congress declared war, the U.S. Navy mobilized its Atlantic fleet. Soon naval destroyers were protecting great convoys of merchant ships carrying men and supplies across the North Atlantic. The American fleet also laid a great mine field in the North Sea to limit the activity of German submarines. Between March and July of 1918, over a million American *"doughboys"* (as U.S. troops were called) landed in France. American manpower, weapons, economic resources, and food supplies ensured an Allied victory.

The Western Front, 1917–1918

The last German offensive. Hoping to win the war before the Allies could be reinforced by fresh American troops, the Germans launched a major offensive to capture Paris in March 1918. Having made peace with the Communist government in Russia, Germany could concentrate its forces on the western front. For weeks, the German army fought French and British forces along the western front. They steadily drove the Allies back, conquering territory and taking prisoners, until they came within 40 miles of Paris. But the German offensive was too late. By May 1918, American reinforcements had reached the front. With American resources, the Allied forces under the leadership of the French Marshal Ferdinand **Foch** [fôsh] began to drive the Germans back.

Central Powers collapse. Suddenly everything fell apart for the Central Powers. Bulgaria surrendered at the end of September, and Turkey gave up a month later. Austria surrendered November 3. Meanwhile, revolution had broken out in Germany. The kaiser abdicated, a republic was created, and the <u>Germans asked for an armistice</u>. On **November 11, 1918,** in a railroad dining car in France, German delegates signed an armistice, to go into effect at 11:00 that morning—the 11th hour of the 11th day of the 11th month. Whistles and sirens sounded and church bells pealed throughout Europe and the U.S. in celebration of **Armistice Day** (now called *Veterans Day* in the U.S.). The Great War was over.

A costly victory for freedom. World War I was a great victory for the forces of freedom, but it was also a very costly victory. World War I brought the greatest destruction in property and people the world had ever seen. It was a modern war, employing trench warfare, airplanes, tanks, machine guns, poisonous gas, and submarines. More than <u>13 million people died</u>, and as many as <u>21 million were wounded</u>. In the aftermath of the war, America began to ship food and medical supplies across the Atlantic. American food relief shipments kept millions of Europeans, including Germans, from starving after the devastation of World War I.

U.S. President Wilson declared that the war was

. . . a war for freedom and justice and self-government amongst all the nations

Armistice November 11, 1918: Parisians and Allied troops celebrate the end of the Great War.

of the world, a war to make the world safe for the peoples who live upon it and have made it their own, the German people themselves included.

He expressed the hope that World War I would be *"the war to end all wars."*

The Peace that Failed

The Conference of Versailles. On January 18, 1919, a peace conference convened at the Palace of Versailles outside Paris. The signing of a peace treaty seemed urgent. The economies of Western Europe were in shambles, and many parts of the continent were experiencing political upheaval. *Communism had taken control in Russia*, and it threatened to spread to other parts of the world. The Conference of Versailles made little progress however, for although it was supposed to achieve a "peace among equals," no representatives from the defeated Central Powers were invited to attend. After two slow months, the leadership of the conference fell to four influential men. The **"Big Four"** included President <u>Wilson</u> of the U.S., Prime Minister David <u>Lloyd George</u> of Britain, Premier Georges <u>Clemenceau</u> [klā′män′sō′] of France, and Prime Minister Vittorio <u>Orlando</u> of Italy.

League of Nations. President Wilson was convinced that the most critical step to maintaining future world peace was the establishment of a League of Nations. He was even willing to compromise on other issues in order to get his League accepted, believing that mistakes made at the peace conference could be corrected later through the League of Nations. Wilson worked hard to get the League covenant drawn up and approved. The covenant specified the aims of the League: "To guarantee international cooperation and to achieve international peace and security."

U.S. President Woodrow Wilson

449

Treaty of Versailles. The result of the peace conference was a series of compromises. The main provisions of the Treaty of Versailles may be summarized as follows:

(1) *German territorial losses.* Germany would be forced to give up all colonies and overseas possessions as well as territory on her northern, eastern, and western borders.

(2) *Demilitarization of Germany.* Germany would be forced to surrender her fleet and reduce the size of her merchant marine. The German army was reduced to 100,000 men, about the size of Belgium's army, and conscription (military draft) was prohibited.

(3) *Reparation and admission of guilt.* Germany was forced to admit full responsibility for causing the war. On that basis, Germany was to pay the entire cost of war damages. A special committee later decided that the total reparations should be about $33 billion.

Many predicted that the Treaty of Versailles would set the stage for another war. When the French Marshal Foch learned that the Rhine was not to be set as a permanent boundary to protect France from Germany, he remarked, "This is not peace. It is an armistice for twenty years."

German bitterness. The Germans had no choice but to accept the Treaty of Versailles, but it left them very bitter toward the Allied nations. It saddled Germany with guilt and with a debt its people could not pay; it placed her in a

EUROPE AFTER WWI
(c. 1918)

Territories Lost by:
Austria-Hungary
Bulgaria
Germany
Russia

position to be easily victimized by extremists and fanatics; and it gave her a new "democratic" government with no sure foundation. The resentment and economic hardship that resulted in Germany because of the Treaty of Versailles helped sow the seeds for World War II.

Peace of Paris. In addition to the Treaty of Versailles, separate treaties were signed with the other Central Powers: Austria, Hungary, Bulgaria, and Turkey. These treaties included the following provisions:

(1) All of the Central Powers were forced to give up land.

(2) Austria and Hungary became separate nations.

(3) The following **new nations** were created: *Finland, Estonia, Latvia, Lithuania, Poland,* and *Czechoslovakia.*

(4) The following **nations were enlarged:** *Serbia* (which became *Yugoslavia* after the war), *Belgium, Italy, Greece,* and *Romania.*

Collectively, the treaties signed at the end of World War I were called the Peace of Paris. Each of the treaties in the Peace of Paris contained the covenant of the League of Nations.

America rejects the League. Ironically for President Wilson, the U.S. was the only victor *not to join the League of Nations.* By the time the Treaty of Versailles was put in final form, many Americans had come to oppose it. Some insisted it was too harsh on Germany, and others feared the entangling alliances it would create. Many Americans feared that the treaty would draw the U.S. into a European war that was none of her concern. By a joint Congressional resolution America officially ended its hostilities against Germany in 1921, but it never ratified the Treaty of Versailles or joined the League of Nations.

CHECK UP

1. Give three important reasons why the United States was drawn to the Allied cause.
2. What tragedy caused the United States to demand the termination of Germany's unrestricted submarine warfare?
3. When did America declare war on Germany? How did American aid ensure an Allied victory?
4. When was an armistice signed by Germany? Where was it signed?
5. What U.S. President wanted to establish a League of Nations? What were the specified aims of the League?
6. What were the three main provisions of the Treaty of Versailles?
7. How did the Peace of Paris affect the nations involved? What new nations were created?
8. What was the only World War I victor *not* to join the League of Nations?

Identify: submarines, airplanes, zeppelins, Zimmerman Note, doughboys, Ferdinand Foch, Big Four

---

The Rise of Communism in Russia

Early History

Origin of Russia. Russia's history began when a tribe of eastern **Slavs** settled in eastern Europe where **Kiev,** the capital of Ukraine, is located today. Later, during the ninth century A.D., this region was invaded by a Viking tribe called the **Russes,** and the region became known as the **Land of the Rus,** or Russia. Around A.D. 990, **Vladimar the Saint** introduced the Russian people to Christianity. Kiev, as a political and a religious center, quickly became the most important city in Russia.

Mongolian rule. About 1240, Russia fell to the **Mongols,** who controlled Russia for nearly 250 years. During this time, **Moscow** rose to power. After the Mongols conquered *Byzantium* (Constantinople, the capital of the old Eastern Roman Empire), a strong Byzantine influence began to be felt throughout Russia, especially through the Greek Orthodox Church. By 1480, Ivan III, prince of Moscow, had driven the Mongols from power. **Ivan III** (ruled 1462–1505) became <u>the first true national leader of a united Russia</u>.

Ivan the Terrible. Ivan IV (ruled 1533–1584) took the title *czar* [tsär: "caesar"], but he was better known as **Ivan the Terrible.** He passed laws tying the peasant farmers to the land. This created a new class of people in Russia—the *serfs*, who were little more than slaves. Thus, at the dawn of the Modern Age, when Western Europe was moving out of the Middle Ages and feudalism was fading away, *Russia was establishing feudalism.* The church at this time became distinctively Russian, and the Greek Orthodox Church became known in Russia as the **Russian Orthodox Church.**

The Romanov dynasty. In 1613, **Michael Romanov** became czar, beginning the Romanov dynasty, which lasted for over <u>300 years</u> (ending in 1917). Under the Romanovs, the czar's power increased and local governments grew weaker as the central government grew stronger. Russian expansion continued, and the government further defined and fixed the status of the serfs.

Peter the Great (1689–1725) called himself *emperor* as well as *czar*, revealing his desire for a great Russian empire and great personal power. He strongly <u>desired that Russia become westernized</u> and break with the centuries-old Byzantine habits. During his reign, Peter traveled in disguise through Western Europe, observing Western ways. He fought a war with Sweden and conquered lands and peoples along the Baltic Sea (the Baltic states) in order to build the port city of **St. Petersburg** to serve as his "window to the west." Open-

Ivan the Terrible

Catherine the Great

ing official relations with other European countries, Peter established Russia among the nations of Europe.

Catherine the Great (1762–1796) <u>also embraced western ideas</u>, especially those of the French philosopher *Voltaire*. At the age of 16, Catherine came to Russia and married Peter III. When Peter became czar in 1762, she deposed him and usurped the throne. Catherine began some reform of the harsh feudal system that subjugated the majority of the Russian people. But the violence of the French Revolution frightened her and cooled her democratic idealism, and she lacked the spiritual discernment to proceed toward republican moderation. Instead, she poured her energy into expanding Russian borders to the Black Sea, forcing many people into the Russian empire against their will. At this time, Russia conquered more of the Ukraine and part of Poland.

St. Petersburg, c. 1885

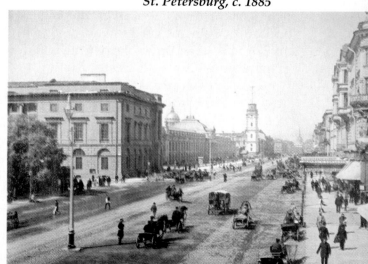

Czar Nicholas I (ruled 1825–1855) oversaw the growth of a huge *czarist bureaucracy* and set up the Russian *secret police* to control the press, the universities, and many other aspects of Russian life. During his reign, Russia added many countries to its empire and forcefully kept several Eastern European countries from breaking away from the empire.

Alexander II (ruled 1855–1881) is known as the *"Czar Liberator"* because in 1861 he supposedly <u>"freed"</u> the serfs. But even though serfs no longer *had* to stay on the land, there was really no place for them to go. The government therefore bought land from the rich and gave it to *groups* of serfs who would form a **commune.** The serfs had to pay for the land in installments. In effect, they were still serfs, but their master was now the czar. Between 1850 and 1900, Russia continued to expand further into eastern Europe, and into central and east Asia.

Alexander II was assassinated in 1881. From that point on, anyone who dared voice dissent was associated with the assassins. His son, **Alexander III** (ruled 1881–1894), determined to crush all oppo-

Czar Alexander II

sition. To ensure that the church would support him, Alexander III made one of his close friends the head of the church. He also instituted strict censorship of the press and of all Russian schools. Alexander III *blamed the Jews* in Russia for his father's assassination. He forced them to live in certain provinces and *subjected them to periodic, organized massacres.* Many Russian Jews emigrated to the U.S. at this time.

Alexander III's son, **Nicholas II** (ruled 1894–1917), wanted to preserve the past during a time when Russia was changing rapidly. The result would be the final collapse of the czarist regime.

GROWTH OF THE RUSSIAN EMPIRE

SWEDEN

RUSSIA

Ural Mts.

•St. Petersburg

•Novgorod

•Moscow

Baltic Sea

DENMARK

•Danzig

Ural R.

•Berlin

•Warsaw

POLAND

Don R.

Volga R.

PRUSSIA

Elbe R.

Vistula R.

•Kiev

Dnieper R.

Dniester R.

•Vienna

Caspian Sea

AUSTRIA

CRIMEA

Danube R.

Black Sea

European Russia, 1689

Territory acquired by Peter the Great

Istanbul•

Territory acquired by Catherine the Great

453

The Rise of Communism

Karl Marx. During the last half of the 19th century, while events were building to the breaking point in Russia, certain extreme political movements arose in Western Europe. The most important of these movements for the future of Russia was **Communism,** or **Marxism,** the atheistic philosophy of the German socialist **Karl Marx** (1818–1883).

As a rebellious student at the University of Berlin, Marx associated with radical students and professors and came under the spell of the religious modernists of Germany who denied the deity of Christ and questioned the authority of the Bible. Though reared in a Lutheran home, he soon denounced Christianity and declared that the course of history would eliminate the upper middle classes and "their" religion and bring the working class to power. Marx said that history is a record of *class struggle* between the <u>wealthy</u> and the <u>poor</u> and *blamed private property as the source of the conflict.* He believed that *economics* (the production, distribution, and consumption of goods) is the overriding driving force in history. But the greatest force in history is the *religion* of the people.

Marx opposed **capitalism,** the economic system based on <u>private ownership and control</u> of business and industry. As long as industries were privately run, he said, the *bourgeoisie* (*the middle class*) and the wealthier capitalists who owned the factories and other means of production would continue to grow rich from the labors of the poor. Marx instead favored **socialism,** the economic system based on <u>state (government) ownership and control</u> of business and industry. He believed that the profits of all production should be distributed according to the principle *"from each according to his abilities, to each according to his need."* Marx taught that the

Karl Marx

change from capitalism to socialism would occur when the *proletariat* (*the working class*) overthrew the bourgeoisie who controlled the government. Marx tried to get people to believe that representative government in capitalist countries is just a "committee of the bourgeoisie."

Once in power, said Marx, the proletariat will set up what he called the *"dictatorship of the proletariat."* But this would *supposedly* be only a temporary arrangement. Eventually, said Marx, the state will wither away, and there will come into being a stateless, classless, perfect condition—*beyond* socialism—called **Communism.** This perfect condition has never come about in any country, of course, and it never will, but many people have fallen into the hands of merciless Communist dictators in their attempts to achieve it.

Marx claimed that in this perfect society, man would no longer feel the need for religion, which Marx called the *"opiate of the people,"* (something that makes them content with less than satisfaction in *this* life because they expect happiness only in the next). Obviously Marx did not understand Christianity at all, for though the Christian does indeed look forward to eternity in Heaven, he knows that God wants men to do their duty in this life to hold back the forces of evil and that only a person who is in the will of God can know true happiness in *this* life.

Socialism and Communism. As we have said, socialism is an economic system in which the government, rather than individuals, controls a nation's businesses and industries. Socialists believe that the individual is unimportant when compared to the welfare of the group. They insist that the government must strictly regulate and control a nation's resources in order to ensure that everyone receives an equal share of the wealth. Communism is a form of socialism which requires a violent, bloody revolution in order to set up a totalitarian dictatorship that dominates the personality and property of its citizens by means of physical and psychological terror. The main difference between socialism and Communism lies in their methods of reform: *what socialists seek through legislation, regulation, and taxation, Communists seek through violent revolution.* Both philosophies enslave the people of a nation in a system that deprives them of their freedoms and property.

The Communist Manifesto. When Marx completed his university studies in 1841, he proclaimed that it was now necessary "to recognize as the *highest divinity, the human self-consciousness* itself." In 1843, Marx went to Paris, where he met Friedrich **Engels** (1820–1895), the only close friend and associate he had. Engels's father was a hardworking and prosperous textile manufacturer, but Engels despised the discipline of his father's home and shared Marx's radical views. Like Marx, he believed that mankind is the high point of biological and social evolution and constitutes the only "deity."

The humanism of Marx and Engels is the foundation of Communist ideology.

Marx and Engels eventually returned to Germany, where they established the Communist League. When revolution broke out in Germany in 1848, they took advantage of the turmoil to issue *The Communist Manifesto,* a pamphlet which laid out a program for Communist revolution. The *Manifesto* advocated the violent overthrow of all established authority and called for the following measures: (1) the abolition of private property; (2) the redistribution of wealth through heavy, progressive income taxes; (3) a centralized federal bank; (4) government control of all means of communication and transportation; (5) government ownership of all means of production and all natural resources; (6) the abolition of unemployment through social welfare programs; (7) the redistribution of the population (from cities to rural areas and vice versa); and (8) mandatory state-sponsored and state-supported education. It closed with a stirring call to battle: "The proletarians have nothing to lose but their chains. They have a world to win. Working men of the world, unite!"

Das Kapital. After the failure of the 1848 revolution in Germany, Engels retired to England to manage one of his father's factories. The income from his "filthy capitalism" kept both Engels and Marx from starving. *Marx, who later proclaimed himself the champion of the working man, never did an honest day's work in his life.* He and his wife and their six children lived in a squalid London apartment because Marx refused to work. While his wife helplessly watched three of their children die in infancy without proper food and medical care, Karl Marx sat in the library of the British Museum trying to solve the problems of the world. Any money that came into his hands (most of it from Engels), he spent for travel, liquor, and tobacco. Two of the three Marx children who survived childhood eventually committed suicide.

While his family struggled to survive, Marx devoted himself to the study of economics, history, and philosophy. Out of this research came what he considered to be his greatest intellectual triumph, *Das Kapital,* which was first published in 1867. Whereas *The Communist Manifesto* laid down a practical program for Communist revolution, *Das Kapital* offered a theoretical foundation for Communist ideology. In it, Marx applied Darwin's idea of evolution to his political theories in a feeble attempt to give them a "scientific" basis. He argued that if man is the product of biological evolution, Communism was the ultimate product of a social evolution by which the human race would achieve perfection.

The spread of socialism and Communism. In Western Europe, Marx's ideas played an important role in developing the **international socialist movement.** Marx thought that his ideas would be best received in the industrialized, capitalistic countries of Europe. Socialist and Communist organizations and parties did indeed spring up in Western Europe during the last half of the 19th century. In 1864, Marx himself founded the International Workingman's Association, or **First International,** which met in Geneva, Switzerland, and later in other European locations.

Socialist, Marxist ideas eventually enjoyed considerable influence in Western Europe in the 20th century. As it turned out, however, the first complete triumph of Communism would come not in an advanced, thoroughly industrialized Western European nation but in backward Russia, where centuries of autocratic extremism had paved the way for revolutionary extremism. As the 20th century began, the Russian government had, like every tyranny in history, sown the seeds of its own destruction.

CHECK UP

1. How did Russia get its name?
2. What title did Ivan the Terrible take? What new class of people did he create in Russia?
3. Who founded the Romanov dynasty? How long did it last?
4. What czar strongly desired that Russia become westernized? What port city did he build on the Baltic Sea?
5. What czar set up the Russian secret police?
6. Which czar was known as the "Czar Liberator"? Why? How did he die?
7. What did Karl Marx believe about history? What did he want people to believe about democracy?
8. Why did Marx oppose capitalism? What economic system did he favor instead? How did he describe the rise of the perfect Communist state?
9. What did Marx call religion? Explain. How did he misunderstand Christianity?
10. What are Marx's two most famous works? Briefly describe each.
11. Where did the first complete triumph of Marx's ideas come? What had paved the way for the acceptance of Communism there?

Identify: Slavs, Kiev, Vladimar the Saint, Mongols, Moscow, Ivan III, Russian Orthodox Church, Catherine the Great, Alexander III, bourgeoisie, proletariat, Communism, Friedrich Engels, First International

---

The Fall of the Czar

Czar Nicholas II was hated by most literate Russians. He lived in splendor, claiming he had the right to rule as he pleased, while other countries were adopting modern ideas about politics and progressively making representative democracy the basis of their government. As the 20th century dawned, Russia was still in the Middle Ages, and most Russians lived like feudal serfs. Inevitably, the great body of the Russian people were going to throw off their bonds. But would they achieve freedom, or would they get new, perhaps *worse* bonds? Organized resistance to the czar began to grow.

Nicholas II lost prestige in 1905 because of two events: (1) the **Russo-Japanese War,** in which Russia lost by trying to expand too far; and (2) the **October Revolt,** when the czar crushed an uprising of Russian workers who demanded reform. In desperation, Nicholas issued the **October Manifesto** (1905), creating the **Duma,** an elected legislative body with limited powers. But Russia had gone too far to alter her course.

World War I proved to be the breaking point for the czar. Russia's war effort was being handled by incompetents, and the war went badly for Russia. The economy plummeted; crops failed; millions faced starvation. The land was ripe for revolution.

The Russian Revolution. In February 1917, food riots erupted in St. Petersburg, the second largest city and home of the royal family. Soldiers sent to break up the riot refused to fire on the crowds and joined the uprising themselves! To restore

Czar Nicholas II: *with Czarina Alexandra and their family, 1905.*

law and order, the Duma set up a **Provisional Government** resembling a Western representative democracy. In March, the Provisional Government asked the czar to abdicate (resign), and he immediately complied. Russia seemed to be moving from an absolute monarchy to a democracy. But the Provisional Government had one big problem: World War I. As the war continued to sap Russia's finances and morale, the popularity and authority of the new government declined rapidly.

Lenin and the Bolshevik Revolution. As conditions grew worse, the **Bolsheviks,** a group of Communist revolutionaries, began to win new followers. The Germans supported the Bolsheviks and began to smuggle exiled Communist leaders, including **Nikolai Lenin,** back into Russia. Lenin quickly rose to power among the Bolsheviks and began to flood the Russian trenches with anti-war *propaganda* (ideas intended to further one's cause or to damage an opposing cause). He also created a Bolshevik *paramilitary force* (a private, often secret military force) known as the *Red Guards* to stir up trouble. As a result of Communist propaganda and terrorism, the Provisional Government was toppled on November 6, 1917, by the **Bolshevik Revolution.** Thus, Lenin became the undisputed leader of the first Communist state in history.

It is vital to remember that the Bolsheviks overthrew not the czar but a basically democratic government that was trying to protect individual freedom. Through force, violence, and the power of persuasion, the Bolsheviks overthrew the only hope Russia had for a truly representative government.

The Reign of Lenin (1917–1924)

One of the first things Lenin did was to end Russia's involvement in World War I in 1917 by making peace with Germany. He then focused on establishing a Communist **totalitarian state** (a government that *controls every area of its citizens' lives*). In this, Lenin faced a great challenge: How could a few thousand Bolshevik radicals impose Communism upon 160 million Russians? When he allowed the Russian people to go to the polls in their first and only general election, they voted overwhelmingly against the Bolsheviks: of 645 positions, only 225 Bolsheviks were elected to the Russian legislative assembly. <u>The people were clearly anti-Communist</u>. Lenin was so frustrated that he ordered his Bolsheviks to forcibly disband the assembly.

The "Red Terror." The solution to Lenin's problem lay in the words of Karl Marx: "There is only one means to curtail, simplify, and localize the bloody agony of the old society and the bloody birth-pangs of the new, only one means—*the revolutionary terror.*" Thus Lenin created a secret police organization called the **Cheka** to bring the Russian people under the heel of Communism by arrest, torture, or death. In czarist Russia, the secret police could make arrests, but people received a public trial. Lenin's secret police arrested, tried, condemned, and imprisoned or executed its victims without public trial. By 1920, Lenin's Cheka had <u>set up the world's first concentration and slave labor camps</u>, and at least *50,000 Russians had been executed.* The "Red Terror" thus became a permanent fixture of life in Communist Russia.

Civil war. Still, opposition to Lenin and the Bolsheviks refused to die. Between 1918 and 1921, Russia was torn by civil war. Those who opposed the Communists were called **White Russians;** those who favored Communism were called **Red Russians.** The White Russians were defeated by the *Red Army.* During the civil war, the Bolsheviks murdered Czar Nicholas II, his wife, and their five children, who had been held prisoner since the revolution.

Nikolai Lenin

Totalitarian control. To establish his Communist regime, Lenin made several far-reaching changes:

(1) The government seized all land.
(2) The government nationalized all banks and major industries.
(3) The government forced all workers to join Communist-controlled trade unions and denied them the right to strike.
(4) The government rationed all food and consumer goods and suppressed private trade.
(5) The government confiscated all church lands.

Lenin also tightened the Bolshevik grip on Russia in other ways, brutally crushing freedom in all forms, including freedom of speech, freedom of the press, and freedom of religion. "Enemies of the state" were imprisoned or executed. *Human life had no value;* anyone who posed even the slightest threat to the Communist regime was killed without hesitation.

Control of education. Lenin knew that by controlling the minds of students he could raise up a generation of loyal Communists. Thus, Communist principles were methodically drilled into the heads of students, who were taught that capitalism and religion are evil. *The Communists sought to destroy the family unit,* taking the children out of the home at an early age to train them in Communist dogmas. The Communist goal was to make people believe that they were supposed to completely submerge themselves in the Communist state, that leaders could do whatever they felt was for the good of the society as a whole without regard for individual human welfare. Never in the history of the world had there been anything as obviously un-Christian, immoral, and contrary to the laws of God as Russia's Communist regime.

International terrorism. In 1919, Lenin organized the **Third International,** a terrorist organization dedicated to spreading Communist revolution throughout the world and establishing a worldwide Communist state. Soon the deceit and violence of atheistic Communism began spreading throughout the world.

New Economic Policy. By 1921, the application of Communist dogma to Russian agriculture and industry had proved disastrous. Faced with the possibility of mass starvation and economic ruin, Lenin adopted a form of state capitalism which he called the **"New Economic Policy"** (NEP). He weakly explained the NEP as a "temporary retreat" from Communism to allow the Russian economy to recover. *"It is necessary sometimes,"* he declared, *"to take one step backward so we may take two steps forward."* The NEP allowed for some private business and attracted much-needed foreign money to invest in the Russian economy.

The Soviet Union. Many Western observers hoped that Lenin's NEP signalled the end of the Communist Revolution in Russia, but they soon realized that the NEP was merely a "breathing spell" before the next phase of the revolution. In December 1922, Lenin created the **Union of Soviet Socialist Republics** (the **U.S.S.R.** or **Soviet Union**) to bring all of the non-Russian nationalities under one centralized Communist regime.

At the height of its power, the Soviet Union included 15 "republics," covered $1/7$ of the earth, and had a population of nearly 300 million people, making it a powerful home base for international Communism. This vast Soviet empire was ruled from the Communist Party headquarters at the **Kremlin** in Moscow.

The Reign of Stalin (1927–1953)

Stalin's rise to power. The death of Lenin in 1924 unleashed a bitter power struggle between two chief rivals: **Leon Trotsky** and **Joseph Stalin.** Trotsky was Lenin's chosen successor, but no one realized Stalin's ruthless determination. Through brilliant political maneuvering, Stalin deposed Trotsky in 1927. Trotsky fled to Mexico, where he was finally murdered in 1940 by a Communist assassin.

Stalin was one of the most brutal rulers of all time. He was personally responsible for the deaths of millions of Russians. Stalin would tolerate no opposition: anyone (whether an old friend or an entire city of people) who got in his way was exterminated.

Stalin's economic policy. In 1928, Stalin replaced the NEP with the first **Five Year Plan.** His goal was to transform the Soviet Union from a backward agricultural country into an industrial and military superpower. The entire Russian economy would be run by an elite group of Communist leaders who rigidly imposed their will on the Russian people.

While building up state-controlled industries, Stalin **collectivized** Russian agriculture, forcing small, private farms to band together into large collective farms supervised by appointed managers. All crops were to be yielded to the Soviet government for distribution. Russian farmers resented the confiscation of their lands and many burned their crops rather than surrender them. Communist troops and police effectively crushed all opposition. Millions of peasants were driven from their lands and either killed or exiled to Siberia. Other problems arose when too much was demanded of farmers: the soil was worn out quickly, and severe famine resulted, especially during 1932–1933. Although Stalin concealed the magnitude of the famine from other countries, mil-

THE SOVIET EMPIRE AT ITS HEIGHT

EAST GERMANY
RUSSIA
CZECHO-SLOVAKIA
POLAND
BELARUS
ESTONIA
LATVIA
LITHUANIA
HUNGARY
ALBANIA
ROMANIA
UKRAINE
BULGARIA
MOLDOVA

R U S S I A

GEORGIA
ARMENIA
KAZAKHSTAN
MONGOLIA
AZERBAIJAN
TURKMENISTAN
UZBEKISTAN
KYRGYZSTAN
TAJIKISTAN

C H I N A

Union of Soviet
Socialist Republics
Soviet Allies

Joseph Stalin

lions of Russians starved to death. *At least 10 million Russian peasants died in Stalin's forced collectivization of Russian agriculture, joining the more than 7 million who had died under Lenin's harsh program.*

Political paranoia. Stalin lived in constant fear of being overthrown and in the mid-1930s instituted a reign of terror known as the **Great Purge,** rooting out anyone who posed even the slightest threat to his authority. Stalin cleaned house even in the Communist party, expelling about

1 million members. Many high-ranking officials were tried on trumped-up charges and executed.

A land enslaved. On the eve of World War II, Russia was truly a land enslaved. The ages of Russia's tragic history of tyranny closed around the people in a threatening deathgrip on the human spirit. They were to continue as enslaved people for many years, and their Communist leaders would succeed in enslaving many other peoples throughout the world.

--- CHECK UP ---

1. Describe Russia at the time of Czar Nicholas II.
2. How did Czar Nicholas II lose prestige?
3. Describe the effects of World War I on Russia.
4. Who led the Bolshevik Revolution? How did he encourage unrest in Russia?
5. What type of government did the Bolsheviks overthrow? What kind of state did Lenin establish?
6. How did Lenin force Communism on the Russian people?
7. List five major changes Lenin made to establish his Communist regime.

8. How did the Communists use education?
9. When did Lenin create the Soviet Union? Why?
10. What two chief rivals struggled for power after Lenin's death? Who won the struggle, and what became of his rival?
11. How did Stalin deal with opposition?
12. What was the result of Stalin's forced collectivization of Russian agriculture?

Identify: October Manifesto, Provisional Government, Bolsheviks, Cheka, White Russians, Red Russians, Third International, New Economic Policy, Kremlin, Five Year Plan, Great Purge

460

CHAPTER 22 REVIEW

MULTIPLE CHOICE   Write the letter of the answer that best completes the sentence.

1. The man who led Prussia in the unification of Germany was _____.
   a Victor Emmanuel II
   b Otto von Bismark
   c Kaiser Wilhelm II
   d Archduke Francis Ferdinand

2. _____ began a program to build a naval fleet to rival the British navy.
   a Victor Emmanuel II
   b Otto von Bismark
   c Kaiser Wilhelm II
   d Archduke Francis Ferdinand

3. The assassination of _____ by a Serbian revolutionist sparked World War I.
   a Victor Emmanuel II
   b Otto von Bismark
   c Kaiser Wilhelm II
   d Archduke Francis Ferdinand

4. _____ led Arab revolts against Turkish rule in the Arabian Peninsula.
   a General Paul von Hindenburg
   b Colonel T. E. Lawrence
   c General Allenby
   d Winston Churchill

5. The Gallipoli Campaign was the strategy of _____, the First Lord of the British Admiralty.
   a General Paul von Hindenburg
   b Colonel T. E. Lawrence
   c General Allenby
   d Winston Churchill

6. _____ was the German Foreign Minister whose note to the German delegate in Mexico enraged Americans.
   a Arthur Zimmerman
   b Marshal Foch
   c Vladimar the Saint
   d Winston Churchill

7. The American President during World War I was _____.
   a Theodore Roosevelt
   b Woodrow Wilson
   c Grover Cleveland
   d Calvin Coolidge

8. _____ was the first true national leader of a united Russia.
   a Ivan I   *c* Ivan III
   b Nicholas II   *d* Alexander IV

9. Czar _____ better known as "Ivan the Terrible."
   a Ivan I   *c* Ivan III
   b Ivan II   *d* Ivan IV

10. Czar _____ set up the Russian secret police to control the press, the universities, and many other aspects of Russian life.
    a Alexander II   *c* Alexander I
    b Ivan I   *d* Nicholas I

11. The czar known as the "Czar Liberator" was _____.
    a Nicholas IV   *c* Ivan II
    b Alexander II   *d* Alexander IV

12. Czar _____ blamed the Jews for his father's assassination and subjected them to periodic, organized massacres.
    a Ivan IV   *c* Alexander III
    b Ivan II   *d* Alexander IV

13. _____ was czar of Russia at the time of the Bolshevik Revolution of 1917.
    a Nicholas IV   *c* Nicholas II
    b Nicholas III   *d* Nicholas I

14. Karl Marx said that history is a record of class struggle between the wealthy and the poor and blamed _____ as the source of the conflict.
    a the church   *c* the government
    b the family   *d* private property

15. _____ assisted Marx and helped support him.
    a Friedrich Engels *c* Nikolai Lenin
    b Joseph Stalin   *d* Karl Marx

16. Bolshevik leader _____ founded the first Communist state in history.
    a Friedrich Engles *c* Nikolai Lenin
    b Leon Trotsky   *d* Karl Marx

461

CHAPTER 22 REVIEW (CONTINUED)

COMPLETION *Choose the correct term to complete each sentence and write the letter in the blank.*

a capitalism
b proletariat
c Great Purge
d doughboys

e Modernism
f *Titanic*
g Communism
h *Lusitania*

i Third International
j bourgeoisie
k Bolsheviks
l League of Nations

m St. Petersburg
n totalitarian state
o socialism
p Moscow

1. The philosophy of ____ (religious liberalism) began in Germany in the late 19th century.

2. The British luxury liner ____ sank off the coast of Ireland after being hit by torpedoes from a German submarine.

3. U. S. troops were called ____ in World War I.

4. President Wilson was convinced that the most critical step to maintaining future world peace was the establishment of a ____.

5. Peter the Great built the city of ____ to serve as his "window to the west."

6. ____ was the atheistic philosophy of the German socialist Karl Marx.

7. The economic system based on private ownership and control of business and industry is called ____.

8. Marx referred to the middle class as the ____.

9. The economic system based on state ownership and control of business and industry is called ____.

10. Marx referred to the working class as the ____.

11. The ____ were a group of Communist revolutionaries who overthrew the Russian government in 1977.

12. A ____ is a government that controls every area of its citizens' lives.

13. The ____ was a terrorist organization dedicated to spreading Communist revolution and establishing a worldwide Communist state.

14. Stalin's reign of terror in which he rooted out anyone who posed even the slightest threat to his authority was known as the ____.

TIME LINE CHALLENGE *Choose the letter of the correct date for each of the events listed below.*

1613	1848	1853–1860	1861	1867	1871–1890	1914	1917	1918	1922
A	B	C	D	E	F	G	H	I	J

____ 1. Victor Emmanuel II becomes first king of Italy

____ 2. World War I begins when Austria declares war on Serbia

____ 3. Bolshevik (Communist) Revolution in Russia

____ 4. "Era of Bismark"

____ 5. Romanov dynasty begins

____ 6. *Communist Manifesto* distributed in Germany

____ 7. *Das Kapital* published in England

____ 8. World War I ends with the Treaty of Versailles

____ 9. Soviet Union created

MATCHING *Match the description with the correct term.*

a Battle of Verdun *g* Triple Entente
b White Russians *h* Triple Alliance
c Allies *i* Central Powers
d Peace of Paris *j* Battle of Jutland
e Red Russians *k* Treaty of
f Battle of Somme   Versailles

_____ 1. France, England, and Russia

_____ 2. Germany, Austria, and Italy

_____ 3. Triple Entente and their allies

_____ 4. Triple Alliance and their allies

_____ 5. the most important naval battle of the war

_____ 6. the treaty that forced Germany to admit full responsibility for the war

_____ 7. all of the treaties signed with Central Powers at the end of the war

_____ 8. those who opposed Communism in the Russian Civil War

_____ 9. those who favored Communism in the Russian Civil War

CONCEPTS TO CONSIDER *On a separate sheet of paper, answer the following questions using complete sentences.*

1. How was America drawn into World War I? What advantages did American assistance give the Allies? Why did America refuse to join the League of Nations?

2. What did Karl Marx believe about capitalism and religion? Explain how he was wrong about both.

3. Define the terms *socialism* and *Communism*. What is the main difference between the two systems?

4. What changes did Lenin make in Russia? How did these changes rob the people of their freedom? How did Lenin try to brainwash Russian children?

5. What was the result of Stalin's forced collectivization of Russian agriculture?

MAP SKILLS *Use the maps on pages 443 and 450 to answer the following questions.*

1. Did Greece join the Allies or the Central Powers during World War I?

2. What nations remained neutral?

3. What territories did Russia lose in World War I?

4. What territories did Germany lose?

5. Name two new nations formed from the territorial losses of Austria-Hungary.

23
Before and During
World War II
(1920–1945)

Between the World Wars
(1919–1939)

Failure of Peace

Attempts at peace. World War I dashed the hopes of many people for a perfect, peaceful world. In the 1920s, the peace obtained at Versailles began to crumble. The **League of Nations,** which was supposed to ensure international justice, met a major obstacle at its founding—<u>the United States refused to join the League</u>. Many Americans firmly believed that America's best policy at that time was to stay completely out of European affairs, to remain isolated.

The U.S. had clearly emerged from World War I as the *most powerful nation of the world*. The Allies found themselves greatly in debt to America financially, and also in a way that could not be measured in monetary terms: for America's aid in delivering Europe from tyranny. <u>The world looked to the U.S.</u>—with its wealth, technology, and international prestige—<u>for leadership</u>. The League of Nations could expect to accomplish little of lasting importance without the U.S. as a member.

Hatred and debt. In Europe, the international hatred that had led to World War I was quickly rekindled in the 1920s.

One major issue was the high war debt that Germany was expected to pay. The huge debt made the Germans bitter toward the rest of Europe, and Germany's inability to pay made the Allies suspicious of her good intentions. Germany's financial woes brought mass inflation and an eventual collapse of the German economy. *By 1923, Germany had defaulted on its debt payments.* The cycle of German-Allied hatred continued, and many Germans began to long for revenge.

Tension with France. Relations between Germany and France were especially tense. To insure itself of receiving proper reparations, France moved into the rich industrial Ruhr Valley of Germany in 1923 with the aid of Belgium and Italy. At the same time that France took advantage of Germany, she feared the growth of a newly organized and revitalized German empire in the future. Thus, France formed a series of alliances against Germany, signing mutual protection pacts with Belgium (1920), Poland (1921), Czechoslovakia (1924), Romania (1926), and Yugoslavia (1927). The Germans watched with contempt as they saw anti-German pacts being signed around them. Many Germans began to look for a leader who could deliver them from their enemies and from their disgrace.

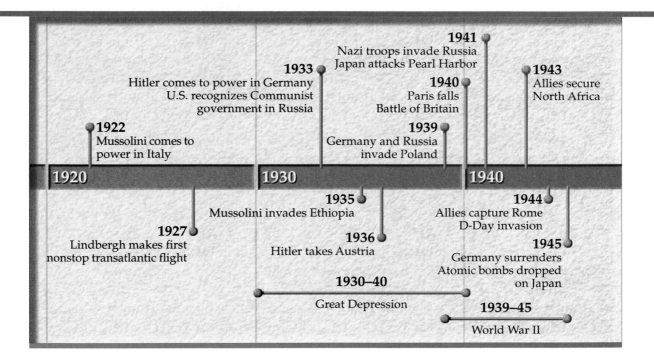

1941
Nazi troops invade Russia
Japan attacks Pearl Harbor

1933
Hitler comes to power in Germany
U.S. recognizes Communist
government in Russia

1940
Paris falls
Battle of Britain

1943
Allies secure
North Africa

1922
Mussolini comes to
power in Italy

1939
Germany and Russia
invade Poland

1920   **1930**   **1940**

1935
Mussolini invades Ethiopia

1944
Allies capture Rome
D-Day invasion

1927
Lindbergh makes first
nonstop transatlantic flight

1936
Hitler takes Austria

1945
Germany surrenders
Atomic bombs dropped
on Japan

1930–40
Great Depression

1939–45
World War II

Troubles in Europe. After World War I, a mood of despair developed in the hearts and minds of many people, especially scholars, writers, and artists. Their acceptance of religious liberalism left a void in their hearts and minds. Historical events seemed to destroy previous hopes, and, for many, faith—whether in God, man, or the future—no longer seemed possible. Rather than turning to the God of the Scriptures, they looked to themselves and their surroundings and were filled with despair.

Many European nations, including England, France, and Spain, experienced economic depressions and political unrest in the 1920s. But conditions were especially desperate in Italy and Germany. In despair, the Italian and German people looked for strong leadership and fell into the hands of despicable tyrants.

Mussolini and fascist Italy. Italy's involvement in World War I had drained it morally and economically. Although Italy had emerged a victor in the war, she had gained very little for her victory. As the economy continued to decline, the Italians suffered from inflation, strikes, unemployment, and hunger. Within four years of the armistice, five Italian premiers were chosen and ousted. Italy looked for a strong leader to deliver the nation from her woes.

This leader emerged in the form of Benito **Mussolini** [mōōs′sȯ·lē′nȇː 1883–1945], a socialist newspaper editor. Following World War I, Mussolini organized the *fascist party* in Italy, promising to take firm control of the struggling government and thereby save it from falling to Communist control. **Fascism** is <u>a form of socialism</u> which *allows people to keep their private property but takes away their freedoms.* The fascists were at first considered radical and were largely ignored. But as conditions in Italy grew worse, fascist party membership continued to grow. In 1922, Mussolini and his fascists marched on the city of Rome. Upon their arrival in Rome, King Victor Emmanuel III invited

465

Benito Mussolini

Adolf Hitler

Mussolini to form a new government. Mussolini became a strong figure in the new government and soon had dictatorial powers. He ruthlessly crushed his opposition and took steps to build Italy into a major military and political power.

Hitler and Nazi Germany. In the final defeat of Germany by the Allies, the German government had collapsed. In its place, the Weimar Republic was established. Under the Weimar government, the German economy slowly recovered and, by the late 1920s, even began to prosper. Yet many Germans were still discontent and bitter over previous economic woes from the burdensome war debts. In this atmosphere of unrest, **Adolf Hitler** came to prominence. Following World War I, Hitler, a veteran of the war, joined the German Workers party—a small extremist group that was nationalistic, antidemocratic, and anticapitalistic. Soon the group took the name **National Socialist German Workers' Party,** or "Nazis." Like Fascism, **Nazism** is a form of socialism, but it relies more heavily on *terrorist aggression, fanatical racism,* and *antidemocratic nationalism.* Under Hitler's leadership, the Nazis staged a revolt against the government. The revolt failed and Hitler

went to jail. While in prison, he wrote *Mein Kampf* (*My Struggle*), an autobiography and exposition of Nazi thinking. By 1925, Hitler was out of prison and spreading the philosophy of *Mein Kampf,* which contended that the *Germans were the noblest race* and were *destined to rule the world.* In 1933, Adolf Hitler became the chancellor of Germany. Soon he would be an outright dictator, and his policies would force the nations to fight a second world war.

Philosophies Clash

Anti-Christian thought. Many people in the 20th century began to be influenced by the ideas of German thinker Friedrich **Nietzsche** [nē'che: 1844–1900] and Danish philosopher Sören **Kierkegaard** [kĭr'ke-gôr: 1813–1855], who formulated *existentialism,* the viewpoint which denies that there is any truth or ultimate reality and therefore says that man must make his own meaning. Nietzsche declared that *"God is dead,"* and Kierkegaard said that all man can do is take a *"leap of faith"* into the great unknown. Another prominent thinker, Sigmund **Freud** [froid: 1856–1939], formulated the system known as *psychoanalysis,* which says that subconscious forces or drives determine a man's actions, rather than reason, faith, or conscious feeling. *Behavioral psychology* also became popular; in its most extreme form, this idea denies that man even has a soul. It ignores thinking and reason and man's relation to God and focuses on man's physical behavior, basically viewing him as just another animal. People who held to existentialism, psychoanalysis, behavioral psychology, or religious liberalism were easy prey for Marxist philosophy. Intertwined in all of these movements, of course, was Darwin's false teaching of evolution.

Defenders of truth in America. In America, these anti-Christian ideas were fought by firm, Bible-believing Christians who held to the <u>fundamentals</u> of the faith—*the inspiration and inerrancy of Scripture, the deity of Christ, His virgin birth and miracles, His blood atonement for sin, His bodily resurrection, and His personal return.* **J. Gresham Machen** (1881–1937), the great Princeton scholar, brilliantly defended the Bible against the attacks of the liberals. He showed that Modernism is anti-Christian and anti-intellectual. He also spoke out against the new liberalism in politics that threatened to take away individual responsibilities and freedoms. Another brilliant teacher and writer of this period was **R.A. Torrey** (1856–1928), who had been exposed to liberalism during his studies at Yale Divinity School and at German universities. D.L. Moody helped Torrey to take a firm stand on the fundamentals of Christianity, enabling him to lead many people from skepticism to faith in Christ. **Billy Sunday, Gypsy Smith, G. Campbell Morgan,** and many pastors and Bible teachers continued to proclaim the truth of the Bible and bring people to Christ. **Harry Rimmer** (1890–1952) fought Modernism in the universities by refuting the error of evolution. These men did much to keep the U.S. from collapsing into immorality and emptiness.

America through the Twenties

Era of optimism. In America, the 1920s was a decade of optimism and great expectation for the future. Having escaped the destruction that World War I brought to Europe, Americans certainly had much to be optimistic about. The war had stimulated industry and agriculture and had increased the nation's exports almost from the beginning. As the war-torn nations of Europe now attempted to rebuild their economies, they looked to America for food and supplies. <u>America became the leading industrial nation and the financial center of the world</u>. American politics of the 1920s reflected the optimism of the times. The country was prospering and seemed to promise a future of endless prosperity for all.

Christians certainly had reason to be optimistic because *spiritual revivals and mass evangelism swept the country in the Twenties.* A number of evangelists held mass crusades, but none were more famous or received more visible results than **Billy Sunday** (1862–1935), the converted baseball hero.

The optimism of the Twenties is perhaps best represented by the triumph of **Charles Lindbergh,** who <u>made the first non-stop transatlantic flight in 1927</u>. The 25-year-old "Lucky Lindy" made the flight from New York to Paris in his *Spirit of St. Louis* in $33^1/_2$ hours. The world proclaimed Lindy a hero. His successful flight symbolized the success of the American system—its economics, technology, and freedom. Lindbergh proved to the world what a nation of free men can accomplish.

Era of prosperity. The optimism of America in the Twenties was undergirded by the prosperity of the decade. From 1923 on, the economy continued to prosper as new industries, particularly the auto industry, expanded rapidly.

The *automobile* became a symbol of the prosperous Twenties. Throughout the decade, more cars appeared on highways as more people could afford them. The auto-

Charles Lindbergh

1920s Automobile

mobile revolutionized America: not only did it completely change transportation in the country, but it <u>promoted more jobs and more prosperity</u>. It benefited steel and paint production, rubber processing, petroleum refining, and road building.

Growing industrial development meant more jobs and better pay for more Americans. Money began to flow more and more freely. As people earned more they were able to spend more, and as they spent more they created more profits for more industries.

Easy credit. Much of the prosperity of the Twenties was based on easy credit. The Federal Reserve Bank kept interest rates low, making it easy for businesses and individuals to borrow money. This policy <u>encouraged people to go into debt</u>. Many ordinary people bought new homes, cars, and even appliances on credit, making small monthly payments instead of paying the full price at the time of purchase. As long as people could buy on credit, factories kept busy and jobs were plentiful.

A frivolous decade. As America basked in the prosperity of the Twenties,

its people enjoyed a decade of frivolity. Thanks to the Industrial Age, Americans had more free time and more money to spend than ever before. In this decade so appropriately called the **"Roaring Twenties,"** they found plenty of ways to spend their new wealth on entertainment and leisure.

CHECK UP

1. What major obstacle did the League of Nations encounter at its founding?
2. Why did the world look to America for leadership during the 1920s?
3. How did Germany's inability to repay her war debt affect her relations with other nations?
4. How did Benito Mussolini come to power? When? What type of government did he organize in Italy?
5. What is Nazism? Who organized the Nazis in Germany?
6. Name three anti-Christian thinkers, and explain their erroneous viewpoints. What does behavioral psychology deny?
7. List some of the fundamentals of the Christian faith. Name six defenders of the faith.
8. How did the automobile revolutionize America?

Identify: *Mein Kampf*, Billy Sunday, Charles Lindbergh, "Roaring Twenties"

The Great Depression (1930–1940)

Hoover becomes President. When **Herbert Hoover** was elected to the American Presidency in 1928, it seemed that the Roaring Twenties would last forever. In his inaugural address, Hoover described America as "bright with hope." But in less than a year, America was plunged into the worst economic depression the nation had ever experienced—the **Great Depression.** In 1929, the stock market crashed and investors lost *$30 billion* in a matter of weeks. The stock market crash effectively shut off the supply of credit that had sustained the economic boom. Thousands of banks closed, and many factories cut down on production or shut down altogether. By 1932, one in every four workers—13 million people—was unemployed. Alarmed by socialist propaganda from the media and certain liberal politicians, many Americans *blamed President Hoover for the Depression and looked for a change in leadership.*

Roosevelt becomes President. In the Presidential election of 1932, the Republican party supported President Hoover's program and nominated him to run for a second term. The Democrats nominated New York governor **Franklin Delano Roosevelt (FDR).** Roosevelt criticized Hoover's program and called for firm, aggressive action to cope with the economic woes of the day. In his nominating speech, FDR declared, *"I pledge myself to a new deal for the American people."* Convinced that something must be done, the American people elected Franklin Roosevelt by a landslide.

The New Deal. In spite of some successes, the New Deal had a devastating effect upon America's political and economic well being. The New Deal introduced the U.S. to socialism, the economic system in which the government controls business and industry. In every nation that has incorporated socialism as a way of life, it has proved to be a self-defeating system that takes away individual productivity, responsibility, and ultimately individual freedom.

By 1939, after six years of government job programs, regulation, and extensive spending, over 9 million workers remained unemployed. The New Deal did little to help the economy and, in some cases, actually prolonged the Depression. FDR's programs marked the beginning of government interference in many aspects of the economy and people's everyday lives.

Recognizing Communist Russia. FDR helped strengthen Communism in the Soviet Union and ultimately around the world. Diplomatic relations had been severed between the U.S. and Russia since the Communist Bolshevik Revolution in 1917. But President Roosevelt wanted to trade with Russia, so in November 1933,

The Great Depression: Throughout the U.S., soup kitchens, bread lines, and shelters sprang up to meet the needs of the poor. Most were sponsored by churches and private charities.

469

U.S. President Franklin Delano Roosevelt: *addressing the American people by radio.*

the U.S. recognized the Communist government of the Soviet Union. By recognizing the Soviet government, the Roosevelt administration made it possible for the U.S. and other Western nations to trade with Russia. It also enabled the Communists to gain loans and technology from the West.

Effects of the Depression around the world. The Great Depression soon spread to Asia, Europe, and other parts of the world, bringing great hardship to millions of people. Suffering from unemployment and other economic problems, many began to accept the socialistic propaganda that brought Mussolini and Hitler to power.

World War II (1939–1945)

Hitler and the Third Reich

The Depression brought perhaps the greatest economic hardship to Germany, which by the mid-1920s was just beginning to recover from World War I. Desperate for economic recovery and fearing a Communist takeover, the German people were easily swayed by the promises of prosperity and protection coming from **Adolf Hitler.**

Hitler comes to power. Hitler had already come to power as chancellor of Germany by 1933. At first, he was the head of a *coalition* (combination of political parties) government; his Nazi party did not hold a majority in the **Reichstag** (the legislative assembly of Germany). In March 1933, just before a new election, the Nazis burned the Reichstag building and blamed it on the Communists. This *discredited the Communist party and gave the Nazis a majority* after the election. Next the Nazi majority in the Reichstag voted to give Hitler power to make laws by his own decree. In 1934, Hitler assumed the total power as *"Der Führer"* (the leader) of Germany. Hitler called his new government the **Third Reich** (Third Empire), claiming the First Reich had been organized by Otto the Great in 962 A.D. and the Second Reich had been organized by Otto von Bismarck in 1871. In 1938, the top German military leaders were defamed and forced to resign, and Hitler took direct control of the German army himself.

Nazi optimism for Germany. Hitler's rise to absolute power was attained with the consent of the majority of the German people. Hitler was a genius as a leader of men. His domineering personality persuaded people to look to him for leadership. His moving speeches convinced the masses that he understood and sympathized with their economic and social needs; he was the man to deliver Germany from its economic and political woes. Unemployed men became faithful and enthusiastic **storm troopers** (members of the Nazi militia), and many young people joined the **Hitler Youth.** Hitler provided the Germans with jobs and a sense of patriotism. Almost before the world realized what was happening, Hitler had become the leader of a newly optimistic, enthusiastic, and thoroughly deluded German people.

German economy and expansion. The professed goal of the Nazis was to get people back to work and get the economy moving again. Hitler did much to rebuild the German economy, largely by rebuilding the German military machine. Many men

Hitler Speaks: Thousands of German troops listen as Adolf Hitler speaks at the Nuremberg Rally in 1936. Germans were dazzled by their country's military might.

Nazi Abuse of the Jews: Jews wearing the star of David are expelled from their homes

were employed in military service, and both men and women were employed in the munitions plants. Public works projects were undertaken to get other unemployed people back into the workforce. But foremost in Hitler's mind was always German expansion; he intended for Germany to conquer. His motto became: *"Today, Germany; tomorrow, the world."*

Nazi persecution of the Jews. Most notorious of Hitler's schemes was his attempted annihilation of the Jewish race. Hitler's personal, intense hatred of Jews made them the logical object of Nazi fury. While Hitler claimed that the Germans were the noblest race, he asserted that the Jews were the lowest and most despicable of the races. He accused the Jews of being pacifists, disloyal citizens, and selfish capitalists who controlled the German economy for their own benefit. He insisted that through intermarriage the Jews were corrupting the purity of the noble German race.

By 1933, German Jews were being severely persecuted. At first, Jewish shops were boycotted, and Jews were removed from positions of political and cultural leadership. In 1935, the Jews were stripped of their civil rights. By the time World War II broke out, many Jews had left the country. After 1939, law forbade Jews to emigrate from Germany. In the course of Hitler's regime, <u>millions of Jews and other Europeans were put to death</u>. The world would not know the extent of Hitler's cruelty until after the war was over.

Hitler's hatred of Judaism was matched by his hatred of Christianity. "One is either a German or a Christian," he said. "You cannot be both." He exclaimed:

The religions are all alike, no matter what they call themselves. They have no future—certainly none for the Germans. Fascism, if it likes, may come to terms with the Church. So shall I. Why not? That will not prevent me from tearing up Christianity root and branch, and annihilating it in Germany.

from *Therefore, Stand,* by Wilbur M. Smith

Another World War in the Making

Turmoil in Europe. By the mid-1930s, Europe was in turmoil as depression stirred unrest and unscrupulous politicians took advantage of the situation. Benito Mussolini had already come to power in Italy before the Depression set in, but the Depression helped convince Italians of the need for strong government and thereby strengthened his dictatorship.

Italy invades Ethiopia. In *October 1935*, Mussolini invaded Ethiopia. The brave emperor of Ethiopia, **Haile Selassie** [hī′le sĭl·lä′syĕ], appealed to the League of Nations for help, but it did nothing. By May 1936, the Italians had conquered Ethiopia.

Germany arms the Rhineland. No sooner had Hitler come to power in 1933 than he withdrew Germany from the League of Nations, making the League's proposals for extended peace virtually worthless. He also ended Germany's World War I reparation payments, renounced the Treaty of Versailles, and— against the treaty's provisions—began rearming Germany. In *March 1936*, in direct violation of the Versailles treaty, German troops marched into the Rhineland, Germany's western territory, which, according to the treaty, was to remain disarmed for the safety of all Europe. In the same year, <u>Mussolini and Hitler formally joined forces</u> by organizing the *Rome-Berlin Axis.* Germany and Italy would soon be known as the **Axis Powers.**

Spanish Civil War. Also in 1936, a long period of political unrest in Spain broke into the Spanish Civil War (1936–1939). Mussolini and Hitler, both eager to see a fascist state on the doorsteps of France, gave aid to the revolutionary forces led by General Francisco **Franco.** Mussolini provided troops, and Hitler provided weapons. The Communists, always ready to step in when a nation is experiencing unrest, also lent aid. Franco saved Spain from Communism by establishing his own dictatorship in 1939, which lasted until his death in 1975.

Hitler takes Austria. When Germany rearmed the Rhineland in 1936, Hitler declared, "We have no territorial demands to make in Europe." His actions soon proved otherwise. In *March 1938*, German troops marched into neighboring Austria. An independent Austria quickly and quietly ceased to exist.

The slicing of the Sudetenland. Next, Hitler turned his attention to the Sudetenland, an area of Czechoslovakia bordering on Germany. Hitler told the British Prime Minister **Neville Chamberlain,** a leading voice in Europe for peace and conciliation, that he wanted the Sudetenland out from under Czech control because its population was predominantly German. In *September 1938*, a conference was held at the Nazi headquarters in **Munich.** It was attended by Hitler, Chamberlain, Mussolini, and Édouard Daladier [dȧ′lȧ′dyȧ′] of France. No representative of Czechoslovakia was present. At this infamous meeting, it was decided that chopping up Czechoslovakia for the sake of European peace was legitimate. The surrender of the Sudetenland to Hitler was agreed upon, and Hitler insisted that he had no further demands in mind.

"Peace in our time." Prime Minister Chamberlain returned to England to proclaim that the Munich Conference had obtained "peace in our time." Most of Europe seemed satisfied with this assurance of peace, even though it was at the expense of little Czechoslovakia. The leading nations of Europe were content to sacrifice part of Czechoslovakia to save themselves from Hitler's wrath. But at least one Englishman saw the folly of appeasing the ambitious, ruthless, German tyrant. Winston Churchill issued a solemn warning:

> And do not suppose that this is the end. This is only the beginning of the reckoning. This is only the first sip, the first foretaste of a bitter cup which will be proffered to us year by year unless, by a supreme recovery of moral health and martial vigor, we arise again and take our stand for freedom as in the olden time.

Hitler conquers Czechoslovakia. In *March 1939*, only six months after the Munich Conference, German troops marched into Czechoslovakia and took over the entire country. Churchill's prophecy was already beginning to be fulfilled.

Plans for Poland. Hitler's next target was Poland, but he feared incurring the wrath of *Joseph Stalin,* the Communist dictator of Russia. Thus, in August 1939, he signed a non-agression pact with Stalin, the **Nazi-Soviet Pact,** which included a secret agreement to jointly invade Eastern Europe and divide the land between them. On *September 1, 1939,* Germany invaded Poland. Two days later, both England and France declared war on Germany. **World War II (1939–1945)** had begun.

CHECK UP

1. What happened to the stock market in 1929? What was the result?
2. Name the 1932 Presidential candidates and their parties. Who won the election?
3. How was the New Deal unsuccessful?
4. How did Roosevelt help strengthen Communism?
5. How did the Depression affect Europe and Asia?
6. What office did Adolf Hitler hold in Germany by 1933?
7. How did Hitler come to power as *Der Führer* of Germany?
8. What was Hitler's most notorious scheme? Explain his view of Jews. How were the German Jews persecuted?
9. How did Mussolini and Hitler take part in the Spanish Civil War? Why?
10. What countries had Hitler conquered by the spring of 1939?
11. What was the Nazi-Soviet Pact? With whom did Hitler sign it?
12. Why did England and France declare war on Germany?

Identify: Great Depression, Reichstag, *Der Führer,* Third Reich, storm troopers, Hitler Youth, Haile Selassie, Axis Powers, Neville Chamberlain, Munich

---

Early Years of the War (1939–1941)

Blitzkrieg. The invasion of Poland was the world's first experience of *blitzkrieg* (German word for lightning war). Like a flash of lightning, Nazi forces smashed all Polish resistance before it had a chance to organize. By September 17, Poland had fallen to the Germans and Russians.

Stalin takes the Baltics and Finland. During the winter of 1939–40, Stalin forced the Baltic states (**Estonia, Latvia,** and **Lithuania**) to allow Russian military bases and troops within their borders. **Finland** attempted to resist Russia but, after a valiant fight, was crushed.

Hitler sweeps across the continent. In April, the Nazis invaded **Denmark** and **Norway.** Denmark fell within hours, but Norway held out until May. **Holland** fell in 5 days, and **Belgium** in 18. Even before resistance had been crushed in Holland and Belgium, German troops began their assault on northern France. The German blitzkrieg was so swift and overwhelming that the British and French troops who had assembled in northern France to block the Nazi advance were soon pushed to the coast at the little port of **Dunkirk** on the English Channel. It seemed certain the entire allied army would be forced to surrender to the merciless Nazis. But in a daring and courageous effort never to be forgotten, the British **Royal Air Force** *(RAF)* held off the Germans long enough for hundreds of small British crafts of all kinds, both military and civilian, to ferry 300,000 troops across the Channel to safety in Britain.

The fall of Paris. Once Dunkirk had fallen, the surrender of France was only a matter of time. The city of Paris fell on June 14, 1940. A new conciliating government, headed by 84-year-old Marshal Henri **Petain,** came to power and immediately asked Hitler for an armistice. France was forced to bow to purposefully humiliating defeat. In the same railroad dining car in which Germany had signed an armistice in 1918, the Germans forced France to accept an armistice on June 22, 1940.

Some patriotic Frenchmen escaped to Great Britain, where they organized a **Free French government** under the leadership of General **Charles de Gaulle.** The Free French government adopted as its symbol the red cross of Lorraine, used by Joan of Arc in her fight to liberate France centuries before. In the safety of England, de Gaulle trained French liberation troops and continued to assist the Allies throughout the war.

The Battle of Britain. With France under the Nazi boot, Hitler focused on Britain. Hitler and his air force commander, Marshal Hermann **Goring,** were confident they could destroy Britain's Royal Air Force and demoralize the British people by approximately one month of constant air attacks. Then, according to their plan, a German task force would cross the English Channel to force Britain into surrender. But the Nazis underestimated the resolve of the British people.

German Troops March Triumphantly into Paris

Shortly after the fall of Norway in May of 1940, Neville Chamberlain resigned, and **Winston Churchill** became prime minister of Great Britain. Prime Minister Churchill realized that the only hope for preserving freedom in Europe was to make a valiant stand against Germany. Hitler unleashed his bombers against England in *July 1940,* beginning the *London Blitz,* or the **Battle of Britain.** For three months, the Nazis bombed the city of London mercilessly (10,000 bombs fell on the city in September alone). But the Royal Air Force (RAF)

German Bombers: flying over the English Channel on their way to the British Isles.

Winston Churchill: In public appearances during the war, Churchill was frequently seen giving his famous V for "Victory," urging the British on to triumph.

destroyed so many German planes that Germany gave up daytime bombing raids on Britain and resorted to nighttime raids only, to take advantage of the cover of darkness. England lost 915 planes to Germany's 1,700. By destroying so many German bombers, the RAF gave Great Britain a chance to defend herself against her ruthless enemy. Churchill expressed the gratitude of the British people to their air force by saying, "Never in the field of human conflict was so much owed by so many to so few."

The courage of the British airmen was matched by that of the citizens of London. After evacuating their children to the relative safety of the countryside, the people of London prepared for the worst. Throughout the London Blitz, they remained steadfast, hiding in bomb shelters during air raids and going about their business when the bombers were gone. Churchill and his government also remained in London. The brave prime minister toured the ruins—sometimes with tears in his eyes, but often flashing his famous "V" for victory hand sign—encouraging the British people to carry on. Many lost their lives, but few ever lost the courage or determination to fight.

Conquests in Eastern Europe. By October 1940, Hitler had abandoned his plan for an invasion of England. For the next several months, through the spring of

1941, Hitler concentrated on **Yugoslavia** and **Greece.** In April, he succeeded, and both nations fell within a span of about three weeks. Later, in the winter of 1941–1942, Hitler took **Romania, Hungary,** and **Bulgaria.**

Invasion of Russia. When Hitler gave up on taking England, he turned his attention to Russia, just as Napoleon had done under similar circumstances over a century earlier. Despite the non-aggression pact Hitler had signed with Stalin, <u>Nazi troops invaded Russia on June 22, 1941.</u> This single event would be a determining factor in world history for the next 50 years. With Russia at war with Germany, Churchill and Roosevelt now considered Stalin their ally against Hitler. *The U.S. would send billions of dollars worth of weapons and other supplies to Stalin over the next few years*, enabling the Communists to drive the Germans out of Russia. Unfortunately, this aid would also help Stalin enslave Eastern Europe after the war.

For the first three months, the invasion of Russia went remarkably well. By October 1941, the Nazis had advanced as far as Leningrad in the north, and they had conquered the Baltic states and the Ukraine. Then Hitler made the same blunder Napoleon had made; he decided to attack Moscow just as winter was setting in. Strained supply lines and the bitter cold of the Russian winter proved to be too much for the Germans. Stalin's forces, used to the cold, gained the upper hand, and Hitler was forced to abandon his invasion of Moscow. Meanwhile, on the other side of the globe, events were taking place in the Pacific that would bring the U.S. into the war and ultimately lead to the fall of Hitler's evil Third Reich.

American Interest in the War

American neutrality. The U.S. emerged from World War I confident, prosperous, and powerful. During the 1920s, most Americans did not want to get involved in world affairs. The American people regretted their active involvement in World War I; they had gained very little from the war and had lent huge sums to countries that were now unable to repay them. So America turned from Europe and enjoyed being separate during the 1920s. During the 1930s, *America was too concerned about the Great Depression to pay much attention to Europe.*

In 1939, Americans opened their newspapers to learn that Europe was once again at war. As the war progressed, American manufacturers began producing more and more weapons. But this time, war material was sold on a strictly cash basis—Europe had not paid its debt from the last war; why lend them any more? Most Americans wanted to see the Allies win the struggle with Germany, but they wanted to view the game from the sidelines and not get involved.

Many Americans hoped this war would be over before it really started. But then France fell, and Germany began the London Blitz. *Now only Britain stood between Germany and America.* Churchill

vowed that the British would never surrender, but Americans listened to Hitler's vows of world conquest and began to get worried. How long could England last?

"Arsenal of Democracy." President Roosevelt believed that America should help Great Britain in its fight for survival. In December 1940, he declared that America should be an "Arsenal of Democracy." He pleaded with Congress to help England:

Let us say to the democracies: We Americans are vitally concerned in your defense of freedom. We are putting forth our energies, our resources and our organizing powers to give you the strength to regain and maintain a free world. We shall send you in ever-increasing numbers, ships, planes, tanks, guns. That is our purpose and our pledge.

Congress responded in March 1941 by passing the *Lend-Lease Act,* which allowed war material to be given to England on credit. American factories were converted to wartime production and a great fleet of ships began taking much needed war supplies to England. True to his pledge, President Roosevelt sent "in ever-increasing numbers, ships, planes, tanks, guns."

Stabbed in the back. Germany was furious. How could America call itself neutral and supply England with weapons? As 1941 drew to a close, tempers flared. German submarines began firing upon American merchant ships, and these ships began firing back at the German subs. Everyone thought for sure that Germany would draw America into the war. But as it happened, America entered the war when it was stabbed in the back—stabbed by a knife held by Japan.

Attack on Pearl Harbor (1941)

It was no secret that Japan and the U.S. were enemies. Relations between the two powers had been deteriorating for years. For centuries, Japan had been a land of mysteries; few Europeans or Americans had ever been there. In the 19th century, Japan had opened its doors to trade with the West and to Christian missions. But the Japanese, who greatly love their traditions and ancient customs, resented the foreigners and their strange ways. They dreamed of establishing an empire in the Orient and driving out all Western influences.

Militaristic Japan. In 1937, Japan invaded China and began waging an undeclared war on that vast land. Japan had become *militaristic,* relying upon military might to accomplish its goals. The official head of the Japanese government, **Emperor Hirohito,** had no real authority; instead, the reins of power were held by such men as **General Hideki Tojo** and a few others who called for Japanese conquest of China and the Pacific. Military leaders convinced the Japanese people that they were under divine protection and could not be defeated. On *September 27, 1940,* Japan signed the *Tripartite Treaty* with Germany and Italy, joining the Axis Powers.

"Moral embargo." The Japanese invasion of China disturbed the American people. For years, the U.S. and China had been close allies. Many Americans were alarmed by the increasingly hostile nature of Japan's leaders and by her powerful military. When Nationalist Chinese leader **Chiang Kai-shek** [jē·äng′ kī′shĕk′] asked the U.S. for assistance, President Roosevelt declared a "moral embargo" on Japan, cutting off all oil exports to the nation. He also began to strengthen American defenses in the Pacific, fortifying the Philippines and other islands. The center of activity was the naval base at **Pearl Harbor, Hawaii.**

A knockout blow. Japan saw the embargo and the military buildup as a threat. Japan asked to be left alone; America refused, insisting that Japan withdraw from China. As the embargo began to hurt the Japanese economy, Japan decided to push America out of the Pacific. But Japanese military leaders warned that a long war with America would result in a Japanese defeat: *the war must be won quickly.* Believing that a knockout blow must be dealt to the Americans at the very beginning, they decided to launch a sneak attack on Pearl Harbor. By *destroying America's Pacific fleet, the Japanese would render the U.S. unable to fight back.* America would be forced to surrender! Even as Japan's diplomats were talking peace in Washington, Japanese aircraft carriers were heading for Hawaii.

Pearl Harbor. On Sunday morning, December 7, 1941, *the Japanese made a surprise attack on the U.S. naval fleet and airfield at Pearl Harbor.* On that quiet Sunday morning, some people at Pearl Harbor were having breakfast; some were getting ready for church; some were away on shore leave; a few were at their positions, cleaning their anti-aircraft guns as a matter of routine. The guns were clean, but the ammunition for them was locked away below deck.

Just before 8:00, waves of planes swooped down out of the sky. One sailor thought they were just army planes showing off; but then the lead plane released its bombs and a loud alarm sounded—"AIR RAID! NO DRILL!"

America in the war. When the pilot of the lead plane, *Mitsuo Fuchida,* saw the battleships below him in neat, unprotected rows, he knew the attack was a complete surprise and he radioed his men to make the most of their advantage. The Americans sprang to action, but it was too late. For two hours Japanese bombs, torpedoes, and machine-gun fire rained down on Pearl Harbor. In those two hours, the *U.S. lost more ships than it had lost during World War I.* The Navy lost 18 ships, including 8 battle-

Devastation at Pearl Harbor: *The Japanese attack on Pearl Harbor, December 7, 1941, crippled the U.S. fleet and freed Japan for conquests in Asia and the South Pacific.*

ships; 170 airplanes were destroyed on the ground. Over 3,500 servicemen had been killed or wounded. Japan lost only 29 of their 359 raiding planes. Confident of victory, Japan immediately declared war on the U.S. and Great Britain.

War declared. On December 8, President Roosevelt asked Congress for a declaration of war: "Yesterday, December 7, 1941, a date which will live in infamy, the United States of America was suddenly and deliberately attacked by naval and air forces of the empire of Japan." Congress responded with an overwhelming vote for war. Three days later, Germany and Italy declared war on the U.S., and the U.S. declared war on Germany and Italy.

Mistaken Japanese. Japan thought that their attack on Pearl Harbor would destroy America, but they soon found that they had failed to anticipate three important things: **(1)** The U.S. aircraft carriers were at sea during the raid on Pearl Harbor and thus escaped harm. **(2)** The raid failed to destroy the repair facilities and fuel reserves at Pearl Harbor. **(3)** Most important, the sneak attack on Pearl Harbor united the American people as nothing has before or since. The entire nation banded together to face their foes with but one goal—to defeat the Axis Powers. The Japanese had not crushed America at all; instead, they had—in the words of a

Japanese admiral—*"awakened a sleeping giant, and filled him with a terrible resolve."*

CHECK UP

1. What countries fell to the Nazis before the British troops arrived?
2. What happened to Paris? Where was the armistice with Germany signed?
3. Who became Britain's prime minister in 1940? What did he realize was the only hope for preserving freedom in Europe?
4. What part did the RAF play in the Battle of Britain? What was the outcome?
5. Why did Hitler's invasion of Russia fail? How did it benefit Stalin?
6. How was America an "Arsenal of Democracy" in the early years of the war?
7. Why were Americans particularly concerned when France fell?
8. How did Germany respond to American aid to England?
9. What incident caused America to enter the war?
10. Name the military leader who held the reins of power in Japan. What region did he want to conquer?

Identify: blitzkrieg, Dunkirk, Free French government, Charles de Gaulle, London Blitz, Emperor Hirohito, Tripartite Treaty, Chiang Kai-shek, Mitsuo Fuchida

The War in Africa and Europe (1941–1945)

The war in Africa. In May 1942, a team of Axis soldiers called the *Afrika Corps* swept across North Africa. Under the skilled leadership of **General Erwin Rommel** (1891–1944), the Afrika Corps marched across Libya and into Egypt. The Nazis were on the verge of seizing the Suez Canal, Britain's link to the oil reserves of the Middle East, when they began to run out of supplies, particularly fuel. The British staged a counteroffensive, and Rommel was <u>forced to retreat</u>. British troops led by **General Sir Bernard Montgomery** pushed all the way to **Tripoli,** in Libya. While the British were marching westward, American forces under **General Mark Clark** marched eastward from Morocco and Algeria. Rommel was caught in the middle. In <u>May 1943</u>, the *Afrika Corps surrendered to the Allies,* and North Africa was secure. Now the Axis powers were confined to the European continent; an important segment of the war had ended.

A third front. When the London Blitz failed in 1940, *Hitler had unleashed his fury on the Soviet Union.* The Russians called upon their allies to start a second front in Europe to divide Germany's forces. Plans were already being made for an Allied invasion of France, but Churchill suggested a third front—a <u>strike at Germany through Italy</u>, which Churchill called the "soft underbelly of the Axis." The Allies in North Africa, just across the Mediterranean Sea from Italy, took advantage of their position and launched an attack in July 1943. The *Italians,* sensing their coming defeat, *removed Mussolini from power.* The Allies <u>captured Rome</u> on June 4, 1944. A few months later, the Italian peninsula was freed from Nazi occupation.

The invasion of Hitler's Europe. Meanwhile, the best military minds of the Allies planned an assault against Hitler's

General Sir Bernard Montgomery

Europe. The invasion *had* to succeed: if not, the war might be lost. American **General Dwight D. Eisenhower** was chosen to head up the invasion. The Germans had heavily fortified the coast of France and were confident that any Allied attempt to invade Europe would fail.

D-Day. On <u>June 6, 1944</u>, the **D-Day invasion** began as thousands of Allied troops hit the heavily fortified beaches of *Normandy* in *northern France,* launching <u>the largest amphibious assault</u> (from ships and other seaborne transports) <u>in history</u>. While shiploads of men crossed the English Channel, planes and gliders carried troops deeper into France. Within a few weeks, about 1 million Allied troops were fighting in northern France. Despite fierce opposition from the Germans, the Allies continued to push eastward. Every step forward brought them that much closer to Berlin. Twenty days after D-Day, Cherbourg, France, fell, giving the Allies a harbor where ships could bring men and supplies.

The race to Berlin. The Allied invasion of France carried on with speed. With swift tanks, American armies under **General George S. Patton** and **General Omar Bradley** pushed the Germans back. By late August 1944, the Allies had *liberated Paris.* The tide of the war was turning. The British and Americans marched on Germany from the west, and the Russians marched on Germany from the east. From

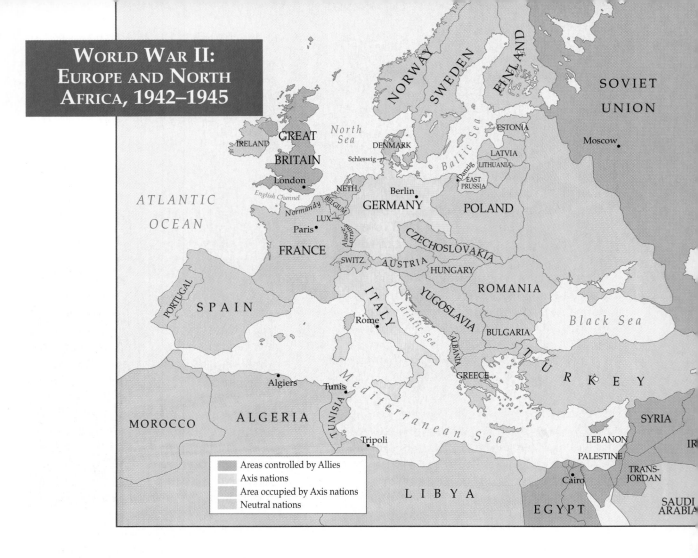

Areas controlled by Allies
Axis nations
Area occupied by Axis nations
Neutral nations

December 1944 to January 1945, the Germans launched their *last great offensive in the West,* known as the **Battle of the Bulge.** But after fierce fighting, the German effort failed, and the Allies began the race to Berlin. Allied bombing raids became more frequent as the Allies approached Berlin. Bombers knocked out German war factories and railroads, further weakening Germany's defenses.

Waning German war effort. Earlier in the war, many German officers had decided that Hitler was a lunatic who was driving Germany toward ruin. Some of them felt that for Germany's sake Hitler should be removed from the scene. On July 20, 1944, a bomb exploded in Hitler's quarters, but the bomb failed to kill the

Führer. Hitler was enraged that his own generals had tried to kill him. Many executions followed; even the well-known Rommel was forced to commit suicide for his part in the plot. From that time on, the German war effort deteriorated. The generals disliked Hitler and wanted to find an honorable way to end the war. Hitler distrusted his generals and accused them of treachery, disloyalty, and incompetence.

Mussolini's end. The end was coming. Italian patriots captured Mussolini and shot him. An angry crowd kicked and spat upon the once-powerful fascist dictator; then they hung his body upside-down in the public square for all to see.

V-E Day. Adolf Hitler lived like a mole 50 feet below Berlin in a bomb-proof

General Dwight D. Eisenhower: *giving the order of the day to the first assault of paratroopers to invade continental Europe, June 1944.*

D-Day, June 6, 1944: *50,000 men and 12,000 vehicles were put ashore on the coast of Normandy to begin the invasion of German-held territory.*

bunker. He was a shattered man, his health and sanity failing fast. On April 30, 1945, Adolf Hitler committed suicide, even as Russian troops were fighting in the streets of Berlin. On May 7, **1945,** Germany surrendered. The next day, May 8, was declared **V-E Day** (*V*ictory in *E*urope Day); people everywhere celebrated. But the war was not quite over. Germany and Italy had been defeated, but Japan was still in the battle.

The War in the Pacific (1941–1945)

After the attack on Pearl Harbor, the Japanese swept across the Pacific, attacking *Guam, Wake, Midway,* and other important American bases in the Pacific. After capturing Guam and Wake, the Japanese made an all-out assault on the *Philippines.* Despite a valiant effort by American troops in the Philippines, the islands fell in early 1942. The fighting at *Bataan* (a Philippine peninsula) and *Corregidor* (a small Philippine island) was especially tragic.

Bataan Death March. When surrender became unavoidable, President Roosevelt ordered **General Douglas MacArthur** to leave the Philippines so that he would not be captured. MacArthur escaped at the last possible moment. When Bataan and Corregidor finally surrendered, over *60,000 Americans became prisoners of the Japanese.* These men were forced to walk 70 miles to prison camps. During the march, many died from hunger, disease, and brutal treatment from the Japanese. More than 10,000 American soldiers died in the **Bataan Death March.** The cruel march angered the Americans and made them even more determined to win a complete victory.

*General
Douglas
MacArthur*

Among those who shared that determination, none was more determined than General MacArthur. He had wanted to stay in the Philippines with his men; now, as he returned to duty elsewhere, he *promised the Philippines:* **"I shall return."**

American hardship. The war in the Pacific was difficult, and America lost many battles in the beginning. The *"territory" was an entire ocean—the Pacific;* therefore, naval battles were important. When land battles did occur, the *"battlefields" were often tiny islands* heavily fortified by the Japanese. Soldiers had to fight in swamps, in dense jungle, or on sharp coral rocks. It was a miserable war for both sides. For Japan, the war was an effort to defend the territory it had obtained; for America, it was an effort to push the Japanese back to Japan and whip them soundly.

Important battles. Victories for America came slowly. As soon as the U.S. Navy could recover from the wounds inflicted at Pearl Harbor, the Pacific fleet met the Japanese navy at the **Battle of Coral Sea** in May 1942. This battle is remembered as the first naval battle in history in which the enemy ships never even saw each other—the battle was fought entirely by planes launched from aircraft carriers. The U.S. won the Battle of Coral Sea and followed it up with a victory at the **Battle of Midway** in June 1942. This crucial battle broke the back of the Japanese navy. American losses were slight, but four Japanese aircraft carriers now sat on the ocean floor. **Midway** ended Japan's domination of the Pacific and turned the tide of the war.

MacArthur returns. In October 1944, American troops under the command of General MacArthur landed in the Philippines. MacArthur had kept his promise to return and liberate the islands. In the **Battle of Leyte Gulf,** *Japan lost almost all of its remaining ships and planes.*

"Island hopping." With the Japanese navy and air force weakened, the American army began to wage land battles in the Pacific. The strategy they followed was known as "island hopping," which meant occupying an island, using it as a base to prepare for an assault on the next island, and moving steadily toward Japan. The

Return to the Philippines: *General Douglas MacArthur wades ashore in the initial landings to take the Philipines from the Japanese. By doing so he kept the promise he made to the Filipinos when he was forced to flee: "I shall return."*

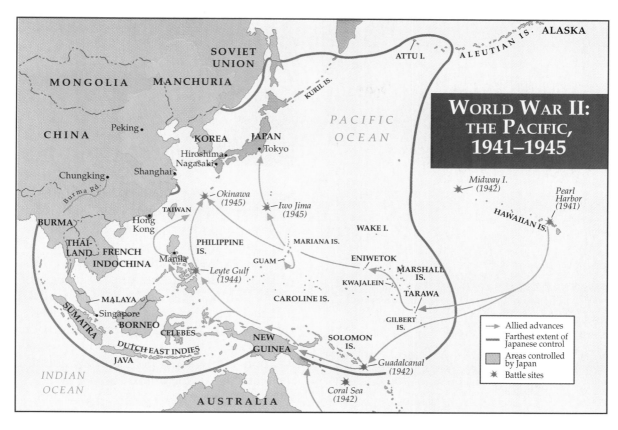

WORLD WAR II: THE PACIFIC, 1941–1945

Legend:
→ Allied advances
— Farthest extent of Japanese control
Areas controlled by Japan
✶ Battle sites

islands fell one by one, but not without long and hard fighting on such islands as *Guadalcanal, Tarawa, Saipan, Tinian, Iwo Jima,* and *Okinawa.*

No Japanese surrender. Island fighting was deadly, and casualties were heavy for both sides. One big problem that American soldiers faced was that <u>the Japanese absolutely refused to surrender</u>. They believed that it was their sacred duty to defend their homeland to the death. To surrender would bring dishonor. Therefore, they would keep fighting even when there was no hope for victory. Many of them would rather commit suicide than surrender. Under such circumstances, a battle would continue until *all* the Japanese troops had been wiped out. Very few prisoners were taken.

Iwo Jima Memorial: The Iwo Jima Memorial in Washington, D.C., honors Marines who have given their lives for their country. It is patterned after a photograph of Marines raising the American flag over Iwo Jima in February 1945.

483

President Harry S Truman

Hiroshima: *The atomic bomb destroying part of Hiroshima, Japan*

Kamikazes. By April 1945, U.S. forces had come within striking distance of Japan. Bombers could take off from Saipan and bomb Japanese cities. Surely now the Japanese would surrender. After all, to continue fighting would mean major battles on Japanese soil. But the Japanese still believed that their homeland was under divine protection and that surrender was dishonorable. They were ready to fight until the last soldier fell. Soon *kamikazes, suicide planes loaded with explosives,* began to crash into American ships, killing hundreds of American sailors.

The atomic bomb. President Roosevelt was reelected to a fourth term as President in 1944, but on April 12, 1945, he died of a stroke. Vice President **Harry S Truman** became President. General MacArthur and others told President Truman that only an immediate and unconditional surrender on the part of Japan would prevent the loss of millions of lives. The Allies pleaded with the military leaders of Japan, but the Japanese leadership insisted that their people would rather die than surrender. In the U.S., scientists had been working for several years on a new secret weapon. Only a few people knew about the existence of the **atomic bomb,** which was perfected in early **1945.** A decision had to be made: should this bomb, the most destructive weapon ever created by man, be used in the war against Japan? Its use could kill hundreds of thousands. But calculations showed that a full-scale invasion of Japan might cost over a million lives. Finally, in order to save the lives of thousands of American soldiers and countless Japanese, President Truman made the painful *decision to drop the atomic bomb.*

Surrender. The *first atomic bomb* was dropped on the city of **Hiroshima** [hē′rȯ·shē′mȧ] on <u>August 6, 1945.</u> Within minutes, the city was wiped out and 90,000 people were dead. When Japanese military leaders still refused to surrender, a *second bomb* was dropped on **Nagasaki** [nä′gä·sä′kĕ] three days later, killing 40,000 people. Finally, the Japanese government surrendered. On September 2, 1945, **V-J Day** (*Victory in Japan Day*), General Douglas MacArthur accepted the surrender of the Japanese military leaders

Japanese Surrender: *Aboard the battleship USS* Missouri, *September 2, 1945, Namoro Shigomitso signs the Japanese surrender document on behalf of his government and his emperor.*

on the deck of the battleship USS *Missouri* in Tokyo Bay. In a speech to those present, he marked the end of World War II— "Today the guns are silent."

American assistance in Japan. General MacArthur became the military governor of Japan. Though the Japanese people felt utterly humiliated in their defeat, MacArthur had great respect for them and encouraged relief efforts and economic development. He also realized that Japan's real need was moral and spiritual. He wrote: "The more missionaries we can bring out here [to Japan], and the more occupation troops we can send home, the better." At MacArthur's request, the Pocket Testament League distributed 10 million Japanese Bibles.

Aftermath

Death and destruction. World War II was finally over. Worldwide, nearly **60 million** died, and millions more were wounded. Many soldiers came home to cities that had been reduced to rubble by bombs and artillery. Practically all of Europe was a smoldering ruin, and both Japan and Russia had sustained heavy damage as well. Only America came through the war unscathed.

The Holocaust. As Germany and Italy were liberated, the dreadful horrors of Nazi rule were exposed to the world. The

Europe in Ruins: *Ruins of downtown Ulm, Germany. All the buildings except the cathedral were demolished by heavy bombing.*

Allies were shocked by what they found in Germany. Hitler had huge *concentration camps* built for the express purpose of *exterminating the Jewish race as well as Germans and others who resisted him.* Some of these camps had gas chambers in which thousands of men, women, and children were killed with poison gas. Great ovens were used to cremate (burn) the corpses of dead prisoners. Yet those who died quickly were the fortunate ones; some prisoners were used in cruel medical experiments which led to a slow, painful death. Those prisoners who survived had suffered untold horrors at the hands of the Nazis; many of them were starving. For the first time, people saw how monstrous Hitler and his Nazi regime had been.

Some of the largest concentration camps were at **Treblinka, Dachau,** and **Auschwitz.** Two million people were gassed and cremated, and another 25,000 worked to death, at Auschwitz alone. When Jews arrived at Auschwitz, they were

Grim Reminder of the Holocaust: An oven used to destroy bodies of prisoners slain by Nazis.

Victims of Nazi Cruelty: *On April 12, 1945, General Eisenhower, on a tour of the Third Army front, walks around a cluster of corpses representing the remains of many of the inmates of the German concentration camp at Gotha, Germany.*

stripped of their belongings and given uniforms. Much of their clothing was shipped back to Germany for resale. During one 6-week period, German clothiers received 222,269 men's suits and underclothes, 192,652 sets of women's clothing, and 99,922 children's outfits. Such statistics reveal the great number of men, women, and children who suffered and died in the Nazi death camps. Altogether, more than **6 million Jews,** as well as many Germans and other Europeans, were systematically slaughtered by the Nazis between 1934 and 1945. This horrible slaughter is remembered today as the **Holocaust.**

Freedom preserved. Thanks to the Allies, such horrors were put to an end. The peoples of Germany, Italy, and Japan were freed from their dictators. The war showed that men everywhere would sacrifice everything—even their lives—to protect their homelands and preserve their freedoms.

CHECK UP

1. Name the generals who stopped German General Erwin Rommel and secured North Africa for the Allies.
2. What was the third front suggested by Churchill for the Allied attack on Germany?
3. What events led up to Mussolini's downfall?
4. Name the American general chosen to head up the D-Day Invasion. Where did the Allies stage their assault on Hitler's Europe?
5. What battle was Germany's last effective stand against the Allied advance?
6. Explain how German officers were involved in the deterioration of the German war effort.
7. When did Germany surrender? What was V-E Day? Was the war over?
8. What was unusual about the Battle of Coral Sea?
9. What super-secret weapon was perfected in 1945? Who made the decision to use this weapon? Why?
10. What had the Nazi death camps been used for? How many Jews were murdered by the Nazis?

Identify: Bataan Death March, Battle of Midway, Battle of Leyte Gulf, island-hopping, kamikazes, Hiroshima, Nagasaki, V-J Day, Holocaust

CHAPTER 23 REVIEW

MULTIPLE CHOICE   Write the letter of the answer that best completes the sentence.

1. The philosophers ____ and Sören Kierkegaard formulated existentialism.
   a Sigmund Freud
   b Friedrich Nietzsche
   c J. Gresham Machen
   d Hermann Goring

2. ____ developed the system known as psychoanalysis.
   a Sigmund Freud
   b Friedrich Nietzsche
   c J. Gresham Machen
   d Sören Kierkegaard

3. The great Princeton scholar, ____, brilliantly defended the Bible against the attacks of the liberals.
   a Harry Rimmer
   b J. Gresham Machen
   c R.A. Torrey
   d G. Campbell Morgan

4. ____ fought Modernism in the universities by refuting evolution.
   a Harry Rimmer
   b J. Gresham Machen
   c R.A. Torrey
   d G. Campbell Morgan

5. ____ made the first nonstop transatlantic flight in 1927.
   a Sigmund Freud
   b R.A. Torrey
   c Harry Rimmer
   d Charles Lindbergh

6. The U.S. President who pledged himself to a "new deal" for the American people was ____.
   a Harry Truman
   b Herbert Hoover
   c Franklin D. Roosevelt
   d Dwight D. Eisenhower

7. Patriotic Frenchmen organized a Free French government in Britian under the leadership of ____.
   a Charles de Gaulle
   b Hermann Goring
   c Winston Churchill
   d Henri Petain

8. General ____ led the Nazis across Libya and into Egypt.
   a Erwin Rommel   c Mark Clark
   b Mitsuo Fuchida   d Omar Bradley

9. The American General ____ was chosen to head up the D-Day invasion in France.
   a Douglas MacArthur
   b Dwight D. Eisenhower
   c George S. Patton
   d Omar Bradley

10. The ____ was the Germans' last great offensive in the West.
    a Battle of Britain
    b Battle of the Bulge
    c Battle of Midway
    d Battle of Leyte Gulf

11. President Roosevelt commanded General ____ to leave the Philippines.
    a Douglas MacArthur
    b Dwight D. Eisenhower
    c George S. Patton
    d Omar Bradley

12. The Battle of ____ was the first naval battle in history in which the enemy ships never saw each other.
    a Britain   c Midway
    b Leyte Gulf   d Coral Sea

13. The Battle of ____ ended Japan's domination of the Pacific and turned the tide of the war.
    a Britain   c Midway
    b Leyte Gulf   d Coral Sea

14. In the Battle of ____, Japan lost almost all of its remaining ships and planes.
    a Britain   c Midway
    b Leyte Gulf   d Coral Sea

15. The ____ was the largest amphibious assault in history.
    a Battle of the Bulge
    b attack on Pearl Harbor
    c D-Day Invasion
    d London Blitz

CHAPTER 23 REVIEW (CONTINUED)

COMPLETION *Choose the correct term to complete each sentence and write the letter in the blank.*

a Pearl Harbor   *e* Nazi-Soviet Pact   *i* Fascism
b kamikazes   *f* Third Reich   *j* Holocaust
c automobile   *g* Nazism   *k* New Deal
d Tripartite Treaty   *h* blitzkrieg   *l* concentration camps

1. _____ is a form of socialism which allows people to keep their private property but takes away their freedoms.

2. _____ is a form of socialism that relies on terrorist agression, fanatical racism, and antidemocratic nationalism.

3. The _____ became a symbol of the prosperous Twenties.

4. The _____ introduced the United States to socialism.

5. Adolf Hitler called his government the _____.

6. Joseph Stalin and Adolf Hitler signed a treaty called the _____, which included a secret agreement to jointly invade Eastern Europe.

7. The invasion of Poland was the world's first experience of _____, or lightning war.

8. Japan signed the _____ with Germany and Italy, joining the Axis Powers.

9. On December 7, 1941, the Japanese made a surprise attack on the U.S. naval fleet and airfield at _____.

10. _____ were suicide planes loaded with explosives.

11. Many Jews and others who resisted Hitler were exterminated in German _____.

12. The horrible slaughter in which over 6 million Jews, as well as many Germans and other Europeans, were murdered is called the _____.

TIME LINE CHALLENGE *Choose the letter of the correct date for each of the events listed below. Answers may be used more than once.*

1930	1933	1935	1936	1939	1940	1941	1943	1944	1945
A	B	C	D	E	F	G	H	I	J

_____ 1. Paris falls

_____ 2. Mussolini invades Ethiopia

_____ 3. Germany and Russia invade Poland (World War II begins)

_____ 4. Great Depression begins in the U.S.

_____ 5. Allies capture Rome

_____ 6. Bombs dropped on Hiroshima and Nagasaki

_____ 7. Nazi troops invade Russia

_____ 8. U.S. recognizes Communist government in Russia

_____ 9. Hitler takes Austria

_____10. Allies secure North Africa

MATCHING *Match the description with the correct name.*

_____ 1. fascist leader in Italy
_____ 2. Nazi leader in Germany
_____ 3. famous American evangelist
_____ 4. President during the Depression
_____ 5. legislative assembly of Germany
_____ 6. emperor of Ethiopia
_____ 7. Germany and Italy
_____ 8. leader of revolutionary forces in Spain
_____ 9. Britain and France
_____10. military leader in Japan

a Haile Selassie
b Billy Sunday
c Reichstag
d Adolf Hitler
e Allied Powers
f Francisco Franco
g Hideki Tojo
h Axis Powers
i Benito Mussolini
j Herbert Hoover
k Mitsuo Fuchida

CONCEPTS TO CONSIDER *On a separate sheet of paper, answer the following questions using complete sentences.*

1. Contrast the state of the rest of the civilized world with that of America in the 1920s.
2. Why did the Great Depression spread from America to the rest of the world?
3. How did World War II differ from World War I? Why do you suppose the number of deaths and casualties were higher in the second war?

MAP SKILLS *Use the maps on pages 480 and 483 to answer the following questions.*

1. Which European nations remained neutral in World War II.
2. Which side controlled the Middle East?
3. Name three important battles that took place in the Pacific in 1942.

24
The Cold War Era
(1945–1980)

HIGHLIGHTS
United Nations • Cold War
Communism in China • Korean War • Communism in Cuba
Berlin Wall • Vietnam Conflict • Détente • Space Age

New Threats to World Peace

Failure of the United Nations

After the use of the atomic bomb in World War II, many people believed it essential to establish a permanent world peace organization, for fear that a nuclear war would destroy civilization. Thus, the **United Nations** (UN) was organized in **1945** and was invited to build its headquarters in **New York City.** Fifty nations signed the UN charter in San Francisco, and other nations later joined.

Time has proven that the UN *has been unable to maintain world peace and cooperation*, and often it <u>has aided the spread of world Communism</u>. The organizers of the UN did not realize that international war and unrest cannot be eradicated from a world filled with men possessing a sinful, selfish nature.

Cooperation with Communists

After the Communists came to power in 1917, *the Russian people lost many personal freedoms* they had previously enjoyed. Atheism replaced the church; incomes decreased; food shortages mounted; stores became empty of goods; travel was curtailed; and the people were practically cut off from the rest of the world. As the Communist government grew intolerably repressive, Russian living standards lagged behind American and Western European living standards.

The U.S. and most of Western Europe opposed Russian Communism. But when the Nazis invaded and drew Russia into World War II, *the Allies felt that cooperation with Russia's leader,* **Joseph Stalin,** *was essential to defeating Hitler*. By the time the war was over, Russia had extended her influence and system of Communism over a vast area of Europe.

United Nations Building in New York City

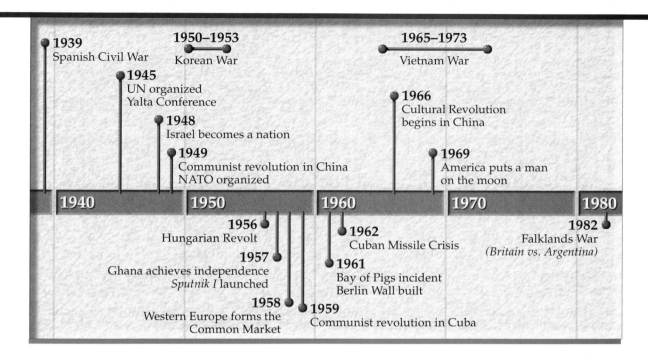

1939
Spanish Civil War

1950–1953
Korean War

1965–1973
Vietnam War

1945
UN organized
Yalta Conference

1966
Cultural Revolution
begins in China

1948
Israel becomes a nation

1949
Communist revolution in China
NATO organized

1969
America puts a man
on the moon

1940   **1950**   **1960**   **1970**   **1980**

1956
Hungarian Revolt

1962
Cuban Missile Crisis

1982
Falklands War
(Britain vs. Argentina)

1957
Ghana achieves independence
Sputnik I launched

1961
Bay of Pigs incident
Berlin Wall built

1958
Western Europe forms the
Common Market

1959
Communist revolution in Cuba

A strange partner. After World War II, it became Russia's policy to see how much territory she could seize in Eastern Europe. *The Allies, by joining hands with the Communists, let Stalin take over Eastern Europe.* Communist Russia was a strange partner for England and the U.S., the great leaders of democracy. When Roosevelt and Churchill gave in to Stalin's demands for control of Eastern Europe, Stalin verbally agreed to establish representative governments and permit free elections in Eastern Europe as soon as possible after the war. But <u>Stalin did not keep his promise</u>. The world paid a high price when the tyrant Stalin was enlisted to help defeat the tyrants Hitler and Mussolini.

Problems at Yalta

Churchill's caution. In the last days of the war, President Franklin Roosevelt and Prime Minister Winston Churchill had discussed what would happen in Europe and Asia after the defeat of Nazi Germany and Japan. Churchill was very *suspicious of Joseph Stalin;* he feared that Stalin might try

to move Communist troops into areas liberated from Germany and Japan. But FDR accused Churchill of trying to hold on to the British Empire, while Stalin encouraged nationalist and socialist revolutions in the African and Asian colonies. FDR

Churchill, Roosevelt, and Stalin at the Yalta Conference, 1945

491

and his advisers believed that democratic socialism was the solution to the problems of the lesser developed nations of the world.

Stalin's brutality. Churchill's fears were well-grounded, however. It was not widely known at the time, but Stalin's Communists had murdered far more than Hitler's Nazis. Stalin was actually the biggest mass murderer in history. In the late 1920s and early 1930s, over *10 million people* who resisted Communism were starved to death, executed, or exiled to Siberia. In the 1940s, an untold number of Christians, Jews, and rival political and military leaders were tortured and killed by Stalin's secret police.

Roosevelt's mistake. Great Britain was economically and physically exhausted by the war; only the U.S. could stop the advance of Communism. But FDR and his advisers were tired of fighting and were willing to compromise with Stalin. In a meeting at **Yalta** [yôl'tə], a seaside resort on the Russian coast of the Black Sea, in early 1945, *Roosevelt let Stalin have his way.* In return for Stalin's promise to enter the war against Japan, and to compensate him for damage done to Russia by the German invasion, Roosevelt *gave the Communist dictator a large chunk of* **Poland** and allowed him to encourage a pro-Communist government in Poland itself. The Free Polish government-in-exile in London was abandoned.

Roosevelt also *allowed Stalin to keep the rich province of* **Manchuria** and *let him have* **Mongolia** as well, betraying Nationalist Chinese leader Chiang Kai-shek, who had bravely fought both Communist terrorists and the Japanese. Finally, Roosevelt *promised Stalin that all American troops would be withdrawn from Europe* within two years of the imminent Nazi defeat. This promise later had to be cancelled when it became clear that Stalin's Communist troops were not going to leave *Eastern Europe* and stood ready to march into Western Europe.

Communist Domination of Eastern Europe

The **U.S.S.R.** *(Union of Soviet Socialist Republics)* moved quickly in Eastern Europe. It had already claimed **Estonia, Latvia,** and **Lithuania** in 1940. As the Germans were defeated in Eastern Europe, Russia absorbed their territories. Soviet-dominated puppet governments called *"people's republics"* were established in **Poland, Hungary, Romania, Bulgaria,** and **Czechoslovakia.** ("People's republic" is a misnomer, since *Communism is dictatorial* and *not republican* in practice.) **Yugoslavia** and **Albania** established independent Communist governments but maintained close ties to the Soviet Union. **East Germany** became the Soviet-dominated German Democratic Republic in 1949.

The Cold War

With World War II just over, America and Western Europe realized they were facing a new enemy—**international Com-**

"Is that the shirt you worked fifteen hours for?"

In the U.S.S.R., wages were lower and prices were much higher than in the U.S. (cartoon from *We Choose America*)

"Just think, only two to a room!"

In the U.S.S.R., housing was so scarce that families often had to share crowded apartments. (cartoon from *We Choose America*)

munism. No sooner had one adversary of freedom (Hitler) been defeated than another had arisen. By the late 1940s, the free world stood in opposition to the human slavery of international Communism. Nations that fell to Communism were locked into an atheistic dictatorship that denied the people freedom of religion, freedom of speech, freedom of the press, and freedom to travel, especially outside their country.

The U.S. and the Soviet Union became engaged in an ongoing **"Cold War,"** *a war fought not with military weapons but with words and diplomacy.* In this war each side attempted to win allies among other nations through financial aid and other forms of assistance. It was soon a full scale "war" to "win friends" either to the cause of *freedom* or to the cause of *Communism.*

Containment of Communism

Truman Doctrine. When Russian Communism threatened Greece and Turkey, President Truman announced a policy of **containment** in 1947, declaring that *the U.S. would provide economic aid to any free country to help it resist Communist aggression.*

This policy, known as the Truman Doctrine, was meant to keep Communism from spreading to new areas of the world.

Marshall Plan. Also in 1947, Secretary of State George C. Marshall announced that *the U.S. would provide economic assistance to help European nations recover from World War II,* with the stipulation that each nation receiving aid must also be willing to do all within its own power to rebuild its economy. The Soviet Union balked at the Marshall Plan, claiming it would interfere with the sovereignty of European nations, but in reality the <u>Soviets simply did not want the U.S. to gain any prestige in Europe</u>. Russia did not want Europe to recover too quickly from World War II because <u>Communism thrives in misery and poverty</u>.

Molotov Plan. The U.S.S.R. refused to allow Eastern European nations to participate in the Marshall Plan. Instead, it set up its own program. Under the Molotov [mô′lŭ·tôf] Plan, *nations of Eastern Europe would trade raw materials with the Soviet Union in exchange for manufactured goods.* This would supposedly give financial aid to Eastern Europe to recover from the ravages of World War II, but in reality it gave the greatest aid to Russia, by providing her with raw materials and a ready market for her manufactured goods. Industry helped bring a degree of prosperity to Russia, but kept Eastern Europe poor and dependent upon Russia.

NATO. To combat the Communist threat to the free world, NATO (the **North Atlantic Treaty Organization**) was organized in **1949**. Twelve nations signed the NATO pact, pledging that if one member were attacked, all would come to its aid. The original members of NATO were the U.S., Canada, Iceland, Nor way, Great Britain, the Netherlands, Denmark, Belgium, Luxembourg, Portugal, France, and Italy. Greece, Turkey, and West Germany joined later.

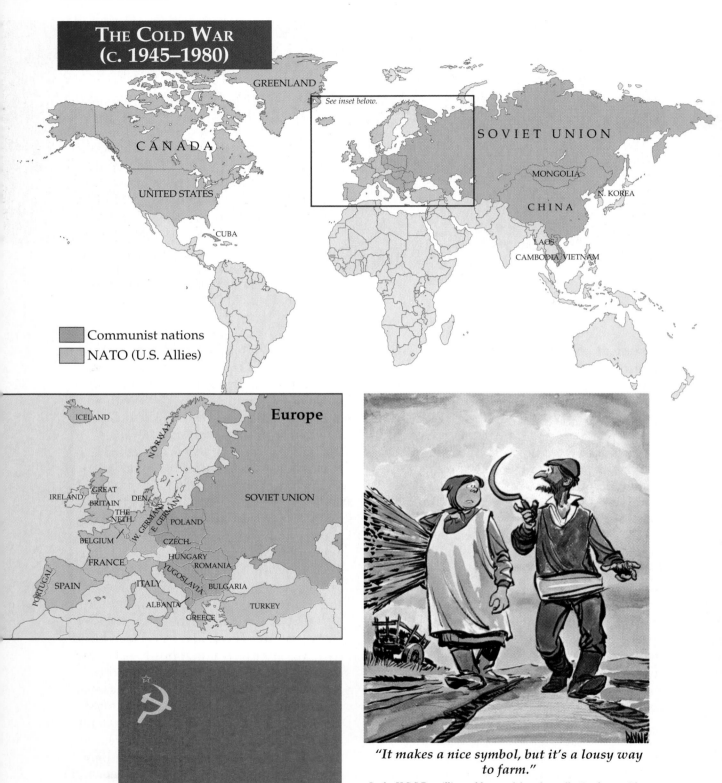

THE COLD WAR (C. 1945–1980)

GREENLAND

See inset below.

CANADA

SOVIET UNION

UNITED STATES

MONGOLIA

N. KOREA

CHINA

CUBA

LAOS

CAMBODIA VIETNAM

Communist nations

NATO (U.S. Allies)

Europe

ICELAND

NORWAY

IRELAND

GREAT BRITAIN

DEN.

THE NETH.

W. GERMANY

E. GERMANY

POLAND

SOVIET UNION

BELGIUM

CZECH.

FRANCE

HUNGARY

ROMANIA

PORTUGAL

SPAIN

ITALY

YUGOSLAVIA

BULGARIA

ALBANIA

GREECE

TURKEY

Soviet Flag

PAYNE

"It makes a nice symbol, but it's a lousy way to farm."

In the U.S.S.R., millions of farmers labored on collective farms with old-fashioned equipment, and the Soviets still had to import food from the West to feed the nation. (cartoon from *We Choose America*)

"Everyone who applies for an exit visa gets it."

The U.S.S.R. greatly restricted travel, especially outside the country. (cartoon from *We Choose America*)

Chiang Kai-shek: *led Chinese Nationalists in their fight against the Communists and finally established a Nationalist government on the island of Taiwan.*

The Common Market. The domination of Eastern Europe by the Soviets forced the nations of Western Europe to cooperate much more closely with each other than they had in the past. In **1958,** Western Europe formed the Common Market (**European Economic Community** or EEC). The original members were France, West Germany, Italy, Belgium, the Netherlands, and Luxembourg. In 1973, Great Britain, Ireland, and Denmark joined the Common Market. In 1981, Greece joined, and in 1986, Spain and Portugal became members of the Common Market.

China: Communist Takeover

One of the greatest disasters for the cause of freedom was the Communist takeover of China in the late 1940s. As early as the 1920s, Communist forces wanted to take control of China's government, but Nationalist forces were able to maintain the traditional government of China. The leader of the Communist revolutionaries was **Mao Tse-tung** [mou′ dzŭ′dŏong′, also spelled *Zedong*: 1893–1976]. The Nationalist government was headed by the Christian statesman **Chiang Kai-shek.** During World War II, the Communist and Nationalist forces had made a shaky alliance to fight off the threat of imperial Japan. But no sooner was Japan defeated than fighting broke out in 1945 between the Communist and Nationalist forces. Chiang Kai-shek's Nationalist army made a respectable stand against heavy odds, but Mao Tse-tung's Communist forces were armed with confiscated Japanese artillery and plenty of aid from the U.S.S.R. <u>The Soviet Union was eager to see Communism triumph in China</u>. By **1949,** Chiang's army was forced to flee to the tiny Chinese island of **Taiwan** (Formosa).

Chiang Kai-shek established a free **Nationalist** government on Taiwan, and Mao Tse-tung and Chou En-lai [jō′ ĕn′lĭ′] established a Communist regime, called the **People's Republic of China,** on the Chinese mainland. For a number of years, the U.S. continued to recognize Chiang's government as the rightful government of all China, but by the 1970s, the U.S. and most of the world recognized *two separate Chinas.*

Soviet aid to Communist China. The U.S.S.R. helped Mao Tse-tung's government establish itself. In many ways, these two Communist systems were much alike.

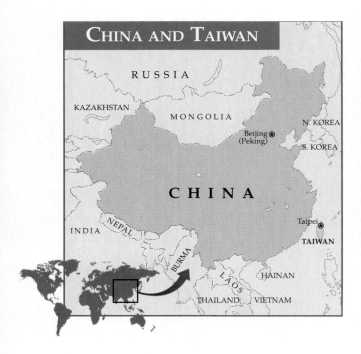

CHINA AND TAIWAN

Poster of Mao Tse-tung: *Throughout China, posters of Chairman Mao reminded the people of their cruel dictator.*

Chinese Communists patterned their government after Russia—civil rights were non-existent and elected officials were puppets of the Communist Party. The totalitarian Communist state's political "education" was accomplished through secret police, mass arrests, executions, slave labor, and the elimination of all opposition to the new government.

Competition for world domination. Since the U.S.S.R and China stood for the same basic principles of Communism, one would expect them to have a close alliance. Indeed, for a time the Chinese were eager to accept the aid and advice of the Russians. But by the mid-1950s, a breech in the friendship was evident. China was going its own way, developing its own brand of Communism. The Soviet Union had helped create its own rival power. Russia had given birth to a new Chinese regime capable of mobilizing ¹/₄ **of the world's population.** Both Russia and China had aspirations to rule the world. They agreed it should be a Communist world, but they disagreed as to who should be in charge. By 1960, Russian-

Chinese cooperation was only nominal. If either regime were to rule the world, the other would have to be eliminated.

The "Great Leap Forward." In 1957, Mao admitted that in the first five years of the revolution some ***800,000 opponents*** had been <u>executed</u>. From 1958 to 1960, Mao conducted a program known as the Great Leap Forward. Under this program, *people were forced to work in factories or on large collective farms.* Food production fell so drastically that as many as ***15 million people*** may have <u>starved to death</u>. Mao's party undertook *a planned program to control every area of Chinese life,* just as Stalin's party undertook to control every area of Russian life.

"Cultural Revolution." In 1966, Mao decided to launch a full-scale "Cultural Revolution" <u>to cleanse China of all Western and foreign influences</u>. Encouraged by the Communist Party, students and young people formed gangs called the ***Red Guards*** which filled China's city streets with noisy demonstrations, marches, and protests, and *attacked Chinese intellectuals and professionals.* By 1979, the Red Guards

had <u>murdered</u> an estimated ***400,000 people.*** Millions more were beaten and terrorized. One famous concert pianist had his fingers smashed with a hammer for playing European classical music. Many doctors, nurses, lawyers, teachers, scientists, and other professionals were imprisoned and tortured; others were forced to work at menial jobs, sweeping streets, digging ditches, and doing hard labor on collective farms. University classrooms, art museums, libraries, and private homes having western-style furniture were vandalized. Books, furniture, and valuable works of art were destroyed. The Academy of Sciences virtually shut down when 150,000 techni-

cians were condemned for believing in scientific methods taught in Europe and the U.S. While most of the *free world moved up in its standard of living, Communist China, Russia, and other Communist countries went backward in their standard of living.*

China's Millions: *Mao Tse-tung and his Communists killed millions of people in China.*

CHECK UP

1. When was the United Nations organized? Why? Where are its headquarters?
2. Describe Russian society after Communism took over.
3. Why did the U.S. and Western Europe cooperate with Stalin during World War II?
4. What did Stalin promise to do after the war? Did he keep his promise?
5. Who met together at the Yalta Conference in 1945? What was decided at this conference?
6. Why is "people's republic" a misnomer?
7. What kind of government was established in Yugoslavia and Albania? What did East Germany officially become in 1949?
8. Describe the Cold War between the U.S. and the Soviet Union.
9. How did President Truman plan to prevent Communism from spreading to new areas of the world? What was his plan called?
10. Why was NATO organized? List the 12 nations that originally signed the NATO pact. Which nations later joined NATO?
11. What great disaster for the cause of freedom in Asia occurred in the late 1940s? Who led the Chinese Communists? Who led the Chinese nationalists?
12. What was the "Cultural Revolution?"

Identify: containment, Marshall Plan, Molotov Plan, Common Market, Taiwan, People's Republic of China, totalitarian, Great Leap Forward, Red Guards

Japan: A Triumph for Capitalism

Between 1945 and 1952, General *Douglas MacArthur* served as the *military governor of occupied Japan*. The Japanese traditionally worshiped their emperor and their ancestors; many also practiced Shintoism (nature worship) and Buddhism. MacArthur encouraged <u>Christian missionaries</u> to come and solve Japan's spiritual problem—the need for "spiritual regeneration." One of the fruits of that missionary effort was the conversion of *Mitsuo Fuchida,* commander of the squadron of Japanese planes that bombed Pearl Harbor on December 7, 1941. Fuchida came to know Christ in 1950.

General MacArthur also encouraged Japan to develop a <u>democratic government</u> and a <u>free-enterprise economy</u>. American business planners helped modernize Japanese industry. As the U.S. had hoped, Japan gradually assumed the role of an economic powerhouse in Asia and, by raising the economies of all non-Communist Asia, hindered the spread of Communism in the region. By the 1980s, Japan had become a *major economic power, not only in Asia, but in the world.*

The Korean War

In the 1950s, Communist aggression spread to **Korea,** and the Cold War boiled into open conflict. After Japan's defeat in 1945, Korea was divided into two zones; **North Korea** (overseen by the U.S.S.R.) and **South Korea** (overseen by the U.S.). In South Korea, the people established a democratic republic, but *in North Korea the Soviet Union interfered with free elections and saw to it that a Communist government was set up.* This made it impossible to unify Korea into one nation.

In **1950,** North Korean troops crossed the **38th parallel** boundary line, and invaded South Korea. The UN sent troops, *largely American forces,* to help the South Koreans protect themselves against Com-

munist aggression. The UN forces were headed by American **General Douglas MacArthur,** the World War II hero who had kept his promise to recapture the Philippines from the Japanese. MacArthur and his troops successfully drove the North Koreans back across the 38th parallel.

When Chinese Communists came to the aid of North Korea, sending in troops and supplies, <u>General MacArthur wanted to</u> bomb China's military bases along the Yalu River and thereby <u>gain victory in the Korean War</u>. But *President Truman feared offending Communist China and the U.S.S.R.* He and General MacArthur both persisted in their opinions until President Truman finally *relieved* General MacArthur of his command.

In **1953,** an armistice was reached, returning the situation to what it had been before the war. Korea remained divided with a *Communist government in North Korea* and a *free government in South Korea.* Thus the Korean War ended in a **"stalemate"** (nothing gained by either side).

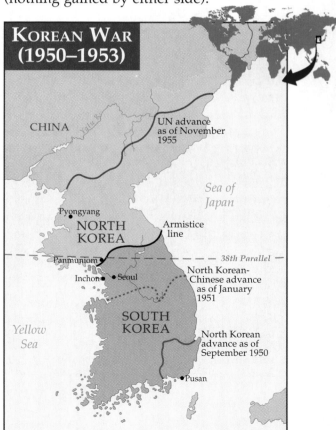

KOREAN WAR (1950–1953)

CHINA

UN advance as of November 1955

Sea of Japan

Pyongyang

NORTH KOREA

Armistice line

Panmuniom

— 38th Parallel —

Inchon • Seoul

North Korean-Chinese advance as of January 1951

SOUTH KOREA

Yellow Sea

North Korean advance as of September 1950

• Pusan

Korean War: U.S. troops depicted in a painting by H. C. McBarron.

General MacArthur came home from Korea an American hero. He was cheered and greeted by thousands of Americans in parades and assemblies. He received a standing ovation from the U.S. Congress when he spoke to a joint session and reminded them that "War's very object is victory," that indeed there is **"no substitute for victory."** He went on to tell Congress that "history teaches with unmistakable emphasis that *appeasement but begets new and bloodier war.*" MacArthur insisted that if we did not fight the Communists in Asia, we would have to fight them later in some other part of the world. Unfortunately, his opinion was ignored in the shaping of American foreign policy, and thousands of American servicemen would later die on Asian soil in Vietnam.

Pueblo seized. Relations between the U.S. and North Korea remained shaky for decades. This tension was illustrated in January 1968 when North Korea seized an American naval ship, the *Pueblo,* in the Sea of Japan. North Korea claimed that the crew of the vessel was spying in North Korean waters, but the U.S. denied the charge. One American serviceman was killed in the capture of the ship, and the other *82 crewmen were held captive for nearly a year* while U.S. diplomats negotiated with the North Koreans. The hostages were finally released in 1968 when the American diplomats signed a written statement *falsely admitting* that the *Pueblo* had been in North Korean waters. The ship itself was never returned to the U.S. Many Americans saw the *Pueblo* incident as evidence of American leadership's weakness toward Communism.

Communism Spreads to the Americas

A false hope for peace. Meanwhile, Soviet Communism spread to other parts of the world. Soviet leader Joseph Stalin died in **1953** and was replaced by **Nikita Khrushchev** [krōōsh′chôf], who in 1956 denounced Stalin's gruesome tactics.

499

Khrushchev gave the false impression that Soviet Communism was "mellowing"—softening in its tactics—and that it no longer aspired to rule the world. This *"de-Stalinization"* of Russia gave the free world false hope that the danger of Communism had lessened. Khrushchev spoke of **"peaceful coexistence"** between Communism and the free world.

Communism in Cuba. But any hope of stopping Communism where it already existed in the world was soon crushed. In **1959,** after years of *guerilla warfare* (revolutionary surprise attacks by a small volunteer army), **Fidel Castro** (1927–) overthrew the Cuban dictator Fulgencia **Batista.** The U.S. had shunned Batista's dictatorship and hoped that Castro's regime would be democratic. The people of Cuba trusted Castro, but they soon discovered that Castro's revolution was backed by Russia and that he was an avowed *Communist.* Batista's dictatorship had been exchanged for a repressive Communist dictatorship. <u>The Cuban revolution was the first Communist revolution in the Americas</u>. Communism was now at the doorstep of the U.S.

Knowing that Communism must be actively opposed, in **1961** the U.S. government supported an invasion of Cuba by

Fidel Castro

Cuban rebels who hoped to overthrow Castro's regime. Unfortunately, the invasion was thwarted at the **Bay of Pigs** when President **John F. Kennedy** *failed to keep his promise to supply air cover to the Cuban patriots.*

In **1962,** it was discovered that *the Soviets had established ballistic missile bases in Cuba.* President Kennedy ordered a blockade of Cuba and demanded that the Soviet Union withdraw all missiles from Cuba. The Soviets reportedly complied, and the **Cuban Missile Crisis** was alleviated.

South America. <u>Cuba became the base for Communist activities throughout Latin America</u>. With aid and encouragement from Cuba and the U.S.S.R., Communists became active in a number of nations in Central and South America. The dominant religion of Latin America, *Roman Catholicism,* also exerted a strong influence on the governments of Central and South America, and it continues to do so today.

In 1967, with the help of the U.S. Central Intelligence Agency (CIA), **Bolivia** put down a bloody Communist uprising led by the Cuban leader Che Guevera [chā gä·vä′rä]. Communists and organized criminals soon started a large illegal drug industry in Bolivia. In 1970, Salvador Allende, a Communist, was elected to head the government of **Chile.** By the end of 1973, the Chilean government had collapsed, and Allende was dead. By the 1990s, Chile had a democratically-elected government and a growing free-enterprise economy.

Brazil, the largest country in Latin America in both land and people, is often called the "Sleeping Giant." Brazil possesses great natural wealth in the undeveloped *Amazon River* basin. Economic problems and Communist threats caused the military to take control of the Brazilian government in 1964. Under the military government, an educated middle class developed and foreign investment encouraged new industrial growth. In the 1980s, Brazil made efforts to "privatize" or turn inefficient state-run industries over to private companies. By 1990, the military had returned the government to civilian rule.

Central America. In 1979, the dictatorship of Anastasio *Somoza* in **Nicaragua** was overthrown by a group known as the **Sandinistas.** The Somoza family had ruled Nicaragua for many years, and the people had suffered under this corrupt government. The Sandinista movement originally included many sincere people who wanted to restore justice to the government, but Communist agents from the Soviet Union and Cuba infiltrated the movement. They organized a Communist guerrilla (rebel) army and armed it with weapons. When these armed rebels took control, Somoza was forced to flee the country. Meanwhile, U.S. President Ronald Reagan began to give aid to the **Contras,** *freedom fighters who tried to liberate their country from the Communist Sandinistas.* By 1990, the Soviet Union and Cuba were no longer in a position to assist the Communists, and a new president, who claimed to be a moderate and to oppose Communism, had been elected.

Communist activity in Nicaragua spread to neighboring **El Salvador.** The Salvadoran government requested military assistance from the U.S. to put down Communist forces. This aid increased greatly under President Reagan, and in the early 1990s a peace agreement was signed. By then, the Communists could no longer rely on help from Nicaragua, Cuba, or the Soviet Union.

The nation of **Panama** contains the *Panama Canal,* the *important shipping channel built by the U.S. to connect the Atlantic and Pacific Oceans.* This vital waterway is included in the 10-mile-wide Canal Zone, which is owned and maintained by the U.S. to assure the proper operation and military protection of the canal. The nation of Panama has received generous revenues from the U.S. for use of this land since the canal opened in 1914.

In 1977, President **Jimmy Carter** *signed a treaty promising the Panamanians full control of the canal by the year 2000.* Many Americans expressed concern that a possible Communist takeover of Panama would threaten the safety of the canal.

In late 1989, President George Bush ordered American troops into Panama to liberate the people and protect U.S. interests from the unpopular dictator, **Manuel Noriega** [nôr·yä′gä]. Noriega not only terrorized the people of Panama but also smuggled illegal drugs into the U.S. After American forces captured Noriega and brought him to the U.S. for trial, the people of Panama held elections for a new leader.

To help promote the political and economic stability of this beautiful, tropical land, the U.S. and other free nations have

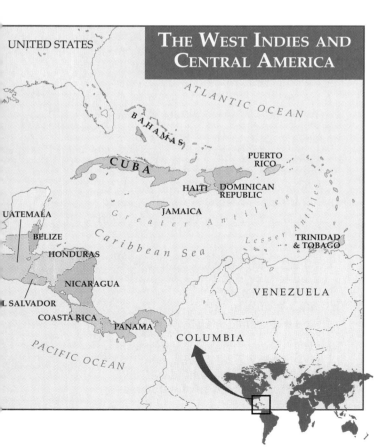

THE WEST INDIES AND CENTRAL AMERICA

UNITED STATES

ATLANTIC OCEAN

BAHAMAS

CUBA

PUERTO RICO

HAITI   DOMINICAN REPUBLIC

JAMAICA

Greater Antilles

Lesser Antilles

TRINIDAD & TOBAGO

Caribbean Sea

GUATEMALA

BELIZE

HONDURAS

NICARAGUA

EL SALVADOR

COASTA RICA

PANAMA

COLUMBIA

VENEZUELA

PACIFIC OCEAN

501

encouraged democratic government and the development of international banking and tourist resorts.

Communist tactics. In the rest of Latin America, Communists have not yet succeeded in seizing power outright, but they have been influential in shaping the overall policies of a number of governments, especially in the poorer countries of Central America. Generally, *their tactic has been to stir up violence and revolution in order to create chaos in which desperate people will turn to Communism for relief.*

Revolts by Soviet Satellites in Eastern Europe

The Eastern European countries became merely Soviet **satellites** *(nations supposedly independent but technically under the dominance of another)*. These satellite Communist countries suffered far greater than any of the European colonies suffered during the colonial era. In 1946, Winston Churchill coined the phrase **"iron curtain"** to describe the Soviet domination of Eastern Europe. The suppression of personal, religious, and political freedoms, added to the poverty of the people, caused some to rebel against Communism, making it difficult for the Soviet Union to hold together its European empire.

In the late 1940s, **Yugoslavia's** leader, **Marshal Tito** [tē′tŏ], rebelled against the Molotov Plan, realizing it would allow Russia to prosper at the expense of its Soviet satellites. The people of **Poland** revolted in 1953 and again in 1956; as a result, Poland gave voters more choice in elections and more independence than the Soviet Union. In 1956, the **Hungarian Revolt** was put down only when Russian tanks and troops poured into Hungary to aid the Communist government and to punish the revolutionaries, putting their leaders to death. In 1968, the Soviets sent tanks into **Czechoslovakia** to stop a trend toward greater freedom for the people.

Soviet Tanks in Budapest, Hungary

CHECK UP

1. What three things did General MacArthur encourage in Japan?
2. What made it impossibe to unify Korea into one nation?
3. Why did President Truman relieve MacArthur of his command in the Korean War?
4. Explain General MacArthur's views on victory in war. Did his opinions change American foreign policy?
5. Who became the leader in Russia after Stalin's death? What impression of Soviet Communism did he give the world?
6. Who overthrew the Cuban dictator Fulgencia Batista? When? What kind of regime did he establish?
7. Who overthrew the Somoza family in Nicaragua? When?
8. What dictator terrorized the people of Panama and smuggled illegal drugs into the U.S.?
9. What tactic have the Communists used to take over the poor countries of Central America?
10. How did Winston Churchill describe Soviet domination of Eastern Europe?

Identify: Mitsuo Fuchida, 38th parallel, stalemate, *Pueblo*, guerilla warfare, Bay of Pigs, Cuban Missile Crisis, Contras, Panama Canal, satellites

Western Europe in the Cold War

Great Britain, France, Germany, and Italy were the **major powers** in Western Europe during the Cold War. The economic assistance provided by the Marshall Plan helped rebuild these European powers, and by the 1960s, they exceeded prewar levels of economic production. But many Western European countries *adopted socialist forms of government*, and *Communism infiltrated many of their governments*, some to a greater degree than others.

Troubles in Germany. The Cold War first became evident in Germany. Shortly after the close of World War II, Germany found itself divided into two zones. The American, British, and French sectors became **West Germany,** and the Russian sector became **East Germany.** The city of **Berlin**, located in East Germany, was also *divided into eastern and western sections.* For over a year, between 1948 and 1949, <u>Russia closed off the road</u> across East Germany <u>to West Berlin</u>, isolating West Berliners from the free world. But through *"Operation Airlift,"* Western powers saved the people of West Berlin by *flying in food and supplies for over a year.* Russia eventually abandoned the blockade.

In **1961,** the Communists built a wall to keep East Berliners from escaping to West Berlin. (Two million East Germans had fled to the West since 1949 to escape the horrible living conditions of Communism.) *It was the first time in history that a wall was built to keep people inside their own country* rather than to keep enemies out. The **Berlin Wall** was a grim reminder of the enslavement of men under a Communist system.

West Germany. Chancellor **Konrad Adenauer,** a traditional Roman Catholic and a staunch conservative politician,

Operation Airlift: *Western powers brought food and supplies to the blockaded city of 2½ million West Berliners for over a year. Children eagerly waited for the planes.*

DIVIDED GERMANY

DENMARK
SWEDEN
Baltic Sea
North Sea
West Berlin East Berlin
THE NETHERLANDS
WEST GERMANY
Berlin
EAST GERMANY
POLAND
BELGIUM
Bonn
FRANCE
LUX.
CZECHOSLOVAKIA
Munich
SWITZ.
AUSTRIA
HUNGARY
ITALY
YUGOSLAVIA

Iron Curtain
American zone
British zone
French zone
Russian zone

Francois Mitterrand

Berlin Wall: U.S. President John F. Kennedy and German Chancellor Konrad Adenauer at the Berlin Wall, 1963.

provided the leadership necessary for West Germany to recover from its wartime defeat. Adenauer promptly *moved Germany toward a vigorous free market economy.* By 1955, the country was producing more goods and services than the entire nation had in 1936 under Hitler's national socialism. Altogether Germany absorbed 10 million East German refugees who fled Communism.

France. As the largest country of Western Europe, France emerged from World War II with its cities and industries badly damaged and with *Communists controlling one of its largest political parties* and chief labor unions. Between 1946 and 1954, France lost important overseas possessions in Indochina, beginning with **Vietnam,** which fell to Communist Ho Chi Minh.

In 1958, **Charles de Gaulle,** leader of the Free French government during World War II, became president of France. After de Gaulle's death in 1970, France moved toward a *socialist state.* In 1981, **Francois Mitterrand** of the *Socialist Party* became president. Miterand, France's longest-serving president, led the French government until 1995, when a conservative became president.

Italy. After World War II, Italy began a slow recovery under the leadership of

conservative statesman Alcide De Gasperi. By his death in 1954, Italy had had more than *30 coalition governments.* Communists began to gain more power in government and some organized into terrorist **Red Brigades,** which kidnapped and murdered premier Aldo Moro in 1978.

Public outrage over Communist violence resulted in a push for law and order; in 1980, a new government was formed. A number of Italy's largest corporations remained in private hands and the economy improved markedly in the 1980s and 1990s.

Great Britain. After World War II, Great Britain fell under the influence of the Labour Party, which introduced state-controlled schools, compulsory national health insurance (socialized medicine), nationalized industries, wage and price controls, and a host of other social programs.

The Conservative Party returned to power in 1951. Under the Conservative prime ministers Winston **Churchill,** Anthony **Eden,** and Harold **Macmillan,** British industry improved in the 1950s and early 1960s. Morality, however, declined drastically in post-war Britain, and churches were generally empty on Sunday. The nation that once sent Christian missionaries all over the world became a mission field, with only a fraction of the population attending church.

In 1979, Conservative **Margaret Thatcher** became <u>Britain's first woman prime minister</u>. Thatcher became the most influential British prime minister since Winston Churchill. Margaret Thatcher remained prime minister until 1990, making her the *longest-ruling leader of Britain in the 20th century.* She promoted high moral standards and private ownership of property. Thatcher believed that able-bodied people should work for their living rather than accept government handouts. Taxes were lowered for the first time in decades, and employers kept more of their profits, enabling them to expand businesses and hire more workers. Great Britain, which had been hopelessly in debt as a social welfare state, began to regain some of her prosperity as welfarism became less popular.

Margaret Thatcher faced a foreign crisis in 1982 when *Argentina* invaded the British colony of the *Falkland Islands;* suddenly several thousand British citizens, mostly sheep herders from Scotland, were living under military rule of an Argentine

dictator. Prime Minister Thatcher appealed to the patriotism of the British people, and in response, thousands of Britons volunteered to go fight for English liberty in the Falkland Islands. The luxury ocean liner *Queen Elizabeth II* was converted into a troop ship. Soon the Royal Navy, Air Force, and Marines were ready to do battle. The U.S. agreed to use its spy satellites to help the British in the war. After a series of naval, air, and ground battles, the Argentine forces were defeated. Freedom was restored to the Falklands, and a tide of patriotism rolled across the British Isles. Many Argentines saw the foolishness of the **Falklands War** and demanded an end to their military dictatorship.

The Falklands War: *British marines raise the Union flag over Port Howard, West Falkland, signifying the end of the Falkland conflict.*

Margaret Thatcher

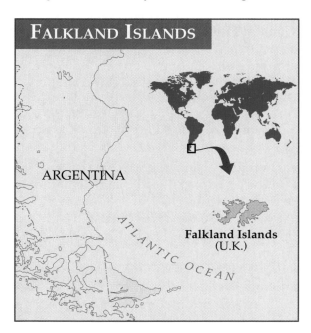

FALKLAND ISLANDS

ARGENTINA

Falkland Islands (U.K.)

ATLANTIC OCEAN

505

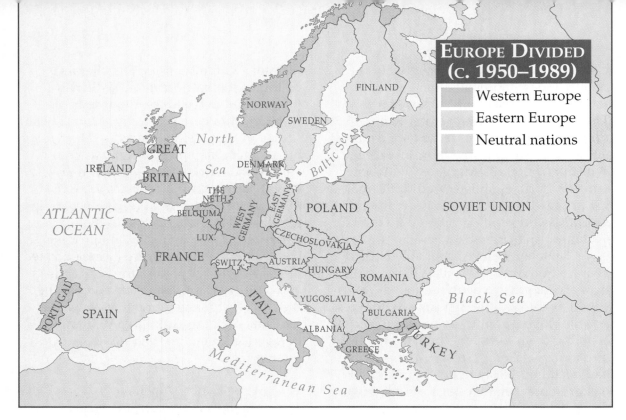

Holland. The country of Holland (the Netherlands), known for its cleanliness, hard work, and law and order, underwent radical changes in the 1960s and 1970s. *Socialist groups* took over the government, and a huge welfare state developed. Despite government interference, several international Dutch corporations increased their productivity and profits in the 1980s.

Switzerland. The small Alpine nation of Switzerland remained *neutral* in **World Wars I** and **II**, and refused to join the UN, even though the UN European headquarters were located at *Geneva.* Switzerland today is a federal republic of 23 cantons where <u>direct democracy</u> is still practiced. Two of the most important ingredients of Switzerland's economic prosperity and financial stability are the *small size and the low cost of Swiss government.* All male citizens of Switzerland must serve in the Swiss military, which is well-trained to defend the country.

Spain. In 1931, Spain (a strong Roman Catholic country) became a republic, but it was soon dominated by socialist and Communist parties. Conservatives became alarmed at the growing Communist influence and the destruction of traditional Spanish life.

A group of army leaders proclaimed a revolution against the Spanish government to save the republic, and in 1936 they named **General Francisco Franco** as their leader. In 1939, Franco's forces, the Nationalists, supported by Germany and Italy, won the **Spanish Civil War** against those aided by the Soviet Union.

Franco managed to keep his shattered country *neutral* in **World War II.** In 1953, Spain and the U.S. agreed to a 10-year economic and military pact. With U.S. help and under Franco's rule, Spain achieved one of the world's highest rates of economic growth during the 1950s and 1960s. In 1975, Franco's successor, Prince **Juan Carlos,** encouraged moderation and democratic rule during periods of political unrest. Spain continues to be less of a unified nation and more of a collection of strong, independent regions. In 1978, the Spanish voters approved a new *democratic* constitution.

Portugal. Portugal had a military dictatorship from 1926 to 1974. Law and order broke down in 1974 when the Communist Party dominated the government and the economy. For years, Portugal had concentrated its economic efforts in its African colonies, but by 1986 Portugal had surrendered its colonies. In 1989, free market reforms boosted the economy, but the country remained poor.

Scandinavia. After World War II, the Scandinavian nations—**Norway, Sweden,** and **Denmark**—adopted *socialistic* governments, and *most Scandinavian churches ceased to preach the gospel.* The economies of the Scandinavian countries grew rapidly from 1945 to 1970, but the decline in public morality and religious faith and the growing cost of welfare finally took its toll. High taxes and dependence on the state for daily needs caused a decline in the work ethic and further eroded moral restraint. Low worker productivity, rebellious youth, and a growing national debt caused many Scandinavians to doubt the effectiveness of socialism.

The Middle East

Lebanon, Syria, and Jordan. In 1945, France granted independence to Lebanon and Syria. In 1946, Jordan became independent of Britain. The new nations struggled to establish Western-type governments, but because they had little experience to fall back on, they were open to Soviet influence.

Israel. The history of Israel goes back to Bible times. In 70 A.D., the Romans destroyed the Temple at Jerusalem, and the Jews were forced to flee the land of Palestine to countries all over the world. <u>The Jewish people were without a country or national government for almost 2,000 years</u>. It is amazing that such a dispersed people would retain their national identity and not be absorbed into other nations for that period of time. (This verifies the Bible's prophesies regarding Israel in future events.)

In 1922, the League of Nations placed the affairs of Palestine into the hands of *Great Britain.* Britain announced intentions of making **Palestine** a home for Jews, allowing them to settle there in large numbers. Between World War I and World War II, there was frequent violence between Jews and Palestinian Arabs. The **Holocaust,** suffered by the Jews in World War II, convinced the world that Britain's plan should be carried out. Since no proposed political system was satisfactory to both Jews and Arabs, it was decided to *split Palestine* and *create a separate Jewish state.*

In May **1948,** <u>Israel became a nation</u> under the leadership of David **Ben-Gurion.** Christians throughout the world saw this as a major step in the unfolding of God's prophetic plans for Israel in the last

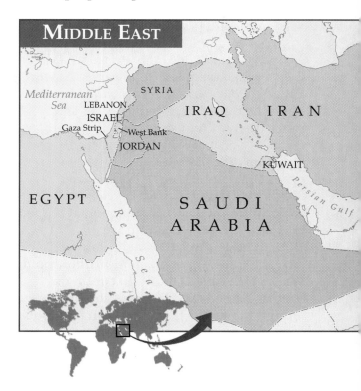

MIDDLE EAST

507

Birth of the State of Israel: *Prime Minister David Ben-Gurion reading the Israeli "Declaration of Independence."*

days. Wars erupted between Israel and its Arab neighbors in 1948, 1956, 1967 (Six Day War), and 1973 (Yom Kippur War). Border disputes continue to occur frequently. In 1979, at Camp David, U.S. President Jimmy Carter persuaded *Egyptian* leader, Anwar **Sadat** [sə·dät'], and *Israeli* Prime Minister Menachem **Begin** [bā'gĭn]to agree to a peace treaty. *This was the first time in history that Jews and Arabs sat down at a peace table.*

Arab oil embargo. In 1960, the oil-producing nations of the Middle East formed **OPEC** (Organization of Petroleum Exporting Countries), a monopoly designed to control the supply and price of oil. In 1973, the U.S. came to Israel's defense against Arab aggressors in the Yom Kippur War, which caused OPEC to cut off oil exports to the U.S. Oil prices shot up around the world as the **Arab oil embargo** created an *oil shortage.* As a result, Americans made efforts to increase fuel efficiency while exploring new fields for gas and oil outside the Middle East.

Iran and Iraq. In 1979, a revolution encouraged by U.S. liberals deposed the ***Shah of Iran,*** who strongly opposed Communism. Iranian rebels under the Ayatollah **Khomeini** [kō·mā'nĕ], a powerful Muslim religious leader, captured the American embassy in Tehran, the Iranian capital, and took American diplomatic personnel hostage. The *hostages remained in Iran for 444 days* before their release in 1981.

Iran and Iraq fought each other from 1980 to 1988. Their conflict spilled over into the Persian Gulf, and the U.S. had to use its naval power to assure the safe passage of oil tankers in the region.

The Third World Emerges

In the years following World War II, as European colonialism was breaking up, European colonies in Africa and Asia became independent nations. This created a **Third World,** *neutral nations not yet aligned with either freedom or Communism.* Both the U.S. and the U.S.S.R. attempted to win these nations to their side. This created a new theater for the Cold War as Communism spread to many Third World countries.

Independence for India

Britain led all of Europe in abolishing colonialism. Even before World War I, Mahatma **Gandhi** [mə·hät'mə gən'dē: 1869–1948], a Hindu nationalist and spiritual leader trained in London, had been working for India's independence. After World War I, he was joined by Jawaharlal **Nehru** [jə·wä'hər·läl nā'rōō: 1889–1964]. Gandhi advocated **"passive resistance,"** or "civil disobedience," as a peaceful but forceful method for India to get what it wanted from Britain. He led numerous labor strikes and hunger strikes and encouraged the native Indians to stage protest marches in areas where British law forbade them to go. Both Gandhi and Nehru were jailed for their leadership in civil disobedience, but their following continued to grow.

England was in a weakened condition following World War II and was ready to relieve itself of the burden of colonialism. Since there was much dissension in India between Hindus and the Muslim minority, it was <u>decided to divide India into two separate countries</u>—**India** *for Hindus* and **Pakistan** *for Muslims.* Pakistan was subdivided into **East Pakistan** and **West Pakistan.** India and Pakistan both became independent members of the British Commonwealth of Nations in 1947. Most other British colonies eventually followed the example and became Commonwealth nations. With Indian encouragement, East Pakistan declared its independence in 1971, becoming the new nation of **Bangladesh.**

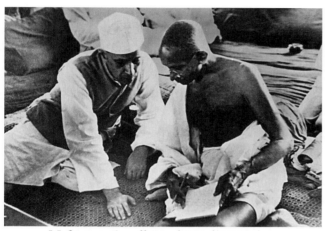

Mahatma Gandhi and Pandit J. Nehru

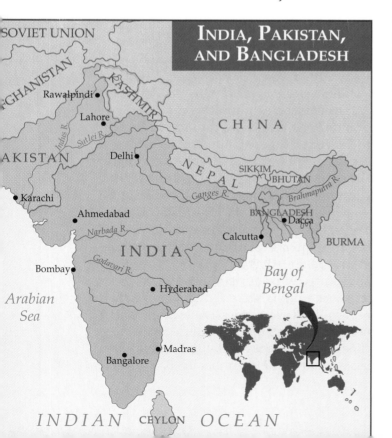

INDIA, PAKISTAN, AND BANGLADESH

CHECK UP

1. Where did the Cold War first become evident? What two zones did Germany find itself divided into? What East German city was also divided?
2. Name France's longest-serving president. What years did he serve? What political party did he represent?
3. Who was Britain's first woman prime minister? What war did Britain win in 1982?
4. Who won the Spanish Civil War? When?
5. What type of government did the Scandinavian nations adopt after World War II?
6. What was Britain's plan for Palestine? What convinced the world that the plan should be carried out? Why was Palestine split?
7. When and under whose leadership did Israel become a nation?
8. What was significant about the peace treaty signed between Egypt and Israel in 1979? Name the officials who signed the treaty and the U.S. President who negotiated the treaty.
9. What Muslim leader came to power in Iran in 1979? For how many days did the American hostages remain in Iran?
10. What are Third World nations?
11. Name two Indian leaders who encouraged civil disobedience against British rule in India.
12. Why was India divided into two separate countries? Name the divisions.

Identify: Operation Airlift, Berlin Wall, Konrad Adenauer, Charles de Gaulle, Red Brigades, Juan Carlos, Palestine, OPEC, Arab oil embargo, Bangladesh

Independence for African Nations

In 1957, **Ghana** (Gold Coast) became the first black African nation to achieve its independence. Ghana's leader, *Kwame Nkrumah* [ĕn·krōō′mə] wanted to form a socialist confederation, or alliance, of all African nations. In 1966, Nkrumah was ousted in a military revolt; he later helped establish the Organization of African Unity (OAU). By the late 1960s, British, Dutch, and French colonialism in Africa and Asia had broken up, and most of the former colonies had become independent countries. Independence for these new countries was fraught with problems, creating an open invitation for Soviet Communism to exert its influence. The U.S. sought earnestly to help these new nations establish democratic governments and at the same time win Third World allies for the cause of freedom.

When the Cold War spread to Africa, the struggle against Communism was particularly evident in **Angola, Mozambique, Zimbabwe** (Rhodesia), **Ethiopia, Somalia,** and **South Africa.**

The Vietnam Conflict

The greatest blow to the U.S. in its fight against world Communism came in Southeast Asia. Following World War II, this entire region was in chaos as European nations granted their colonies independence and encouraged them to establish democratic governments. Throughout Southeast Asia, Communists worked unceasingly to establish dictatorships in these former European colonies. For the U.S., the real problem came in **Vietnam.**

Outbreak of conflict. France recognized the independence of Vietnam in 1948. However, the French opposed the plan of Russian-trained **Ho Chi Minh** [hō′chē′mĭn′]to establish a Communist dictatorship there. As a result, civil war raged in Vietnam between Ho Chi Minh's Communist forces (backed by the U.S.S.R.

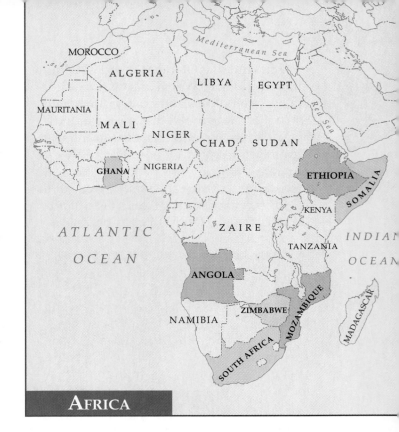

AFRICA

and Communist China) and democratic Nationalist forces (backed by the French). By 1954, the French resistance to a Communist takeover had collapsed. In an international agreement, Vietnam was temporarily divided at the **17th parallel.** *North Vietnam was to be ruled by Communists,* and *South Vietnam was to be ruled by Nationalist forces.*

U.S. enters conflict. In 1950, President Harry Truman sent military aid to help the French keep their hold on Indo-China and to prevent Chinese Communists from taking over Southeast Asia. According to the "domino theory," if Indochina fell to Communism, so would the remainder of Southeast Asia. In the late 1950s and early 1960s, North Vietnamese Communists began to invade South Vietnam in increasing numbers. By 1962, the U.S. was giving substantial support to South Vietnam: American pilots were flying over Vietnam, and military advisers were training and directing Vietnamese ground forces in defensive operations. By the time he was assassinated in November 1963, President

John F. Kennedy had sent over 16,000 military advisers to South Vietnam. The U.S. hoped to set an example by stopping Communist advancement in Vietnam.

Gulf of Tonkin incident escalates war. The conflict (*technically not a war because a state of war was never declared*) was stepped up in 1964 when two U.S. destroyers were *allegedly* fired upon by North Vietnamese torpedo boats in the Gulf of Tonkin. After this reported incident, Kennedy's successor President **Lyndon B. Johnson** ordered air strikes against North Vietnam. <u>In 1965, marines became the first U.S. combat troops sent to Vietnam</u>. By 1968, more than 500,000 American troops were in Vietnam. America was involved in a full-fledged war (still technically *undeclared*) to defend freedom and human dignity in South Vietnam against the Communists of North Vietnam.

No victory. Soon Russia and Communist China came to the aid of North Vietnam. The advantage of the North Vietnamese was their *large numbers, knowledge of the terrain,* and supply of *weapons from the Soviet Union and China.* As the war dragged on, American lives and money continued to be spent on foreign soil with no apparent hope of victory.

The war divided the American public into **"hawks,"** who *supported the fight against Communism,* and **"doves,"** who were *soft toward Communism.* At home, American morale and patriotism reached its lowest ebb. Patriotic Americans were disgusted with "draft dodgers," young men who fled to Canada or Europe to avoid being drafted into the military, and felt that liberal political leaders were helping the Communists by *mismanaging the war.* They criticized government leaders for the "no-win policy." They realized that U.S. leaders were not allowing the military to do what was necessary to win the war.

FBI Director J. Edgar Hoover warned that <u>Soviet influence was growing on</u>

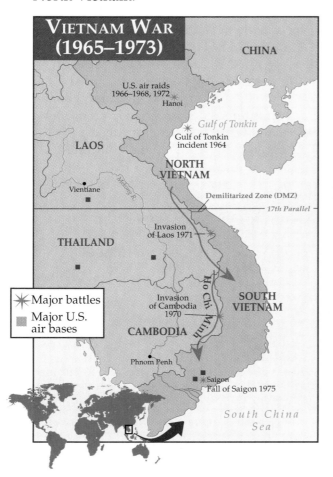

Vietnam War: U.S. Marines take cover behind a tank after Viet Cong snipers open fire on them.

college campuses and in high-ranking government circles. Flag-burning (of American flags), protest marches, and riots on college campuses outraged most loyal American citizens, as did Jane Fonda (Hollywood actress), who made radio propaganda for the North Vietnamese and posed for pictures beside North Vietnamese anti-aircraft guns while Americans were being killed in battle and tortured in prisons. It became evident that *without the American President's support to step up the war, there was no way for American troops to win a victory in Vietnam.*

U.S. withdraws; South Vietnam falls. Americans wanted either a victory or an end to American men fighting and dying in Vietnam. Thus President **Richard Nixon** decided to get the U.S. out of Vietnam. In **1973,** *after eight years of a no-win war,* South Vietnam, the U.S., and North Vietnam signed a cease-fire agreement, and the U.S. removed its combat troops from Vietnam. Some 56,800 American troops died in Vietnam, another 303,700 were wounded, and 780 were missing in action. Vietnam was *America's first no-win war.*

As U.S. military personnel returned home, a wave of patriotic fervor swept across the nation. Cheering Americans showed their heart-felt appreciation to the servicemen who bravely fought in Vietnam. Many Americans were saddened as prisoners of war told of their long inhumane treatment in **Hanoi** [hä·noi′] **prisons.** (Hanoi was North Vietnam's capital.)

No sooner were American troops out of Vietnam than the North Vietnamese Communists launched a new assault against South Vietnam. On April 23, 1975, President Ford officially announced the end of American involvement in Vietnam, ordering the evacuation of U.S. civilians and embassy personnel. On April 30, 1975, **Saigon** [sī·gŏn′], South Vietnam's capital, *fell to Communist forces, and the Communists gained complete control of Vietnam.* The cause for containing Communism in Southeast Asia was lost. MacArthur's warning about Korea proved to be true in Vietnam.

After South Vietnam fell, the Communists quickly extended their control to **Cambodia** and **Laos.** Despite the Communists' promise not to harm the people of South Vietnam, thousands were killed, imprisoned, and tortured. In Cambodia, the Communists destroyed private property and slaughtered families, murdering over 2.5 million men, women, and children.

Vietnam War Vets: American troops returning from Vietnam are greeted with a ticker-tape parade in San Francisco.

Confessions of Robert McNamara

In 1995, *twenty years after the Vietnam War*, Robert McNamara, secretary of defense during the war, published his book *In Retrospect* in which he confessed that he and the Presidents he advised (Kennedy and Johnson) had made wrong decisions and that American soldiers had died because of their wrong judgment. McNamara opposed taking the military offensive in Vietnam; he repeatedly argued against bombing and invading North Vietnam. He *supported the anti-war protesters,* saying "I respected these students' right to dissent and the spirit in which most of them did so." But he was careful to keep his "no-win policy" from the American people.

McNamara *did not believe in achieving a military victory over Communism* in Vietnam; he hoped for a compromise with the Communists based on a diplomatic solution, which was what the Soviet Communists hoped for. In January 1966, he told presidential adviser Averell Harriman that "an acceptable military solution was not possible and therefore we should get in direct touch with the North Vietnamese and Vietcong [Communist guerrillas] to work out the best settlement obtainable."

McNamara, the State Department, and President Johnson *acted against the advice of America's military leaders.* In March 1967, the leader of U.S. ground forces in Vietnam, General William C. Westmoreland, requested permission to invade Laos and Cambodia to disrupt Communist supply lines, expand the number of allowable bombing targets in North Vietnam, increase the naval mining of Northern ports, and launch an amphibious invasion of the North. But McNamara opposed these tactics, claiming they "posed an unacceptable risk of confrontation with the U.S.S.R."

In August 1967, during a Senate hearing called to investigate the mishandling of the war in Vietnam, Senator Thurmond of South Carolina addressed McNamara on his policy of containment: "Mr. Secretary, I think it is a statement of *placating the Communists.* It is a statement of *appeasing the Communists.* It is a *statement of no-win.*"

It is regretful that while American soldiers were dying in Vietnam, McNamara was concerned about upsetting the Soviets. What American "hawks" suspected proved to be true—that top officials forced the U.S. military to fight with their hands tied behind their backs. McNamara's public confession 20 years after the war brought waves of protest from many Americans.

Communist threat spreads in Southeast Asia. In the 1960s, a Communist revolt was put down in Indonesia. The **Philippines** struggled against Communist and Muslim terrorists throughout the 1980s and into the 1990s. The Philippine government was forced to expend many valuable resources protecting itself from Communist takeover.

Period of Détente

After the Vietnam War, America entered a period of détente with the Russians. (**Détente** [dā·tänt'] is *a lessening of tension or hostility between nations*, a trying to work out differences through talks, treaties, etc.) The U.S. tried to use bargaining power and treaty-making to deal with the Soviet Union and Communist China.

*Alexander
Solzhenitsyn*

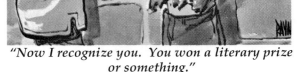

*"Now I recognize you. You won a literary prize
or something."*

In the U.S.S.R., artists and writers who criticized the government were
imprisoned or exiled to Siberia. (cartoon from *We Choose America*)

The age of détente was symbolized by President Nixon's goodwill tour of China in 1972 and subsequent opening of trade relations with China. Détente was an attempt to build cordial relations with the Communist world. The U.S. government concentrated on disarmament treaties with the Communists, rather than maintaining powerful military defenses.

Warning to the West. In 1975, the famous Russian writer **Alexander Solzhenitsyn** [sôl′zhe·nēt′sĭn], imprisoned in the Soviet Union for exposing the cruelties of Communism, was exiled to the West. He warned Americans not to be fooled into thinking that détente would bring peace. Solzhenitsyn said:

> The Communist ideology is to destroy your society. This has been their aim for 125 years and has never changed; only the methods have changed a little. When there is détente, peaceful coexistence and trade, they will still insist: The ideological war must continue. And what is *ideological war?* It is a focus of *hatred*, it is continued repetition of the oath to *destroy the Western world.*

Détente in Communist China. The death of Mao Tse-tung in **1976** precipitated a *power struggle* between **Mao's widow** Chiang Ch'ing [also spelled Jiang Qing] and the Communist Party's former general

secretary **Teng Hsiao-p'ing** [also spelled Deng Xiaoping]. Mao's widow wanted to continue the Cultural Revolution (1966–1976), but she overstepped her power when she demanded complete obedience to herself rather than the Communist Party. Teng placed her on *public trial* and sentenced her to prison.

The dangers of détente became evident when Communist China was admitted to the UN in 1971. In 1978, the U.S. formally recognized Communist China as *the only legal government of China.* It dismayed many U.S. citizens to end the American commitment to freedom in the Republic of China (Taiwan). The Communist Chinese leader, Teng Hsiao-p'ing, agreed to allow *foreign investment* in China.

What Price Freedom?

Appeasement of Communism. It is unfortunate that the U.S. (the major world power) and other free nations did not take firm, aggressive action to stop the spread of Communism immediately after World War II and especially after the Korean and Vietnam wars, rather than letting the Cold War drag on to an era of détente. The designs of Communism upon the world were no secret in the late 1940s. Winston Churchill saw clearly the aims of Stalin even before World War II was over in Europe. He urged President Roosevelt to send the Allies to conquer all of Germany before the Russians had a chance to take it. But President Roosevelt said, "no . . . lest we offend the Russians."

The price of procrastination. Had the U.S. taken aggressive action to stop the spread of Communism, she would not only have avoided the threat of Communism on her own shores, but she would have also spared herself another embarrassing problem in dealing with Third World nations. Most of these nations are backward in culture and are not ready to handle democratic government, which requires a moral, educated, and informed majority of citizens.

Most of the Third World nations that have not fallen to Communism are ruled by dictators or some other type of repressive regime. If the U.S. supports such regimes, she is accused of being an enemy of the people and being hypocritical about believing in democracy. On the other hand, *the alternative to supporting the old regime is to allow Communist forces to take control.* In Vietnam, the Nationalist government was not as democratic as the U.S. thought desirable, but Communism was the alternative. In Iran, the U.S. became embarrassed over supporting a Shah who was not as democratic as might be wished. The alternative proved to be a tyrannical religious dictator backed by Communist resources. These are two examples. If world Communism had been "nipped in the bud," there might well be a better alternative in such situations.

The Space Age: A Tribute to Freedom

There is no question that a system of freedom is far superior to a system of slavery. In the 1960s, America gave the world an astounding example of what free men living in a free nation where there is respect for human dignity can accomplish. In that decade, America put a *man on the moon.*

Sputnik I. In 1957, Americans became extremely apprehensive about the future of America's defense and prestige when the Soviet Union launched *Sputnik I,* the *world's first man-made satellite.* The Soviet Union had a head start in the race to take man into outer space. Would America catch up? How would the space race affect America's ability to defend itself against foreign attack?

Moon walk: triumph of free men. Americans determined to catch up and beat the Soviets in the race to put a man on the moon. In 1961, President Kennedy committed the U.S. to land a man on the moon before 1970. Immediately, the U.S. began trial orbits of men in space. By 1966, the world agreed that the U.S. had achieved equality with the Soviet Union in the space race. But Americans were not satisfied with equality.

With these words, *"That's one small step for man, one giant leap for mankind,"* American astronaut **Neil Armstrong** stepped onto the surface of the moon on July 20, **1969.** A new summit of human achievement had been reached in the history of the world.

A nation of free men worked together to plant Neil Armstrong's feet on lunar soil. The government, of course, played a large role. But individual voters elected the leaders of that government, and hardworking individual taxpayers paid the cost. Individual scientists and engineers—most of them working for private companies—designed the equipment. Private industry built the equipment. Eventually hundreds of businesses in every state were harnessing the initiative and energy of thousands of individuals into one grand national effort to land a man on the moon and return him safely to Earth. In a sense, not one man but an entire nation went to the moon.

The Apollo program was a milestone for human freedom and dignity as well as a triumph for modern science, economics, and politics—all of which are products of individual human freedom. *The United States had proved what free men can accomplish.* A nation of free men can certainly be victorious over the evil of tyrannical world Communism if they put their minds to it and demonstrate a will to win.

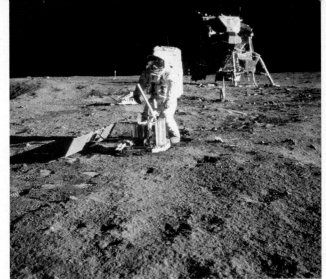
1969 Lunar Landing

CHECK UP

1. What was the first black African nation to achieve its independence? What organization did Kwame Nkrumah establish?
2. Into what two sections was Vietnam divided? Who ruled each section?
3. What event in 1964 caused President Johnson to order air strikes against North Vietnam? When did the first American combat troops arrive?
4. What nations came to the aid of the North Vietnamese Communists? Why did American morale continue to decline?
5. When and under what President were American troops removed from Vietnam? What then happened to South Vietnam?
6. Who wrote a book confessing that he and the Presidents he advised had made wrong decisions during the Vietnam War?
7. What is détente?
8. Name the two key figures in the power struggle that followed Mao Tse-tung's death in 1976.
9. When did the U.S. formally recognize Communist China and abandon the Republic of China (Taiwan)?
10. Why does the U.S. sometimes support repressive regimes in Third World nations?
11. What event in 1957 gave the Soviet Union a head start in the space race?
12. What nation was the first to land a man on the moon? Explain how, in a sense, not one man but an entire nation went to the moon.

Identify: Ho Chi Minh, John F. Kennedy, "hawks" and "doves," Alexander Solzhenitsyn

---

CHAPTER 24 REVIEW

MULTIPLE CHOICE Write the letter of the answer that best completes the sentence.

1. The leader of the Communist revolutionaries in China was _____.
   a Chiang Kai-shek
   b Ho Chi Minh
   c Mao Tse-tung
   d Chiang Ching

2. The American general who said there is "no substitute for victory" was _____.
   a George S. Patton
   b Arthur Douglas
   c Douglas MacArthur
   d Fidel Castro

3. Joseph Stalin was replaced by _____, who gave the false impression that Soviet Communism was mellowing.
   a Nikita Krushchev
   b Karl Marx
   c Konrad Adenauer
   d Alexander Solzhenitsyn

4. The Cuban revolutionary who overthrew the dictator Fulgencia Batista and established a Communist regime was _____.
   a Konrad Adenauer
   b Manuel Noriega
   c Nikita Krushchev
   d Fidel Castro

5. The Panamanian dictator _____ terrorized the people of Panama and smuggled illegal drugs into the U.S.
   a Konrad Adenauer
   b Manuel Noriega
   c Nikita Krushchev
   d Fidel Castro

6. The Chancellor of Germany, _____, moved Germany toward a vigorous free market economy.
   a Konrad Adenauer
   b Manuel Noriega
   c Nikita Krushchev
   d Fidel Castro

7. The Socialist _____ became France's longest-serving president.
   a Konrad Adenauer
   b Charles de Gaulle
   c Francois Mitterrand
   d Juan Carlos

8. Margaret Thatcher was the first woman prime minister of _____.
   a Great Britain   c Denmark
   b France   d Sweden

9. Nationalist forces led by _____ won the Spanish Civil War.
   a Konrad Adenauer
   b Charles de Gaulle
   c Francisco Franco
   d Juan Carlos

10. Israel became a nation under the leadership of _____.
    a Robert McNamara
    b David Ben-Gurion
    c Douglas MacArthur
    d Fidel Castro

11. The powerful Muslim religious leader whose followers took American diplomatic personnel hostage was _____.
    a Ayatollah Khomeini
    b Mahatma Gandhi
    c David Ben-Gurion
    d Juan Carlos

12. The Hindu nationalist and spiritual leader who worked for India's independence from Britain was _____.
    a Ayatollah Khomeini
    b Mahatma Gandhi
    c David Ben-Gurion
    d Juan Carlos

13. The leader of the Communist forces in Vietnam was _____.
    a Chiang Kai-shek   c Mao Tse-tung
    b Ho Chi Minh   d Chiang Ching

14. U.S. President _____ ordered air strikes against North Vietnam.
    a Jimmy Carter
    b Lyndon B. Johnson
    c John F. Kennedy
    d Dwight D. Eisenhower

15. U.S. President _____ pulled American troops out of Vietnam.
    a Richard Nixon
    b Lyndon B. Johnson
    c John F. Kennedy
    d Dwight D. Eisenhower

16. Secretary of Defense _____ advised Presidents Kennedy, Johnson, and Nixon during the Vietnam War.
    a Douglas MacArthur
    b David Ben-Gurion
    c Robert McNamara
    d Fidel Castro

THE COLD WAR ERA

CHAPTER 24 REVIEW (CONTINUED)

17. Russian author _____ warned Americans not to be fooled into thinking that détente would bring peace.
    a Nikita Krushchev
    b Winston Churchill
    c Konrad Adenauer
    d Alexander Solzhenitsyn

18. American _____ was the first man to walk on the moon.
    a Robert McNamara
    b Neil Armstrong
    c Alexander Solzhenitsyn
    d Mitsuo Fuchida

COMPLETION *Choose the correct term to complete each sentence and write the letter in the blank.*

a Bay of Pigs
b Third World
c Yalta Conference
d *Sputnik I*
e iron curtain
f *Pueblo*
g Ghana
h Marshall Plan
i Berlin Wall
j Cold War
k Molotov Plan
l Red Guards
m OPEC
n Truman Doctrine

1. Decisions made at the _____ resulted in the Soviet Union gaining a large chunk of Poland.

2. The _____ was not fought with military weapons but with words and diplomacy.

3. The _____ promised American economic aid to any free country to help it resist Communist aggression.

4. The _____ said that the U.S. would provide economic assistance to help European nations recover from World War II.

5. Under the _____, nations of Eastern Europe would trade raw materials with the Soviet Union in exchange for manufactured goods.

6. Students and young people called _____ filled China's streets with Communist demonstrations in the "Cultural Revolution."

7. The _____ was an American naval ship seized by North Korea in the Sea of Japan.

8. The invasion of Cuban rebels was thwarted at the _____ when President Kennedy failed to supply air cover to the patriots.

9. Winston Churchill coined the phrase "_____" to describe the Soviet domination of Eastern Europe.

10. The _____ was erected to keep East Berliners from escaping to West Berlin.

11. In the early 1960s, the oil-producing nations of the Middle East formed _____, a monopoly designed to control the supply and price of oil.

12. The _____ consists of neutral nations not yet aligned with either freedom or Communism.

13. _____ was the first black African nation to achieve its independence.

14. _____ was the world's first man-made satellite.

MATCHING Match the description with the correct term.

a "doves"
b Contras
c 17th parallel
d Saigon
e United Nations
f guerilla
g Sandinistas
h détente
i satellite
j Taiwan
k "hawks"
l 38th parallel
m Palestine

_____ 1. world peace organization

_____ 2. free China

_____ 3. divides North and South Korea

_____ 4. overthrew Somozas in Nicaragua

_____ 5. freedom fighters

_____ 6. member of a rebel army

_____ 7. "independent" nation actually dominated by another nation

_____ 8. home of the Jews

_____ 9. divided North and South Vietnam

_____10. Americans against Communism

_____11. fell to Communists in 1975

_____12. lessening of hostility between nations

CONCEPTS TO CONSIDER On a separate sheet of paper, answer the following questions using complete sentences.

1. Describe the Cold War.

2. When and how did Communism come to the doorstep of the United States?

3. How might history have been changed if the U.S. had taken firm, aggressive action to stop the spread of Communism after World War II?

MAP SKILLS Use the maps on pp. 494 and 509 to answer the following questions.

1. Name the two largest Communist nations during the Cold War.

2. What was the only Communist nation in the Western Hemisphere?

3. Name the bay that lies east of India and south of Bangladesh.

TIME LINE CHALLENGE Choose the letter of the correct date for each of the events listed below. Answers may be used more than once.

1945	1948	1949	1950–53	1957	1961	1965–73	1966	1969	1973
A	B	C	D	E	F	G	H	I	J

_____ 1. Vietnam War

_____ 2. Berlin Wall built

_____ 3. Israel becomes a nation

_____ 4. Communists take over mainland China

_____ 5. UN organized

_____ 6. NATO organized

_____ 7. U.S. puts first man on the moon

_____ 8. Korean War

_____ 9. Yalta Conference

_____10. Ghana achieves independence

25
Era of Change
(1980–1995)

HIGHLIGHTS

Ronald Reagan • Collapse of Soviet Union • Persian Gulf War
European Union • South Africa • Bill Clinton

The Reagan Era

New Leadership in England and America

In Great Britain, the 1979 election of Prime Minister **Margaret Thatcher** promised a return to more free enterprise capitalism, traditional values, and a strong stand against Communism. In the United States, the 1980 election of President **Ronald Reagan** held similar promise, not only for America but for many other nations as well. Reagan took a strong stand against the tide of socialism, immorality, crime, drug abuse, abortion, and Communism threatening the free world. During his administration, the debate between political Liberals and Conservatives was clearly defined: President Reagan represented the Conservatives, while the news media was strongly biased toward the Liberals.

President Reagan

National recovery. When Reagan assumed office in 1981, inflation and unemployment were both rising. Within months, inflation was temporarily under control and unemployment began to decrease as the nation experienced an economic recovery; there was also a return to patriotism and traditional morality. President Reagan won reelection in 1984 by

U.S. President Ronald Reagan

the *greatest margin in American history (49 states),* demonstrating that a majority of Americans were tired of the Liberalism and the secular humanism that were destroying the nation's moral and spiritual foundations. Reagan's strong leadership and concern for traditional values gave many people new hope for America's future, but many remained watchful, knowing that the country's greatest need was spiritual revival.

Sound economics; strong foreign policy. Sound conservative thinking flourished during the Reagan years, complimented by a strong foreign policy. Reagan stressed that: **(1)** budgets should be balanced and **(2)** trade and business should be *free from government interference.* Liberals labeled these concepts **"Reaganomics,"** not realiz-

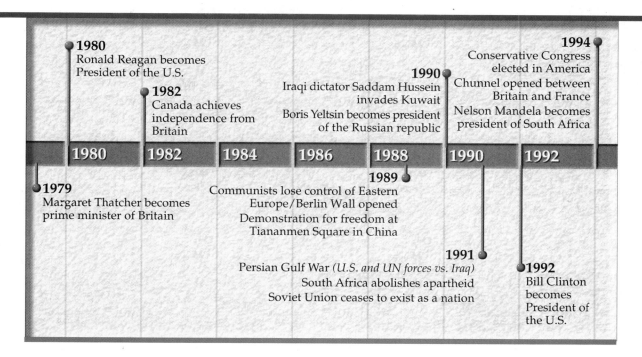

1980
Ronald Reagan becomes
President of the U.S.

1982
Canada achieves
independence from
Britain

1990
Iraqi dictator Saddam Hussein
invades Kuwait
Boris Yeltsin becomes president
of the Russian republic

1994
Conservative Congress
elected in America
Chunnel opened between
Britain and France
Nelson Mandela becomes
president of South Africa

| 1980 | 1982 | 1984 | 1986 | 1988 | 1990 | 1992 |

1979
Margaret Thatcher becomes
prime minister of Britain

1989
Communists lose control of Eastern
Europe/Berlin Wall opened
Demonstration for freedom at
Tiananmen Square in China

1991
Persian Gulf War (*U.S. and UN forces vs. Iraq*)
South Africa abolishes apartheid
Soviet Union ceases to exist as a nation

1992
Bill Clinton
becomes
President of
the U.S.

ing that these were part of the traditional principles that made America great. The Reagan years were the <u>longest period of continuous economic growth since World War II</u>, with lower taxes and less government regulation.

Reagan restored the strength of the U.S. Army, Navy, and Air Force, enabling the nation to exercise peace through strength. He believed in stopping Communism before it could attack and enslave a country; this idea was known as the **Reagan Doctrine.** His policies gave hope and active support to people around the globe in their struggle against Communism. The Reagan years represented **(1)** *traditional values,* **(2)** *less government regulation of private property,* and **(3)** *a return to patriotism and military strength.*

Standing up to Communism. The Communist dictator, Fidel Castro, continued to threaten the Caribbean region while holding his own people captive with threats and terrorism. In 1980, Castro allowed some 120,000 Cubans to flee to the U.S. in what became known as the **Mariel**

Boatlift. In 1983, Reagan learned that Castro planned to take over the island nation of **Grenada** in the West Indies and use it as a <u>military base to invade the mainland of South America</u>. A small force of Cuban military men had already arrived in Grenada when the Grenadians and other Caribbean islands called on the U.S. for help. To prevent a full-fledged Communist invasion, Reagan sent American troops to Grenada to defend the people. The Grenadians gratefully welcomed the American soldiers to their island. With the help of armed forces from neighboring islands, U.S. forces quickly rounded up the Cubans and shipped them back to Cuba.

The liberation of Grenada was just one example of Reagan's strong foreign policy. He supported anti-Communist and anti-terrorist operations around the world by arming freedom fighters in **Nicaragua** and **Afghanistan** (invaded by Russia). He also punished Libya's radical leader Muammar Al **Qaddafi** for acts of terrorism and sent American war planes to bomb targets in **Libya.**

End of the Cold War

Changes in Eastern Europe

The Reagan Presidency (1981–1989) set into motion a chain of historic events. Under his leadership, America strengthened her defenses and pursued research in space-age technology with renewed vigor. Reagan knew that America's progress in the development of *laser weaponry* alarmed the Soviets, especially the **Strategic Defense Initiative (SDI),** a system of space-age weaponry designed to destroy enemy missile warheads in flight. <u>Reagan equipped the American military with technological marvels that the bankrupt Soviet economy could not match.</u>

Poland's Solidarity. The renewed strength of America's stand against Communism encouraged the people of Poland. In the 1980s, a movement of Polish nationalists calling themselves **Solidarity** stood up to the Soviets. Led by Lech **Walesa** [vä·lĕn′sə], Polish workers refused to work until their demands for more freedom were met. In response, the Communists declared **martial law** (military rule) in Poland and rounded up members of Solidarity to be imprisoned, tortured, and executed. Reagan expressed support for Solidarity, and Pope John Paul II, from Poland, denounced the Communist Party and called for the liberation of Poland.

As the situation in Poland grew tense, Soviet troops prepared to invade. Suddenly, the Soviet leader **Mikhail Gorbachev** [gôr′bə·chôf′] announced a *dramatic change of Communist policy.* Gorbachev agreed **(1)** to reduce Soviet weapons strength, **(2)** to free the enslaved nations of Eastern Europe, and **(3)** to stop encouraging revolution and bloodshed throughout the world. In return, the U.S. and other free nations promised to help the Soviet Union rebuild its economic and political system on a democratic, free enterprise model—a plan the Soviets called **Pere-**

Polish Solidarity Leader Lech Walesa

stroika [pĕr′*e*·stroi′kə], which means *"restructuring."* The Communists also adopted a foreign policy known as **Glasnost** [glăs′nŏst], which means *"openness,"* claiming that they wanted world peace and had no plans to conquer other countries.

"One step backward." The Communists' change in tactics showed their desperation; they were adopting Lenin's advice: *"It is necessary sometimes to take one step backward so we may take two steps forward."* The <u>economy</u> of the Soviet Union was on the <u>verge of collapse</u> and <u>food shortages</u> were common. Realizing their weakness and hoping to catch up and surpass the U.S. at a future date, the Communists loosened their control over Eastern Europe in order to get **money** and **technology** from the U.S. and Western Europe.

Iron Curtain is lifted. By **1989,** the <u>Communists had begun to lose control of Eastern Europe</u> as the countries realized their freedom movements would not be crushed by Soviet troops. The peoples of Eastern Europe rose up against Communism desperately wanting freedom from Communist oppression. Some wanted to reform Communism and move toward democratic socialism, and others wanted free market capitalism. Persecuted ethnic and religious groups, including Christians, wanted freedom to openly worship and express their beliefs. All were united in the feeling that the Communist system was cruel and repressive and destroyed individual freedoms.

Opening the Berlin Wall: East Germans gather near the Brandenburg Gate to watch a crane remove part of the Berlin Wall.

Berlin Wall comes down. Events moved quickly; in June, those opposing Communism gained control of the **Polish** parliament. **Hungary** declared its independence in October; **Czechoslovakia** rose up against the Communists in November. On November 17, 1989, half a million residents of **East Berlin** marched in the streets demanding freedom. The East German police were overwhelmed. Finally, in November *1989, the Communists opened the* **Berlin Wall,** and millions of Berliners took to the streets to celebrate as young Germans beat down sections of the wall with sledge hammers.

East and West Germany were reunited on October 3, 1990. The tearing down of the Berlin Wall and the reunification of the two Germanys created a wave of patriotism and excitement among Germans. But decades of Communist rule had so destroyed the economy of East Germany that prosperous West Germany would be burdened for many years trying to raise the living standards of the East Germans.

Romanian Revolution. The overthrow of Communism in Romania resulted in the violent execution of the cruel dictator Nicole **Ceausescu** [chou·shĕs′kū] and his wife. Romanians had experienced 25 years of suffering under Ceausescu. In 1971, after the Ceausescus visited Mao's China and North Korea, they returned to Romania to begin their own version of "Cultural Revolution."

To hasten industrialization, the Romanian Communist government borrowed heavily from the West. Much of the money was wasted. By the 1980s, forced to repay these debts, Ceausescu severely rationed food supplies and cut energy consumption. People were cramped into tiny apartments and allowed only 2 to 4 hours of heat in 45° winter temperature. Many children and older people became ill or died. Ceausescu also set up state nurseries and sold children to adoption agencies in Western Europe. The secret police terrorized anyone who voiced opposition. Meanwhile, the Ceausescus built a luxurious palace and lived like royalty.

Romanian Revolution: (right) Freedom demonstrators in Bucharest take cover as the Romanian army exchanges fire with pro-Ceausescu forces. (below) Romanians watch as a statue of Lenin is pulled down in Bucharest.

Ceausescu hated Christianity and began a program to wipe out the Christian faith by destroying churches and the family. He planned to bulldoze 7,000 Romanian villages, destroying all the churches. The people were to settle in "agro-industrial" centers, and the churches would be replaced by community centers called "Hymns to Romania," permitting only atheistic worship of the state.

The revolution in Romania began in mid-December 1989 in **Timisoara,** the second largest city in the country. The consistent evangelical preaching of a Presbyterian pastor infuriated the secret police and sparked the first public protest against Communism in 45 years of Communist rule. Outside the doors of his church, a small, courageous band of members silently gathered to block the access to the building and thereby protect their pastor. Seeing that they were outnumbered, the secret police left to get reinforcements. They

returned to find that over 1,000 people had gathered outside the church. The Christians that had gathered were no match for the armed secret police, however, and the pastor was arrested and forcibly taken to the mountains for interrogation.

Word spread throughout the community of what had happened outside the Presbyterian church. As a result, 100,000 people demonstrated in the city square. The pastor of the First Baptist Church, Peter Dugulescu, addressed the crowd, raising a voice of opposition to Communism and its atheistic ideology. After speaking, he called upon the crowd to kneel in public prayer. The multitude fell on their knees and publicly prayed the Lord's Prayer; then, standing to their feet, they cried in unison, "God is alive!" The secret police responded with gunfire. Children and young people made a dash for the Orthodox Cathedral at the far end of the city square. Under gunfire and running for their lives, they made it to the top of the stairs of the building, only to find that the Orthodox priests had closed the doors. Over 100 children and young people gave their lives that day for God and for the freedom of their country. The Romanian Revolution was sealed in blood.

When news of the killings in Timisoara reached the capital of Bucharest, the people took to the streets shouting "Down with Communism." Ceausescu called out the army, but the *soldiers refused to obey the Communist officers.* Eight days later, the dictator and his wife were shot by a firing squad.

Romanians hoped for a better future without Communism. Christians from the West found the Romanians hungry for the Word of God, and by 1995 many Christian ministries were operating in Romania.

Winds of freedom. Between 1990 and 1991, the Baltic Republics of **Lithuania, Latvia,** and **Estonia** declared their independence from the Soviet Empire. *By 1991, every East European nation considered itself independent of the Soviet Union.* The winds of freedom had swept across the Soviet Union and broken it up.

Members of the underground church (secret believers), persecuted for their faith, were released from prisons and allowed to openly worship and witness for Christ. Many American Christians sent Russian Bibles to the Russian-speaking countries and others visited Eastern European

countries to minister to the spiritual needs of the people. God gave an abundant harvest of souls in these countries, where atheism and Communism had ruled for so many years.

The End of the Soviet Empire

The Communists lost their grip on Eastern Europe and appeared open for peace and free market reform; as a result, a wave of false euphoria, or unrealistic hope and joy, swept across the globe. Many world leaders declared that the Cold War was over and that the UN could achieve world peace. There was much talk of a one world government. In 1990, the Communist leader Mikhail Gorbachev was awarded the Nobel Peace Prize.

Collapse of the Soviet Union. In May 1990, **Boris Yeltsin,** a reformer, became the President of the Russian republic in a popular election. By December **1991,** eleven of the former Soviet Republics had banded together to form the *Commonwealth of Independent States.* The <u>Soviet Union ceased to exist as a nation</u>.

Russian President Boris Yeltsin

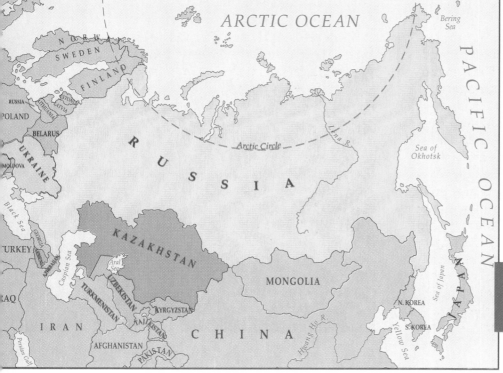

COMMONWEALTH OF INDEPENDENT STATES

Troop reductions in Europe. Meanwhile, the U.S. and Russia agreed to a limited troop withdrawal from Europe. Soon Russia withdrew troops from Eastern Europe, and the U.S. withdrew troops from Western Europe. In the Strategic Arms Reduction Treaty (START) of 1991, the U.S. and Russia agreed to destroy some of their nuclear weapons.

China Crushes Freedom

The winds of freedom blew into Communist **China.** In the spring of 1989, university students in China challenged the Communist regime. A million students and workers gathered in Beijing's **Tiananmen Square** in a *great demonstration for freedom.* The demonstrators erected a large replica of the Statue of Liberty to express their desire for freedom. The world watched and waited to see how the Chinese Communists would respond. As most conservatives expected, <u>the Communists sent soldiers to crush the freedom demonstrations</u> in Tiananmen Square. Many people were killed, and others were jailed. The world was once again reminded of the cruel oppression of Communism.

In Reagan's Shadow

President George Bush. The Reagan Administration's *buildup of American military* defenses greatly aided in the collapse of Soviet Communism, and Reagan's *support of private enterprise* caused an economic boom that further weakened the appeal of Communism. <u>Reagan's strong foreign policy was the major political cause of the end of the Cold War and the collapse of Communism's stronghold in the Soviet Union.</u>

The American people overwhelmingly elected Reagan's Vice President, George Bush, to the Presidency in 1988 with Dan Quayle as Vice President. The decade of the 1990s opened with President Bush proclaiming that the world was poised on the brink of what he called a **New World Order.** President Bush promised to continue the direction that Reagan had begun, and he promised not to raise taxes.

Growing debt. Bush was plagued by a growing *national debt* resulting from years of runaway spending by a Democratic

Demonstrations in Tiananmen Square (Beijing, China)

U.S. President George Bush

Congress. Thinking that the collapse of the Soviet Union signaled a "new world order" for global peace, <u>President Bush cut the defense budget</u>, but this did little to help the national debt and threw many people out of work.

Seeing no other alternative, President Bush finally <u>agreed to raise taxes</u> in order to keep the government from going further into debt. It was soon evident that the extra tax money would not be used to reduce the national debt, because *Congress continued to increase government spending.* Conservatives felt that Bush should have

known that raising taxes only encourages more government spending.

The Persian Gulf War (1991)

Trouble in the Middle East. While world leaders were distracted with events in Eastern Europe, a major crisis developed in the Middle East. In August 1990, **Saddam Hussein** [sä·däm′ hōō·sän′], dictator of **Iraq,** invaded the tiny, oil-rich kingdom of **Kuwait.** Hussein planned to make all the Arab nations surrounding the Persian Gulf subservient to him. President Bush compared Saddam Hussein to Adolf Hitler— *both dictators were determined to conquer innocent people and steal their wealth.*

Europe and Japan feared Hussein because he threatened their oil supplies; other Arab nations and Israel feared that they would be Hussein's next victims. When Israeli secret agents discovered that Hussein was close to developing an atomic bomb, President Bush convinced the UN to send troops to liberate Kuwait and protect the other Arab nations.

Operation Desert Storm begins. As in past actions, the U.S. provided most of the

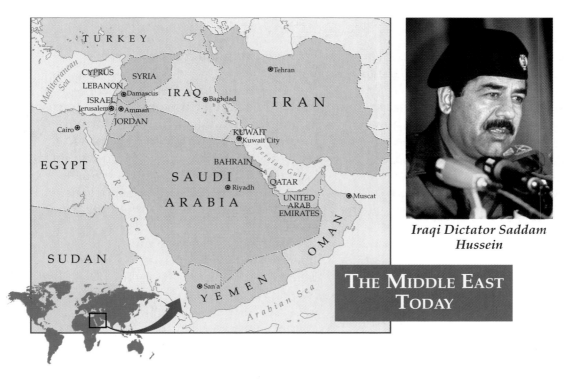

Iraqi Dictator Saddam Hussein

THE MIDDLE EAST TODAY

527

General Colin Powell (left) and
General Norman Schwartzkopf

UN military muscle. About 500,000 American troops, including air force and navy units, were shipped to Saudi Arabia to liberate Kuwait. Once President Bush obtained the support of Congress, **Operation Desert Storm** began. UN forces took the offensive and began round-the-clock bombing of Iraqi troop positions. New technology, including highly accurate *"smart bombs"* and *cruise missiles,* enabled the air force to select and destroy military targets without harming Iraq's civilian population. The "high-tech" weapons developed and stockpiled during the Reagan Administration overwhelmed the Iraqi military.

Great American generals. President Bush insisted that the war in the Persian Gulf be <u>directed by military men rather than by politicians</u>. He realized that soldiers know better than politicians how to fight and win a war. The President placed **General Colin Powell** in command of Operation Desert Storm. *For the first time since World War II, the American President and Congress followed the counsel of a military commander.* As Chairman of the Joint Chiefs of Staff, Powell was second in military command only to the President. He served as the spokesman for the military, explaining to the American people exactly what UN forces were doing in the Middle East. At all times, he insisted on

taking the offensive and pushing toward total victory to liberate Kuwait with the loss of as few lives as possible.

Because General Powell had to remain in Washington, D.C., **General Norman Schwartzkopf** [shwôrts′kŏf] was appointed to lead the troops into combat. General Schwartzkopf inspired great devotion and bravery in his men. He kept the American public and the world aware of the daily events of the war through *television briefings,* beamed by satellite into every corner of the world. He often stated that his main goal in combat was to "minimize risks and save soldiers." Unlike the Vietnam War, the *Gulf War had the support of all Americans* and most countries of the world.

Invasion and victory. On February 24, **1991,** American, British, and French forces, assisted by Saudi and Egyptian forces, invaded Iraq, while Israeli forces stood ready to assist. The army of Iraq crumbled before General Schwartzkopf's brilliant moves on the battlefield, and thousands of Iraqi troops surrendered or fled the Allied advance.

Within a few days, Kuwait had been liberated and Saddam Hussein had retreated to a bunker in Baghdad. The allied troops did not pursue Hussein any further because the liberation of Kuwait, the primary objective, had been achieved.

Operation Desert Storm was a great triumph for the American military and the cause of freedom. The <u>war lasted only 2½ months</u>—from January 16 to April 6, 1991—making it <u>the shortest war in U.S. history</u>.

CHECK UP

1. Who helped return Great Britain to free enterprise capitalism, traditional values, and a strong stand against Communism? Who was elected President of the U.S. in 1980?

2. What was "Reaganomics?" What did Liberals fail to realize about Reagan's principles of government?

3. List three things the Reagan years represented.

4. How did America liberate Grenada in 1983?

5. What dramatic change in Communist policy was implemented by Mikhail Gorbachev? How did this change reflect Lenin's advice?

6. Why did the Communists lose control of Eastern Europe?

7. When were East and West Germany reunited? How did the Germans react to reunification?

8. Explain how the Soviet Union ceased to exist as a nation.

9. How did university students in China show their desire for freedom? How did the Communist government respond?

10. Why did President Bush cut the defense budget? Why did he agree to raise taxes?

11. What was the purpose of Operation Desert Storm? Who was placed in command of the American military? Who was appointed to lead the troops into combat?

12. How long did the Gulf War last?

Identify: Reagan Doctrine, Mariel Boatlift, Muammar Al Qaddafi, Strategic Defense Initiative, Solidarity, Lech Walesa, Perestroika, Glasnost, New World Order

---

More Changes around the World

Europe and Asia

Commonwealth of Independent States. In the summer of 1992, the disintegration of the old Soviet empire continued to create new problems throughout Europe and Asia. As rival ethnic groups struggled for more independence and territory, fighting broke out in many areas. In the southwestern parts of the Commonwealth, republics with predominantly Muslim populations aligned themselves with the Arab nations of the Middle East. A violent civil war in former Yugoslavia split that nation into several new countries.

The European Union. In the 1990s, the European Parliament was given more power to enact wide social legislation. In 1994, the European Economic Community (Common Market) became known as the **European Union (EU).** Austria joined the EU in 1994, and Finland and Sweden joined in 1995.

Nationalistic differences remained strong, however, and not all Europeans approved of this plan to establish a "United States of Europe." Former British Prime Minister Margaret Thatcher insisted that "willing and active cooperation between sovereign states is the best way to build a successful European community." She warned of the "suppression of nationhood" as larger nations or coalitions of nations dominated the European Parliament. The push toward European unity was complicated when the Eastern European nations, freed from Soviet control, asked for admittance into the European Union. A united Germany worried some who feared too much German domination in a European Parliament. In 1994, the people of Norway rejected membership in the EU.

The Chunnel. The most visible symbol of increased European unity was the

EUROPE TODAY

completion of a **31-mile-long tunnel**, called the **"Chunnel,"** *beneath the English Channel*, linking Great Britain from France. Work began on the Chunnel in 1987 as workers on either end of the channel began to drill through the chalky rock beneath the sea. Using laser technology, French and British engineers steered giant drills,

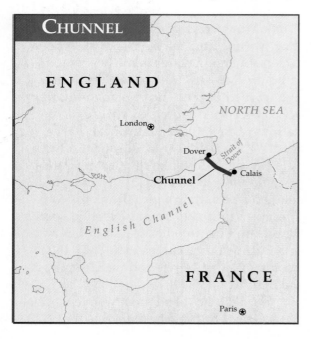

CHUNNEL

enabling them to meet each other only 4 inches apart. On December 1, 1990, the two work crews met and shook hands 150 feet beneath the bottom of the sea. In **1994,** the first high-speed train raced through the Chunnel, *cutting the travel time of 7 hours between London and Paris to less than 3 hours.* The Chunnel is a marvel of modern technology.

The Americas

Canada. Canada, the *world's second largest country,* achieved complete independence from Great Britain in **1982.** Queen Elizabeth II of England continues as Canada's official head of state, but the *real political power* in Canada rests in the hands of the Canadian **prime minister,** the leader of the majority party in Canada's House of Commons.

The key trends in post-war Canadian history were

(1) the move toward *socialism,* which became prevalent under Prime Minister Pierre E. **Trudeau** of the Liberal Party, who held power most of the time from 1968 to 1984.

(2) the rise of the **Quebec Separatist Movement.** During the 1960s, the *French Canadians of Quebec Province began demanding separation and independence from English-speaking Canada.* In 1965, in spite of Conservative opposition, Canada adopted a new **maple leaf flag** that completely omitted any symbol of ties with Britain in order to appease French Canadian separatism. In 1977, French became the official language of Quebec, making Canada a *bilingual* nation. Those residents of Quebec who favor making Quebec a separate nation are known as *separatists,* but they have failed to gain the majority of political power in the province.

(3) the quest for **national unity.**

By the 1990s, a trend toward more free enterprise and more political power to the individual provinces contributed to Canada's prosperity. **Kim Campbell,** a member of the Progressive Conservative Party, became Canada's *first woman prime minister* in 1993.

Regional distinctions are very strong in Canada. Although most Canadians live in the provinces of **Ontario** and **Quebec,** *much of the nation's wealth comes from the oil, minerals, timber, and farm products from the* *western provinces and the territories.* Thus, the provinces have insisted on more freedom to control their political and economic affairs.

In 1993, Canada joined the U.S. and Mexico in ratifying the North American Free Trade Agreement **(NAFTA),** calling for the elimination of trade restrictions among these three countries.

Kim Campbell: Canada's first woman prime minister

Canadian Flag

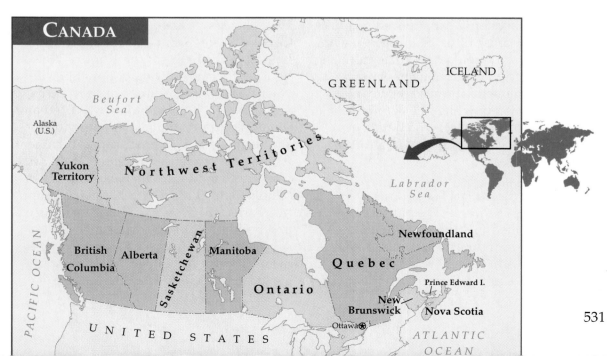

Mexico. Mexico, a democratic republic, has been controlled by one party since 1929, but mismanagement of the economy has increased opposition to that party. The Mexican economy is heavily socialized with government control (tight regulation) of major industries. A recent trend toward more free enterprise has been partially successful. Large oil reserves were discovered in 1974. Mexico soon became the *fourth largest producer of oil* in the world— behind the Soviet Union, the U.S., and Saudi Arabia.

The government used the oil money to fund the welfare system and prop up inefficient state-owned industries. Many foreign investors lent Mexico money to develop its economy. When the price of oil fell in the 1980s, the Mexican economy went into a crisis, unable to pay off its foreign loans. The Mexican government was forced to sell off some of its state-owned industry and began a campaign to attract foreign investment by allowing more free trade. In 1993, Mexico joined with the U.S. and Canada in the North American Free Trade Agreement. Most tariffs and other trade barriers among the three nations were eliminated.

Periodic economic disasters have gripped Mexico in recent years. In 1995, the Mexican economy experienced serious difficulties because of its inability to make payments on its foreign debt. The troubles were linked to socialistic business practices by the government. International bankers agreed to a plan in which the *U.S. Treasury would lend Mexico money,* which further weakened the U.S. dollar on foreign currency exchanges.

Africa's Struggle for Freedom
Communist threat. The nations of Africa continued to struggle with discredited socialist economies and political and religious strife in the 1990s. The collapse of the Soviet Union reduced the amount of terrorist activity, but Communists continued a bloody civil war in **Angola** and **Mozambique.** Communist-inspired violence also continued in **Namibia,** which became independent of South Africa in 1990. In all of these conflicts, the UN took the side of the Communists.

More war and bloodshed. The rise of Islamic militants threatened civil war in **Algeria** and the **Sudan.** Conflicts created by intertribal warfare, Communist and Muslim terrorists, and witchcraft cults resulted in much bloodshed. The U.S. withdrew its peace-keeping troops from **Somalia** in 1994 after 18 Americans were killed. In 1995, at least 500,000 people died in the country of **Rwanda** when the Hutu tribe attacked the mostly Christian Tutsi people. In contrast, the new government of **Zambia** (1995) responded to Christian missionary activity and committed itself to rebuilding its economy on Biblical principles.

South Africa. The struggle against Communism in South Africa centered on the activities of the *African National Congress* (ANC) and on its leader, activist **Nelson Mandela.** At first, the ANC was a peaceful civil rights protest group, but in 1949 it developed close ties with the *South African Communist Party* (SACP). In 1961, the ANC joined forces with the Communists to form a terrorist group known as the Spear of the Nation. Nelson Mandela became its first commander-in-chief and *organized Marxist violence throughout Africa.* In 1964, Mandela was tried and sentenced to prison for planning violent acts against the South African government. Among the evidence presented at the trial was a note in Mandela's handwriting: "The people of the South African Communist Party will destroy capitalist society and build in its place socialism."

The Soviet Union promoted Communism in South Africa because of its strategic location. South Africa lies on the *world's busiest sea lane*, with over 25,000 ships a year passing the Cape of Good Hope. It is also a *storehouse of rare minerals* that are needed for the military defense and economic security of the U.S. and her allies. Communist control of South African resources would endanger the security of the U.S. and Western Europe.

In the 1980s, the U.S. Congress joined the UN in **trade sanctions** against South Africa to protest the racial policy of *apartheid*, which segregated blacks and whites. The sanctions caused widespread suffering and unemployment, especially among black South Africans, weakening the legitimate government's attempts to achieve gradual reform while resisting Communism. To end the trade sanctions, the South African government released Nelson Mandela from prison in 1990 and agreed to share power with the ANC. South Africa <u>abolished apartheid</u> in 1991.

On the day of his release from prison, Mandela stood behind a podium draped with the flag of the South African Communist Party, declaring, "I salute the South African Communist Party. . . . We are heartened by the fact that the alliance between ourselves and the party remains as strong as it always was." Within weeks, Mandela received the 1990 Lenin Peace Prize, awarded by the Supreme Soviet of the U.S.S.R.

In the 1994 elections, the ANC gained control of the South African parliament and <u>Nelson Mandela became the first black president of South Africa</u>. Mandela campaigned with Communist leaders and was often photographed raising a clenched fist—the victory salute of Communist terrorists. Upon his election, he quickly appointed Communist party members and "democratic socialists" to cabinet posts in the new government.

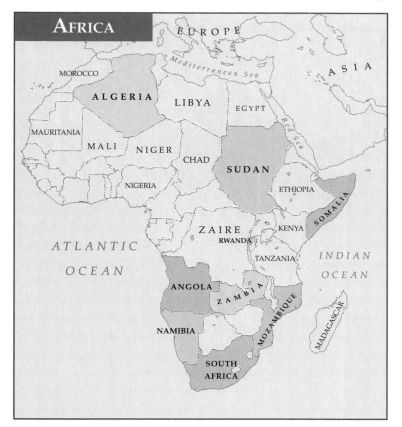

Nelson Mandela: South Africa's first black president

Asia and the Pacific Rim

By 1995, the most dynamic and rapidly growing economies in the world were in Asia, especially the **Pacific Rim,** *those regions directly bordering the Pacific Ocean.* The Pacific Rim nations of Japan, South Korea, Taiwan, and Singapore have become role models for the success of free enterprise capitalism in Asia. More than <u>50 percent of the world's trade</u> is now conducted in the Pacific Rim region. Australia and New Zealand do most of their foreign trade with these nations. The coastal cities of mainland China have also benefited under the current plan of the Communist government to allow more private enterprise in China.

After Japan, the four most prosperous economies in the Pacific Rim are known as "the Little Tigers"—Singapore, Taiwan, South Korea, and Hong Kong. **Singapore,** a former crown colony of Britain, has become a financial center for Southeast Asia. Adhering to a free enterprise system of competition and private property, **Taiwan** has also prospered; there is a strong Christian community on the island. Though threatened by Communist North Korea, **South Korea** has a thriving economy and a stable, democratic government. **Hong Kong,** a colony of Britain since 1842, has been a center of business and commerce in the Pacific Rim for many years. Through an agreement between Britain and Communist China, Hong Kong was scheduled to become a possession of Communist China in 1999. Although the Chinese promised to continue Hong Kong's free-enterprise economy, many of the colony's residents made plans to emigrate.

By the 1990s, **Thailand, Malaysia,** and **Indonesia** all practiced free enterprise capitalism, encouraging small family-owned businesses.

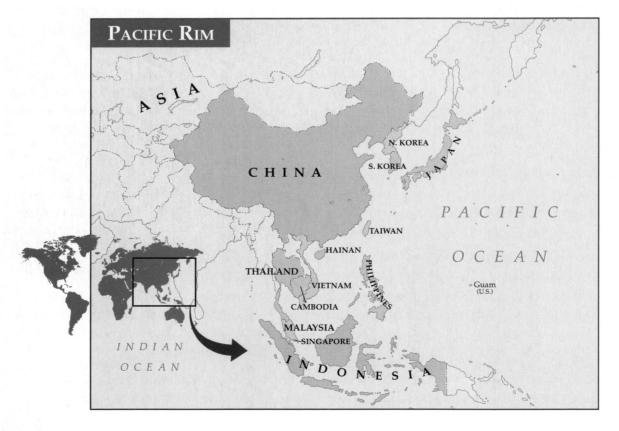

PACIFIC RIM

U.S. President Bill Clinton with wife Hillary: presenting their plan for national health care (socialized medicine).

Speaker of the House Newt Gingrich

The United States

The Clinton Presidency. As socialism seemed to weaken its grip on Eastern Europe and the former Soviet Union, it strengthened its grasp on the American people when Democrat **Bill Clinton** won the Presidential election of 1992 with only 43% of the vote; the remaining 57% was divided between President George Bush and independent candidate Ross Perot, who campaigned as a Conservative. When the election results came in, telecasts showed Perot and his staff celebrating Clinton's victory. By splitting the conservative vote, Perot put Clinton, a strong Liberal, into the White House.

National Health Care. The centerpiece of the first term of the Clinton administration was First Lady Hillary Clinton's plan for *national health care* (socialized medicine). Conservatives warned that the average person would pay more taxes and become more dependent on the government while receiving sub-standard health care—the hallmark of socialized medicine in every country that has it. Congress debated it and finally

defeated the plan. The Clinton administration succeeded in raising taxes and promoting abortion, homosexuality, gun control, and more government programs.

1994 Congressional elections. Voter dissatisfaction with the Clinton administration and the Congress was evident during the 1994 Congressional elections when for the first time since the Eisenhower Administration (1950s), the *Republicans gained a majority in both Houses of Congress* in the midterm Congressional elections. The American people made known their displeasure concerning big government programs. Speaker of the House, Georgia Congressman **Newt Gingrich,** led the drive for a *Contract with America*, promising to lower taxes, reform welfare, and return more political decision making to state and local governments. The more **conservative Congress** wanted individual states to assume more responsibility for government programs. Many Americans wanted less government interference in their lives, lower taxes, and a return to traditional values in the home and school.

Events in Europe (c. 1900–1995)

British Isles	France	Germany
1914–1918 Great Britain and the Allies win World War I.	**1914–1918** France joins with the Allied nations in World War I.	**1914–1918** Germany is defeated by the Allies in World War I; the German Empire ends.
1922 The Irish Free State is established.	**1939–1944** France joins with the Allied nations in World War II, until defeated and occupied by Germany.	**1919** Weimar Republic is established.
1931 The Commonwealth of Nations is recognized.	**1946** The Fourth Republic is set up under a new French constitution.	**1934** Nazi dictatorship begins under Hitler.
1939–1945 Great Britain and the Allies win World War II.	**1949** France joins NATO.	**1939–1945** Germany is defeated by the Allies in World War II; Hitler's dictatorship ends.
1946 Labour Party begins to implement welfare state in Great Britain.	**1954** France withdraws from Indochina.	**1945** Allied Big Four divide Germany into four military occupation zones.
1949 Ireland becomes a republic and leaves the Commonwealth of Nations.	**1957** France joins the European Common Market.	**1948–1949** Russian blockade of Berlin fails to make Allies leave West Berlin.
1951 The Conservative Government led by Winston Churchill rules Britain.	**1958** The Fifth Republic begins under a new constitution, and Charles de Gaulle is elected president.	**1949** East and West Germany adopt separate constitutions.
1955 Ireland joins the European Common Market.	**1960** France explodes its first nuclear bomb.	**1955** East and West Germany are declared independent.
1956 Great Britain, France, and Israel invade Egypt but are influenced by other countries to abandon the campaign.	**1966** President de Gaulle withdraws French troops from NATO.	**1961** Berlin Wall is built by Communists to keep East Germans from escaping to West Berlin.
1973 Britain becomes a member of the European Common Market.	**1969** De Gaulle resigns as president of France.	**1967** East Germany limits its citizenship to East Germans.
1979–1990 Conservative Margaret Thatcher is prime minister of Great Britain.	**1981–1995** Socialist Francois Mitterand is president of France.	**1973** East and West Germany sign a treaty for closer dealings between the two nations.
1982 Britain defeats Argentina in the Falklands War.	**1995** Conservative Jacques Chirac becomes president of France.	**1974** United States and East Germany establish diplomatic relations.
1990 Conservative John Major becomes prime minister of Great Britain.		**1989** Berlin Wall is torn down.
1994 The Channel Tunnel ("Chunnel") links Britain and France.		**1990** East and West Germany reunited as one nation.

Conflicting Views

The greatest political event in the latter part of the 20th century was the collapse of Communism in Eastern Europe and the former Soviet Union. The political, economic, and moral failure of Communism was finally exposed to the world. But Communism is far from dead. Communists still rule in China, the world's most populated nation, and Communists still have strong influence on many other countries of the world. Indeed, Christians in Russia feel that Communists still control events in Russia.

Gorbachev's Prophecy

Communist reformer Mikhail Gorbachev insisted that the Cold War was over and that world history had entered a new era. He urged the unification of Western and Eastern Europe in "our common European home." On May 6, 1992, Gorbachev spoke to a crowd of more than 10,000 people at Westminster College in Fulton, Missouri—the very spot where Winston Churchill had warned of the onset of the Cold War in 1946, coining the phrase "iron curtain" to describe the Communist domination of Eastern Europe. Gorbachev declared the Cold War to be officially over,

Italy

1915–1918 Italy fights in World War I on the side of the Allies.

1922 Fascist Benito Mussolini is appointed premier of Italy.

1927 Mussolini becomes dictator of Italy.

1940 Italy fights in World War II on Germany's side.

1942 Italy surrenders to the Allies and declares war on Germany.

1947 Constitution for the Republic of Italy is adopted.

1962 Coalition between Christian Democrats and Socialists, *opening to the left*, is signed.

1970s Elected Communist officials control many Italian local governments.

1976 Vatican agrees to revision of 1929 agreement, thus depriving Roman Catholicism of its "state religion" status.

1976 Communists gain parliamentary posts through elections.

1978 Aldo Moro, Christian Democrat leader, is assassinated.

1994 Conservative coalition comes to power.

Scandinavia, The Netherlands, and Switzerland

1905 Norway becomes an independent nation.

1914–1918 Norway, Sweden, and Denmark remain neutral during World War I.

1914–1918 The Netherlands remains neutral throughout World War I.

1920 The League of Nations has its first meeting in Geneva.

1940 Germany invades and then bombs Holland; Holland surrenders.

1940–1945 All Scandinavian countries remain neutral during World War II. German troops occupy Norway and Denmark.

1945 The Netherlands joins the United Nations.

1945 Norway joins the United Nations.

1949 Norway and Denmark join NATO.

1957 The Netherlands aids in the formation of the European Common Market.

1959 Norway, Sweden, Denmark, and Switzerland along with three other nations, form the European Free Trade Association.

1971 Swiss women gain the right to vote in federal elections.

1973 Denmark joins the European Common Market.

1975 Sweden adopts a new constitution that greatly lessens the king's power.

1995 Sweden joins the European Union (Common Market).

Spain and Portugal

1910 A republic is instituted in Portugal.

1914–1918 Portugal is allied with England against Germany in World War I; Spain remains neutral.

1931 King Alfonso XIII flees the country; Spain becomes a democratic republic.

1936–1939 General Francisco Franco emerges as dictator of Spain after the Spanish Civil War.

1939–1944 Portugal and Spain remain neutral during World War II.

1950s and 1960s Spain experiences a boom of economic growth.

1969 Prince Juan Carlos, grandson of Alfonso XIII is named by Franco as heir to the Spanish throne.

1973 Admiral Luis Carrero Blanco, appointed by Franco to be head of government, is assassinated. Carlos Arias Navarro is his successor.

1974 A military coup topples the undemocratic regime; the new leaders promise to restore democracy to Portugal.

1986 Spain and Portugal join the European Common Market.

1989 Portugal moves toward a free enterprise economy.

---

stating that the world was no longer divided between the East and the West, but "between the rich and the poor countries of the North and South." He said, "We live today in a watershed era. . . . One epoch has ended and a second is commencing." The "new era," he continued, would be one of global "interdependence," with environmental cooperation, disarmament, and economic sharing.

Solzhenitsyn's Warning

In 1994, the exiled Russian writer Alexander Solzhenitsyn returned to Russia. His message was far different from Gorbachev's. Solzhenitsyn insisted that the

Former Soviet Premier Mikhail Gorbachev

only hope for the world was a spiritual rebirth. He was not happy with what he saw in Russia. Solzhenitsyn's message was the same as it had been in 1983:

> While I was still a child, I recall hearing a number of older people offer the following explanation for the great disasters that have befallen Russia: **"Men have forgotten God;** that's why all this has happened." . . . *And if I were called upon to identify briefly the principle trait of the entire twentieth century, . . . I would be unable to find anything more precise and pithy than to repeat once again: "Men have forgotten God."*

The Hope of the World

Despite all the problems of our present world, the Christian knows that Christ is the center of all history, for one day He will return to rule the world with righteousness and peace. In the meantime, knowing that victory is ultimately ours—knowing that every earth-shaking event is part of His plan, we must continue to be salt and light to a needy world, carrying the gospel to the ends of the earth.

The Modern Age (1500 to the present) has seen a tremendous increase in knowledge of all kinds. Books have multiplied; art and music have increased; science has flowered and given us an infinity of technological devices that we can use for our advancement or our destruction. Representative government has spread to many parts of the world, but dictatorial governments have spread as well.

England, along with America, proved to the world during the Modern Age that pure <u>representative democracy, when it is accompanied by spiritual revivals and national righteousness, is probably the best form of human government</u> man has yet seen. However, if the people in a democracy are not governed by righteous principles, even that form of government will eventually crumble and turn against true liberty.

History has shown that democracy, when the circumstances are not right for it, often ends in tyranny, socialism, and anarchy. The problem begins when the authority of God is questioned. If God's principles are not accepted as binding on a nation that wants to be democratic, then the only "absolute" becomes the will of the people:

> Democracy, which began as a means of preventing tyranny, may tend toward allowing the most powerful tyrants of all to rule, because people in a democracy tend to trust their leaders as merely those who carry out the will of the people.
>
> Why is it that even democracy, good as it is, cannot in the long run bring "peace and good will to men"? The answer lies in the nature of man. Man is, by nature, a sinner, and he does not want to be governed by God or by anyone else. Even the best form of human government will come to an end. Only when Christ returns and personally rules the earth "with a rod of iron" shall mankind know a form of government that is established in peace and *always* administered in righteousness.
>
> We must continue to defend our representative form of government against the tyranny of Communism and socialism. We must always remember, however, that the **hope of the world does not lie in a system of government.** True political freedom will not last in any society that defies the principles of the Word of God. The fruits of liberty are wonderful, but if they are cut off from their historical root—obedience by men and nations to the Word of God—they will quickly spoil.
>
> The **hope of the world lies in God** and in his servants who will obey Christ's command to "occupy till I come."

Samuel J. Andrews, *Christianity and Anti-Christianity in Their Final Conflict.*

538

CHECK UP
---

1. What was the most visible symbol of increased European unity? How is it a marvel of modern technology?

2. Who has the real political power in Canada? What three trends did Canada follow after the war?

3. Where do most Canadians live? Where does most of the nation's wealth come from?

4. What was discovered in Mexico in 1974 that greatly increased the country's wealth?

5. Why did the Soviet Union promote Communism in South Africa? How did the U.S. Congress and the UN weaken the South African government and help the Communists rise to power?

6. What is the Pacific Rim? What are "the Little Tigers?"

7. What was the centerpiece of the Clinton administration? What did Conservatives warn would happen if this plan were implemented?

8. What happened in 1994 that proved voter dissatisfaction with the Clinton administration and the Congress?

9. What has to accompany representative democracy to make it the best form of government?

Identify: European Union, Kim Campbell, Somalia, Rwanda, apartheid, Newt Gingrich, Nelson Mandela, African National Congress

CHAPTER 25 REVIEW

MULTIPLE CHOICE   Write the letter of the answer that best completes the sentence.

1. British Prime Minister _____ brought hope of a return to more free-enterprise capitalism, traditional values, and a strong stand against Communism.
   a Boris Yeltsin   *c* Margaret Thatcher
   b Lech Walesa   *d* Kim Campbell

2. The Polish Solidarity movement led by _____ stood up to the Soviets.
   a Boris Yeltsin   *c* Margaret Thatcher
   b Lech Walesa   *d* Kim Campbell

3. Soviet leader _____ announced a drastic change in Communist policy in the late 1980s.
   a Lech Walesa
   b Mikhail Gorbachev
   c Boris Yeltsin
   d Saddam Hussein

4. The dictator of Iraq who invaded the tiny oil-rich kingdom of Kuwait was _____.
   a Lech Walesa   *c* Boris Yeltsin
   b Sadam Hussein   *d* Colin Powell

5. President Bush placed _____ in command of Operation Desert Storm.
   a Norman Schwartzkopf
   b Newt Gingrich
   c Nelson Mandela
   d Colin Powell

6. _____ was appointed to lead American troops into combat in the Persian Gulf War.
   a Norman Schwartzkopf
   b Newt Gingrich
   c Nelson Mandela
   d Bill Clinton

7. Kim Campbell was the first woman prime minister of _____.
   a Canada   *c* Mexico
   b Great Britain   *d* Romania

8. _____ became the first black president of South Africa in 1994.
   a Norman Schwartzkopf
   b Newt Gingrich
   c Nelson Mandela
   d Bill Clinton

Chapter 25 Review (continued)

9. President _____ helped socialism strengthen its grasp on the American people.
   a Norman Schwartzkopf
   b Newt Gingrich
   c Nelson Mandela
   d Bill Clinton

10. Speaker of the House _____ led the drive for a Contract with America, promising to lower taxes, reform welfare, and return more political decision making to state and local governments.
    a Norman Schwartzkopf
    b Newt Gingrich
    c Nelson Mandela
    d Bill Clinton

MATCHING Match the clue with the correct nation.

a	Somalia	f	Poland
b	China	g	Singapore
c	Romania	h	Soviet Union
d	Germany	i	Grenada
e	Mexico	j	Canada

_____ 1. invaded by Cuba

_____ 2. Solidarity

_____ 3. reunited in 1990

_____ 4. Nicole Ceausescu

_____ 5. Commonwealth of Independent States

_____ 6. Tiananmen Square

_____ 7. second largest country

_____ 8. oil discovered

_____ 9. U.S. withdrew peace-keeping troops

_____ 10. financial center of Southeast Asia

COMPLETION Choose the correct term to complete each sentence and write the letter in the blank.

a	Glasnost	f	Reagan Doctrine
b	Strategic Defense Initiative	g	prime minister
c	Operation Desert Storm	h	European Union
d	"Reaganomics"	i	Solidarity
e	Perestroika	j	apartheid

1. President Reagan's principles of government were labeled _____ by the Liberals.

2. President Reagan's belief that Communism should be stopped before it could attack and enslave a country was called the _____.

3. The _____ was a proposed system of space-age weaponry designed to destroy enemy missile warheads in flight.

4. Polish nationalists who stood up to Communism called themselves _____.

5. The plan to rebuild the Soviet Union's economic and political system on a democratic, free enterprise model was called _____.

6. The Communists' foreign policy known as _____ claimed they wanted world peace and had no plans to conquer other countries.

7. America's plan to liberate Kuwait from Saudi Arabia was called _____.

8. In 1994, the European Community became known as the _____.

9. Although the Queen of England is Canada's official head of state, the real political power in Canada rests in the hands of the _____.

10. The policy of racial segregation in South Africa was known as _____.

*TIME LINE CHALLENGE Choose the letter of the correct date for
each of the events listed below. Answers may be used more than once.*

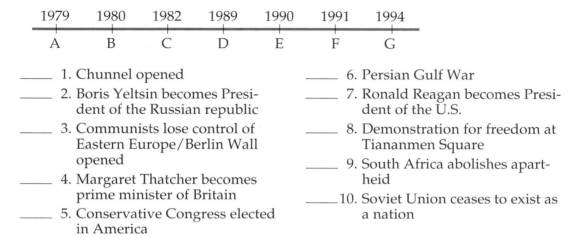

1979   1980   1982   1989   1990   1991   1994

A   B   C   D   E   F   G

_____ 1. Chunnel opened

_____ 2. Boris Yeltsin becomes President of the Russian republic

_____ 3. Communists lose control of Eastern Europe/Berlin Wall opened

_____ 4. Margaret Thatcher becomes prime minister of Britain

_____ 5. Conservative Congress elected in America

_____ 6. Persian Gulf War

_____ 7. Ronald Reagan becomes President of the U.S.

_____ 8. Demonstration for freedom at Tiananmen Square

_____ 9. South Africa abolishes apartheid

_____ 10. Soviet Union ceases to exist as a nation

*MAP SKILLS Use the maps on pages 525 and
530 to answer the following questions.*

1. Name the largest member of the Commonwealth of Independent States.

2. Which nation is the second largest member of the Commonwealth?

3. Name the three former Soviet republics along the Baltic Sea that did *not* join the Commonwealth.

4. Which former Yugoslavian republics border the Adriatic Sea?

5. Which former Yugoslavian republic is the largest?

6. Name the two new nations formed when Czechoslovakia split.

7. What Eastern European nations border the Russian Republic?

*CONCEPTS TO CONSIDER On a separate
sheet of paper, answer the following
questions using complete sentences.*

1. How did the Romanian Revolution begin? Where? When?

2. How did the Persian Gulf War differ from the Vietnam War?

3. Why would the Communists want to control South Africa? How did they gain influence and power in the South African government in 1994?

4. Contrast Gorbachev's and Solzhenitsyn's views concerning world peace. Which do you believe is more accurate? Why?

The 20th century began with great promise for mankind. The progress and accomplishments of the previous century led many to believe that the world could only get better. Little did anyone realize that on the horizon loomed two of the greatest wars the world had ever known.

By the late 19th century, the seeds of Modernism had taken root in Germany. Modernist theologians in German universities denied the basic doctrines of Christianity, including Christ's deity, man's sin nature, and the reality of Heaven and Hell. Rejecting the authority of the Bible, they exalted their own reasoning above God's Word and taught that the Bible was a collection of myths and legends with a few historical facts. As a result of Modernist influences in German churches and universities, Germany was spiritually dead, much like the rest of Europe. When people turned from faith in God, they fell prey to political revolutionaries and ultimately to tyranny. Most Englishmen and Americans were spared from these anti-Christian influences because of the preaching of evangelists and Bible teachers.

This spiritual coldness mixed with the spirit of revolutionary nationalism that troubled the European continent in the late 19th century, creating a tension among the powers of Europe. In July 1914, this tension sparked World War I (1914–1918), the first war to be fought on a global scale. On one side stood the Central Powers (Germany, Austria-Hungary, and their allies) and on the other side stood the Allies (Britain, France, Russia, and their allies). For three years, the British and French attacked Germany from the West while the Russians attacked from the East, dividing Germany's forces between two fronts. Then, in 1917, the Bolshevik Revo-

lution established a Communist state in Russia, and Communist leader Nikolai Lenin signed an armistice (cease-fire) with Germany, allowing the Germans to concentrate their troops on the western front. Just when it seemed that the Allies were doomed, the U.S. joined the war. American manpower, weapons, economic resources, and food supplies ensured an Allied victory, and in November 1918, Germany surrendered.

World War I was a great victory for the forces of freedom, but it was also a costly victory. It had brought the greatest destruction in property and people that the world had ever seen. World War I was perhaps the first modern war, employing trench warfare, airplanes, tanks, machine guns, poisonous gas, and submarines. A total of 13 million people died, and millions more were wounded.

Many hoped that World War I would be "the war to end all wars." At the Conference of Versailles, the Allied Powers drafted a treaty ending the war and establishing a League of Nations to maintain world peace. However, the harsh terms of this treaty caused much bitterness and resentment in Germany, sowing the seeds for another world war.

While Europe was struggling to recover from World War I, Nikolai Lenin was busy building a Communist totalitarian state in Russia. Soon the government controlled every aspect of the people's lives. Communism, the atheistic philosophy of German socialist Karl Marx, robbed the Russian people of their freedoms and destroyed the Russian economy. Through terror and torture, Lenin forced Communism on Russia and smaller, neighboring countries, creating the Union of Soviet Socialist Republics (U.S.S.R. or

Soviet Union). His successor, Joseph Stalin, strengthened the Communist grip on Russia and oppressed the people even more than his predecessor had oppressed them. At least 10 million peasants died in Stalin's forced collectivization of Russian agriculture, joining the more than 7 million who had died under Lenin's harsh program. On the eve of World War II, Russia was truly a land enslaved.

To review the second world war, we must return to the 1920s. In America, the twenties was a decade of optimism and great expectation for the future. Having escaped the destruction that World War I brought to Europe, Americans certainly had much to be optimistic about. The war had stimulated industry and agriculture and had increased the nation's exports almost from the beginning. As the war-torn nations of Europe now attempted to rebuild their economies, they looked to America for food and supplies. The U.S. became the leading industrial nation and the financial center of the world. As America basked in the prosperity of the twenties, its people enjoyed a decade of frivolity.

In 1929, the optimism of the Roaring Twenties suddenly vanished, and the U.S. was plunged into the worst economic depression the nation had ever experienced—the Great Depression. Banks closed, factories shut down, and many people lost their jobs. Alarmed by socialist propaganda from the media and certain liberal politicians, many Americans blamed President Hoover for the Depression and looked for a change in leadership. As a result, Franklin D. Roosevelt became President in 1933. FDR promised to solve the nation's economic problems, pledging himself to a "new deal" for the American people. However, in spite of government job programs, regulation, and extensive spending, the Depression continued. Roosevelt's New Deal did little to help the economy and, in some cases, actually prolonged the Great Depression. Furthermore, it introduced the U.S. to socialism, instituting a measure of government control over American businesses and industries. The New Deal had a devastating effect upon America's political and economic well being.

As the Great Depression spread to Asia, Europe, and other parts of the world, it brought great hardship to millions of people. Suffering from unemployment and inflation, many began to accept the socialistic propaganda that brought Mussolini and Hitler to power. Fascist dictator Benito Mussolini actually came to power in Italy in the 1920s; the Depression only strengthened his socialist state. In the early 1930s, Nazi leader Adolf Hitler took advantage of the Depression to take control in Germany. Both dictators established socialist states and built up their military forces to prepare for national expansion. The aggression began in 1935 with the Italian invasion of Ethiopia. By the spring of 1939, Germany occupied Austria and Czechoslovakia. Then Hitler and Stalin signed a non-aggression pact and jointly invaded Poland in the fall of 1939. In response, Great Britain and France declared war on Germany, and World War II began.

In the early years of the war, Hitler conquered most of Western Europe and divided Eastern Europe with Stalin. Only Britain withstood the Nazi onslaught. When the London Blitz failed, Hitler turned on his ally Stalin and invaded Russia, only to fail in this effort as well.

Meanwhile, events were taking place in the Pacific that would bring the U.S. into the war and ultimately lead to the fall of Hitler's evil Third Reich.

On December 7, 1941, the Japanese attacked the American naval base at Pearl Harbor, Hawaii. This unprovoked attack shocked Americans and aroused the country for war. The U.S. declared war on Japan; and Germany, allied with Japan, promptly declared war on America. For the next four years (1941–1945) World War II raged across the face of the globe. The U.S., Great Britain, and their allies won the great conflict. Hitler committed suicide in a bunker beneath Berlin, and Japan surrendered only after the U.S. dropped atomic bombs on two of her cities. After the war, the world discovered the full extent of Nazi tyranny in the death camps of the *Holocaust,* where millions of Jews and others were murdered. As a result of this tragedy, Israel was established as a homeland for the Jewish people and became a nation in 1948.

The League of Nations, established after World War I to ensure world peace, had failed to do its job. With the threat of the atomic bomb, many believed it essential to establish a permanent peace organization. Thus, the United Nations (UN) was organized in 1945. The United Nations failed to maintain world peace, however, and often aided the spread of world Communism.

As America and Western Europe emerged from World War II, they faced a new enemy—international Communism. Led by the U.S., the free world opposed the human slavery of Communism supported by the Soviet Union and Communist China. A *Cold War,* a war fought not with military weapons but with words and diplomacy, developed in which both sides attempted to win allies among the newly emerging *Third World* nations of Africa and Asia.

An *Iron Curtain* descended across the European continent when the Soviets refused to withdraw their troops from Eastern Europe and forced these nations to adopt Communist governments. While the U.S. helped to rebuild a strong and free Western Europe through the Marshall Plan and the NATO military alliance, the Soviet Union exploited Eastern Europe, eventually ruining the economies of these enslaved nations as well as its own through socialist inefficiency.

Capitalism scored many victories against Communism, but a foreign policy known as *containment* allowed Communism to spread to other parts of the world. As the Cold War continued and sometimes heated up into military conflicts, containment proved to be a weak and ineffective policy. In 1949, Communist Mao Tse-tung took control in China and began to build a totalitarian regime like that of the Soviet Union. From China, Communism spread to North Korea in 1953 and North Vietnam in 1954. Later, after a long, hard struggle, South Vietnam fell to Communism in 1975. On the other side of the globe, Communist Fidel Castro took control of Cuba, establishing the first Communist regime in the Americas.

In the 1960s and 1970s, a philosophy of secular humanism caused spiritual and economic decline in the U.S. and Western Europe. The great progress and prosperity of the free market system, which put a man on the moon in 1969, was not accompanied by a spiritual revival. Declining moral standards led to a breakdown of the family, a lack of the Protestant work ethic, and a decrease in patriotism. Communists working under the cloak of "democratic socialism" created a vast social welfare state in Western Europe, and these ideas spread to the U.S. Socialism hindered economic growth and hurt the military readiness of the free world.

By the late 1970s, Communism was on the march throughout the world. Soviet military power grew and Communist-inspired revolutions wracked Africa, Asia, and parts of Latin America. The only true military victories for freedom were in the Middle East, where Israel, supported by the U.S., prevailed over its foes in a series of border wars. Fearing a further decline of freedom, living standards, and morality, conservatives in the U.S. and Western Europe began to take political action.

In Great Britain, the 1979 election of Prime Minister Margaret Thatcher promised a return to more free enterprise capitalism, traditional values, and a strong stand against Communism. In the United States, the 1980 election of President Ronald Reagan held similar promise, not only for America but for other nations as well. Reagan took a strong stand against the tide of socialism, immorality, crime, drug abuse, abortion, and Communism threatening the free world. He restored the strength of the American military and repudiated the failed policy of containment. Reagan believed in stopping Communism before it could attack and enslave a country. In Grenada, Nicaragua, and Afghanistan, the U.S. helped the people resist Communism. While President Reagan equipped the American military with technological marvels which only a capitalist nation could produce, the Soviet nation bankrupted itself in a vain attempt to catch up.

In desperation, the Communists changed their tactics. Hoping to catch up and surpass the U.S. at a future date, the Soviet Union loosened its control over Eastern Europe in order to get money and technology from the U.S. and its allies. By 1989, the Communists had lost control of their empire; the countries of Eastern Europe achieved independence, and the Berlin Wall came down. By 1991, the Soviet Union had ceased to exist as a nation.

With the apparent collapse of Communism in Europe and a stunning American-led UN victory over Iraq in the Gulf War, U.S. President George Bush declared the Cold War over and the beginning of a New World Order. But Communists still controlled China, and many Christians in Russia felt that Communists still controlled events in that land as well. Indeed, the movement toward world disarmament, economic interdependence, and world socialism promoted by the United Nations continues largely unabated.

Yet there is still cause for hope. Many former Communist lands are at least temporarily open to the gospel, and many nations continue to enjoy the benefits of representative government and free-enterprise capitalism. Most important, **God continues to work among men and nations, blessing those that follow after righteousness.** We must remain vigilant in safeguarding our nation against the tyranny of Communism and socialism, realizing that the hope of the world lies not in military might or political leaders, but in our obedience to the Word of God.

INDEX

Page numbers for illustrations are printed in *italic* type.

A

Abraham, 12, 22
Act of Union, 413
Adolphus, Gustavus, 223, *224*
Africa, 418–427, *419, 425,* 510, *510,* 532
Age of Enlightenment, 333–334
Albert, Prince, 410, *410*
Alexander the Great, 82–83, *83*
Alexandria, Egypt, 83
Alfred the Great, 238, *238*
Allies (WWI), 444
Allies (WWII), 473–476, 479–480
America (see also *United States, The*), 264–274
American Declaration of Independence, 311
American War for Independence, 310
Anglo-Saxons, 237–238
Antony, 97
Apostles, 134–139
Aquinas, Thomas, 182, 364
Arab oil embargo, 508
Arabia, 148, 151
aristocracy, 75
Aristotle, 80, *81*
Armistice Day, 448, *449*
Armstrong, Neil, 515
Ashurbanipal, 57
Asia, 275–290, 534, *534*
Assyrian Empire, 46, 56–58, *56*
Athanasius the Great, 420
Athens, 77–79
atomic bomb, 484
Augustine (Saint), 238
Augustine (of Hippo), 181
Australia, 428–429, *428*
Axis Powers, 472, 477

B

Babel, 9
Babylon, 9, 19
Babylonian Empire, 19–21
Bach, Johann Sebastian, 214, 394, *394*
Bacon, Francis, 364
Bangladesh, 509
Barton, Clara, 431, *431*
Bastille, 337
Bataan Death March, 481
Battle of Hastings, 239

Battle of Nations, 345
Battle of Tours, 152, 161
Bay of Pigs, 500
Beethoven, Ludwig van, 396, *397*
Begin, Menachem, 508
Bell, Alexander Graham, 384, *384*
Ben-Gurion, David, 507, *508*
Berlin Wall, 503, *504,* 523, *523*
Bible, 135–136
Bismarck, Otto von, 352, *352,* 441–442, *442*
Black Death, 184
Bloody Mary (see *Mary Tudor*)
Boer War, 426
Boers, 424, 426
Bohemian Brethren, 204
Bolshevik Revolution, 445, 457
Bonaparte, Napoleon, 342, *342*
Booth, William, 430, *430*
Bradford, William, 295
Bradley, General Omar, 479
British Commonwealth of Nations, 429
British Empire, 408, 410, 415, *415,* 429
British North America Act, 429
Buddhism, 278, 285–286
Bunyan, John, 405
Bush, President George, 501, 526–528, *527*
Byzantium (see *Constantinople*)

C

Cabot, John, 273
Cabral, Pedro, 233, 272
Cabrillo, Juan, 270
Caesar Augustus, 97–98, *98*
caliphs, 151
Calvin, John, 214–215, *215,* 325
Campbell, Kim, 531, *531*
Canaan, 22
Canada, 429, 530–531, *531*
Canute the Dane, 238
Capet, Hugh, 228
capital punishment, 8
capitalism, 454
Carey, Lott, 320
Carey, William, 288, *288,* 302, 416
Carlos, Prince Juan, 506
Carmichael, Amy, 416, *417*
Carnegie, Andrew, 386, *387*
Carter, President Jimmy, 501
Carthage, 48, 92

Cartier, Jacques, 272, *273*
Carver, John, 298
Castro, Fidel, 500, *500,* 521
catacombs, *138*
Catherine the Great, 452, *452*
Ceausescu, Nicole, 523–525
Celts, 237
Central Powers, 444
Ch'in dynasty (China), 282
Chaldean Empire, 46, 58–60, *58*
Chamberlain, Neville, 472
Champollion, Jean Francis, 27
Charlemagne, 162–163, *162,* 227
Charles I (England), 255, *256*
Charles Martel, 161
Charles V (Holy Roman Emperor), 212
Chaucer, 182
Chiang Ch'ing, 514
Chiang Kai-shek, 477, 495, *495*
China (see also *Taiwan*), 280–284, 289, 495–497, *496*
China (Communist), 495–497, 526
Christendom, 145, 224
Christian IV (Denmark), 223
Christianity, 114–122, 134–138, 430–432
Chunnel, 529–530, *530*
Churchill, Winston, 443, 445, 472, 474–475, *475,* 491–492, 504
Clark, General Mark, 479
Claudian emperors, 116
Cleopatra, 97
Clinton, President Bill, 535, *535*
Clovis, 160–161, 227
Cold War, 492–515
Colosseum, 94
Columbus, Christopher, 264, *264,* 266–268
Common Market, 495, 529
Commonwealth of Independent States, 525, *525,* 529
Communism, 454–460
Communist Manifesto, The, 455
Confucianism, 281, *281*
Congress of Vienna, 347
Constantine, 122, *123*
Constantinople, 123
Constitution, U.S., 312–313
Contras, 501
Cook, Captain James, 428
Copernicus, Nicolaus, 365, *365*
Coronado, Francisco, 270, *270*
Cortes, Hernando, 269, *270*
Council of Constance, 179, 180, 203, 204

Council of Nicaea, 144
Council of Toulouse, 178
Counter-Reformation, 221
Creation, 4–7
Cromwell, Oliver, 257–258, *257*
Crowther, Samuel Adjai, 427, *427*
Crusades, 153–155, *154, 155,* 185
Cuba, 500
Cuban Missile Crisis, 500
Cultural Revolution, 496–497
Cyrus the Great, 61–63, 73

D

D-Day invasion, 479, *481*
da Gama, Vasco, 233, 268, *268,* 287, 420
da Vinci, Leonardo, 187–188
Daniel, 59
Dante, 182
Darius I, 62, 73
Darius III, 64
Darwin, Charles, 373–375, *373*
Das Kapital, 456
David (King of Israel), 44
de Balboa, Vasco, 269, *270*
de Champlain, Samuel, 272
de Gaulle, Charles, 474, 504
de la Salle, Robert Cavalier, 272
de León, Ponce, 269, *270*
de' Medici, Giovanni, 185
de Médicis, Catherine, 327, *327*
de Médicis, Marie, 330
de Soto, Hernando, 270, *270*
de Tocqueville, Alexis, 274, 315, *316*
de Verrazano, Giovanni, 272
democracy, 76
détente, 513
Dias, Bartholomeu, 233, 266
Diocletian, 120
direct democracy, 77
dispersion, 12
Disraeli, Benjamin, 410, 411, *411,* 426
Drake, Sir Francis, 251, *251,* 273, *273*
Dunant, Jean-Henri, 431, *431*
Dutch Republic (see *Netherlands, The*)

E

East India Company (British), 279, 416
Eastern Europe, 475, 492, 502, 522–525

Eastern Roman Empire, 123
Edict of Milan, 122
Edict of Nantes, 329, 333
Edison, Thomas, 384, *385*
Edward VI, 247
Edward VII, 432
Edwards, Jonathan, 303, *303*
Egypt, 26–37, *28,* 426
Einstein, Albert, 369, *369*
Eisenhower, General Dwight D., 479, *481*
Elizabeth I, 248, *249*
Elizabethan Age, 253
Engels, Friedrich, 455
England (see also *Great Britain*), 236–261
English Bill of Rights, 260
English Civil War, 257
English Reformation, 244–247
Erasmus, Desiderius, 207–208, *207*
Ethiopia, 420, 424
Etruscans, 89
European Economic Community (see *Common Market*)
European Union, 529
Eusebius, 122
evolution, 6, 373–375

F

Falklands War, 505, *505*
fascism, 465
Ferdinand and Isabella, 232, 267
Ferdinand II (Holy Roman Emperor), 223
Ferdinand, Archduke Francis, 442, *443*
fertile crescent, 12, 14–15
feudalism, 165–171
Finney, Charles, 319, *319*
Flavian emperors, 116, 117
Flood, 7, 8
Ford, Henry, 384, *385*
Forum (Roman), 89
Foxe, John, 248, *249*
France, 227–228, 324–352, 473–474, 504
Franco, General Francisco, 472, 506
Franco-Prussian War, 352
Franks, 159–165, 227
French Revolution, 334–342
Freud, Sigmund, 466
Fulton, Robert, 383

G

Galilei, Galileo, 365, *365*
Genghis Khan, 283
George III, 307, *307*
Germany, 218–220, 222–224, 347, 441–442, 503–504, *503,* 523
Ghana, 510
Ghandi, Mahatma, 508, *508*
Gingrich, Newt, 535, *535*
Gladstone, William, 411, *411,* 412
Glorious Revolution, 260
Gorbachev, Mikhail, 522, 536–537, *537*
Great Awakening, 303–305
Great Britain (see also *England*), 307, 408–433, 474–475, 504–505
Great Depression, 469–470, *469*
Great Pyramids, 33
Great Silk Road, 282
Great Sphinx, 33, *33*
Great Wall of China, 282, *282*
Greece, 68–84
Gutenberg Bible, 207
Gutenberg, Johann, 198, 206–207, *206*

H

Hammurabi, 19–20, *20*
Han dynasty (China), 282
Handel, George Frederick, 214, 395, *395*
Hanging Gardens of Babylon, 59, *59*
Hannibal, 93, *93*
Hapsburgs, 212, 222
Harris, Townsend, 289, 417
Harvey, William, 371
Hatshepsut, 33
Haydn, Franz Joseph, 396, *396*
Hellenistic Age, 83
Henry IV (France), 328, *329*
Henry the Fowler, 183
Henry VII (England), 244
Henry, VIII (England), 244, 246–247, *246*
Hinduism, 277–278
Hirohito, Emperor, 477
Hiroshima, 484, *484*
Hitler, Adolf, 466, *466,* 470–476, 480–481
Hittite Empire, 48, *49*
Ho Chi Minh, 510

Holland (see *Netherlands, The*)
Holocaust, 485–486
Holy Roman Empire, 183–184
Homer, 70, *70*
Hong Kong, 283, 534
Hoover, President Herbert, 469
Hudson, Henry, 273
Huguenots, 325–329, 330, 333
humanism, 6, 18
Hundred Years' War, 242
Huss, John, 180, *180*, 203–204
Hussein, Saddam, 527–528, *527*
Hussites, 180, 204

I

India Act, 416
India, 277–279, 288, 508–509, *509*
Indonesia, 286–288
Industrial Revolution, 376–389
Inquisition, 180–181, 205, 221
Ireland, 413–414, *414*
Irenaeus, 139
Isaiah, 62
Islam, 148, 151–153, 155
Israel, 22, 40–46, *45*, 507–508
Israel (Northern Kingdom), 46
Italian Renaissance, 199, 206, 392
Italy (see also *Roman Empire)*, 440,
    444, 465–466, 472, 479–480, 504
Ivan the Terrible, 452, *452*

J

James I, 254, 294
Japan, 284–285, 289–290, 477–478,
    482–485, 498
Jerome, 178
Jerusalem church, 137
Jesuits (Society of Jesus), 221
Jesus Christ, 98–100, 114, 126, 134–
    135
Joan of Arc, 242, *243*
John I (England), 240
John I (Portugal), 232
Johnson, President Lyndon B., 511,
    513
Joliet, Louis, 272
Jonah, 58
Joseph, 23, 26, 37
Joshua, 42
Judah (Southern Kingdom), 46
Judson, Adoniram, 320
Julius Caesar, 95–97, *95*, 237
July Monarchy, 349
July Revolution, 349

K

Kennedy, President John F., 500, 511,
    513, 515
Kepler, Johannes, 365, *365*
Khomeini, Ayatollah, 508
Khrushchev, Nikita, 499–500
Kierkegaard, Sören, 466
Knox, John, 215, 249
Koran, 150–151
Korea, 285–286, 289
Korean War, 498–499, *498, 499*
Kublai Khan, 283

L

Lancastrian dynasty (England), 243
Lawrence, T. E., 445
League of Augsburg, 332
League of Nations, 449, 451, 464
Leif Ericson, 264
Leipzig, Battle of (see *Battle of
    Nations*)
Lenin, Nikolai, 445, 457–459, *458*
Liberia, 424
Lincoln, President Abraham, 315, *315*
Lindbergh, Charles, 467, *468*
Livingstone, David, 422–423, *422, 423*
Lollards, 179, *179*
Louis XIV, 330–332, *332*
Louis XV, 334
Louis XVI, 334, *334*, 336–340
Loyola, Ignatius, 221
Lusitania, 446
Luther, Martin, 199, 208–214, *209, 213*

M

MacArthur, General Douglas, 481,
    482, 498
Machen, J. Gresham, 467
Machiavelli, 188–189
Magellan, Ferdinand, 269, *270*
Magna Carta, 240–241
Magna Graecia, 89
Magyars, 164
Mandela, Nelson, 532–533, *533*
Mao Tse-tung, 495–497, *496*, 514
Margrete of Denmark, 230
Marie Antoinette, 336, *337*, 341
Marquette, Jacques, 272
Marshall Plan, 493
Martyn, Henry, 288
Marx, Karl, 454–456, *454*
Mary I (England), 248
Mary Stuart (see *Mary, Queen of Scots*)
Mary Tudor (see *Mary I*)
Mary, Queen of Scots, 249
Maurya Empire, 278

Mayflower Compact, 297–298
Mecca, 148–150
Mein Kampf, 466
Mesopotamia, 16
Mexico, 532
Michelangelo, 188
Middle East, 2, 12, 507–508, *507*, 527–
    529, *527*
Milton, John, 405
Minoans, 69
Mitterand, Francois, 504
modern science, 362, 364–376
Modernism, 440
Moffat, Robert, 423, *424*
Mogul Empire, 279
Mohammed, 148–152
Molotov Plan, 493
monarchy, 75
monasticism, 175–176
monotheism, 17
Montgomery, General Sir Bernard,
    479, *479*
Moody, D. L., 319, *320*
Moors (Muslims), 164, 231, 232
Moravians, 204, 300
Morgan, G. Campbell, 467
Morrison, Robert, 289, *289*, 417
Morse, Samuel, 384
Moses, 26, 36, 40
Mount Olympus, 70
Mount Sinai, 40, *40*, 42
Mount Vesuvius, 117, *118*
movable-type printing press, 198,
    206–207
Mozart, Wolfgang Amadeus, 396
Müller, George, 430, *430*
Muslims, 150–155, *153*
Mussolini, Benito, 465, *466*, 471–472,
    479, 480
Mycenaens, 69

N

Nabopolassar, 58
NAFTA, 531–532
Nagasaki, 484
Nahum, 58
Napoleon III, 349, *349*
Napoleonic Wars, 340–342
NATO, 493
Nazism, 466
Nebuchadnezzar, 58–60
Nehru, Jawaharlal, 508, *508*
Nelson, Lord Horatio, 343
Nero, 116, *116*
Netherlands, The, 226–227, 250–251,
    506
New Babylonian Empire (see
    Chaldean Empire)
New Zealand, 428–429, *428*

Newton, Sir Isaac, 367, *368*
Nicene Creed, 144
Nicholas II, 453, 456–457, *457*
Nietzsche, Friedrich, 466
Nightingale, Florence, 431, *431*
Ninety-five Theses, 210
Nixon, President Richard, 512–513
Nkrumah, Kwame, 510
Noriega, Manuel, 501
Norman Conquest, 238–239
Normandy, 164, 230
Northern Renaissance, 206–208, 392

O

Octavian (see *Caesar Augustus*)
oligarchy, 75
Olympic games, 72, *72*
OPEC, 508
Operation Airlift, 503, *503*
Operation Desert Storm, 527–529
Otto the Great, 183, *183*
Ottoman Turks, 152–155

P

Pacific Rim, 534, *534*
Pakistan, 509
Palace of Versailles, 331, *331*
Palestine, 100, 153–154
Panama Canal, 501
Pantheon, 90
Papal States, 162
Parliament, British, 241–242,
Parthenon, *71*, 84
Patriarchs, 22
Patton, General George S., 479
Paul (Apostle), 116, 134, *134*, 139, 141
Pax Romana, 98
Peace of Alais, 330
Peace of Augsburg, 220, 222–223
Peace of Paris, 451
Peace of Westphalia, 223–224
Pearl Harbor, 476–478, *478*
Peasant's Revolt, 218–219
Peloponnesian War, 79
People's Republic of China (see *China, Communist*)
Pepin the Short, 161–162, 227
Pericles, 77, *77*
Perry, Commodore Matthew, 289, 417
Persian Empire, 61–64, *61*
Persian Gulf War, 527–529, *527*
Persian Wars, 73–74
Peter the Great, 452
Peter (Apostle), 116
Petition of Right, 256
Petrobrusians, 202

pharaohs, 30
Philip II (Macedonia), 81, *82*
Philip II (Spain), 272
philosophers (Greek), 80
Phoenicia, 46, 48
Pietism, 299
Pilgrims (see *Separatists*)
Pizarro, Francisco, 269
Plantagenet dynasty (England), 240
Plato, 80, *81*
Poland, 522–523
polis, 71
Polo, Marco, 266, *266*
polytheism, 17
Pompey, 95
Pope Gregory the Great, 158, *159*
popes, 140, 143–144
Portugal, 232–233, 507
Powell, General Colin, 528, *528*
Prince Henry the Navigator, 232, 266
Protestant Reformation, 199, 208–210, 392
Protestant work ethic, 377
Prussia, 441–442, *442*
Pueblo incident, 499
Punic Wars, 92–93
Puritans, 255, 294

R

Raikes, Robert, 302
Raleigh, Sir Walter, 273
Ramses II, 33, *33*
Raphael, 188
Reagan, President Ronald, 520–522, *520*
Reconquista, 231
Rembrandt (van Rijn), 400, *400*
Renaissance (see also *Italian Renaissance*), 185–189
representative democracy, 77
Republic of China (see *Taiwan*)
republic, 90
Richard the Lion-Hearted, 154, 240
Richelieu, Cardinal, 330, *330*
Rimmer, Harry, 467
Roaring Twenties, 467–468
Robespierre, Maximilien, 340, *341*
Rockefeller, John D., 386, *387*
Roman church, 137–145, 177–178, 180–181, 183–184
Roman Empire, 98–99, *99*, 116–126, *121, 124*
Romanian Revolution, 523–525, *524*
Romanov dynasty (Russia), 452
Rommel, General Erwin, 479
Roosevelt, President Franklin, 469, *470*, 491–492
Rosetta Stone, 27
Rousseau, Jean-Jacques, 334

Russia (see also *Soviet Union*), 451–460, *460*, 475–476, 525–526

S

Sadat, Anwar, 508
Saladin, 154
Salvation Army, 432
Sandinistas, 501
Sargon the Great, 16
Saul (King of Israel), 44
Scandinavia, 229–230, 507
scholasticism, 181–182, 363
Schütz, Heinrich, 214, 394
Schwartzkopf, General Norman, 528, *528*
Scottish Reformation, 249
Second Great Awakening, 317
Selassie, Haile, 472
Seljuk Turks, 153
Senate (Roman), 91
Sennacherib, 58
Separatists, 294–295
Sepoy Rebellion, 416
Septuagint, 99
Shakespeare, William, 96, 253, *253*, 404
Shalmaneser V, 57
Shinar (see *Sumer*)
Shintoism, 284
Simons, Menno, 215
slave trade, 421–422, *421*
Smith, Adam, 378, 387, *388*
Smith, Gypsy, 467
socialism, 454
Socrates, 80, *80*
Solidarity, 522
Solomon (King of Israel), 44
Solon, 77
Solzhenitsyn, Alexander, 514, *514*, 537–538
South Africa, 424–426, *424*, 532–533
Soviet Union, 459–460, *460*, 490, 492–493, 496, 499–500, 502, 522–523, 525–526, 532
Spain, 230–232, 506–507
Spanish Armada, 251–252
Spanish Civil War, 472, 506
Sparta, 76–77, 79–80
Spener, Philipp, 299, *299*
Spurgeon, Charles Haddon, 432, *432*
St. Bartholomew's Day Massacre, 327
St. Francis of Assisi, 177, *177*
Stalin, Joseph, 459, *460*, 473, 490–492
state churches, 219–220, *220*, 233
Stuart dynasty (England), 254–256, 260
Suez Canal, 426
Sumer, 9, 10, 12–19

Sunday, Billy, 467
Swiss Confederation (see *Switzerland*)
Switzerland, 214, 225–226, 506

T

Taiwan, 495
Taoism, 281–282
Taylor, J. Hudson, 289, 417, *417*
Ten Commandments (Decalogue), 41, *41*
Teng Hsiao-p'ing, 514
territorial churches, 220
Thatcher, Margaret, 505, *505*, 520
theocracy, 41
Theodosius I, 123
Third International, 459
Third Reich, 470
Third World, 508
Thirty Years' War, 223
Thutmose III, 35
Tiananmen Square, 526, *526*
Tiglath-pileser III, 56
Tito, Marshal, 502
Tojo, General Hideki, 477
Torrey, R. A., 467
Trafalgar, Battle of, 343
Trajan, 118
Treaty of Paris, 311
Treaty of Verdun, 163–164
Treaty of Versailles, 450–451
Triple Alliance, 442
Triple Entente, 442
Trotsky, Leon, 459
Truman, President Harry S, 484, *484*, 493, 498
Tudor dynasty (England), 243–254

Tutankhamen, 34, *34*
tyranny, 75

U

U.S.S.R. (see *Soviet Union*)
United Nations, 490, 492, 533
United States, The, 306, 308–320, *318*, 476–478, 481–484, 535
Ur, 12

V

V-E Day, 481
V-J Day, 484
Vesalius, Andreas, 370
Victor Emmanuel II, 440
Victoria, 408–411, *409, 410*
Victorian Age, 410
Vietnam War, 510–513
Vikings (Norsemen), 164, *165*, 229
Voltaire, Francois, 334
von Hindenburg, General Paul, 445, *445*
von Metternich, Prince, 347
Vulgate, 178

W

Waldensians, 202
Walesa, Lech, 522, *522*
Wars of the Roses, 243
Washington, President George, 310, 313, *313*
Waterloo, Battle of, 346
Watts, Isaac, 395, *395*

Wesley, Charles, 300
Wesley, John, 300, *300*
Wesleyan revival, 300–301, 377
Western Europe, 228–229, 350–351, 473–475, 536–537
Whitefield, George, 300–301, 304, *305*
Wilberforce, William, 301–302, *302*
Wilhelm I, 441
Wilhelm II, 442, *442*
William III and Mary II (England), 260
William of Ockham, 182
William the Conqueror, 238–239, *239*
William the Silent, 250, *250*
Williams, Sir George, 430
Wilson, President Woodrow, 448, *449*
World War I, 442–451, *443*
World War II, 473–486, *480, 483*
Wright, Wilbur and Orville, 385, *385*
Wycliffe, John, 179, *179*, 202–203

X

Xenophanes, 80
Xerxes, 64, 73

Y

Yalta Conference, *491*, 492
Yeltsin, Boris, 525

Z

Zimmerman Note, 448
Zwingli, Ulrich, 214, *215*

CREDITS

The "Chronology of Bible History" is reprinted from *The Simplified Pronouncing Edition of the Bible,* copyright 1942 by A. J. Holman Company.

Maps on the following pages were adapted from Mountain High Maps images copyright ©1993 Digital Wisdom, Inc. and Mountain High Map Frontiers images copyright ©1994 Digital Wisdom, Inc.: cover, x, 8, 132, 200–201 background, 271, 313, 318, 326, 419, 442, 460, 494, 496, 498, 501, 503, 505, 507, 509–511, 527, 530, 531, 533, 534.

Photo/illustration credits are listed top to bottom, left to right on each page. Locations are noted by t–top, b–bottom, r–right, c–center, l–left. Some photos are used courtesy Corel Corporation. All maps and other illustrations or photos not credited are the property of the publisher. The abbreviation GRC is used throughout for The Granger Collection, New York.

i—NASA; ii—SEF/Art Resource NY, GRC, Farrell Grehan/Photo Researchers Inc.; iii—George Haling/ Photo Researchers Inc., ABB, GRC, GRC, Scala/Art Resource NY; iv—Scala/Art Resource NY, GRC, Collection of the New-York Historical Society; v—GRC, GRC, NASA—br; 2—tl: University Museum at University of Pennsylvania, tr: SEF/Art Resource NY; 3—t: NASA , bl: GRC, bc: Farrell Grehan/Photo Researchers Inc., 7—Fred J. Maroon/Photo Researchers Inc.; 8—NASA; 16—Scala/Art Resource NY; 17—SEF/Art Resource NY, GRC; 18—The University Museum of the University of Pennsylvania; 20—l: GRC; 27—Farrell Grehan/Photo Researchers Inc.; 29—Bernard Pierre Wolff/Photo Researchers Inc.; 30—GRC; 31—GRC; 32—The Bettmann Archive, GRC; 33—Fred J. Maroon/Photo Researchers Inc., GRC; 34—GRC; 36—GRC; 40—GRC; 47—ship: The Bettmann Archive; 48—l: Paolo Koch/Photo Researchers Inc., br: GRC; 49—t: The Bettmann Archive; 54—GRC, GRC, George Haling/Photo Researchers Inc.; 55—courtesy of the Oriental Institute of the University of Chicago; 57—The Bettmann Archive; 59—The Bettmann Archive; 60—Frank and Helen Schreider/National Geographic Image Collection; 64—GRC, courtesy of the Oriental Insitute of the University of Chicago; 68—GRC; 69—Herve Donnezan/Photo Researchers Inc.; 70—GRC, The Bettmann Archive; 71—r: GRC; 72—detail from Greek vase ca. 530 B.C. from The Metropolitan Museum of Art Rogers Fund 1914 (14.130.12), GRC; 77—Scala/Art Resource NY; 80—Scala/Art Resource NY; 81—Scala/Art Resource NY; 82—The Bettmann Archive; 83—Scala/Art Resource NY; 90—Scala/Art Resource NY; 93—GRC; 94—l: GRC; 95—The Bettmann Archive; 98—GRC; 115—Scala/Art Resource NY; 116—Giraudon/Art Resource NY, GRC; 117—GRC; 119—bl, r: GRC; 122—l: GRC; 125—George Haling/Photo Researchers Inc.; 132—t: Vanni/Art Resource NY, bl: Scala/Art Resource NY, Mona Lisa: GRC; 133—t, br: GRC; 134—Rembrandt van Rijn: *The Apostle Paul* (detail), Widener Collection, © 1995 Board of Trustees, National Gallery of Art, Washington; 136—University Museum of the University of Pennsylvania; 142—Yale University Art Gallery—Dura-Europos Collection, Scala/Art Resource NY; 143—